NATURAL LAW AND LAWS OF NATURE IN EARLY MODERN EUROPE

Natural Law and Laws of Nature in Early Modern Europe

Jurisprudence, Theology, Moral and Natural Philosophy

Edited by

LORRAINE DASTON and MICHAEL STOLLEIS

Max Planck Institute for History of Science, Berlin

Max Planck Institute for European Legal History, Frankfurt-am-Main

ASHGATE

Published by
Ashgate Publishing Limited
Wey Court East
Union Road
Farnham
Surrey GU9 7PT
England

Ashgate Publishing Company
Suite 420
101 Cherry Street
Burlington, VT 05401-4405
USA

Ashgate website: http://www.ashgate.com

British Library Cataloguing in Publication Data
Natural law and laws of nature in early modern Europe :
jurisprudence, theology, moral and natural philosophy
1.Natural law – History 2.Jurisprudence – Europe – History
3.Science – Europe – Philosophy – History
I.Daston, Lorraine, 1951– II.Stolleis, Michael, 1941–
340.1'12'094

Library of Congress Cataloging-in-Publication Data
Natural law and laws of nature in early modern Europe : jurisprudence, theology, moral and natural philosophy / edited by Lorraine Daston and Michael Stolleis.
p. cm.
Includes bibliographical references.
ISBN 978-0-7546-5761-3 (alk. paper)
1. Natural law—History. 2. Law and ethics—History. 3. Science and law—Europe—History. 4. Religion and law—Europe—History. 5. Law—Europe—Philosophy—History. I. Daston, Lorraine, 1951– II. Stolleis, Michael, 1941–

K455.N36 2006
340'.112—dc22

2006002164

ISBN: 978 0 7546 5761 3

Mixed Sources
Product group from well-managed forests and other controlled sources
www.fsc.org Cert no. SA-COC-1565
© 1996 Forest Stewardship Council
FSC

Printed and bound in Great Britain by
MPG Books Ltd, Bodmin, Cornwall.

Contents

Preface and Acknowledgements

This volume is the result of an interdisciplinary and international collaboration stretching over several years. The authors met twice (and, in some cases, three times) in order to discuss the themes of the book and drafts of individual papers together and then modified their essays in light of these discussions. The density of the internal cross-references within the volume bear witness to these spirited and stimulated discussions, which took place in a friendly Babel of French, German, and English, with some Latin thrown in for good measure.

We are deeply grateful to the institutions whose support and hospitality made these discussions possible: the Deutsche Forschungsgemeinschaft, the Stiftung zur Förderung der wissenschaftlichen Forschung an der Universität Bern, the Schweizerische Akademie der Geistes und Sozialwissenschaften, the Universität Bern (Switzerland), the Werner-Reimers-Stiftung (Bad Homburg, Germany), the Max Planck Institute for European Legal History (Frankfurt-am-Main, Germany), and the Max Planck Institute for the History of Science (Berlin, Germany). Dr Josephine Fenger at the Max Planck Institute for the History of Science prepared the final manuscript with intelligence and care. We thank all most heartily for their generosity, patience, and assistance.

Notes on the Contributors

Editors

Lorraine Daston is Director at the Max Planck Institute for the History of Science in Berlin and Visiting Professor at the Committee on Social Thought, University of Chicago. Her publications include *Classical Probability in the Enlightenment* (1988); with Katharine Park, *Wonders and the Order of Nature, 1150–1750* (1998); and edited volumes on *Biographies of Scientific Objects* (2000), *Things that Talk: Object Lessons from Art and Science* (2005) and, with Katharine Park, *The Cambridge History of Early Modern Science* (2006).

Michael Stolleis was until 2006 Professor for Public Law and History of Law at the University of Frankfurt. Since 1992 he has also directed the Max Planck Institute for European Legal History. He has been awarded both the Leibniz Prize of the Deutsche Forschungsgemeinschaft (1991) and the Prize of the International Balzan Foundation (2000). Michael Stolleis is a member of the Academy for German Language and Poetry. His books include *Stato e ragion di stato nella prima età moderna* (1997); *Law under the Swastika: Studies on legal history in Nazi Germany* (1998); *Histoire du droit public en Allemagne 1600–1800* (1998); *Public Law in Germany 1800–1914* (2001); and *L'Œil de la loi* (2006).

Authors

Jean-Robert Armogathe is Professor for the History of Scientific and Religious Ideas at the Ecole Pratique des Hautes Etudes (Sorbonne) in Paris. He belongs to the Centro di Studi su Descartes e la Filosofia del Seicento (University of Lecce, Italy). Among many contributions to the intellectual history of early modern Europe (especially on Descartes), his recent publications include *L'Antéchrist. Exégèse et politique à l'âge classique* (2005); *La nature du monde* (2007); and, as co-editor with V. Carraud, *Bibliographie cartésienne (1960–1996)* (2003).

Gerd Graßhoff is Professor for History and Philosophy of Science at the Faculties of both Sciences and Humanities at the University of Bern, Switzerland. His books include *The History of Ptolemy's Star Catalogue* (1990); with H. Treiber, *Naturgesetz und Naturrechtsdenken im 17. Jahrhundert. Kepler – Bernegger – Descartes – Cumberland* (2003); with M. Baumgartner, *Kausalität und Kausales Schliessen* (2003); with B. Eastwood, *Planetary Diagrams for Roman Astronomy in Medieval Europe, Ca. 800–1500* (2004); *Theodore von Kármán – Flugzeuge für die Welt und eine Stiftung für Bern* (2004); with T. Lampert, *Ludwig Wittgensteins Logisch-philosophische Abhandlung: Entstehungsgeschichte und Herausgabe der Typoskripte und Korrekturexemplare* (2004); with A. Hentschel, *Albert Einstein: 'Those Happy*

Bernese Years' (2005); with T. Lampert, *Paul Engelmann: Psychologie graphisch dargestellt* (2005); with A. Stückelberger, *Klaudios Ptolemaios: Handbuch der Geographie* (2006); and *Wittgenstein's World of Mechanics* (2006).

Sachiko Kusukawa is Tutor and Director of Studies in History and Philosophy of Science at Trinity College, Cambridge. Her books include, *The Transformation of Natural Philosophy: the case of Philip Melanchthon* (1995); *A Wittenberg University Library Catalogue of 1536* (1995); as co-editor, *Philosophy in the Sixteenth and Seventeenth centuries: Conversations with Aristotle* (1999); and *Transmitting Knowledge: Words, Images, and Instruments in Early Modern Europe* (2006).

Catherine Larrère is Professor of Philosophy at the University of Paris 1-Panthéon-Sorbonne (France). Her publications include *L'Invention de l'économie. Du droit naturel à la physiocratie* (1992); with Raphael Larrère, *Du bon Usage de la nature* (1997); and *Actualité de Montesquieu* (1999). In addition, she has published numerous papers (some of them in English) on two main issues – political philosophy and the history of political and economical ideas; and the ethics and politics of environment.

Klaus Luig is retired from the faculty of Law of the University of Cologne where he was Professor of Private Law, Roman Law, and History of Private Law in Modern Times. His books include *Zur Geschichte der Zessionslehre* (1966); a collection of essays under the title *Römisches Recht, Naturrecht, Nationales Recht* (1998); and *'...weil er nicht arischer Abstammung ist' – Jüdische Juristen in Köln während der NS-Zeit* (2004).

Ian Maclean is Professor of Renaissance Studies in the University of Oxford and Senior Research Fellow of All Souls College, Oxford. He is a Fellow of the British Academy. His books include *Woman Triumphant: feminism in French literature 1610–52* (1977); *The Renaissance Notion of Woman: a study in the fortunes of scholasticism and medical science in European intellectual life* (1980); *Meaning and Interpretation in the Renaissance: the case of law* (1992); *Montaigne philosophe* (1996); *Logic, Signs and Nature in the Renaissance: the case of learned medicine* (2001), *Le Monde et les hommes selon les médecins de la Renaissance* (2006); an edition of Girolamo Cardano's *De libris propriis* (2004); and a translation of René Descartes' *Discours de la methode* (2006).

Heinz Mohnhaupt, jurist and legal historian, is emeritus fellow of the Max Planck Institute for European Legal History in Frankfurt am Main. His research – documented in numerous publications – is now focused on the theory and practice of legal sources (above all, forms of legislation and jurisdiction), the history of constitutions and of legal terms, the history of comparison in the natural and human sciences; especially of the sixteenth to twentieth centuries.

Andreas Roth is Professor of Private Law and History of Law in the Johannes Gutenberg-University of Mainz; he was formerly Assistant Professor in the

Institute of History of Law in the Wilhelms-University of Münster. His books include *Kollektive Gewalt und Strafrecht. Die Geschichte der Massedelikte* (1989); *Kriminalitätsbekämpfung in deutschen Großstädten* (1997); *125 Jahre Amtsgerichte in Rheinland-Pfalz* (2004); and *Grundriss der Deutschen Rechtsgeschichte* (11th edition, 2006).

Sophie Roux is maître de conférences at the Université Grenoble II and a member of the Institut universitaire de France. Her publications as an editor include *Retours sur l'Affaire Sokal* (2006); with S. Carvallo, *Du Nouveau dans les sciences* (2006); with W.R. Laird, *Mechanics and Natural Philosophy before the Scientific Revolution* (2008); and, with M. Bucciantini and M. Camererota, *Mechanics and Cosmology* (2007). In collaboration with E. Festa, she is currently working on a critical edition, translation and commentary of the two versions of Galileo's *Le Mecaniche*.

Jan Schröder is Professor for German Legal History and Civil Law in the Eberhard-Karls-Universität Tübingen and an ordinary Member of the Academy of Sciences and Literature Mainz. His books include *Wissenschaftstheorie und Lehre der 'praktischen Jurisprudenz auf deutschen Universitäten an der Wende' zum 19. Jahrhundert* (1979); with Gerd Kleinheyer, *Deutsche und Europäische Juristen aus fünf Jahrhunderten* (4th edition 1996, Japanese edition 1983, Chinese edition 2005); *Justus Möser als Jurist* (1986); *Recht als Wissenschaft* (2001); and *Verzichtet unser Rechtssystem auf Gerechtigkeit?* (2005).

Friedrich Steinle is Professor of History of Science and Technology, and executive director of the 'Interdisciplinary Centre of Science and Technology Studies: normative and historical perspectives' at the University of Wuppertal (Germany). His research interests concern the history and philosophy of science, with a special focus on experiment, and case studies from the seventeenth to the nineteenth centuries. His books include *Newtons Manuskript 'De gravitatione'* (1991) and *Explorative Experimente: Ampère, Faraday und die Urspünge der Elektrodynamik* (2005); and he is co-editor, with M. Heidelberger, of *Experimental Essays – Versuche zum Experiment* (1998) and, with J. Schickore, of *Revisiting Discovery and Justification. Historical and philosophical perspectives on the context distinction* (2006).

Hubert Treiber is Professor of Administrative Sciences at the Leibniz University of Hannover (Germany). His publications include: as co-editor with Karol Sauerland, *Heidelberg im Schnittpunkt intellektueller Kreise* (1995); with Leonie Breunung, *Die Vollzugsorganisation als Entscheidungsfaktor des Verwaltungshandelns* (2000); with Gerd Graßhoff, *Naturgesetz und Naturrechtsdenken im 17. Jahrhundert* (2002); as editor and commentator, *Paul Rée: Gesammelte Werke 1875–1885* (2004, Supplementa Nietzscheana, vol. 7); with Heinz Steinert, *Die Fabrikation des zuverlässigen Menschen. Über die 'Wahlverwandtschaft' von Kloster- und Fabrikdisziplin* (2005); with Leonie Breunung, *Recht als Handlungsressource kommunaler Industrieansiedlungspolitik. Zum Gebrauch und Verzicht von Recht bei ungleicher Machtverteilung* (2005); and 'Der "Eranos" – Das Glanzstück im Heidelberger Mythenkranz?', in W. Schluchter and F.W. Graf (eds), *Asketischer*

Protestantismus und der 'Geist' des modernen Kapitalismus. Max Weber und Ernst Troeltsch (2005).

Anne-Charlott Trepp is currently guest professor at the Department of History, University at Göttingen. From 1994 to 2004 she was research scientist at the Max Planck Institute for History at Göttingen. Her books include *Natur als religiöse Praxis. Zum Verhältnis von Natur und Religion in der Frühen Neuzeit* (in press) and, as editor, *Antike Weisheit und kulturelle Praxis. Hermetismus in der Frühen Neuzeit* (2001) and *Im Zeichen der Krise. Religiosität im 17. Jahrhundert* (1999).

Catherine Wilson is Professor of Philosophy at the Graduate Center of the City University of New York. She specializes in seventeenth- and eighteenth-century history and philosophy of science. Her books include *Leibniz's Metaphysics* (1989); *The Invisible World* (1995); *Descartes's Meditations* (2003); and *Epicureanism at the Origins of Modernity* (2008).

Introduction

Nature, Law and Natural Law in Early Modern Europe

Lorraine Daston and Michael Stolleis

Natural Laws and Laws of Nature

This collection of essays began in a shared puzzlement among a group of historians of law and of science: was the efflorescence of natural law in both European jurisprudence and natural philosophy from circa the mid-sixteenth through the mid-eighteenth centuries merely a coincidence? Was the fact that so many early modern authors seemed to use terms such as *ius naturale* and *lex naturalis* (or *lex naturae*) roughly as synonyms and, perhaps more significantly, to use the same qualifying adjectives, such as 'certain' and 'universal', to modify the 'laws' from both realms just so much linguistic confusion? Or did these disciplinary traditions develop within a common conceptual matrix, in which theological, philosophical, and political arguments converged to make the analogy between legal and natural orders compelling? If so, what were the implications of this common matrix for the understanding of natural laws in each discipline? This book attempts to give preliminary answers to these questions, on hand from examples drawn from the history of law, science, philosophy, and theology.

To our knowledge, this is the first concerted attempt to address these questions from the standpoint of all these historical specialties. There exist impressive historiographies that examine the emergence and influence of natural law concepts in early modern jurisprudence and science,[1] respectively; there have also been some notable attempts to relate these developments to their theological and political backgrounds.[2] But, as historian of science John Henry has recently remarked, to date the historiographies 'of these two concepts of laws in nature have been largely

[1] The literature in both fields is too large to be comprehensively listed here, but for the history of law see Pollock 1922, Krause 1949, Tuck 1979, Ilting 1983, Stolleis 1987b, Pagden 1987, Bastit 1990, Haakonssen 1996, Brett 1997, Tierney 1997, Westerman 1998, Luig 1998, Scattola 1999, Hochstrasser 2000, Hunter 2001, Hunter and Saunders 2002, Hochstrasser and Schröder 2003; and for the history of science and philosophy, Zilsel 1942, Needham 1969, Milton 1981, Ruby 1986, Steinle 1995, Horowitz 1998, Milton 1998, Roux 2001, Henry 2004.

[2] Oakley 1961, Oakley 1984a, Oakley 1984b, Shapin 1981, Funkenstein 1986, Osler 1994, Oakley 1999.

separate'.[3] Given the formidable complexity of both fields, this separation is not surprising; hence the problem cries out for an interdisciplinary collaboration. The authors of the essays contained in this collection met twice (and in some cases, three times) to discuss their drafts with the entire group; the internal system of references (designated in the text [NAME]) bears witness to these interactions. Although the resulting book does not achieve a panoramic synthesis of all aspects of natural law in early modern Europe, it does reframe the problem. Generalizing from the individual essays, this introduction indicates the points where legal, scientific, philosophical, and theological views intersected and suggests directions for further enquiry. The volume as a whole is meant to be the first, not the last word on a new area of research.

The Problem

'Natural law' is an essential element of the conceptual vocabulary of modern science and philosophy; the term is also prominent, if perhaps less central, in modern jurisprudence. The term has ancient antecedents in both jurisprudence and natural philosophy, but only in the seventeenth century did it suddenly thrust itself onto centre stage in both realms. For at least a half-century, historians of law and science have wondered why the concept of natural law should have climbed to such rapid eminence in jurisprudence and natural philosophy in early modern Europe, after centuries of relative quiescence. They have wondered in parallel, both in the sense of lines never meeting but also following one another closely. In both law and science, historians have drawn attention to ancient roots and medieval precedents. Historians of law cite Aristotle in the *Nicomachean Ethics*, Cicero in *De legibus*, Romans 2:13–15 in the New Testament, Gratian in the *Decretum*, Aquinas in the *Summa theologiae* – all speak of a natural law that has normative force and is variously derived from universal human nature (in some formulations, such as that of Ulpian, what humans have in common with animals), the dictates imprinted by God in the human heart, or the participation of rational creatures in the divine *lex aeterna*.[4] For their part, historians of science point to Seneca's reference to a possible 'law' of comets in the *Questiones naturales*, Pliny's call for a 'law' of the maximum elongation of Venus and Mercury from the sun in the *Historia naturalis*, Roger Bacon's 'law' of refraction, and the *lex contradictionis* of thirteenth-century logic as evidence of a long lineage for the natural law concept in the sciences.[5]

But these long genealogies have complicated rather than simplified the historical problem of explaining the surge of natural law thinking in the early modern period: if the vocabulary and conceptual resources that went with it had been available for centuries, even millennia, why wait until the seventeenth century to exploit them on a grand scale and – the central question of this book – exploit them at the same time and the same places (and sometimes by the same people) in both jurisprudence and natural philosophy? It is this question of timing, as well as of intellectual

[3] Henry 2004: 74n.

[4] For a compact account of these sources, see Ilting 1983.

[5] Ruby 1986.

preconditions and implications, that has preoccupied the most recent historical treatments of the topic.

Various plausible explanations have been advanced. Historians of natural law and natural right theory in jurisprudence argue that these doctrines could be wielded as weapons in Reformation–Counter-Reformation polemics[6] and that they further promoted the interests of absolutist monarchies intent on overriding local customary law by centrally promulgated codes.[7] Others have suggested that the shock of academic scepticism, compounded by the evidence of the diversity of human custom reported by travellers to the Far East and the Far West, obliged jurists to seek more stable foundations, especially for international law.[8] Historians of science adduce the prominence of voluntarist theology among some of the leading figures in the Scientific Revolution, such as René Descartes, Robert Boyle, and Isaac Newton, and the corresponding emphasis on God as lawgiver to nature.[9] None of these claims is undisputed, and none of them comes to grips with the problem of *conjunction* in jurisprudence and natural philosophy: is it, for example, simply a further coincidence that the voluntarist theology first advanced in the fourteenth century by Duns Scotus and William of Ockham should be revived in natural philosophy at the same time Protestant jurists were eager to undermine the divine justification for natural law?

For historians of science, the perplexity is deepened by the apparent unsuitability of the terminology of law to describe inexorable, universal natural regularities. First, as sixteenth- and seventeenth-century writers on the subject repeatedly pointed out, it was difficult to understand how inanimate matter could be said to 'obey' laws in any but a metaphorical sense.[10] Second, laws, notoriously prone to inconsistency, variations, and violations, would seem a poor model for the allegedly immutable regularity of the natural order, resulting in an uneasiness that surfaced in protracted late seventeenth-century debates about miracles [Roux] and in early eighteenth-century contrasts between the well-ordered natural and comparatively unruly human realms [Larrere].[11] Third, early modern natural philosophers and, especially, mathematicians had a well-established, highly differentiated, alternative terminology which they could and often did use to describe natural regularities, including *regula*, *axioma*, *hypothesis*, *ratio*, *proportio* [Maclean, Steinle].[12] Why then turn to the problematic *lex*, and why did this term spread so quickly and so widely in the latter half of the seventeenth century?

One difficulty in tracing the terms *ius naturale*, *lex naturalis*, or *lex naturae* over centuries and millennia is that significant shifts in meaning can be overlooked. Hence not only the words themselves and the contexts in which they are applied, but also their lexical fields – the terms often used in association with the target terms – must be included in the philological dragnet. Careful attention to the semantic clusters

6 Hunter and Saunders 2002: 3.

7 Stolleis 1987a: 23.

8 Tuck 1987: 109f., Westerman 1998: 130; but cf. Tierney 1997: 321.

9 Milton 1981, Milton 1998.

10 Wilson 1987.

11 See, for example, Montesquieu [1748] 1845: 5.

12 Steinle 1995.

that accrete around these words in the early modern period reveals some intriguing patterns, albeit with disciplinary variations. Laws in both jurisprudence and natural philosophy were surrounded by a swarm of terms that were used mutually to define and modify one another, including *regulae*, *aphorismi*, *principia*, *maximae*, *ordo*, *hypotheses* [Maclean]. Many of these terms (aphorism, maxim, rule) referred to succinct statements of certain precepts, a suggestive anticipation of the standard version of the natural law in natural philosophy, which can almost always be stated in a single sentence or equation. Originally in astrological contexts, but increasingly in natural philosophy more broadly, words are used (for example, *fatum*) that suggest an ironclad determinism. In both jurisprudence and natural philosophy, laws aspire to 'certainty', in both epistemological (the degree to which they are known) and ontological (their unexceptioned reliability) senses [Mohnhaupt, Graßhoff]. Some luminaries of seventeenth-century natural philosophy, including Galileo, Mersenne, and Pascal, made almost no use of law terminology, preferring the mathematical vocabulary of axioms, theorems, hypotheses, and propositions to denote regularities. In both France and England, the 1660s seem to mark a sharp break, with 'law talk' diffusing broadly not only among natural philosophers affiliated with the Royal Society of London and the Paris Académie Royale des Sciences [Steinle], but also among philosophers and theologians such as Malebranche and Arnauld [Roux]. In several early modern disciplinary contexts, the terminology of law and its cloud of related terms was used to blur distinctions – between the natural and the moral, the descriptive and the prescriptive, the providential and the determined – in ways that were quite convenient for intellectuals trying to cope with an avalanche of novelties – geographical, religious, scientific, and political [Maclean]. These ambiguities were, if anything, magnified by the centrality of a providential order of nature, in which the order of nature had a soteriological as well as a philosophical significance [Trepp].

Given the diversity and complexity of contexts, there is unlikely to be any simple answer to the question as to why natural law became a concept to conjure with in either early modern jurisprudence or natural philosophy, much less in both; moreover, disciplinary and contextual specifics surely played a weighty role in both cases. But on the basis of the essays gathered in this volume, it is possible to single out several areas in which commonalities, interactions, and convergences between the two natural law traditions illuminate both.

We shall treat these under the rubrics of 'Order', 'Hierarchy', 'Epistemology', and 'Cause'. Taken together, these concepts sketch the contours of a shared, if often implicit framework for natural laws in early modern European natural philosophy, jurisprudence, moral philosophy, political theory, and theology. Natural laws in all these domains invoked an order legislated for the entire universe by a supreme authority (rather than immanent in specific natures); they stood at the apex of a hierarchy of regularities and ordinances, the latter being ideally derived, even deduced, from the former; most seventeenth-century thinkers believed natural laws could be discovered by reason alone, but by the turn of the eighteenth-century, more and more turned to empirical investigation of either nature or diverse cultures to find them out; natural laws forged the link between cause and effect in both the moral and natural realms. Natural laws were above all associated with a conceptual programme of foundationalism and universalism, the bedrock of an order that rested upon a few postulates – whether self-evident to reason or gleaned from wide experience – and that was valid everywhere and always. In jurisprudence, these issues were intertwined with far-reaching changes concerning the legitimation of laws; the overview essay by Michael Stolleis [Stolleis] should be read in tandem with this Introduction for a panoramic view of these developments.

Order

There are many ways of conceiving both social and natural orders, of which 'universal legality' is only one. And even among those who deployed the term 'law' to describe both orders, there is considerable latitude in what they meant by the term. So, for example, Stoic philosophers spoke of one single law of nature, in contrast to seventeenth-century notions of particular phenomena linked by general laws [Larrère]; the order defined by specific natures (including human nature), which stamp each thing with an ontological identity, or by the semina or essences postulated by some early modern Protestant natural philosophers [Trepp], contrasts with that formulated as a mathematical relationship between objects made of undifferentiated matter [Wilson], though both may invoke the language of 'laws'. Even if the sample is narrowed to late seventeenth-century natural philosophy, it is possible to find side-by-side (for example, in the pages of the *Philosophical Transactions of the Royal Society of London*) instances of 'law' used to refer to fundamental regularities derived from metaphysical first principles (for example, laws of motion) and to empirical correlations among observables (for example, between lunar phases and the weather) [Steinle, Daston]. Although variations in usage are not so striking in jurisprudence (if only because 'law' is too central a concept in this context to permit such liberties), here also significant shifts in meaning occur in the course of the early modern period: for example, from the requirement that a law must by definition be just to the more modest stipulation that it simply be an authoritative command [Schröder], with concomitant shifts in the legitimation of laws [Stolleis, Mohnhaupt].

Despite this variability, it is nonetheless possible to discern some aspects of an order of natural laws peculiar to the early modern period and common to both jurisprudence and natural philosophy. Although none of these features is present in every single case, together they sketch the outlines of a distinct kind of order, defined by certain, universal, and fundamental laws. In most, if not all cases this order is providential as well as predictable: that is, it has been instituted to fulfill divine purposes, whether or not further divine interventions subsequent to the creation are countenanced or not.

The phrase 'certain law' as a desideratum occurs frequently in both legal and scientific literature throughout the early modern period. Sixteenth-century jurists complain repeatedly that man-made laws were 'uncertain' – that is, confused, variable, and/or obscure – and many understood natural laws as the guarantors of certainty for all laws, including positive law [Mohnhaupt]. When Nikolaus Copernicus sought a 'certain law' to explain why the inner planets were never observed very far from the sun, he was not only echoing Pliny, but also drawing a contrast between 'certain laws' that simply saved the phenomena, as Ptolemaic 'hypotheses' had, and those that were additionally true [Graßhoff]. Laws could be certain in the sense that they could be specified with clarity and precision, that they held in each and every case, and/or that they were true. These three criteria converged in Leibniz's attempts, as jurist, mathematician, and natural philosopher, to derive a code of laws from human nature (or even from the laws of motion in mechanics), laws which would enjoy the same degree of certainty as mathematics or physics [Luig]. Although Leibniz may have been unusual in spanning several disciplines and in his conviction of the unity of *ius naturale* and *lex naturalis*, he was not anomalous in associating natural laws in both domains with certainty.

Leibniz was also typical in asserting that, in jurisprudence, natural law trumped positive law (although the former may need to be supplemented by the latter) [Luig]. Although some sixteenth-century writers, such as Melancthon, reserved the terminology of 'law', with its resonances of certainty, for the celestial realm in which the regular motions of the stars and planets were unperturbed by generation or corruption [Kusukawa], there was a strong tendency in both jurisprudence and natural philosophy to assert universal jurisdiction for natural laws, as opposed to other, more local, laws and regularities. This had always been explicit in ancient Roman and medieval accounts of natural law in jurisprudence, despite somewhat differing rationales: the *Digest* (D.1.1) stated: 'Natural law [*ius naturale*] is that which nature teaches all animals.' In Roman law of the republican era, however, universality did not necessarily imply that natural law superseded civil law in cases of conflict between the two: slavery was, for example, admitted to be contrary to natural law but nonetheless wholly legitimate according to civil law.[13] It was under the influence of Christian doctrines of natural law as divine edict, reinforced by stoic teachings of nature's pre-eminence, that universality came to imply superiority in a hierarchy of norms; Augustine's arguments against sodomy as an affront to God as the author of nature anticipate that many of his readers would find it counterintuitive to assert that a crime *contra naturam* should be punished even in those locales where it had long been sanctioned by custom [Roth].[14] Medieval Christian sources, most famously Aquinas in his account of natural law as the participation of rational creatures in God's eternal law [Armogathe], consolidated not only the universality but also the precedence of natural law over positive law in jurisprudence. Seventeenth-century theorists of natural law in natural philosophy adopted these precepts of universality and precedence.

They also assumed that natural laws were fundamental laws, in the sense of assuming that other, more local laws could be derived from them. This was not a necessary implication of universality and precedence; it was conceivable that natural laws and municipal laws (as Robert Boyle called regularities of more limited purview) might simply exist side-by-side, as *ius gentium* did with local custom. The impulse to systematization, with natural law supplying the first principles, was notably strong in both seventeenth-century jurisprudence and natural philosophy. In the case of jurisprudence, this impulse often took the form of codification of

13 Thomas 1991: 203.

14 Augustine 1912: III.8, 1:127–133.

laws, and it is suggestive that natural philosophers who were legally trained, such as Francis Bacon and Leibniz, were often involved in such attempts [LUIG].[15] The sense of 'derivation' was however subject to variation. Leibniz seems to have believed that his derivations of a code of law enjoyed demonstrative certainty, and may have had as a model Descartes' derivations of physical consequences from the 'laws of motion' in the *Principia philosophiae* (1644). Richard Cumberland seems to have entertained similar ambitions for his attempts to derive a code of natural laws of the moral realm from a mechanistic account of the rewards and punishments built into the world by God [TREIBER]. The rigour of particular derivations was challenged by contemporaries, but the model of a foundation of axioms or principles or natural laws– whether in jurisprudence or natural philosophy – upon which was erected an elaborate edifice of consequences proved irresistibly attractive in precept, however often it failed in practice.

Hierarchy

Foundationalist arguments by definition assume a firm base which supports their conclusions. Not all forms of legitimation in either jurisprudence or natural philosophy make this assumption: in both Aristotelian and certain other strands of early modern natural philosophy, regularities were conceived in terms of observable generalizations and the essential natures of species [WILSON, TREPP]; Roman law was justified by imperial authority [STOLLEIS]. It is hence a noteworthy aspect of natural law doctrines in the early modern period that so many of them were set forth in foundationalist terms. In these self-consciously systematic systems, the 'laws of nature' played a role analogous to the axioms and postulates in Euclidean geometry: they were the undeniable basis and departure point for all the derivations that followed. As noted above, there was considerable latitude in how the derivations proceeded, although claims for rigour or even necessity were frequently advanced, by Hobbes in the *Leviathan* no less than Descartes in the *Principia philosophiae*. But, regardless of the character of the initial axioms or laws and the actual mode of derivation, all of these systems aspired to a kind of inverse pyramid structure, in which the greatest number of conclusions (be they natural phenomena or directives for human conduct) flowed from the fewest number of natural laws – a structure reminiscent of ancient atomist systems like those of Epicurus and Lucretius [WILSON].

Although God was often invoked as the legislator who decreed these laws [STOLLEIS, ARMOGATHE], whether of motion or of self-preservation, the ways in which natural laws related to their consequences in early modern jurisprudence and natural philosophy diverged sharply from the model of divine creation. The Christian God created and sustained the world by the imposition of laws by fiat, an act of will that accomplished and legitimated all that followed. In contrast, early modern natural law theorists of all stripes were at least as concerned with the process of derivation of 'all that followed' as they were with the specification of the laws themselves. The laws were often controversial, as in the case of Descartes' laws of collision or

[15] Steinle 1995: 331–333.

Grotius's principle of human sociability, and there were heated debates between rationalists and voluntarists as to how much freedom God enjoyed in the choice of which laws to impose [Roux]. But the viability of a system also depended on which consequences were asserted to follow from these laws and how they were asserted to follow. Because natural philosophers (Descartes) and jurists (Leibniz) of even the most deductive cast were forced to admit that natural laws alone were insufficient to explain the variability observed in both the natural and moral realms [Daston, Larrère], they created hierarchies within their systems, in which fundamental natural laws had to be supplemented by more specific rules in order to be applied to specific cases.

Jurists within a scholastic tradition had long been accustomed to imagining a hierarchy of divine, natural, and positive law [Stolleis] and to harmonizing or modifying universal laws to accord with local circumstances.[16] What is striking about the seventeenth-century use of natural law talk in natural philosophy is the degree to which the legal language of a hierarchy among laws was taken over lock, stock, and barrel. Sixteenth-century natural philosophers had formulated ideas of hierarchy without recourse to such legal metaphors, as in the case of the Paduan philosopher Jacopo Zabarella's distinction between universal natures (which impose ultimate goals on things in general) and particular natures (which conserve the individual thing) [Kusukawa]. When Boyle wished to express a similar idea approximately a century later, however, he appealed to a 'scale of causes', in which the fundamental 'laws of nature' (in this case, the laws of motion and impact that applied to all bodies) were extended by means of 'municipal laws' governing the various different kinds of bodies.[17] This terminology echoed that of Bacon's talk of universal 'laws of nature' versus mere 'habits' (*consuetudines naturae*) that governed locally, and it is perhaps not so surprising that a trained jurist like Bacon would reach for such metaphors [Steinle]. Leibniz, another natural philosopher with a legal background, also wrote of the relationship between individual laws (that is, the natures of individual substances) and the universal laws of nature [Roux]. But these cases of individual multidisciplinarity do not explain the appeal of this legalistic way of understanding the hierarchy of causes among later natural philosophers like Boyle, whose usage of the vocabulary of natural laws owed at least as much to Descartes' *regulae sive leges naturae* of motion and impact,[18] derived from God's immutability, as to Bacon.

Other ways of talking about the relationship between levels in the hierarchy made a distinction between the universal and fundamental 'laws' of nature (usually equated with the laws of motion, following Descartes) and the lower-level phenomenological 'rules' that described specific phenomena. The English natural philosopher and astronomer Edmund Halley, for example, distinguished between the 'Laws of Staticks' and the 'General Rules' that accounted for regular patterns in the prevailing winds [Daston]. Especially among Fellows of the Royal Society of London in the late seventeenth century, there was, however, a tendency to use 'rule', 'principle', and 'law' as rough synonyms for one another, thereby erasing distinctions among

16 For example, Conring's 1670 letter to Leibniz: see Hochstrasser 2000: 48.

17 Steinle 1995: 337.

18 Descartes [1644] 1982: II.xxxvii, VIII-I: 62.

levels in the hierarchy. Savants at the Paris Académie Royale des Sciences, perhaps following the lead of their head, Christiaan Huygens, preferred locutions such as *règle*, *principe*, and *proposition* to *loi*, albeit with a similar penchant for stratification of levels of generality [STEINLE]. In his epoch-making *Principia mathematica philosophiae naturalis* (1687), Isaac Newton used the term 'law' to refer both to axiomatic principles and empirical regularities [STEINLE], thereby promoting the trend, already strong among other members of the Royal Society, to enlarge the scope of law talk in natural philosophy and to blur the levels of the hierarchy, which an earlier, more differentiated vocabulary of 'universal' and 'municipal laws' or 'laws' and 'rules' had picked out. By the mid-eighteenth century, 'natural law' had become the blanket term in natural philosophy for almost any kind of regularity, whether fundamental or not; in natural law jurisprudence, it retained pride of place, but lost divine authority as jurists became increasingly reluctant in the period c. 1650–1800 to appeal to God as the direct source of law [SCHRÖDER, LARRÈRE].

Epistemology

One reason for the jurists' hesitation in this matter was doubt about the ability to know God's will without revelation. The question of how humans come to know natural law was one posed with growing urgency by both jurists and natural philosophers in the course of the seventeenth century, especially by those who subscribed to voluntarist theologies that blocked attempts to constrain divine choice by reason. By no means all natural law theorists upheld divine will over reason – Leibniz was a notable and influential opponent of the voluntarists on both legal and natural philosophical fronts [LUIG, ROUX]. Even among the professed voluntarists, it was possible to appeal to God's immutability and benevolence as a guarantee of human ability to know natural laws by reason alone, as Descartes did. Nonetheless, the image of *Deus legislator*, reinforced by biblical exegesis, remained powerful throughout the seventeenth century, as did the assumption that natural laws must somehow be promulgated [ARMOGATHE]. Hence Boyle, who otherwise followed Descartes rather closely in his conceptions of how universal laws of motion grounded the rest of the mechanical philosophy, protested against Descartes' a-priori derivation of the laws of impact as a denial of divine free will.[19]

Within the Thomist tradition in jurisprudence, access via reason was built into the very definition of natural law as the participation of rational creatures in God's eternal law by means of 'natural light' [SCHRÖDER, ARMOGATHE], a phrase that turned up suggestively in several key seventeenth-century philosophical texts, including Descartes' *Principia philosophiae*.[20] Indeed, the claim that law was reason implanted by nature reached back to Cicero.[21] Although he turned it to very different ends, Hobbes also appealed to reason as the source of *lex naturalis*, defined as 'a Precept, or generall Rule, found out by Reason, by which a man is forbidden to do, that, which is destructive of his life; or taketh away the means of preserving same; and to omit,

[19] Steinle 1995: 338.

[20] Descartes [1644] 1982: I.xx, VIII-I: 12.

[21] Cicero 1994: I.v.18, 317.

that, by which he thinketh it may be best preserved'.[22] According to Descartes, the laws of motion were known in a fashion analogous to mathematical truths: although neither was necessary in an absolute sense (God might have chosen otherwise), they were nonetheless imprinted by God in the human mind and were hence necessary for us [Roux, Steinle]. This line of thought could lead to a subtly different epistemology of natural law, especially in jurisprudence: natural laws might be derived by the a priori exercise of reason from human *nature*, but not necessarily from human *reason*, resulting in a kind of psychologism of mental universals. It was a short step to Samuel Pufendorf's rejection of innate natural laws (relativizing Romans 2:15 as merely figurative) and insistence on the importance of the cultivation of the soul (*cultura animi*) in formulating such complicated concepts. As Leibniz recognized, the rationality of natural law in jurisprudence was endangered by all such arguments based on human nature, even if they were themselves rationalist in approach (rather than empirical, proceeding from ethnographic evidence).[23]

One might argue that such psychological construals of human nature as the source of natural law were empiricist in spirit, even if they did not actually involve investigation of data. Genuinely empirical arguments, proceeding from the large and growing corpus of ethnographic reports available to early modern Europeans as a result of the voyages of discovery, appear to have been rare in natural law jurisprudence. In the sixteenth century, the practices of other cultures were cited in the controversy over whether bigamy was a crime against nature [Roth]. But by the mid-seventeenth century, if ethnographic evidence was cited, it was usually to undermine the claim that something like universal natural laws of human conduct existed, as in the case of John Locke [Daston]. Montesquieu took the diversity of human customs to contradict the claims of moral philosophers like the Abbé Saint-Pierre that natural laws governed the moral realm with the same necessity as they ruled that of physical nature [Larrère].

In natural philosophy, the shift from rational to empirical inquiry into the laws of nature began in the 1660s and gathered force thereafter [Steinle]. In some quarters, metaphysical or theological reasons could be given for this a posteriori approach, as in the case of Nicholas Malebranche's occasionalist claim that, since things do not have constant natures, natural laws can only be discerned as constant relations [Roux]. But the principal source of pressure came from the growing ambitions of natural philosophical inquiry itself, intent on subsuming ever more phenomena under natural laws, including such unpromising domains as the weather, even at the cost of devaluing natural laws into mere empirical regularities [Steinle, Daston]. As already noted, this expansionist programme also eventually subverted the foundationalist hierarchies so characteristic of natural law approaches to both jurisprudence and natural philosophy in the first half of the seventeenth century. In the same way that the jurists' reluctance to ground natural law in divine edicts led to a collapse of natural law legislated by God into positive law by the late eighteenth century [Stolleis, Schröder], so the drive within natural philosophy to embrace the most variable phenomena within the framework of natural law led to a collapse

22 Hobbes [1651] 1985: I.xiv, 189.

23 Hochstrasser 2000: 80–89.

of divinely ordained natural laws discoverable by reason into Humean constant correlations.

Causes

In both early modern jurisprudence and natural philosophy, natural laws became ever more closely associated with causes of both human conduct and physical effects. These transformations profoundly modified earlier understandings of natural law, with implications for conceptions of order and epistemology. The term law implied a lawgiver, who commanded or imposed (an ambiguity created by extending natural laws to inanimate objects) edicts upon subjects, *Deus legislator* [ARMOGATHE]. Because the medieval legal model of natural law, at least in its Thomist articulation, assumed the insight and consent of rational creatures, there was no further need for an additional causal account of how the laws came to be obeyed. Although violations of natural laws were possible, as in the case of crimes *contra naturam* [ROTH], they were by definition aberrations from reason. Moreover, both Aristotelian and Christian providentialist understandings of chance tended to thwart exclusively deterministic accounts of causes in the natural as well as the moral orders. Chance was defined not just as the absence of a cause, but as the absence of a final cause, that is, as lacking an end, and could therefore (paradoxically by modern lights) be used as a near-synonym for 'blind necessity'. Providentialist attacks on Epicurean philosophy were aimed at contingency *and* necessity, both equally repellent to a view of the universe in which everything had a divine purpose, as well as material and efficient causes [WILSON, KUSUKAWA]. Finally, the sciences in which the language of 'certain laws' had figured most prominently since at least the thirteenth century, namely the mathematical sciences of astronomy and optics,[24] had been mostly divorced from natural philosophy, which sought the causes of natural phenomena.[25]

Hence it was an innovation of the first magnitude to connect natural laws with causal explanations, whether these appealed to the hidden springs and principles of human nature or to the physical forces between moving bodies. In astronomy, Copernicus seems to have self-consciously abandoned Ptolemaic mathematical 'hypotheses', which accounted for the observed motions of heavenly bodies but made no claim to physical reality, for true 'certain laws', a distinction Johannes Kepler pursued with a vengeance in his quest for an explanation of the orbit of Mars [GRAßHOFF]. Descartes' laws of motion and impact were meant to supply the causes of the phenomena explained in the *Principia philosophiae*, not just the mathematical presuppositions from which results in rational mechanics might be deduced, in the manner of the Latin demonstrations of Galileo's *Discorsi* (1638). Analogously, more psychological accounts of natural laws, such as Hugo Grotius' and Pufendorf's appeals to human sociability, sketched a causal account of why and how natural laws operated in the world and were at the same time pointedly noncommital about divine origins and enforcement. But, even among jurists who retained God as the *fons et*

---

[24] Ruby 1986.

[25] Henry 2004: 92.

origo of natural law, such as Cumberland and Leibniz, the derivation and operation of the laws invoked causal factors – a built-in system of rewards and punishments in Cumberland's case and the laws of motion in that of Leibniz – that went beyond divine fiat [Treiber, Luig].

Natural laws had become the glue that joined cause and effect in both the natural and moral realm. One sign of their causal character was the debate joined on several fronts – theological and natural philosophical – in the late seventeenth and early eighteenth centuries over miracles [Roux]. Since at least the thirteenth century, it had been conceptually possible, if not entirely unproblematic, to imagine God's extraordinary providence superseding his ordinary providence, and in any case medieval natural philosophers had deemed not only supernatural but also preternatural occurrences to be beyond their explanatory writ.[26] Once natural laws were conceived to be themselves causally efficacious, it was more difficult to comprehend how God could suspend his own dictates, without compromising the order of the entire universe. Even staunch voluntarists like Boyle and Newton ended up conceding that, although God could in principle intervene in the causal nexus of natural laws, he rarely if ever did so – Boyle going so far as to assert that the uniformity of natural laws was a higher priority for God than the welfare of his creatures [Daston]. And once natural laws in jurisprudence were equated with the causes of human conduct, the category of crimes *contra naturam*, which were perverse rather than miraculous, began to lose its coherence, eventually melting into the rest of criminal law [Roth].

In the early decades of the eighteenth century, jurists and natural philosophers made an ever sharper distinction between the natural and moral realms, and between the kinds of regularities that governed each. Although the moral sciences of the Enlightenment might seek their Newton in Montesquieu or Hume [Larrère], nothing like Newton's 'axioms or laws of motion' and the consequences that were believed to flow inexorably from them were envisioned. The more stringent understanding of causal connection that had been the issue of the union between natural philosophy and the mathematical sciences seemed ill-suited for the looser regularities of human conduct. 'Natural laws' in jurisprudence and 'laws of nature' in natural philosophy came to seem more and more like homonyms rather than synonyms. Yet resonances between the two persisted, still clearly audible in the late eighteenth-century declarations of universal rights issued by the American and French Revolutions, which invoked the authority of the natural order to reform the moral order. These were the faint echoes of a shared history.

[26] Daston and Park 1998: 109–134.

Chapter 1

From Limits to Laws: The Construction of the Nomological Image of Nature in Early Modern Philosophy

Catherine Wilson

Introduction

By the mid-eighteenth century, it was common to represent Nature, considered as an object of theoretical inquiry, as a collection of laws and law-governed entities. According to the Comte de Buffon: 'La Nature est le système des lois éternels etablies par le créateur, pour l'existence des choses et pour la succession des êtres.'[1] The identification of knowledge of nature with knowledge of nature's laws prompted inquiry into dependencies of the most qualitative and speculative forms: laws of the union of soul and body, laws of compensation spanning the physical and moral realms, and laws of historical evolution.[LARRÈRE]. The subsequent entrenchment of the law concept in the philosophy of science over the next two centuries was profound, even with the loosening of its deterministic connotations with the introduction of statistical mechanics and thermodynamics.[2] The view that scientific explanation – including explanation in the social sciences and even in history – implied deduction from general laws gave support to a picture of scientific inquiry as specially dedicated to the discovery of previously unknown laws of the natural and social world,[3] and the historiography of science reflected this understanding.

The representation of nature as a domain ruled by or constituted by its laws is undoubtedly related to seventeenth-century discoveries in what Thomas Kuhn has designated as the classical or mathematical sciences – astronomy, optics, statics and hydrostatics, and music, to which mechanics and dynamics were later added.[4]

---

[1] The naturalist G.-L.L. Buffon (1707–1788) and S.A. Tissot (1728–1797), an author of popular medical works ('La nature est l'existence des choses soumise a des lois universelles'), are quoted prominently in *Larousse Encyclopédie générale* 1982: XI (2), 860, which defines Nature as 'puissance, force active, crée ou non, qui a etabli l'ordre de l'univers, et qui le conserve en vertu de certaines lois'. For an overview of definitions of nature and associated contests, see Leinkauf 2000.

[2] The probabilistic revolution in a number of fields is detailed in Gigerenzer et al. 1990.

[3] Hempel and Oppenheim (1948) proposed that to explain an occurrence was logically to deduce it from premises containing at least one law of nature.

[4] Kuhn 1977.

Within a hundred years, Kepler's three rules of planetary motion, Galileo's law of falling bodies, Descartes' laws of motion and his rules of collision, emended by Huygens and Wallis, Snell's law of the refraction of the light ray, Boyle's law of gases, and Newton's inverse-square law make their debuts. They are held to confirm, in the first instance, the wisdom and power of the Creator; later, the genius of their discoverers.

The concept of a law of nature has several paradoxical features that belie its seeming robustness. Contemporary philosophers of science regard the laws of nature as well-confirmed general statements about the behaviour or properties of some type of entity, or as well-confirmed general statements relating two or more variables or constants. Unlike a mere accidental generalization, a law of nature is thought to have counterfactual implications, and to presuppose certain idealized conditions free of interference. But why call such logically, semantically, and pragmatically unusual statements 'laws' when the laws of the land – the original laws of human experience – do not possess these characteristics? And how were our early modern predecessors, who had no explicit understanding of these logico-linguistic niceties, able to characterize some statements correctly as stating laws of nature?

Another difficulty is this: On the one hand, we are inclined to believe that it was not always known that there *were* laws of nature and that scientific inquiry is a search for fundamental laws. Historically, there have existed a number of conceptions of systematic inquiry into nature, for example, Aristotelian or Paracelsian, or Baconian, that were formulated without reference to the discovery of laws of nature, but instead by reference to discovery of logical relations, or essences, correspondences, or 'Forms'. The existence of laws and their importance in scientific discourse was a fact that, like other facts, had, it seems, to be discovered by experimentation with the possible forms of science, by a process of trial and error with respect to the aims and methods of inquiry. On the other hand, the nomological conception of nature seems to be an invention and not a discovery at all. Inanimate objects, as was first pointed out by Lactantius in the fourth century, cannot enter into civil relations. The notion of a universal *physical* law of nature must be a metaphor, not to be taken literally. But how can the lawfulness of physical nature be both the outcome of a lengthy historical experiment with different styles of inquiry and the imposition of the imagination?

This essay will try to shed light on these questions by offering a historical account of the introduction of the law of nature concept in the seventeenth century, showing how its separate and independent strands came together in certain texts to fashion the nomological image of Nature expressed in the definitions above. These separate strands consisted of the appreciation of natural regularities, the posit of a providential supervisor, the hypothesis of qualitatively undifferentiated basic units of matter (atoms, corpuscles), the rejection of chance or hazard, and – critically – the discovery that not just the actions of *light*, but also those of its supposed antithesis, *matter*, could be described by quantitative and relational 'rules'. In view of its tangled origins, it is not surprising that the very idea of a law of nature has never managed to extricate itself from the charge that it is philosophically incoherent.

Order without Laws in Ancient Natural Philosophy

The notion of a law of nature appears only rarely and not programmatically in ancient writings.[5] There are several likely explanations – terminological and conceptual – why 'nature' and 'law' do not take up nearby places in ancient texts, despite the interest of philosophers in natural necessity and in observed regularities.

First, it is often pointed out that the ancients were impressed by the distinction between *physis* and *nomos*: the realm of the natural and the realm of the normative, and a salient feature of laws for the ancients (with the exception of Stoic natural law, mentioned below) was that they were not universal, but local and conventional.[6] But the *physis-nomos* distinction explains at best a terminological gap. The absence of a law-concept, called by whatever name, needs a different sort of explanation. Might not the recognition of the fact that fire tends to move upwards and a stone downwards be considered as an acknowledgment of lawlike behaviour, even if formulated in the language of *physis* or potentials? Aristotle after all observed that, while some occurrences are 'spontaneous' or 'due to chance', others 'always come to pass in the same way, and others for the most part'.[7]

Another contributing reason for the absence of a law-concept in ancient natural philosophy is that for Plato, Aristotle and the Stoics, the distinction between ideal order and rough actuality is conceived as a distinction between celestial and the terrestrial realms, not between observations made within controlled experiments and passive observation, nor between mathematical models and data-sets. Orderliness descends from higher to lower and is lost as one moves from higher causes to lower effects. The regular motion of the heavenly bodies causes the regular (but still slightly unpredictable) succession of the seasons; the seasons bring about the (still more unpredictable) weather; and the weather influences the (very unpredictable) growth of crops and increase of flocks.

Epicureanism, the original 'mechanical philosophy,' rejected top-down accounts of order, but it did not furnish an exception to the generalization that ancient natural philosophy does not mediate order through laws. As A.A. Long points out, later Epicureanism is deterministic and form-preserving in its overall intention. Lucretius frequently refers to nature under the description '*certa*', best interpreted as 'definite', for example, *certa ratio, certa semina, certa genetrix, certum tempus* and so on.[8] At the same time, the atomists were motivated to downplay the theme of natural order to strengthen their theological scepticism.

The atoms, according to Epicurus, move with equal speed regardless of size provided they meet with no obstruction or resistance. Their actual motions are a (seemingly unpredictable) function of upward and lateral motions on account of

---

5 Bobzien 1998: 373.

6 So Aristotle contrasts (with some qualifications) the local conventions of justice with the ubiquitous power of fire: 'Whereas … fire burns [us] both here and in Persia, rules of justice seem to vary …' (Aristotle 1963: 1134). The Hardie and Gaye translation of this passage imposes the anachronistic term 'law of nature'. The ascription to Aristotle of a law-based philosophy of science was once common; see Whitehead 1933:142–147.

7 Aristotle 1930: 196b.

8 Long 1977.

collisions and a downward motion due to weight. Collision between the atoms does not affect their speed. However, 'weight' and 'obstruction' do.[9] As might be expected, Epicurus' astronomy was less impressive than his terrestrial meteorology. He insisted in his *Epistle on Physics* that 'in the sky revolutions, solstices, eclipses, risings and settings and the like, take place without the ministration or command, either now or in the future, of any being who at the same time enjoys perfect bliss along with immortality'.[10] He conjured up mechanisms, processes of friction, pressure, tearing, compression, collision, and congelation – useful for explaining thunder, lightening, rain, hail and snow, but useless in accounting for the pathways of celestial objects in the night sky. Nor did Epicurus insist on the uniformity of nature. Other worlds may be dissimilar to ours, he thought, with different plants and animals.[11]

The system of Titus Lucretius Carus developed in his Latin poem of c. 55 BCE, *De rerum natura* and presumed to follow a lost treatise of Epicurus', employed the order concepts noted by Long, but defended mechanism and materialism without any substantial help from the concept of a law of nature. In this treatise known to and cited by every early modern philosopher of note, Lucretius provided a comprehensive account of physical, psychological, and even historical phenomena, encompassing colour vision, the weather, epidemics, the formation of government and the social contract, dreams, love, and death, as well as describing the origins of our world and all the other worlds in the cosmos. All phenomena supervene on the motions of atoms, and the philosophical fundamentals of matter and motion are discussed at some length. Lucretius followed his predecessor in maintaining that '[The atoms] must be carried with equal speed, although not of equal weight, through the unresisting void.'[12] (He remarked, displaying a more quantitative perspective than his master, that 'all weights naturally thrust downward; but when a blow is added, the velocity is doubled, and that first impulse grows heavier…'[13]) At the same time, Lucretius was an indeterminist or at least vague about the motion of individual atoms: 'Motions have some cause other than blows and weights.'[14] Both he and Epicurus ascribed to them a swerve, not only to preserve the mind's freedom, but lest their overall tendency to move downwards eventually bring the universe to a condition of stasis.[15] Though the manifest order supervenes on the motions of the atoms, there is no latent order, only 'secret and unseen motions.'[16] '[T]his world was made by nature, and the seeds of things themselves of their own accord, knocking together by chance, clashed in all sorts of ways, heedless, without aim, until at length those combined which, suddenly thrown together, could become in each case the beginnings of mighty things …'[17]

---

9 Diogenes Laertius 1931: (2) 593.
10 Ibid.: (2) 607.
11 Ibid.: (2) 605.
12 Lucretius 1975: 114.
13 Ibid.: 519.
14 Ibid.: 117.
15 Ibid.: 119.
16 Ibid.: 105.
17 Ibid.: 177.

How is it possible that such motions can produce a visible, stable order? Why isn't the universe simply a confused, structureless chaos, as is suggested by the image of the minute particles in '*solis radiis turbare videntur*'?[18] Although his poetic imagination was captured by variety and change, the problem of the basis for the order of nature was clearly worrying to Lucretius, for he had many ingenious solutions to it.

One of his responses was to deny the supposed phenomenon to be explained. The universe is not after all as orderly as some suppose; it does not show the markings of a divine creative intelligence and has rather a good deal of ugliness and ungainliness.[19] Every bit of observed structure is temporary; and, from the perspective of the universe, short-lived. All objects, from monuments to human minds to entire worlds, come into being from a chaotic swirl of material and dissolve again into particles.[20] A second form of response involves selection: unstable or nonfunctional forms are quickly eliminated; those adapted to their surroundings persist longer.[21]

Lucretius' other answers were structural. Combinations of a few atoms seem to provide a framework on which other atoms can hang, like objects caught in a net, or trapped in a filter, or swept up in a whirlpool, or stuck on like snow to a snowball. Or, stable forms emerge from seeds that are initially differentiated and that can give rise only to particular types of beings. In this context, Lucretius referred several times to 'laws'.

> We see that all things bred from fixed seeds by a fixed mother are able to conserve their kind as they grow. Assuredly this must come about in a fixed way [*certa ratione*] … Do not think that animals only are held by these laws [*legibus*], for the same principle holds all things apart by their limits [*eadem ratio disterminat omnia*]. For just as all things made are in their whole nature different from one another, so each must consist of first-beginnings differently shaped … Since the seeds are different, different must be their intervals, passages, connexions, weights, blows, meetings, motions …[22]

A fourth answer was that 'each thing has limited power and a deep-set boundary mark' [*ratione atque alte terminus*],[23] and a fifth answer is that patterning is a

---

[18] Ibid.: 105: '[S]uch turmoil [as is seen in the motes in a sunbeam] indicates that there are secret and unseen motions also hidden in matter.'

[19] Ibid.: 395.

[20] Ibid.: 411: 'For certainly neither did the first-beginnings place themselves by design each in its own order with keen intelligence, nor assuredly did they make agreement what motions each should produce, but because, being many and shifted in many ways they are harried and set in motion with blows throughout the universe from infinity, thus by trying every kind of motion and combination, at length they fall into such arrangements as this sum of things consists of …'

[21] Ibid.: 445f.

[22] Ibid.: 151.

[23] Ibid.: 385. Cf. ibid.: 49: '[A] limit has been fixed for the growth of things after their kind and for their tenure of life, and … it stands decreed what each can do by the ordinances of nature, and also what each cannot do, and … nothing changes, but all things are constant to such a degree that all the different birds show in succession marks upon their bodies to distinguish their kind …'

consequence of the *foedera naturae*: '[T]he various kinds of plants and the corn and the luxuriant trees, which even now spring in abundance from the earth, nevertheless cannot be produced interwoven together, but each thing proceeds after its own fashion, and all by fixed law of nature [*foedere naturae certo*] preserve their distinctions.'[24] But only in the following passage is there even a hint of the modern notion that the appearances – whether orderly or disorderly to human eyes – at the manifest level are a function of the fixed behaviour of invisible entities:

> In whatsoever motion the bodies of the first-beginnings are now, in that same motion they were in ages gone by and hereafter they will always be carried along in the same way, and the things which have been accustomed to be born will be born under the same conditions; they will be and will grow and will be strong with their strength as much as is granted to each by the laws of nature [again: *per foedera naturai*].[25]

The nearest approach to the modern conception of nature as lawful was to be found in Cicero's writings. By way of making his case for a benevolent Providence in his critique of Epicureanism in *De natura deorum*, Cicero employed the language of administration, rule, subjecthood and obedience that the later Christian opponents of atomism found so congenial. He remained wedded to the notion that perfect order pertains to the celestial regions only, not to the realm below the moon:

> In the heavens therefore there is nothing of chance or hazard, no error, no frustration, but absolute order, accuracy, calculation and regularity. Whatever lacks these qualities, whatever is false and spurious and full of error, belongs to the region between the earth and the moon … and to the surface of the earth.[26]

It is not *nature*, Cicero emphasized, that 'rules the sky, sea and land'. On the contrary, 'Nothing exists that is superior to god; it follows therefore that the world is ruled by him; therefore god is not obedient or subject to any form of nature, and therefore he himself rules all nature.'[27] On Cicero's conception, sky, sea and land are all 'obedient and subject'. The elements of which they are composed do not, however, perform stereotyped actions, any more than the builders of a beautiful edifice do; they are commanded to do whatever is necessary to ensure the outcome. Accordingly, the visible order does not supervene on a hidden one. 'Thus the parts of the world are held in union by the constant passage up and down, to and fro, of these four elements of which all things are composed. And this world structure must either be everlasting in the same form in which we see it, or at all events extremely durable.'[28]

The Stoics posited laws of nature in an ethico-legal sense, rules of right conduct and statements of rights that they held pertained to all humanity and were superior in force of obligation to any positive and merely local law. Civil laws, in their view, borrowed what authority they had from the natural law, as opposed to the force

---

24 Lucretius 1975: 451.

25 Ibid.: 119.

26 Cicero 1951: 177.

27 Ibid.: 197. Cicero does however refer to nature as 'ruling'; hence the suspicion of Christian commentators that Stoicism is simply pantheistic nature-philosophy. Cf. ibid.: 205.

28 Ibid.: 205.

of magistrates and rulers. Laws of nature in this sense included the obligations to abstain from theft, murder, and unusual sexual practices, to obey one's superiors, honour one's parents, feed one's children, assist the needy, and to practise charity and fidelity.[29] Though the hypothesis that the natural law concept as it applied to the moral realm was somehow 'transferred' to the physical realm is an attractive one, there is scant direct evidence for it. The laws of nature in the moral sense appear to belong to a separate strand of intellectual history. Though Hobbes, for example, maintained that he was articulating a civil science parallel to natural science, he did not take advantage of the opportunity to draw a parallel between his moral laws and, say, the Galilean laws of motion. The 'Lawes of Nature' he cites in *Leviathan* (Chs. XIV, XV), are somewhat original statements of rights and obligations: resources should be shared equitably, people ought not to be insulted, and so on. His opponent, Richard Cumberland, *De legibus naturae* (1672), similarly understood the laws of nature merely as obligations, objecting to Hobbes's omission of benevolence and piety. A later 'backward' conceptual transfer from the physical to the moral realm can be more easily demonstrated. When Locke raised the possibility that there might be novel moral and civil regulations for human reason to discover, he did so by appealing to the new notion of nature as a realm ordered by laws.[30]

The Fathers of the Early Church followed the Ciceronian line on Providence, joining in the attack on Epicurean conception of nature. Lucretius' *foedera naturae* was sharply criticized by Lactantius as implying an inconceivable intentionality in inanimate things: 'Then, by what pact, by what agreement do they come together among themselves that something may be formed of them? If they lack sense, they are not able to come together with such order, for it is not possible for anything but reason to bring about anything rational.'[31] Since causal power is transmitted from greater to lesser, it is impossible that such small and feeble entities as atoms are can be responsible for much of anything. 'Nor is it likely, indeed, that lesser and lowly things have power of control and that greater and supreme things do not.'[32] The 'peculiar and fixed natures' of things, according to Lactantius, are *their own* laws: '[I]t is clear that nothing is produced from the atoms since every single thing has its own peculiar and fixed nature, its own seed, its own law given from the beginning.'[33]

In summary, ancient and early medieval philosophers perceive sublunary nature as orderly, and as subject to occasional disorders. They disagree on whether the orderliness proceeds from wisdom and intelligence or is the result of time and chance, and those who reject time and chance sometimes present wisdom and intelligence as immanent in natural things, sometimes as downstream products of

29 See Aquinas 2000: 775.

30 Locke 1954: 117: 'All things observe a fixed law of their operations and a manner of existence appropriate to their nature … This being so, it does not seem that man alone is independent of laws, while everything else is bound.' Von Lyden notes Locke's debt to Nathanael Culverwel, *Discourse of the Light of Nature* (1652); see ibid.: 40.

31 Lactantius 1964: 211. This popular work went through 86 editions between 1461 and 1739.

32 Lactantius 1965: 83–84.

33 Ibid.: 79.

superior causes. Where subordination and obedience link nature to the gods or to a God, this relationship is not mediated by laws.[34]

Laws of Nature in the Revival of the Mechanical Philosophy

Sachiko Kusukawa suggests that the introduction of a law-concept through the word 'lex', but also the words 'regula' and 'ordo', into pre- Scientific Revolution natural philosophy textbooks in the fifteenth and sixteenth centuries can be seen as 'attempts to establish and map out a Providentially designed universe that eliminated the randomness of Epicurean atomism on one hand, and the Stoic chain that bound God to secondary causes on the other' [Kusukawa]. The divine regimentation of inanimate particles within the revived corpuscularian philosophies of the seventeenth century addressed one aspect of the problem of orthodoxy, as well as one aspect of the problem of explanatory adequacy.

The correction of the moral-theological deficiencies of classical atomism, as it displaced Aristotelian hylomorphism through the efforts of Sennert, Bacon, Descartes and Gassendi, was a pressing task.[35] Neo-corpuscularianism presented an explanatory challenge and a metaphysical opportunity. The challenge was to explain why corporeal nature, if its substances consisted of 'matter' uncontrolled by any superior principle such as 'form,' and devoid of powers, tendencies, appetites, and unregulated by final causes, was not a chaos. Perhaps because Lucretius was a poet, not a philosopher engaged in a dialectic with Aristotle, he had not perceived the seriousness of this problem, but the self-described modern philosophers facing the authority of the Schools could not afford to ignore it. The corresponding opportunity was the prospect of unifying top-down and bottom-up accounts of the origins of the visible order and displaying appropriate theological credentials, that is to say anti-Epicurean ones. The Christian-Ciceronian dogma that order descends from the superior to the inferior could be happily married to the Epicurean dogma that order is a feature of the manifest image grounded in the incessantly planless activities of tiny unintelligent particles. With the help of a law concept, one could be a corpuscularian, a mechanist even, and yet deny Lucretius' disturbing and socially pernicious claim that 'nature is free and uncontrolled by proud masters and runs the universe by herself without the aid of gods'.[36]

The Stoic God rules, but not by imposing laws. This raises the question why the Christian God works through laws, and it was the Islamic-Judaeo-Christian God's special role as semi-effective moral lawgiver to humans that has been taken by historians as providing the conceptual resources for the new role of perfectly effective lawgiver to physical bodies.[37] Francis Oakley's claim for the theological origins of the concept of a physical law of nature is supported by the presence of fleeting references in St Augustine and a well-developed law concept in St Thomas, one in

[34] Dennis des Chene (1996: 201) notes that the term law of nature occurs infrequently and never in an empirical sense outside a Cartesian context in the Coimbran commentators.

[35] On the revival of ancient atomism, see Newman 1996; also Luethy 1997: 24–34.

[36] Lucretius 1975: 179.

[37] Oakley 1961a; see also Foster: 1934.

which the human subjection to divine moral law is considered as one aspect of law-obeying tendencies in created things generally.[38] While human beings are incapable of imposing laws on inanimate objects that have neither reason nor understanding, this is not true of God who 'commands the whole of nature',[39] through the 'imprint of inner sources of activity'.[40] Oakley argued that 'When Descartes spoke of God's having imposed laws upon nature, all he really had to do … was to transfer from the moral order into the realm of natural philosophy the well-established theological doctrine of an omnipotent Legislator God …'[41]

The thesis that the modern concept of a law of nature has theological origins has not gone unchallenged. Jane Ruby[42] found writers using the term 'law' as well as 'rule' in a recognizably modern sense from the thirteenth century onwards in optics, astronomy, and mathematics, without a surround of theological language, suggesting that the concept of a law of nature had a secular history. But Ruby's findings do not establish the irrelevance of theology. They are consistent with the hypothesis presented above: the discovery of exact formulas in the classical sciences – particularly geometrical optics – is a separate strand of the nomological picture, along with theological absolutism and the rejection of chance.[43]

But which agents are ordered by laws and what are examples of the laws that order them? Even before the mathematizing innovations of Kepler, Galileo, and Descartes took hold, Protestant writers greeted the notion that God devolves power by instituting laws favourably [Stolleis, Kusukawa]. Richard Hooker, in the *Laws of Ecclesiastical Polity* (1593) distinguishes three kinds of law 'laid up in the bosom of God and eternal', to wit, Celestial law, governing the Angels, Reason, which 'bindeth creatures reasonable in this world', and Nature's law, which 'ordereth natural agents'.[44] Oakley quotes the Gassendist Walter Charleton as referring to the 'severe Laws of Nature with which God has bound up the hands of his Creatures, limited their activities and punctually consigned them their several provinces'.[45] According to Culverwel in 1652, 'God has set a Law to the waves, and a Law to

---

38 Thus Augustine: 'The ordinary course of Nature in the whole of creation has certain natural laws in accordance with which even the spirit of life … has its own appetites' (quoted from *The Literal Commentary on Genesis*, in Lindberg 1986: 37. Cf. Aquinas 2000: 9: '[T]he eternal law rules and measures everything subject to God's providence … But the rational creature is subject to God's providence in a more excellent way than other things … [T]he natural law is simply rational creatures' participation in the eternal law.'

39 Ibid.: 29.

40 Ibid.

41 Oakley 1961a: 441.

42 Ruby 1995: 300ff.

43 The specific role of voluntarism is defended by Oakley 1961a: 438ff. See also Deason 1986. Cudworth claimed that the revival of Epicurean and Democritean atomism was linked with voluntarist theology, according to Oakley (Cudworth was a critic of both; see Treiber). However, a convincing case for the role of voluntarism outside Ockhamist science has yet to be made.

44 Hooker 1975: 114. In a much-quoted passage, Hooker continues 'that obedience of creatures unto the law is the stay of the whole world' (ibid.).

45 Quoted in Oakley 1961a: 444, from the *Darkness of Atheism*, Ch. 4, sect. 5.

the windes; nay, thus clocks have their lawes, and Lutes have their Lawes, and whatsoever has the least appearance of motion, has some rule proportionable to it.'[46] Yet several well-known philosophers of the seventeenth century seemed to have only a vague, if imposing, idea of a law of nature with no direct links to the new successes of the mathematical sciences. Gassendi asserted that Epicurus was wrong to make chance the fashioner of the world, but he did not introduce laws of nature as a replacement for chance; indeed, in a voluntarist spirit, he insisted that God's absolute power is inconsistent with any kind of natural necessity.[47] Galileo described nature as 'inexorable and immutable; she never transgresses the laws imposed upon her, or cares a whit whether her abstruse reasons and methods of operation are understandable to men'.[48] But he did not enlighten us further as to the details of these laws. Nor did John Locke, imitating Cicero in asserting that:

> it is by his order that the heaven revolves in unbroken rotation, the earth stands fast [*sic*]and the stars shine, and it is He who has set bounds even to the wild sea and prescribed to every kind of plants the manner and periods of germination and growth; it is in obedience to His will that nothing is so unstable, so uncertain in this whole constitution of things as not to admit of valid and fixed laws of operation appropriate to its nature …[49]

Drawing on the optical-mechanical notion of a fixed pathway followed by a body free of constraint – a light ray or a falling cannonball – Descartes was the first philosopher to be explicit about what the laws of nature actually *say*, as opposed to what types of natural entities – 'all creatures', winds, waves, lutes, the moon, the clouds, the rain, 'natural agents', clocks – are subordinated to God. Lactantius' notion of an *individual* law pertaining to the 'peculiar and fixed' essence of a body has no place in corpuscularian theory. The laws of nature, according to Descartes, as well as the rules of mechanics, describe inanimate matter, macroscopic as well as microscopic bodies [Roux]. A body is an ensemble of particles of matter that happen to be moving together or resting together. No federation or mutual recognition amongst corpuscles is necessary to explain cohesion or form. The Epicurean hypothesis that there are numerous different *cosmoi* with different forms inhabiting them is welcomed, but at least the laws of nature, if not the rule of mechanics, are everywhere the same, following from the immutability of God.

The similarities between the Lucretian and Cartesian programmes of explanation are striking. So are the differences in many details. Cartesian mechanism does not posit indivisible atoms or corporeal souls, or use material films and images to explain perception and dreams. The transmission of nonmaterial impulses through a *plenum*, rather than the knocking of particles, or their entry into or exit from the brain, is the basis of such important effects as vision, hearing, and voluntary motion. Nevertheless, Descartes appropriated and introduced into natural philosophy the Lucretian idea of a self-creating cosmos that emerges from a state of chaos, bringing forth worlds with plants, animals, and even men. Like Lucretius, he tried to make this scenario

46 Culverwel 1978: 20.

47 Osler 1994: 51ff.

48 Galileo, 'Letter to the Grand Duchess Christina', in Galileo 1937: 182.

49 Locke 1954: 109.

plausible by indicating that the time scale and the quantity of matter available are vast. But he insisted that laws, not chance, bring structure out of chaos:

> Even if we were to suppose the Chaos of the Poets, that is to say, a total confusion of all the parts of the universe, one could always demonstrate that [by means of the laws of nature] this confusion should gradually give way to the order which is at present in the world, … because it is not appropriate to the sovereign perfection that is in God to make him the author of confusion but rather of order …[50]

Descartes partitioned laws and rules in an attempt to clarify the respective roles of God and Nature. Thus:

> By Nature I do not understand some Goddess, or some other imaginary power; I make use of this word to signify matter itself … under the condition that God continues to preserve it in the same way he created it. For it follows necessarily, solely from the fact that he continues thus to preserve it, that there must be many changes in its parts which cannot … be attributed to the action of God, because that action never changes, and which I therefore attribute to nature. The rules, according to which these changes take place, I call the 'laws of nature.'[51]

In this manner, the rules of mechanics were identified with those of nature; so that, as Friedrich Steinle remarks, the term 'law' was reserved by Descartes for his conservation principles, supposed to derive from divine immutability. By contrast, the animal spirits in the arteries are carried 'selon les regles des Mechaniques qui sont les memes celles de la nature'.[52] The tendency to shift arbitrarily between 'rule' terminology and 'law' terminology noted by Steinle in connection with Huygens and Mariotte, is consistent with the introduction of the new formulation 'rule of nature' [Steinle]. The law-term is taken up and extended by Descartes' successors, careless of his theological subtlety, to cover what were formerly mere rules, that is, the principles of collision mechanics.

Descartes recognized that the rules describing the motion of bodies do not manifest themselves to casual observation. The confident assertion of a stable and unvarying latent order of nature that cannot be appreciated by those wedded to their senses, and the adaptation of our minds to the discovery of that order, underwrote his natural philosophy. Order is unavailable to sense-perception for two reasons. First, all particles or parts of matter, whether macroscopic or microscopic, are subject to motion-deflecting interference. Second, microscopic particles cannot be seen. Yet it is because objects (many of them invisible to our eyes) would move in fixed paths under ideal conditions of noninterference and would interact in a determinate manner under ideal conditions that they are said to follow rules even under ordinary conditions. 'In most of the motions we see in the real world we cannot perceive that the bodies which begin or cease to move are pushed or stopped by some other bodies.' But that gives us no reason to think that the rules of inertia and conservation of motion are not being followed exactly. '[Even] if everything our senses ever

50 Descartes 1964–74: IX-2, 159–60.

51 Descartes 1964–74: XI, 37.

52 Descartes 1964–74: VI, 54, 55.

experienced in the real world seemed manifestly contrary to what is contained in these two rules,' he continues, reason forces him to posit them in the 'new world' identical in its appearances to ours that that God could have made.[53] The atomists indicated that there were pathways their primordial particles, would follow were they unimpeded, recognizing that they met with obstructions and barriers that deflected them. But the optical-mechanical notion of a determinate pathway did not inform their conception of atomic motion. A twofold process of abstraction – from surface phenomena to a precise characterization of latent reality, and from latent reality as it was imagined to be to a precise characterization of its idealization – was beyond the conception of the ancient atomists. Though Descartes is not usually considered a great experimentalist, his metaphysical commitment expressed in his *Principles* to a latent order unavailable to causal observation reinforced the Baconian methodology of constructing nature-vexing artifices and isolating variables. Gassendi, by contrast, though an active experimentalist and an influential atomist, was not concerned to project the same nomological image in his writings.

Robert Boyle, who took his providentialism from Cicero and Lactantius, and his mechanical philosophy from the chemists, Descartes, and Gassendi,[54] declared a programmatic commitment to the rule of law in inanimate nature. In his *Free Inquiry into the Vulgarly Received Notion of Nature* (1685), Boyle maintained that Nature could be considered simply as 'the system of the Corporeal works of God'.[55] He kept up the attack on the pagan notion of Nature as a Goddess with autonomous powers. Synthesizing to the best of his considerable ability, he claimed that God 'settled such *Laws* or Rules of local Motion among the Parts of the universal *Matter*, that, by his ordinary and preserving Concourse, the several Parts of the Universe, thus once completed, should be able to maintain the great Construction, or *System* and Oeconomy, of the mundane Bodies, and propagate the Species of *Living Creatures*'.[56] God's task, according to Boyle, was to 'dispose that chaos or confused heap of numberless atoms into the world … to establish the universal and conspiring harmony of things, and especially to connect those atoms into those various seminal contextures upon which most of the more abstruse operations and elaborate productions of nature appear to depend.'[57]

> According to their [the Epicureans'] *Hypothesis*, whilst their numberless *Atoms* wildly rov'd in their infinite *Vacuity*, they had nothing belonging to them, but *Bigness*, *Figure*, and *Motion*: And 'twas by the Coalition or Convention of these *Atoms* that the World had its Beginning. So that, according to them, it was not *Nature* but *Chance* that framed the World: … and this course, though casually fallen into & continu'd without Design is that, which, according to their Hypothesis, ought to pass for *Nature*.

If the Epicureans had found an atomism without laws credible, should we not find far more credible, Boyle seemed to be asking, atomism under the hand of God?

[53] Descartes 1964–74: XI, 42–3.

[54] Via Water Charleton, the transmitter and proponent of Gassendi in England.

[55] Boyle 1685: 38.

[56] Boyle 1685: 78.

[57] Boyle 1744: I, 452.

Doubts, Exceptions, and Exclusions

From the philosopher's point of view, it was still unclear why a Cartesian universe was not a chaos on the phenomenal level. Why should it follow from the fact that bodies of whatever size, including the smallest parts of matter, are determined by God to move in certain pathways or to remain at rest, depending on precisely stated conditions, that any empirical generalization whatsoever obtains in the phenomenal world? And because the species are not created according to divine prototypes, or maintained within limits and goalposts, the Cartesian theory of the world gives us no reason to believe that our present animals, vegetables, and minerals – or even creatures with human bodies like ours – or for that matter, oceans and mountains like ours, have been here for any length of time and will survive into future epochs rather than being replaced by other creatures and features that are mechanically possible. These deficiencies prompted a good deal of philosophizing over the problems of cosmic maintenance, a subject treated in the Leibniz–Clarke correspondence of 1715–16, as well as over the problems of reproduction and species-fixity in minerals, plants and animals. The speculations of cosmologists, geologists, and natural historians in the eighteenth century are addressed to the questions of the formation and succession of celestial and natural objects, from nebulae to crystals, to living creatures.

Just how difficult the Cartesian conception of a law of nature was to understand in philosophical terms, and how difficult the Cartesian nomological image was to accept as a full account of nature, can be seen from Boyle's writings. In his *Free Inquiry*, Boyle rejected as 'improper and figurative', and as inconsistent with the 'General Fabrick of the World', any reference to laws received from the Creator by individual creatures.[58] And he revisited the problem of how laws could be imposed on inanimate objects, conceding nevertheless that:

> [T]here is oftentimes some Resemblance between the orderly and regular Motions of inanimate Bodies and the Actions of Agents, that, in what they do, act conformably to Laws. And even I sometimes scruple not to speak of the Laws of Motion and Rest that God has established among things Corporeal, and now and then to call them, as men are wont to do, the *Laws of Nature* ...[59]

To speak strictly, he continues, a *Law* is 'but a *Notional Rule of Acting according to the declar'd Will of a Superior*' and ''tis plain that nothing but an Intellectual Being can be properly capable of receiving and acting by a *Law*'.[60] An arrow does not act by a law when it is shot from the bow, but by 'an External, tho' well-directed Impulse'.[61] It is nevertheless acceptable to conceive bodies as acting according to laws: Nature, he says, ought to be defined as '*the Aggregate of the Bodies, that make*

[58] Boyle 1685: 41–42.

[59] Ibid.: 40–41.

[60] Ralph Cudworth takes up this familiar point: '... their [the Mechanick Theists', i.e. Cartesians'] *Laws of Nature* concerning *Motion* are Really nothing else, but a *Plastick Nature*, acting upon the Matter of the whole Corporeal Universe'. See Cudworth, *True Intellectual System of the Universe* (1678) I:III:37, in Patrides 1969: 294.

[61] Boyle 1685: 43.

up the World ... considered as a Principle, by virtue whereof, they Act and Suffer according to the Laws of Motion prescribed by the Author of Things'.[62]

Boyle's commitment to the mechanical philosophy was not as thoroughgoing as his programmatic writings suggest. He acknowledged, like the majority of his contemporaries, the possibility of direct interventions into the course of nature by God and by good and evil spirits, as well as by the human will. More significantly from the perspective of the history of science, he departed from Cartesianism by treating explanation by reference to laws as different in kind from explanation by reference to multi-corpuscular fit and interaction, which he regarded as different in turn from explanation by reference to general or 'cosmicall' causes. A pluralist in the theory of explanation, Boyle listed amongst the 'more catholic and primary causes of things' 'either certain primitive, general, and fixed laws of nature (or rules of action and passion among the parcels of the universal matter); or else the shape, size, motion, and other primary affections of the smallest parts of matter, and of their first coalitions or clusters, especially those endowed with seminal faculties or properties; or … the admirable conspiring of the several parts of the universe to the production of particular effects …'[63] He denied that the prescription of laws by God is sufficient for the original production of the visible order: 'I do not at all believe, that either these *Cartesian laws of motion*, or the *Epicurean casual concourse of atoms*, could bring mere matter into so orderly and well-contrived a fabrick as this world.'[64]

Boyle insisted that the Aristotelian and scholastic axioms pertaining to the superficial order and uniformity of nature are false. It is untrue that 'Nature does nothing in vain', that 'Nature always acts for the best' that 'Nature takes the shortest routes' and that 'Nature abhors a vacuum'.[65] His explanation for why phenomenal generalizations so often fail accorded with the Cartesian point that real-world objects interfere with one another. The phenomena we observe depend on the confluence of the actions of a number of agents, and complex aggregates do not behave in ways true to their types. On the practical level, the contribution of accessories presumably explains the success and failure of experiments and cures and the existence of monsters and exceptions. Intentionally or not, Boyle's interpretation of surface-level indeterminacy and disorder is put in terms of the failure of inter-object helping behaviour reminiscent of the Lucretian *foedera*.

> [A]n Individual Body, being but a Part of the World, … needs the Assistance or Concourse of other Bodies … to perform divers of its Operations and exhibit several *Phenomena's*, that belong to it. This would quickly and manifestly appear if, for instance, an Animal or a Herb could be removed into those Imaginary Spaces the School-men tell us of beyond the World; or into such a place, as the Epicureans fancy their *Intermundia* … For, whatever the Structures of these Living Engines be, they would as little without the Co-operations of external Agents such as the *Sun, Aether, Air* &c., be able to exercise their Functions, as

---

62 Boyle 1685: 71.

63 Boyle 1744: I, 444.

64 *Origin of Forms and Qualities*, in Boyle 1991: 70. On Boyle's theory of generation, see Anstey 2002.

65 Boyle 1685: 58ff.

> the great Mills, commonly used with us would be to Grind Corn, without the assistance of Wind or running Water. [66]

The dependency of life on air, for example, can be experimentally demonstrated.

The semi-Cartesian image of nature that dominates Boyle's programmatic writings was important to present and represent, for it functioned as a hedge against accusations of futility directed against Royal Society science. In Steinle's terms, pre-Newtonian references to the discovery of laws of nature conferred a 'higher dignity' on experimental practice that was only sporadically successful and that was vulnerable to criticisms on the grounds of being frivolous entertainment, as well as materialistic impiety [Steinle]. At the same time, qualifications of the nomological picture had their own motives and uses [Daston]. Philosophical scepticism about the sufficiency of the laws of nature is pronounced in More, Cudworth and Newton; it seems to be a trademark of English philosophy. Locke concluded dimly that 'The Things that, as far as our Observation reaches, we constantly find to proceed regularly, we may conclude, do act by a Law set them; but yet by a Law, that we know not; whereby, though Causes work steadily and Effects constantly flow from them, yet their *Connexions* and *Dependencies* being not discoverable in our *Ideas*, we can have but an experimental Knowledge of them.[67] The Leibniz–Clarke correspondence set a Continental philosopher, fully committed to the sufficiency of laws and well-defended against the objection that God is thereby tied to the chain of secondary causes, against an Empiricist who insists that God's agency descends to individual salutary acts.[68]

Because the term 'law of nature' was a term of art, woven of many strands, it was strong, but also subject to unravelling. The nomological image of nature and its prescriptive implications, as philosophical analysis of the deductive nomological theory of science and its presuppositions has shown, is something of a mirage.[69] From a historical perspective, the theological strand was the first to fray. Hume suggested that nomological necessity could only correspond to a sentiment we share with animals, not to the apprehension of a supersensible ordinance. For eighteenth-century materialists like Baron Holbach, the laws of nature were not God's commands but replacements for them. In the nineteenth century, the notion that the pathways of the fundamental units of matter are determinate, nothing being left to chance, came uncoupled from the notion of a fundamental equation in statistical mechanics.

More recently, even the central importance formerly attached to mathematical equations, as opposed to mathematical models in a more general sense, for the understanding of natural processes has been challenged. We increasingly recognize that the articulation of quantitative laws of nature in seventeenth-century science corresponds to only one aspect of mathematicization in the theoretical representation

---

[66] Ibid.: 79–80.

[67] Locke 1975: 560.

[68] Daston argues that scepticism about laws is an index of the Baconian commitment to empiricism and a mark of rebellion against a closed Aristotelian science. See Daston 1992; and Daston and Park 1998.

[69] Criticism began in Scriven 1961 and Scriven 1962. The same line of argument was developed extensively in Cartwright 1983: esp. chap. 3.

of physical reality. This realization hardly detracts from our admiration of the experimental and conceptual accomplishment involved in the fabrication of the nomological image.

Chapter 2

Expressing Nature's Regularities and their Determinations in the Late Renaissance

Ian Maclean

For the new science of the seventeenth century, law is a complex term when associated with nature, as can be seen from other contributions to this volume. It is generally thought of as independent of the human mind; it determines a regularity in nature; it is applicable without exception; it is not necessarily dependent on a version of metaphysics or an overarching theory, and can relate to isolatable aspects of nature [GRAßHOFF].[1] One route to the discovery of laws of this type was the meticulous chronicling of natural particulars and variability.[2] This inductivist route to the discovery of laws can be distinguished both from a (broadly Cartesian) deductivist approach through the establishment of clear, intuitively irrefutable principles from which laws would derive a rational and necessary character, and a heuristic approach, in which the law-statements made would be no more than the product of the human imagination. In a very rough and ready way, these alternatives can be mapped back on to much earlier medieval debates about universals: the inductivist route is Aristotelian in character in that it presupposes that laws are discoverable *in re*; the deductivist approach is realist and Platonic, in that it presupposes that laws in some sense precede the phenomena in which they manifest themselves and are *ante rem*; and the heuristic approach is one in which a nominalist attitude to universals makes the laws which humans derive from the particulars of experience *post rem*.[3]

---

1 This strict definition of a law of nature can be taken a little further: if we follow Stafleu 1999, we can add to mind-independence the characteristic of universality (it must relate to all of the aspect of nature to which it applies); furthermore, no given thing can be law-less, even if the law which governs it is not known; finally, the laws are inseparable from the subjects which they govern.

2 Daston 2000b: 4. She adds a third point: '[for Oresme], habit, deviation and the causes responsible for both were in principle all manifest to the senses. In contrast, seventeenth-century natural laws were in principle inviolable, and operated at the level of subsensible "latent configurations" or "mechanisms". Whereas fourteenth-century regularities – nature's habits – had been the phenomenological effect of natural causes, seventeenth-century regularities – natural laws – were themselves the hidden causes of phenomenological effects.' It is my view that, prior to the seventeenth century, causes were not necessarily believed to be manifest to the senses; the causes of illness were not so perceptible, and great distance, which is given (in the standard example of a demonstration quia) as the cause of the twinkling of the stars, is also not sensible in any straightforward way.

3 Stafleu 1999.

These alternatives were consciously grappled with by late Renaissance thinkers, but in different terms.

Before the emergence of 'law of nature' as a significant phrase in Latin and in various vernaculars in the latter half of the seventeenth century, 'ius naturale' and 'lex naturae' or 'leges naturae' occur as collocations, and aspects of the complex of meanings attributed to the phrase are expressed in other ways.[4] In this essay I shall explore the broad lexical field of the late Renaissance encompassing law and nature in collocation, which includes the following terms: 'theses', 'hypotheses', 'theoremata', 'schemata', 'dogmata', 'leges logicae', 'praecepta', 'praecognita', 'praemissa', 'aphorismi', 'maximae [sententiae]', 'axiomata', 'necessaria', 'principia', 'ordo', 'constitutio', 'cursus', 'ratio', 'proportio', 'causae', 'normae', 'regulae', 'regimen', 'elementa', 'fatum'.[5] I shall first investigate this lexical field in respect of its usage in combination with other terms and in specific disciplinary contexts; I shall next turn to the concepts of law and nature current in the late Renaissance, and examine some of the issues arising from them which reveal how different they are from the concepts which appear in the later seventeenth century: the question of exceptions, the forces which are said to act on nature, the location of their regularity (either in the human mind or in nature itself), and the related issues of logical and physical necessity and of prescription and description. In conclusion, I shall venture one or two general observations about the differences in usage and semantic content between the earlier and later periods. This essay does not claim to be an exhaustive discussion, but rather a survey of some issues symptomatic of the differing philosophical agendas of thinkers at either end of the seventeenth century.

I

The first issue to consider is the occurrence of combinations of these terms. A confluence of law-connoting terms is found in many contexts involving nature, from classical times onwards,[6] of which the following are two examples (all italics are mine):

> Laws of nature are notions of principles and conclusions drawn from them, congruent with the eternal and unchangeable norm of the divine mind, about the governance of morals [*Leges* naturae sunt notitiae *principiorum* practicorum et conclusionum ex his extructarum, de regendis moribus, congruentes cum aeterna et immota *norma* mentis divinae].[7]

---

4 At the same time, in different (moral and literary) contexts, the terms 'physis' (nature) and 'nomos' (law) are also seen as mutually exclusive, as instinct is to humanly ordained convention: see Morrison 1977: 594.

5 It was also possible simply to refer to 'natura universalis' and evoke its regulatory features by the use of verbs: see Gilly 1977–79: 105–106 (citing Zwinger).

6 For example, Cicero, *Academica*, 2.46.140: 'fontem omnium bonorum in corpore esse, hanc *normam*, hanc *regulam*, hanc *praescriptionem* esse naturae, a qua qui aberravisset, eum numquam quid in vita sequeretur habiturum'.

7 Melanchthon 1834–60: 16.227–228. Scattola 1999b: 874, compares this passage to Aquinas 1955, *Summa theologiae*, 1a 2ae 100,1. Cf. Melanchthon 1834–60: 13.150–151, and

> The components of the noun 'physiognomy' are physis (nature) and gnōmē (rule), as if you were to say the law or rule of nature, that is to say, that through a norm or ordinance of nature, such and such affections of the soul would follow from such and such form of the body [Physiognomia nomen ex φύσις *natura* et γνώμη *regula* compositum est, quasi *legem* vel *naturae regulam* dicas, ut scilicet quadam naturae *norma ordinatione*que ex tali corporis forma tales animae affectiones consequantur].[8]

One of the reasons for terms to occur in conjunction may be that none has the full range of desired connotations (Melanchthon wants to stress both the origin of nature's laws, and their status as moral principles); another may be, conversely, that all of them have too many connotations, and need to have their sense further modified by the presence of other words with similar semantic force (Porta feels that the translation of 'γνώμη' by 'regula' needs further restriction by a stress on the prescriptive associations of 'norma' and 'ordinatio'). Such usage reveals that these writers are aware of the dual sense of law, as regularity and ordinance. The awareness shown by late Renaissance thinkers of the problems inherent in the terminology they were constrained to use belies their characterization by anti-Aristotelians (including Bacon, Galileo and Descartes) as uncritical somnambulists unwittingly stumbling about in contradiction, word-spinning and mental confusion.[9] These thinkers carefully spell out different meanings of terms employed in the same philosophical school, thereby following the practice of the metaphysical lexicon of Aristotle (*Metaphysics*, v, 1012b 34ff.).

Other terms given in the list above have plural meanings, deriving from the usages attributed to different ancient schools of thought; this is noted by the writers of various philosophical and discipline-specific lexica of the late Renaissance. A pertinent example is provided by the term 'axioma'. There was much enthusiasm shown for Euclid and geometrical method in the Renaissance; the 'mos geometricus' is sometimes described as the best approach to any field of knowledge, and figures such as Cardano write versions of dialectics based on it.[10] One might therefore expect that the Euclidean usage of 'axioma' would be a strong candidate to describe fundamental, mind-independent, universal laws in any discipline. In Aristotelian philosophy too, 'axioma' has the sense of self-evident proposition (*Posterior analytics*,

---

21.686: 'legem naturae esse notitiam legis divinae naturae hominis insitam'; also Goldammer 1991: 20: 'das Mittelalter und die frühe Neuzeit kennen ferner [ausserhalb experientia] keine "Naturgesetze" wie sie heute geläufig sind, deren Entwicklung die mathematische Formulierung von Beobachtungen und experimentellen Ergebnissen mit Hilfe von Messen und Wägen voraussetzt. Der Begriff "lex naturae" ist theologischer und philosophischer und bezieht sich auch auf äussere "Naturvorgänge"'.

8 Porta 1593: 56. Cf. Kepler, *Epitomes Astronomiae Copernicanae liber primus* (1621), quoted by Graßhoff 2000: 3: 'Unde est dicta Astronomia? Ab Astrorum, id est motuum, quibus astra moventur, lege seu regimine, ut Oeconomia a regenda re domestica, Paedonomus a regendis pueris.' For other examples, see Goclenius 1609: 323, quoted below, note 24, and Zabarella 1590a: 559–564, quoted below, note 25.

9 See Maclean 1998.

10 Cardano 1663: 1.293–308.

72a 17, 75a 41, 76b 14; *Metaphysics*, 997a 11).[11] However, in Stoic philosophy, its meaning is rendered by such Latin words as 'dictum', 'edictum', 'proloquium', 'ecfatum' 'profatum', and these do not evince a high scientific status in Renaissance natural philosophy, where they can be associated with weak induction.[12] Goclenius explicitly spells out these two conflicting senses in his *Lexicon philosophicum* of 1613.[13] The conjunction of both meanings can be found in certain contexts, such as jurisprudence, where axioms are described as 'the principles of disciplines and certain undemonstrable propositions which are current in common sense and common thinking'.[14] The persistence of the Stoic meaning raises the issue of the location of laws of nature, whether in the human mind or in nature herself; this was, as we shall see, explicitly explored by late Renaissance thinkers.

A further factor affecting the uptake of the terms listed above is their discipline-specific nature. This is revealed by statements about equivalences; or the use of the same term with different senses in different disciplines. Equivalences of law-like terms across a number of disciplines are set out by a lawyer (Matthaeus Gribaldus alias Mopha) in the following passage:

> We see that our predecessors have collected together out of the whole context of the laws *regulae* which are as short as possible, such as are to be found in the Digest title *De regulis iuris antiqui*, and broadly also in the tract we have called *Axiomata iuris* ... what jurists call *regulae*, theologians call *summae*, logicians *theses* or *positiones*, doctors *aphorismi*, yet others *epitomae*, *enuntiata* or *axiomata*.[15]

'Regula', which seems on the face of it to be the most obvious candidate to express the notion of regularity, is here coloured by its association as a legal term with 'summa' in theology, 'thesis' in dialectics and 'aphorismus' in medicine,[16] all of which carry strong implications of rules imposed on a discipline by the human mind.

---

11 Sachiko Kusukawa has pointed out to me that Melanchthon uses the phrase 'axiomata physica' in MS Vatican Pal. Lat. 1038, fol. 2 ('Physicae seu naturalis philosophiae compendium'); see also Kepler quoted by Barker 1997: 360: 'quae certa et apud homines confessa essent ea speciali nomine AXIOMATA dictitarunt'.

12 Glucker 1995: 131–132 (the meaning as given in Stephanus); Porzio 1598: 138: 'quae sunt veluti proloquia solum opus habent tenui inductione'.

13 Goclenius 1613: 135–136.

14 Spiegelius 1569: s.v. axioma: 'disciplinarum principia et propositiones quaedam indemonstrabiles, quae in communi sensu conceptuque versant[ur]'; cf. s.v. natura: 'civilis auctoritas latius porrigit naturae axiomata accommodat negociis, et dispensat secundum immensam varietatem unicuique'.

15 Gribaldus 1541: 393r, cited by Herberger 1981: 235: 'maioribus nostris visum est ex toto legum contextu *regulas* quam brevissimas colligere: quales habentur in titulo Regularum iuris [D 50.17] et latissime in nostro tractatu quem *Axiomata* iuris inscripsimus ... Jurisconsulti *regulas*, Doctores *summas*, Dialectici *theses* seu *positiones*, Medici *aphorismos*, aliqui *epitomas*, nonnulli *enuntiata* sive *axiomata* vocant'.

16 See also Herberger 1981: 236–237 (quoting da Monte's claim that the dogmas of medicine are preferable to those of law not only because they are not tyrannical (i.e. prescriptive).

II

The term 'regula' leads us on to a more general consideration of the concepts 'law' and 'nature'. In jurisprudence, 'regula' relates to the stipulative force of law, by which rules are laid down and exceptions are made. A 'regula' is a second-order generalized version of a number of 'leges', as we learn from D 50.17.1: 'a rule is what briefly sets out the matter in question; the law should not be derived from rules, but the rule should be made out of the existing law'.[17] A rule is, as it were, a 'harmony' or 'concert', whereas a law is only 'a single voice'.[18] Although the terms 'generaliter' and 'regulariter' are used to indicate that which must necessarily and in all circumstances be the case, the medieval jurist Irnerius in his gloss on *Institutes* 1.3 states that 'it is not absurd to find something which does not fall under the rule'.[19] He does not mean by this that the rule is not of universal application, but that it remains a rule even when exceptions have been stated, provided that they are all made explicit; the full version of the well-known maxim that the exception proves the rule (nowadays used in precisely the opposite sense to that accorded to it in the sixteenth century) reads 'the exception confirms that the rule applies to all cases not excepted'.[20] There is a potential sophism here, which is explored by later medieval logicians and lawyers.[21] The equivalent in medicine of these juristic usages of 'rule' and 'exception' is the looser concept of genus.[22] For medicine, there can be exceptions within a genus: this usage is found also in natural philosophy and in grammar, as Goclenius and Binsfeld testify: there 'regulariter' indicates what happens in most cases.[23]

---

[17] D 50.17.1 (Paulus): 'Regula est quae rem breviter enarrat: non ex regula ius sumatur, sed ex iure quod est, regula fiat'.

[18] Hotman 1569: s.v. regula: 'Differt ... Lex a Regula: quod illa dicitur, quam populus certo et cognito omnibus iure constituit: Regula vero, quam Iurisconsulti ex pluribus legum capitibus notatis inter seque comparatis elicuerunt: ut non omnino incommode dicere possumus, leges esse tanquam voces, et sonos singulos: Regulam vero esse tanquam harmoniam et concentum.'

[19] 'Non est absurdum aliquid extra regulam inveniri': *Glossa* ad Inst. I.3, quoted by Otte 1971: 95.

[20] The most sophisticated Renaissance discussion of the maxim 'exceptio firmat regulam in casibus non exceptis' (which is much cited throughout the medieval period) is in *Commentarii* 1593: 10ff. (by Philippus Decius), whose paraphrase of the maxim runs: 'licet exceptiones sint contra regulam in casibus exceptis, tamen in aliis casibus non exceptis exceptiones firmant regulam'.

[21] In the sophisma 'omnis homo praeter Socratem excipitur', the 'prejacent' proposition ('omnis homo excipitur') includes Socrates if he is a man: see Kretzmann 1982: 224–231. This logical problem is also discussed by the medieval jurist Placentinus (ad D 50.17.1, quoted by Otte 1971: 215–216).

[22] See Maclean 2000a. On division based on similarity/dissimiliarity decisions see Galen, *De placitis Hippocratis et Platonis*, ix.

[23] Goclenius 1613: 572 (s.v. 'regulare'): 'ortus Pleiadum et Styadum regulariter affert pluvias'; 'natura fit plerunque ut congruant temperamenta, inclinationes, actiones et eventus'; Binsfeld 1596: 273: 'ut Grammatici loquuntur, nulla regula tam firma [est] quae non patitur exceptionem'.

The medical usage of 'regulariter' reflects a feature of the concept of nature which divides the late Renaissance sharply from the later seventeenth century. Only in contexts in which a distinction is made between 'universal' nature[24] and 'particular nature[s]' is it usual to find passages in which the former of these described as consistent and rule-governed, as a way of explaining the double status of phenomena like putrefaction and death as both natural (*qua* part of universal nature) and preternatural (in given individual cases).[25] A more conventional view of sublunary nature at the time characterizes it as manifestly variable, infinitely diverse, and subject to regularity only in the majority of cases.[26] Francis Bacon acknowledges this by demanding that 'nature erring' – not only in the case of monsters, but also in that of miracles and rare events – be included in any account of nature so that 'fundamental and universal laws' might be framed.[27] His contemporaries and

---

[24] Goclenius 1609: 323, refers to 'natura universalis' by a conjunction of terms similar to the examples given above: 'ordo rerum omnium seu omnium causarum inter se, cum dependentia ab uno principio primo, unde statutus est singulis rebus, proprius cursus, propria lex. Haec lex interdum dicitur fatalis, id est fatis determinata, vel ipsum fatum.'

[25] For example, Zabarella 1590a: 559–564: 'Propter haec omnia, quae hactenus considerate sunt, ego puto non esse hic recipiendam propriam misti naturam, sed potius naturam universalem, quae nil aliud est, quam ordo rerum omnium, seu omnium causarum certo quodam ordine dispositarum cum pendentia ab uno primo principio, unde statutae singulis rebus sunt propriae leges, quae praeteriri nequent; natura igitur propria misti nollet putrescere, nec modo ullo interire, at natura universalis statuit eam esse interitui obnoxiam, et tandem interire:Secundum hanc considerationem dixit Aristoteles in initio 1 lib. de Ortu et interitu, interitum esse naturalem, id est, secundum leges naturae universalis, quae statuit omne genitum esse aliquando interiturum: sed in contex. 3 lib. 4 Meteorolog. consideratio Aristotelis est particularior quam ibi; nam in initio 1 de Generat. etiam combustio misti dicitur interitus naturalis, quatenus est rei corruptibilis, et fit a causa naturali et naturaliter agente? nil enim aliud per fatum potest intelligere, nisi legem a natura universali constitutam de modo, quo quaelibet res generetur, et intereat. Sententiam hanc Pomponatius et recentiores illi sub nube vicerunt, et proxime ad veritatem accessisse videntur; quam etiam plene essent assequuti, si naturam particularem ab universali, quam Aristoteles in memorato loco respexit, seiunxissent, non enim dixit putrefactionem esse secundum misti naturam, sed secundum naturam absolute, nempe secundum leges naturae universalis hanc proprie significat id, quod Pomponatius dixit, secundum cursum naturae, nempe universalis, seu etiam dicamus naturae particularis, quatenus subita est legi naturae universalis, a qua mistum, quatenus mistum est naturalis propensio ad putretudinem; non enim a propria natura dirigitur ad putrescendum, sed a constitutione naturae universalis, quae talem esse eius interitum statuit. Hanc puto esse rei veritatem? sicuti combustio est ea ratione naturalis, quatenus fit a causa naturaliter agente, neque ob id fit, quin dicatur alia ratione esse misto interitus violentus, quatenus non est secundum legem naturae universalis; ita dicendum est de illis, quae in locis calidissimis et frigidissimis intereunt alio modo, quam per putretudinem; etenim patiuntur quidem a causis naturalibus, sed non intereunt res modo, quo natura statuit universaliter mista esse apta interire, scilicet per dissolutionem in elementa; quanquam hoc naturae decretum recipit impedimentum ob aliquam violentiam praeoccupantem misti interitum, sicut etiam Aristoteles dixit.' I am grateful to Sachiko Kusukawa for pointing this passage out to me.

[26] On the variability of nature, see Siraisi 1994; on diversity and infinity in nature, see Maclean 2000a.

[27] See Daston and Park 1998: 227–228; Maclean 2002a:236–251.

predecessors on the other hand elaborate means of describing and dealing with natural events which exclude the rare and the monstrous. Their sublunary nature is 'nature for the most part', and is a complex of forces and functions. It is a producer and a generative internal principle (in the forms of 'vires', 'virtutes', 'facultates'); a product (the hylomorphic being, with its internal principle of movement and rest), and a process (also in the form of cause, 'vis' or function).[28] 'Ordo' and 'ordinaria vis' or 'potestas' are frequently encountered in descriptions of nature *qua* producer; 'cursus' in descriptions of nature qua process.[29] Another way of expressing this combination is through the metaphysical distinction between act and potency; nature is both active as 'forma informans' and passive in respect of the necessity which governs it, and which can thwart its purposes: 'many things happen by necessity (of a material or formal kind) which are not brought about by the intention of nature'.[30] This should not lead, however, to epistemological despair; as Theodor Zwinger points out, just as one swallow does not make a summer, so one exception does not wholly weaken man's grasp of the principles by which nature operates.[31] Such a view does no more, however, than displace the problem; now it becomes important to distinguish between what is trivially exceptional (such as having six fingers rather

---

[28] Galen, *Methodus medendi*, i.9, Galen 1821–33: 10.71.

[29] Blair 1997: 51 (quoting Bodin); Alsted, cited by Camerarius 1626–30: 142 (ii.4); Scaliger 1592: clxxxviii, ccclix.11 'Ordo' and 'cursus' are not easily used to describe rules; the former is strongly coloured by its association with 'methodus', from which it is distinguished by most logicians and dialecticians. Where method is a mode of invention (of the already known and of the yet to be discovered), order is principally a pedagogical tool for the clear exposition of materials, and is clearly the product of the mind, not a patterning inherent in nature: see Gilbert 1960; also above, note 24.

[30] Arnisaeus 1613: 150, attributed to *Physics*, ii.9, 200a 10ff.: 'multa fiunt ex necessitate quae non fiunt ex eius intentione'; Lenoble 1968; Daston and Park 1998: 209; Sennert 1650: 1.14; Porzio 1598: 150–151 (on Deus, 'electio', 'casus' and art as principles of action in nature). See also *Physics*, ii.9, 201 32ff.; *De generatione animalium*, iv.4, 770b 10ff.: 'a monstrosity ... belongs to the class of things contrary to nature although it is contrary not to Nature in her entirety, but only to nature in the generality of cases. So far as concerns Nature which is always, and by necessity, nothing occurs contrary to that ... Unnatural occurrences are found only among those things which occur as they do in the generality of cases, but which may occur otherwise.' See also ibid., ii.5 197b 33ff; ii.6 199a 11–15. Examples of this necessity (in the case of the generation of monsters) are the lack or excess of matter; the active quality in semen; the effect on the embryo of its environment (the womb) or of the mother's imagination; and heaven in either the form of demons or divine punishment: Toletus 1615: 75–77. Cf. Piccolomini 1600: 224: 'conspicuus egressus ex ordine lege communi recessus ab instituto Naturae ob materiae impedimenta'; Argenterio 1610: 500: 'morbi non ea ratione dicuntur esse praeter naturam, ut monstra, quae agentia naturalia non sibi proponunt, tanquam finem sui operis, sed ex errore aliquo contingunt'. Weinrichius 1595: 54–55; Waldung 1611 (on *cas-limites*); Céard 1996; Roger 1997: 68ff. 'Causae' can be used to describe regularities in nature, but the term is mainly used to designate the classes of predispositions, preconditions or triggering agencies rather than the local manner of their regularity; a similar remark could be made of 'elementa': cf. also Piccolomini 1600: 106: 'principium causa et elementum sunt voces satis affines, et frequenter una pro altera usurpatur'.

[31] Zwinger cited by Gilly 1977–79: 155.

than five: a divergence which can be dealt with by the theory of 'latitude of forms'[32]) and what is so contrary to nature that it must indicate intervention by a higher agency. The Renaissance understanding of miracles and portents, both of which are said to infringe the 'leges naturae', depends on this distinction, which is very difficult to make with any precision.[33]

III

This brings me to the question of forces which act on nature, and might be considered as law-like either because they ordain what happens, or because they impose a necessity on the sublunary world which can give rise to observable regularities. In treatises on natural principles, a number of instances are seen to be able to act on nature, conceived of as matter (the elements), or matter and form combined: these are the creator God; the stars, and other denizens of superlunary nature, such as divine intelligences, demons and the devil; fate; the human will, through the action of man on his own nature and on external natural processes.[34] Superlunary nature is often connected with Neoplatonist astrology. The perfect movement of the spheres, a 'lex fatalis' whose origin is the 'animae sphaerarum', is given to humanity to contemplate, and from such contemplation to deduce its effects on the sublunary world. If it is accepted that the stars determine sublunary nature, then the natures of animals can be said to be determined by them (a claim fundamental to the discipline of physiognomy); humans are only not fully determined in this way because they have free will, which they can exercise to overcome such astral determinism.[35] Superlunary nature is associated with unchanging laws which can be observed in action by the human intellect. As Kusukawa points out, Melanchthon uses 'lex' to refer to laws of planetary motion, as most certain, true and ordained by God. He also attributes to the influence of the stars on sublunary affairs the same degree of certainty, as does Cornelius Gemma.[36]

The intervention of God (or fate) in nature is something which is discussed in various ways. According to Goclenius, fate for Aristotle is 'nothing other than Nature, or a law constituted by universal nature governing the way in which everything comes into being and passes away'; for some Stoics, and for theologians, it is divine providence; for other Stoics, it is the 'the connection between the first cause and secondary natural and voluntary causes'; there is also the 'fatum physicum', namely

---

32 For 'latitudo formarum' in anatomy, see Siraisi 1994.

33 Aquinas and Zacchia cited by Maclean 2002a: 271–272.

34 See Porzio 1598: 150ff; Vicomercatus 1596: 139ff.

35 Cardano 1663: 2.417: 'animalia voluntate carent et astrorum constitutioni subiiciuntur'; see also note 40; Ficino 1559: 55v: 'animae sphaerarum movent sphaeras per legem fatalem'; Hellerus 1548: A3v: 'deinde cum in tanta motuum coelestium varietate certissimae tamen leges, ac regulae motuum reperiantur: absurdum est dicere pulcherrimam illam harmoniam ac vicissitudinem sapientissime a divina mente constitutam in motibus corporum coelestium, certo usu carere'.

36 Gemma 1575: 1.133: 'verum caelestis influxus in meteoris significationes secundum naturae leges saepe certissimas habet'.

the 'series of natural causes, that is, the conjunction of the stars with temperaments and inclinations, not however entailing simple necessity or removing the freedom of the will'.[37] Goclenius goes on to distinguish between 'naturale' ('that which depends on the ordained principles of universal and common nature') and 'fatale' (' that which occurs beyond the common causes of nature by divine will');[38] in both definitions, it is matter (or matter and form) which is subject to inexorable laws, but a space is left for divine intervention and voluntary human action.[39] There are clear statements about God's constant activity in nature around this time which have voluntarist or even occasionalist implications.[40] All these considerations tend to reinforce the association of superlunary nature with absolute and perfect regularity, and sublunary nature with regularity only for the most part.

IV

Clearly, it is very difficult, given the late Renaissance view of sublunary nature as admitting exceptions, to formulate laws satisfying the conditions set out later in the seventeenth century. It is also clear to many late Renaissance thinkers that the account of nature on which they rely could be at least in part determined by man's limited grasp of nature rather than by nature itself; 'mens est mensura rerum', as the tag has it.[41] This issue arises in many disciplinary usages in the distinction there

---

[37] Goclenius 1613: 571:'fatum nihil aliud est quam Natura vel lex a natura universali constituta de modo, quo quaelibet res generetur et intereat'; 'connexio causae primae cum secundis naturalibus et voluntariis'; 'series causarum naturalium, id est copulatio stellarum cum temperamentis et inclinationibus, non inferens tamen simplicem necessitatem, aut tollens libertatem voluntatis'. See also Melanchthon 1581: 253–296; Piccolomini 1600: 60; Cardano 1663: 1.143 calls fate a 'futurorum ordo et successus causarum'.

[38] Goclenius 1613: 573: 'quod pendet ab ordinatis universae communisque naturae principiis';'quod praeter vel supra communes naturae causas divina voluntate contingit'.

[39] Piccolomini 1600: 60: 'nam imbecillitates, interitus, senium, sequuntur conditionem materiae et nobis lege naturae ac Fato competere dicuntur'. The same desire to show a materially determined propensity and the human ability to overcome this is found also in physiognomy at this time: Gratarolo in Indagine 1603: 216: 'omnibus animalibus commune est agere vel pati ab inclinatione naturali, quae in brutis impetus, ita in hominibus propensio dicitur (ut in cholerico est ad iram inclinatio) ... Inclinationes ergo istae in hominibus morum atque affectuum semina dicuntur, quoniam ratione regulari possunt; in brutis vero mores et affectus, quoniam sensibus et appetitu vivunt. Ex quidem patet Physiognomiam scientiam esse necessarium, quo per ipsam praedicimus aptitudines naturales et affectus vel mores: quo vero per ipsam praedicimus affectus vel mores actuales, nec est scientia necessaria, nec firma: verum quia homines plerunque vivunt sensu, et non nisi sapientes vivunt ratione, ideo physiognomia est scientia praedicandi mores actuales et effectus ut in pluribus, quoniam plures appetitunt et sensu vivunt, quam ratione, quam etiam ob causam Bias Prienaeus dicebat plures esse malos quam bonos.'

[40] See Melanchthon 1581: 45–53, 253–296; Peucer 1580: 340v; Garcaeus 1584: 7; Hucher 1602: **6v, quoted by Maclean 2002a: 90.

[41] Galen, *Ad Thrasybulum*, Galen 1821–868; Crusius 1615: 13 (quoting Zabarella, *De naturae constitutione*, v): 'qualiter res in essendo, taliter se habent in cognoscendo'; Sennert 1676: 179, quoted by Eckart 1992: 157: 'res mensurant cognitionem nostram, non contra;

made between the rules or laws of an art and the laws governing the subject-matter of the art. The former relate to pedagogical contexts; the latter to nature itself, which may not be knowable in the same way. There are a number of words connected to the precepts of a discipline: 'theses', 'hypotheses', 'theoremata', 'schemata', 'dogmata', 'leges logicae', 'praecepta', 'praecognita', 'praemissa', 'aphorismi', 'maximae [sententiae]'. This group of words represent one of three orders or conditions of knowledge, or a mixture of the three: (i) that which is logically required for speculative knowledge ('scientia') to be possible in a given field; (ii) that which is derived from indubitable knowledge or experience (defined as 'what is perceived by all through the senses'[42]); (iii) that which has been generated as a set of rules which have been found to be usefully applicable. 'Theses', 'hypotheses', 'theoremata', 'schemata', 'dogmata' can be set out in forms which resemble scientific laws (there are good examples of this in Keckermann); their content is not however usually claimed to be mind-independent.[43] In the case of the first two of these terms, their use in forensic rhetoric may affect their meaning;[44] 'schemata' and 'leges logicae' are often associated with Ramist presentation of information, which does not always aspire to philosophical rigour.[45] 'Praecepta' are rules of a given discipline which are applicable and may be trusted by practitioners, but which are usually thought to be derived from principles borrowed from natural philosophy.[46] 'Praecognita' and 'praemissa' are similarly those pieces of information which must be known before a disciplinary discourse can be operated.[47] Such 'praecognita' or 'principia' are usually

---

neque quia nos ita cogitamus, res ita se habent, sed quia sic se habent, ita eas cognoscimo, cum recte cognoscimus'. For the opposite view, see Nicholas of Cusa 1983: 5.172: 'sic omnis rei mensura vel terminus ex mente est; et ligna et lapides certam mensuram et terminos habent praeter mentem nostram, sed ex mente increata, a qua rerum omnis terminus descendit'; Bacon 1878: 210–211 (*Novum Organum*, i.41), stressing that sense perception as well as the mind imposes measures on man. Zwinger (cited by Gilly 1977–79: 144), in talking about the method of enquiry into nature, suggests that the opposition of perception and objective nature may not be as great as is generally thought: 'quid vero erunt leges [methodi] istae? Nimirum quas Natura suggerit atque dictat Ratio effingit et imitator.'

[42] Biesius 1573: 158r, refers to 'certa demonstratio' as 'omnibus nota principia demonstrationum omnium, quae axiomata vocant: ut totum esse quavis sua parte, de rebus omnibus affirmationem vel negationem esse veram'; he further glosses 'certa' as 'quae sensu bene constituto ab omnibus percipiuntur'. Also Aquinas, *Summa theologiae*, 1a 2ae 112.5: 'certitudinaliter' is glossed as both 'indemonstrativa universalia principia' and 'conclusiones demonstrativa'.

[43] Keckermann 1614: *passim*. On 'dogmata', see Herberger 1981. Mandelbrote 2001: 92, has an illustration of Newton's manuscript revisions to the first edition of his *Principia*, in which on p. 402 he has changed the heading 'hypotheses' to 'regulae philosophandi'.

[44] Maclean 1992: 77.

[45] For example, Scribonius 1584; Magirus 1596.

[46] Maclean 2002a: 133f.

[47] The relevant Aristotelian doctrine is to be found at the beginning of the *Posterior Analytics* (i.1, 71a12ff), where 'praecognitio' is divided into (i) prior knowledge of fact, (ii) prior knowledge of the meaning of a term, and (iii) prior knowledge of both; and all such prior knowledge is distinguished from the actualization of potential knowledge, which is what occurs when we engage in reasoning. 'Praecognitio' is often linked to the 'principia' of

said to be specific to disciplines: those of physics are supplied by metaphysics and are both logically and ontologically necessary; those of medicine are supplied by natural philosophy, and have the same status.[48] 'Aphorismi' are brief accounts of the procedures to be followed or the inferences drawn from given sets of circumstances which may allow for a general account of knowledge to be drawn up, but may not. It seems that the Hippocratic corpus was interpreted as though the choice of aphoristic form was a deliberate strategy on the part of the author to provide guidance in specified sets of circumstances, and to avoid building general systems of diagnosis, prognosis and therapy; the use of 'maximae [sententiae]' in political discourse is similar.[49] As such, both terms are unsuitable to describe general laws, and like the rest of the terms in this group, may not even offer any explanatory force, being no more than prescriptive.

Implicit in the use of these terms is the fact that they combine mind-independent with mind-dependent elements. Zwinger addresses this issue through the opposition of 'nature' and 'art'; the latter representing the imposition of mental categories on the former. Between the two he places 'exercitatio': a practice (including experiment and empirical discovery) which confirms the mind-independent status of nature and recognizes at the same time man's active engagement with it, yielding results which have some degree of certainty, even if the weakness in man's sensory and ratiocinative powers has to be acknowledged.[50] The distinction between intra-mental and extra-mental laws is also articulated at this time in terms of the debate of the existence of universals and the nature of truth.[51] A related problem is the distinction

any discipline, which are 'neither derived from anything else, nor from each other, but from which all else is derived'; see also Sennert 1650: 1.7: 'neque ex aliis sunt, neque ex se mutuo, sed ex quibus omnia': Aristotle, *Physics*, i.5, 188a 27–28; Galen, *Methodus medendi*, i.4, K 10.33–34.

48 'Praecognitio' is a word with different senses according to discipline: in medicine it can mean both prognosis and prior knowledge of theory, in physics it can indicate the presuppositions taken over from the superior discipline metaphysics (form, matter, privation; act and potency, etc.) Ingolstetter 1596: A1; Lemosius 1598: 1r.

49 Maclean 2002a: 113–114; Malvezzi 1635.

50 Zwinger cited by Gilly 1977–79: 204; Hellerus 1548: D3v: 'ea enim est nostrae cognitionis imbecillitas, ut nullam artem, quam humana industria excogitavit et tradidit absolutam possideamus. Interim plusquam scepticae impudentiae ac dementiae est, nihil certitudinis philosophiae relinquere.'

51 Grawerus 1614: 17 (on the distinction between the 'veritas objecti' and a double notion of correspondence): 'adaequatio notionum in intellectu cum rebus et orationum cum notionibus, ita ut oratio consentiat cum notionibus animi, notio animi cum re ipsa extra animum vere existente'; Martini 1593: B4v (arguing that philosophy is a 'mentis habitus' not 'extra mentem'): 'si nullus sit homo capax artis, et per consequens nulla hominis mente ars, ubi tuae artes habitabunt? An apud ideas Platonicas? Vel in Utopia simul cum vestra philosophia? Ut si nullus sit sutor in rerum natura ubi erit ars sutoria?' See also Aquinas *De veritate*, 2,1 ad 4 (on scientia as either 'in deo' or a 'habitus conclusionis'); Maclean 1992: 74 (on Scaliger); and Case 1599: 9.41 (truth is in things qua subjects; in propositions qua signs; and in minds, qua terms); Eckart 1992: 156 (on Sennert); Herberger 1981: 93–94 (quoting Galen, *De optima secta*, ii, K 1.108–110);see also Keckermann 1614:1 596–1600.

between epistemology and ontology, as can be sensed from Piccolomini's definition of cause as 'a principle on which effects depend ontologically and epistemologically', and his related claim that 'principia' (ἀρχαί) are both necessary presuppositions or preconditions, and postulates; the sense is always made clear by the context; they can be either 'ex [rei] natura' or 'ex parte nostra'.[52] The full implications of this for experimental philosophy, in which the causal propositions derived from effects need to be very cautiously framed, will only be worked out in the latter half of the seventeenth century.[53]

It is pertinent here to add a note on the use of the word 'certitudo' in the late Renaissance, in view of such collocations as the following: 'naturae lex, ordo et intentio [sunt] res certae'; 'nullus praeter naturam affectus homines corripit nisi certis praecurrentibus signis ille indicatus fuerit'; 'certissima signa de mutatione temporum'; 'agricultores, ac medici in re certiore saepius praedicendo falluntur';'coniectura ex rebus certissimis'; 'signum certius'; 'certae leges'; 'certa principia artis'; 'certa sensuum obiecta'; 'praecepta [physiognomiae] non [sunt] ita simpliciter categorica, sed cum conditionibus certis intelligenda'.[54] Both 'certitudo' and 'veritas' are subject to the distinction between what is a mental object and what is mind-independent;[55] and both relate not only to 'scientia' (knowledge based on causes or arguments from necessity) but also to 'opinio' ('probable' knowledge).[56] In the case of the latter, authors speak of premisses, laws and conclusions which are 'certiores' or certissimae', 'veriores' or 'verissimae'; and they recognize that the same degrees can be found in necessity.[57] 'Certus' denotes both 'fixed' (which leaves unanswered the question: by what or by whom?) and 'reliable'. This means the

52 Piccolomini 1600: 105–106: 'principium ex quo effecta pendent secundum esse et secundum cognitionem'. Principles can be associated with axioms as in the title of Thomas White's work *Euclides physicus seu de principiis naturae staecheidea*, London, 1657. See also Maclean 1996: 59–60.

53 See Sprat 1667: 101–103: 'The first *Danger* that I shall observe in [dogmatizing] is an over–hasty and praecipitant concluding upon the *Causes*, before the *Effects* have been enough searched into ... [The Philosopher] pitches upon some *particular* object ... [makes] some guesses at its Causes ... begins to mould some General *Proposition* upon it ... and meets with more and more proofs to confirm his *judgment*. But now ... he carelessly admits whole crowds of Testimonies, that seem in any way to confirm that *Opinion*, which he had before establish'd.'

54 Case 1599: 13; Diocles 1972: 2v; Gratarolo 1554; Ficino 1576: 1616; Memm in Siraisi 2000: 11; Timpler in Freedman 1988: 422; Melanchthon 1834–60: 13.194; Liddel 1628: 512; Severinus 1571: 2 (also on 'geometricus mos'); Keckermann 1614: 1590.

55 Horst 1629: 4 distinguishes between 'ratio rei' which is 'theoricum, quod opere naturae et non nostro productione est' and 'ratio intellectus', 'inquantum ipse rem quamlibet utcumque speculativam reddere potest'; Bernardus 1605: s.v. certitudo, on Alexander of Hales, *In Metaphysicam*, i: 'certitudo duplex: alia oritur ex natura rei, alia ex parte nostra ... certitudines diversae sunt in diversis scientiis'.

56 On the sense of this usage, see Maclean 2000a: 230.

57 Piccolomini 1600: 104 (on a horse being 'necessary' for a long journey, as opposed to a stone 'necessarily' falling); Hawenreuter in Zabarella 1597: 3r: 'verissimis demonstrationibus et perpetuis et necessariis praeceptis'. Galen's division of knowledge (in *De locis affectis* i.1, K 8.18–19) into [i] 'exquisita notitia', 'certissimae notae' and indubitatae indices'; [ii]'artificiosa

selection of phrases given above, which have been taken from a variety of natural-philosophical and medical texts, are doubly ambiguous; not only may they refer to the mind's grasp on reality, or reality itself; but they may also refer to different degrees of reliability.

V

The ambiguity of these phrases relates also to the relationship between logical and physical necessity in respect of law-like statements. If the universe is rationally conceived, then there will be congruence between these two forms of necessity. This can be sensed as a presupposition in Aristotle's *Physics* and in most of the ancient commentaries written on it; an example of argumentation based on this presupposition is the demonstration in book 3 that there cannot be infinity in nature. It seems that thinkers such as Melanchthon accepted this presupposition and even derived a form of rationalist ethics from it.[58] Newton's editor Roger Cotes, on the other hand, was to see this assumption as presumptuous, because it limits the power of the creator deity and fails to take account of the design of the universe:

> Without all doubt this world, so diversified with that variety of forms and motions we find in it, could arise from nothing but the perfectly free will of God directing and presiding over all. From this fountain it is that those laws we call the laws of nature have flowed, in which there appear many traces indeed of the most wise contrivance, but not the least shadow of necessity. These therefore we must not seek from uncertain conjectures, but learn them from observations and experiments. He who is presumptuous enough to think that he can find the true principles of physics and the laws of natural things by the force alone of his mind, and the internal light of reason, must either suppose that the world exists by necessity, and that the same necessity follows the laws proposed; or if the order of nature was established by the will of God, that himself, a miserable reptile, can tell what was fittest to be done.[59]

It is clear from this that Newton is nearer to an Aristotelian position in which sense impressions are prior to conceptions, than a Platonic anamnestic one. It is clear also that this position leaves the possibility of what might be termed 'nomic

---

coniectura'; and [iii] 'pura ignorantia' is an example of the conjoining of epistemological and ontological.

[58] See Kusukawa 1995; Scattola 1999b.

[59] Newton 1972: 33: 'Neutiquam profecto potuit oriri mundus, pulcherrima formarum et motuum varietate distinctus, nisi ex liberrima voluntate cuncta providentis et gubernantis dei. Ex hoc igitur fonte promanarunt illae omnes quae dicuntur naturae leges: in quibus multa sane sapientissimi consilii, nulla necessitatis apparent vestigia. Has proinde non ab incertis conjecturis petere, sed observandi atque experiendi addiscere debemus. Qui vere physicae principia legesque rerum, sola mentis vi et interno rationis lumine fretum, invenire se posse confidit: hunc oportet vel statuere mundum ex necessitate fuisse, legesque propositas ex eadem necessitate sequi: vel si per voluntatem dei constitutus sit ordo naturae, se tamen homuncionem misellum, quid optimum factum sit, perspectum habere'. I have taken the translation from Stafleu 1999: 94.

occasionalism' open (that is, the regular and consistent intervention at will of the creator, who constitutes the source of all change, in his creation).

We have already noted that necessity governs nature in a certain way in an Aristotelian system; it is (besides an intrusive deity) the highest governing instance; as the proverb has it, 'necessity has no law'.[60] It is however uneasily tied up with logic and the human will. According to Goclenius, there are two meanings of necessity: 'that without which something cannot exist, as in the case of a man without a soul'; and 'that without which something does not apply consistently or as aptly, as in the sentence "it was necessary for the son of God to be incarnated for the redemption of mankind"'.[61] It is both logically and physically impossible for a man to be without a soul; the same necessity is referred to in the Cambridge disputation of 1639 on the proposition 'eccentric orbits are posited necessarily' (necessario ponuntur orbes eccentrici), and the later one (of 1650) on the proposition 'the law of nature is indispensable' (lex naturae est indispensabilis). Necessity's connection with both material determinism and the human will is shown in the worked example in Goclenius on the proposition 'the necessity of dying is innate to man through (1) the established law of nature in the form of the consumption of radical moisture or something harmful being suffered or (2) sin'.[62] Piccolomini also points out that 'necessarium' is either 'pro vere' or merely 'difficulter aliter se habere' (see above, note 57). It can be 'in re ex suppositione' or 'in re absolutum'; his examples of the latter sound like laws of nature (the example, borrowed from Aristotle, of 'absolutum coactum' is 'a stone necessarily rising when thrown upwards by someone'; the example of 'absolutum secundum naturam' is 'a raised-up stone necessarily falling if not held up by someone').[63] But 'necessaria' have both strong metaphysical and logical connotations, being related to entailment (a man must be an animal), impossibility (a man cannot be a stone) and possibility, in which both non-existence and existence are conceivable (a man may, or may not be, a writer).[64] We are back to a conception of nature whose potency does not lead to a necessary act; and to a world-view which links theological issues of freedom with determinism of matter.

VI

I come finally to the association of regularity with prescription. The terms '[naturae] lex, leges, ius' are used quite frequently and in various disciplines, and they evince these awkward juxtaposed connotations. The legal force of prescription may be sited

60 'Necessitas legem non habet': cited by Binsfeld 1596: 342.

61 Goclenius 1613: 751: 'sine quo aliud esse non potest, ut homo sine anima'; 'sine quo non convenienter, seu tam apte esse non valet, sicque ad redimendum Genus humanum necesse Dei filium incarnari'.

62 Ibid.:'moriendi necessitas inest homini ex (1) lege Naturae instituta propter consumptionem humidi radicalis [aut] ex passioni nocente' [vel] (2) peccato'.

63 Piccolomini 1600: 219; 'ut necesse est lapidem tendere sursum, dum a proiiciente impellitur'; 'ut lapis elevatus et non detentus necessario descendit'. See also Zabarella 1586–87: 5.44f. The Aristotelian locus is *Posterior Analytics*, ii.11, 95a 3ff.

64 The example is taken from Lohr 2000.

at one remove in God, who passes on a command to nature, or to mankind in the form of laws which the deity alone can override; or it may betoken God's direct intervention into his creation. In jurisprudence, 'ius naturale' is distinguished from 'ius civile' and ius gentium' in the first law of the Digest (D 1.1.1); this is the law which nature teaches all animals and hence is common to all creation; even the 'principes' of civil law are subject to it.[65] It is said to constitute both a constraint (in that it is the determinant of human nature) and a sort of liberty, in contradistinction to the law laid down by human societies.[66] It is also the basis of civil authority, which expands on the axioms of nature and accommodates these to the infinite diversity of the world.[67]

Sennert may well write that 'it is not for us to prescribe rules to Nature, but to describe that same Nature from itself',[68] but in fact most of the uses of 'natural law' deliberately conjoin the prescriptive with the descriptive.[69] God ordains that the universe should be as it is; the laws by which it is governed are his, but are self-operating regularities guaranteed by a version of immanent teleology.[70] The term 'law' here combines associations of legislation (it is ordained by an agency of some kind) with regularity (it describes, inter alia, physical phenomena which can be relied upon to stand in a constant relation one to another). It is this which *prima facie* makes adoption of the term after the second half of the seventeenth century seem awkward. But it may be that this combination of associations is seen as an advantage by some thinkers, for it dispenses with the need to locate law-giving either in the divine mind as it first constituted nature, or in a constantly interventionist God, to whose occasional action all phenomena and events in the world can be attributed, or in a superlunary nature acting on the sublunary, or in a material sublunary nature.

VII

It might tentatively be concluded from the above that in the whole semantic field in which the earlier usages of 'laws of nature' is to be found, description and

---

65 Schickhard 1615: 45, 260, 267.

66 The 'law of liberty' is of course a biblical phrase (James 1:25; 2:12).

67 Spiegelius 1569: s.v. natura: 'civilis auctoritas latius porrigit naturae axiomata accommodat negociis et dispensat secundam immensam varietatem unicuique'. The Ciceronian use of 'norma' covers both prescriptive and descriptive rules, and the same combination of senses is found in Renaissance contexts: 'vitam ad certam rationis normam dirigere': *Pro Murena*, 2,3; *Academicae quaestiones*, 2,46,140, quoted above; 'natura norma legis est', *De legibus*, 2,24,178 etc.

68 Sennert 1650: 1.179: 'verum non nostrum est naturae leges praescribere; sed ex ipsa natura natura describenda. An earlier use of 'lex naturae' to indicate regularity of phenomena and nothing more is found in Zabarella 1590a: 559–564: see above, note 25.

69 Scaliger 1592: clxxxviii and ccclix.11, in referring to 'ordinaria Dei potestas', link the prescriptive and the descriptive clearly.

70 See Donne 1953–62: 3.229: 'God's ordinary working is by Nature, these causes must produce these effects: and that is the common law; He goes sometimes above that, by Prerogative, and that is by miracle, and sometimes below that, as by custome, and that is Fortune, that is contingency; Fortune is as far out of the ordinary way, as miracle.'

prescription work in conjunction with each other; and that the discursive elaborations of 'law of nature' evince a blurring of the distinctions between teleological and non-teleological, metaphysical and physical, general and local, ontological and epistemological which, although awkward to the modern eye, suits the purposes of post-Aristotelian students of nature.[71] This field is, as has already been noted, to some degree discipline-specific; the reasons for the eventual preference shown for the term 'lex' over others in the later seventeenth century (notably 'regula' and 'axioma') may well be to do with, inter alia, unwanted residues of discipline-specific senses. The concepts of 'law' and 'nature' change significantly in the course of the seventeenth century; 'law' comes to be associated with what is independent of the human mind, whereas late Renaissance thinkers continue to speculate whether nature's regularities are no more than the product of their own perception of them; 'nature' comes to be seen as including the preternatural, whereas before it could be looked upon as an agency permitting exceptions, whose regularity applied only in the majority of cases. These changes in the semantic content of the terms may indicate also a change in the questions driving any enquiry into the sublunary and superlunary worlds; what was mainly of interest to natural philosophers in the late Renaissance was the speculative question of essence rather than the productive issue of nature's modes of operation, whereas after 1660, laws governing matter are of particular interest because their identification and understanding will facilitate the manipulation of nature itself.

[71] For example, Cardano 1663: 1.98 (alluding to Plotinus): 'Quod si quae futura sunt, praevisa sunt a Deo, etiam ordinata sunt: si ordinata a Deo, iusta etiam sunt: Deus enim iustissimus est, si iusta, queri non debemus, ne Deo adversari videamur. Etenim non ille iustitiam suam indignatione statuit in poenam, ut homines: sed unicuique quod expedit, et quantum expedit, tribuit. At non nunc nos ex providentia Dei eam scire possumus, quam ex fati ordine ac constitutione, cuius auctor Deus ipse est, haec a Deo instituta esse.'

Chapter 3

The Legitimation of Law through God, Tradition, Will, Nature and Constitution

Michael Stolleis

I

> Ordinary law-givers offer us laws to regulate society–laws, subject to change like the minds of those who make them, and of the people who obey them: those talk only of general, immutable, and eternal laws, which, without exception, are obeyed with order, regularity, and absolute exactness in the immensity of space. (Montesquieu, 1923: 223–224)

Just what the 'legitimation' of law actually means may depend on what is agreed, either tacitly or explicitly, by the speakers. Given the vagueness of the term, it allows scope for a considerable number of possible variations. In the following, however, a broad outline will suffice – along the lines of regarding the legitimation of law as a possible indication of the various arguments that proved most persuasive at any given time to contemporaries asking such questions as 'Where does law come from? Why is it valid? To whom does one turn or to what does one take recourse in order to justify law?' In this respect, much has been said about the 'grounds' or 'foundations' of law. It is a metaphor indicative of something that is not, in itself, law, but which underpins law, lending it validity and, as it were, making it 'right' or 'just'. On closer inspection, there are two sides to this: on the one hand, it describes the kind of authority that lends emphasis and vitality to a premise, backing it up, and threatening sanctions for failure to comply with it, while on the other hand, in a more specific sense, it has to do with a qualitative leap that turns any such premise into a legal norm or rule of law. This latter aspect presumes the possibility of distinguishing between premises in such a way that those based on convention are described as custom or bonos mores, whereas the others take on the quality of legislation. If such a distinction is made, or rather, agreed upon, it must also be possible to determine which are the characteristics that make a premise into a rule of law. Here, too, there are conventional views – such as the view that the prevailing authority should be public, state, or perhaps even divine, and that norms should be designated 'law' by dint of general agreement. Whether or not this necessarily involves the potential threat of sanctions on grounds of the violation of norms has long been a point of contention and has been debated time and again by way of example of certain sanction-free norms or international law.

In the same vein, it is widely believed that, in the oldest cultures, it was the gods, a single god or (in monotheism) God who 'gave' law to humankind, by writing it in their hearts (Romans 2:15) or by revealing it in divine scripture.

Admittedly, this presupposes a theogony – a developed realm of gods or a theological concept of the divine derived from it. Yet even before that, there were surely other, earlier eras in which law-giving gods acting with deliberation were still unknown. For this reason, it would seem more plausible to turn to cultural anthropology or ethnology in order to determine stages of development in which an environment inhabited by animals, plants, spirits and ancestors was regarded as an established 'order' that included humankind. Given a lack of distinction between law and religion, it seems misleading to describe 'law' – still unrecognizable as such – as being based on 'religion'. Where the human world and the natural world were one, deviations from that which was considered 'right' were healed ritually, and nature was dialogically involved in the process. In this respect, in so far as we can have any insight at all into prehistory or can presume to draw any ethnological analogies, basic patterns of ritual response to repeated 'deviations' (homicide, adultery, theft) began to emerge. If we were able to ask our prehistorical forebears about the legitimation of such rituals, we would probably be told that any breach of the established order was inherently dangerous and that it had to be healed. The order itself may have been handed down by ancestors or deduced from an animistic perception of the natural world – in the case of Pygmies, the 'forest'.[1]

Perhaps it is for this reason that the age-old question as to whether law developed out of religion and was originally legitimized by it is actually somewhat misleading in that it invariably presupposes separate systems of norms that did not initially exist in such clearly distinct forms. At any rate, it may be observed that the more strongly anthropomorphic images of deities took shape, the more clearly the concepts of 'law' and 'justice' applying to human society became linked to these gods. Soon, certain gods were considered specific guardians of law and judgment – gods to whom places of jurisdiction were dedicated, gods who were invoked when it came to the violation of accepted norms. The terms 'right' (*recht*, *droit*, *diritto*) and 'just' (*juste*, *justus*) associated with good deities, show law as something approved by the gods or by God. In the words of Psalm 99, 'The Lord reigneth; let the people tremble: he sitteth between the cherubims; let the earth be moved. The Lord is great in Zion; and he is high above all the people. Let them praise thy great and terrible name; for it is holy. The king's strength also loveth judgment ...' (Ps 99: 1–6). Luther summarizes this as 'Im Reich dieses Königs hat man das Recht lieb [In the realm of this king, law is cherished]'.

The prologue of the *Sachsenspiegel* from the first third of the thirteenth century succinctly states: 'Gott ist selber Recht. Darum ist ihm Recht lieb' ['God himself is law. Therefore is law dear to him'][2] and continues with the admonition that all those ordained by God to pass judgment should ensure that they judge in such a way that God's wrath and his judgment be merciful upon them ['Das Gottes Zorn

---

1 Turnbull 1984; Wesel 1985.

2 'Got ist selber recht. Dar umme ist im recht lip'.

und sein gericht gnädiglich über sie gehen möge'].[3] God is thus the omnipotent legislator. He is the source and legitimation of law; a natural law separate from God is inconceivable. All earthly judges are themselves ultimately subject to God's Last Judgment. In functional terms, this meant not only that law – particularly penal law – was divine and thus immune to change, but it also reinforced the status of the lawcourt or tribunal as an institution with a divine mission.

The identification of divine law and natural law is an expression of a theocratic order. In advanced civilizations, this requires the existence of a 'holy scripture', a bookish culture and an educated clergy engaged in interpreting God's divine law and order on earth. The distinction, still valid in canon law, between *ius divinum*, *ius naturale* and *ius positivum* (*aut civile aut gentium*)[4] postulates a correlation between even the smallest details of legislation and the fundamental principles of *ius divinum*. Law constitutes a clearly structured pyramidical hierarchy of norms supported by the ecclesiastical claim to order. Given that God is the creator and lord of nature, natural law is in harmony with *ius divinum*; it is the same everywhere, because it follows the same 'natural instincts' (*quod ubique instinctu naturae ... habetur*). Accordingly, ius positivum can be corrected and amended to comply with the tenets of *ius naturale*. The legitimation of even simple canon law thus derives from *ius divinum*, just as a ray of light from above illuminates everything.

II

This view is idealistic. Historically speaking, in the High and Late Middle Ages in Europe, the strategies for the legitimation of law were far more complex. Legitimation through ancestral tradition was still very much alive and blended with God's will. According to the *Sachsenspiegel*: 'Diz recht en habe ich selbir nicht erdacht,/ ez haben von aldere an uns gebracht / Unse guten vorevaren [I did not conceive of this law myself / older persons have brought it to us / our good forebears]'.[5] Law was thus legitimized by tradition; it was the order by which people lived and it constituted what was 'right'. In an era of highly evolved theology, this notion of what was 'right' was consolidated by invoking God. By combining the topoi of legitimation, all manner of variations were possible: in 1525, rebellious peasants appealed to local 'customs, usage and justice'[6] and then legitimized their position through 'divine and natural law' which now seemed directly accessible to them in the New Testament as a result of the Reformation. They described this renewed invocation of *ius divinum* and *ius naturale* as 'divine jurisprudence'[7] – and did so with a sentiment fuelled more by enthusiasm than by irony.

Alongside local law and canon law legitimized by tradition and theocracy, international Roman law took hold from the thirteenth century onwards. From the universities of Northern Italy, it spread throughout Latin-speaking Europe and

[3] 'daz gotis zorn unde sin gerichte genedicliche obir se gen muze'.

[4] *Decretum Gratiani*, c.1.D.1.

[5] Prologue to the *Sachsenspiegel*, 151–153.

[6] Blickle 1998: 77ff.

[7] Ibid.: 80, 100.

established itself as a new paradigm over older legal strata,[8] sometimes even replacing these older structures completely because of the higher social prestige conferred as much by its greater rationality as by the new artificial language in which it was couched. In spite of invoking God in the enforcement of the Corpus Iuris Civilis in the year 533,[9] Roman law actually took its legitimation from imperial authority. A sharp distinction was made between divine perfection on the one hand and, on the other hand, human imperfection and mutability (*humana condicio*); for, according to the legislator, 'Nature desires to bring forth ever new forms',[10] which explains the need for a worldly legitimation of law in the name of 'peace' and 'order'. The term 'nature', according to *Digesten* (Dig. 1.1.3), covers all living creatures (*animalia*), human beings, the animals of the earth and the birds of the air, and all things that swim in the water. Even the wild animals, it is expressly stated, live according to natural law. The laws created by humankind (*ius publicum, ius gentium, ius civile*) deviated from natural law, developed historically,[11] were functional and mutable, and were legitimized in the sixth century by the imperial will that decreed them valid.

III

The reception of worldly Roman law conveyed a notion of temporality that was reflected in the fact that the faculties of jurisprudence were entirely independent of the faculties of theology. This, in turn, spawned a third topos of legitimation: the will of the authorities. Their will was manifested for the first time by the jurist popes of the thirteenth century, who began to rule a world church through the carefully targeted application of ius positivum.[12] The same development continued with the city authorities basing their municipal rights and new 'gute Policey' [good policies] on their will, and, by the Late Middle Ages and early modern era, with the landowning classes consciously shaping their territories and applying a will to reform.[13] As Ernst Kantorowicz has pointed out, they were, to a greater or lesser degree, drawing upon a repertoire of absolutist formulae from the classical world, most notably the formulae of *princeps legibus solutus* and *quod principe placuit, legis habet vigorem*.[14] Even for Roman law, whose legislators had by now been dead some thousand years, efforts were made in the sixteenth century to construct an act of legislation by a German emperor based on 'will' (the Lotharian Legend).[15] In other

8 Kiefner 1990.

9 Constitutio 'Dedoken' (*Digesten*), Preamble and No. 10 on the implementation of imperial power through God, 'that it may decide the ever arising questions for the people who require it and thus counter the inconstancy of human nature (*physis*) and include it in fixed rules and laws (*nomoi kai horoi*)'. Also Constitutio 'Imperatoriam' (*Institutionen*).

10 'multas etenim formas edere natura novas deproperat', Const. Tanta 18.

11 Dig. 1.2 on the emergence of Roman law and the genealogy of legal scholars.

12 Gagnér 1960.

13 Stolleis 1990; Stolleis 1996.

14 Kantorowicz 1957; Wyduckel 1979.

15 Conring 1643. On the Legend of Lothar, see Luig, 1983.

words, in the spiritual and temporal field throughout Europe from the High Middle Ages to the Early Modern Era, we can discern a process in which the legitimation of law shifted from the notion of theologically determined truth (veritas) to that of secularized will (voluntas), and, with that, from eternal law to a continuously adapted positive law.[16] In the mindset of the early modern age, this law approximated natural law because it appeared to be a timeless ratio scripta. What is more, being 'imperial law', it bore a sacred aura.[17]

We thus see two lines of justification, both of which focus on legitimation through will. One of these is rooted in the animistic notion of a natural world inhabited by spirits to be feared, in which all things 'occur' and in which humans seek to defend themselves from danger by means of magic. In the course of the history of religion, the will of the gods emerges behind this nameless occurrence. Nuomina become gods. Gods have a will, or multiple wills; they are wrathful, vengeful and determine the lot of humankind. As this polytheism increasingly gave way to monotheism – leaving aside the close parallels to Islam or, from a Christian viewpoint, the pagan residues and the cosmos of saints – the just will of the trinitarian God increasingly became the source and legitimation of law.[18] This, to repeat a point already made, is the product of highly evolved scholastic theology as practised by Thomas Aquinas or Aegidius Romanus.[19]

The second line of justification focused on will is that of Roman law. Although, in principle, it goes back to the will of the Roman people, it is in fact, from Augustus to Justinian, the will of the (god-like) emperor.[20] Here, too, we find the apotheosis of a divine being into a legislator whose justice, wisdom and omniscience mean that he cannot but decree 'right law'.

As the foundations of Christianity were increasingly undermined in the sixteenth and seventeenth centuries by the formation of different confessions and by successive wars of religion, so too did modern politics and the rule of law determined by principalities become increasingly emancipated from prescribed religious content.

In terms of political thought, an orientation towards the vera natura delle cose essentially began with and through Machiavelli.[21] Experience and observation served to decode the 'nature' of the political world. God no longer played a role. What Machiavelli observed was the mechanism of temporal power, dominated by virtù and fortuna. Natural law in the sense of this new 'politics' was based on the 'probability' of the behaviour of political powers as documented by historical example (historia docet).

At the same time, there was an erosion of the Christian element in the justification of law. The invocation of God in the preambles to a growing volume of communal and territorial acts of legislation became increasingly formulaic, with an undercurrent betraying the will of a worldly god, or Leviathan, whose legendary maxim 'auctoritas

16 Gagnér 1960.

17 Krause 1952.

18 Mittelstras 2000.

19 Zumkeller 1980.

20 Kunkel and Schermaier 2001: 103f., 167f.

21 Cantimori 1976; Buck 1985; Skinner 1981; Münkler 1982.

non veritas facit legem' succinctly expressed this change in the foundations of legitimation. In theory, the state could also ordain something that was unjust, and it would nevertheless be law. 'Truth' and 'justice' were thus no longer the defining characteristics of positive law. Law was valid because it had been decreed valid. Thus, as Pascal put it, different truths could prevail on either side of the Pyrenees. Content became relative and no longer qualified law as 'right'.

This rather pointed comment is intended only to indicate the general direction of developments, rather than implying that there was already any explicitly formalistic legal positivism in the seventeenth century. This was certainly not the case, even for Hobbes, who did not give up the concept of natural law. Rather, we find in the seventeenth and eighteenth centuries a number of legal strata existing concomitantly. The law of custom, legitimized by tradition, still played an important role at both local and imperial levels (as *Reichsherkommen* or 'imperial origin').[22] Mediaeval Roman law (*usu sensim receptum*),[23] which had gradually taken hold, was considered a superior and generally reasonable system of law, even if those interpreting it could not reach a consensus. Aside from this, there was all manner of positive law based on the authority of those in power, and thus drawing its legitimation from 'sovereignty' – a sovereignty that was simply defined as the capacity to issue orders. Imperial laws were based on consensus, having the character of an agreement between the Emperor and the empire, and were thus based on a dually binding will.[24]

What these various legitimized forms of positive law had in common was that they were 'human', established, positive norms. Their religious background, that is to say their metaphysical claim to 'justice' and 'truth', paled in the course of time, from the sixteenth to the eighteenth century. Legal norms, produced in evermore rapid succession, soon became increasingly secularized, until they eventually oriented themselves exclusively towards a temporal purpose. Montesquieu then recommended that the legislators observe the 'nature' of the states they ruled,[25] and repeatedly spoke of 'the nature of the thing' but also spoke of the law of nature as human nature,[26] and of natural law in the sense of what people, and peoples, at all times, spontaneously accepted as reasonable.

This brings us to the use of language in the eighteenth century, when natural law was at its height. From the last third of the seventeenth century, every university had its chair of natural law, and a flood of theoretical publications on the subject of natural law followed. This began in the 1680s, peaked in the mid-eighteenth century and did not really peter out completely until well into the nineteenth century. Jurists looked to these publications to learn the general principles of law (legal theory), thereby acquiring a normative social theory (social philosophy, sociology of law)

---

22 Roeck 1984; on the role custom in the hierarchy of legal sources of usus modernus, see Oestmann 2002: 118ff.; Oestmann 1998.

23 Conring 1643.

24 Mohnhaupt 2000.

25 Radbruch 1938: 168; Mohnhaupt 2003.

26 Cf. The last letter of Montesquieu 1923, in which Roxane, languishing in the seraglio, confesses her unfaithfulness to her faraway master Usbeck and self-confidently declares that she has 'corrected your laws by those of nature'; in other words, she has overcome human injustice in a legal form through natural law.

and the ability to structure and unify the perplexingly intricate volume of positive law (politics).

Consequently, there is no such thing as 'the' natural law; instead, in the course of some 150 years, the success of natural law was based on a wide variety of religious, theoretical and political approaches and motifs. Initially, in the sixteenth and seventeeth centuries, natural law was linked to the theological context of late mediaeval scholastics and reform teachings [1]; then, from about 1650, on systems of *more geometrico* that were largely detached from moral theology [2]; thirdly, the Enlightenment systems of natural law emerged with their distinction between law and morals and their critique of Absolutism [3]; and fourthly, following Kant and the French Revolution, there were forms of natural law based either on revolutionary or on liberal and constitutional argumentation [4]. In each of these phases, though the arguments put forward for the 'law of nature' were made in different and often contradictory contexts, the notion of a 'law of nature' proved semantically irresistible, appearing as it did to guarantee security and superiority. Invoking the 'law of nature' seemed to brook no contradiction. Anyone who did contradict automatically put themselves in the position of a blasphemous rebel 'against God and Nature'.

The rise of natural law can be explained primarily by three key changes in the European world. They are fundamental transformations of the geocentric world view and the theoretical revolution in the natural sciences, the religious crisis in Europe that triggered a relativization of the theological monopoly on truth, the political rise of absolutism and the emergence of the nation state at the cost of feudal rule and the power of the estates and cities.

The Scientific Revolution from the mid-sixteenth century onwards – in mathematics, physics, astronomy and medicine, to name but a few disciplines – directly affected jurists as the constructors of a normative world. The emergence of 'natural sciences' shaped by 'laws', set forth in a 'Book of Nature'[27] inevitably posed the question as to whether such laws might not also be found in the social order. A formerly hermetic, God-given world of heaven and of inhabited and uninhabited nature, including the social order, fell apart. With the mathematization of the world, the 'laws of nature' became both ineluctable and at the same time calculable. Jurists were faced with the challenge (much as they later would be in the nineteenth century) of creating certain and calculable rules for the social realm. To this end, they made deductions from supreme principles, attempted to mathematize Roman law (Leibniz), and generally took a *more geometrico* approach to evidence: major premise, minor premise, conclusion. As in the social philosophy of the seventeenth century, this meant, in principle, turning away from God. God became the clockmaker watching the clock from afar as it ticked to its inherent laws. He still remained prima causa, but no longer had the 'will' to intervene, even if he could. Natural law thus came to

[27] Alunni 1982. The documentation of the Tenth Annual Meeting of the Arbeitskreis für Barockforschung: 'Artes et Scientiae. Repräsentationen neuer und alter Sichtweisen von "Natur" in der frühen Neuzeit' (ed. Barbara Bauer), held at Wolfenbüttel in 2000, has not yet been published. Of particular relevance to the context of this essay is Thomas Leinkauf's paper 'Zwei konkurrierende Verständnisweisen von "Natur": qualitativ und quantitativ, aus einheitsmetaphsischer Sicht und im experimentellen Zugriff'.

be perceived as something that could apply even without God, as in Grotius' famous maxim of *etiamsi daremus*.[28]

The religious crisis of the sixteenth and seventeenth centuries had weakened the claim to certainty made by religion and its exegetes. 'Silete theologi in munere alieno' became the call of the jurists,[29] and a little-known German author, leaning on Justus Lipsius, developed his 'Politick' with explicit disregard for the 'gelehrten Theologen Zanck und ohneinigkeit' ['the learned theologians Strife and Disunity'].[30] The authority of the theologians disintegrated, even in the university hierarchy. God was cited, as ever, but the confessional aspects were gone. By the end of the eighteenth century, the world was perceived increasingly deistically and even pantheistically.[31]

The third main reason for the rise of the topoi 'Law of Nature' and 'Natural Law' was their dual potential for political instrumentalization – not only by nascent Absolutism but also by its opponents.

Given the *more geometrico* form of natural law, the early modern principality, which was to become the paradigm of the era,[32] had at its service a whole battery of arguments which permitted the modernization and unification of the fragmented mediaeval legal world. The outlines of the first attempts at codification, which occurred around this time, were based both on Roman law and on natural law. It was no longer the consensus-based model of 'head' and 'limbs' that held sway, but the notion of the 'state as machine' functioning according to the rules of the natural sciences.[33]

On the other hand, the opponents of absolutism based their arguments on the evocative topoi of natural law and the laws of nature. However much a tyrant might be able to do, he would always be constrained by the limitations of the laws of nature and natural law. Even a 'godless' tyrant was physically part of nature and thus, by analogy, of the social order. He, too, was therefore subject to elementary obligations. Theorists never tired of stressing this point and applied subjugation to the 'laws of nature' as functionally as any constitutional obligation *avant la lettre*. A natural law that emphasized 'liberties' could become charged with revolutionary sentiment and thereby brand prevailing law itself as unjust.[34]

In this way – in eighteenth century Germany at least – arguments based on the 'law of nature' were available for all political interests. Disregarding the ever-weakening tradition of a genuinely Christian natural law, the secularized natural laws made deliberate use of the argumentative advantages resulting from the oscillation between the 'natural law' of the scientists and the pessimistically or optimistically interpreted notion of 'human nature' and the empirically or intuitively grasped 'nature of the

28 St.Leger 1962; Hervada 1983.

29 Albericus Gentili (1552–1608). See Schmitt 1950: 91ff.

30 Kreps 1620: 13.

31 On the vehement resistance to pantheism still current at the end of the eighteenth century, see Mauthner 1912.

32 On the diversity of forms of rule in practice and on the problems of considering time in the context of the model of absolutism, see Asch 1996; Schilling 1999.

33 Stollberg-Rilinger 1986.

34 Klippel 1976.

thing'.[35] Prior to Kant's epistemologically critical insights, this oscillation between normative and descriptive statements was still possible. When the normative intent was clothed in the vestments of what was already called for by dint of 'nature', the commandment took on the character of the ineluctable. Vice versa, nature lost its traits of the chaotic and the threatening when it manifested itself not only as pure Being (*Sein*) but as ordered and certain Being (*Sein*) determined by a higher will.

A century later, in the last third of the nineteenth century, the brilliant achievements in the natural sciences and successful technical progress led to a paradigmatic situation in the field of jurisprudence similar to that which had existed in the seventeenth century. From now on it was no longer positive law (*ius*) – or the 'law' (*lex*) – that was to be made inviolable *more geometrico*; instead, leading jurists hoped for the discovery of evolutionary laws of legislation analogous to the 'laws of nature'. For example, Franz Liszt, the expert in penal and international law, hoped for a development of the law 'according to laws that function with the force of natural law. Even if we are unfortunately not in a position to prove these laws with the same clarity as natural laws. And if the development of international law is the same as the development of state law, if the same basic laws govern the development of legislation between states, then we can, with absolute certainty, posit the thesis that the development of international law must occur in the same way as the development of state law.'[36]

The fields of natural science in which the jurists so optimistically sought their metaphors and analogies are those that demonstrated a spectacular degree of success. In the mid-nineteenth century, it was chemistry (Rudolf von Jhering),[37] and physiology,[38] and finally, to an increasing degree, the theories of evolution, which catapulted age-old patterns of international historical development (primitivism, barbarism, civilization) into the general consciousness, and even the popular press, with enormous force. At the same time, they provided an explanation of the biological foundations of human nature – now at last without reference to God. A form of legal ethnology that blossomed and operated worldwide at the same time as comparative law appeared to supply the empirical material for the 'natural law of legislation'.[39] The jurists – for the most part little versed in questions of philosophy, scientific theory and natural sciences – succumbed once again to the illusion that they could alleviate their chronic lack of any scientific basis by borrowing from the natural sciences. The natural scientists remained sceptical. In 1862, Hermann von Helmholtz wrote that the commandments and laws of theology and jurisprudence, unlike natural law, did not 'contain the generalization of a wealth of facts. However, as in the application of a natural law to a given case, there is also a subsumation beneath the grammatical, juristic, moral and dogmatic commandments in the form

[35] From now on, law is also considered in relation to the 'nature of things': Montesquieu, for instance, claims near the beginning of *Esprit* that laws are 'relations, ... that necessarily result from the nature of things'.

[36] Herrmann 2001: 189ff.

[37] Behrends 1993.

[38] Treiber , 1998: 172ff.

[39] Kiesow 1997.

of a conscious logical conclusion.'[40] This common factor, however, did not bear up and it could not prevent the still ongoing process of a drifting-apart of natural sciences and arts into 'two cultures' (C.P. Snow). As I see it, the Neo-Kantianism and empiricism of the Vienna Circle, including the Vienna School of Hans Kelsen, put an end, for a while at least, to the somewhat naive analogies drawn by jurists.

From then on, the basic underlying differences between the laws of jurisprudence and the laws of natural science could no longer be overlooked. They were aimed at different domains (Is and Ought): the sciences taking recourse to different methods (experiment, understanding) and being different in practice (natural laws can be disproved as falsifiable hypotheses, whereas judicial laws are not falsifiable but are based on political decision and are therefore culturally variable).[41] For this reason, natural laws required no legitimation; they either held up against experimental attempts at falsification or they did not. Judicial laws, on the other hand, were more dependent than ever on legitimation in a world in which it was no longer enough to invoke God, tradition, 'truth', the 'nature of the thing', the 'common weal' or 'Western values' in order to justify restricting liberty or freedom.

The problem of the legitimation of legal norms in modern democratic industrial societies whose legal and political structure is written into a constitution will not be addressed here. A temporal order that declares metaphysical bonds or obligations (*religio*) to be a private matter can certainly no longer justify law by invoking a higher being or a socially binding 'truth' derived from nature and its laws. We have become accustomed to underpinning the validity of norms by referring to 'higher-ranking' norms – which, in a constitutional state, means by referring to the constitution and to prevailing international law. In order to justify its validity, Kelson referred to a fictitious 'basic norm'. However, it can also be said that a constitution is valid because the people to whom it applies have recognized it in fact within the process of communication. Here, too, we are faced with the paradox that Is and Ought are separate, but do coincide at a certain interface – which, in this case, is 'recognition'.

All that we now demand of 'valid' or prevailing law is that it has been established by the correct process (in accordance with meta-rules on which a consensus also had to be found, including meta-rules on how that consensus should be determined) and that it does not contradict the contents set forth in the constitutional texts. Whether or not this is the case can be determined only by means of a decision which, in turn, concludes a process of communication about the 'meaning' of the constitutional text.

IV

As far as the legitimation of law is concerned, the most crucial innovation of the last two centuries in continental Europe was the notion of the written constitution[42]. It

---

40 Helmholtz 1968: 17ff. Also Treiber 1998.

41 Dreier 1999: 286.

42 Mohnhaupt and Grimm 2002.

has been the actual 'legal source' of prevailing law ever since. The law of God and the law of nature (both in the religious form and in the evolutionary-idealistic form of the nineteenth century) have disappeared. Nature is in the hands of empiricists whose task is not to produce normative rules that can be legitimized. Legal norms are legitimized by references to the text of the constitution. Constitutional judges are entrusted with its interpretation. They are expected to find in it solutions for the greatest and smallest problems that concern the nation.

The issue as to how the constitution itself is legitimized remains unresolved. The usual response is: through the act of creating a constitution-giving assembly which in itself represents the will of the people. If one further asks who legitimizes the constitution-forming assembly, one arrives – as in a creation myth told backwards – at chaos and the spirit presiding over it. Out of the chaos of revolution, forces of order must have arisen to decree their fiat lux, dividing the firm from the fluid and creating the first institutions or using (de-legitimized) remains of earlier statehood in order to create a law of suffrage for the constitution-forming assembly. However different the historical processes may have been, the question as to the origins of the chain of legitimation concluded in an act of decision-making so assertive that it transformed power into law. Because of this freedom to act and to do so with a will to legislate, the original act of creating legislation resulted in law from which further law could be derived [Armogathe].

The strong parallels between this process and the theological chain of legitimation are patently obvious. After Jesus' baptism in the Jordan, we are told, 'and lo, the heavens were opened unto him, and he saw the Spirit of God descending like a dove, and lighting upon him: and lo a voice from heaven, saying, This is my beloved Son, in whom I am well pleased.' (Matthew 3:16–17). From this point onwards, God acts through his chosen people and all his acts are legitimized by this first solemn accreditation. In this respect, the constitution as a source of legitimation for laws and individual decisions is the modern 'word of God'. It is not 'natural law', but a higher order, made sacred by its historic origins and dignitas of content, which a secularized society, a world without gods, evidently cannot do without.

Chapter 4

The Concept of (Natural) Law in the Doctrine of Law and Natural Law of the Early Modern Era

Jan Schröder

Below I will examine the concept of the positive law in general (lex) and of the law of nature (lex naturae/naturalis) in jurisprudence and philosophy from the sixteenth century to the late eighteenth century. The examination will concentrate on German academic writings but also include various non-German authors, in particular at the beginning of the early modern era.

PART 1: 1500–1650 – THE UNIFORMITY OF THE CONCEPT OF LAW

1.I Jurisprudence

1.I.1 Law [lex][1]

(a) Adopted Roman law [ius]

The jurisprudence of the sixteenth century borrows almost without exception from the sources of Roman law adopted in Germany. Various definitions of law [lex] are to be found therein. The most well-known is a Digest passage: D. 1, 3, 1: 'A law is a general rule, a decision of intelligent men, a coercive measure against injustice committed wilfully or unknowingly, and a joint promise to the citizenry'.[2] A second definition is contained in the Institutions of Justinian. It refers to the (Roman) constitutional requirements of a law (I. 1, 2, 4): 'A law is what is decided by the people of Rome at the request of a senatorial magistrate, such as a consul'. Finally, passage D. 1, 3, 2 brings together certain quotations from authors of the ancient world according to which the law is 'an inspiration and gift of God' (Demosthenes), 'King over all divine and human things ... a standard for right and injustice' (Chrysippus), and so on.

[1] No comprehensive history of the (legal) concept of law exists at present. See, in the meantime, Mohnhaupt 1972: 188–239; Krawietz 1974: esp. 481–484; Grawert 1975: 863–922; Link 1987: 150ff.; Ebel 1988; Bastit 1990; Schröder 2001: 13 ff., 105, 200–202.

[2] Translation [into German] here and below in accordance with: *Corpus Iuris Civilis* (pp. 1990 et seq.).

As far as I can ascertain, most German jurists of the sixteenth and early seventeenth century adopted these definitions without criticism.[3] They do not, however, provide a great deal of clarity. At any rate, the definition of the law as a general rule ('commune praeceptum') was probably widely accepted.

(b) Independent definitions

Certain attempted definitions which deviate from Roman law are more informative. Around 1550 the French jurist Franciscus Connanus (Connan) describes the law as a 'general, just and good command of higher authorities aimed at protecting the community'.[4] In the 1560s, positive law ('lex civilis') is to be found described by the German/Dutch jurist Matthäus Wesenbeck as a 'virtuous ordinance of lawful authorities'.[5] Around the same time Johannes Schneidewin, his predecessor in the Wittenberg chair, called the law a 'statement on morals, made by a magistrate, which prescribes the virtuous and prohibits the shameful'.[6] Somewhat later (1589) the great French systematist Hugo Donellus (Doneau), who worked latterly in Altdorf, writes that the law is 'an ordinance aimed at the general public which orders or permits that which is correct and prohibits the opposite'.[7] In 1625, Hugo Grotius provides a similar definition, stating that the law is 'a rule relating to moral acts which requires that which is correct'.[8] In that respect 'correct' ('rectum') means 'that which is per se virtuous and just or that which is of benefit to all or the majority in the state concerned'.[9] Finally, the Lutheran statesman and state theorist Theodor Reinkingk (1619) writes that laws in the state 'are nothing other than virtue and a way of life expressed in particular written rules'.[10]

To me, two characteristics of the concept of law in the very early modern era appear to stand out clearly: Firstly, the law is – as indeed it is also in Roman law – a rule, an order, an ordinance. Secondly, however, it is also just and virtuous, or at least expedient. If it is not just etc., it is not a law.[11]

---

[3] Zasius 1550: col. 17, no. 2, p. 11; col. 364 'lex est com.', p. 184; col. 365 'Nam Demosthenes', no. 1, p. 185; Bocer 1588: disp. 1, no. 17 et seq., p. 9; Obrecht 1603: p. 1, disp. 1, no. 58 et seq., p. 3; Althusius 1649: lib. 1, cap. 14, no. 16, p. 40; cap. 64, no. 7, p. 220; cap. 80, no. 4, p. 283; Meier 1657: lib. 1, tit. 3, no. 2, p. 15; Harpprecht 1658: on Inst. 1, 1, 3, nos. 2–4, cols. 72 et seq.

[4] Connanus 1562: lib. 1, cap. 8, no. 7, p. 44.

[5] Wesenbeck 1582: lib. 1, tit. 3, no. 2.

[6] Schneidewin 1575: lib. 1, tit, 2, § Ius autem civile, para. 6, p. 16.

[7] Donellus 1589: lib. 1, cap. 5, § 1 p. 25 (Concept of Law [ius]); § 2, p. 25 (a 'constitutio' is also a 'lex').

[8] Grotius 1625: lib. 1, cap. 1, § 9, p. 34.

[9] Donellus 1589: lib. 1, cap. 5, § 6, p. 28.

[10] Reinkingk 1651:, lib. 2, classis 1, cap. 1, para. 1, p. 786.

[11] Around 1600 only a few authors deviate from this view. Cf., however, Kirchner 1608: disp. 2, th. 5, fol. B 3v; Vultejus 1614:, lib. 1, cap. 2, p. 2: 'A law is an ordinance or command of those who have the authority to legislate'; Besold 1618: 1618, lib. 2, cap. 2, no. 29, p. 616.

1.1.2 Natural law[12]

(a) Adopted Roman law

Most jurists take Roman sources as a basis also in the doctrine of the law of nature ('lex naturae') or 'natural law' ('lex naturalis'). They speak only of the 'law of nature' ('*ius* naturale') and describe as such 'that which nature has taught all living beings, that is to say not only men',[13] namely the union of the male with the female sex and the procreation and upbringing of children. In Roman law any other international law is referred to as 'ius gentium', that is, the 'law of nations'. However, the academic legal writings of the sixteenth century do not adhere to this narrow concept of the law of nature. Instead, they also attribute to the law of nature a proportion of 'international law', namely 'primary' international law.[14] Only secondary 'international law' is clearly delimited from the law of nature, that is to say, for example, the law of property, of slavery, of war and so forth. Since primary 'international law' is essentially equated with the Decalogue, in this regard the jurists' law of nature covers the same area as contemporary philosophical/theological law.

Definitions of the 'law of nature' (lex naturalis) among jurists appear to be rather few and far between. However, they clearly did not draw a strict distinction between 'lex naturalis' and 'ius naturale'[15] and consequently I am also able to include definitions of the latter. The following definitions are to be found among the Wittenberg jurists. Melchior Kling (1542) states 'natural law [ius naturale] consists of general rules which are inscribed in the human mind by nature and which set out the best and most perfect way of life'.[16] Schneidewin's definition is almost the same: namely, 'knowledge or general rules, instilled in the human mind by nature or by God, which set out, through good morals, the best and most perfect way of life'.[17] According to Wesenbeck, it is 'knowledge (or the concept? [notitia]) of practical principles, and the conclusions drawn therefrom, governing the guidance of morals consistent with the eternal and invariable direction of the divine spirit'.[18] In the view of Grotius, 'the law of nature [ius naturale] is the doctrine of proper reason

[12] A comprehensive history of the term 'law of nature' ('lex naturae', 'lex naturalis') likewise does not, from a legal point of view, exist from the sixteenth to the eighteenth century, as far as I can ascertain. Isolated references are to be found in academic writings on the law of nature. As regards the older law of nature, see: Kaltenborn 1848; Krause 1949; Welzel 1962; Specht 1984: cols. 576–582; Hügli 1984: cols. 582 et seq.; Seelmann 1997; Scattola 1999; Schröder 2001: 9–12, 100–104. The academic writings on the new law of nature after 1650 are countless. See, for example, in addition to the above, Wieacker 1967: 249ff.; Röd 1970; Klippel 1976; Ilting 1978: 245ff. (esp. 278ff.); Stolleis 1988: 268ff.; Peterson 1992: 7–35; Luig 1998: 133ff.; Grunert 2000; Hochstrasser 2000; Hunter 2001.

[13] Dig. 1, 1, 3: 'Ius naturale est, quod natura omnia animalia docuit'. Similarly, Inst. 1, 2 pr.

[14] Cf., for example, Zasius 1550: 10; Wesenbeck 1582: on D 1, 1, para. 15.

[15] Equation of the two, for example, in the case of Zasius 1550:, col. 380, p. 192 (para. 3): 'the reason for natural and divine law' ('ratio legis seu iuris naturalis & divini.').

[16] Kling 1542: lib. 1, tit. 1, para. 11, p. 3.

[17] Schneidewin 1575: lib. 1, tit. 2, 'Quid est Ius naturale?', para. 1, p. 10.

[18] Wesenbeck 1582: lib. 1, tit. 1, para. 15. This is followed by two other definitions which, in my view, do not differ in this regard.

which shows that an act … is morally shameful or necessary and thus prohibited or prescribed by God as the creator of nature'.[19]

In these definitions of the 'lex naturalis' (or 'ius naturale') the general characteristic of the rule or order in the concept diminishes yet further in comparison with the general concept of law (lex). The law of nature (ius naturale) is now primarily the knowledge of the system of values or this system of values itself (prior to Descartes no distinction is drawn between subject and object in the knowledge process!) and the entire collection of rules and principles on proper conduct. As Grotius, for example, emphasizes, they also reveal a divine commandment or prohibition but only as a consequence and in a secondary manner. However, this concept of law almost devoid of any 'command' still differs from physical law in that it relates only to human action and not to the regularities of the rest of nature. As far as I can ascertain, a more comprehensive meaning of the 'law of nature' ('lex naturae'), which goes beyond human conduct, was not even considered by the jurists.

1.II Catholic Philosophers and Theologians

1.II.1 Law [lex]

Comments on the law (lex) and the law of nature (lex naturalis) are also to be found among the moral theologians at the beginning of the early modern era since there was still no distinction between the law of nature and morals prior to Christian Thomasius (1705). The Catholic theologians discuss the concept of law generally in conjunction with Thomas Aquinas's teachings in the 'Prima secundae' of the *Summa Theologiae*. Initially, Aquinas described the law as 'a particular rule and measure of acts' ('quaedam regula et mensura actuum')[20] and then subsequently provided the definition ' an ordinance of reason for the common good, made known by those who have care of the community' ('quaedam rationis ordinatio ad bonum commune, ab eo qui curam communitatis habet, promulgata').[21] Thus, here too there are the two characteristics of the concept of law already familiar to us: namely, the characteristic of the rule or ordinance and the characteristic of correct, rational content which refers to a system which lies beyond the specific rule. However, Aquinas emphasizes the second element, in particular in the earlier definition, very much more than the first.

The two characteristics of the concept are also to be found among the Spanish Late Scholastics. However, there appears to be a tendency to emphasize more clearly the element of order and the deliberate laying down of rules. For example, Domingo de Soto writes in the words 'and rule' ('et praeceptio') after Aquinas's words 'ordinance of reason'.[22] Therefore, to him the word 'ordinance' ('ordinatio') does not express clearly enough the nature of the law as a rule. In 1612, Francisco Suárez provides the following definition: 'A law is a general, just and constant rule which is

---

19 Grotius 1625:, lib. 1, cap. 1, § 10, p. 34. Cf. also Reinkingk 1651: lib. 2, class. 2, cap. 2, para. 3, p. 788.

20 Aquinas, *Summa Theologiae*, II 1, quaest. 90, art. 1 on 1.

21 Ibid.

22 De Soto 1569: quaest. 1, art. 1, p. 2.

made sufficiently known.'[23] Luis Molina describes the 'lex humana' as an 'order of the highest authority in the State'.[24] Gabriel Vasquez speaks of a 'rule to which acts must conform so that they be just'[25] but requires that this rule be deliberately laid down. In addition, however, the other characteristic of the law, namely just content, is also maintained for the most part.[26]

1.II.2 Law of Nature

Thomas Aquinas described the law of nature (lex naturalis) as 'participation of the rational creature in eternal law'.[27] To him, eternal law was, for its part, the 'essence of divine wisdom by which it guides all acts and movements'.[28] Thus, to Thomas Aquinas the law of nature was knowledge of the principles of correct action and in this regard the nature of law as an order was very much of secondary importance.[29] The Catholic theologians of the sixteenth and early seventeenth century clearly still operate within this framework. Domingo de Soto declares that the law of nature (lex naturalis) is impressed and imprinted into our souls.[30] It is the knowledge 'of the principles which are known, without discussion, through the natural light per se' such as, for example, the Golden Rule.[31] Francisco Suárez describes the lex naturalis as the law 'which is inherent in the human mind for distinguishing the virtuous and the shameful'.[32] However, he stresses that it is also a divine rule not only a standard for good and evil.[33] By contrast, Gabriel Vasquez does not wish to speak of a 'lex naturalis' but of a 'ius naturale' since ius naturale is devoid of the element of will.[34] Furthermore, he describes lex naturalis or ius naturale as the 'first natural rule governing the acts of rational creatures'.

Finally, to Luis Molina the law of nature is 'nothing other than a capacity to reason itself, instilled in us by nature, through which we discern certain principles, known per se, both in speculative and practical matters'.[35] This definition is noteworthy in that it appears to classify the 'speculative', theoretical, that is to say also physical,

---

[23] Suárez 1612: lib. 1, cap. 12, § 4, p. 54.

[24] Molina 1614: disp. 46, para. 31, col. 1699.

[25] Vasquez 1620: on quaest. 90, art. 1, disp. 150, cap. 3, para. 22, p. 5.

[26] Only in the case of Molina is none of this to be found in the definition of human law ('lex humana'). Cf. also Lessius 1605: lib. 2, cap. 2, dubitatio 1: 'lex, quae est regula iusti in genere'.

[27] Aquinas, *Summa Theologiae*, II 1, quaest. 91, art. 2, on 1.

[28] Ibid.: quaest. 91, art. 1.

[29] Aquinas does not include physical law in his definition of natural law and therefore I do not set out his doctrine of the law of irrational nature here (see, in that regard, Armogathe, Chapter 16 in this volume).

[30] De Soto 1569: quaest. 4, art. 1, p. 10.

[31] Ibid.: quaest. 3, art. 1, p. 8.

[32] Suárez 1612: lib. 1, cap. 3, § 10, p. 9.

[33] Ibid.: lib. 2, cap. 6, § 5, p. 105 ('Lex naturalis non solum est indicativa mali, et boni, sed etiam continet praeceptionem et prohibitionem utriusque'); cf. also § 13, p. 108.

[34] Vasquez 1620: disp. 150, cap. 3, para. 22, p. 5.

[35] Molina 1614: tom. 6, disp. 47, para. 3, col. 1701.

principles as natural law. However, Molina is the only Catholic author whom I have studied who goes so far.

Overall, these definitions are consistent with those of the jurists. The law of nature contains knowledge of the principles of correct action or these principles themselves. The characteristic of order or commandment in the concept is less evident. At least one Late Scholastic, namely Luis Molina, places even the 'speculative' principles, that is to say also the physical regularities, under the concept of the law of nature.

1.III Protestant Philosophers and Theologians

I will restrict myself to the three authors who are important as regards the development of the law of nature (ius naturale).[36] In 1546, Philipp Melanchthon described moral philosophy ('philosophia moralis') as the part of divine law (lex) which dictates external actions. The judgment on this is born in man. It is the law of nature (ex naturalis) and human nature has no more outstanding gift than this knowledge.[37] Later he again states that virtues are dominated by the power of judgment ('iudicio mentis'), that is to say by knowledge ('notitiis') which guides them, and this knowledge consists of 'principles or practical conclusions, rules familiar from nature known as the laws of nature which guide virtuous acts towards God and men'.[38]

Thus, as with the Catholic theologians and the Wittenberg jurists, who were probably influenced by Melanchthon, we again find the idea that the law of nature contains knowledge of the principles of good and evil action (or these principles themselves). Physical law is also included even more clearly than by Melanchthon by one of his pupils, the Danish philosopher and theologian Niels Hemmingsen (Nicolaus Hemmingius). Hemmingsen defines the law of nature as 'the certain knowledge, imprinted in men by God, of the principles of *knowledge* and action … so that man *knows*, desires, chooses and does what is right and avoids the opposite'.[39] Thus, he refers to as the 'law of nature' – as does Luis Molina just under fifty years later – not only the principles of action but also those of knowledge, and consequently appears to include in the concept of law not only practical but also theoretical and thus physical knowledge. However, he makes no further observations on the matter.

The Protestant jurist Benedict Winkler,[40] an outsider, goes one step further in his textbook of the law of nature of 1615. He is the only author whom I have studied who also expressly places physical law under the term 'law of nature'. Winkler describes

---

36 I cannot examine here the differences of opinion within Protestant doctrine. Cf., for example, Scattola 1999: 90ff., on the denial of the existence of the law of nature by Matthias Flacius Illyricus.

37 Melanchthon 1546: lib. 1, pp. 157ff.

38 Ibid.: p. 198.

39 Hemmingius 1564: fol. C 2r/v (emphasis added).

40 Little is known about Winkler (1579–1648). In 1615 he was a lecturer in Leipzig, in 1616 he received his doctor's degree in Basle, and subsequently he became the deputy syndic and syndic of the imperial town of Lübeck (Landsberg 1898: 449). Kaltenborn (1848) drew attention to him again in the nineteenth century (section 2, pp. 45ff.).

law in the strict sense of the word as 'the reason (way?) which orders (governs?) and guides a particular move' (ratio 'quae certum motum imperat ac gubernat').[41] He contends firstly that the law of nature is one common to all bodies and beings ('lex naturae communis'). However, he argues secondly that there is also a human law of nature ('lex humana naturae'), namely 'the principle and rule of the movement and rest of human action and it is in this that we seek the law of nature of men'.[42] Winkler returns repeatedly to this distinction between the general and human law of nature. Eating and drinking form part of the law of nature but to the sensual (general) and not to the rational (human)[43] law of nature, and where man ignores reason 'he is guided by the general, not the human, law of nature'.[44] Thus, Winkler also recognizes a 'law of nature' (lex naturae) in the scientific, physical sense, which is unconnected with law (ius) and ethics.

1.IV Summary

Our collection of definitions shows that, at the beginning of the early modern era, law (lex) has a broad range of meanings from order or *commandment* to a rational and just *system* (or knowledge of this system). However, for most authors, both elements of the concept exist in both positive and natural law. Positive human law is not only the commandment of a legislator, it must also be just – natural law is an expression of a just system behind which, however, there is also ultimately a legislator, namely God. In this respect it is possible to speak of a uniformity of the concept of the law at the beginning of the early modern era. In the same way as human law, the law of nature is primarily a law *of morality or of law*. The jurists and theologians or philosophers cited here describe physical regularities as laws only in isolated cases and 'per analogiam'.

PART 2: 1650–1800 – THE DISINTEGRATION OF THE CONCEPT OF LAW

As far as I can ascertain, the following changes can be observed between 1650 and 1800. Human law becomes a mere order or commandment which is no longer necessarily just (2.I). Conversely, God as legislator increasingly disappears from the natural law of law/morality (2.II.1, 2.II.2) with the result that positive and natural law contrast sharply with one another. Finally, the 'law of nature' takes on the meaning of a physical law (2.II.3). Three different attempts at formulating a general definition of law correspond to these three stages of development. However, in my view, they no longer cover the entire range of the new concept.

---

41 Winkler 1615: lib. 2, cap. 1, p. 66 with reference to lib. 1, cap. 4. The passage is clearly not printed in Kaltenborn.

42 Winkler 1615: lib. 1, cap. 7, p. 56.

43 Ibid.: lib. 1, cap. 10, p. 61.

44 Ibid.: lib. 1, cap. 7, p. 57.

2.I The Concept of Human (Positive) Law

The earlier view had been that human law was not only the commandment of a legislator but also always rational or at least expedient. This additional element disappears in the course of the seventeenth century, having already been abandoned earlier in isolated cases. Civil (positive) laws are, according to the famous definition by Thomas Hobbes, now only 'orders of those who have supreme authority in the State in respect of the future actions of citizens'[45] and, in the view of Samuel Pufendorf, 'decrees of the supreme ruler which impose on the citizens that which they shall and shall not do in civic life'.[46] Such laws no longer necessarily have to be rational or expedient. They may, as Pufendorf expressly states, arise from the 'naked arbitrariness' of the legislator.[47]

This concept of positive law becomes established in Germany both in the academic writings on natural law[48] and on positive law,[49] and remains uncontested until the end of the eighteenth century. The other contexts surrounding this incipient positivism need not be considered here. A role was certainly played by the fact that, following the schism and the resulting religious and civil wars, any system, even an arbitrary one, appeared to be better than the protracted dispute over actual legal/moral truth.

2.II The General Concept of Law and the Law of Nature

2.II.1 Law as a Commandment or Order

With the concept of positive law the concept of the law in general had to change. In an initial stage in the development of the doctrine of the law of nature after 1650 this change is to the effect that *law* [lex] is now construed in general as an order of a superior, namely a legislator, and, moreover, as an order which no longer has to also be rational or expedient, as had previously been the case. However, it remains the case that 'law' is understood as meaning only moral and not physical law. Therefore,

---

45 Hobbes 1642: chap. 6, no. 9, p. 222: 'Leges civiles ... nihil aliud sunt, quam ejus, qui in civitate summa potestate praeditus est, de civium futuris actionibus mandata'.

46 Pufendorf 1673: lib. 2, cap. 12, § 1.

47 Pufendorf 1672: lib. 2, cap. 3, § 24, p. 163.

48 Ibid.: lib. 8, cap. 1, p. 742; Thomasius 1688:, lib, 1, cap. 1, no. 28, p. 6 (human and divine laws); Thomasius 1705:, lib. 1, cap. 5, § 3, p. 146; Heineccius 1738:, lib. 2, cap. 8, § 152; Wolff 1750: § 1068, p. 665, cf. also § 39, p. 20; Achenwall and Pütter 1750:, § 689; Kant 1798: 44, Sect. B 1: 'positive [statutory] law which arises from the will of a legislator'.

49 Böhmer 1704: lib. 1, tit. 1, § 14, p. 10; Ludovici 1725: lib. 1, tit. 3, § 1, p. 8: 'Law is a rule, laid down by the bearer of majesty, to which the subjects must adjust their actions' ('Lex est regula a superiore maiestatem habente praescripta, iuxta quam actiones subditorum instituendae'); Glück 1797, 1, book 1, tit., § 4, p. 45; Höpfner 1803: § 19, p. 48; cf. also § 18, p. 47. See also the *Codex Maximilianeus Bavaricus civilis* (1756), part 1. chap., § 3: 'Although law [ius] has various meanings, in this case it means a law [lex], that is to say a commandment of a supreme ruler, which, in matters concerning the common good, is imposed upon the subject'.

law in general is now only 'a decree by which a superior obliges a subordinate to act in accordance with his instructions'[50] or 'an order of a ruler who obliges his subordinates to adjust their actions to that order'.[51]

That means that the authors on natural law also continue to regard the *law of nature* (lex naturalis) as a divine order. Hobbes takes the view it is true that 'in accordance with strict language usage' law is 'only the word of the person who orders others to do or not to do something by right'. Therefore, the natural laws listed by him are 'not in fact laws since they arise from nature itself'. However, where they are 'laid down by God in the Holy Scriptures, as the following chapter will show, they are in fact laws since the Holy Scriptures are the word of God who rules over all with supreme right'.[52] Pufendorf even regards Hobbes's reservation that the law of nature must be revealed at some point in the Bible as a superfluous 'subtlety' since 'one knows from the dictates of reason not only that compliance with the laws of nature is beneficial to mankind, but also that God intends and commands that mortals guide their actions by them'.[53] Various other authors in the late seventeenth and early eighteenth century continue to take the view that the law of nature is a divine commandment and therefore automatically fits into a general concept of the law as the order of a legislator.[54] Nonetheless, an important difference in comparison with the sixteenth century lies in the fact that the law of nature is no longer 'written in the heart' of man but can be discerned only through reason.[55]

---

[50] Pufendorf 1672:, lib. 1, cap. 6, § 4, p. 71: 'In genere autem lex commodissime videtur definiri per decretum, quo superior sibi subjectum obligat, ut ad istius praescriptum actiones suas componat'.

[51] Thomasius 1688:, lib. 1, cap. 1, § 28, p. 6. Cf. also Glafey 1723: 81: '... one can describe a law / as an order of a sovereign / which obliges his subjects / to live in accordance with his will'; Heineccius 1738: lib. 1, cap. 1, § 9: law is 'the will of a superior being which prohibits or prescribes certain actions under pain of punishment'.

[52] Hobbes 1642: chap. 3, § 33. There is a slight difference in chap. 14, § 4, where Hobbes defines natural law as that 'which God has made known to all men though his eternal word inborn in us, that is to say through natural reason ...'

[53] Pufendorf 1672:, lib. 1, cap. 6, § 4.

[54] Thomasius 1688:, lib. 1. cap. 2, § 97, p. 50: 'Natural law is a divine law which is written in the hearts of all men and which obliges them to do what is necessarily consistent with the rational nature of man and not to do what is contrary thereto'; Glafey 1723: 177 ('The other kind of divine laws are those which/ are promulgated thus through reason/ and known as jus naturae') ibid., 207, 213 (The law of nature [ius naturae] is a 'genuine law [lex]' since God wanted man 'to act in accordance with the rule of nature' and had revealed [it] through reason'); Heineccius 1738: lib. 1, cap. 1, § 10 (God is certainly also a 'ruler' and he is the author of the law which must serve as a standard for all men), and § 12 ('Therefore, the law of nature is the embodiment of the laws which immortal God himself has made known through just reason'). Probably also Gundling 1747: 6: The law has its name 'a ligando' and 'takes something from our freedom' and in the case of the laws of nature this restriction of freedom comes from God: 'In the same way as our nature comes from God, our leges naturales can come from nowhere else than from God'.

[55] Pufendorf 1672: lib. 2, cap. 3 § 13, pp. 145ff.; Thomasius 1688: lib. 1, cap. 2, §§ 66–69, pp. 44ff.; Wolff 1738:, §§ 259–261, pp. 204–207; *Zedlers Grosses vollständiges Universal*

However, around and after 1700 there are also authors on the law of nature who no longer wish to speak of a *law* (lex) of nature precisely because the law of nature (ius naturae) is, in their view, incompatible with the concept of law (lex) as an order or commandment. For example, although in 1705 Christian Thomasius still adheres to the concept of the law (in the narrow sense) as the order of a ruler or master,[56] he now wishes to classify the law of nature more as pieces of advice ('consilia'), than orders, that is to say no longer as laws in the strict sense.[57] Even Johann Jacob Schmauß, an outsider in terms of natural law, who bases the entire law of nature on the natural instincts of man, doubts that ius naturae has the character of lex: 'Although the instinctus naturales of men can, to a certain extent, be compared with laws [leges], and are thus also named' this is merely done 'improprie' (that is, improperly). 'A lex proprie dicta (i.e. a law properly called) and as construed by all jurists presupposes a sovereign and ruler who imposes on his subjects laws and ordinances by which they are to live.' However, in a state of nature a man will regard God not as a legislator 'but rather as his creator who has given him such a nature'.[58]

2.II.2 Law (lex) as a Binding Body of Rules

In the second stage of development, too, *'law'* (lex) is generally still understood as meaning the law of law or morality and not physical law. However, the predominant trend is now effectively to form the concept of law in such a way that the feature of the legislator can be abandoned. Even prior to the mid-eighteenth century a concept of law arises in the doctrine of natural law which follows from the earlier definition of Hugo Grotius[59] and which is propagated principally by Christian Wolff. In the first part of his *Philosophia practica universalis* of 1738, Wolff describes a law (lex) as 'a rule in accordance with which we are obliged to determine our actions'.[60] Thus, the obligatory force of the law now becomes the decisive criterion.[61] This new concept of the law remains firm for several decades, not only in the actual Wolff school but also among influential and extensively read eclectics such as Achenwall and Höpfner. The wordings used vary,[62] but it remains the case that the decisive feature of law is the creation of an obligation alone and no longer the ordinance of a legislator.

---

aller Wissenschafften und Künste, vol. 23 (1740), cols. 1094–1098. Cf. also, in that respect, Hochstrasser 2000: 85ff., and Daston (Chapter 14 in this volume).

56 Thomasius 1705: lib. 1, cap. 5, § 3, p. 246.

57 Ibid.: lib. 1, cap. 5, § 34, p. 152.

58 Schmauß 1754: 528ff.

59 Grotius 1625: lib. 1, cap. 1, § 9, p. 34. See above in footnote 8.

60 Wolff 1738: § 131, p. 115: 'Lex dicitur regula, juxta quam actiones nostras determinare obligamur'.

61 Although this feature of 'obligation' (obligatio) created by law [lex] is also to be found in earlier definitions of law of our era, at that time it was always linked to the idea of an order or commandment of a legislator: Pufendorf 1672: lib. 1, cap. 6, § 4, p. 71; Thomasius 1688: lib. 1, cap. 1, § 28; Glafey 1723: 81; Heineccius 1738: lib. 1, cap. 1, § 9.

62 Vattel 1747: 4 (like Wolff); Claproth 1749: § 51, p. 29: 'A body of rules through which an obligation is made known to us is known as a law'; Achenwall 1774: § 13, p. 13 ('a body of rules which expresses an obligation … is referred to as a law'); Höpfner 1780: § 8, p. 5 ('A

Therefore, an important reason for the new concept of law lay in the fact that the *law of nature* (lex naturalis) was no longer regarded as a divine commandment. Wolff himself no longer sees an adequate basis for the law of nature in God but in the essence and in the nature of man and of things.[63] He considers that God is the author of the law of nature but is not the supreme principle from which it is derived (principium demonstrandi).[64] The other authors who concur with Wolff's definition of law also eliminate God from their definitions of the law of nature.[65] The idea that the will and commandment of God is the actual basis of the law of nature is discussed (in part extensively) and rejected. For example, Emer de Vattel in his much cited 'Essay on the Principles of Natural Law' ('Essai sur le fondement du droit nature …') states that any attempt to prove that God's will is the basis of natural laws must ultimately be attributable to the nature of man and of things.[66] Similar statements are to be found among the other authors on the law of nature. God has not revealed the law of nature to us directly (in the same way as the 'positive divine law' of the Bible) and therefore 'how should I know that God so wishes?'[67] We believe we know 'that God's will in relation to men is that they should live cheerfully and contentedly … However, the question then arises as to which is the correct path to human happiness? In this regard no one can, without invoking a revelation, refrain from carrying out the examination which we have conducted, that is to say he must acquaint himself with his nature and consider the consequences of his actions. He will thus discover what constitutes his true pleasure and displeasure',[68] 'one need look only at the nature of man'.[69] Thus, these authors do away with God as the

body of rules which expresses an obligation is known as a law'); Nettelbladt 1785: § 111, pp. 57ff.: 'Moral law in the broadest sense is any rule in accordance with which we are obliged to determine our actions'.

63 Wolff 1738: § 135, p. 117: 'A natural law is one which has sufficient basis in the essence and nature of man and of things.'

64 Ibid.: § 273, p. 215.

65 Vattel 1747: 4: 'the natural laws are, in particular, those which oblige us by nature or whose basis is to be found in the essence and nature of man and in the essence and nature of things in general'; Montesquieu 1748: book 1, chap. 2 , p. 12: The laws of nature 'are so called because they spring solely and entirely from our character'; Claproth 1749: 33: 'When one perceives them (i.e. laws) from the nature of man and of the other things by which we are surrounded, one refers to them as natural laws'; Achenwall 1774: § 49, p. 42: a law is a body of rules which express an obligation and 'an obligation which man can discern from philosophical principles is referred to as a natural obligation'; Höpfner 1780: § 20, p. 13: 'A natural law is that which expresses a natural obligation'; Nettelbladt 1785: § 111, p. 58: A law is a 'rule' and 'if one accepts that this rule is laid down by nature, the law is referred to as natural law'.

66 Vattel 1747: 9ff.: 'How do these authors (i.e. those who attribute the laws of nature to God's will) know that God and no other has imposed a particular law on men ?' They presuppose that God can give men only the most appropriate laws. 'But how do they discern the most appropriate laws? They observe the nature of man and of things ...'

67 Darjes 1762: 259.

68 Claproth 1749: 42.

69 Schmauß 1754: 455. Likewise probably also Montesquieu 1748: book 1, chap. 1, p. 10 (page numbering cited in accordance with Ernst Forsthoff's 1992 German translation). Cf.

legislator of the law of nature and thereby remove the idea of a legislator from the concept of law in general.[70]

The provisional assessment (prior to the beginning of the Kantian era in which physical law also comes into play) is that positive and natural law have separated from one another. They are now no longer connected by the feature of an order or even of a rational or expedient system. Positive law is a commandment, but not necessarily a rational one. Natural law is rational, but not a commandment. The new concept, which presupposes common interest, that both types of law at least establish an obligation barely conceals the break-up of the concept of law. It no longer even covers a specific feature since an obligation can be established not only by a law but also by a treaty. Certain contemporaries clearly also recognized this fact.[71]

2.II.3 Law as Necessity (the Inclusion of Physical Laws in the Concept of Law)

(a) Concept of law in general

During the third stage of development, which primarily covers the final two decades of the eighteenth century, German jurists too discover the *law* (lex) of irrational nature, namely physical law. Prior to this, references thereto are only rarely to be found among them. At any rate, as early as 1723 Glafey states: 'Physicists and physicians use this word (i.e. lex) generally/ where they speak de ordine naturali/ in accordance with which it is lex naturae/ that the sun orbits the earth in 24 hours ...'[72] However, Glafey himself retains the conventional terminology of jurists, in accordance with which law is to be understood as meaning only law or morality.

also Achenwall 1754: § 2, p. 5.

[70] For example, Vattel 1747: 31; Claproth 1749: 31, 43 and 46; and Höpfner 1780: § 8 note (1), p. 5, expressly reject the requirement of a 'superior' or legislator in respect of the concept of law. Schaumann 1792: note 5 on § 108, p. 76, appears no longer able to explain the contrary view: 'Is the concept of a legislator necessarily linked with the concept of law? Why is it so in the case of so many, in particularly the old, teachers of natural law that they answer this question in the affirmative?').

[71] For example, in attempting to demarcate law from treaty Nettelbladt (1785) repeatedly returns to the criterion of 'provision', even though, in concurrence with Wolff, he clearly no longer regards God as the legislator of the law of nature. cf. the continuation of the passage cited in footnote 62 above: 'However, in the strict sense in which it [i.e. a law] differs from an agreement, a piece of advice, a dogma, an instruction or a commission, it is a general rule imposed on us all in accordance with which we are obliged to determine our free actions.'

[72] Glafey 1723: 96ff.: 'However, just one also calls the normal course of nature legem naturae/in the same way one speaks of dying as legem naturae exsolvere, or paying nature its due/ a meaning which, however, must be understood in moral and not in physical terms/ thus, in this sense one can indeed accord animals a (!) legem naturae. Physicists and physicians use this word generally/ where they speak of de ordine naturali/ in accordance with which it is lex naturae/ that the sun orbits the earth in 24 hours. However, they use this expression primarily where they speak of marvels which they call dispensationem or suspensionem legis naturalis/ under the title of which a famous Englishman by the name of Connor wrote an entire treatise' (96 et seq.). Also where animals are reared they act 'according to their instinct in a physical manner'. I thus term this behavior such/ because no law exists in this respect/ and in the absence thereof no act can be referred to as moral' (97).

The first jurist to include physical law – and also sociological laws [LARRÈRE] – in the general concept of law appears to have been Montesquieu in 1748 ('Laws in the broadest sense of the word are relationships which necessarily arise from the nature of things'[73]). As far as I am aware, the first German jurist to make a similar attempt is Wolff's pupil Joachim Georg Darjes in 1762. In his view, law 'in the general sense' is 'a proposition in accordance with which the varia are to be bound together or which is homogeneous, a general body of rules in accordance with which consequence can be explained in the effects of a force. Accordingly, lex sensationis is such a proposition from which we can explain consequence in our sensation.'[74] However, in the case of Darjes this general concept of law is scarcely conveyed in comparison with his concept of law or morality ('truths which teach us what is just and unjust, what is right and wrong'[75]) and Darjes develops no further criteria for distinguishing physical law from the law as such.

A uniform new concept of the law which also takes account of physical law and a clear demarcation of law or morality from physical law probably first became established as a consequence of Kant's influence. Kant states that 'rules, in so far as they are objective (of necessity adhere to knowledge of the subject-matter) are referred to as laws'.[76] It is in this sense that law is now also defined generally in the legal-philosophical academic writings on the law of nature of the late eighteenth and early nineteenth century. 'The standard (norm) of a provision is known as a rule and a rule with the character of generality and necessity, a law (lex).'[77] 'A law is nothing other than a body of rules in which a necessity is expressed'[78] and so on.

(b) Concept of the law of nature

According to Kant, laws are 'either laws of nature or of freedom'.[79] The laws of freedom are moral or juristic.[80] This is more or less consistent with modern linguistic

---

73 Montesquieu 1748: book 1, chap.1, p. 9.

74 Darjes 1762: 77ff.

75 Ibid.: 51.

76 I. Kant (in J. and W. Grimm, *Deutsches Wörterbuch* IV, I, 2, col. 4073 sub 6).

77 For example, the philosopher J.C.G. Schaumann (1792: § 105, p. 73). Also on the philosophical side, for example, Jakob 1802: § 16, p. 8: 'A law generally expresses the necessity of particular provisions'; Hoffbauer 1804: § 1, p. 3: 'Laws in general (or in the broadest possible sense) are rules stating that something is necessary on a particular condition'. A somewhat different view is taken by Abicht 1792: § 1, p. 1: 'The ... stipulated, invariable reasons of effect ... [are referred to as] the laws of force. These laws together constitute the essence or nature of force.'

78 For example, the jurist K.H. Gros (1815: § 5, p. 3). Also on the legal side, Hufeland 1795 § 3, p. 1: 'A law (lex) is a general rule relating to the necessity of actions (where 'actions' can be not only behaviour controlled by will but also natural occurrences': § 4, note 1, p. 2); Schmalz 1795: 28: 'Changes which are brought about by the power of things themselves we call actions in consideration of these things; and the definition of their possibility or necessity we call laws'; Thomas 1803: § 8, p. 4: 'A law in the general sense is an absolute, general and necessary norm'; Bauer 1808: § 3, p. 2: 'A law is ... a general and necessary rule.'

79 Kant 1785: preface, p. IV.

80 Kant 1798: 6.

usage. The '*law of nature*' is now (perhaps for the first time in the long history of the concept thereof) no longer law per se or morality but the physical law of irrational or non-freely-acting things. However, this fundamental change of meaning meant that there was no longer any usable designation for the former 'natural law' (in contrast with positive law). Kant still refers to it as 'natural law' where he has to demarcate it from positive law.[81]

The legal-philosophical doctrine around 1800 also concurs with Kant in this respect. 'Laws whose sphere lies in the field of the concept of nature are referred to as laws of nature (physical laws). Those which relate to subjects of the concept of freedom, however, are referred to as laws of freedom (moral laws).'[82] Therefore, everywhere the 'law of nature' is not the law itself but rather physical law. Where the intention is to designate the non-positive in contrast to the positive law known previously as the 'law of nature', it is generally referred to as 'natural' law, as it is by Kant.[83] However, there are also a number of authors who no longer use the word 'law' (lex) at all in relation to non-positive law (ius) but speak only of the 'law of nature' (ius naturae)[84] and thus prepare the way for modern linguistic usage in this respect too.

Finally, as regards the concept of the 'law of nature' (ius naturae) or 'natural law' (lex naturae/naturalis), it is still the case that it is no longer derived from a (divine) legislator but from nature or reason. The philosophical legal doctrine is 'a system stemming from reason'[85] and the 'law of nature can also be referred to as the law of reason because law is based on the rational nature of man'.[86]

---

81 Kant 1798: 24: 'External laws (i.e. laws of freedom)' 'are those in respect of which the obligation can be discerned a priori by reason even in the absence of external legislation … natural laws, by contrast, which are not binding at all in the absence of external legislation …, are referred to as positive laws' (emphasis in the original). As regards earlier attempts to demarcate the law of law and physical law in English and French academic writings, see Roux and Steinle (Chapters 12 and 13 in this volume.

82 Schaumann 1792: § 107, p. 74. See also in philosophical academic writings: Abicht 1792: 39 ('laws of freedom', the law of nature clearly does not occur); Jakob 1802: § 1, p. 1 (laws of nature/ laws of freedom); Hoffbauer 1804: § 1, p. 3 (natural laws/ positive laws). And in legal academic writings: Hufeland 1795: §§ 4, 11, p. 1, 4 (natural law/ moral law); Schmalz 1795: 36 ('moral laws', natural law clearly does not occur); Thomas 1803: § 8, p. 4 (natural law/ practical law); Bauer 1808: § 3, pp. 2ff. ('natural laws, physical laws' / 'moral laws or laws of freedom'); Gros 1815: § 12, p. 7 ('physical' / 'moral' laws).

83 Hufeland 1795: § 498, p. 240; Thomas 1803: § 9, p. 5; Bauer 1808: § 231, p. 264; Gros 1815: § 42, p. 26. However, natural laws in a different sense are still spoken of by Hoffbauer 1804: § 2, p. 4; and 'laws of natural law' are spoken of by Schaumann 1792: § 585, note 4, p. 324.

84 I have not found the word 'law' (lex) in relation to the law of nature (ius naturale) in connection with demarcation from positive law in Tafinger 1794; Heydenreich 1794; Schmalz 1795; or Jakob 1802.

85 Kant 1798: preface, p. III.

86 Gros 1815: § 42, note, p. 26. Cf. also Tafinger 1794: § 9, p. 4 (moral laws are provided by 'practical reason'); Heydenreich 1794: 33 ('legislation of reason'); Jakob 1802: § 9, p. 5 ('provided through the concept of human nature'); Thomas 1803: § 9, pp. 4ff. ('founded … directly in reason'); Hoffbauer 1804: § 66, note 1, p. 50 ('The reason for the validity of laws of

All in all, the following are united under the term 'law' [lex] in the late eighteenth century: (1) physical laws (the only laws which are now designated 'natural laws' [leges naturales], (2) non-positive laws derived from reason (law of nature [lex naturae/naturalis]) and (3) positive laws based on the commandment of a legislator. They all supposedly display the feature of expressing a 'necessity'. However, what is 'necessary' must apply always and everywhere, and this clearly is not true of positive law[87] which is regarded by contemporaries precisely as 'empirical ... accidental ... historical'.[88] Therefore, in the third stage of development of the concept of law between 1650 and 1800, it becomes clearer than before, in my view, that the concept of law has broken up and can no longer be reduced to a uniform formula. There is no longer any inner link between imperative positive law and rationally deduced moral and natural law which cannot be attributed to a legislator.

2.III Considerations in summary

Between 1650 and 1800 the old concept of the law as a rational system established by God or inherent in man disintegrates. Positive law becomes a mere order or commandment of the legislator which no longer has necessarily to be rational or expedient.

Natural law and morality become a mere product of reason from which God as legislator is eliminated in the same way as he is from physical law, which is regarded as the 'law of nature' per se as of the end of the eighteenth century. Only the 'necessity rule' remains as a common feature. In terms of key words, the reasons for the change in the concept of law can be designated as *positivization* or 'emptying of value' (of the human law of law) and *secularization*[89] (of moral and natural knowledge).

As regards the general concept of the law, it is conspicuous that the development is towards it being guided no longer by positive law but by the law of nature (in the Kantian and modern sense). However, I also consider that it is now completely impossible to form a new uniform concept. The attempts nevertheless to formulate a general concept of law, which were made in quick succession between 1650 and 1800, merely highlight the crisis surrounding the concept of law. It has broken down into the components order and commandment, on the one hand, and observed or deduced regularity, on the other (albeit that there is also no overwhelming evidence that the authors of the late eighteenth century had become aware of this break-up). In my view, there have to be general doubts as to whether the disparate phenomena of the positive law and the law of nature can be brought forcibly together under a single meaningful term at a time when positivist and secularized thought prevail.

---

law can lie only in reason'); Bauer 1808: § 20, pp. 19ff. ('The sole source of the law of nature lies in practical reason').

87 It is also occasionally regarded thus by the authors on natural law used here such as Schaumann 1792: § 585, note 4, p. 324: 'since they are determined with the aid of politics by variable circumstances and conditions, and laid down by men, positive provisions cannot, by nature, have the generality and invariability of moral laws'.

88 Hugo 1817: § 24, pp. 21ff.

89 Welzel 1962: 107, speaks of the 'replacement of transcendence by the immanence of laws'.

Chapter 5

'Lex certa' and 'ius certum': The Search for Legal Certainty and Security

Heinz Mohnhaupt

Introduction: The Problem of Certainty in the Natural Sciences and Humanities

The extent to which the investigative methods of one particular scientific discipline can be usefully transferred to another is a question that has often been posed in the past – and continues to be relevant even today. The scope for interaction between scientific disciplines or for one discipline to influence another depends on the receptivity of the methodology involved. When we look at the relationship between the natural sciences and the humanities, this applies in particular to the interaction of the former with the discipline of jurisprudence. In an age which believed in the unity of sciences – 'universitas' and 'unitas scientiarum' – this seemed a much more natural question to ask than nowadays. Ever since the idea of a single God of creation and a uniform plan of creation lost credence, the – formerly virtually unknown – boundaries between the humanities and the natural sciences have developed into clearly-drawn lines of demarcation. The question whether there is a fundamental difference between the natural sciences and the humanities, or whether these two areas of academic enquiry can be merged into a single, uniform view of the sciences, has today been sidelined by the more specific conclusion that ongoing attempts to differentiate individual disciplines within the natural sciences mean, for example, that even here it is hardly even possible to speak in terms of unity. The idea of the unity of a specific scientific discipline such as physics is today even regarded as problematic and difficult to sustain.[1] The existence of Max Planck Institutes for 'Biophysical Chemistry' or 'Terrestrial Microbiology' are examples of a process of differentiation that puts the question of the 'unity of the sciences' into a new perspective. This shows just how complex and multi-faceted the question of the 'unity of the sciences' has become, particularly if we include in the concept of 'unitas scientarum' not just all the disciplines in the natural science but also the humanities. This has implications for the receptivity of the humanities to methods derived from the natural sciences. In the eighteenth and particularly the nineteenth centuries, the examples of mathematics and physics exercised a considerable pull on approaches to thinking and working in the humanities,[2] and raised hopes that the

---

1 Hüttemann 1998: 209–222.

2 Stephanitz 1970: 2s.

degree of certainty and proof called for in the 'exact' sciences could be transferred to individual disciplines within the humanities. Included amongst these was the science of jurisprudence.

During the Enlightenment, individuals had little compunction about asking and investigating whether and how methods could be borrowed from the natural sciences. Göttingen constitutional law expert Johann Stephan Pütter, in 1767, differentiated between two ways in which other disciplines could influence or have an impact on jurisprudence – adaptation and application of other 'sciences' as 'supplementary aids', and the combination of jurisprudence with individual disciplines from the natural sciences.[3] Amongst the aids, 'without which no-one can make progress in the sciences' Pütter included for lawyers above all 'geography, chronology, genealogy and numismatics'.[4] Amongst the other sciences that 'are necessary and useful to a legal expert in addition to his own field' Pütter puts in an encyclopaedian manner the 'mathematical sciences' on his list 'above all others'. Their usefulness for the legal expert is of a methodological nature. It consists in 'tidying the mind so as to learn to think, deduce and furnish proof in an orderly fashion'.[5] Next on his list of 'necessary sciences' for jurisprudence experts are, in this order, logic, metaphysics, practical philosophy and morality, physics and other 'beautiful sciences'. Physics, which he puts in fifth place, is regarded as useful 'for erudite learned persons', particularly for legal experts with regard to 'cameral affairs' ... 'including some knowledge of chemistry, anatomy etc.'[6] From a utilitarian Enlightenment perspective comes the need for 'sciences that are combined of several sections of law'. Pütter calls these 'assemblies of the legal sciences', 'which seem to easily lead to the emergence of completely new sciences'.[7] However, of more significance in our context is the 'linking of jurisprudence' with other unrelated sciences in such a way that 'often, in practice, one merges with the other and thus, through a process of mixing, new sciences come into being'.[8] Such combinations of disciplines, for example, make up the 'art of legal interpretation', 'legal mathematics', 'legal medical science' and 'legal divinity'.[9] Daniel Nettelbladt saw the main utility 'that one discipline is offered by others' as being in the 'influence' that 'one area of scholarship can have on another'.[10] In concrete terms this means: 'One discipline exerts an influence on another when it contributes to the clarity or certainty of another.'[11] With 'clarity or certainty' we come to the central concept that is to be investigated in this paper, a possible element that natural law or natural scientific laws have in common with man-made law. We shall look at the use of 'lex certa', 'ius certum', and 'certitudo' as common criteria for postulating the basically scientific nature of both types of law. Amongst the disciplines 'in which others have an influence and therefore are useful',

3 Pütter 1767: 58–65, 42–45.
4 Ibid.: 58, 60.
5 Ibid.: 62.
6 Ibid.: 64.
7 Ibid.: 42s.
8 Ibid.: 43 (§ 78).
9 Ibid.: 43–45.
10 Nettelbladt 1750: 111.
11 Ibid.: 111, note a.

Nettelbladt includes 'above all positive jurisprudence' and he investigates influences on this, using the philosophy of Christian Wolff and his 'mathematical approach to teaching'.

The Relationship between Natural Laws and Man-made Laws ('Rechtsgesetze')

If we are to define or illuminate the relationship between natural and man-made laws ('Rechtsgesetze'), we first require a clear definition of these two categories. Such a definition does not, however, exist – as both have been variously defined according to the particular era and context – in other words, both have a long and separate history. It is unlikely to prove possible to reach any general definitions – but nevertheless some sort of attempt has to be made. A survey of the problem does not result in uniform findings, as nowadays 'there is no clear definition' of 'what natural laws actually are' [12] and 'why in the Nature there are such things as laws at all'.[13] However, it is possible to say that the concept of the law of nature refers to relationships within the natural world that of themselves display a degree of constancy and regularity.[14] The state of things – for example in the universe – determines the necessary relationships, the quality and quantity of events.[15] Under equal conditions, things that are equal behave in the same way – at all times and in all places. This is often taken as a logical basis – the principle of identity – for all laws of Nature. It is generally based on experience – though this is not absolutely required. These laws of Nature are established by things and their relations with one another.[16] They are quantifiable – Christian Wolff calls them 'mensurabiles'.[17] Quantifiability is regarded as a prerequisite for a natural relationship to be susceptible to formulation as a law with any certainty, security and consistency.[18] Mathematics represents their application.[19] The laws of nature are impersonal,[20] and this crucially distinguishes them from man-made laws. With this in mind, Hegel differentiated between 'Laws of Nature and Laws of Right' (Rechtsgesetze):[21] 'The Laws of Nature quite simply exist, and apply as they are: they do not suffer degeneration … The criteria for these laws lie outside us.' 'Rechtsgesetze', on the other hand, are 'made' – usually man-made – and are not absolute. 'Positive jurisprudence' therefore 'often has to deal only with contradictions'.[22]

12 Vollmer 2000: 205, 236.

13 Hampe 2000: 251.

14 Cf. Müller 1973: 569; Eisler 1910: 423.

15 Krajewski 1968: 95s.

16 Eisler 1910: 423.

17 Wolff 1736: 561.

18 Stephanitz 1970: 3.

19 Müller 1973: 572, 574.

20 Eisler 1910: 424 (with further literature and source references).

21 Hegel 1902: CLXXXVIII.

22 Ibid.: CLXXXIX.

The concept of the man-made law ('Rechtsgesetz') is central to all consolidated social systems and at the same time is a prerequisite for any attempt to create 'systematic' scientific disciplines.[23] Evidence of this fact is provided by the diversification and proliferation of the terms 'laws' and 'legislation' since the sixteenth century.[24] A 'Rechtsgesetz' aims to lay down obligations, and 'describe what should happen'.[25] It is created by human beings and focuses above all on their actions and behaviour, but also on the ordering of things and regulation of matters.[26] It has to take into account its anthropological determination in terms of those who are subject to it and its chronological determination in terms of the matters it regulates. For this reason, information has to be provided about it and it has to be generally known. In the real world past and present, the contents of laws cannot take the form of rigid norms but rather have to constantly re-adapt to the particular reality they exist in.[27] This means that one characteristic of a 'Rechtsgesetz' – in contrast to a law of Nature – is a certain mobility at the expense of the desired security and certainty. When it comes to the question of certainty and security of regulation, laws of nature and man-made laws have one point in common, for – as Hufeland puts it – 'the concept of law always includes related concepts of firmness, inviolability and strength'.[28] Thus, in the eighteenth century, attempts were frequently made to draw parallels between laws of Nature and man-made laws. 'Every regulation of action is, in the broadest sense, a law. A rule becomes a moral law when the actions it determines relate to our freedom. We therefore use the word "law" both for inanimate and animate things. One speaks of laws in optics, as one does in mechanics etc.'[29]

The concepts of these two types of law converge in the certainty – 'certitudo' – of lawfulness, with the aim of using the laws of Nature as a model and guarantor of certainty for man-made laws. This was the great attraction of the laws of Nature – the scope they offered to remove the 'arbitrariness' of man-made regulations for – as Hegel put it – 'one is often forced by the arbitrariness of life to have recourse to observation of Nature and to use it as a model'.[30] Wilhelm Arnold, in 1865, praised Lotze's successful attempt[31] 'to treat Nature and the Humanities from a uniform, common perspective' and to use the opportunity offered by the fact 'that exact research in ... the ... natural sciences ... can, in a transmuted form, also be applied to historical investigations'. Arnold was referring here to the 'method' of always 'starting from what is concrete and positive ... which suits the jurists'.[32]

These voices from the nineteenth century were merely continuing – with increasing reference to the natural sciences – an approach that had already been

---

23 Fischer 1985: 9, 21.

24 Cf. Gagnér 1960: 54ss.

25 Affolter 1904: 22.

26 Cf, the definition given by Thomasius 1705: 9: 'Lex est jussus imperantis obligans subjectos, ut secundum istum jussum actiones suas instituant.'

27 Wieacker 1967: 613; Müller 1973: 576.

28 Hufeland 1785: 6.

29 Paalzow 1781: 7: 'Von den Gesetzten überhaupt. Vom Naturgesetz.'

30 Hegel 1902: CLXXXIX.

31 Lotze 1856–64, volume 1.

32 Arnold 1865: XXIs.

pursued in earlier times: using the ideal of the unity of scientific disciplines as a source of insights and a basis for practical progress. Comparisons between the natural sciences and the law focused on the similarities of the objects of research in both disciplines. 'The jurists ... are also researchers of Nature – they are researching the natural laws of civil society.'[33] This was what Emerico Amari had in mind when he spoke, in 1857, of the 'constants of social physics' and the 'biology of laws'. [34]

Hand in hand with the idea of 'certitudo', comes its opposite: 'incertitudo'. The concept of 'incertitudo iuris' was much discussed by legal scholars in the seventeenth and eighteenth centuries and provided the starting point for the search for legal certainty. 'Certitudo' and 'incertitudo' help decide 'truth' in science and thus also help define the concept of science itself.

'Certitudo' (Certainty) as a Principle of Scientific Understanding

The search for certainty ('certitudo') is a general goal of scientific understanding – and at the same time represents a basic desire to have a firm basis for understanding and knowledge.[35] Modern philosophy speaks in this context of 'certism',[36] which, after 'critical rationalism', represents a reason-based philosophy that only admits what is 'certain' in order to keep theory as free as possible of 'uncertainty'.[37] In 1733, Christian Wolff even expressed this desire in the following words: 'From my youth onwards I have had a yearning for certainty of understanding', especially that certainty that 'serves the happiness of the human race'.[38] He was concerned 'to recognise truth as truth and ... learn to apply it'. The Enlightenment saw reason as the source of this certainty.[39] The ancient and medieval worlds, viewed 'certainty' differently: In his *Phaidros*, Plato calls 'clarity and security (or consistency)' (σαφὲς καί βέβαιον) the goal of all understanding.[40] For Thomas Aquinas, certainty of understanding is required for knowledge: '... ad scientiam requiritur cognitionis certitudo, alias non est scientia sed opinio vel credulitas ...'[41] From the certainty of the principles is derived the certainty of knowledge, 'quod certitudo scientiae tota

33 Zachariae 1829: 27 (wrongly cited as p. 43).

34 Amari 1857: 258.

35 Cf. also Nettesheim 1526; Lessing 1778: 9: 'Ich hungere nach Überzeugung so sehr, daß ich, wie Erysichthon, alles verschlinge ...'

36 Cf. comments on this concept in: Prechtl and Burkard 1999: 88.

37 This approach is extremely controversial nowadays. Albert (1991) criticizes this 'certism' as being legal thinking applied to questions of understanding. Even 'mathematics appears to be no island of certainty in a sea of our otherwise fallible understanding' (ibid.: 55). Cf. also Gamm (1994: 100ss.), who puts forward the theory that all knowledge is uncertain. Along the same line Luhman (1978: 144, 146) speaks of the variability of legal structures: 'Positive law can no longer be claimed to be invariable and therefore has to replace those certainties that lay in the social embedding of the old law.'

38 Wolff 1733: Vorrede (I).

39 Eisler 1910: 434.

40 Cf. Szlezák 1993: 51s.

41 Aquinas 1988: 8 (De veritate XI, 13).

oritur ex certitudine principiorum: tunc enim conclusiones per certitudinem sciuntur quando resolventur in principia; et ideo hoc quod aliquid per certitudinem sciatur, est ex lumine rationis divinitus interius indito quo in nobis loquitur Deus ...'[42] The basis of understanding here is seen as the faculty of reason implanted by God in human beings. But Thomas offers empiricism as a tool for establishing certainty when he associates 'certitudo' with natural movement, 'quod lapis certitudinaliter tendit deorsum': a stone falls downwards with certainty. 'And it does this on account of the infallibility derived from the certainty of understanding' ('propter infallibilitatem quam habet ex certitudine cognitionis ...') that precedes the instinctual or natural tendency.[43]

The example of the natural sciences is found later in Newton and David Hume. Descartes derives certainty from observation and elimination of doubt: 'm'assurer'. He examines the 'incertitude des propositions' according to 'raisonnements clairs et assurés', in order to come to a 'conclusion assez certaine' – even if the end result is merely to exclude certainty: 'qu'elle ne contenait rien de certain'.[44] David Hume's search for certainty involves liberation from prejudice, and impartiality of judgement 'is the only method, by which we can ever hope to reach Truth, and attain a proper Stability and Certainty in our Determinations'.[45] He examines the relationship of cause and effect from observation of Nature and derives from these 'Laws of Nature',[46] which, however – and this is his finding – display differing degrees of certainty: 'from the highest Certainty to the lowest Species of moral Evidence'.[47] Deriving general statements from individual empirical cases, however, is regarded by Hume only as having habitual rather than logical legitimization. He focuses on the 'Uncertainty' of 'Certainty' and for the first time specifically he makes dubious traditional understanding of the laws of the natural sciences. A further relativization can be found in Johann Lambert: 'The certainty of the whole of human understanding dissolves in the question of the correctness of the terms.'[48] Behind this lay an older principle of scientific understanding formulated by Romei as follows: '... dalla buona diffinizione nasc(e) la soluzione di tutti i dubbi che occorrano nella scienza.'[49] Identifiable ancient authorities on whom Romei bases his statement are Cicero's *De officiis* (I 2,7) and Plato's *Phaedrus* (263a–264).

---

42 Aquinas 1988: 30 (De veritate XI, 1. Art., 13).

43 Aquinas 1955: 305s. (*Summa theologicae* I–II questio 40, ad tertium). On the same example in the argumentation of Melanchthon cf. Kusukawa, Chapter 7 in this volume.

44 Descartes 1908: 65.

45 Hume 1748: 233.

46 Ibid.: 132, 140.

47 Ibid.: 175.

48 Lambert 1761, quoted here after Arndt 1971: 152.

49 Romei 1586, quoted here after: Cox (1992): 100. Romei is here following Cicero's definition in *De officiis* lib. I, 2/7.

'Ius certum' in Roman Law

'Certitudo' in law and legal affairs can be related to and supported by legislation, jurisprudence and jurisdiction. In particular we find it being demanded of legislation – 'incertitudo legislatoribus numquam placet'[50] – and as a model of the mathematical method for law in general. 'Certitudo' represents, on the one hand, an ideal of justice and, in the commonly-cited contrasting concept of 'incertitudo', indicates a criticism of the inadequate certainty of the law and its application which is contained in the old Roman concept of 'ius controversum' or what is today known as 'controversial law' (strittiges Recht).[51]

In Roman law, under the Justinian *Corpus Juris Civilis*, 'ius certum' and 'lex certa' are identified as characteristics of law in contrast to its original uncertainty (D. 1.2.): 'Initially the people ordered their own affairs without a fixed system of law and without fixed laws. Everything was administered by the King alone' ('... populus sine lege certa, sine iure certo primum agere instituit, omnia a regibus gubernatur'). 'Jus' is the more comprehensive term for law, 'lex' the more restricted. The lack of a system of law and fixed legislation is circumscribed as 'incerto iure et consuetudine aliqua' (D. 1.2.3). By contrast, in the case of fixed legislation, the term used is 'certo iure utimur' (D. 2.11.10). Even when a law exists, it can become uncertain as a result of interpretation by a lawyer and thus requires certainty anew – 'quaerere, disputare' results in a 'ius controversum, ius dubium, ius varium'.[52] It can be returned to the status of 'ius certum' by the 'auctoritas' of the 'peritissimi', as non-controversial law 'sine dubio multo maxima est'.[53] The goal is 'interpretatio certa'.[54] 'Interpretatio' is, however, only regarded as permissible when the wording of the law is unclear. This means, conversely, that where the words are clear in their meaning there may be no interpretation. For this rule, Hostiensis significantly used the typical formulations 'certus' and 'incertus'. In the case of 'verba certa: tunc a significatione verborum recedendum non est'.[55]

The ideal of 'certitudo' or legal certainty dominates the whole process of producing and implementing legislation. To preserve 'certitudo', even a customary and declared interpretation may not be relinquished: 'Minime sunt mutanda, quae Interpretationem certam semper habuerunt' (D. 1.3.23). Budaeus adds the demand that the pronouncements of lawyers should at last become certain and secure: '... ut certa fixaque aliquando iurisconsultorum dogmata essent ...'[56] For, as Budaeus asks, when will there be an end to disputes if there are no secure and recognized decisions by lawyers?: 'Alioquin quis erit finis litium, si nulla certa fuerint, semelque recepta iurisconsultorum decreta.'[57]

---

[50] Oldendorp 1548: 'Incertitudo' (not paginated).

[51] Schwarz 1951: 201ss.

[52] Cf. Bona 1987: 127–129.

[53] Cicero, *De oratore*, I, 241s.

[54] Lantella 1987: 228.

[55] Hostiensis 1537: fols. 299, 299v: 'Que est distinctio verborum; Qualiter verba dubia interpretantur'; on this see Schott 2001: 165–171.

[56] Budaeus 1557: 10.

[57] Ibid.: 8; cf. on this subject Herberger 1981: 229.

This approach, involving famous jurists deciding on controversial issues, was consistently criticized and rejected as being a non-rational 'argumentum ab auctoritate' right up to the age of the Enlightenment. The 'authority'-argument was revealed as being arbitrary in the seventeenth and eighteenth centuries. The new concept of science required logical proof, even in the field of jurisprudence. Strategies for achieving certainty were discussed and exchanged, but the ultimate goal of 'certitudo' remained constant.

For relationships under the law of obligations to be valid, 'certitudo' has, to this day, remained a crucial prerequisite, providing for the necessary specification of the obligation involved: 'certum vocatur, si apparet, quid, quale, quantum sit id, de quo quaeritur.'[58] Where there is uncertainty, there can be no conviction and certainly no execution of a judgement: 'Ubi incertitudo ibi nulla condemnatio, multo minus executio.'[59]

Under the Roman *Corpus iuris civilis*, a link to the 'certitudo' of a law of Nature could only be ascertained in one case: 'cum per rerum naturam certum fuerit ...; nec rerum naturam intuendam, in qua omnia certa essent' (D. 5.1.28.5). This involved the share of an inheritance claimed by an heir at a stage when it was not yet clear how many siblings (with whom the claim would have to be shared) would be produced by the mother, who was still pregnant. Sabinus and Cassius were of the opinion that one should not refer to Nature, given that it was already certain that only one further son would be born, even if the future event was as yet unknown.

For solving the case, certainty according to the laws of Nature and uncertainty with regard to the facts remained independent of each other.

'Lex certa' in the Natural Sciences and Law

Newton's use of the term 'lex certa' is well known.[60] According to this, empirical facts achieve the status of a 'lex certa', when they lead to a regular and unambiguous result.[61] Newton differentiates degrees of certainty on the basis of his empirical observations, for example of light waves.[62] He uses the terms 'Laws', 'Common Rules' and 'Necessary Laws'.[63] Through experimentation he establishes stability and constancy, and at the same time asks whether it is in fact possible 'quicquam certi in ulla scientia determinare possit'. His basic question is 'how certainty can be obtained in any science'.[64] For him, too, nothing is 'so certain as mathematical demonstrations'.[65] This was a view held equally by lawyers and philosophers – including Descartes – during the Enlightenment.

---

58 Jacobus 1595: 18; Oldendorp 1548: 'Certum est' (s.p.).

59 Knorr 1680: 171.

60 See also the ideas of Steinle, Chapter 13 in this volume.

61 Newton 1978: 100, 102.

62 Ibid.: 95, 110, 111.

63 Ibid.: 149, 152, 318.

64 Ibid.: 99, 106.

65 Ibid.: 114.

One important element in creating 'certitudo' in law or a 'ius certum', is the conversion of unwritten customary law – 'lex non scripta' – into written form – 'lex scripta'. In legal language, 'ius certum' is used much more commonly than 'lex scripta', but the two are closely related. 'Lex scripta' represents, particularly in the late Middle Ages, the recording in written form of what was originally unwritten law, thereby converting it into a written text of evidential value, guaranteeing the necessary clarity, security and certainty for legal and court proceedings. Thus the authenticity of the law was textually secured. The lack of a 'scriptura certa vel authentica' was removed by the creation of a legal code. The Castilian 'Libro del Alcalá' of 1348 speaks in this context of establishing 'leyes ciertas'.[66] Theory formulated the principle: 'Omne ius scriptum est certius et nobilius iure non scripto.'[67] In this way, the law became a secure basis for decision-making and thus also predictable for those seeking justice. As a text it was thus raised to the status of 'ius certum', though it unavoidably lost some of its certainty as a result of legal interpretations. Francis Bacon perceptively stressed this when he raised 'certitudo' to the level of a demand for justice.

In the third chapter of the eighth book of his *De augmentis scientiarum*, Bacon devotes one title to the question 'De prima dignitate legum, ut sint certae'. Without a 'lex certa' there can be no justice. He compares the 'incerta vox' of the 'tuba' with the 'incerta vox' of the 'lex'. Judges, he says, should only be allowed limited scope for interpretation. 'Optimam esse legem, quae minimum relinquit arbitrio iudicis: Id quod certitudo eius praestat.'[68] He differentiates between two kinds of 'incertitudo': (1) when no law exists, and (2) when the law is ambiguous and unclear ('ambigua et obscura'). The 'remedium', according to Bacon, is to have recourse to 'similia' and 'usus exemplorum', or to jurisdiction 'ex arbitrio boni viri'. This 'remedium', however, is more indicative of a certain helplessness with regard to legal 'incertitudo' – perhaps also a realization of its inevitability – than of a feasible route to achieving 'certitudo' in law. References to the laws of Nature and their 'certae propositones' are not found in Bacon, although the term 'Law of Nature' can be found in his writings and this can be defined in the modern sense of a rule that is comprehensive, absolute and constitutive for Nature: 'ex lege naturae universalis'.[69] For Christian Wolff, on the other hand, 'certa lex' has a different meaning – in depicting 'ars inveniendi' it has the character of a method according to which the 'inventor certa lege progrediatur'.[70]

Mathematical Certainty in Philosophy and Law

Since the seventeenth century, writers have created and variously discussed a link between the laws of Nature and man-made law via mathematics. Ever since classical antiquity, geometry and arithmetic have been attributed with the highest

---

66 Cf. Wolf 1981: 156.
67 Quoted after Scholz 1973: 136.
68 Bacon 1740: 249.
69 Schramm 1981: 197, 204.
70 Cf. Arndt 1971: 145.

degree of certainty. Mathematical 'certitudo' was also transferred as a method of understanding to other areas of science and linked to the theological question of truth. The mathematical certainty theorem began to predominate. Cusanus (Nikolaus von Kues) stated: 'Nihil certi habemus nisi nostram mathematicam.'[71] This constituted 'incorruptibilis certitudo' par excellence[72] and was postulated with regard to the understanding of divine truths: 'Quod mathematica nos iuvet plurimum in diversorum divinorum apprehensione.'[73] Mathematics guaranteed a high degree of certainty in the observation of perceptible objects: '... firmissima videmus atque nobis certissima, ut sunt ipsa mathematicalia.'[74] In this context, Kues refers explicitly to the traditions of classical antiquity, quoting Boethius: 'neminem divinorum scientiam, qui penitus in mathematicis exercitio careret, attingere posse.'[75] In his *Pensées sur la religion*, Pascal takes the same 'mathematical approach' in order to uncover 'vérités inconnues': '... et je n'ai pour cela qu' à expliquer la methode que la géométrie y observe: car elle l'enseigne parfaitement.'[76] The application of mathematics even in the humanities is supposed to result in demonstrability and certainty of decisions – even with regard to 'vérités des sciences morales et politiques', whose susceptibility to the 'certitude ... des sciences physiques' and the 'certitudes mathématiques' were stressed, with considerable faith in progress, by Condorcet in 1785.[77]

Descartes praises mathematics because of the security and certainty of the proof it offers: 'cause de la certitude et de l'evidence de leurs raisons'.[78] Only mathematics, according to him, have been able to find secure grounds and proof – 'quelques raisons certaines et evidentes'. Descartes saw mathematical method – 'certitude aux règles de l'arithmetique' – as offering the same scope for solving difficulties in other sciences 'as it provided me with in algebra'.[79] The universality of mathematical methodology – in the sense that it was transferable to other scientific disciplines – is expressed in the very term 'mathesis universalis'. Descartes regarded it as the ideal procedure for solving problems, and one whose universality enabled it to be transferred to other problems.[80] However, he was only talking about the natural sciences, even if his rules on methods can be taken as a model.

The four methodological rules described by Descartes in his *Discours de la méthode* – the principle of evidentiality, the principle of dividing a problem into individual parts, the principle of grading one's approach according to increasing degrees of difficulty and the principle of complete enumeration – constitute the starting point for a methodology based on 'mathesis universalis'.[81]

---

71 Cf. Eisler 1910: 434.

72 Kues/Cusanus (1448) 1970: 44.

73 Ibid.: 40.

74 Ibid.: 42.

75 Ibid.

76 Pascal (1662) 1991: 390.

77 Quoted here after Solnon 1994: 531.

78 Descartes 1908: 41, 55.

79 Ibid.: 57.

80 Cf. Arndt 1971: 48.

81 Arndt 1978: 60.

The link between 'mathesis universalis' and jurisprudence is made by Christian Wolff, who attributes an 'indubitable certainty' to mathematics, which means 'without mathematics our understanding cannot become properly clear'.[82] Only mathematics, according to Wolff offers 'the most precise and complete understanding that can be achieved'.[83]

Wolff practises 'the mathematical approach to pedagogy' – to use his term – in all his lectures:

1. never using terms without an unambiguous explanation and account of the grounds for proof;
2. never referring to a principle without previously demonstrating the proof for it;
3. linking the declarations and statements taken from these and deriving deductions.[84]

He calls this the 'demonstrative method'[85] and uses the physical laws of gravity as an example.[86]

Wolff does not deny that even without the demonstrative method 'one can achieve a well-grounded understanding of law despite not presenting the truths contained therein in relation to one another as one can be demonstrated by the other'.[87]

However, he stresses the 'usefulness' of the mathematical method of teaching 'in jurisprudence' 'if the civil laws taught at university were to be incorporated into such an order as one has its cause in the other'. Agreements and contradictions could be identified in this way. 'One would learn the general maxims on which laws are founded and accordingly in other cases where no law exists one would be able to determine what is right … Indeed, one would be able to incorporate many laws in more general ones …'[88] Thus he identifies rationalization criteria that were to become significant for the debate on codification in the Age of Enlightenment. But as a formalized technique of deduction they were soon subjected to criticism.[89] Nevertheless Wolff convincingly identified his method as that of 'demonstrative certainty'.[90] Proof was regarded as demonstration, so that 'everything that is correctly demonstrated is equally certain ...'[91] The 'geometrical truths' signified for Wolff a method of understanding of 'indubitable certainty', so that everything that 'is demonstrated in a geometrical manner is as certain as we are ourselves.'[92] For Wolff, the natural sciences demonstrated what the mathematical method can

[82] Wolff 1716: Vorrede (IV).
[83] Wolff 1978: 120.
[84] Wolff 1733: 52s.
[85] Cf. also Stephanitz 1970: 88.
[86] Wolff 1733: 103.
[87] Ibid.: 112.
[88] Ibid.: 119s.
[89] Stephanitz 1970: 84ss.
[90] Wolff 1733: 123.
[91] Wolff 1751: 5 (§ 8).
[92] Ibid.: 5 (§ 9).

achieve. And similar success could be expected for law. Wolff's aim is 'ut ceteras quoque disciplinas ad aliquem certitudinis gradum evehere tentarem'.[93] In his search for security and certainty in law and for the training of jurists, however, mathematics retained its strong suggestivity – without its methodology being precisely transferable to jurisprudence.[94]

For David Hume, too, mathematics offered scope to discover 'certain Laws – established by Nature in her operations'.[95] Hume is thinking here of the 'Law of Motion', which is discovered through 'Experience'. The degree and correctness of every movement is laid down 'by the Laws of Nature ... with such Exactness' and demonstrates the 'precise Idea of Necessity'.[96] Hume also stresses 'the great Advantage of the mathematical Sciences above the moral', because the former are always 'clear and determinate ... without Ambiguity or Variation'.[97] For this reason, he claims, it is necessary 'in Metaphysics' to achieve 'a greater Clearness and Precision in philosophical Reasonings', in order to rule out 'Ambiguity and Obscurity'.[98] This meant that the basic difference between the natural sciences and the humanities had been described in terms of the amount of 'Certainty' achievable – but it did not remove that difference.

Thomas Hobbes assumes the same difference between the two areas of discipline and contrasts the 'certitudo' of physics and geometry with the unpredictability of human emotions: 'Cognita enim, pari certitudine, ratione actionum humanarum, qua cognoscitur ratio magnitudinum in figuris, ambitio et avaritia quarum potentia falsis vulgi circa jus et injuriam opinionibus innititur, inermes essent, fruereturque gens humana pace adeo constante ...'[99] So long as the methods and criteria of the natural sciences were not transferable to the humanities in terms of 'certitudo' – and this included jurisprudence – the desirable degree of scientific certainty could not be achieved in these disciplines. Hobbes, too, attributed a greater degree of rationality to the mathematical sciences compared with jurisprudence: '... but I say, that the great masters of the mathematics do not so often err as the great professors of the law'.[100] 'Reason' and 'experience' could always be named as universal and universally useable criteria, but they could not lead to equal degrees of certainty and valid truths in the humanities and the natural sciences.[101] In the argumentation of Richard Cumberland who, on the one hand praises 'certitudo Mathematica' as a transferable model and, on the other, relativizes its applicability for 'certitudo in regulis vitae, ac morum',

---

93 Wolff 1735: 6.

94 Thomasius 1710: 51–153; Kestner 1699: 81s.: 'Matheseos usum in vita civili longe maximum, eumque nulli non commendandum esse, tam certum quam certissimum ...'

95 Hume 1748: 56.

96 Ibid.: 132.

97 Ibid.: 99.

98 Ibid.: 101s.

99 Hobbes 1647: 'Epistola dedicatoria' (VI).

100 Hobbes 1962: 3.

101 Various examples of the grades of 'certitudo' from 'certa' to 'certissima lex' and of 'certitudo' and 'veritas' are provided by Maclean and Graßhoff (Chapters 2 and 9 in this volume); cf. also above on Hume and Newton notes 47 and 62.

this basic difference between the two disciplines is brought out clearly.[102] Hugo Grotius had already cited Aristotle in his apt decription of this aporia and discrepancy between the natural and ethical sciences: 'Verissimum est quod scripsit Aristoteles,[103] in moralibus non aeque, ut in mathematicis disciplinis certitudinem inveniri: quod eo evenit, quia mathematicae disciplinae a materia omni formas separant, et quia formae ipsae tales plerumque sunt, ut nihil habeant interiectum, sicut inter rectum et curuum nihil est medii. At in moralibus circumstantiae etiam minimae variant materiam, ... unde ambiguitas saepe incidit, ut in crepusculo … Et hoc est quod ait Aristoteles, quid cui anteponendum sit difficilis saepe est iudicatio.'[104]

'Incertitudo iuris' and the Limited Influence of the Methodology of the Natural Sciences

If one examines legal texts for the reception of the methods of the natural sciences or at least for attitudes towards the achievement of 'certitudo' in the field of law, little evidence is forthcoming. Complaints about the uncertainty of the law – 'de incertitudine iuris', as it is called in tracts and countless dissertations – predominate, and have fuelled calls for legal reforms ever since the sixteenth century.[105] Various terms are used to describe the much-criticized 'incertitudo' of the law and legal system: 'confusio tanta', 'ambiguitas', 'multitudo jurium, 'dissensio inter doctores', 'magna disputatio', 'varietas jurium singulorum', 'obscuritas in legibus', 'controversia iuris'.[106] These characterizations refer both to received Roman law and to the indigenous 'ius patriae' – as well as the confusing rivalry between these two levels of law. The reluctant conclusion drawn is frequently: '... ut videas amice lector, nihil esse in jure nostro non ambiguum'.[107] Conring blames this on the incalculable number of legal cases and the lack of any order in these: '... cum in tanta Prudentiae nostrae incertitudine propter casuum innumerum numerum nihil certi fere sperare …'[108]

The reasons for this 'incertitudo' are examined and identified: removing all the contradictions in the laws is regarded as an impossible task while human beings still exist; the scope and validity (auctoritas) of received Roman law, and, as a result, its 'vis legis', are uncertain.[109] In 'disciplinis moralibus' no 'certitudo' can be found, like in other disciplines, 'inprimis mathematicae'. Also 'de meteoris nonnisi verosimilem cognitionem habemus'.[110] Ernestus states, in 1718, that only some aspects of mathematics – which he regards as an extremely clear science – have

[102] Cumberland 1683: 182–184; cf. TREIBER (Chapter 10 in this volume).

[103] There reference is to Aristotle's *Nicomachean Ethics*: I, 1 (1094 b, 10).

[104] Grotius 1626: 436; cf. Otte 1979: 194–196.

[105] Cf. Schiemann 1998: 162–165; Diestelkamp 1977: 30s.

[106] Ernestus 1718: 6, 12, 22; Gribner 1715: Cap. IV; Conring 1695: 224; Thomasius 1713: Praefatio (4, 6–12).

[107] Conring 1695: 224.

[108] Conring 1663: Thesis I.

[109] Gribner 1715: IV; Ernestus 1718: 4–8.

[110] Ernestus 1718: 5.

been dealt with hitherto in the disputations led by doubt.[111] The structural difference between those natural sciences that operate on a formal logical basis – geometry and mathematics – and jurisprudence, which is value-oriented and aims at ordering social life, is recognized but not dealt with in depth in these writings. 'Certitudo' as a scientific ideal, however, remains a concept that links jurisprudence and the natural sciences. This also comes out clearly in legal language.

A link to the natural sciences exists in comparisons and in a metaphorical language – though this does not make any direct borrowings from the 'certitudines' or laws of the natural sciences. The human body is compared to a clockwork, and the blood circulation system is interpreted as the mechanics of life.[112] The concept of space in physics and of bodies in space is used as a parable for the stratification of society and the status of the individual within society. But conclusions regarding 'certitudo' are not made. 'Certitudo' should be achieved through decisions by the legislators or by jurisprudence,[113] through authoritative judgements on controversial issues and by the laying down of definitions[114] – in other words by activities within the discipline of jurisprudence and by jurisprudence itself.

Codification and 'ius certum'

In the Age of Reason the most significant instrument for achieving legal certainty and security is regarded as the systematic codification of the law.[115] Order of material and form of laws; the removal of obsolete legal traditions; the systematic creation of legal texts and logical derivations that make it possible to close gaps in the law and remove uncertainties in texts by clear definitions; simplicity combined with linguistic comprehensibility and precision in the national language[116] are the ideal goals of codification during the Enlightenment. A legal norm can only achieve its aims if 'et recta, certa ac constans, et cum obligatione ... coniuncta sit'.[117] Only certain and uniform legislation makes it possible to achieve uniform and certain jurisdiction. And it was precisely the latter that suffered from uncertainty and unpredictability. In France, d'Agusseau – Louis XV's chancellor – described this in terms 'd'incertitude et d'instabilité qui est presque inséparable de tous les ouvrages humains'.[118] The optimism of the Enlightenment that everything was susceptible to rational planning thus also included the ultimate 'plannability' and predictability of the law by means of comprehensive, general and standardized legislation. Behind all this there also lay a belief in the feasibility of individually and collectively shaping society through legislation. In an age of law based on reason, the main role of legislation was to

[111] Ernestus 1718: 4.

[112] Heineccius 1738: 21s. (§§ XXVIII, XXIX).

[113] For example, Thomasius 1713: 4 to 18.

[114] Gribner 1715: XXII.

[115] Summarized by Dölemeyer 2000: 1005–1007.

[116] Schott 1983: 121–146.

[117] Heineccius 1738: 44 (§ LX).

[118] Quote here after Solnon 1994: 614.

secure civil peace, civil liberties and, above all, legal certainty.[119] If one examines, for example, the Prussian *Project des Corporis Juris Fridericiani* of 1749 against the background of this theoretical aspiration to codification, then it becomes clear that the very title of this legal code reflects the entire range of important topoi of the 'certitudo'-discussion.[120] The Code is consistently related to the question of and demand for 'ius certum'. As indicated by the very title of the law, 'provincial state law' is based on 'reason and provincial constitutions' and 'Roman Law is integrated into a natural order and subjected to systematisation according to the three Objectis Juris: the General Principles based on Reason are established for every Objecto and the necessary Conclusiones, dependence on many Laws, deduced therefrom: All Subtleties and Fictiones, and also what is not applicable to the German System are left out: All dubious laws found in the Roman laws or made by the Doctoribus are decided on, and in this way a Jus certum and universale established in all its provinces.'

The 'Reader's Introduction' to the law, with its nine or more pages divided into 34 paragraphs also concerns itself with the topic of 'ius certum'. A historical section explains 'that the Romans never had Legal Certainty'. And the conclusion drawn from this is: 'thus it can be said with some Authority that even in the German Reich there has never been, up to the present day, such a thing as "ius certum"' (§ 17). The *Project des Corporis Juris Fridericiani* regards itself as a realization of 'ius certum', so 'this Province Law justifiably can be called a Jus naturae privatum' (§ 30). The reference to 'Jus naturae' contains the idea of a natural order based on Reason that underlies the 'Principia Juris Naturalis' (§ 30). The intention is to secure a foundation of deduction on which the necessary 'conclusiones' can be based and thus guarantee a secure 'universal system' (§ 28). In a language itself characterized by certainty, the conviction is underlined that this ensures legal certainty based on the Roman scheme of 'personae, res, actiones': 'This is certain that according also to Natural Reason no law remains that is not covered by these three Concepts; and that there can be no Controversy that cannot be decided on this basis – as will emerge from the System itself' (§ 28 II).

This codification was, accordingly, based on the assumption that 'all Casus are covered by the 'Principiis'' (§ 29). Cases of doubt were to be solved through 'ratio legis'. If there was still no clear 'ratio vera et unica legis' in the sense of 'certitudo', then the court had to 'bring the Rationes pro et contra to the Justice Department, which ... will decide the Dubium: and such Decisiones should be annually put into Print' (§ 29). The legal certainty that was thought to have been achieved through codification was on no account to be undermined by interpretation. Jurisprudence and jurisdiction were to be excluded from the task of interpretation. If a 'dubium' arose, then it had to be returned to the status of a – putative – 'ius certum' by a

[119] Cf. Krause 1988: 12–13; cf. also Zeiller 1806: 40: 'The purpose of civil legislation is to provide the citizens with certainty (i.e. a clear knowledge) and security regarding their private rights. This is the basis on which the characteristics, appropriateness and quality of a civil code must be judged.'

[120] Used here: *Project des Corporis Juris Fridericiani*, 2nd edn, 1750.

decision of the Justice Department on the basis of the advice of the permanent 'State Legal Committee'.

This was a task for the legislator, in the shape of the enlightened absolute ruler, and was not to be overturned or questioned by legal or political individuals working in parallel – that is, by jurisprudence experts, judges or other estates in society. The optimism of the Enlightenment, with its belief in rational planning, was not, however, able to generally stabilize the basic structural weakness of the law. Finality, certainty and security in law could not be achieved even with the aid of borrowings from the natural sciences, with their regularities and certainties. But they nevertheless remained an ideal. The 'mathematicization' of the law foundered on the historicity and time-bound nature of the changing tasks faced by the law and the need to adapt and vary its instruments in societies and states that are continuously evolving. The law is not neutral and devoid of values, like a law of causality in the natural sciences. Legislation, as part of the legal order, is determined by the human will – the individual will of a sovereign prince or the 'volonté générale' of a sovereign nation – and determines and constitutes the particular social order of a state community. That is why the range of juridical concepts in the form of the *lex* or regulative statements on equality are not the same as the concept of laws in the natural sciences. The latter are observable, more or less fixed rules, whereas man-made laws have a social purpose and function.[121] This fundamental difference does not exclude the possibility that the idea of mathematical certainty can, at times, have an impact on the humanities and even on jurisprudence. This manifests itself in historical terms in the concept of 'ius certum'. But as the legal system has to work with concepts that are value-related and lack mathematical clarity – permitting, for example, general clauses that deliberately allow for a degree of discretion in decision-making – those responsible for applying the law cannot reach conclusions that are based exclusively on formal logic and are devoid of value-judgements. Nevertheless, the constant desire for 'certitudo iuris' will remain an element in the essential concept of justice.

[121] Cf. also Stephanitz 1970: 8s.

Chapter 6

Crimen contra naturam

Andreas Roth

Introduction

> If there is any doctrine in the field of morality which can be set out in the same way as a physical doctrine, it is certainly the doctrine of punishments since there is virtually no matter relating to punishments where it is not possible to draw conclusions relating to the duty to punish precisely from the duty of a good doctor.[1]

Although I do not wish to question the legitimacy of this assertion by Thomasius, it does at least give an indication of the self-evident nature of criminal law theory in the mid-eighteenth century. The older law of nature assumed that criminal law could be justified without recourse to divine authority. Initial signs thereof are to be found in Hugo Grotius and the subsequent commentaries on Grotius. Punishment per se is henceforth legitimized by the law of nature. This development away from theologically-based to natural law-based justification of punishment does not constitute new knowledge and has already frequently been taken as a topic in the history of law.[2] However, the manner of the new reasoning is interesting in itself over and above the departure from the purely divine legitimization of human punishment. In the quotation Thomasius speaks of a 'physical doctrine'. The scientific concept is used to characterize 'the doctrine of punishment'. This raises the question whether, on account of such terminological similarity, corresponding borrowings were also made in substantive terms. For example, did the biological view of nature influence the assessment of human actions as contrary to the law of nature? Was there a specific human nature whose transgression was unnatural and thus liable to punishment? Was there, consequently, a 'crimen contra naturam'? These questions, which thus far have not been the subject of academic examination, will be considered below using contemporary legal and theological writings and it is in this context that the concepts in the title of this essay are to be understood:

---

1 Thomasius 1688: vol. 3, chap. 7, n. 56.

2 Cf. Fischl 1913; Schmidt 1968: 164.

Crimen

In its narrow meaning[3] 'crimen' means crime or punishable act.[4] In this respect the title deals with the question whether specific conduct transgresses nature and for that reason must be liable to punishment. Thus, what is under consideration is the justification for regarding certain acts as criminal on the basis of nature. This is where the considerations will focus.

The term 'crimen' can also mean a rule of criminal law itself. In that case the expression 'crimen contra naturalem legem' describes a criminal offence which, for its part, transgresses nature. What is meant here are the attempts, in particular of the so-called 'more recent law of nature', to correct existing positive criminal law by means of arguments based on the law of nature. This aspect will be addressed briefly at the end of the essay.

Natura

The term was used in a wide range of ways in the modern era. On the one hand, it was used in the Aristotelian sense, that is to say stemming from the semantic sphere of the word *physis*, thus describing the essence which is characteristic of a particular thing.[5] On the other hand, however, the word is often also used in accordance with its Latin root (*nasci* = innate) and, since High Scholasticism, often independently of theology. In research it is widely held that a mechanistic concept of nature[6] has become accepted since Hobbes. Although it is certainly possible to see a development in the use of the term 'nature', the use made of the word in the seventeenth and eighteenth centuries is by no means clear. Different concepts of nature occur in the works of the same author, such as in the case of Leibniz who subscribes to the new thinking guided by law (lex) in physics, but derives law (ius) from the rational nature of man. Nor is a uniform view to be found among jurists. Pufendorf, who distinguishes between the entia moralia and the entia physica, equates the former with natural laws which, although they can be arrived at from observing man, cannot be derived from the nature of man.[7] By contrast, Thomasius supported precisely the latter view which is based on a purely physical factor.[8]

The following examination is not based on any particular concept of nature. Instead, the historical use of the term is adopted and in each individual case an attempt is made to convey the meaning intended by the authors. Therefore, the scholars concerned are not selected by whether or not they can be assigned to a particular school of thought on the law of nature. For example, where reference is

3 As regard the broad meaning, whereby 'crimen' means criminal law in very general terms, see the words of the early modern era prefixed by 'Kriminal-' in *Deutsches Rechtswörterbuch* 1974: 1578ff.

4 Georges 1972: crimen.

5 Aristotle, Phys II 1, 193 a.

6 Kaulbach 1984: 469ff., and the references contained therein.

7 Pufendorf 1672: book 2, c 1 § 2.

8 Thomasius 1688: I 4 § 29.

made below to an older or more recent law of nature, this is merely intended as an indication for the benefit of the reader and does not mean that a category has been found for the relevant topic under discussion. Nor has the sole decisive factor for the choice made been the departure from criminal law guided by God which took place in the natural law era.[9]

Specific Crimes against Nature

The *Constitutio Criminalis Carolina* of 1532 was still entirely influenced by a criminal law legitimized through God. This applies also to the majority of criminal law scholarship of this era[10] and in particular to the practice of the early modern era which was largely guided by this code.[11] However, as early as the sixteenth century, and more so subsequently, natural law-based justifications appeared in addition to theological justifications for individual criminal offences. Derivations from nature are to be found most often in the case of morality offences.

Article 116 of the Carolina Code

Sodomy

Conceptually, this offence is the only one to use transgression of human nature as a characteristic of the criminal act. The heading reads 'Punish the unchaste, for they act against nature'. The offence laid down in Article 116 of the Carolina Code, which is described as 'unnatural sexual practice' and was still to be found in the German Criminal Code under the heading 'Sodomy' until 1969, is certainly religious in its origin.[12] The religious and moral character of the article of the Carolina Code is undisputed and the first commentaries on the Carolina Code, such as those by Georg Remus[13] and Nicolaus Vigelius,[14] are accordingly based solely on the Old Testament. However, Justin Gobler,[15] also a commentator on the Carolina Code, and Jose Damhouder, in his textbook, suggest a view based on the law of nature as early as the mid-sixteenth century: 'this, however, goes far beyond the aim of nature ...'[16] Although this timeworn link with nature remains current in the sixteenth century,

---

9 Although the question at issue is how far the theological legitimization of criminal law was superseded by a new way of thinking guided by science, the complete exclusion of the earlier thinking based on the law of nature would obscure any possible continuity. Thus, also of interest is the question whether or not initial thoughts are perhaps to be found in Late Scholasticism which were subsequently adopted and developed further even though the authors at that time still perhaps supported the view of criminal law originating solely from God.

10 Schmidt 1968: 161ff.

11 Sellert and Rüping 1989: 199.

12 Cf. Moses 1: 19, 5; Moses 2: 22, 18; Moses 3: 18, 22.

13 Remus 1594: 107.

14 Vigelius 1603: 237.

15 Gobler 1543: 93.

16 Damhouder 1565, c 96 § 1.

albeit without being set out in detail, in the seventeenth century the reformed French theologian Amyraut goes one step further. He takes biology as a basis for justifying the existence of the offence: 'If different animal species do not mix with one another, man can be allowed to do so even less.'[17]

Observation of the animal world is used directly to demonstrate the prohibition of certain forms of human behaviour. The conclusion is simple. Zoological fact is equated with a normative order of nature which is directed at men.

If one looks at the rest of the academic writings on criminal law of the seventeenth and eighteenth centuries, it is conspicuous that almost all authors henceforth cite nature in the biological sense as justification for liability to punishment. Referring to Article 116 in his *Meditationes*, Böhmer states that it 'is based on sexual intercourse contrary to the order of nature'[18] and by 'ordo naturae' he probably means the order of the animal world to which humans evidently also belong.

Both quotations are consistent with the view of the period which perceives man not merely as a being of creation, but primarily as part of biological nature. This makes it possible to infer from the observation of animal behaviour a law applicable a fortiori to humans. Böhmer refers to Leyser's commentary according to which sodomy 'is an act where a desire develops that is other than that assumed by nature'.[19] In the second paragraph Böhmer goes on to state that:

> Nature not only requires sexual intercourse from both sexes, but also teaches all living beings the way in which this is performed. Where a person deviates in this regard, where a sex loses its place or the pleasure of love takes on a different form, the act is disorderly, unnatural and more than bestial.[20]

In the case of most authors there is an attempt to draw conclusions applicable to criminal law from a specific consideration of the biological creature 'man'. Nature is perceived as a factor and man as a part thereof. Domingo de Soto states that 'the law of nature is what nature teaches all creatures'.[21] No grounds are stated for this approach since the authors consider the conclusion reached to be too self-evident. This is also typical of findings which are (apparently) gained directly from nature.

Homosexuality

Particular attention was paid to same-sex love, in particular between men, in Article 116 of the Carolina Code. Homosexuality is also meant for the most part in the above quotations: 'be it a man or beast in the same or peculiar sex'.[22] It is often referred to in the same breath as sodomy. Clasen writes: 'where any man engages in shameful

[17] Amyraut 1648: 88 (quoted according to Erle 1952: 60).

[18] '... constitit in concubitu contra ordinem naturae'.

[19] '... est actus, quo libido alia, quam natura monstrat via, expletur'.

[20] Böhmer 1770: 'Natura ad coitum non modo utrumque sexum requirit, verum etiam modum, quo ille consummatur, omnia animalia docuit. Qua in re si quis aberrat, si sexus perdit locum, vel venus in aliam formam mutatur, actus est inordinatus, praeternaturalis, et plusquam bestialis.' Similarly Ludovici 1716: 151; cf. also Pufendorf 1672: 1.6 c 1 § 4).

[21] De Soto 1569: 4. Sent dist 33: 'Ius naturae est, quod natura omnia animalia docuit'.

[22] Frölichsburg 1741: 255.

and unnatural intercourse with a man or a woman does so with another woman, such conduct, it is said, is contrary to nature'.[23] Whereas uniform grounds, derived mainly from the Bible, were stated for the various forms in which the offence was committed into the seventeenth century, statements are to be found among the authors of the modern era which are aimed solely at homosexuality. An example thereof is Amyraut who argues that nature has created two sexes.[24] Whilst this consideration is rather superficially based on anatomy, others go further. Pufendorf, for example, takes the instinct to reproduce as a basis[25] and includes human behaviour in that regard. A similar approach is adopted by Christian Wolff who likewise considers that in this regard conclusions relating to criminal law can be drawn from such biological observations:

> Since the sexual organs of both sexes enable mankind to reproduce so that it does not perish and, moreover, human beings have, in the same way as other animals of nature, an instinct to use their sexual organs in such a manner …[26]

Man is seen as a creature belonging to nature which, like it, is accessible to scientific knowledge. 'Natural science' is the physical anthropology of that period. Not only anatomy and its functions but also specific instincts are 'researched' and used as norms. According to Wolff's comments in the general part , the prohibition of the opposite follows, by contrary inference, from this precept.[27]

Referring to Fröhlichsburg, Johann Fröhlich speaks in his commentary (on the Carolina Code) of 'unnatural mixing of the flesh' and regards sodomy and homosexuality as a transgression of the 'natural inclinations of man'.[28] The distinctions that he draws (several pages later) in respect of the various forms of offence show that he uses this expression to derive the offence from the specific consideration of human characteristics. For example, he takes the view that sexual relations between Christians and Jews or Moslems must also be subsumed under this provision, but specifically emphasizes that 'such conduct does not run counter to nature'.[29] By contrary inference, one should probably take him at his word as regards homosexuality.

At the end of the eighteenth century, Fredersdorff still puts forward similar arguments in relation to 'excesses in the exercise of the reproductive instinct'. In his case the derivation from nature is explained in somewhat greater detail. To him, nature is 'the order imposed on man in consideration of his continuation and all his powers and the expressions thereof'.[30] The directions on how man's powers are to be

---

[23] Clasen 1685: p. 459: '... si quis masculus cum masculo, aut femina cum alia femina turpem & contranaturalem congressum facit: quales dicuntur contra naturam luxuriari.'

[24] Amyraut 1648: 92.

[25] Pufendorf 1660: obs. 4, § 8.

[26] Wolff 1754: § 854.

[27] Ibid.: §§ 49, 51. However, Wolff makes no express comment on liability to punishment.

[28] Frölichsburg 1741: 255.

[29] Ibid.: title 7.

[30] Fredersdorff 1790: 56.

used also lie in the natural determination thereof. Where the boundary is exceeded, man is frequently punished automatically by the nature of this own body (he cites drunkenness as an example). With regard to sexual excesses he states that

> the voluptuous pleasure connected with the reproductive instinctive, without any intention to procreate [is forbidden] because it is not consistent with the intention for the natural instinct. That intention is reproduction.[31]

Function of the arguments

Perhaps the justification of liability to punishment by means of nature was so well received because in the case of homosexuality the 'criminal act' infringed no tangible legal interest and thus made it difficult to provide grounds for it independent of theology. On the other hand, the existence of a relevant penal provision was too self-evident for the tenor of new arguments to be limited to that. Moreover, these arguments had the advantage not only of covering the two above-mentioned forms of offence (bestiality and male homosexuality), whose liability to punishment was already laid down in the Bible, but also same-sex love among women, which is not referred to specifically in the Scriptures but to which the Carolina Code was applied. In addition, the commentators extended Article 116 to include masturbation, even though this was not covered by the wording of the law. The grounds cited in Fredersdorff appear to be aimed at the latter. Wolff is clearer still: 'the sin of masturbation is forbidden by the law of nature and thus not permitted by nature.[32] Perhaps it is no coincidence that with the extension of the possible forms of offence new considerations are also to be found in relation to the grounds for liability to punishment and therefore the interest in unlawfulness under natural law satisfied a practical need.

Furthermore, the arguments addressed here must also be viewed in their socio-political context. Reference is hereby made to the persecution of homosexuals in respect of which Pius V in 1566 and the Spanish in the final third of the sixteenth century can be cited as examples.[33] Obviously homosexuality was not only condemned morally, it was also perceived as a quantitatively relevant phenomenon, even though the sources are extremely vague in this regard. At any rate, it must be assumed that the fear of its spread was the cause of the persecution.

Finally, a further cause was probably the hostility to sex on the part of the church which accepted sexuality at most within marriage. Accordingly, the criminal laws of the modern era contain extremely harsh punitive sanctions which are quite far removed from the Roman law otherwise adopted which was much more lenient in this regard.[34] The church's intolerance of any extramarital sexuality explains why the view of sex at that time was characterized by a division into the natural (that which is conducive to procreation) and the unnatural (that which is contrary to procreation) which related principally to same-sex sexual intercourse.[35]

---

[31] Ibid.: 71ff.

[32] Wolff 1754: § 854.

[33] Cf. also the eighteenth-century example in Aries 1984: 91.

[34] Mommsen 1899: 703.

[35] Hergemöller 2000: 75.

Bigamy (Article 121 of the Carolina Code)

The prohibition of bigamous marriage occupied not only the authors on criminal law but above all the theologians. In the early modern era matrimonial law was primarily canon law and not the reserve of secular lawyers. Precisely the reverse, the influences of theology on criminal law were enormous in this respect.

The theologians

The requirement of monogamy was one of the most discussed issues of the theology of the early modern era.[36] Although there was agreement that the principle of monogamous marriage also required a corresponding prohibition, a specific entitlement of the wife to marital fidelity did not exist under Mosaic law and could be established at most in accordance with the New Testament view of marriage.[37] The polygamy of the patriarchs, which had been tolerated in the Old Testament, was the reason why the patristics discussed this matter intensively and sought various justifications (divine promissio, tolerantia or dispensatio from a prohibition which existed in principle).[38] It is therefore no wonder that, contrary to the orthodox Lutheran doctrine of the unity of natural and divine law, new grounds were sought in Spanish Late Scholasticism[39] without the biblical origin of the prohibition being denied in each case. At any rate, polygamy often provided an illustration of the divergence of natural and divine law. The compatibility of polygamous marriage with divine law was conceivable but any prohibition required grounds, particularly since, on account of Luther's and Melanchthon's consent to the bigamous marriage of Landgrave Philipp,[40] a known case existed.[41]

Corresponding arguments, based in part on biological and in part on psychological considerations, are to be found as early as the sixteenth century. Both the Catholic Domingo de Soto[42] and the Danish Protestant Hemmingsen, whose book on marriage was in broad circulation in the seventeenth century,[43] take the view that no one can promise something which is impossible. No man is capable of committing himself as completely equally to several wives as he is to one.[44]

Therefore, the union of one man with more than one woman is contrary to nature. Moreover, Hemmingsen considers that nature demonstrates this fact in the make-up of the different bodies and the 'performance of procreation' which can be brought about only by the joining together of *two* bodies 'for procreation is performed by the

---

36 Cf. Schwab 1995: 141–77; Buchholz 1987: 71–91; Koch 1983: 266ff.

37 Matthew 19:4.

38 As regards the discussion in the Middle Ages, cf. Mikat 1984: 1818. In the view of Augustinus, polygamy was not contra naturam (ibid.).

39 For example, de Vitoria 1557: 479; cf. also in that respect Schwab 1995: 176f.

40 The famous confession of the two reformers is published in part in Mikat 1988: 15.

41 In that regard, see Rockwell: 1904.

42 De Soto 1569.

43 As regards Hemmingsen (Hemmingius), see Tamm 1983: 47–56; Mikat 1988: 37ff.

44 Hemmingsen 1572: 37f.: '... fieri non potest, ut unus vir peraeque obligari possit pluribus uxoribus copula …'.

joining together of two bodies'.[45] The fact that this argument was ill-founded, as it ignored the possibility of successive unions, posed no obstacle. It appears that it was merely important to have an argument stemming from nature.

In defence of polyandry, the 'heretical outsider' Ochino[46] stated in a similarly superficial manner, with reference to the human body, that it 'is, however, not unnatural, but proper for a body to have several parts'.[47] Furthermore, the reply by his great adversary Theodor Beza, Calvin's successor,[48] countered – using the same metaphor – by arguing that two noses on the same head was just as impossible as one nose serving two heads.[49] The human body is both the object of examination and the subject of more or less appropriate comparisons.

Psychological considerations are used to point out the senselessness of polygamous marriage which, it is claimed, results necessarily in jealousy among the wives and thus destroys domestic peace.[50] The counter-argument that polygamy can have favourable effects on procreation is countered with the natural limits on male capability.[51] Here too biological arguments are put forward.

Also evident are the concerted efforts in this respect made by the Protestant theologians who clearly wish to distance themselves from Luther's view, such as, for example, the orthodox theology professor Calov (latterly of Wittenberg) who in his monograph derives the prohibition from the principle of the invariable law of nature.[52]

An interesting aspect of the theological discussion is that the arguments of Late Scholasticism prepare the ground for the later authors on the law of nature[53] because its advocates seek grounds for liability to punishment which lie outside the Bible. Even though for them the conclusion was foregone, the formulation of the opposite standpoint opens up the way to different views and makes possible an open discussion within which biological and psychological observations form part of the fixed repertoire.

The jurists

As mentioned above, the jurists look up to the theologians in this regard, as is the case, for example, where Georg Remus' commentary on the Carolina Code cites verbatim

---

45 '... perficitur enim generatio ex duorum corporum complexu ...' He makes extensive use of the principle of equality as an argument: 'Ius naturae est, ut nemo faciat alteri, quod sibi nolit fieri. Cum ergo maritus nolit uxorum suam pluribus misceri viris, debet et ipse una uxore contentus esse. Cum autem hoc ius analogem violatur, vis fit legi naturae, et iniuria alteri coniugem.'

46 Buchholz 1987: 74.

47 Ochino, quoted in Koch 1983: 273: '... neque vero monstrosa, sed decora est, unius corporis esse plura membra.'

48 With regard to him, see Mikat 1988: 27ff.

49 Koch 1983: 273.

50 Beza 1571: 11.

51 Ibid.: 24.

52 Mikat 1988: 40ff.

53 Schwab 1995: 150.

the tract of the leading Calvinist Beza.[54] However, as early as the beginning of the seventeenth century, Arnisaeus, who considers that polygamous marriage infringes the primary law of nature, cites the limited resources of male capacity to substantiate his view.[55] In a similar manner to the theologians, the jurists think along the lines of natural boundaries. In their view, the inability to support any number of children by several women constitutes a ground for prohibition. Psychological considerations are also put forward as grounds for the purposes of marriage. Polygamy makes the sensible raising of children impossible and mutual conjugal love is significantly impaired. The inability to have an inner spiritual union with several wives is also cited.

However, many advocates of the law of nature distance themselves from the idea that polygamy is contrary to the law of nature. Grotius already took this view,[56] and the legal writers of the eighteenth century generally no longer regarded polygamy as contrary to the law of nature.[57] Instead, this was a graphic example of the divergence of the penal provisions of divine law and the law of nature.[58] Knowledge from other disciplines is also cited as proof of the compatibility of bigamy with the law of nature. A fundamental argument for this view was the ethnographic observation that polygamous marriage was practised by other peoples (Grotius cites the Teutons, the Persians and the Egyptians) and therefore a view of monogamous marriage open to generalization could not be taken as a basis.[59]

To sum up, although the prohibition on bigamy can be cited as evidence of a 'crimen contra naturam', it also provides a graphic example of the limitations on attempts at making inferences from nature and of the ephemeral nature of the relevant arguments.

Incest (Article 117 of the Carolina Code)

A number of theological authors cited the law of nature as grounds for the eligibility for punishment of incest – also a topic of family law. Hemmingsen, who was mentioned above, observes, as early as the sixteenth century, that marriages among relations would prevent the natural extension of love beyond a narrow circle and thus breach a principle of nature.[60] As a further argument he states that the elevation and dignity of ancestors would suffer as a result of marriage between relatives. Attempts to derive specific grounds are difficult. At any rate, the term used in practice, that is to say 'Blutschande' (defilement of the blood), indicates that the eligibility for

[54] Remus 1594: 108.

[55] Arnisaeus 1613: 1 c, sectio III no. 11.

[56] Grotius 1625: vol. 2, p. 49.

[57] Fredersdorff 1790: 340.

[58] Struve 1663: book 23, title 2; Böhmer 1741; Leyser; and the references contained therein, in Mikat 1988: 52ff.

[59] Pufendorf 1672: book 4 chapter 1 §§ 15 et seq. Thomasius, who considered that both forms of bigamy were consistent with the law of nature, was quite radical in this respect (Thomasius 1685: § 23). As regards polyandry, this was an outrageous theory since up until then it had been regarded as extremely unnatural.

[60] Hemmingsen 1572: 80.

punishment has a biological cause even though the most frequent cases (between father-in-law and daughter-in-law)[61] involved no blood relationship at all.

The authors on criminal law also use nature as an argument: 'from which shame and natural modesty shrink back, so to speak'.[62] In their case, the interest in providing grounds based on the law of nature is sometimes quite simply the penalty. Since Article 117 of the Carolina Code does not lay down the penalty specifically but with reference to imperial law ('as laid down by our forefathers and imperial laws'), it was disputed whether the death penalty was permissible in the event of a transgression. Blumblacher points out that in many previous cases such crimes had been punished not by death but by 'birching and banishment'.[63] The advocates of the death penalty concluded that, if adultery was eligible for the death penalty, the crime of incest, which they regarded as more serious, was a fortiori eligible and they used the argument that it was contrary to the law of nature to support their view. Damhouder, for example, stated:

> since such vice is contrary to nature itself, that is to say that not only human beings, who are gifted reason and created by God, but also unreasoning animals have an abhorrence thereat.[64]

Comparison with the animal world is again used as an argument. Others, such as Blumblacher for example, expressly opposed this view based on the law of nature, primarily, however, to argue against the death penalty as a standard punishment.

A number of authors were also uncertain on this matter and reached different conclusions. For example, a prohibition on sexual intercourse between ascendants and descendants is asserted and natural modesty is stated as the grounds.[65] However, as regards marriage between siblings and sexual intercourse between distant relations, these same authors question this inference from the law of nature, clearly because no firm grounds exist. Nevertheless, in a large number of quotations it is possible to sense that something unnatural is to be seen in such behaviour, as, for example, in the case of Amyraut:

> If we also fail to hear the voice of nature in this matter loudly and clearly, we must conclude that the reason is not the weakness of her voice but the numbness of our senses.[66]

And, in 1783, Globig and Huster wrote in their award-winning work:

> the love of parents towards their children is contrary to carnal love, in the same way as two poisons of a different kind which drive one another away … Thus, one can see that this degree of incest really does run counter to nature.[67]

---

61 Rublack 1995: 182.

62 Clasen 1685: 463: '... aqua pudor & vercundia naturalis quasi abhorret.'

63 Blumblacher 1670: 255.

64 Damhouder 1565: c 94 no. 2 (cf. Blumbacher 1670: 254); Berlich 1739: part 4, p. 177.

65 Pufendorf 1660: 1.2 obs. 5 §§ 5, 6; Wolff 1754: § 895.

66 Amyraut 1648: 227 (Erle 1952: 69).

67 Globig and Huster 1969: 247.

Conclusion

There are probably several reasons why the (biological) nature of man is put forward as an argument precisely in the case of morality offences. On the one hand, sexuality as a biological factor is the subject of scientific observation at this time. In the modern era, natural history is extended to the human world and man becomes the subject of examination both in anatomical and biological terms.[68] Since he was no longer regarded solely as God's creation but as a being belonging to nature, comparison with the animal world was also obvious: 'If there were no animals, the nature of man would be even more incomprehensible.'[69] Although there was still no anthropology in the modern sense of the word in the seventeenth century, clearly there existed a strong interest in investigating 'man' as a creature of instinct and declaring his sexuality 'natural'. This created the basis for the grounds set out. Their function is to make up for the absence of specifically harmed legal interest since, without recourse to divine authority, morality per se was too non-specific to provide grounds for an infringement.

On the other hand, the ideas set out above could be seen as reactions to the increasing liberality of the Renaissance which emphasized corporeality in fashion and sensuality in art. At that time nature was also stated as grounds for greater permissiveness vis-à-vis the predominant hostility towards sexuality. In the new literary genre of the novella there were many authors who deal with the subject of incest.[70] In the literature of the seventeenth century love between siblings stands for positive, fervent passion.[71] Homosexuality is increasingly taken as a topic as well. In this respect the theological and legal arguments might also have been a response to the corresponding literary permissiveness.

Murder of relatives

The Carolina Code sets out no specific definition of the murder of relatives. Nevertheless, an offence referred to as 'parricidium' was adopted from Roman law as a classification of murder in the early modern era. In respect of such a crime classical Roman criminal law provided for the extreme and bizarre punishment of drowning in a sack.[72] The Carolina Code merely contained a provision which punished the killing of 'closely related friends' in exactly the same way as the killing one's own master.[73] It was not disputed that the killing of parents by one of their own children constituted the most sinful homicide offence.[74] However, the question of whether or not the classical Roman punishment should still be applied in the seventeenth

68 Moravia 1977: 17ff.

69 Buffon 1956: 370ff.

70 Beutin 1990: 430.

71 Rublack 1995: 176; von Braun 1989: 85; however, this topic does not become widespread until 1800.

72 Mommsen 1899: 643ff.; this punishment was subsequently upheld by Constantine.

73 Article 131.

74 Cf. Fröhlichsburg 1741: 174.

century was disputed.[75] The particular respect which children naturally showed their parents was cited as a ground for greater eligibility for punishment in comparison with 'ordinary murder'. Whether the increased punishment applied only to so-called 'natural' children raised within marriage or also to an illegitimate child was unclear. In that regard, Blumblacher stated:

> Whose opinion it is that nature does not distinguish between children produced from a marriage and illegitimate children and scarcely distinguishes between own children and rather that nature or love for own children is transgressed equally by killing on the part of own children or illegitimate children in exactly the same way as killing on the part of the children produced from a lawful marriage.[76]

In the view of Böhmer, the decisive factor is common blood.[77] Fröhlichsburg takes the view that 'it must make no difference whether the father is a legitimate or only natural father, for this atrocity is founded in nature'.[78] In this regard it is not the socio-biological ties but the genetic link, which is obviously attributed with a magical effect that is perceived as nature. The predominant view was that an adoptive relationship was not covered, nor that between stepfather and stepchild;[79] presumably because of the lack of any genetic link. On the other hand, the existence thereof in the case of the illegitimate child gave rise to an increased punishment. This is surprising when one considers that at that time the kinship of the illegitimate child, at least in respect of its father, was held in low regard or even denied.[80] Nevertheless, society believed that the killing of one's own father had to be made taboo. The above-mentioned authors share the view that a father–child relationship is established by the production of an illegitimate child which, although scarcely taken into consideration in the family law of that time,[81] demands respect and protection in criminal law by nature, that is to say the patriarchal dictate of blood.

Suicide

The eligibility for punishment of suicide was a highly contentious issue. Article 135 of the Carolina Code provided for the confiscation of property in the event that an accused person sought to evade sentencing by killing himself. The commentaries on this provision sometimes take as a basis man's natural survival instinct. The above-mentioned Fredersdorff states the following grounds for this penal provision:

---

75 In Saxony it was considered that it should: Carpzov 1635: Quaestio 8 no. 15.

76 Blumblacher 1670: 290: 'Cuius ratio est, quod Natura liberos ex Matrimonio procreatus & inter liberos naturales tantum, ac spurios non distinguat, adeoque per occisionem filii naturales aut spurii, Natura vel amor naturales erga liberos aequi violatur, quam per occisionem filii ex legitimo Matrimonio procreati.'

77 Böhmer 1770: 552.

78 Fröhlichsburg 1741: 175.

79 Ibid.: 176; Quistorp 1796: 409.

80 Stryck 1706: diss. 7, chap. 2, §§ 33 et seq.

81 Schmitz 2000: 49ff.

> The great love of life imbued in man, which is rarely destroyed by pain, sorrow or age, is strong evidence of the intention of him who created man thus and of the intended steadfastness of this natural law.[82]

Christian Wolff infers the prohibition on suicide from man's duty to achieve perfection of his own body.[83] However, since only he who is offended may punish (§ 93), Wolff probably does not mean that the prohibition carries any liability for punishment. The restraint, which is not exercised by Wolff alone, may be connected with the fact that, viewed from a historical perspective, the relevant provision of the Carolina Code constitutes a decriminalization in that it laid down the general exemption from punishment for suicide and provided for confiscation of property in only one exceptional case. This is probably the reason why the most important authors on the law of nature did not classify suicide as contrary to natural law.

Opposite Trends

The attempt to re-legitimize criminal law as a whole inevitably entailed, sooner or later, an effort to attain a higher level of abstraction which had to run counter to the derivation of individual crimes from the specific contemplation of nature.

Since the seventeenth century, writers on the law of nature, who start from a positive view of man, have sought to draw conclusions in respect of criminal law and, in part, also specifically in respect of individual crimes. For example, if one assumes that man is a social being with 'appetitus societatis', acts which run counter to this must be classified as contrary to the law of nature. Although nature is put forward as a basis for the social instinct, punishments are legitimized, according to Grotius, on the basis of the criterion of ensuring social peace.[84] However, on specific issues he remains closely attached to an empirical concept of nature, as demonstrated above. Pufendorf is the first to replace the theocratic view of crime by a (almost) completely secularized theory of crime. Pufendorf accepts the natural freedom of man only in regard of the primordial state and considers that upon entry into society law is conveyed through the social contract. At the decisive point at which the law of nature is put forward as an argument he speaks of 'legem naturalem' and 'jure naturali'.[85] The very formation of the concept reveals the different methodology. Not 'nature' but the 'law of nature' becomes the criterion. Although the law of nature becomes the ground for the crime only through the social contract, Pufendorf infers the legitimization for punishment not from prior consent but directly 'ex iure naturae'.[86] Under the law of nature the punishment is a purely purposive punishment which is justified not by the nature of the offence but by its benefit to the community.[87] This explains Pufendorf's reluctance to infer individual criminal offences from the

---

82 Fredersdorff 1790: 74.

83 Wolff 1754: § 112, read in conjunction with § 51.

84 Grotius 1625: book 2, chap. 20 (Punishments).

85 Pufendorf 1682: book 1, c 3, § 9.

86 Pufendorf 1672: 769.

87 Ibid.: 776ff.

law of nature. He is rarely as specific as Grotius concerning precise conclusions relating to punishable conduct, but mainly restricts himself to the paramount factors: legitimization of the punishment, justification of individual types of punishment, calculating the level of punishments, and his now famous imputation doctrine. The individual crimes are – apart from a few exceptions – a matter for the civil legislator. There is no longer any 'crimen contra naturam'.

Limits of Criminal Law 'Stemming from Nature'

From early on, arguments based on the law of nature were cited not only to provide grounds for but also to limit State punishment: for example, Grotius rejects punishment for acts which are inevitable by human nature (inevitabilis naturae humanae).[88] Since, in his view, the classification of acts as a crime can be justified by the law of nature only where this serves to ensure social peace, he emphatically rejects morality offences where he deems such peace not to have been breached, as is so in the case of, for example, incest or cohabitation involving adultery. Criminal provisions of the latter kind are consistent only with divine law and are also anticipated by it.

Whereas such ideas can be observed only at certain points in the era of the older law of nature, it is a characteristic of the period of the more recent, post-1780, law of nature, with its switch towards a substantive notion of crime, that its advocates have less in mind the grounds for positive law than the restriction of State legislation. In this context, 'crimen contra naturam' means that positive criminal law transgresses nature or the law of nature. It is widely held that the more recent law of nature differs from the older law in that it ceases to be based on an order dictated by nature but makes human rights the basis of considerations.[89] However, life, freedom and property are not inferred as empirical theorems but recognized, in the wake of the Enlightenment and the French Revolution, as central human rights which have to be respected not only by the State but also by individuals.

Even before the publication of the *Metaphysics of Morals* Fichte deduces criminal law from a categorical imperative in the *Grounds of Natural Law*.[90] Coercive law has to have an effect such that the perpetrator is able to foresee, with mechanical necessity, that the infringement of his rights affects him in the same way that he has infringed others' rights. These grounds also automatically contain the restrictions on the power of sentence. Violations against the self or transgressions against social morality are ruled out as ineligible for punishment. It is also in this era that punishments for homosexuality become more lenient for the first time. The Feuerbach view that the offence should be punished only where it involves the seduction of minors[91] is reflected in the Bavarian Criminal Code of 1813 which was influenced by him.

It must be assumed that Kant has had an influence in this respect and this has already been suggested in research. The view set out is indeed based on the separation

88 Grotius 1625: book II, chap. 20 no. 19.

89 Cf. Klippel 1976: 178ff.

90 Fichte 1797: 66.

91 Feuerbach 1847: 719.

of legality and morality which was laid down in the *Metaphysics of Morality*.[92] Since rational laws independent of any motivating forces which might exist and internal determinative grounds are aimed solely at external compliance, the concept of law is very narrow. This naturally applies to criminal law as well. In this respect nature as an empirical object has disappeared completely from the grounds for criminal law.

92 Kant 1797: 353ff.

Chapter 7

Nature's Regularity in Some Protestant Natural Philosophy Textbooks 1530–1630

Sachiko Kusukawa

> 'Everything that is rare is appreciated, but what is an everyday occurrence comes to be regarded as commonplace.' If the stars did not rise during every single night or in all places, how great a gathering of people there would be for this spectacle! Now not one of us even opens a window because of it.
>
> Martin Luther on *Genesis* 2:21[1]

Within the Latin Western tradition of natural philosophy built on Aristotelian views, nature's regularity – that it occurs always or most of the time – was an uncontroversial part of the definition of nature. Some Protestant textbooks in the sixteenth century showed a renewed interest in the regularity of nature and began to use the word 'lex' – out of many other terms available for expressing orderliness in the period [Maclean] – to express such regularity. My aim in this paper is to examine the Protestant context of ideas about nature's regularity.[2] I focus on three Protestant authors whose textbooks dominated the period between 1530 and 1630: Johannes Bernhardi Velcurio (d. 1534), Philip Melanchthon (1497–1560) and Johannes Magirus (d. 1596).[3] The frequency of reprinting, the variety of printing locations, annotations in extant copies and other evidence suggest that these textbooks circulated beyond the local institutional markets: in England, for instance, John Whitgift (d. 1604; better known as tutor to the Bacon brothers) was buying Velcurio's textbooks for his students in Cambridge in the 1570s; Melanchthon's textbook was adopted widely in Protestant areas, and the more famous readers of Magirus' textbook included

---

1 Luther 1955–76, vol. 1: 126f.

2 For recent studies on the religious contexts of studying nature, see Cunningham 1991; Lindberg and Numbers 1989; Bellucci 1998; *Sciences et religions* (1999); Helm and Winkelmann 2001; Hellyer 2005.

3 There are 22 known printings of Velcurio's textbook between 1537 and 1595; Melanchthon's commentary on the *De anima* (two editions) was printed 36 times between 1540 and 1595, and his *Initia doctrinae physicae* 20 times between 1549 and 1587; at least 15 imprints are known for Magirus' *Philosophiae Peripateticae* between 1597 and 1629 (Lohr 1988a: 236, 256, 474). For the variety of texts and textbooks used in universities, see Kirchhoff 1889; Schmitt 1988: 792–804; Reif 1969; and Des Chene 1996. A good collection of early modern philosophy textbooks exists in Pembroke College, Oxford (for which, see Chandler 1891); I thank the librarian, Naomi van Loo, for granting me access to these texts.

John Evelyn (1620–1706) and Isaac Newton (1642–1727).[4] I wish to argue that the Protestant obsession with Providence led to an increasing emphasis on the regularity of nature within the Aristotelian tradition, with inspiration from other sources. In stark contrast to later developments [Wilson], abhorrence of Epicureanism as the negation of natural *and* moral orders was the other side of the coin of this obsession. The Protestant tradition, of course, shared much with the Catholics, including the idea of God as legislator [Armogathe]. Furthermore, the compendium format of natural philosophy textbooks was not unique to Protestants. Nor was it the case that Protestant authors referred exclusively to 'confessionally correct' commentators. Indeed, they shared a common ground and assumption in the underlying Aristotelian tradition and were equally ready to apply humanist insights to their expositions. Nevertheless, Protestant authors may generally be identified with following in one way or another Luther's distinction between 'Law and Gospel' and for expressing a strong interest in God's providence.

Luther famously drew a distinction between Law and Gospel, between knowledge necessary for human life but insufficient for salvation, and the saving message of the crucified Christ which could only be understood through reading the Bible; humans were powerless to become spiritually meritorious, either by deed or by knowledge unaided by the Holy Spirit. The corollary was to acknowledge human incapacity and instead to attribute everything to God himself and glorify him in the way he created and maintained everything. This implied a renewed emphasis on acknowledging the normal course of providence, rather than the abnormal, as Luther wrote on Genesis. As is well known, Luther's justification by faith alone was a position logically compatible with the nominalist distinction between *potentia ordinata Dei* and *potentia absoluta Dei*, between what God has done and what God can do; nominalists held that the relationship between the two was contingent, which led to the voluntarist position that this world and matters of salvation were dependent on the will of God alone.[5] Voluntarism indeed goes a long way towards explaining the contours of philosophies of seventeenth-century thinkers like Gassendi, but it must be noted that not all voluntarists or nominalists believed in the use of natural philosophy; nor were their natural philosophies identical.[6] Several of the Protestant authors who wrote about natural philosophy in the sixteenth century, however, *did* draw a line between human and soteriological knowledge, between Law and Gospel. In this process, philosophy was invariably declared as not the Gospel and its grounds for certain knowledge had to be re-established, but the basic assumption remained that nature was something created and maintained by God.

---

[4] For Whitgift's book purchases, see Gaskell 1979; and for the circulation of textbooks by Velcurio and Melanchthon in sixteenth-century Oxbridge, see Kusukawa 2002a. Evelyn's copy (1638) is in the British Library (shelfmark Eve.a.58), with few annotations; for Newton's notes on Magirus, see Newton 1661: 16r–26v (summarized in McGuire and Tamny 1983: 15–17).

[5] Oberman 1987; Oakley 1961a; Milton 1981.

[6] For Gassendi, see Osler 1994. For a cautionary note about the identity of 'nominalists' and 'Ockhamists', see Courtenay 1995.

Johannes Bernhardi Velcurio

Velcurio was a lecturer in natural philosophy at Wittenberg and an early supporter of Luther. He died in 1534, and the textbooks that bear his name were all posthumously printed.[7] Although Velcurio did not use 'lex' to denote regularity of nature, his compendium, as the first Lutheran textbook on natural philosophy, showed emphases and trends that were continued by later textbook writers.

Velcurio's textbook treated the whole of Aristotelian natural philosophy, encompassing topics such as God, his Providence, principles, causes, and motion in general. Velcurio's treatment of Aristotelian topics was supplemented with those of other classical and later authors – he drew upon Cicero's works, especially the *De natura deorum*, Aulus Gellius' *Noctae Atticae*, Lactantius' *Institutiones divinae*, the works of Theophrastus, Dioscorides, Pliny the Elder, Theodore Gaza, Albertus Magnus, Georgius Agricola, Alessandro Benedetti and Jacopo Berengario da Carpi.

The book was arranged by way of headings, using a topical version of Aristotle's questions for finding definitions in the *Posterior Analytics* (II, i). Nature signified various things, but, properly speaking, it was the principle of motion and rest; it may be divided into prime infinite nature (God) and finite nature ('physica'), and it is in the latter sense that nature should be understood; whether such a nature exists or not was a risible question, tantamount to doubting one's own existence.[8] Nature was then defined 'as a principle and cause of motion and rest in a natural thing in which it exists *per se* and not *per accidens*' (*Physica* II).[9] Velcurio added next that it was 'a power exciting necessary motions in bodies, whose order reveals which effects follow on from which cause' (*De natura deorum* II);[10] and that it was also some perpetual and certain power placed necessarily in natural things and set up by God in such a way that it supplies matter and form to those natural things with a certain course, virtue and example; and adds accidents to them and conserves the norms of the essence ('regula essentiae') in their bodies.[11] The additional elaborations underscore the importance of causation and God as the creator and conserver of nature. Since Velcurio believed that God could be known only a posteriori,[12] investigating causes through their effects became the sole means of a philosophical knowledge of God.

Velcurio, however, was clear that this God of natural philosophers was different from the God of the theologians, to whom alone belonged discussions of God's goodness, mercy and faith.[13] Salvation and damnation were classified under 'fate',

---

7 Velcurio 1537: 1–4, includes the 'author's preface, but contains only the commentary on the *De anima*; Velcurio 1538 appears to have been edited by a student, A2vf.

8 Velcurio 1540: 14v.

9 Ibid.: 14v–15r: 'Natura est principium et causa motus et quietis, in re naturali, cui primum per se et non per accidens inest.'

10 Ibid.: 14v–15r.

11 Ibid.: 15v: 'Rursum, natura est vis quaedam perpetua, et certa, rebus naturalibus insita necessario, et sic instituta a Deo, ut eis certo cursu, virtute, et exemplo suam materiam, formamque suppeditet, atque accidentia sua ipsis superaddat, et cuiusque essentiae regulam conservet in corporibus.'

12 Ibid.: 56r.

13 Ibid.: 8r.

one of the four secondary causes (the others being nature, fortune and will).[14] In effect, the human will is excluded from acting as the cause of spiritual justification or damnation. These are formulations consistent with Luther's insistence on the distinction between the salvific message and human knowledge. Another implication of this distinction was the suspicion against metaphysics as the science of divine being: Velcurio limited the usefulness of metaphysics to the part that taught the primary principles, common axioms and propositions of other disciplines.[15] But emphasizng the limits of human knowledge did not mean obscurantism for Velcurio, as he argued for certainty in philosophy through the three 'didactic' principles in logic, physics and ethics, innate to humans.[16] That things cannot be true and false at the same time is an example of a logical principle; physical principles are statements such as 'everything that can be generated is corruptible'; and moral principles are divinely endowed as the 'law of nature'. Following Cicero, Velcurio understood 'law of nature' to contain distinctions between right and wrong that have been endowed to all human beings by God, and to which all humans must assent.[17] Velcurio's only discussion of 'lex naturae' in his textbook thus turns out to be traditionally moral and Ciceronian.

Ciceronian also in inspiration was Veclurio's lengthy description of the taxonomy of causes.[18] Causes were divided into the primary, infinite cause (God) and secondary, finite causes. The latter were in turn divided into fate, nature, fortune or will. These were the four main secondary causes which depended on God as the primary cause and on which all other special or individual causes depended.[19] Drawing on Chrysippus, fate was defined as a perpetual order of causes and events, depending on the providence of God as a primary cause, imposing inevitable necessity on fatal things.[20] Nature was the principle and cause of motion and rest in things that have that principle in themselves *per se* and not *per accidens*.[21] Fortune was accidental causes of events which happened to things, neither always nor most

---

[14] Velcurio 1540: 13v.

[15] Ibid.: 6r. For metaphysics as the science of divine being, see Lohr 1988b.

[16] Velcurio 1540: 250vf.

[17] Ibid.: 242r: 'In genere quidem Lex est sententia, qua bona praecipiuntur, et mala prohibentur. Ius autem est auctoritas et facultas faciendi, quod secundum leges. Verum triplex est lex, scilicet naturalis, quam Iurisconsulti vocant Ius naturale et Ius gentium: et Lex Divina, quae in sacris literis traditur: et Lex Humana, quae Iure civili aut Canonico Scripto, vel consuetudine recepta continetur. Et iuxta Ciceronem, Lex naturae est ratio summa, insita in hominis natura, quae iubet ea quae facienda sunt, prohibet contraria. Vel lex naturae est sententia communis, cui omnes homines pariter assentiuntur, insculpta nobis a Deo, pertinens ad mores formandos. Referuntur ergo ad legem naturae principia practica, id est, sententiae communes, omnibus notae, de moribus: et item conclusiones elicitae ex illis principijs; talia sunt decem praecepta Decalogi, item praecepta similia ex libris Ethicorum quoque…'

[18] See Sharples 1995 for Cicero's taxonomy of causes.

[19] Velcurio 1540: 8v.

[20] Ibid.: 9v–10r: 'Fatum est connexio et perpetuus ordo causarum et effectuum, dependens a providentia primae causae, hoc est Dei, et imponens necessitatem rebus fatalibus inevitabilem.'

[21] Ibid.: 14v–15r.

of the time, but rarely, and with deliberation and purpose.[22] Will was the power of the soul which sought good and refused bad, as understood by reason.[23] Natural causes were further divided into material, formal, efficient and final causes. Causes could also be divided into internal or external; universal or particular; *per se* or *per accidens*; proximate ('propinqua') or remote; necessary or contingent; constant and certain or inconstant or uncertain; non-complex or complex; active or potential; or subordinate or non-subordinate.[24] A further six ways of subdividing efficient causes and five ways of dividing final causes were listed; hierarchies and sequential connections amongst these causes were noted; and Velcurio provided a further eight rules ('regulae') to help determine the proper cause of things or events. For instance, not all antecedents are causes, as the *aurora* preceding the day cannot be the efficient cause of day; singular causes are frequently impeded, while common and universal causes cannot be.[25]

The taxonomy of causes contained in Velcurio's textbook was in fact wider in scope than was needed for studying nature. Within the Aristotelian canon, it was of course standard to compare nature with other kinds of causes such as chance or luck, but what is worth nothing is that Velcurio seems to have covered the gamut of causes through which God governs his entire creation through providence. Following Cicero's definition in the *De natura deorum*, Velcurio defined the providence of God as the divine reason by which God foreknows all future events that happen necessarily or contingently.[26] Indeed, providence was a kind of book in which everything necessary and contingent was written.[27] By mapping out God's governance of the universe through a taxonomy of causes, Velcurio wanted to defend God's providential plan against two extreme classical positions: the Epicurean position that God or his providence does not exist and the stoic position that would have God's providence chained necessarily to secondary causes.[28] Velcurio thus explicitly set nature within the larger 'book' of providence.

Velcurio also divided nature, one of the necessary causes, into universal and particular. Universal nature could be divided into 'mathematical physica' and 'common physica'. By 'mathematical physica' Velcurio meant the study of the heavens and their powers emitted onto inferior things, studied geometrically. Heavenly bodies were nobler than the other bodies and had nobler and more perfect motion, namely

22 Ibid.: 53v.

23 Ibid.: 239vf.

24 Ibid.: 38v–41r.

25 Ibid.: 42rf. Cf. Cicero, *Topica* 58–64.

26 Velcurio 1540: 10r: 'Providentia Dei est ipsa divina ratio, in summo omnium principe Deo constituta, qua is cuncta praeterita, et futura, videt et praecognoscit, hoc est, Providentia Dei est scientia Dei certa, in eius mente concepta ab aeterno, de his quae olim facta et unquam futura sunt, necessario, vel non necessario et contingenter.'

27 Ibid.: 12r: 'Itaque providentia Dei est tanquam liber quidam, in quo consignata, et conscripta sunt omnia, necessario, vel contingenter facta, aut futura unquam, et alias, vocatur voluntas, praedestinatio, praescientia, dispositio Dei, qua vult, et disponit rerum necessitatem vel contingentiam.'

28 Ibid.: 9v.

uniform circular motion which is exceptionally regular.[29] This perpetual celestial motion was, according to Velcurio, divine rather than natural, because its efficient cause was the prime mover, God.[30] 'Common physica' was the general principle of conservation of species in the sublunary world: just as man begets man, and a pear tree is produced from a pear tree. These effects, Velcurio stressed, were necessary, not contingent, and could not be otherwise unless this 'common course of nature' was interrupted miraculously by some kind of fate.[31] Thus, 'fate' in the sense of a necessary connection between cause and effect (which cannot be otherwise) applies to nature in general, and could therefore be called 'physical fate', though it could not be applied to the connection between superlunary and sublunary events ('astrological fate').[32] Velcurio also defined particular nature as that which exists in individual things, giving rise to particular effects, but did not discuss it in terms of regularity.[33]

For Velcurio, the study of nature was thus a causal investigation of the common course of nature, created and maintained by providence, and his taxonomy of causes showed that this providential government of God was neither random nor deterministic. In many ways Velcurio was following the traditional, Aristotelian, essentialist view of change in which the focus of inquiry was the normal course of nature which occurred always or most of the time. He acknowledged two types of regularity, the perpetual motion of the heavens and the conservation of species in the sublunary world. He also emphasized universal nature as a necessary cause by calling it 'physical fate', and thus underscoring a strong sense of regularity. He did not, however, claim any strong causal connection or regularity between superlunary and sublunary events.

Studying God's work has been an essential feature of natural philosophy since the thirteenth century, and in this respect Velcurio's textbook is still within this tradition and shares much with its Catholic counterparts, such as the work by a contemporary, best-selling Catholic author, Frans Titelmans (1502–37).[34] It is worth noting, however, the different concerns reflected in these textbooks. Titelmans, a Franciscan, wrote a textbook on natural philosophy for the expeditious instruction of novices in his order: the textbook proceeded by summaries of Aristotle's arguments in the *libri naturales* in twelve books, each book ending with a hymn in praise of the omnipotent God. A meditation on the passions of Christ at the end of the section of the five senses is a clear mark of Franciscan spirituality.[35] In comparison, Velcurio's project focused on one aspect of divinity, namely providence.

---

29 Velcurio 1540: 84r.

30 Ibid.: 84rf.

31 Ibid.: 16rf.

32 Ibid.: 9rf.

33 The destruction of individual natures after the Day of Judgement is, however, discussed in Velcurio 1540: 16v.

34 For the invention of natural philosophy as a God-orientated enterprise, see French and Cunningham 1996. There are 35 imprints known for Titelmans' textbook between 1530 and 1596 (Lohr 1988a: 457f.). Relatives of the Lyonnais printer Rouillé sold Titelmans' works to the clergy in Spain (Davis 1966: 86).

35 See also Titelmans 1572: 171r–172r. Some editions, for example Titelmans 1552, do not carry the hymns. For Titelmans, see now also Lines 2008.

Philip Melanchthon

Melanchthon wrote two textbooks on natural philosophy that were used widely across Europe: the *Commentarius de anima* (1540 onwards, later revised as *Liber de anima*) and the *Initia doctrinae physicae* (1549 onwards). In many ways Melanchthon draws on Velcurio's textbook: he too used topical headings in a question-and-answer format, beginning with God, providence, contingency, the world, heavenly bodies, all the way down to humans. Providence was defined as a knowledge by which God perceived and foresaw things, maintained universal nature, saved the just and punished the wicked. This Melanchthon called knowledge of Law about God.[36] He also defended providence against Epicureanism and stoicism,[37] describing providence through three types of necessity and two types of contingency. The three types of necessity were: absolute necessity, physical necessity and necessity of consequence. Absolute necessity was that whose contrary is impossible (for example, God exists, God is just); physical necessity was a way of operation ordained to natural causes (for example, the course of the sun), which cannot be otherwise unless interrupted by God;[38] and necessity of consequence was the necessary occurrence of things on account of preceding causes, even if those causes were contingent to the nature of the subject, for instance events that occur by divine decree (such as the resurrection of the body). Contingency was of two kinds: one was due to the great variety and fluidity of matter – since clouds can be agitated in a variety of ways without a certain stable law ('certa et stabili lege'), it is contingent to the nature of clouds that it rains in Leipzig and not in Nuremberg;[39] the other type of contingency was due to the freedom of will in making (non-spiritual) choices.

Providential design was also reflected clearly in Melanchthon's definition of nature: to Aristotle's definition of nature as the cause of motion and rest of a thing in which it exists principally, not accidentally, he added the stoic definition that nature was 'fire' skilfully proceeding towards generation, because it signified that all species were ordained by some architectonic mind to procreate like from like. This additional definition spelt out the skilful Creator behind the workings of nature.[40] Melanchthon was also clear that knowledge of God thus attained through philosophy was not the same as knowledge of God attainable through faith and Scriptures: philosophy could never discover the saving message of the Gospel or affirm the truth of theological doctrine.[41] The distinction of Law and Gospel was reflected further in Melanchthon's *Commentarius de anima* in the discussion of the human will as wholly incapable of spiritually meritorious choice, and in the Scriptural justification of the immortality of the soul.[42] Indeed the diminished capacity of Fallen Man was

36 Melanchthon, *Corpus Reformatorum* (1834–60), 28 vols (CR hereafter): 203.

37 CR 13: 205.

38 CR 13: 207–209. 'Necessitas physica est modus agendi ordinatus in causis naturalibus, quo modo non interrupto, a Deo, non possunt illae causae aliter agere, ut Solis cursus dicitur necessarius, quia mutari non potest, nisi divinitus' (CR 13: 207).

39 CR 13: 208.

40 CR 13: 303f.

41 CR 13: 190f.

42 Kusukawa 1995: 87–100.

recalled in the opening lines of the *Initia doctrinae physicae*: natural philosophy was an inquiry into the series, qualities and motion of all corporeal bodies in nature, the causes of generation, corruption and other motions, in so far as is possible for humans in their weakness.[43]

But against those who said that nothing could be known for certain or those who suspended the certainty of senses and judgment, Melanchthon was adamant that certainty should be sought despite such human weakness. This certainty of philosophy was established on religious grounds – God had wished that there should be certain, firm and immutable knowledge for correct life.[44] Drawing on stoic ideas again, Melanchthon posited three kinds of certainty necessary for philosophical reasoning that was endowed by God to all human beings: principles ('prolepsis'); universal experience ('aisthesis'); and the understanding of syllogistic consequences ('gnosis') (derived from principles and experience).[45] A fourth criterion, divine revelation, is available for believers only.[46] Principles are propositions that can also serve as the starting point of various arts and sciences. For Melanchthon, both scientific (for example, the whole is greater than its part) and moral propositions, also called 'leges naturae' (for example, it is wrong to kill one's parents), should be equally certain as innate principles. Universal experience is of knowledge of things in nature (for example, fire is hot) which is certain if its opposite would lead to the destruction of the nature concerned. The third criterion, knowledge of syllogistic reasoning, means that the certainty that rules of logic yield are divinely guaranteed. These innate criteria are certain, immutable and correspond to some eternal rules ('aeternam regulam') in the divine Creator.[47] As with Velcurio, divinely endowed innate knowledge thus guaranteed the certainty and knowability of philosophy.

Melanchthon then also rehearsed various divisions of causes from Plato, Galen, and others more extensively than Velcurio had done.[48] The classification of causes showed the hierarchy and order of causes, which in turn pointed to a single prime cause.[49] Melanchthon then reduced causes *per accidens* (fortune and chance) to six causes *per se*.[50] These were: God; good angels or evil spirits; temperament; various inclinations of the stars; human mores; and instability of matter. Investigation into

---

[43] CR 13: 179.

[44] CR 13: 181.

[45] CR 13: 186.

[46] For the fourth criterion, see CR 13: 150f., which may also add conviction to knowledge arrived at through reason alone, such as that the immobility of earth: 'Ratio deprehendit terram stare immotam, et solem moveri. Sed cum idem divinitus traditum esse audimus, firmius adsentimur' (CR 13: 152).

[47] CR 13: 301: 'Addatur et haec ratio: cum impossibile sit intelligentem naturam a bruta oriri, non existit humana natura ex atomis sine mente aliqua et casu, cum humana natura non solum sit intelligens, sed etiam universaliter habeat insitas noticias firmas et immutas, ut numeros et leges naturae, quas congruere ad aliquam aeternam regulam in mente conditrice necesse est.'

[48] CR 13: 306–318. Cf. CR 13: 673–685.

[49] CR 13: 202: 'Cum enim physicus inveniat causas esse ordinatas, necesse est unam primam infinitae potentiae esse. Nam si plures essent primae, nullus ordo esset causarum.'

[50] CR 13: 319f.

causes *per se* was important for Melanchthon because it showed that the world could not have come into existence without a mind.[51] In fact there could be other causes *per se* which were not yet grasped by humans.[52] Melanchthon's point here was that regularity and certainty of God's order existed even for seemingly accidental events - they only seem accidental, contingent and irregular to Fallen Man, who has imperfect knowledge.[53] Melanchthon thus acknowledged a gap between ontological and epistemological certainty.

Interestingly, Melanchthon claims certainty and regularity for astrology. This was possible because he posited as innate 'universal experience', a shortcut that guaranteed much of certain knowledge of nature.[54] One should not, for instance, spend too much time looking for demonstrations for why fire heats, but content oneself with 'universal experience' that it is so, because God had ordained things so.[55] Many examples indicating the same effect could be the basis of accepting it as a general description. Even if everything is not exhaustively investigated, what is experientially (and endoxically) true may be treated as true ('vera') and certain ('certa') knowledge ('cognitio').[56] Universal experience thus allows humans to accept what God has ordained without the certainty of causal investigation or a substantial definition; it kick-starts investigations into nature, because these descriptions can form the starting point of further inferences: we see the sun always moving by a very certain law ('certissima lege'), so we may affirm that the sun is not a vapour thrown up by the earth, for such vapours exhaled from the earth would scatter in a variegated manner into the air. The regularity of the sun's movement, known from experience, makes it unlikely that the sun could be made of matter with such unstable behaviour.[57] Melanchthon explicitly acknowledged universal experience to be a medical form of generalization, which was also 'universal' and 'regular'.[58] Generalization from experience and probable knowledge could be expected of astrology, just as it could be expected of medical knowledge. Manilius' 'certa stant omnia lege' may be too strong because not all events are governed by the stars, but

[51] CR 13: 328.

[52] CR13: 320.

[53] Cf. how Goclenius 1609: 320, explains (referring to Melanchthon) how the same event can be seen as fatal or fortuituous, according to God's counsel or human judgement.

[54] CR13: 186.

[55] CR 13: 189.

[56] CR 13: 187, 195.

[57] CR 13: 194.

[58] CR 13: 333: 'Cum natura uno et eodem modo agat, postquam multa exempla congruere compertum est, recte inde extruitur universalis. Hoc modo et Medicus suas universales constituit. Non colligi omnes singulares experientiae de Cichorio, cuius magnus usus est in febribus, possunt, et saepe effectio eius impeditur, sed tamen consensus multorum exemplorum, quia natura uno modo agit, vim speciei ostendit. Ita de astris recte dicimus, universales experientias esse, quas recitavimus de Solis et Lunae effectionibus: item de insignibus coniunctionibus, quia compertum est, similes esse effectiones plerunque. … *Ac talis experientia vere dicitur universalis, aut certe regularis*, ut supra de positu stellarum diximus, qui efficit corpus *dunamei noseron*, ut cum Luna Marti et Saturno in sexta domo iuncta est, aut ex vicino circumsessa est.' My italics.

the effects of the sun and the moon were, according to Melanchthon, as reliable as the effects of chicory. Universal experience allowed Melanchthon to assume *virtual* regularity and necessity of events that were largely probable, a step that Velcurio had not taken.

Nature's regularity and the Creator are intertwined throughout Melanchthon's *Initia doctrinae physicae*. It contained a rough summary of Ptolemy's *Almagest*, with some up-to-date corrections, incorporating Copernican parameters. Astronomy was normally considered a separate discipline from natural philosophy but Melanchthon thought its inclusion was justifiable.[59] Ptolemaic astronomy allowed Melanchthon to point out how planetary motions that seemed chaotic and 'wandering' were in fact regular and followed quite certain laws ('leges certissimae') ordained by God.[60] The task here was not just to ascertain that all the planets were created ('condita') and arranged ('ordinata') with stable laws ('certis legibus'), but to understand *why* they were created and arranged as such.[61] Not only the beauty, but also the permanence of celestial bodies and their laws of motion ('leges motuum') arranged with great counsel rendered it unlikely that they were created in vain ('frustra').[62]

Melanchthon used 'lex' to describe regularity of nature only in connection with celestial motion; as already noted, he was also capable of using the term 'lex' in the traditional, moral sense – the phrase 'leges naturae' was used to denote innate knowledge of ethical behaviour;[63] he also pointed out that there was no point of having law if there were no choice.[64] Melanchthon's use of 'lex' for regularity only of celestial bodies may well be due to his belief that greater certainty was yielded by the celestial bodies because they are not subject to generation and corruption as the sublunary bodies were.[65] At present, there is no direct evidence, however, to connect this use of 'lex' by Melanchthon with his reading of Copernicus' works.[66] Melanchthon's earliest use of 'lex' for planetary motions dates to 1531 and I think

---

59 CR 13: 292. Cf. Velcurio's reluctance to cross disciplinary distinctions in Velcurio 1537, 3. For disciplinary boundraies of astronomy, see Westman 1980.

60 CR 13: 229: 'Quanquam enim leges motuum certissimae sunt, et mirando consilio Dei ordinatae, tamen sic [planetae] adpellantur, quia singulae stellae in his septem orbibus diversos motus habent, congrediuntur et rursus discedunt ex congressibus aliae aliis longius.' My insertion.

61 CR 13: 180: 'Postremo peragrata universa natura corporali, discernere ab ea divinam architectatricem omnium rerum, et hanc coram contueri, et in ea causas legere, cur ita sint condita, ordinata, et septa certis legibus omnia, cum non sit consentaneum homines tantum ad ingentes miserias huius vitae nasci, an alius portus restet diurturnus, aut aeternus, et qualis sit illa aeternitas.'

62 CR 13:179: 'Non est enim versimile haec pulcherrima corpora in coelo, frustra condita esse, praesertim cum et maneant eadem, et leges habeant motuum magno consilio ordinatas.'

63 CR 13: 197. Bauer 1951.

64 CR 13: 209.

65 CR 13: 186f.

66 As suggested by Ruby 1986: 356. Melanchthon's knowledge of Copernicus' *De revolutionibus* by 1549 (when the *Initia doctrinae physicae* was published) is indisputable; and indeed he seems to have known of Copernicus much earlier, see Kusukawa 1995: 172f.

it unlikely that Melanchthon's derivation of 'lex' is exclusively Copernican.[67] Given Melanchthon's interest in astrology, it is more likely to come from a source such as Manilius, whose use of the word 'law' for regularity he explicitly referred to (as in fact too deterministic for astrology). Melanchthon was also interested in the regularity of nature in the sublunary world, for which he used the word 'regula'.[68] For Melanchthon, perpetual conservation of species was an illuminating testimony that this world did not come into existence by chance.[69] The fact that the same laws of motions and the same species endure rendered impossible a chaotic world of atoms crashing into one another by chance.[70] Regularity on the other hand, did not imply stoic fate, that is that God's will is tied to secondary causes, since God is most free to do anything or alter secondary causes.[71]

In the coverage of topics and succinct discussions of them, the *Physicae, seu de naturæ philosophia institutio* of Cornelius Valerius (1512–78) is similar to Melanchthon's *Initia doctrinae physicae* and the *Liber de anima*.[72] Valerius' defence of astrology and astronomy compares especially well to Melanchthon's, but Valerius does not adopt probable generalizations or show any particular concern to establish regularity as evidence of God's providential government. He did not deny providence, but he used the word 'lex' only for innate, moral knowledge.[73]

Melanchthon's obsession with regularity of nature and his refutation of Epicurean chaos *ad nauseam* stem from how he saw the function of natural philosophy. As a philosophy, the fact that its certainty was based on the three innate criteria, universally endowed by God to all humans, provided that philosophy with the possibility of achieving agreement among unbelievers.[74] More significantly for Melanchthon, natural philosophy demonstrated the first principles of *moral* philosophy: moral philosophy took from natural philosophy its starting point like a 'hypothesis' that humans were created for a certain purpose, and this purpose was obedience to the divine order, which included secular governments and magistrates.[75] This was an important point to make for magisterial Reformers like Melanchthon, who saw evangelical radicals, the *Schwärmer*, as jeopardizing reform because of their

67 Melanchthon 1999: 105–112.

68 CR 13: 393–395.

69 CR 13: 350: 'Conservatio perpetua specierum, id est, quod manent eaedem species, et quod in singulis similia procreantur, bos a bove, leo a leone, illustre testimonium est, hunc mundum non extitisse casu, quia si temerario concursu atomorum natae res essent, non diu manerent eaedem species, et ex bove homines aut volucres nascerentur. Necesse est autem aliquam sapientem, aut regularem causam esse huius perpetui ordinis.'

70 CR 13: 301: 'Et facilis est refutatio, impossibile enim esset manere easdem leges motuum et species certas omnibus temporibus, si confusio atomorum subinde alios mundos gigneret.'

71 CR 13: 329.

72 At least ten editions are known of the *Physicae seu de naturae philosophia institutio* from 1566 (Voet 1982, vol. 5: 2301f.). The first edition (900 copies) was sold to booksellers for 1¼ st. per copy (Voet 1969–72, vol. 2: 389).

73 Valerius 1567: 21, 121 (on lex naturae).

74 For the point of forcing non-believers to agree, see Kusukawa 1997.

75 *Erotemata dialectics*, CR 13: 650.

seditious claims.[76] The orderliness of nature, which excluded any possibility of randomness (ontologically), was required in order to support moral and political orders; but the orderliness of nature must not lead to moral determinism, and hence the regularity of nature was always set within a larger view of God's providential universe. Nature was thus an authority for moral philosophy, and it was a universal authority in that even unbelievers had to agree that this divinely instituted order must be preserved. Melanchthon's use of Aristotelian philosophy to establish regularity of nature thus directly supported his effort to establish Roman (rather than Mosaic) law for social and political order.[77] Political and natural orders were also conflated by Georg Liebler (1524–1600) in his *Epitome philosophiae naturalis*: just as in a great city where discordant and contrary elements converge to a summary law ('summam legem') and produce peace rather than sedition, so everything in nature came to be by the most certain and immutable law ('certissima et immota naturae lege'), in a wondrous and not-random way; to regulate mores and life is to imitate this wondrous order of nature or perpetual justice of nature ('perpetuam naturae iusticiam').[78]

Melanchthon's textbooks spawned further commentaries, and several later commentators followed his formulations of *lex naturae* and innate knowledge.[79] The textbooks by Velcurio and Melanchthon circulated widely in Europe during the sixteenth century and became the basis for other textbooks. Although providential nature served primarily as a moral authority for Melanchthon, the focus on providence was picked up by many of his students who studied nature in a variety of fields, including botany, as a way to trace the vestiges of God and his providence.[80] The regularity of nature confirmed God's providence, thereby providing believers with fortitude and consolation during trying times. Proclamation of providence became signs of martyrdom; and the workings of providence could come to serve polemical needs.[81]

In the second half of the sixteenth century, there developed a greater variety of textbooks written by Protestant authors, with a smaller run of editions, and catering more for local needs, such as Johann Ludwig Hawenreuther's (1548–1618) textbooks for the Academy at Strasbourg, Henricus Gutberleth's (1572–1635) for Herborn, Clemens Timpler's (1563/4–1646) for Steinfurt and Bartholomaeus Keckermann's (1571–1609) for Gdansk.[82] The variety also reflects the contours of various struggles

---

[76] Kusukawa 1995: 62–74.

[77] For Melanchthon's interest in Roman law, see Kisch 1967. For the moral authority of nature, see Daston 1998a.

[78] Liebler 1566, α6rf.

[79] For Melanchthon's 'lex naturae', see now Scattola 1999a: 28–76; for commentators on Melanchthon, see Stigelius 1570, Strigelius 1590, Snellius 1596 and Magirus 1603. His formulation of innate knowledge was followed in Zanchius 1602: 799f. For Niels Hemmingsen, see Scattola 1999a: 880.

[80] Kusukawa 1995: 175–188; for Melanchthon's students and followers, see now Scheible 1997. Wildenberg 1548 is very closely based on Velcurio. Cf. vernacular Protestant literature about nature; see Crowther-Heyck 2003.

[81] Kolb 1987: 148–156; Walsham 1999.

[82] For Strasbourg, Hawenreuter 1594 and Schindling 1977; for Herborn, Gutberleth 1613 and Hotson 2000: 15–39; for Steinfurt, Timpler 1605 and Freedman 1988, vol. 1: 34–65;

within the evangelical camp and the deepening of confessionalization in the second half of the sixteenth century. Melanchthon's authority especially became problematic after the Interim among the 'gnesio-Lutherans'. The distinction between Law and Gospel came to be applied in a variety of ways. For instance, Christoph Scheibler (1598–1653) mapped the distinction between Law and Gospel onto natural theology/ metaphysics and Biblical hermeneutics.[83] Those such as Daniel Hofmann (1540–1611) who were pessimistic of post-lapsarian human knowledge, argued that pagan (unrevealed) philosophy could never aspire to a true, Christian philosophy and claimed that instead natural philosophy had to be erected anew, based on the Bible.[84] Knowledge of Law thus became subservient to the Gospel. In turn it was not obvious how such 'pious' philosophies could function outside the group of the 'faithful'. In an age when questions such as who could read the Bible properly and what was the correct way to read it were hotly contested, it is unclear whether 'unbelievers' could properly comprehend 'pious philosophy' without proper faith. Such 'pious' natural philosophies, then, had limited use for polemics or universal persuasion, but probably had more to do with bearing witness to one's faith. While nature became the object of study and sign of the faithful, logic and metaphysics became the fields in which solutions for the differences between Lutherans and Calvinists were sought.[85] In these contexts, it was the works of Julius Caesar Scaliger (1484–1558) and Jacopo Zabarella (1533–89) that became the major source of inspiration for these textbook writers.[86]

Johannes Magirus

Johannes Magirus studied at Padua under Zabarella and Archangelus Mercenarius (d. 1585), and took his doctorate in medicine from the University of Marburg in 1585, after which he spent some time at Fritzlar until 1591, when he became the professor of natural philosophy at Marburg.[87] The University of Marburg maintained Lutheran orthodoxy until 1605, when it became the Reformed university of the Hessen-Kassel territories for the next twenty years (Marburg returned to Lutheranism between 1624 and 1645).[88] Magirus died in 1596, and all his publications are posthumous. In 1597, appeared his textbook on natural philosophy: *Physiologia peripatetica*, which was used at Marburg. Later printings in Wittenberg, Geneva and London indicate that there was a market for it beyond Marburg. It was frequently published with Caspar Bartholin's *Enchiridion metaphysicum* in the seventeenth century.

---

for Gdansk, Keckermann 1613 and Freedman 1997.

83 Lohr 1988b: 628f.

84 Blair 2000 and Petersen 1921: 263–270.

85 Lohr 1988b: 629f. For the 'return' of metaphysics in Protestant schools, see now Leinsle 1985.

86 Jensen 1990, Kusukawa 2002b, Maclean 2002b.

87 Lohr 1988a: 235f. Hermelink and Kaehler 1977: 210. Natural philosophy had been taught continuously at Marburg since 1533 (Gundlach 1927: 386).

88 Hermelink and Kaehler 1977: 213–220.

Instead of a topical or catechetical arrangement, Magirus' textbook lists a series of definitional statements under each chapter, followed by detailed scholia on those statements. The scholia function to show how other authorities (classical, patristic, medieval or contemporary) have argued for the positions cited in the statements, and how others have been erroneous or misguided in holding different positions. This reflects the 'irenic' stance of the Marburg philosophers at the turn of the century who believed that true positions could be reached by a synthesis of various positions rather than through vitriolic polemics. Magirus drew on numerous authorities: Zabarella, Mercenarius, Scaliger, Thomas Erastus, Jacob Schegk, Francesco Vimercato, Gasparo Contarini, Hermolao Barbaro and Franceso Patrizi, as well as Velcurio and Melanchthon.

Magirus' discussion of nature indicates his familiarity with late sixteenth-century debates by physicians. For instance, nature has a wider signification than things *secundum naturam*, because disease, which in a sense is in the nature of the body, is not according to nature, as a disease destroys a natural thing.[89] The definition of praeternaturals as those which, even if they are not following the prescription of nature, exert no great power, but delay the course of nature in some way, echoes Jean Fernel's definition.[90] Things *contra naturam* happen against the common course of nature such as a stone being thrown upwards (*Posterior Analytics*, II, xi).[91] To this, Magirus adds another category, 'hyperphysica', to emphasize the transcendence of God's actions, as Timpler had done.[92] Hyperphysical events were beyond nature; they occur by an extraordinary and sublime power such as God or angels, rather than through a natural one, and they include creation, miracles, and the perpetual motion of celestial bodies.[93] Fortuituous events were reduced to six causes, following Melanchthon.[94]

Magirus explicitly discussed 'lex' in the section on putrefaction, citing Zabarella's position that putrefaction was natural because it followed the 'laws' of universal nature.[95] The problem of whether putrefaction was natural arose because although it seemed to be a necessary corollary for all things that were generable, some philosophers such as Pietro Pomponazzi (1462–1525) had thought that this

89 Magirus 1642: 8.

90 Ibid.: 'Praeter naturam vel *para phusin* dicuntur ea, quae tametsi non sunt ex praescripto naturae, illi tamen nullam vim insignem inferunt, sed aliquo modo retardant; ut foedus ictericorum color, geminus nasus in facie, sex digiti in manu'. Magirus 1642: 19, refers directly to Fernel, though it could have been mediated via Argenterio (Maclean 2002a: 253f.).

91 Magirus 1642: 8. Cf. Valerius' example of a stone falling down as *secundum naturam*, a stone thrown up as *contra naturam* and a stone being hurled across a level plane as *praeter naturam*, in Valerius 1567: 10.

92 Timpler 1605: 66.

93 Magirus 1642: 8.

94 Ibid.: 25.

95 Magirus 1642: 137f.: 'Sed cur dicatur [= putrefactio] naturalis, magnae sunt controversiae. Zabarella naturalem dici ait, ratione naturae universalis, secundum cujus leges mixtum necessario dissolvitur in elementa, quae putrefactio dicitur, qua tota compages et concretio mixti dissipatur.' My interpolation.

was against nature, as putrefaction led to the destruction of nature itself.[96] Zabarella explained putrefaction as being within universal nature, but against the singular nature of mixed bodies. Universal nature was defined as the order of all things and of all causes arranged in a certain order, depending on the prime principle, which in turn imposed special laws ('propriae leges') on individual things. Universal nature decrees nature to be subject to destruction, but it is not the nature of singular things to seek their own putrefaction.[97] According to Zabarella, universal nature imposes the ultimate goal on things, but in following that decree, particular nature seeks first to exist, conserve and maintain itself as an individual.[98] Thus, universal and particular natures were now connected with a legal metaphor by Zabarella: there exist universal, inviolable laws of nature, as well as more special, violable decrees applicable to singular nature.

The significance of Zabarella's formulation was not lost on Magirus' mentor, Rudolf Goclenius Sr. (1547–1628)[99] who dominated philosophy teaching at Marburg and spearheaded many philosophy projects to be published from Frankfurt. As an irenicist, he sought to synthesize and unify philosophy through various publications by himself and others; his famous *Philosophical lexicon* was designed to resolve philosophical differences in support of Reformed positions.[100] His *Philosophicus conciliator*, a manual for training theologians in disputation, characteristically began with the distinction between philosophy and the saving message of Christ. Then Goclenius applied Zabarella's distinction between universal and particular natures to monsters: monsters were not beyond universal nature; only beyond particular nature. Universal nature, following Zabarella, was called 'lex' by Goclenius; he then equated universal and particular nature with God's universal and special providence, and then called the law of universal nature 'fatal'.[101] Goclenius elsewhere explicitly

---

[96] Maclean 2002a: 254–256.

[97] Zabarella 1590b: 559.

[98] Ibid.: 88f.

[99] For Goclenius' debt to Melanchthon, see Stiening 1999.

[100] See for instance, Goclenius 1613: 412 on the hypostatic union; 359 on good works; 469–71 on 'supra naturam'.

[101] Goclenius 1609: 323ff.: 'An aliquid fiat contra naturam?

Nihil est praeter (a) naturam, ne monstra quidem, Scal. ex. 10. s. 25	Praeter (b) naturam multa sunt. idem.
Conciliatio	
(a) Universalem, quae dicitur a philosophis, praeter fatum, praeter fati determinationem, praeter Dei singularem providentiam.	(b) Particularem: seu cum impedita est externo: vel, praeter naturam, id est, praeter potestatem Dei ad motus ordinarios: praeter modum et legem eis a natura constitutum.

Explicatio

… Naturam universalem definio cum Zabarella, ordinem rerum omnium, seu omnium causarum inter se, cum dependentia ab uno principio primo, unde statutus est singulis rebus, proprius cursus, propria lex. Haec lex interdum dicitur fatalis, id est, fatis determinata, vel ipsum fatum (lex a natura universali constituta cuiuslibet rei). At Scaliger fatum definit vim ordinatarum inter se causarum atque effectionum, idque facit duplex: unum commune in tota serie naturae, ut fatale est aestate calere: et ver esse, cum sol est in ariete, id est, summe naturale, et ita necessarium, ut non habeat causam, nisi primam causam: alterum proprium,

equated nature with fate, and described fate itself as 'law'.[102] He attributed this idea of physical fate, not as a single cause, but as a series of efficient and material causes, to Velcurio and Melanchthon.[103] Whereas Melanchthon used 'lex' to describe regularity of heavenly motions only, Goclenius here extended it, with the help of Zabarella, to sublunary changes.

I have argued that the first Protestant textbook on natural philosophy by Velcurio set nature in God's Providential governance, strengthened the sense of the necessity, and thus regularity, of nature in terms of 'physical fate'; two types of regularity were acknowledged in the heavens and in the conservation of species, without using the word 'lex'. Melanchthon's textbook which drew on Velcurio, strengthened the concept of 'physical fate' by allowing probable generalizations to be virtually universal and regular; he used the word 'lex' for the regular laws in the heavens, and the word 'regula' for sublunary conservation of species. Importantly for Melanchthon, providentially designed and governed nature was absolutely crucial to support a *moral* philosophy that conserved political orders. Some later authors picked up this connection between natural and moral regularities, while others saw it more as signs of faith. Magirus (and his mentor Goclenius the Elder) followed Zabarella in using 'law' for the regularity of universal nature and 'decrees' for special nature. Celestial motions and conservation of species in the sublunary world evinced the regularity of universal nature (or nature *in genere*), while particular nature conserved the individual. Universal nature and special nature, furthermore, corresponded to universal and special providence respectively.

Nature as cause, regularity of nature, essential definitions, fate and chance had all been part of the philosophical equipment of the Latin Western commentary tradition of Aristotle, which also drew on Ciceronian, stoic and Christian traditions.[104] Some Protestant authors focused and underscored certain parts of this tradition, and made God's providence central to their view of nature. This focus on providence distinguishes most Protestant textbooks from their Catholic counterparts – as Liebler put it, his natural philosophy was more about understanding creatures in the

---

quod versari potest circa minutiora, ut cum dico, hoc mihi fatale est.
Particularis natura est cuiuslibet rei propria, ab universali ei assignata.
Natura universalis, seu universe sumpta, prae ceteris quaerit conservationem, perpetuitationem et propagationem specierum.
Particularis praecipue vult conservationem et durationem individui: deinde vero speciei.
Officium universalis naturae est, finem ultimum rebus, ad quam tendant, statuere. Naturae autem particularis, jussa decretaque quodammodo illius exequi.' Cf. Goclenius 1613: 741 and 708–715 (monsters).

[102] Goclenius 1613: 571: 'Fatum a fando dictum est, iussum, dictum, decretum quoddam. 1. Aristotele. Fatum nihil aliud set, quam Natura vel Lex (seu decretum) a natura universalis constituta de modo, quo quaelibet res generetur et intereat'. Cf. Goclenius 1591: 96f.

[103] Goclenius 1613: 574.

[104] For the eclectic origins of medieval interpretations of Aristotle's *Physics*, see Lang 1992.

Creator, than the Creator through creation.[105] This, of course, did not stop Protestant authors from using formulation of laws of nature by non-Protestant authors, such as Zabarella.[106]

Philosophy as knowledge of Law, not Gospel, furthermore, meant for some Protestant authors that its certainty had to be guaranteed – by innate knowledge endowed by God or by returning to Mosaic principles. Later, seventeenth-century authors would place certainty in God's creation. An almost exclusive focus on providence in natural philosophy drove these authors to establish the regularity of nature increasingly through taxonomy of causes,[107] probable generalizations, and use of the word 'law'; this, at least in the case of Melanchthon, was necessary in order to prevent 'Epicurean' moral disorder, though again, it must be noted that the connection between God's natural and moral orders was not unique to Protestant natural philosophy itself, as can be seen in the works of Catholic commentators of this period who wrote on liberty and rights.[108] My point here is that the Protestant focus on providence led to a relatively greater emphasis on the regularity of nature. By the end of the sixteenth century, the idea of a 'law' of (universal) nature as inviolable and ordained by God was thus fairly commonplace among Protestant authors.[109] This implies that the concept of 'lex' in natural philosophy is not unique to the new philosophies of the seventeenth century discussed in this volume [Steinle, Treiber], nor to an English brand of voluntarism. Indeed, seeking Providence in nature remained an important theme of the Protestant tradition, especially in the physico-theologies that investigated the variations and the details of nature [Trepp].

---

105 Liebler 1561: 20: '… non per creaturas Creatorem, sed in Creatore creaturas cognoscere valeamus.' Cf. the title in Titelmans 1530: 'de consideratione rerum naturalium earumque ad suum creatorem reductione'.

106 Cf. Brosserius 1546: 28v.

107 Cf. also Newton on the taxonomy of causes of Daniel Stahl's *Axiomata philosophica*; see McGuire and Tamny 1983: 17f.

108 Brett 1997. Not all Protestant textbooks were interested in providence either: for example, Lonicer 1540.

109 For example, Case 1599: 13. For Case, see further Schmitt 1983b.

Chapter 8

Natural Order and Divine Salvation: Protestant Conceptions in Early Modern Germany (1550–1750)

Anne-Charlott Trepp[1]

In the early modern period, 'Nature' became a key point of reference on the most diverse social and cultural planes. In an early modern culture strongly shaped by religious ideas and practices, nature came to assume particular significance in the field of religion itself.[2] In this essay I would like to show first how 'Nature' became a central medium of early modern attributions of meaning and concepts of salvation, and second how these religious patterns of interpretation in turn determined concepts of 'Nature' and its 'order'. I will be concerned here not with patterns of order in the sense of natural laws, but rather with alternative concepts of order.

Beginning in the mid-sixteenth century, the notion of the impending end of the world, which was particularly intense among Lutherans, and the revival of spirituality meant that 'Nature' increasingly became an object of salvific hopes. In connection with the question of the 'Last Things' and the search for spiritual certainty about God, a close, at times causal relationship was posited between Nature or Creation – understood as a second source of divine revelation alongside the Scriptures – and the longed-for deliverance from this world. The interpretation of nature in terms of salvation was associated not just with a religious charging of the natural world, and to some extent also a sacralization of nature, but also with a central interest in deciphering the salvific 'facts' that God conveyed through nature. In this respect, the soteriological interpretation of nature within Protestantism furnished significant impulses for the observation and study of nature. In the seventeenth century, nature was gradually disentangled from these all-encompassing spiritual and eschatological schemes. Nature suffered no loss of religious valence in the process; what did change were its religious meanings and the ways in which people regarded it.

In the course of the seventeenth century, acute expectations that the end of the world was at hand disappeared. At the same time, many Lutheran theologians came to believe that eschatological renewal did not represent an event of Creation as a whole, and that the old world would not be miraculously transformed into a new one

[1] I would like to thank Hermann Geyer, Johanna Geyer-Kordesch and Peter Hanns Reill for intense discussions and fruitful criticism.

[2] On this and the following theses, see the more detailed discussion in Trepp (in press).

at the end of days. This did not, however, render the creaturely world theologically meaningless. The less people expected an eschatological transformation of Creation as a whole and a transfiguration in the hereafter, the more important it seems to have become to derive experiences of salvation from Creation, that is, from nature itself. The secularization of nature (with secularization understood here as a gradual dwindling of all-encompassing and absolute theological explanations rather than the elimination of theological and religious interpretations more generally) was thus accompanied by a naturalization of religion or religious concepts and vice versa.

The meaning of changing ideas about salvation among Lutheran Protestants for their understanding of Nature has received little attention up until now.[3] In the early modern period, the allegorical perception of Nature as a network of essentially interrelated similarities and concordances, in which each thing (in its quality as a sign) was the bearer of multiple meanings was replaced by an unambiguous, empirical, naturalistic viewpoint orientated towards the concrete individual phenomena of Nature (in certain realms of knowledge homogeneity and uniformity were also becoming increasingly central [Daston]).[4] Changing spiritual and eschatological expectations played a key role among the factors that contributed, however indirectly and diffusely, to this development. This relationship will not be presented here as a mono-causal or directly causal developmental process. Instead, I will examine specific contexts and tendencies within time periods and religious tendencies.

Particularly in the seventeenth century, those who shaped and promoted nature-orientated attitudes and practices were not Lutheran scholastic theologians, with their Aristotelian views of nature derived mainly from the work of Philipp Melanchton (on their perspective, see Kusukawa), but rather reform-orientated theologians critical of the church, whose ideas on theology and natural philosophy went back in part to pre-Reformation traditions. In these reform-orientated groupings 'Nature' took on central religious significance and developed into a distinct form of religious practice. In the seventeenth and early eighteenth centuries they not only developed the innovative theological concepts; it was also they – and not the 'orthodox' clerics more strongly orientated towards academic and controversialist theology – who took the leading role in interpreting and studying nature, along with likeminded Christian laypersons (Johannes Kepler and Matthias Bernegger belong to the latter group; on them, see Graßhoff and Treiber).[5] And yet some of the theologians who *also* sought orientation outside confessional doctrine maintained close ties with the emphatically dogmatic theologians; the boundaries between the *mainly* heterodox and the *mainly* orthodox were fluid, and were drawn with varying strictness by contemporaries themselves, especially since German Lutheranism never possessed a decision-

[3] Previous studies have concentrated mainly on millenarianism, which was particularly widespread in England. See in particular the classic study Webster 1975: XVI; see also his more recent reflections: Webster 1986: 192–217; and Oster 1994: 137–148; Greyerz 2001: 205–217.

[4] On the various aspects of this transformation see Maclean 2002a: 236ff.; Daston 2000a: 17ff.; Daston and Park 1998: esp. chaps 4 and 6; Harrison 1998; Bono 1999; Meier Reeds 1991: 28ff.; Funkenstein 1986: 28ff.

[5] For more detail, see Trepp (in press).

making body responsible for doctrine across territorial frontiers.[6] To that extent, the doctrinal models of 'the' orthodox and the concepts of nature and religion prevalent among reform-orientated theologians had ample opportunities for mutual influence.

A certain diversity of belief within Lutheranism is also evident in the varying accentuations of notions of Providence (cf. KUSUKAWA; on the Catholic tradition, see ARMOGATHE). Apart from specifically salvific visions, ideas about how divine Providence guided events in the world, and could in turn be recognized in those events, were central to defining the interest in nature. One can distinguish here between more strongly actualistic and more sapiential-ordinative doctrines of Providence. According to the actualistic view favoured by Reformation theologians, particularly Luther, God brought about every event, down to the smallest detail, through his actions and according to his will. The sapiential-ordinative model, in contrast, emphasized more strongly 'the mediation of God's efficacy through the existential and natural order that had been set up according to his wisdom'[7] (on central aspects of genesis, see ARMOGATHE and WILSON). We will see that in the first view, attention tended to be focused on the diversity and individual facts of nature, while the second stressed more nature's regularities and autonomy.

I will discuss these specific interpretative contexts of 'nature and religion' using the examples of three men from outside the ranks of the famous natural philosophers of their respective eras. Johann Arndt, Johann Rist and Friedrich Christoph Lesser all devoted their main energies to their profession as pastors. With the exception of Lesser, who was an important representative of the physico-theological movement, they were not known to contemporaries for their natural philosophical discourses. It is worth noting that both Arndt and Rist were also practising physicians, while it is likely that Lesser's first choice of profession would have been medicine rather than the church. However individual these men and their ideas were, it is precisely their status as amateur natural historians that constitutes the representative moment for (male) members of a 'progressive' educated middle-class stratum, which largely distanced itself from scholastic dogma and its accompanying educational and religious practices. They laid out their concepts of nature in theological works intended primarily for devotional purposes and written in German. In this respect the significance of such scientific amateurs for the dissemination of contemporary knowledge can scarcely be overestimated.

Apart from an analysis of their devotional writings, I will try to provide some idea of the living conditions and experiences of people in the early modern period. The specific forms of religiosity and concepts of nature cannot, after all, be adequately understood without examining the particular experiences and perceptions of those who interpreted them. They, too, determined how individuals concretely adopted and generally also reinterpreted religious models and ideas about nature, particularly when these were increasingly experiences of catastrophe, as was the case during the Thirty Years War. It was precisely in those instances where nature was viewed as

---

6 Kaufmann 1998: 79ff.

7 See Bernhardt 1999: 45. My treatment of the doctrine of Providence largely follows Bernhardt's profound study.

part and expression of divine Providence that the aspect of coping with contingency attained central significance.[8]

Johann Arndt (1555–1621)

Aside from the Bible and Luther's *Kleiner Katechismus*, Johann Arndt's *Vier Bücher vom wahren Christentum* (Four Books of True Christianity) is considered by far the most widely disseminated and read work of German Protestantism. This devotional work, whose volumes appeared between 1605 and 1610, had already gone through 64 printings by 1670 and 240 by the end of the eighteenth century. It was also translated into nearly all European languages.[9] In his theology, Arndt synthesized the mysticism and spiritualism of earlier forms of piety and tried to integrate them into the Protestant faith. Although his work did not go undisputed among churchmen, it provided the decisive impulses for the spiritual movement that was forming in the seventeenth century, which as one of the strongest forces in the Lutheranism of that period not only prepared the ground for Pietism, but also influenced reform-minded theologians more generally, including the proponents of orthodoxy.[10] Despite its uncommon popularity and the remarkable importance accorded to the interpretation of Nature in the *Vier Bücher*, the work has, in contrast to the *oeuvre* of Jakob Böhme, for example, received scant attention from scholars interested in the relationship between nature and religion at the period. This despite the fact that Arndt – who like Böhme had not studied theology, but *had* studied medicine[11] – unlike Böhme combined concepts from natural magic, or Paracelsian hermetic notions, with practice as a physician.[12]

Arndt's chief objective was to renew Christian life and overcome the dominion of so-called sham Christianity (*Scheinchristentum*). Faith should be centred not on pure doctrine but on 'active exercise' and 'living experience'. Arndt confronted the 'mere imputation of righteousness', that is, justification by faith alone, with a mystical and spiritual path of renewal for the 'inner human being'.[13] His concept of a mystical and decidedly practice-orientated piety was a reaction to external as well as internal problems facing the Lutheran church. While Lutheranism was increasingly on the defensive in its power politics from the second half of the sixteenth century onward, it was becoming evident within the church that the much-preached word in the congregation had missed its mark.[14] On the one hand, this was a result of the threatened ossification of Protestant teachings into orthodoxy. In order to promote confessional doctrinal distinctions, university studies emphasized not pastoral but disputational theology. On the other hand, the centrepiece of Protestant teaching, the

8 For a general account, see Luhmann 1992: 182ff.

9 Wallmann 1990: O19.

10 Brecht 1993: 185, 194.

11 Schneider 1991: 133–175; Feingold 2002: 79ff. overlooks that, until the beginning of the seventeenth century, this 'career' could also lead to clerical office.

12 He also acted as a physician while he was a pastor; Schneider 1995: 94f.

13 Brecht 1993: 134ff.

14 Sträter 1995: 1.

doctrine of justification, had proved from the beginning to be difficult to convey.[15] Justification by faith alone, which negated any form of justification by works (*Werkgerechtigkeit*) and placed believers in the paradoxical situation of the *simul iustus et peccator*, was obviously too complicated and too intellectual to become an 'understood, let alone a lived reality'.[16] Above all, we need to ask to what extent the doctrine of justification was available to early modern people as a permanent experience of faith that could also be called upon in difficult, existentially threatening and even crisis periods; and to what extent it was able to offer them adequate life security. Some scholars have pointed, not without reason, to the latent problem of an absent assurance of salvation, particularly within Lutheran teaching.[17]

The Protestant church's failings became all the more seriously apparent as it had to prove itself in an era ridden with catastrophe and crisis. Beginning in the final decades of the sixteenth century, people throughout Europe saw their living conditions worsen.[18] The reasons for this development lay in a complex fabric of demographic, economic, political, social and cultural factors, as well as climatic changes that set in around 1570.[19] In addition to the frightening confrontations between confessions and intimidating internal enmities, Europeans were increasingly confronted with poor harvests, waves of price increases for basic goods, and famine, which in turn almost always opened the door to epidemics such as plague and dysentery that claimed massive numbers of the lives, albeit with an impact that varied along regional and social lines. These already critical circumstances were terribly exacerbated by the Thirty Years War. The fact that witch persecutions began in the late 1570s and reached an initial high point around 1600[20] was doubtless no coincidence, any more than was the veritable boom in hermetic and, more broadly, natural magic, and mystical teachings and practices. The extent to which the learned and educated of the era adopted nature mysticism and theosophical notions is evident not just in Rosicrucian writings, which have received much scholarly attention, and the ensuing debate in the second half of the seventeenth century, but even before that in the work of churchmen such as Johann Arndt.

While the first three books of *Wahres Christentum* were intended to instruct readers in 'Understanding God in the Soul', the fourth book (*Liber Naturae*), which elucidated the six-day work of Creation, aimed in analogy at 'Understanding God from Nature'.[21] The 'great world-book of Nature' could serve to convince any person that 'we are obligated to love God, because of His great love, which He shows and proves to us through all creatures'.[22] God's concern for Creation should make us aware that the world was made for and on behalf of humanity.[23]

---

15 Brecht 1993: 116ff.

16 Sträter 1995: 1.

17 See Axmacher 1989: 289ff.; for a different view see Wallmann 1999: 29.

18 On this see Lehmann 1980: 105–114; see Parker and Smith 1978; for Germany see also Schilling 1994: 372–396; Press 1991: 29ff.

19 Lehmann 1986: 31–50; Lamb 1982: 201–320; Pfister 1985: I, 119ff.

20 Schulze 1987: 273ff.; Schilling 1994: 388.

21 For a thorough account, see Geyer 2001a.

22 Arndt (1610) 1851: IV, II, Beschluß 3.

23 See Weber 1978: 176, 179.

For Arndt, divine Providence was fulfilled in the wise and systematic order of Creation, which God constituted, preserved and guided according to his will in his teleologically ordering wisdom.[24] In keeping with his primarily sapiential-ordinative notion of providence, he accorded a central role to evidence of an order of Creation and its regularity. The order of Creation is, however, not a mechanistic, but rather an organic and animate one, in which God is not just the origin and transcendent counterpart to the world, but also 'fills' it quite literally with his 'spirit' or 'breath'. He is immanent in the world, without being taken up into it.[25] Just as the human soul permeates the body with life, God fills the world with his presence in the sense of an *anima mundi*.

By following the teleology installed within it by God, Nature refers to God and his systematic work of Creation. At the same time, however, Nature remains hidden and secret in its essence and function. For it contains not just the (visible) signs of God's systematic work of Creation, but also harbours within itself the path to redemption and salvation. The creaturely world bears within itself the 'evidence' of redemption.[26] The path of salvation is, however, visible only to those who have followed the path of faith leading to rebirth traced by Arndt (in books I–III of his *Wahres Christentums*). They have enlightened access to the whole of Creation. According to a hermetic theosophy and mysticism, the 'Book of Nature' and the 'Book of Grace' (the Holy Scripture) mesh tightly.[27]

In Arndt's cosmos, the earthly and heavenly worlds were inextricably linked (in a relationship of microcosm and macrocosm). Everything was interconnected 'in a hidden and invisible manner, as on an invisible chain'. Arndt expanded the originally (neo-)Platonic and hermetic idea of the 'golden chain', which was adapted within Christianity, into an 'aurea catena naturae et providentiae divinae' which incorporated the aspect of Providence. In this idea, God is connected with all of his creatures, down to the lowliest among them, in a slowly graduated chain of being.[28] The *catena aurea* was the basic principle with which God in his *providentia* preserved and permeated the cosmos.[29] 'The Lord God speaks of the entire wise order of Nature, and begins from above, a prima caussa [*sic*].[30] For he has 'decreed that the lower must receive the powers and influences of the higher', which are connected to each other by a 'wondrous consonance and kinship', that is, by sympathetic-harmonic forces.[31]

A central medium used by God to guide the world and its creatures was the heavenly body or its 'natural influences'. The *semina* or *astra* – named for their origins as 'hidden living stars' – were the bearers of hidden powers and brought forth all life according to the will of the Creator.[32] They were conceived as spiritual rather than material, and in turn had their origins in God. Arndt describes how these 'seminal

24 On this see Bernhardt 1999.

25 Geyer 2001a: III, 244ff.

26 Arndt (1610) 1851: IV,I,1,30; see Geyer 2001b: 100.

27 On this see Geyer 2001a: esp. I and II.

28 Arndt (1610) 1851: IV,I,4,36. Cf. Geyer 2001a: III 33ff.

29 Geyer 2001a: III, 38.

30 Arndt (1610) 1851: IV,I,4,37.

31 Ibid. IV,I,3,30.

32 Geyer 2001a: III, 43ff.

powers' function in particular detail in his account of God's work of populating the waters on the fifth day. 'The sea and everything in it [has] its order, time and motion implanted by God' just as the other elements do. It has its 'innatas leges motus, innate laws of motion', because it has an 'internal motor' in itself 'and not in another'.[33] 'For how could the Lord God have inserted life and movement into all elements, universaliter et particulariter …?" Nature thus possesses a remarkable autonomy. Its processes rest, however, not on mechanical causes, but on the sympathetic co-operation ('concordance') of forces immanent in nature.[34]

Signatures represented a link between the immaterial *semina* or *astra* as the hidden essence of things and earthly phenomena.[35] They turned all creatures into the bearers of divine messages: 'You will find in every little weed or flower special signs which are the living handwriting and signature of God, with which he draws each plant so artfully, so wondrously, so tenderly according to his hidden power.'[36] As bearers of divine revelation, even the lowliest plants thus become 'witnesses of God's love, benevolence and omnipotence'.[37]

Only those who had been reborn, who had laid aside the old Adam in themselves and re-established in their souls the state of being made in God's image, were capable of deciphering the semiotics of nature in accordance with its actual meaning, something that Adam (before the expulsion from Paradise) had 'understood quite well [how to do] on the basis of his acquired wisdom'.[38] Arndt also draws analogies between nature and religion in order to reveal to his readers how this rebirth might be accomplished. His system of hidden references and correlation of effects corresponded to his thinking in analogies. Arndt interprets the entire visible, creaturely world, like the Holy Scripture, allegorically. He repeatedly draws conclusions from natural to spiritual processes. His analogies are particularly far-reaching in the area of the purification or spiritualization of nature: 'separatio puri ab impuro'. The spiritualization and redemption of the human being parallels the alchemical process of purification in nature.[39]

While the portrayal of natural processes and 'natural signs' runs as a central theme through the entire work, Arndt virtually avoids any mention of the existence of supernatural effects. This is particularly evident in his extensive discussion of solar eclipses.[40] Contrary to the opinion common among theologians that solar eclipses, as harbingers of Judgement Day, must be attributed to supernatural causes, he emphatically supported the view that they were nevertheless natural in origin. All eclipses, he wrote, were 'contrary to Nature and a quality of the heavenly lights'. Since all stars were created to shine, any hindrance to their luminosity, 'their natural effects and powers' must be deemed a defect in their nature. Any deviation from

---

33 Arndt (1610) 1851: IV,I, 5. 16–19.

34 Geyer 2001a: III 53.

35 See also Arndt 1597: chap. 9, and Geyer 2001a: III, 62ff; for a different view, cf. Mager 1998: 41–60; see in general, Maclean 2002a: 199f.

36 Arndt (1610) 1851: IV,I,3,14.

37 Ibid.: IV,I,3,13.

38 Ibid.: IV,I,6,2.

39 See Geyer 2001b: 100.

40 Arndt (1610) 1851: IV,I,4, 54–57.

normality, however, occurred not of its own accord, but was caused by human sinfulness. Only human sin forced God to interrupt the natural course of nature, in order to admonish humankind to change their ways before it was too late, and also in order to punish them. All misfortune was brought about by human sin. The unity of humankind with Creation, underlined by the relationship of microcosm and macrocosm, and man's potential power over Creation, is turned into its negative by Arndt's premise of human sinfulness. 'For the suffering of all creatures, good and evil, is directed towards man, as if to a centre in which all lines of the circle meet … Because the evil of man grows ever greater, the world can no longer bear the heavy weight of sin, and must necessarily perish.'[41] Human wickedness pushed the world towards ruin.

Arndt lived in the certainty that the end of the world was near. The sense of living in the Last Days was particularly marked among Lutherans.[42] On the one hand, the Reformation as a movement of religious renewal could itself be interpreted as a sign of the end of the world.[43] On the other, Luther himself, with his identification of the pope as the Antichrist, had become increasingly convinced that he was living in the Last Days of history that supposedly immediately preceded the return of Christ. For Luther, though, the arrival of the Supreme Judge and the expected end of the world were not terrifying events. In the assurances of salvation that justification provided, Luther awaited the Final Judgement as a 'dear day of judgement',[44] when true believers would gain a 'new heaven and a new earth' (Revelation 21:1) through the 'eschatological re-creation' of the present world.

Beginning in the mid-sixteenth century, expectations of the imminent end of the world intensified still further and changed in character. In the growing yearning for certainty about the signs of the times, particularly the time point of the Apocalypse, the linking of eschatological hopes with revelations of natural magic became ever more self-evident.[45] On the other hand, expectations of the eschatological re-creation of the world more generally increasingly shifted to the question of individual salvation. The salvation of Creation, in contrast, was scarcely addressed anymore. At the same time, Judgement Day increasingly resumed its pre-Reformation character of impending divine punishment – as the day in which decisions would primarily be made about the punishment or reward of the individual.[46] Only for true believers would the Last Judgement bring the longed-for salvation from a world that, in Arndt's view, was already doomed: 'Therefore keep watch and pray for the eternal salvation of the body! It is high time! And wait patiently! Things are not getting any better here.'[47]

Arndt thus repeatedly reminded his readers of the transience and futility of Creation. However beautiful its appearance, however appropriate its functions and

---

41 Arndt (1610) 1851: IV,I,4,55.

42 See Barnes 1999.

43 Kunz 1980: 14.

44 Asendorf 1982: 312.

45 See, more generally, Barnes 1988: 75.

46 Korn 1957: 118.

47 From Arndt's sermons on the ten plagues, cited in Greschat 1968: 171; Brecht 1993, 142.

autonomous its processes, his descriptions always culminate in warnings about recalling its fleeting quality and coming destruction on Judgement Day, accompanied by admonitions to withdraw from it while there was still time. True believers turned away from the 'impure and thoroughly abject earth', so that they might not be 'sullied' by it. The earth appeared as a place of misery and sin, a 'muddy prison, in which even the purest air is filled with earthly foulness'.[48]

Arndt attributed a central salvific function to nature in his theology, for God's *providentia*, love, kindness and omnipotence are also revealed in the creaturely world. Nature can and should be recognized in the order, suitableness and beauty of this world, because in it Nature refers back to and beyond itself towards God.[49] Like a father with his child, God has thrown a beautiful gift to humankind, not so that they might 'remain stuck to the gift', but rather in order to 'draw' and 'attract' them.[50] In the methodical structure and rich meaning of Creation, people should recognize God's work and his concern for humanity, but only in order to detach themselves all the more easily from this world. In Arndt's theology, the meaning of nature, despite its autonomy, lies not in itself,[51] but rather in its capacity to guide and to refer, in its transcendence. True knowledge of nature leads through and beyond the earthly world into the divine world of the hereafter. By analogy, everything in Creation was aimed at continual spiritualization and, consequently, at change. The emphasis on autonomies in Arndt's work does not contradict the continual transformation of Creation, and is also compatible with its apocalyptic destruction. This leads to an apparently paradoxical phenomenon: Arndt promoted the idea of natural laws more radically than the theologians we will address presently, but they had less in common with natural laws in the modern sense.

Johann Rist (1607–1667)

Unlike Arndt, the Wedel pastor Johann Rist did not concentrate in his writings on portraying an all-encompassing order of Creation in a methodically ordered cosmos. His interest was less in the whole and the 'essence' of nature than in its rich variety, details and 'mechanisms'. Rist's concept of Creation was also influenced in individual aspects by hidden, nature-magical microcosm–macrocosm relationships and the corresponding relations of analogy and sympathy. At the same time, he was interested in studying the diversity of nature and in reconstructing natural processes, both alchemical and mechanical.

Rist's treatment and image of nature rested on more strongly actualistic notions of Providence, in the tradition of Martin Luther. In the Lutheran view, God controlled all events in the world through permanent activity. He was not connected to Creation in the essential sense, as in Arndt's work. Instead, his relationship with Creation was rooted solely in his constant works. His relationship with the world was expressed in his continual love and care and his personal concern for his Creation, down to

48 Arndt (1610) 1851: IV,I,2, Schlußgebet.

49 See Krolzig 1988: 24.

50 Arndt (1610) 1851: IV, Vorrede 6.

51 Anders Krolzig 1988: 24ff.; Gruebner 1998: 217f.

the smallest things.[52] Beyond the alternatives of transcendence and immanence, he was omnipresent in his actions, both as an absolute ruler who acted freely according to his will and as an admonishing, punitive and benevolent father. This actualistic concept of Providence determined Rist's relationship to God and his attitude towards nature. He expressed it in his perception of outbreaks of epidemics and the plague and especially in his description and 'processing' of natural disasters. Thus, for example, Rist described the mighty storm of 1648 as a misfortune sent directly by God: 'God Almighty had the winds work their cruel will / ... / The wind was more powerful / for this was the hand of God.'[53] Social catastrophes such as the Thirty Years War were also understood as divine dispensation, as direct punishments by God. The heavier the 'hand' of God weighed upon contemporaries, however, the more intensely they sought to secure his care, especially and increasingly in the areas accessible to their immediate experience.

Rist, who, in addition to theology, had studied medicine and also botany as an auxiliary science, presented his ideas on nature in several works,[54] most extensively in his *Monatsgespräche* (Monthly Conversations). When Rist decided in 1662 to write 'of all manner of remarkable things / in Nature / indeed of all things / to be found under Heaven', he was weighed down not just by the past events of the war – Danish territory had been subject to enemy siege until 1659 – and the most recent outbreak of an unknown epidemic disease, which had claimed 150 lives in Wedel alone. The immediate occasion for writing his *Monatsgespräche* was the death of his wife. Amidst his 'sorest' affliction, as he wrote, he had consciously shifted his focus from earthly to heavenly things.

For his own comfort and edification, but also for the 'useful' instruction of youth, he devised a series of conversations that, in the manner of humanist disputations, explored the question of the optimum: 'What is the noblest ...?' In these conversations, which are orientated less toward actual than toward 'plausible' conversations, he addressed current themes from the fields of nature, art and technology as well as questions of the proper conduct of life in the broadest sense. He was concerned not with a detailed explanation of individual aspects, but rather with entertaining himself and others by conveying knowledge in an edifying manner. His interlocutors were above all members of the 'language or virtue society' he founded, of which Matthias Merian the Younger was also a member. The numerous printings of his work until 1703, as well as the continuation of the *Monatsgespräche* after his death, speak for the success of this series. Rist was known in the republic of letters as a naturalist (*Naturkündiger*).[55] He had made his name long before, however, with his extensive religious and secular literary writings, chief among them his peace dramas. He was a member of the Fruchtbringende Gesellschaft founded in 1617, among other societies. In order to avoid confessional conflicts, the statutes of this strongly Protestant-influenced society, like the Royal Society later, generally forbade the acceptance of theologians as members, with only a few exceptions. Among them

[52] Bernhardt 1999: 42.

[53] Rist 1648: liness 271–274, 292.

[54] For more detail, see Trepp (in press).

[55] Harsdörffer 1651: 306.

were Johann Valentin Andreae, who was admitted in 1646, and Johann Rist who joined a year later. His membership of the Fruchtbringende Gesellschaft points to his irenical, non-denominational stance, which he expressed repeatedly, especially in his writings on peace.

The rejection of war was typical of the humanist-educated reformist pastorate, who like Rist promoted active, true Christianity *(wahres Christentum)* 'in life as well as in doctrine'.[56] In contrast, he sharply distanced himself from disputational theology and its proponents. He wrote disdainfully of 'sick Lutheranism'[57] with its 'numerous Pharisees' and 'scribes',[58] who all too often condemned their own colleagues because of a few 'bad church ceremonies', which at least contributed to blessedness. Rist was convinced that it was 'a thousand times better to sit in a solitary spot / and contemplate the ineffable wonders and works of the Almighty Creator'.[59] Unlike the church and its individual members, and perhaps also in contrast to the Scriptures, the 'Book of Nature' appeared immune to doctrinal disputes, which had proved so fruitless and destructive; for in Nature God's signature was immediately and unmistakably visible (this also included the search for 'general truths'; on this see Daston). It was not least the eschatologically motivated search for hidden truths and signs in nature that had contributed to a marked shift in the relationship between the divine books in the seventeenth century. For Rist, the Book of Nature and the Scriptures were equal as sources of divine knowledge.[60] It even appears that it was only his insight into nature that allowed him to attain a true understanding of the Holy Scripture.[61]

Rist was convinced that a truly Christian life began in this world, and that it must be possible to experience 'true godliness'[62] in this life. Believing this, he sought in a certain sense to anticipate by accumulating knowledge the state of supreme blessedness, which could actually only be fulfilled eschatologically, that is, in the hereafter. His search for 'earthly bliss' (*irdische Glückseligkeit*), as he repeatedly wrote, aimed at the grandeur, variety and utility of Creation, which proceeded from God, and knowledge about it: 'It remains an eternal truth … / that no greater earthly bliss exists under the sun / than to know everything.'[63] For knowing everything *about* Creation was confirmation of God's love and care *for* his Creation.

With his idea that God's love and care were expressed in every single event, Rist was not seeking a universal order in nature, but rather turning his attention to

---

56 Rist (1638) 1982: 6. Like many of his fellow clergymen, Rist supported a renewal of Christianity as called for by Arndt, without, however, sharing the latter's mystical spiritualism or his hermetic theosophy.

57 Rist (1652)1978: 682.

58 Rist (1667) 1976: 70.

59 Ibid.: 75.

60 Nevertheless, in contrast to Arndt he distinguished between the 'Book of Grace' and the 'Book of Nature'. Cf. Feingold's 2002 article on the relationship between clerics and 'nature' or natural philosophy, which however do not go far enough; for another view, cf. Ben-Chaim 2002: 59f.

61 For more detail, see Trepp 2001.

62 Rist (1638)1982: 6.

63 Rist (1663a)1972a: 17.

individual things and experiences. His concept was collection and experimentation. In the conviction that more knowledge about Creation also meant more certainty about the author of that Creation, he soaked up all of the knowledge available to him, the medical ideas of Paracelsus and the natural magic of Athanasius Kircher as well as the insights and concepts of such representatives of the 'new science' as Francis Bacon and Galileo Galilei.[64] In so doing he never adopted a complete system; he did not aim at coherence as we conceive of it. Instead of tracing an all-encompassing order of Creation, he collected natural objects of all kinds, searched for the most diverse plants, which he pasted into his 'living herbarium',[65] planted varied gardens, experimented with telescopes and microscopes, sought the perpetual motion machine, and worked day and night in his laboratory to solve alchemical secrets such as the elixir of life, the panacea or the secret of life itself; but he provided no explanation of the order of nature, the causes of natural processes or the quality of matter. One also looks in vain for a precise description of what he did in the laboratory that he had set up next to his study. He filled entire pages, in contrast, with detailed and highly sensuous descriptions of flowers, ranging from their outward appearance and incidence to their medical and other 'useful' applications. Rist found in each phenomenon, each thing and being in nature, visible evidence of the hand of God.

Whenever he became aware of the abundance and grandeur of the cosmos, Rist was filled with a feeling of great devotion. He was a proponent of the heliocentric world-view although he was convinced that he would be accused of heresy because of it.[66] He had telescopes built in the neighbouring city of Hamburg and used them to observe the constellations.[67] There is no evidence of the oft-mentioned 'Copernican shock' or feeling of loneliness in Rist's case. On the contrary, the fullness and breadth of the cosmos only made him more aware of, and grateful for, God's benevolence, omnipotence and greatness.[68] He experienced a similarly edifying feeling when he observed God's tiniest creatures under the microscope:

> The louse / scarcely smaller to look upon/ than a crab / has such a marvellous form/ of eyes / mouth / feet / fibres / that one may be awed by it / and I once intently observed/ a rather large louse/ hatching two young lice on a plate of glass / how wondrous this was to watch/ no one can truly say or believe/ who has not seen it himself / and / briefly put / one may take as much and as various *pleasure* in these instruments / as one wishes.[69]

Rist repeatedly described the great 'pleasure' he drew from everything he observed in nature. For him, every thing and phenomenon in nature pointed to God, whom he saw in the Lutheran manner as directly present everywhere in Creation.[70] Through

---

[64] He mentions and praises scholars of the most diverse traditions and programmes – with the exception of Aristotelians and Galenists, that is, of scholastics in the broad sense of the term.

[65] Rist (1668) 1976: 415; Rist (1666) 1974: 206.

[66] Rist (1652) 1978: 683f.

[67] Rist (1668) 1976: 404.

[68] Ibid.: 317.

[69] Ibid.: 406 (emphasis added).

[70] Luther (1901) 1964: 133f.; see Frey 1994: 110f.

his direct and permanent activity, God is omnipresent in his Creation, he is always 'there'.[71] This notion of the presence of God in the manifestations of nature guided Rist in his observation and study of nature.

Rist not only recognized in nature God's omnipotence and benevolence but, more urgently still, he sought to assure himself of God's presence in Creation as a sign of his continuing divine love and care. Filled with enthusiasm, he thought he detected 'life' in the sea-grass that he also examined under the microscope. Every sign of 'life' in even the tiniest thing was proof of God's care. 'Notwithstanding that this is a proper and genuine plant; yet I found something in the belly of this sea-mouse / that looked like a natural lung / a liver or the like / so that I began to believe / that these sea-mice lived as starfish do ... as if there were life in them.'[72]

All those natural phenomena that potentially gave evidence that God would grant his creatures new life after death assumed central significance.[73] Luther too had seen in nature symbols of resurrection after death; but while he perceived in nature simply a 'splendidly beautiful parable' of the resurrection of the dead,[74] for Rist observing Creation provided the final certainty necessary for salvation.

> Now I [thank] God Almighty / that the dear springtime is approaching / in which the most splendid plants / herbs and flowers creep forth from the earth / which reveals clearly to me/ not just the great omnipotence of the eternal Creator / every time I merely step into my garden / but also recalls to me so powerfully the universal resurrection of the dead / that I / thanks be to God / *no longer* harbour the least doubt about this otherwise lofty and difficult article.[75]

Rist overcame his doubts about redemption and resurrection after death in a twofold manner: on the one hand, by observing the yearly processes of renewal in nature and, on the other by the transformative processes of alchemy which he himself practised.[76] He has a member of his language society confess to the following:

> It must be an excellent pastime / to be able to bring forth/ all manner of herbs and flowers / from their [own] ashes / so that they are in their perfect bloom and growth / which reveals and *demonstrates* to us so clearly/ the resurrection of the dead / that one would have to be a stone or a block / to harbour any further doubts of this very comforting article of faith in the face of such an excellent natural miracle.[77]

What interested him here was no longer the symbolic interpretation of alchemical processes that had been common for centuries. Rist's message was that the process of alchemical transformation could serve as 'proof' of the Resurrection.

---

[71] Lüpke 1999: 307; Bernhardt 1999: 77pp; see Steiger 1999: 21–41; on the meaning of divine ubiquity, see also Funkenstein 1986: 70ff.

[72] Rist (1668) 1976: 415.

[73] Rist (1663a) 1972a: 31. On what follows see also Trepp 2001.

[74] Cf. the quotation from Luther's Canonika in Kopp 1971: 211; see also Trepp 1999: 485.

[75] Rist (1663b) 1972b: 183 (emphasis added).

[76] See the examples in: Linden 1984: 102–124.

[77] Rist (1668) 1976: 423 (emphasis added).

In the seventeenth century, the question of the resurrection of the individual developed into one of the most urgent issues surrounding salvation. The eschatological interest in Creation, in contrast, diminished considerably.[78] For Rist and his contemporaries, the eschatological complex of resurrection, redemption and perfection no longer referred to all of Creation, but to humankind alone. In an age of war, epidemic and natural disaster, divine judgement appeared omnipresent. In this context, a pastorally inadequate disputational theology and a doctrine of justification that was, in some respects, alienated from life rendered the question of personal salvation increasingly pressing. As a result, the salvation of Creation itself was regarded as secondary, while at the same time it became increasingly important to derive salvific experiences not just from the Scriptures but also from Nature.

In the course of a generally observable growth in the significance of 'fragmentary salvific experiences of the present',[79] Nature also gained in religious evidential value. This reinterpretation in the direction of a religious revaluation of nature was doubtless related, not exclusively but among other factors, to changes in eschatological notions and concepts in the seventeenth century. On the one hand, nature gradually became detached from all-encompassing soteriological concepts, whether in connection with spiritual or eschatological visions. The interest in the salvation of Creation as a whole diminished in favour of a more individualized (not just in eschatological terms) religiosity. The question of the salvific future of the present world was either no longer posed or, as was usual in Lutheran orthodoxy, it was assumed that all things creaturely would be utterly destroyed in the last days, the *annihilatio mundi*. On the other hand, the expectation of the imminent Second Coming lost its intensity. At the beginning of the Thirty Years War, apocalyptic expectations had taken on a virtually explosive character. Judgement Day appeared to be very near indeed. In the course of the war, probably already in the 1630s, however, the intensity of expectations of the Second Coming of Christ ebbed again in Germany.[80] The prophesied struggle between the two churches had not led to the victory of the 'true church', and the Antichrist had not been destroyed by the breath of Christ. Henceforth, apocalyptic expectations played a role mainly in separatist groupings. Such groups, however, awaited less the Last Judgement than the advent of the Millennium.[81] The consciousness of the immediately impending Day of Judgement and the eternal kingdom of God generally began to disappear.[82] The expectation of the imminent Second Coming exhausted itself and become obsolete to a certain extent through the repeated disappointment of predictions.[83] It also seems probable that the Thirty Years War, which even contemporaries saw as exceeding any previous experiences of catastrophe,[84] left people unable to imagine 'concrete

[78] Korn 1957: 21, 24, 107.

[79] Cf. Wintzer 1979: 533.

[80] Barnes 1988: 249ff.

[81] Cf. Wallmann 1995: 390–421.

[82] Kunz 1980: 58.

[83] See Kaufmann 1999: 74; Schneider 1999: 208, n. 88; Koselleck 2000: 24.

[84] See Medick and Krusenstjern 1999: 28ff.

utopias'[85] such as the vision of a new heaven and a new earth[86] or of a chiliastically tinged renewal of society as a whole[87] – such as was apparently significantly more widespread among the educated in England than in Germany, even after the middle of the century.[88]

Dwindling expectations of the imminent end of the world, as well as an evident 'detachment' of Creation from eschatology more generally in favour of an individual eschatology, promoted an unequivocally naturalistic view of Nature. Increasingly disconnected from the all-encompassing salvific schemata, Nature became more readily perceptible in its diverse manifestations and functions and, at the same time, as a direct expression of divine love and care. The observation of nature shifted from an emphasis on ever greater spirituality to its 'unspiritual' materiality, its actual details and processes. Although Rist, rejecting Aristotelian natural philosophy, insisted not just on his own observations and experience, but also on not becoming 'stuck' on the visible surface of things, for him the things of nature did not fundamentally refer to something that lay behind their manifestations. Despite the allegorical descriptions he used and his undimmed enthusiasm for Paracelsus, he quite tellingly does not mention the latter's theory of signatures. Rist's providential interest was not directed at an all-encompassing unity behind things, neither at their allegorical and symbolic 'essence' nor at a universal order underlying all phenomena. Trusting in God's omnipresent care, which extended to even the smallest natural objects and processes, he felt assured of God's nearness in the variety and the individual phenomena of nature.

Friedrich Christian Lesser (1692–1754)

In the course of the seventeenth century, Luther's theology of Creation, which had proceeded from actualistic impulses, was increasingly interpreted within orthodox Lutheran teaching in terms of a sapiential-ordinative doctrine of Creation (in the tradition of Philipp Melanchthon[89]). Representatives of orthodoxy sought to adhere to actualism by tying it more closely to the *ordo* of processes in nature. This

85 Wintzer 1979: 534.

86 It appears that in England eschatology may have continued to be regarded as an all-encompassing event of Creation, as we can see in the second part of Thomas Burnet's Telluris Theoria Sacra of 1689; see Harrison 1998: 142ff.

87 Among German Lutherans, apocalyptic notions appear to have had a different character and taken a different course than they did among English Protestants. While apocalyptic expectations in England increased massively in the 1640s, that is, at the time of the Civil War, they were already waning in significance in Germany. On the one hand, chiliastic ideas had a more widespread influence in England because of their stronger entanglement in denominational politics, and, on the other, they appear to have played a more important role in the thought of educated people and scholars than they did in Germany. The possible influence of the emigration of German chiliasts such as Johann Amos Comenius, who became influential in England, remains to be studied more closely. On eschatological thinking in England, see among others Greyerz 1999: 172ff.; Greyerz 2001; Webster 1982: 48ff.

88 For more detail see Trepp (in press).

89 Kusukawa 1995.

produced the concept of the *providentia ordinatia* in the shape of the *concursus*, which proceeded as an at once steady and actual divine influence on the events of Creation.[90] The concern with eschatological concepts also retreated firmly into the background in the face of a concentration on comprehensible, God-given regular functional contexts in Creation. What mattered was no longer when and how God had decided upon the end of the world. It was important instead to recognize how meaningfully and appropriately the omnipotent and omniscient Creator had set up the world. The question that exercised the minds of educated people was not when evil would gain the upper hand in the world, but what meaning evil might have in the 'best of all possible worlds'. In a certain sense, the question of theodicy replaced eschatological interpretations of nature. These primarily ordinative notions of providence and their corresponding interpretations of nature were addressed above all in the physico-theological movement, which, in its strict definition, spread from England in the late seventeenth century and became a mass phenomenon in Europe around the mid-eighteenth century.[91] Physico-theological literature was particularly widespread in Protestant countries, although its significance in Catholic regions was probably greater than has hitherto been recognized.[92]

The advent of works of natural theology as a sort of mass literature in Germany was accompanied by the beginnings of a definite stabilization of social conditions. Armed conflicts did not end, but were more limited, the Ottoman expansion in the East was halted altogether, climatic conditions began to be normalized, and the witch craze disappeared along with apocalyptic visions and fears. Apocalyptic expectations reached a high point towards the end of the seventeenth century in certain Pietist groupings, whose members however did not expect the absolute destruction of the world but rather the dawn of God's kingdom on earth. Nature was increasingly detached from an orientation towards its fulfilment in the Last Days. In its tangible stability and calculability, human life was, similarly, no longer understood as a transitional phase and preparation for 'actual' life in the hereafter. The intentions of the physico-theologians and their model of nature corresponded to just this experience. Using every conceivable natural object, they sought to convey a single message: that the observation of nature in its wondrous beauty, order and suitableness revealed the omnipotence, greatness and benevolence of the Creator. Physico-theological authors repeatedly emphasized the regularity and functionality in particular with which God in his wisdom had guaranteed the stability of the creaturely world for the use of humankind. Especially in the early days, physico-theologians stressed the functioning of individual natural processes in the cycle of nature as a whole, as in the *Pyrotheologie* or the *Hydrotheologie* of the 'founder' of German physico-theology, the Hamburg polymath Johann Albert Fabricius, published in 1732 and 1734, respectively.

---

[90] Bernhardt 1999: 125ff.,148ff., 187f. For the discussion of contiguous concepts of order, see Wilson (Chapter 1).

[91] On physico-theology, see among others Brooke and Cantor 1998: 141ff.; Wilson 1995: 176ff.; Krafft 1999: 75ff.; Krolzig 1988; Stebbins 1980.

[92] Toellner 1982: 76.

Later physico-theological writings came increasingly to focus on particular natural objects.[93] God's (omnipresent) omnipotence, wisdom and benevolence could be demonstrated using even the smallest and most specific things, that is, particular plants, animals and minerals. To this extent, physico-theology also provided the impetus for a detailed observation and study of nature. In 1724, Friedrich Merz developed a rana-theology, in which he sought to deduce God's omnipotent and benevolent providence from the characteristics and usefulness of frogs and tadpoles. In a similar manner, Ernst-Ludwig Rathlef formulated an acrido-theology in 1748/50, in which he examined locusts, just as Adolf Gottlieb Schirach glorified bees as God's creatures in his melitto-theology of 1767. One of the most prominent proponents of this specialized form of physico-theology was Friedrich Christian Lesser (1692–1754), a pastor in what was then the free imperial city of Nordhausen in the Harz region. Like the other theologians treated here, he was not an orthodox Lutheran, but adhered to moderate Pietist ideas. According to his biographer, he went to Halle to study medicine, but once there was encouraged by August Hermann Francke to take up theological studies.[94] Apart from theology he also attended lectures in physics and visited natural history collections. About twenty years after taking up residence as pastor in Nordhausen and beginning his own naturalist observations and research, which he pursued particularly in the mines and caves of the Harz Mountains, he began to publish his findings. His *Lithotheologie, Das ist: Natürliche Historie und geistliche Betrachtung derer Steine* (Lithotheology, That is, A Natural History and Spiritual Consideration of Stones)[95] appeared in 1735, followed in 1738 by his *Insecto-Theologia* and in 1744 by his *Testaceotheologie*, which was devoted to crustaceans. With unflagging enthusiasm and a rather pedantic pleasure in minute details he sought to collect, study, order and describe the most diverse natural objects. That his work in physico-theology was acknowledged during his lifetime may be inferred not just from the multiple editions and translations of his work[96] but also from his membership of both the Academia Naturae Curiosorum (Leopoldina) and the Academy of Sciences in Berlin.

According to Lesser, knowledge of the natural world was not merely permitted to the clergy but a veritable religious duty: Nature was 'a divine Book, which we should read with industry', and a 'Catechism that teaches us the first letters of a knowledge of God'.[97] He believed it to be a particular duty of clergymen 'to acquire a thorough knowledge of other sciences, particularly the natural sciences'. In keeping with orthodox thought, he distinguished sharply between nature and grace.[98] From a soteriological standpoint, the Holy Scripture or revealed word of grace sufficed. A knowledge of nature had more the character of a preparatory pedagogical attempt to

93 On diversity within the genre, see Brooke and Cantor 1998: 179f.

94 Goetten 1736: II, 546–555. The contribution is based on a short version of the curriculum vitae which Lesser composed on the occasion of his acceptance into the Leopoldina in 1735.

95 Lesser 1735.

96 Lesser's *Insectotheologie* (1738) was translated into French and English.

97 Lesser 1735: Vorrede X.

98 Autobiography of 1735, printed in Lesser 1992: 45.

know God. At the same time, Lesser considered the study of the Book of Nature to be indispensable for attaining a proper understanding of Holy Scripture and a perfect knowledge of God.[99] He supplemented his argument regarding the knowledge of God with a further, apologetic one:[100] only by familiarity with nature and its 'common laws' could clergymen confront 'atheistic scoffers' and credibly explain the 'wonders that occur so frequently in the Holy Scriptures'.[101]

The basic structure of his model of nature is an order resting on 'natural causes' and 'universal laws', instituted by God as its wise 'architect'.[102] Nothing in nature occurred without a reason. Everything had its place and its 'excellent use' within a fundamental functional context, which guaranteed the stability of Creation. The author and guarantor of this harmonious order is God. He has 'his hand in it, albeit not directly, but indirectly through the laws that he has dictated to nature thereby'.[103] Lesser was not, however, trying to defend the God of the Deists, whose nature functioned according to a perfect 'mechanism'[104] requiring no help whatsoever from God. On the contrary, he was anxious to combat this model of providence and nature, which he primarily associated with Descartes. For 'GOD is no mere spectator in nature, who allows everything simply to take its course; rather, his providence very frequently expresses itself in remedies, and restores the proper course of natural causes to their ultimate purpose, so that one can readily see the fingers of the Almighty [at work]'.

God controls the world not directly, in unpredictable and spontaneous expressions of his will, in 'divine decrees' (*Schickungen*) as Rist put it, but rather indirectly, 'through the order of a causal nexus established by him and thus in universal regularity (*providentia ordinata*) and as a uniform influence on the general course of events in the world (*providentia universalis*)'.[105] God's sapiential-ordinative predestination occurs in his active intervention in natural processes. Typically for his time, Lesser wrote of a *concursus*, in which God effects his (actual) influence. He was certain 'that GOD concurs (*concurrire*) in all movements of natural things … Although the natural causes have their own communicated power to act; at the same time GOD nevertheless makes his own contribution to all of their movements'.[106] If one were, in contrast, to assume God's immediate action in nature, there would be a danger of equating God with nature.

> Thus some modern philosophers err in denying all efficacy to natural causes, and argue instead that they were effected by GOD alone … Among the Lutherans in particular the renowned Altdorf professor Johann Christoph Stormius has defended this opinion quite vigorously. However, it is suspect because one can easily arrive at the same view as the

[99] Lesser 1735: Vorrede XII.

[100] On the wider significance of the anti-atheism argument, see Brooke and Cantor 1998: 195ff.

[101] Ibid.: XIX.

[102] Ibid.: 206.

[103] Lesser 1735: 224.

[104] Ibid.: 234.

[105] Bernhardt 1999: 187.

[106] Lesser 1735: 234.

> atheistic Spinosa [*sic*], that GOD and matter at once, as inner causes, constitute the whole world, if one wished to say that GOD effects everything immediately, but matter behaves passively.[107]

In light of the admirable regularities in nature, instituted by God and in which he continually concurs (*concurriert*), a special explanation is required in order to demonstrate from nature God's free will and his fundamentally possible contingent action (on this, see also TREIBER). According to Lesser, one must distinguish between God's 'general and orderly concourse' and his 'specific direction', 'according to which he occasionally and exceptionally steers the natural causes to a particular effect'.[108] Were God, in contrast, to adhere constantly to his 'orderly course', his promises as well as his threats in the Scriptures would be in vain. Thus God hinders the usual course of nature, curtailing its effects in order to punish humankind, or assists nature in order to increase its powers, as in the fruitful years which God sends humanity 'as a particular bounty'.[109] Thunder in particular is deployed by God according to his intentions to the good of the faithful and the detriment of the godless. It, too, can be used to illuminate God's omnipotence, justness and benevolence. For like everything else in nature, thunder brings humankind far more benefits than damage.[110]

In the conviction that everything, even the smallest natural phenomenon, was essential for the steady and harmonious course of nature, like 'patching-stones in a wall',[111] the physico-theologians were interested in even the most paltry and unassuming natural objects. Some scholars have already noted an increasing tendency to demonstrate God's ever-present omnipotence, wisdom and benevolence from the small and the specific, which can be observed above all among German or German-speaking Protestants.[112] If this observation is accurate, it seems likely that Lutheran *Providentia*, which saw divine *procuratio* above all in God's constant presence in Creation, turned its attention to both the varied and the smallest manifestations of divine Providence, as was already evident in Johann Rist's interest in nature in the mid-seventeenth century. (KUSUKAWA, however, regards the Protestant orientation towards divine Providence as the reason for a relatively great emphasis on the regularity of nature.)

What interested Lesser was not the hidden, the unusual and secret, but the visible, the familiar and the everyday.[113] His objective was to look at these phenomena in a new light. For the things that people 'see before their eyes daily, and which seem too small to them, or whose usefulness is not immediately obvious' to them, are all too often passed over with 'culpable inattention'.[114] In even the tiniest living creatures, the visible points to the invisible, in its facticity and not its allegorical significance.

---

[107] Lesser 1735: 228f.

[108] Ibid.: 235.

[109] Ibid.: 238.

[110] Ibid.: 248.

[111] Ibid.: 126.

[112] Brooke 1991: 197; Krafft 1999: 83. A different explanation is suggested in Wilson 1995: 191ff.

[113] Cf. Stebbins 1980: 183ff.

[114] Lesser 1740: Introduction, 1.

For even the insects 'which one can scarcely detect without a magnifying glass, endowed with their attendant joints, skin, muscles, parts, tendons and nerves, which do not exist without reason, and are not formed as they are by accident, in which each minute particle has a function, refer as admirable, scarcely comprehensible works of art to God's eternal power and wisdom'.[115] Through their intense interest in small things, however, Lesser and other physico-theologians also drew the invisible into the realm of the visible. 'It is certain that this splendid invention of the magnifying glass [as the third eye] has led to the discovery of many things, and has introduced us, as it were, to a new world of creatures.'[116] Intensive use of the microscope or telescope, including by clergymen, contributed to the gradually waning significance of the metaphysical dimensions of nature and, ultimately, of the 'Book of Nature'. Nature as the world of the visible and of matter, in contrast, gained in depth and complexity as well as self-contained functionality and stability.

[115] Lesser 1740: 11, 39ff.,58; see more generally Toellner 1982: 78.

[116] Ibid.: 21.

Chapter 9

Natural Law and Celestial Regularities from Copernicus to Kepler

Gerd Graßhoff

Copernican Laws

Copernicus lays out the essential assumptions of his astronomy in chapter four of the first book of *De Revolutionibus*. In the tradition of Ptolemy's astronomy, Copernicus uses a superposition of rotating circles and epicycles to describe the apparent motions of the planets. He justifies these geometrical assumptions by the single statement:

> We must acknowledge, nevertheless, that their motions are circular or composed of several circles, because these nonuniformities recur regularly according to a constant law.[1]

In Latin:

> Fateri nihilominus oportet circulares esse motus, vel ex pluribus circulis compositos, eo quod inaequalitates huiusmodi certa lege, statisque observant restitutionibus.[2]

This is not the only occasion that Copernicus refers to laws. In a short treatise entitled *Commentariolus* which was composed and sent to friends thirty years before the publication of *De Revolutionibus*, Copernicus argues that a specific property of the planetary orbit bears true testimony of a law of motion:

> The same reasoning must be employed also with the other motions of the heavenly bodies, because their apsides, which are likewise fixed in the firmament, with their true testimony make manifest the laws of the motions as well as heaven itself.[3]

For Copernicus, laws imply truth, unlike hypotheses, which can be either true or false. Laws exist even though one might not fully understand them:

> But even though the law involved is not yet sufficiently understood, it is less surprising that all these phenomena can occur on account of the earth's motion.[4]

---

1 Copernicus 1984: 11.

2 Ibid.: 10.

3 Rosen's translation in Copernicus 1985: 84: 'Eadem ratio in aliis etiam motibus siderum habenda est, quod absides eorum et statae sub firmamento motuum leges docent, ac coelum ipsum veraci testimonio.'

4 Rosen's translation, with the exception of 'law' in place of his 'principle' for 'lex'.

The last quotation and the argumentation in chapter four of book I imply a sort of causal reasoning related to laws of nature, since they bring order to the succession of heavenly events. Copernicus uses the term 'law' with reference to specific laws in asserting that the motions of the outer planets follow a different law from those of the inner planets, hence he refers to a different parametrization of a geometrical, epicyclic model of motion.[5]

In the following it will be argued that the introduction of natural laws into astronomy is closely linked with the Copernican revolution and the need to provide a criterion for the differentiation between empirically equivalent astronomical theories. Copernicus' notion of law comes from the early medieval reception of Latin writers on astronomy.

Roots of the Copernican Achievement

Ptolemy's Almagest *and Arabic variations*

Planetary astronomy that could derive positions of the planets by geometrical means developed quite late, in the first century AD with the work of Ptolemy. His *Almagest* reached Europe even later, by the middle of the twelfth century, but technical mastery was only achieved from the fifteenth century on. Ptolemy's models needed to be modified to accommodate changes in the astronomical configurations more than a thousand years after they were constructed. These modifications were cautiously introduced by Islamic astronomers and then slowly transmitted to Europe. Quantitatively they were successful. Planetary positions could be predicted with fair precision by geometrical models. Their theorems were called hypotheses – Ptolemy never referred to them as laws.

Medieval Latin Astronomy[6]

There is another, largely neglected astronomical tradition of importance for both the Copernican revolution and the introduction of the concept of law into astronomy. Throughout three distinct periods, between c. 800 and c. 1600, European astronomers were concerned with planetary motion. This first developed in the ninth century in the course of studying ancient Latin texts on cosmology and astronomy. Beyond the works of Cassiodorus, Isidore, and Bede, none of which either gave adequate guidance for a coherent understanding of planetary astronomy or presented a useful picture of the celestial sphere without supplementary oral instruction, only six Roman Latin texts provided essential knowledge. The descriptions of the celestial sphere and the constellations appeared in Aratus' *Phaenomena*, as translated by Germanicus (and Cicero and Avienus), and in Hyginus' *Astronomia*. The foundations of planetary

5 'Habet enim quisque duos epicyclos, quorum alter alterum defert, propemodum sicut in Luna dictum est, set lege diversa' (Copernicus 1990: 20). Cf. Swerdlow's translation: 'Now each sphere has two epicycles, one of which carries the other in almost the same way as was explained about the moon but by a different rule' (Copernicus 1973: 465).

6 This section reflects the findings of Eastwood and Graßhoff 2003.

astronomy came to Carolingian scholars in Pliny's *Historia naturalis*, Macrobius' *Commentarii in somnium Scipionis*, Martianus Capella's *De nuptiis Philologiae et Mercurii* (book VIII), and Calcidius' *In Timaeum commentarius*. This second group of four works is where we find descriptions of planetary motion.

Written elaborations on astronomy do not appear in this first period as independent texts. However, the history of astronomy has widely neglected the fact that astronomical thought manifested itself in a different form, namely in glosses and diagrams. The medieval scribe used these means of expression to clarify his thoughts and develop astronomical models to explain obscurities in his texts. They appeared first in the margins and were summarized at the end of the text. Finally, complete cosmological images were produced of an entirely different composition from the ones in the much more elaborate astronomical treatises in antiquity. In the ninth century, a group of ten astronomical diagrams was assembled and transmitted as an appendix to the astronomical book of Capella's *De nuptiis*, usually appearing at the very end of the final book, along with similar groups of diagrams for each of the other Capellan books on the quadrivium.

Giving no clue about his source, Martianus Capella went against both Pliny and Macrobius in asserting that the two inner planets circled around the sun rather than around the earth as did the moon, the sun, and the three outer planets. His first statement of this pattern of planetary motion read: 'Along with the Sun and the Moon three other planets circle around the orb of Earth, while Venus and Mercury do not go around Earth.'[7]

The medieval attempt to clarify such a bold statement is best summarized in Figure 1. Here the oval representation of earth is eccentric. The sun is more or less at the centre of the cosmos and Mercury and Venus circle around the sun. Such diagrams, used to represent different phenomena and aspects of planetary motion, persisted as long as they were found useful in teaching to expose questions, or propose theoretical positions. The history of this tradition of planetary diagrams indicates a constant interest in the qualitative explanation of major astronomical phenomena and a coexistence of both qualitative and quantitative planetary theory after the introduction of the Greco-Arabic mathematical tradition of planetary astronomy in twelfth-century Europe. In the sixteenth century the same qualitative tradition continued as a source of approaches to new phenomena and problems. While the Capellan tradition is important in transporting the idea of circumsolar motion, Martianus Capella does not mention 'laws' in his astronomical exposition. This is the case with Pliny.

When we look at the development of astronomical study at schools of the twelfth and thirteenth centuries, many peculiarities emerge. While the translations of Ptolemy's *Almagest* from the Greek in 1160 and from the Arabic by 1175 ought to have set a completely new standard for planetary theory, evidently this standard was not used that soon in schools. At the University of Paris in the first half of the thirteenth century the standard text required for student preparation in the liberal art of astronomy was that of Martianus Capella.

---

[7] Martianus Capella 1983: (193), 323.21–22 (VIII, 854).

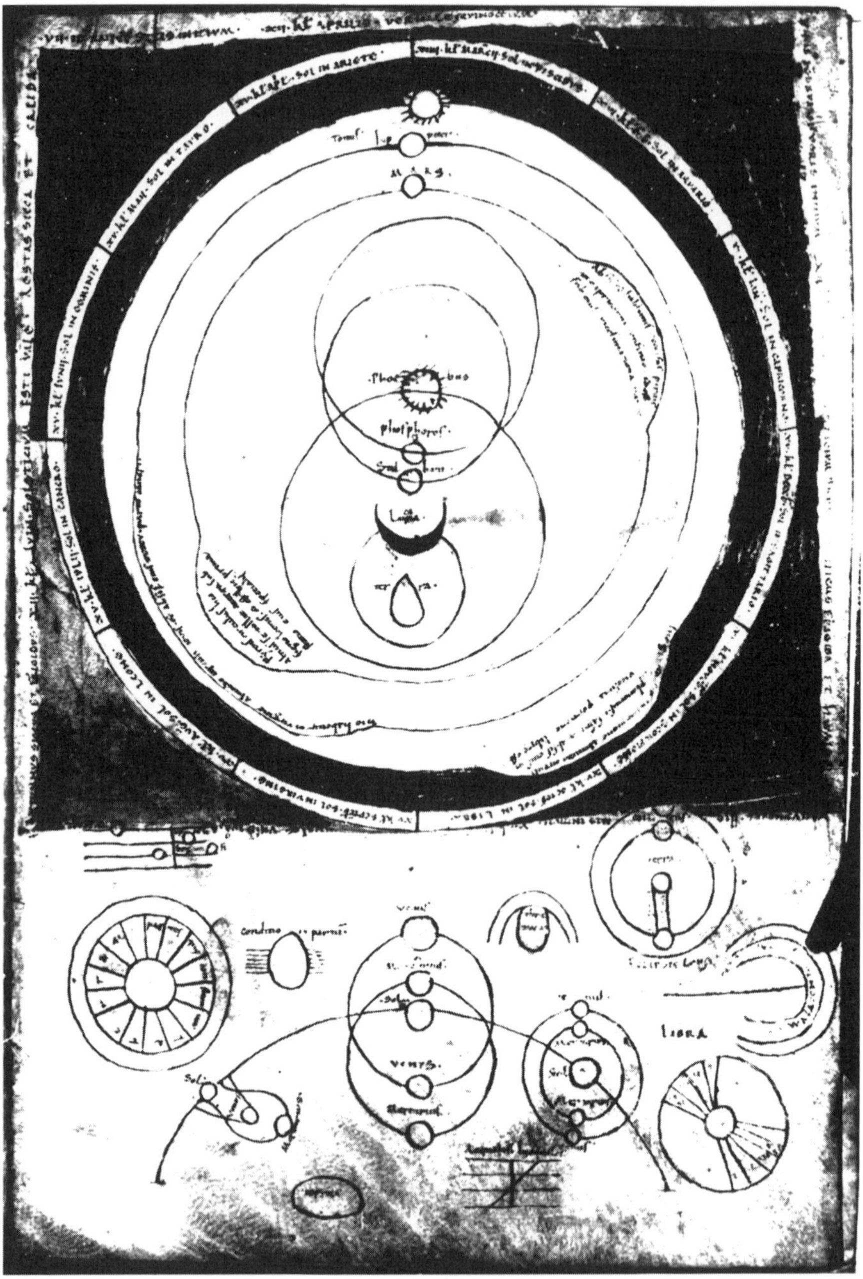

Figure 1 Firenze Biblioteca Laurenziana ms. San Marco 190, f.102r (c. A.D. 1000): constructed planetary model. Reproduced by permission of the Ministero per i Beni e le Attività Culturali. Further reproduction is prohibited.

Merging of Traditions in the Sixteenth Century

Medieval Latin qualitative astronomy and classical Greek mathematical astronomy coexisted independently from each other in the world of scholarly learning throughout the fifteenth and sixteenth centuries. In the history of astronomy the development of theory is typically described as a linear succession from Ptolemaic astronomy, with intermediaries in Arabic astronomy up to Copernicus' heliocentric revolution and Kepler's final abolition of epicyclic models. Contrary to this view, it will be argued that only a synthesis of both astronomical traditions posed the questions leading to Copernicus' heliocentric cosmology. Three theoretical elements come together as the basis of the new mathematical astronomy:

(a) *Geometry as a deductive means* Ptolemaic astronomy is geometrical at its core, perfect for computational purposes. The qualitative medieval tradition lacked any computational possibilities, which made it impossible to derive even the simplest positional information about the celestial bodies. Yet this tradition was rich enough to supply the two further essential elements for Ptolemaic astronomy.

(b) *Explanatory requirement* Pliny required that astronomy should *causally explain* the qualitative astronomical phenomena.

(c) *Specific limits of a circumsolar model* Capella restricts only the two inner planets to circumsolar motion.

The combination of these elements requires three significant changes to be made to both traditions:

1. The inclusion of element (a) into qualitative astronomy requires a strict geometrical reinterpretation of astronomical models. Only geometrically well-defined circles are superimposed to describe planetary motion by their combined rotations about a geometrically defined centre. Capellan diagrams were seen from a stricter geometrical viewpoint, which led to a significant change in the understanding of Capellan astronomy in the sixteenth century.
2. The geometrical interpretation of element (b) specifies that explanations of qualitative astronomical phenomena are provided only if qualitative phenomena can be deduced geometrically from a model.
3. Capellan circumsolar motion of the inner planets provides a model for the explanation of a number of qualitative phenomena, most notably the fact that the inner planets never exceed a certain angular distance from the sun (bounded elongation). These three elements are the basis from which Copernicus undertook his new theoretical enterprise. They appear frequently in *De Revolutionibus*.[8]

[8] Especially in book I there are numerous implicit references to Pliny. Copernicus' own annotated copy of Pliny's *Natural History* is still preserved and can be consulted in the library of Uppsala University. The apparatus of the critical edition identifies some but not all references to Pliny by Copernicus.

Tracing Influences: Capella and Pliny in Copernicus

There are significant traces of such an influence on Copernicus' major work. As a mathematical astronomer Copernicus had to base the geometry of his astronomy on Ptolemy's models. At the time, it was common knowledge that one could transfer such models into empirically equivalent heliocentric models. To do so, Copernicus referred to a reason which he expressed in different ways and by various metaphors: only a heliocentric cosmology could causally explain the bounded elongation of the inner planets – that is, the very fact that Mercury and Venus always move in proximity to the sun. In a very prominent place, in book I, chapter X of *De Revolutionibus*, Copernicus gives credit to Martianus Capella for having shown him the right way to understand the motion of the planets. Capella and other Latin authors had Mercury and Venus circle the sun. Their reason for doing so was, according to Copernicus:

> Existimant enim, quod Venus et Mercurius circumcurrant Solem in medio existentem, et eam causam illo non ulterius digredi putant, quam suorum convexitas orbium patiatur, quoniam terram non ambiunt ut ceteri, sed absidas conversas habent.[9]

Rosen translates this as:

> This is the reason, in their opinion, why these planets diverge no farther from the sun than is permitted by the curvature of their revolutions. For they do not encircle the earth, like the other planets, but 'have opposite circles'.[10]

Rosen's translation is unintelligible. There is no such thing as a 'curvature of ... revolutions'. He ignores the historical background to which Copernicus alludes. Copernicus' explanation for why the inner planets cannot deviate from the sun more than the bounded elongation employs three unusual Latin phrases. They also reveal Copernicus' sources.

1. In contradiction to Rosen's translation, '*suorum convexitas orbium*' states 'the convexity of their orbits', an expression that goes back to Pliny.[11] It is an expression describing the geometrical properties of the orbits as drawn *in a diagram*. The closed orbit of each of the inner planets appears convex from the position of the earth, outside their planetary circles about the sun. On the other hand, the orbits of the outer planets appear concave from the earth, which is inside their circles. Such geometrical premises lead to a simple geometrical proof for the bounded elongation of the inner planets (that they cannot exceed a certain angular distance from the sun): convex orbits exclude the planets' movement in opposition to the sun, since 'convex orbits' always circle about the sun but cannot ever circle about the earth.
2. The phrase '*terram non ambiunt*' is a specific expression from Martianus Capella meaning that the inner planets do not move around the earth.

---

9 Copernicus 1984: 19.

10 Copernicus 1992: 20.

11 Pliny 1938: book II.

3. Finally, '*absidas conversas*' is an expression of special importance. Rosen's translation as 'opposite circles' obscures a complicated background. The expression '*absidas conversas*' does not occur in Capella's text but very prominently in Pliny's *Natural History*, where it is used so unclearly that it elicits a number of unhelpful glosses from medieval commentators. Yet Pliny has nothing to say about a heliocentric motion of the inner planets. He simply repeatedly requires an explanation for their maximum elongation from the sun without providing a geometrical model for such an explanation. Capellan diagrams in their geometrical reinterpretation do add such models.

Copernicus responds to the Plinian demand for qualitative explanation with geometry as its solution. He finds the geometrical solution in Capellan *diagrams*. In the diagram of the three versions for the motion of the inner planets, Pliny's name is attached to a circumsolar motion. By means of the diagram Copernicus could link Pliny's requirement of a causal explanation with a *geometrical* argument that derives the fact of bounded elongation of the inner planets. Pliny could then be cited authoritatively for circumsolar motion. In an argumentative style typical of *De Revolutionibus*, Copernicus uses the rhetorical means of citing known phrases from Latin authorities to perform the synthesis of explanatory requirement and circumsolar motion. The sequence of subjects in *De Revolutionibus* follows that of Ptolemy's *Almagest*. He opens the book with a discussion of whether the heavens are a sphere. While in the *Almagest* Ptolemy carefully develops geometrical arguments for a *rotating spherical* universe and tests his conclusions on a whole range of observational phenomena, Copernicus does nothing of the sort.[12] Instead of recounting observational data and providing geometrical descriptions, he rephrases Pliny as grounds for the view that the universe is spherical.[13] Copernicus could have seen the Capellan diagram while studying astronomy in Italy, in the Florentine manuscript copy of Figure 1 or one of the many triple-version diagrams in circulation. There the connection between Pliny and circumsolar motion is explicit.

Pliny's particular role in the heliocentric transformation is visible in Rheticus' account of the Copernican achievements.[14] Rheticus was professor at the University of Wittenberg and in 1539 travelled to Frauenburg to learn from Copernicus himself about his new astronomy. His *Narratio prima* was the first published account of Copernicus' views. In one section Rheticus summarized the reasons for the preference for the Copernican model. When citing ancient authorities supporting Copernicus' innovation, Rheticus names Pliny and not Martianus Capella in the context of the motion of the inner planets. Rheticus and Copernicus must have talked about the subject, because the name Pliny is not mentioned in the corresponding passage in *De Revolutionibus*. Yet, Pliny does not describe the heliocentric motion of Mercury and Venus as an explanation for their bounded elongation. It is his demand for

---

[12] Copernicus cannot copy Ptolemy's argument since he views the stars as spatially static and all apparent motion as a result of the earth's rotation. Hence, Copernicus has no convincing argument for assuming a celestial sphere.

[13] Copernicus 1984: 7; Pliny 1938: II.2, II.65, 70; Ptolemy 1984: 38.

[14] Rheticus 1982.

such a causal explanation that intrigued both Copernicus and Rheticus in referring to Pliny's work. The methodological preference in the new theory for additional explanatory content is the sole reason behind Copernicus introducing a heliocentric mathematical astronomy. The Copernican theory has no other advantage over its Ptolemaic competitor. It is neither empirically more accurate, nor more economical in its use of circles in the construction of the models.

A few lines after speaking of *absidas conversas*, Pliny declares that astronomy must seek laws in order to explain the peculiar behavior of the inner planets. Only then have we understood why we never observe Venus and Mercury, for example, opposite to the sun. And it is this very reason that let Copernicus execute a standard set of geometrical operations which ultimately ended in the construction of a heliocentric cosmology.

Transforming Geometrical Models into Explanatory Models with Laws

In the Ptolemaic system the planets move on epicycles about the earth (Fig. 2). The earth O is eccentric to the centre C of the large circle, the deferent, on which the epicycle moves with the planet P uniformly in relation to the equant point E. Such models successfully describe the motion of the planets in the zodiac, in particular:

1. The non-uniform velocity of the planets in their orbit about the sun (first anomaly). From a modern perspective this is due to the elliptic shape of the orbit. The epicyclic model accounts for this variation of speed largely by (a) the eccentric position of the earth at O and (b) the introduction of the equant in respect to which the planet moves uniformly on its epicycle.
2. The retrograde motion is a perspectival effect of the terrestrial motion (second anomaly) at opposition to and in conjunction with the sun. It can be modelled by adding the motion of the planet on an epicycle.

Copernicus began his astronomical work by studying Regiomontanus' *Epitome*, in which the geometrical properties of Ptolemy's models are fully explored. For a mathematically trained astronomer it was standard procedure to transform models into equivalent geometries which describe the same apparent motions of the planets. They could be transformed in such a fashion that the planets would move around the sun instead of the earth. This was well known to the astronomers of Copernicus' time. But why should anyone do so, especially since Aristotelian physics would pose severe difficulties in explaining spatial motion on a moving earth? Several oft-cited reasons do not explain Copernicus' preference for the heliocentric theory. Foremost among such reasons are those referring to the equant and to empirical adequacy:

1. It is true that Copernicus was uncomfortable with Ptolemy's use of the equant to model the non-uniform motion of the planets, but this did not provide a reason for a heliocentric transformation. His substitution of additional epicycles for the equant was indifferent to either heliocentric or geocentric arrangement.
2. The demonstrated equivalence of heliocentric and geocentric models with respect to the apparent planetary motion also excludes empirical adequacy

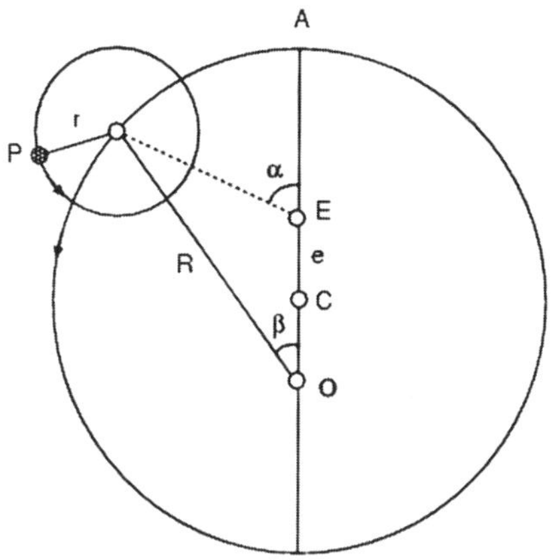

Figure 2 Ptolemy's epicyclic model of planetary motion in ecliptical longitudes.

> as a criterion to decide between the two cosmologies. For any heliocentric model Copernicus might compose, there would always be a geocentric version producing the same apparent motions of the planets.

If neither empirical adequacy nor an apparent violation, via the equant, of Aristotle's principle of uniform motion led Copernicus to design a heliocentric planetary theory, what else could have guided him? Early documents confirm that Copernicus initially worked on transforming Ptolemaic models for the inner planets into their equivalent heliocentric counterparts.[15] Capellan diagrams set the pattern. Their sole advantage was to provide explanations with reference to laws, as required by Pliny, for a number of qualitative cosmological properties. Both models are compared in Figure 3, which is simplified in so far as the geometrical features required for the first anomaly are omitted.

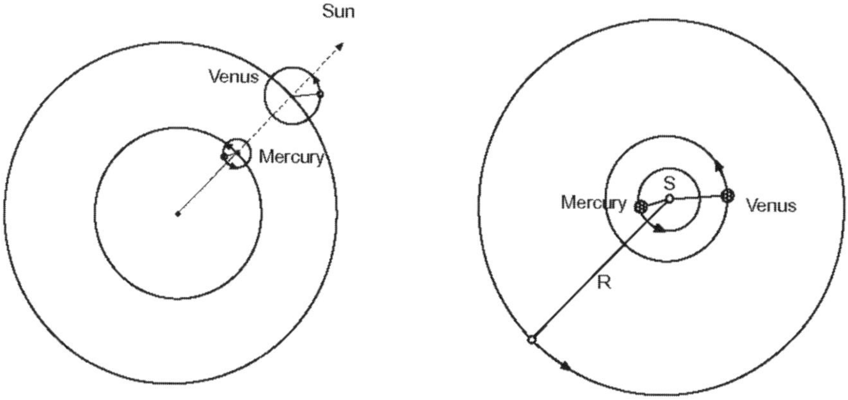

Figure 3 The two empirically equivalent models for the motion of the inner planets: Ptolemaic (left) and heliocentric (right).

[15] Cf. Swerdlow and Neugebauer 1984: 54ff.

The left arrangement is Ptolemaic with the orbits of Mercury and Venus arranged within the circles of the sun. The empirically equivalent model of heliocentric motion is shown on the right. It can be proven geometrically that both models produce the same observational data. Yet only the heliocentric model allows a geometrical proof for the bounded elongation of the inner planets. This is different in Ptolemy's model. His model requires, in addition to the geometrical arrangement, that the centre of the epicycles of Mercury, Venus and the sun lie on one line. The additional requirement is not enforced by geometry. This difference in construction is the sole reason for Copernicus' new cosmology.

Although the medieval tradition visualized Capellan circumsolar motion of the inner planets by a triad of orbital arrangements and identified Capella with the intersecting-circles model, Copernicus mentions neither of the other two arrangements by the Latin authors nor does he attribute intersecting circles to Capella. He silently attributes concentric circumsolar motion to Capella and the other Latin authors together. The medieval alternatives disappear. Laws now gain a specific meaning. They are true hypotheses shaped in geometrical form. Astronomically their shape is circular and a superposition of them explains planetary motion. Empirical conclusions can be derived from them by geometrical means.

Kepler's Continuation of the Copernican Programme

Kepler's close collaboration with his teacher and expert in the Copernican model, Michael Maestlin, while writing the *Mysterium cosmographicum*, is evident from Maestlin's active interest and assistance with the orbital calculations. In his third letter from Graz, Kepler informed Maestlin early on about the envisioned aims of the *Mysterium cosmographicum*[16] and mentioned three arguments in favour of Copernicanism, which he intended to – and eventually did – publish in the work:

> Then I present three reasons which move me to remain true to Copernicus. The first is of an astronomical nature; I confront the assertion that truth sometimes followed from falsehood, which was why it were possible that Copernicus departed from false presuppositions and nevertheless derived from this in an elegant way some truth. I contest this possibility. The second reason is of a physical nature. I undertake to show that from Nature's sources the full scope of the Copernican hypotheses may be proven correct far more than the contrary. The third reason concerns your 'Venus comet'.[17]

In Kepler's view, only geometrical demonstrations can deliver a physical proof as well as Maestlin's determination of the orbit of a comet in the proximity of Venus. Kepler's first argument insists that such proofs are only acceptable when they are based on true premises. The basic principles of an astronomical theory must be true if they are to deliver the causes of natural processes. Such 'first' principles or axioms would be good candidates for what Kepler understood by the word '*lex*'.

---

[16] Kepler promised in the preceding letter to send his work, did not finish in time, and therefore summarized its content for Maestlin.

[17] Kepler 1945: 34f., letter 23, 3 October 1595.

The causal explanation for the retrogressive motions of the planets replaces the heliocentric theory of planetary epicycles by a single circle along which the earth revolves around the sun. A close comparison of Kepler's description of the advantages of the Copernican theory with the advantages of his own theory in the *Mysterium cosmographicum* reveals a surprising parallel.

Unlike the Ptolemaic theory, the Copernican theory can explain the planetary motions, but:

> That is due to the fact that they [the advantages of Copernican theory] say nothing about the causes of the number, magnitude and times of the retrograde motions; they cannot explain why they coincide exactly with the mean position of the sun and the solar motion.[18]

In the first chapter of the *Mysterium cosmographicum*, Kepler defines the goals of his astronomical project as follows:

> At last, in 1595, I threw the full force of my intellectual faculties onto this subject, since I wanted to pass the time free from instruction well and as is proper to my office. There were three things, above all, whose causes I relentlessly examined for why they be such and not otherwise, namely the number, magnitude and motion of the orbits.[19]

Kepler had discovered new geometrical characteristics of the planetary orbits which derive even the number of planets, the size of their orbits and the velocities of the planets along their orbits. His discovery that the geometry of regular bodies explains astonishingly well the size and motions of the planetary orbits around the sun, moreover identifying their number with the number of regular bodies, was for Kepler progress in astronomical theory along the same methodological lines that Copernicus used in superseding Ptolemy's theory. Copernican theory can explain the second anomaly of the planets, the characteristics of the planetary system hitherto unexplained in the *Mysterium*: the number of planets as well as the existing sizes of the planetary orbits and velocities. No overdrawn inclination for Neo-Platonism is needed to lend plausibility to Kepler's astronomical programme for the *Mysterium*. Kepler was still unsure of his astronomical abilities and asked his teacher for support.

> You shall encounter assertions drawn from false principles, assertions lacking any principle. Here and there you shall find me at a loss for want of knowledge of the Copernican astronomy. You may smooth over, alter, strike out, criticize, caution: Howsoever you write me, any letter shall be most welcome to me.

Then Kepler posed physical assumptions about the conveyance of motion from the sun to the planets:

> Let us take the example of light. For light and motion are in any case connected with each other, from their source, as from their action; perhaps light is even the vehicle of motion. Now, in a small circle close to the Sun there is as much light as in a large one far away

[18] Translation from Kepler 1937b: 30.

[19] Ibid.: 20.

> from the Sun. Hence the light on the larger circle is rarer, on the tighter circle denser and stronger. This strength, however, is equally proportional to the circles or the distances. Now, if the conditions are the same in motion (and one cannot think of anything that would fit better), then it would follow that the distance would have a double effect on the reduction of the motion.[20]

This is a formulation of the *distance law*, which Kepler would subsequently implement. According to this principle Kepler calculated the size ratios from the orbital periods of the planets and relayed this to Maestlin in a table which contained his own values for the sizes of the Copernican epicyclic model. But small differences emerged:

> [These differences] do appear very large, but a certain regularity lies therein ... Yet I am still in an awkward position here. One remedy would be to add or substract a little from the mean distances in correction. If you think that this is permissible, we should then have the motions very exactly.[21]

A letter dated 1605 to a former assistant of Tycho, Longomontanus, illuminates Kepler's enthusiasm in tackling the problem of Mars. In this letter Kepler recapitulates the years elapsed since Tycho's death:

> I would now, however, like to give you an account of the use of my time, because You seem to wish it. In the year 1600, I spent most of the time from February until the beginning of May hoping and musing. You know that I had wagered that I would set right whatever was still unclear within eight days.[22]

This letter is extremely revealing. Kepler and Longomontanus were by no means friends. Tycho had removed his longtime assistant Longomontanus from the work on the Martian orbit when Kepler arrived in Prague. Tycho recognized Kepler's much greater abilities, and Longomontanus found himself demoted. After Tycho's death the tensions between Longomontanus and Kepler increased when Tycho's heirs felt cheated by Kepler of the observational data he had taken and used in his research. Longomontanus took the side of the heirs in this conflict. It was in this connection that Kepler wrote to Longomontanus, in order to secure the publication of *Astronomia nova* against the heirs' claims. Kepler's reminder in the first letter to Longomontanus about his wager of completing the theory of the motion of Mars within a week reveals much about his original plan. In view of Kepler's later arduous year-long struggles to find a correct theory for the motion of Mars, this wager is surprising. It certainly cannot be seen as a bet lightly made between friends. What made Kepler so sure that he could finish the work on the Martian orbit in such a short time after working on the *Mysterium cosmographicum*? There is only one plausible answer to this question: Kepler's original plan consisted in nothing other than repeating Maestlin's technique of determining parameters of the epicyclic constructions, only that he would use as a basis not the ephemerides of the Prutenic tables but the actual empirical data of Tycho's observations. Kepler would have still

---

20 Kepler 1945: 38.

21 Ibid.: 39.

22 Kepler 1995: 134f., letter 323.

had to reduce the observations to fit a parametrization of the models. Such a task could indeed have taken about a week to complete.

Scope of Possible Planetary Theories

These first steps reveal Kepler's way of working, which he adhered to throughout the whole period of his work on Martian theory. Few fundamental principles of the astronomical models determined Kepler's constructive latitude in his search for correct explanations of the motions of the planets. They are general, fundamental for his research and do not change throughout his work on the theory of Mars. On the other hand, they are specific enough to limit the scope of possible planetary models quite strongly. The basic type of the Keplerian planetary model has the following components:

- The number of forces working on the planetary orbit is two: the sun and the planet itself. Consequently: two circles describe the kinematic characteristics of this two-force system.
- The centre of the main circle is the location of the real sun as the source of a force that guides the planets around the sun.
- A second circle – the epicycle – represents the action of the second force originating from the planet.
- The velocities of the circular revolutions are variable, depending on the geometrical constellation and the interactions among the physical bodies.

The free parameters of the Keplerian model are thus: the eccentricity or size of the epicycle, the position of the aphelion, and the revolving motions of the free parameters of the basic type of his planetary model. Kepler's astronomical research on Martian theory benefited from the experiences he gained while working on planetary models for the *Mysterium*. Throughout his revolutionary work on the theory of Mars, which included his discovery of the elliptic shape of its orbit and what is now called Kepler's second law, his constructions always remained within the set framework of epicyclic models. Kepler was more clearly aware than Copernicus that many empirically equivalent models could be construed with different geometries. But according to his interpretation, only the true one upheld the underlying principles of motion – these principles describe *natural laws*. I will now briefly sketch the history of the discovery in order to expose the central function of natural laws in Kepler's astronomy.

The Quest for the Right Epicyclic Model

In 1595, right at the outset of his theoretical explorations, Kepler wrote to Maestlin as a fellow traveller, with evident confidence in his basic astronomical assumptions. He had good reasons for it. While performing the calculations for the *Mysterium* he had realized that the actual position of the sun should be chosen as the reference point for the circular orbits of the earth and the other planets. This was at odds with Copernicus, who had the planets revolve around a fictitious point near the sun. Tycho had missed this important detail. Kepler was able to recognize the (unfavourable) consequences of it for all the planetary theories. The mistaken choice of a mean solar position as the point of reference led to unnecessarily complicated geometrical constructions that could not be interpreted as the results of the motive virtues in nature.

After starting to work for Tycho Brahe in Prague, Kepler found that revising the theory of the planets was much more difficult than he had anticipated. By the end of 1601, although confident of ultimate triumph in his astronomical endeavours, he had still not found a suitable parametrization within the geometry of epicyclic theory. Along the way Kepler shed light on the fundamental constructive faults of the accepted planetary theories. It was important that the geometric models should reflect the actual virtues at work in the orbital motions of the planets:

> The inquiry took up these findings and found that the cause of the equant circle is of a purely physical nature but is manifested in geometric ratios. For, as any distance relates to another, so too does the time which the planet stays at the point at that distance relate to the time it stays at the point at the other distance.[23]

The last sentence in his letter, with which Kepler concludes his physical justification, states the distance law. This letter was written just a few months before his insight that no parametrization of an epicyclic model resulting in a circular orbit, no matter how good, is capable of correctly rendering the observed positions of Mars. The few modifications of his basic model involved redefining the point of reference as the actual position of the sun, revising the eccentricity and assigning a fixed spatial position for the planet's orbital plane. In the *Astronomia nova* Kepler reported on a few variations in the Martian orbit that he arrived at after changing the reduction of the empirical data.

An epicyclic theory produces a circular orbit when there is a particular rotation at constant angular velocity. By means of a complicated triangulation, Kepler realized that the Martian orbit was not circular in shape but depressed on both sides. But it was not enough for him simply to reassign a suitable shape for the orbit, such as with an ellipse, an oval, or whatever else one could think plausible. In comprehending Kepler's working method it is crucial to consider his continued attachment to epicyclic models. Only epicyclic models represented the planetary motions as effects of the acting virtues. A correct description of the orbital shapes was for Kepler an incomplete astronomical approach going scarcely beyond mere reproduction of the observational findings. It does not *explain* orbital motion. That is why Kepler did not abandon his model of superimposed circular motions but rather tried to adjust their rotations in such a way that the required orbital elongation would follow as a resultant motion of the epicyclic motions.

He arrived at the first solution, in the form of a resultant oval orbit, by applying simple physical concepts to possible causal interactions and their kinematic consequences on a rotating epicycle on which the planet Mars is set. Along a circular orbit the epicycle does not move continuously over time. So the only change that Kepler initially made was to replace the previous complex rotational motion of the epicycle with the assumption of a rotation at constant angular velocity. The resulting Martian orbit was oval in shape.

Now the real difficulties in calculating the position of Mars began. In constructing a circular orbit it is easy to position the planet on the epicycle as a function of the

[23] Kepler 1937a: 204.

mean anomaly. With an oval, it is quite another story. One cannot determine the rotational angle of the epicycle at the same time as its position along the large circle by direct construction. The solution must be found iteratively.

In search of this new procedure Kepler went down various extremely tedious paths. Recalcitrant calculation errors and methodologically inconsistent geometric preconditions were strewn along the way. Kepler never could be quite certain of his results and frequently repeated the calculations in the same way or thought up alternative procedures in order to recheck his work by numerical methods. The orbital shape was defined by the geometry of the epicyclic construction. That is how Kepler knew the planet's distance on its orbit as a function of the true anomaly. But Kepler did not know *when* the planet would reach this orbital point. For the motion along the orbital curve, Kepler returned to the principle that he had formulated in the *Mysterium* as a consequence of the Copernican hypothesis and had verified many times over while working on Martian theory: the velocity of a planet is inversely proportional to the true distance of the sun (*distance law*). Kepler applied this law to calculate and add together the times necessary for traversing short segments of the Martian orbit. The sum of these small partial times then yields the time at which the planet is situated at a given point on the orbit. In order to avoid calculational errors, the individual summed orbital segments have to be very small. This procedure is so laborious that Kepler thought up a clever alternative: instead of calculating the added times of the individual small orbital segments, he assumed that the dimensions of the covered area between the sun and Mars is directly proportional to the time required to traverse that arc of the orbit. Therefore Kepler just had to calculate the area covered in moving along the orbit to a given point on the oval and thereby immediately obtain the corresponding time (what is today called '*area law*'– Kepler never called it '*lex*').

Kepler himself was still not sure of the validity of the area theorem (to avoid the notion of 'law'). Upon rechecking his calculations discrepancies appeared again and again. He kept wondering whether they were attributable to calculational error or to oversimplifications arising from the use of the *area law*. No matter how Kepler varied his method and checked his calculations, small discrepancies from the observed values remained. The persistence of these small discrepancies transformed his doubts about the calculational method into doubts about the hitherto seemingly so secure hypothesis of a uniformly rotating epicycle driven by the intrinsic virtue of the planet. This hypothesis had to be wrong.

In the previously cited letter to Christian Longomontanus in response to his reproaches for using the Tychonic observations, Kepler reported on the various phases of his work on Martian theory:

> As concerns the tables for the equations, know that I spent the whole of last year, insofar as I was free from illness and worries, solely on calculating the orbital equations of Mars, and I am not ashamed to admit that I have not yet reached my goal. I have a hypothesis, postulated already four years ago, which delivers most accurately the positions of the planet on its orbit. However I do not like it because it is not physical but simply what one would describe as a hypothesis.[24]

[24] Kepler 1995: 135.

284 DE MOTIB. STELLÆ MARTIS

Cap. LVIII.

ſumus mutuari: idem per hanc etiam veriſſimam hypotheſin tentans, falſa methodo, rurſum de rerum ſumma trepidare cœpi. *In linea apſidum, centris* A. B. *ſcribantur æquales circuli* G D. H K. *Sitque* A B *eccentricitas circuli* G D. *Sit autem anomalia eccentri, ſeu numerus graduum ejus, arcus* G D *vel* H K, *per æquipollentiam capitis* III. *Centro igitur* K, *diaſtemate* K D, *quod ipſi* A B *ſit æquale, ſcribatur* L D F *epicyclus, qui ſecabit circulum* G D *in* D, *per æquipollentiam cap.* III. *Ducatur* A K, *& continuetur donec ſecet epicyclum in* L, *ut ſit* L D *arcus ſimilis anomaliæ eccentri* G D *vel* H K. *Et connectatur* B *cum* D. *Ex puncto vero* D *demittantur perpendiculares in* G A, L A, *quæ ſint* D C, D E. Quare per hactenus cap. LVI. demonſtrata, A E citra controverſiam erit juſta diſtantia ad hanc anomaliam eccentri, de qua quæritur, quantum temporis in ea ſit conſumptum. Cumque ejus arcus ſinus verſus G C, ſive poſt multiplicationem, L E ablatâ a G A, prodiderit diſtantiam A E juſtam: ex his indiciis perſuadebar, terminum ipſius A E alterum, quærendum eſſe non in D C linea, quod veriſſimum tamen erat, ſed in D B lineæ puncto I: ut ſi centro A, diaſtemate A E, ducerem arcum E I F, qui ſecet D B in I. Eſſet igitur A I ſecundum hanc perſuaſionem juſta diſtantia, ſitu & longitudine; & I A G anomalia vere coæquata. Manifeſtum eſt autem, quod E I F arcus ſecet D C lineam, loco ſuperiori ſcilicet in F. itaque anguli I A G & F A G differant quantitate I A F.

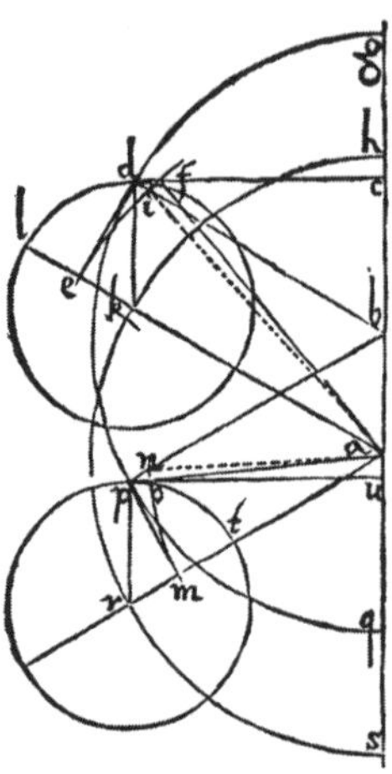

Figure 4 Facsimile of p. 284 of *Astronomia Nova*, chapter 58, where Kepler introduces the construction of the elliptical orbit by means of epicycles. The planet is located in point F, which Kepler puts on epicycle LDF.

Thus Kepler had already found the correct calculational methods for the orbit by 1601. He just lacked a *physical* explanation for the orbit or, to be more precise, its derivation from the *distance law*.

In reporting to Longomontanus that the cause was not yet ascertained, Kepler admitted that despite finding the correct orbital shape (such that he could correctly calculate all the positions of Mars by applying the *area law*), he had not yet succeeded in providing a geometrical construction of this orbital shape by means of an *epicyclic* model. The correlation between the motive virtues and their geometrical expression had not yet been found. Under enormous time pressure – the work had long since been announced to the emperor and money was getting short – Kepler had already started recapitulating his research for the future publication, as the continuation of the letter to Longomontanus reveals. He described exactly what geometrical steps he was taking to explain the newly found orbital shape:

> I have meanwhile assembled all my previous findings in 51 chapters. If I should die, I do know that all of these should be of great usefulness to someone wanting to build upon it. The main content is this: Mars performs on its own a deviation along the diameter of an epicycle. Furthermore it is pulled away by a virtue which extends from the sun into space. Both motions are irregular. The deviation is stronger or weaker, not just following a law dictated by one of the two circles, as for Copernicus, but both the circles themselves move faster or slower in accordance with the apparent increase or decrease in magnitude of the sun's diameter.[25]

The letter reveals that, despite having found the elliptic orbit, Kepler was still looking for an epicyclic construction in which the revolving speeds of the two defining circles were correctly coordinated. He did not even consider his discovery of the ellipse as so important. Kepler was speculating. With the oval hypothesis refuted, it was not so easy to find an epicycle guided by the period and revolving at a constant angular velocity. The rotational motion had to vary in order to produce a new resultant ellipse. But how? Kepler's letter continues with an enunciation of those parts of the physical basis that he believed secure:

> One thing is absolutely certain: A virtue emanates from the sun which affects the planets. The rest is still doubtful but one assumption after another takes me, step by step, closer to my goal. Now you are informed of my progress. Otherwise, perhaps no one else will see these investigations, if not through me personally.[26]

Kepler did *not* pick out an orbital form from among those that appeared to him to be physically permissible by conforming with the few empirically determined orbital points. A correct *causal* planetary theory must be able to derive such an orbit with the aid of epicyclic constructions, for it was only through such constructions that the kinematic consequences of the motive virtues of the sun and the planets were to be found. Kepler sought desperately for a solution. He had already had to submit a manuscript to the emperor in which the oval orbit was still given as the correct solution. On 5 March 1605, Kepler tried for the last time to draw his former teacher Michael Maestlin into the project. After describing the state of his research he anxiously asked again whether it weren't possible to collaborate again. But again, there was no response from Maestlin. In the few weeks that followed Kepler eventually wrung out a solution – better, something that looked like a solution.

It was ultimately accepted, without verification against the observations, for physical reasons. Kepler published the construction in the *Astronomia nova* (see Fig. 4). From point D on the epicycle a perpendicular is drawn on the extension of the distance SN, and on this line point F is constructed which represents the position of the planet. If you assemble the points F for the times of one revolution, an ellipse results as an orbit. Victory at last, so it seems!

---

[25] Kepler 1995: 141.

[26] Ibid: 141.

Four theses sum up the findings so far:

1st thesis *What is known as Kepler's first law does not, in Kepler's view, have a lawlike character because it offers no connection between the causes of motion and the resulting components of motion. It only affects the shape of the orbit, which Kepler could already calculate empirically correctly in 1601.*

2nd thesis *The so-called second law, the area theorem, was regarded by Kepler only as a tool with which the motions of the planets could be calculated much more efficiently than by direct application of the distance law. Through lengthy approximations Kepler calculated that the area theorem approximates very well an iteration of the individual steps of the motion. But he was not sure whether the area theorem could be derived strictly from the distance law.*

3rd thesis *The distance law is, strictly speaking, false, which Kepler did not know. Strictly speaking, it is only valid for two orbital points; for the rest of the motion, however, it is valid to a good approximation.*

Had Kepler thus arrived at the goal he had been desperately seeking since the spring of 1605, namely a strict derivation of the orbital motions from a natural law, the *distance law*? The elliptic orbit results from the intersecting point of the perpendicular from D to the line of apsides (line DC) at point F. But that point does not lie on an epicycle! Nevertheless, Kepler described point F as if it lay on the epicycle LDF ('*scribatur LDF epicyclus*'). According to this description, Kepler made his reader falsely to believe that point F lies on the epicycle.

4th thesis *Owing to this small gap between the construction point F and the epicycle, the strict derivation has failed. The elliptic orbit results only approximately from the two compounded circular motions which are superimposed upon each other according to the distance law. Kepler ignored this small interval and passed over it in his work. The main motive behind the research from 1601 to 1605 on the theory of the Martian orbit was the quest for the correct application of what he considered the true law of nature. In this Kepler did not succeed, a fact that was very well hidden.*

The determination of the fundamental laws was the real objective in Kepler's astronomy. Long after his 'battle over Mars' Kepler's friends asked him to present the complicated arguments in the New Astronomy in a more comprehensible way in the form of a textbook. The resulting work was the *Epitome*, published in numerous parts until 1621. In the *Astronomia nova*, Kepler developed a complex line of argumentation based upon his own history of discovery that only few could follow. The *Epitome*, by contrast, has the question-and-answer structure typical of didactic expositions and attempted a systematic arrangement of astronomical topics along with derivations of the necessary theorems.

Kepler opens his textbook of astronomy with a conceptual definition of the scope of astronomy. In answer to the question why a treatment of celestial phenomena is called *astronomy*, he replies that it deals with the *laws* of the causes of stellar motion:

> Ab Astrorum, id est motuum, quibus astra moventur, lege seu regimine, vt Oeconomia à regenda re domestica, Paedonomus à regendis pueris.[27]

Kepler uses the term '*lex*' frequently. In the fourth book of the *Epitome*, where the laws of planetary motion are introduced, one of the questions demands an example of a '*lex*' and he names the lever law as a paradigm. It has the same mathematical form as the *distance law*.

In a prominent place in the *Epitome* Kepler mentioned that the lever law was valid in physics *and* likewise determined the conveyance of virtues from the motive virtues of the celestial bodies upon the other moving heavenly bodies.[28] The difficulty in erecting astronomical theories lay in identifying the governing virtues and modelling their superposition geometrically. The motive virtues of the earth are, in turn, determined by the *distance law*, only we have to take into account a variety of interactions, as Kepler pointed out in the *Epitome*:

> Cùm verò in principio libelli, quando de Hypothesibus quaestio fuit, legem hanc praescripseris astronomo, vt non quidvis pro libitu ponat, sed positiones suas etiam comprobet Naturae consultis, quaero igitur, num speres te hanc absurdam positionem probare posse, et quibus argumentis?

Kepler regarded the distance law as the law of nature which determines the motions of the planets, also on an elliptic orbit, from which the two 'Keplerian laws' follow approximately. These laws just describe the courses of motion and are therefore *not* called laws by Kepler himself. In Kepler's view, a law distinguishes itself from among other possible empirically equivalent alternative geometrical models in that it reflects what he considered the actual causal relations for the astronomical motions. A principle that delivers this is a natural law.

---

27 Kepler 1991: 21.

28 Kepler 1991: 332.

Chapter 10

The Approach to a Physical Concept of Law in the Early Modern Period: A Comparison between Matthias Bernegger and Richard Cumberland

Hubert Treiber[1]

I

The drawing of any admissible comparison is a useful way of illustrating insights gained, or even of enhancing them. It therefore appears appropriate to make such a comparison between two scholars of whom it may be said that, thanks to the favourable circumstances that both notably enjoyed, they were equally well placed, in their studies on the subject of natural law, to establish a modern physical concept of law, or at least to give an impetus in that direction. Where they differ, however, is in the fact that one of them did indeed make the leap in question, while the other did not. The favourable circumstances mentioned include the degree of familiarity with mathematics that both possessed; this would have been very much to the purpose, since the establishment of the physical concept of law in the early modern period was closely linked to the enthronement of that discipline as the supreme science. The first of the two scholars chosen is Matthias Bernegger (1582–1640), who not only was well acquainted with mathematics and astronomy, but also and above all entered at a relatively early date (apparently from 1605 onwards) into a regular and sustained correspondence with Johannes Kepler (1571–1630). In addition, he translated Galileo's *Systema cosmicum* (1632) from Italian into Latin, then the universal learned language. It is true that Bernegger did not, in his polemic *Tuba pacis*, published in 1621, set out a theory of natural law of his own, as the other scholar to be considered here, Richard Cumberland (1631/32–1718), did in his treatise *De legibus naturae*, published in 1672; but other scholars belonging to Bernegger's Strasbourg School – Johann Heinrich Boecler (1611–72) and Johannes G. Scheffer(us) (1621–79), the authors of well-reputed commentaries on Grotius – did take part in the discourse on natural law that arose in the second half of the seventeenth century in consequence of

[1] My particular thanks are due to Anne Marie Schleebach, Hildegard Cancik-Lindemaier, Maximiliane Kriechbaum, Gerd Graßhoff and Friedrich Steinle; and also to the translator of my text, Anthony Mellor-Stapelberg (Hanover).

the amazing impact made by Grotius's work.[2] Cumberland has been selected because in the above-mentioned treatise he borrowed both from the voluntaristic concept of law[3] developed by Descartes (1596–1650) in his *Principes* (1644) [Roux] and also from the debate on the leges motûs carried on under the auspices of the Royal Society [Steinle]. In fact, Cumberland's involvement in the 'ideas exchange' of the young Royal Society is one indispensable element in the answer to the question as to why he succeeded in making the leap to the new concept whereas Bernegger failed to do so.

However, the charm of making a comparison between Bernegger and Cumberland lies above all in the fact that the former, although a disciple of the topical manner of argumentation and, as an imitator of Lipsius and a card-carrying Tacitist, of his time a practitioner of the cut-and-paste technique of the 'cento', nonetheless came to recognize, as a consequence of his work in translating Galileo, that there was an essential difference between what had been considered in the past to be the ideal way of developing a line of argumentation, and the new way. This was also to play a part in the debate on the 'leges motûs' carried on decades later by Christiaan Huygens (1629–95), William Neile (1637–70), John Wallis (1616–1703) and Christopher Wren (1632–1723) under the aegis of the young Royal Society, and also separates Bernegger from Cumberland to the extent that the latter took up the term 'leges motûs' (together with its synonyms) that was employed in that debate. Even though Bernegger, despite his general openness of mind, remained largely a captive of the manner of thinking to which he and his generation were accustomed, he can nevertheless, not least thanks to the wide range of his qualifications, be regarded as a suitable candidate who might have been capable of forming the innovative analogies that would have led him to make such a leap as is here in question.

II

Irrespective of any detailed analysis of the content of selected texts of Bernegger's, his partiality for the montage technique of the cento with its multiplicity of applications allows him to be presented as a dyed-in-the-wool Tacitist, completely rooted in the ideal of the topical or dialectical manner of argumentation as a method of demonstration. Bünger, in his Bernegger study of 1893, points out in several places what an important role this cut-and-paste technique played for Bernegger. With regard to the speech that Bernegger gave on the occasion of the Reformation Festival of 1617, for example, Bünger comments that he had a 'peculiar manner of patching together a speech out of classical quotations in the manner of a cento,' which he had 'learnt off Justus Lipsius', and which he 'later used even more extensively in his Hypobolimaea [= *Idolum Lauretanum*] and his Tuba pacis'.[4] In his introduction to Bernegger's 'most significant work' – by which he means the 1621 polemic *Tuba*

---

2 Boecler 1663; Scheffer(us) 1693 (originally 1672?). Boecler 1674 was also drawn upon.

3 Steinle 2001: 78f; Specht 2001.

4 Bünger 1893: 160.

pacis – Bünger quotes a passage from the 'Praefatio ad Lectorem',[5] to which he attaches an explanation of his own:

> 'Just as in Plautus the Phrygian gold embroiderers weave a carpet from their shining threads, so have I composed this book out of many thousand passages from the best authors, a laborious and time-consuming task, as it was only with great effort that the words could be fitted to the thought. Fortunately, Seneca and Tacitus and also other authors who are well known to me were frequently to hand, without waiting to be called.' – That is to say: in order to clothe his thoughts in the best form, he created a veritable cento from the ancient classical authors, hoping to have found therein a method that would impress statesmen and princes.[6]

If one casts a glance at the foreword 'Ad Lectorem de Consilio et Forma Nostri Operis' with which Lipsius prefaced his work *Politicorum sive civilis doctrinae libri sex*, later also to be edited by Bernegger, one will find, at the marginalium 'Centonem quendam fecimus', this passage that Bernegger inserted into the preface of his *Tuba pacis*.[7]

At this point something should be said about the montage technique of the cento that has already been mentioned several times. The Latin word cento – 'patchwork garment' – originally indicated a 'blanket composed of colourful patches', and in the figurative sense a poem composed of lines from other famous writings: a 'patchwork poem'. The same technique was also made use of in prose texts. Lipsius in particular made use of this time-honoured 'art', and explicitly applied the term 'cento' to it. The fact that Bernegger, precisely at the time when he was composing his two polemical texts *Idolum Lauretanum* (1619) and *Tuba pacis* (1621), held this cut-and-paste technique in high esteem, applying it in obvious imitation of his admired model Lipsius, can also be deduced from the fact that Julius Wilhelm Zincgref (1591–1635), who was close to him at that time, also made use of the technique in composing his book of emblems in 1619, although without actually naming Lipsius as his model. The passage from the 'Praefatio de Origine et Usu Emblematum' is noteworthy because Zincgref here both recalls the tradition of using this technique and also mentions an important function associated with it: that of recruiting recognized authorities in support of one's own cause. As Zincgref puts it:

> In order, Reader, not to delay you too long, we will tell you just a little about the plan and form of this, our little work. It is, in fact, nothing very new, nor is it without model or example. For – to speak with the most learned man of our century – what could I have done that would have been more profitable than to bring together so many wise sayings that are so finely and so tellingly put, and, as truly as my Saviour (God) loves me, composed for the salvation of mankind? For if I were to say the same myself, would

[5] Bernegger 1624: 3.

[6] Bünger 1893: 176.

[7] Lipsius (1704) 1998: 6v, 7. The expression 'sand without lime' used there is an allusion to a derogatory assessment of Seneca's style by the Emperor Caligula, reported by Suetonius: Caligula 53, 2. My thanks are due to Hildegard Cancik-Lindemaier for kindly communicating this information. The edition procured by Lipsius was published in 1598, the one procured by Bernegger shortly after his death in 1641.

> I ever attain to the same force and credibility? Just as with any kind of projectile, or with a sword, much depends on the hand that guides it, so in the case of a sentence, if it is to strike home, the weight of a powerful and acknowledged authority is most effective. Now such authority lies with the ancient writers, and it is from them that we have drawn what we here present.[8]

The fact that it is Lipsius whom Zincgref means by 'the most learned man of our century' is revealed in the preface to the already mentioned treatise *Politicorum sive civilis doctrinae libri sex*, where the passage which Zincgref borrows without mentioning his source is to be found at the marginalium 'Forma nova nostri operas'.[9] Bearing in mind the function that both Lipsius and Zincgref explicitly ascribe to the cento, namely that only the opinions and statements of recognized authorities (that is, classical authors of the ancient world) can invest an argument with credibility and effectiveness, the montage technique of the cento is indicative of faith in the topical or dialectical manner of argumentation as the ideal method of demonstration and proof. This common form of argumentation among the humanists is also to be found throughout Bernegger's *Idolum Lauretanum* (1619), a polemic text directed against the occurrence known as the 'Miracle of Loreto', by which, it was asserted, the house of the Holy Family had been transported there by angels. Completely in line with the methodology he had been so well versed in since his student days in Strasbourg,[10] Bernegger sets out his argumentation in such a way as to 'derive from the acknowledgement of certain propositions that other propositions deserve also to be acknowledged'.[11] What is meant by such an 'acknowledged proposition' from an authoritative source (éndoxon) can be seen from the frequently quoted definition of Boethius (*De topicis differentiis* I 1180 CD), who here goes beyond the definition to be found in Aristotle (*Topics* A1 (100b21–23)) which is more usually referred to. According to Boethius, an 'acknowledged proposition' is:

> what all hold to be true, or most people, or the wise, and among these either all or most or the best known and most excellent, or what a specialist in his field …, or else what he with whom one is in discussion or he who judges holds to be true.[12]

In addition to dismissing a counter-argument on the grounds that it is a 'fabula' or rejecting an argument by making a counter-assertion without any further reasoning to justify it, Bernegger in his anti-miracle text attempts to weaken the position of his adversaries by making them look ridiculous – above all by questioning the credibility of the sources and authorities they draw upon or by quoting other sources to demonstrate the contrary. Conversely, he strengthens his own position by calling upon generally recognized sources and authorities, the listing of which also underlines his own learnedness. The historical-critical investigations of words that

[8] Zincgref 1993b: 15f.

[9] For the original Latin text of the passage quoted by Zincgref, see Lipsius (1704) 1998: 6v.

[10] Schindling 1977.

[11] Otte 1970: 188.

[12] Otte 1971: 188; Herberger 1981: 29; also Maclean 1992: 76f., who in this connection also emphasizes the requirement that it must be true.

Bernegger repeatedly undertakes are above all clear indications that he is completely rooted in the philological tradition of text comparison and text interpretation. To this extent, 'reality' and 'experience' are to him what texts that have to be interpreted say about them.[13] Thus what Ian Maclean has shown to be a common concern of the historical methods of interpretation used by the humanists and of the kind of text interpretation used by lawyers also applies to Bernegger: he too was interested in 'the relationships between word and concept, between word and intention and the historicity of words'.[14] Even in that chapter of his polemic in which he briefly considers the transportation problems that the angels would have had to overcome, he relies on contradictions within texts and other inconsistencies, and so remains completely 'text-bound' (whereby the texts concerned are, needless to say, ones by acknowledged authorities); his consideration does not extend to any 'reality' existing beyond such texts.[15]

The extent to which Bernegger relies upon the topical method of argumentation can also be seen from the way he treats the passage from Kepler's introduction to his *Astronomia nova* (1609) in which the author explains the ebb and flow of the tides on the basis of the 'Law of Distance' that he had discovered ('The power of motion emanating from the sun declines in proportion to the distance') [GRAßHOFF]. This law plays a central role in all of Kepler's theoretical expositions, although oddly enough the Law of Distance, which Kepler designates as 'lex', is 'not called a "law of nature" by any later author, while those principles that Kepler, rightly from his point of view, does not call laws of nature later become known as "Kepler's Laws"'.[16]

Significantly, the reference to Kepler that is here in question is to be found in the tenth chapter of Bernegger's 1618 edition of Tacitus' *Agricola*, in the form of some remarks commenting on the 'naturae miraculum' of the tides, which are distinguished by the regularity of fixed intervals of time.[17] Bernegger first points out that it cannot be the task of an edition of Tacitus to 'seek out ... the cause of this phenomenon', and then refers to the explanation given by Kepler. However, he quotes merely the two purely descriptive paragraphs from the introduction to the *Astronomia nova*,[18] and does not mention the concept of law that Kepler uses in presenting his 'true doctrine

---

[13] Maclean 1984: 231.

[14] Maclean 2000b: 237.

[15] Bernegger is equally conventional with regard to the nature of proof provided by miracles: in chapter 10 he rejects them as proof, since the miracles said to have occurred at Loreto were either 'alleged by lying and suspect witnesses' or were 'false miracles' which, if the possibility of man-made fraud was excluded, must have been worked by the devil. See Daston 1998: 35f. and 47ff.

[16] See GRAßHOFF, Chapter 9 in this volume.

[17] C. Cornelii Taciti, De Vita Julii Agricolae, Argentorati 1618, sectio V, cap. X: 136–142, esp. 141f.

[18] Kepler 1609: Introductio. The quotation begins with: 'Orbis virtutis tractoriae' ('The field of the moon's power of attraction') and ends with 'nonnulla diversimodè ob diversos Oceani aditus' ('because of the different degrees of access that exist to various seas'). See also Kepler's presentation of his theory of the tides in letters to D. Fabricius (11 October 1605) and Herwart (2 January 1607) in Caspar and van Dyck 1930a: 256f. and 274f.

of gravity', formulated in the light of his 'Law of Distance'.[19] Although Bernegger is to some extent right on target here, Kepler's 'physical reasoning' remains foreign to him. His reference to Kepler remains rooted in a topical manner of argumentation: Kepler is presented as a serious authority and placed side by side with Seneca, whose authority is universally recognized:

> And Seneca at any rate writes in Book 7 ,de benef., ch. 1, that it is of no matter if one does not know what principle (ratio) it is that causes the sea to withdraw and calls it back, even though it would do no great harm to have trespassed upon that which it is not permitted to know; but neither would it be of use.[20]

Furthermore, Bernegger immediately follows up the 'extremely acute judgement, that comes as close as possible to the truth', namely Kepler's theory of the tides, with a proffered conventional explanation:

> Those who nevertheless desire to inquire more carefully into this miracle of nature should consult the writings of the philosophers, who, despite such a great contention of opinions, are nonetheless more or less agreed that that motion [of the tides] is to be ascribed to the moon, since it also, as has been recognised, governs and controls other liquid bodies.[21]

Even where Bernegger, thanks to his general open-mindedness and wide reading, almost happens upon Kepler's Law of Distance, he shows himself to be a Tacitist 'imprisoned' in his conventional manner of thought, who continues to attempt to imitate his great model Lipsius. It was only the work of translating and editing Galileo's *Systema cosmicum* (1632), which he undertook 15 years later, that led Bernegger to the insight that the astronomer was an adherent of a new and different method of argumentation and demonstration from the one that he himself and his generation were grounded in. This insight does not prevent him from putting together for his Galileo edition cento-like texts in which the cento performs the function that it was perceived as having in apologetic literature.[22] Thus Bernegger uses the cento-like assemblies of text extracts that he includes in that edition to demonstrate that Galileo's expositions contradict neither Scripture nor a series of ancient authors whose opinions are recognized as authoritative. Bernegger repeatedly mentions his concern to do this. The title page in particular expresses clearly, with the aid of two quotations elevated to the status of epigraphs, the claim to truth that underlies this method. First, Bernegger quotes Polybius 13, 5, 4–6,[23] and then adds at the

---

[19] It may be assumed that Bernegger knew this passage since it is the section following the one which concludes the extract from Kepler's 'Introduction' that Bernegger had taken into his edition of Galileo's *Dialogue*. See Kepler (1609) 1990: 33f.

[20] The passage from Seneca that Bernegger quotes (*De beneficiis* VII, 1.5) thus gives the movement of the ocean as an example of knowledge that is superfluous as it brings no direct moral advantage.

[21] Bernegger 1618: 141.

[22] *Historisches Wörterbuch der Rhetorik*, vol. 2, col. 149.

[23] The source attribution 'cap. 3' is an error. The quotation translates as follows: 'It seems to me that Nature has exalted Truth to be the greatest Goddess for mankind, and has endowed her with the greatest power. For even though she is sometimes oppressed by all and

bottom of the title page a sentence in Greek which translates as 'Judge everything without prejudgment'.[24] Another passage from the preface to the edition of Galileo[25] emphasizes this concern, while at the same time indicating that Bernegger has realized that Galileo himself is a disciple of a different ideal of proof:

> It is therefore truly meet to wonder at divine providence and to venerate it, which in our time more than in any other is revealing the (secret) inner workings of heavenly creation. For whereas in former days, that doctrine (sententia) was founded upon a number of considerations that were more credible than they were correct in their conclusions, but appeared to shrink back utterly affrighted before the principles of natural philosophy, today those topical arguments (i.e. the generally acknowledged opinions) have, by means of that which lay concealed for centuries, but which the great Galileo, with the aid of the divine invention of the telescope that he has perfected, has discovered in the heavens, become strictly apodictical ones (i.e. strictly proved by scientific method): the mists with which physics (the doctrine of nature) obscured them have been driven away by the bright radiance of the clearest proofs. Truth has prevailed and will continue to prevail, as long those people can be reconciled to us who, like Cleanthes, deluded by unenlightened piety, wrongly consider the decrees or doctrines of Holy Scripture to be undermined thereby.

The mention of Cleanthes – who, as Plutarch[26] reports, accused Aristarchus of Samos of impiety for having proposed a heliocentric model – is likely to be an allusion to Melanchthon. The latter had compared Copernicus to Aristarchus, although naming as his source Archimedes, who does not mention the accusation of impiety reported by Plutarch.[27] As far as the difference between the old and the new methods of demonstration is concerned, Bernegger describes it, in his accustomed terminology, as a difference between topical and apodictical 'argumenta'. It is also notable that he associates this difference with Galileo's 'divine invention of the telescope'. The extent to which he is here already taking cognizance of the phenomenon of seeing mediated by instruments, which bears with it a new understanding of 'experience' (in the sense of mathematically and experimentally constructed experience), cannot be gone into here;[28] but his translation work has at any rate given him the insight, as he informs a former pupil, that what are important to Galileo are 'physical

all the arguments of probability are arrayed on the side of Falsehood, yet nevertheless she somehow penetrates of her own accord into the souls of men; sometimes she shows forth her power immediately, but sometimes also, having long remained obscured, she nevertheless gains the victory in the end and beats down Falsehood through her own strength …' (Polybios 1963: 834).

[24] The Greek quotation, transliterated, is: 'chorís prokrímatos ta pánta krínete'. The phrase 'chorís prokrímatos' ('without prejudgment') is to be found in the New Testament (1 Timothy 5:21). As the primary word prókrima is only found here and does not occur at all in classical Greek, but otherwise only in papyri and in the Justinian Code (with a special legal meaning), it may be assumed that this quotation is a formulation of Bernegger's with which he alludes to this passage in St Paul. For all these details I am indebted to the kind assistance of Hildegard Cancik-Lindemaier.

[25] Bernegger 1635: p. 3, l. 28.

[26] *De facie in orbe lunae* c. 6; Stoic. Vet. Fr. I 500.

[27] Blumenberg 1996: II, 378ff.

[28] Koyré 1998: 67f.

and mathematical proofs'.[29] This appears to him to be something fundamentally different from the form of argumentation that he himself favours, that of relying on the universally acknowledged opinion of recognized authorities and placing a high value on 'dialectics'; as is also demonstrated by his praise of the 'syllogism' in his anti-miracle text.

What distinguishes Bernegger from Cumberland is that he did not go on to present any concept of natural law of his own. Although his polemical text *Tuba pacis* (1621), which was directed against Gaspare Scioppio's (1576–1649) *Classicum belli sacri* (1619) and appeared four years before Grotius' *De iure belli ac pacis* (1625), borrows from Alberico Gentili's *De iure belli libri tres* (1588f.) and displays figures of argument based on natural law, it is nevertheless not possible to identify any systematic exposition of a scheme of thought grounded in the concept of natural law. Boecler and Scheffer, on the other hand, as representatives of Bernegger's Strasbourg school, did take part in the discourse on natural law to the extent that they added publications of their own to the mass of commentaries that had expanded by leaps and bounds as a consequence of the overwhelming response to the work of Grotius. The commentaries written by Boecler and Scheffer do not, however, apply a physical concept of the law of nature[30] despite the high degree of freedom of thought that this genre of literature permits. Thus the commentary is not only an appropriate reaction to the discrete structure of references with their 'unconnected statements by philosophers, historians, poets and orators'[31] which Grotius himself admits to be characteristic of his work. It is precisely this 'discreteness' and 'multi-perspectivity'[32] that make the commentary a suitable medium for creating, 'by the relation of known facts to known points of view, something which is nevertheless new'.[33] The fact that something new can be created in this way, when 'words that are fixed in their contexts ... are transferred to a new context',[34] is demonstrated for example by Descartes' use of the term 'lex' in his *Principes*, as has been demonstrated only recently by Rainer Specht. To the extent that Descartes introduced the expression 'lex naturae' into the 'thematic constellation of concursus divinus, lex aeterna and ordo naturalis', his 'use of "lex" appears quite simply conventional'. This impression is however 'mitigated by two unconventional aspects: firstly by the use of the traditional expression "lex" in

---

29 Cf. the letter of 11 August 1633 to Rebhan, printed in Reifferscheid 1889: 922, where it is said of Galileo: 'Argumentum eius demonstrationes et physicae et mathematicae sunt ...' In 1636 Bernegger publishes the letter written by Galileo in 1615 to the Grand Duchess of Tuscany, Christine of Lorraine (bilingually in Italian and Latin). Here, Galileo uses terms that effectively correspond to the expression 'law of nature': in the Italian original he speaks of 'delle legi impostegli', while the Latin translation reads: 'Contra verò, cum ipsa Natura esse suum immutabiliter servet, nec limites sibi à Deo praescriptos egrediatur ...' (Bernegger 1636: 12). 'Praescribere' and 'le(g)ge' are used synonymously.

30 Bernegger's pupil and son-in-law Johannes Freinsheim (1608–60), who met Descartes in Stockholm and was made to read his *Principes* (1644) by Queen Christina, does not appear to have allowed this to influence him either.

31 Hofmann 1986: 83.

32 Wagner 1996.

33 Weber 1973: 214.

34 Stolleis 1997: 22f.

the new context of a physico-mathematical approach, and secondly by the associated denial of the activity of bodies'.[35]

III

What distinguishes Cumberland, then, is that he develops his own theory of natural law.[36] This is not the place to attempt a comprehensive presentation of his concept of natural law, which is substantially influenced by Stoic ideas; only an outline of his basic concerns can be given. Cumberland's guiding idea is that processes in the realm of inanimate nature and in the field of moral activity are equally subject to universal laws (of nature),[37] which for him are identical with the leges motûs. In this connection Cumberland speaks of a 'system of bodies' which are in a certain state of motion. This results from the interaction of stimuli that obey immutable laws of motion (secundum immutabiles motûs leges), under which nothing of the quantity of motion that God, the 'First Cause', originally created, is lost.[38] According to Cumberland, this view points to the 'principia Physiologiae Mechanicae generalia',[39] which reflect a conception, harking back to Descartes, that may be described as 'mechanistic'.[40] It is Cumberland's concern to be able to determine more exactly and reliably with the aid of these 'principia Physiologiae Mechanicae generalia' – which he believed would also be accepted by Hobbes, against whom his text is primarily directed – what natural law, that is God as the First Cause and supreme lawgiver[41] [ARMOGATHE], prescribes as being morally binding. For this purpose he devises a theory of rewards and punishments which – being on the one hand a direct expression of the divine will, while on the other hand also obeying the immutable

[35] Specht 2001: 75.

[36] Richard Cumberland, who later became a theologian and a bishop and is also said to have been interested in mathematics as a student, studied at Magdalene College, Cambridge, from 1649 to 1656, and probably got to know Descartes' philosophy through Henry More (1614–87), who had initially been an enthusiastic Cartesian (Parkin 1999: 115f., 176, 72ff.). From 1667 onwards Cumberland also had quite close contacts with lawyers who were particularly interested in John Selden (1584–1654), who had developed his concept of natural law in the dispute with Hobbes.

[37] Stoicism acknowledges the possibility of being able to determine divinely inspired morality from the 'observation' of nature. To give a somewhat oversimplified formulation: Cumberland is seeking to propound this principle, which he has gleaned from reading (amongst others) Cicero (for example, *De finibus*, III, 22), more exactly and reliably with the assistance of the 'modern' natural philosophy of his time.

[38] Cumberland 1672 (hereafter DLN) II: 101f., § 15; DLN II: 118f., § 15 (trans.). The parallel to Descartes' 'Principes' (1644) is obvious. Cf. in particular the second part (Descartes 1955: 31ff.), which contains the three laws of nature propounded by him together with the related doctrine of motion. See also Steinle 1995: 323ff. For the use of lex naturae in the *Principes*, see also Specht (2001), who draws attention to the influence of La Flèche and of Suárez, who helped to shape the teaching set out there.

[39] Translated as 'Principles of Mechanical Philosophy' (DLN II: 118, § 15).

[40] Schiemann 1997: 21 and 24 with footnote 16.

[41] DLN V: 324, § 58; DLN V: 299, § 58 (trans.).

laws of motion – allow us to recognize unequivocally which actions or what kinds of moral behaviour are in accord with nature (and therefore obligatory) and which are not. In this way, the rewards and punishments emanating from God, which thanks to their regularity can be discovered with the aid of science and exact methods, not only provide reliable information as to his will, but are also at the same time expressions of divine providence [Trepp]. On the one hand Cumberland adopts Stoic ideas, as transmitted by Cicero, whilst on the other he strictly rejects the atomism expounded by Epicurus,[42] which sees chance and not divine providence as the governing factor [Wilson].[43] This decisive rejection of Epicurus reflects the decisive rejection of Hobbes, whom Cumberland significantly views as an Epicurean.[44]

Even though the explicit reference to Descartes is obvious,[45] Cumberland also names as further authorities for the laws of motion Wren and Huygens, although without stating any precise source – which omission is remedied by the translator of *De legibus naturae*, John Maxwell,[46] who mentions 'Philosophical Transactions'. But even without this note of Maxwell's, there are sufficient passages that demonstrate the regard in which Cumberland held the young Royal Society.[47] Their *Philosophical Transactions* is associated above all with the name of the first secretary of the Society, Henry Oldenburg (1618?–1677), who not only initiated that journal, but also published it himself and on his own responsibility from 1665 to 1677. The link between this periodical and the position of secretary to the Royal Society gave it continuity and made it – thanks to the particular commitment and skill of Oldenburg, who knew how to make a good impression with his self-defined role of promoter

[42] DLN V: 278f., § 41; DLN V: 263f., § 41 (trans.). Cumberland also exercises direct criticism of the ideas expounded by Epicurus in his 'Letter to Herodotus'. See also Meinel 1988. Cumberland may have been influenced here by Descartes, who excludes the existence of a vacuum and links this to a rejection of atomism.

[43] DLN V: 225, § 20; DLN V: 221, § 20 (trans.); and DLN V: § 18 and § 19.

[44] In order to demonstrate that anti-social behaviour such as Hobbes ascribes to the natural state is unnatural, Cumberland appeals, amongst other things, to William Harvey's (1578–1657) study of the circulation of the blood, *Exercitatio anatomica de motu cordis et sanguinis in animalibus* (1628) (DLN II: 112f., § 19; DLN II: 127, § 19 (trans.)). Cumberland declares that, on the contrary, social behaviour is not only advantageous but also corresponds to nature; for as Harvey had shown, he says, passions such as hatred or envy damage the heart and constrict the circulation of the blood, whereas a well-disposed attitude towards one's fellow men has a beneficial effect on the heart and circulation.

[45] Parkin 1999: 151: 'There are more references to Descartes in De legibus naturae than to any other single philosopher apart from Hobbes.' For example, Cumberland several times refers explicitly to Descartes' method of 'Mathesis Universalis' (for example, DLN I: 48, § 9).

[46] The following comment by Linda Kirk (1987: 106) is particularly noteworthy: 'Maxwell is keenly aware of developments in philosophy and science which took place after Cumberland wrote De Legibus Naturae. He explains that the Cartesian world picture has been replaced by that of Newton, but that Cumberland's view of human powers and endeavours, as balanced as the motions of the universe in its plenitude, is not thereby invalidated. This "does not in the least affect our Author's Reasoning" because he has used the hypothesis as an illustration, not as a proof.'

[47] For example, DLN: Prolegomena, § 30; DLN I: 3, § 3.

– into a platform for the 'industrious dissemination of ideas and discoveries'.[48] The contributions published in it were as a rule identical with published letters or extracts from letters from Oldenburg's wide-ranging correspondence, supplemented by reports taken from other comparable journals or by book reviews.[49] In fact, the story of the origin and publication of precisely those articles on the 'laws of motion' (règles du mouvement) associated with the names of Wren and Huygens that Cumberland would ultimately draw upon provides a particularly good illustration of Oldenburg's role as promoter, and emphasizes the very particular significance attributable to 'his' periodical in the 'dissemination of ideas'.[50]

At a meeting of the Royal Society in October 1668, Robert Hooke (1635–1703) had expressed the supposition that 'there might be made experiments to discover ye nature & laws of motion, as ye foundation of Philosophie and all Philosophical discourse', whereupon William Brouncker (c. 1620–84) pointed out that both Christopher Wren and Christiaan Huygens 'had considered that subject more yn many others, & probably found out a Theorie to explicate all sorts of experiments to be made of that nature', as Oldenburg writes in letters to Wren and Huygens. The former replied immediately and stated that 'he had "looked out those papers of Experiments that concerned Lawes of Motion arising from collision of hard bodies," but "found them somewhat indigested as I left them at first. & I could be glad if you would give me a little time to examine them".' Wren did indeed submit a treatise on the subject some time later,[51] which was published in the *Philosophical Transactions* of January 1669[52] together with one by John Wallis.[53] Oldenburg had also written to Huygens, 'asking him to "inform" the Society "when (he) would bring (his) speculations and observations on this subject before the public", and if they were not yet in publishable state to communicate his "hypothesis of motion" to be registered in the Society's books'. This it duly was, together with the contributions by Wren and Neile, after Huygens had given his approval and finally made his manuscript available. Oldenburg sent Wren's article to Huygens and informed him that he had

[48] Hall 1981: 190.

[49] Ibid.: 188.

[50] In relation to the following see Hall 1981: 190f.; also: Hall and Hall 1968, vol. V; Steinle 2001: 81ff.; Steinle in this volume.

[51] Wren 1669.

[52] Hall 1981: 189. The work by William Neile (1637–70) is not in the January number; Friedrich Steinle was kind enough to investigate this at my request. Neile did, however, participate in the debate, which can be reconstructed on the basis of the volume of correspondence published by Hall and Hall in 1968, which also includes (on pp. 519–528) Neile's 'Hypothesis of Motion'. A conspicuously large number of terms are used as synonyms in this debate (both by the different correspondents and also within individual letters): for example, hypothesis of motion, Hypotheses & Propositions of motion, law(s) of motion, (generales) motus leges, law of nature, la loy de la Nature, loix du Mouvement, principles of motion, generalia motus principia, proposition, rules and axioms, rules (of Motion), theoremes du mouvement (et regles), Theorie du mouvement. The debate was thus not concerned with the 'concept of law' as such, but with fundamental principles of the theory of motion (the laws of the collision of bodies).

[53] Wallis 1669.

written to the other authors, calling upon them to comment on his article. When Oldenburg sent the January edition of his periodical, which contained only Wren's and Wallis's contributions, to Huygens in February 1669, the latter was offended and did not reply to several letters from Oldenburg. At the end of March, the latter received a copy of the *Journal des sçavans* containing a summary of the theories presented by Huygens, accompanied by a declaration in which the latter advanced a priority claim. Oldenburg finally mollified Huygens by proposing to reprint his article from the *Journal des sçavans* in the *Philosophical Transactions* with an acknowledgement of the original source of publication.[54]

The synonymous use of the terms 'rule', 'proposition' or 'principle' for 'law'[55] that can be observed in the above-mentioned articles in *Philosophical Transactions* is also typical of Cumberland's *De legibus naturae*. Random examination will show that the expression 'Law(s) of Nature' is used neither consistently nor in a manner that is free from contradictions. Linda Kirk[56] draws particular attention to two versions of the definition of lex naturae that are to be found in the first section of the fifth chapter of first editions of *De legibus naturae*,[57] taking these and other inconsistencies as grounds for assuming that there is a conflict here between a voluntaristic and a utilitarian approach. Whereas the former ascribes the obligatory,

---

54 Huygens and Oldenburg 1669; see also Huygens 1669.

55 Steinle 2001: 82f.

56 Kirk 1987: 31f., 79 and 109f.

57 The original, but later rejected, shorter version is: 'Lex Naturae est propositio natura rerum ex voluntate primae causae menti satis aperte oblata vel impressa, quae actionem agentis rationalis possibilem communi bono maxime deservientem indicat, & integram singulorum foelicitatem exinde solum obtineri posse' (quoted according to Parkin 1999: 108, footnote 64, who omits the à from the ablative natura) – 'The law of nature is a proposition presented to or impressed upon the mind clearly enough by the nature of things from the will of the first cause, which points out that possible action of a rational agent which will most promote the common good and by which alone the complete happiness of individual people can be obtained' (quoted according to Kirk 1987: 31).

The corrected (longer) version, on the other hand, goes on as follows after 'impressa': 'actionem indicans Bono Rationalium communi deservientem, quam si praestetur praemia, sin negligatur, poenae sufficientes ex Naturâ Rationalium sequuntur' (DLN V: 185, § 1) – as quoted later in the text. According to Kirk, this version expresses above all Cumberland's voluntaristic attitude. In the original Latin there is an addition to this version which is neither completely nor faithfully rendered in Maxwell's translation: 'Hujus definitionis pars prior Praeceptum, posterior sanctionem continet: & utraque à Naturâ Rerum imprimitur. Illa autem *praemia poenaeque sufficiunt*, quae tanta sunt, & tam certò distribuuntur, ut manifestò magis conducat ad integram singulorum foelicitatem (quam per Naturam Universi obtinere possunt, & necessariò expetunt) si publico Bono perpetuò serviant, quàm si quicquam in contrarium attentarent' (DLN V: 185, § 5). – 'The first part of the definition contains the precept, the second the sanction and both are imprinted by the nature of things. Those rewards and punishments are sufficient which are so great and so certainly administered that it is obviously more conducive to the complete happiness of individual people (which they can obtain and must desire by reason of the nature of the universe) if they always promote the public good rather than if they were to attempt anything opposed to it' (quoted according to Kirk 1987: 31).

binding character of the leges naturae to the lawgiving will of God, the latter sees in this obligatoriness a consequence of rational action which promotes the public good (bonum commune), and is thus useful.[58] Over and above this, however, there is a further area of conflict between a voluntaristic and a naturalistic conception, since for Cumberland rewards and punishments, while on the one hand a direct expression of the divine will, on the other hand obey immutable laws (of motion) and are thus prescribed by 'nature' (though this too was of course created by God). Cumberland attempts to find lines of argumentation that will take the edge off this conflict. Amongst them are an assumption that God imposes obligations on himself,[59] or the view put forward in the fourth chapter that in the field of practical morality one can, if equipped with sufficient 'prudentia' and experience, make do with a lesser degree of 'moral certainty' [MOHNHAUPT]. Although Cumberland has just reminded his readers that ethical relationships can be understood as physical systems that are subject to the same 'certain' (that is, predictable) laws that also govern the motion of bodies, and although he has just mentioned that the exact methods developed by Descartes, Vieta, Wallis and Ward might also be of service in the 'Science of Morality and Politicks' ('Disciplina moralis & civilis'), he confronts his readers two sections later with considerations that in the field of practical morality, which is subject to 'propositiones practicae' (here translated by Maxwell as 'practical propositions'; the term 'practical dictates' used elsewhere is perhaps more readily understandable), not only depart from those 'exact' methods that afford certainty (even though these are still assigned a model function),[60] but also amount to an admission that, in that field, behaviour must be assumed that is predictable, in other words to be expected, only with a certain degree of probability:[61]

58 Cumberland is trying to demonstrate that the highest individual good is at the same time the highest good for all rationally acting people. As he assumes that the greatest possible well-being of all will lead humankind to the highest level of blessedness, the common good (bonum commune) represents for him a suprema lex in the sense of a 'universal Proposition' which represents the source of all laws of nature (DLN I: 4, § 4).

59 Since it is God's will not to contradict himself, he keeps to the order prescribed by nature (that is, by himself). By making this assumption Cumberland is also able to link moral obligations to the way nature obeys its own laws, without having to regard that as the exclusive source of such obligations. In principle, God could act differently if he wished to.

60 DLN IV: 180, § 4; DLN IV: 185, § 4 (trans.): 'I confess, however, "That *those things* which, in *Morality*, are granted, or *assumed* as known, such as GOD and MAN, their Actions and mutual Relations, are *not so exactly known*, as *those things*, which in *Mathematicks* are *assum'd*, in a fix'd determinate Proportion or Quantity; and that, therefore, the *Conclusions* thence drawn must labour under the *same want of Exactness"*. Yet the *Method*, the *Rules* of Operation, and the *Manner* of drawing Consequences, is the *same*. Nor is *Exactness* necessary for the Uses of Life; as neither is it requir'd, in the Practice of measuring Planes and Solids.'

61 What is however confusing is that Cumberland (DLN IV: 177, § 3; trans.: DLN IV: 183, § 3) also calls these 'practical propositions' 'Laws of Nature' ('Termini autem earum propositionum practicarum, quae Leges naturae dicuntur ...'). It is also confusing that such 'practical propositions' are at the same time also given the status of rules of prudence and experience.

> It is sufficient, in few Words, to *affirm*, 'That in all Affairs, whether private or publick, Mathematicks is the principal *Instrument* of *Certainty* and *Justice* in Action, wheresoever *Exactness* is requisite.' Which I do not advance, with a view to commend *Mathematicks* ..., but to demonstrate the Certainty of the Rules of Life and *Morality*, upon this Account, that Natural *Prudence* almost makes Use of the *Assistance* of a *Science* that is *certain*, or of *self-evident Principles*. To this Head also, I think, may be referr'd, 'That, whereas we know not what shall hereafter happen, we may, nevertheless, know what is possible: And things *possible* may be *compar'd* among themselves; and it may be *certainly* known, not only, which of *two possible* Things will be of *greater* or *less Value*, when they do happen; but, also, which of them may be produce'd by *more*, which by *fewer*, *Causes*, that do now, or shall soon, exist. But that is *more probable*, which may happen *more ways*, and its *Chance* or *Expectation* is of *greater Value*.' Now it is of great *Consequence*, in the Management of Affairs, 'To know certainly the *Probability*, and *Value*, of the Hope of the several Things, or Effects, we have occasion to consider.' For *such* is the condition of human Life, that we must lay out *almost* our *whole* Labour, our *Expence* often, nay expose *Life* it-self to *Danger*, for the *Hope* of such Things, as conduce to the Preservation or Happiness of our-selves, or of others, altho' that Hope be *probable* only, *not certain*; ... That skill of investigation by *Analysis*, which all Men exercise *naturally*, teaches how to weigh these things very well; how the Value may be farther ascertain'd by *Analysis*, improv'd by Art, the famous *Huygens* hath finely shewn in his *Calculations of the Chances of the Dice*, which you may find at the End of *Schooten's Miscellaneous Mathematical Exercitations*. – It is an *Observation* pertinent to this Head, 'That, as in *Matters of Prudence* we must *sometimes try several Ways, before we can know certainly, whether the Affair shall succeed*, according to our Wish, in this or that manner? Or whether we can all obtain what we hop'd for?'[62]

The above reading of Cumberland's arguments, which also seem to point to a hierarchy of types of law, is supported by his mention of Huygens,[63] which at first sight appears unusual. Unusual because the term 'probabilitas', as Hacking[64] points out, is 'Janus-faced' – that is, has both an aleatory and an epistemic dimension (in the sense of a coherent and convincing assessment of the degree of credibility of uncertain statements). Lorraine Daston is, however, able to demonstrate that Huygens had elaborated 'a calculus of expectations rather than of probabilities' after the pattern of the 'hazardous contracts' drawn up by lawyers, which aim to secure calculable conditions for partners engaged in risky ventures with regard to how the amount of the venture can be shared fairly among the partners when the outcome of the transaction is uncertain.[65] In addition, Daston draws attention[66] to the fact that the formulation 'ordered stages of (moral) certainty' that was common currency in circles close to the young Royal Society should by no means be confused with a 'full

62 Cf. DLN IV: 187f., § 4. Latin original: DLN IV: 182f., § 4.

63 The reference is to Huygens' treatise 'De ratiociniis in alea ludo' of 1657. The mathematician Schotanus [Frans van Schooten the Younger (1615–60)], had introduced Huygens to the mathematics of Descartes. The work mentioned is *Exercitationum mathematicarum libri quinque*' (1657). With regard to Huygens, see also Hacking 1975: 92–101 and Shapiro 1983: 3–6, 27ff. (Figure 1), 37–44 and 277n.

64 Hacking 1975: 12.

65 Daston 1988: 11–15; 19ff. The model was the aleatory wager agreement (sponsio).

66 Ibid.: 38.

continuum of degrees'. The idea behind it is rather to provide, in view of the fact that absolute certainty is unattainable, a certain degree of 'probability' or expectation that a particular course of action is morally correct, to the extent that it is governed by prudence and (knowledge gained from) experience.

Despite all his fondness for invoking the leges motûs, which are of course presumed to be immutable and therefore binding, Cumberland is also concerned with the issue of the (degree of) obligatoriness of the 'practical dictates', a question that also involves that of the binding nature of (natural) laws, if only because Cumberland mixes up these terms. The question of the degree of obligatoriness is after all commonly linked to that of the reason for the obligation. The discussion of these questions appears to draw upon *De legibus, ac Deo legislatore* (1612), a treatise by Suárez (1548–1617), which Cumberland probably became acquainted with through reading a text by Nathaniel Culverwell (1619–51)[67], *An Elegant and Learned Discourse of the Light of Nature* (1652).[68] The utilization, though admittedly sparing, of certain particular key terms[69] and a small number of key passages[70] allow the assumption that Cumberland was impressed by Suárez's distinction between 'lex indicans' and 'lex obligans'. This terminological distinction is concerned with the issue 'as to whether a law derives its binding nature from the will of the lawgiver or from the moral rightness of its content, which is to be ascribed to the sphere of the intellect'.[71] By posing this question Suárez seeks to make it clear that practical reason is perfectly capable of judging what is good and what is evil in any particular case, but that this theoretical knowledge as to what should be done and/or left undone only attains to its obligatory nature through a lawgiving will. This applies equally to the law of nature, which 'is a true and real divine law, the lawgiver being God'.[72] To Suárez, then, every law, and thus also the lex naturalis, aspires to create an obligation that is expressed in the will of the lawgiver (lex obligans), whereas mere knowledge of the matter that is to be observed (lex indicans) 'does not yet create an obligation, but at most indicates that such is to be presumed'.[73] For Cumberland, there are consequences arising out of this view. It is already inherent in his ambitious attempt to conceive the lex naturae and the physical laws of nature as a unity that they should divide into two areas ('worlds') with varying degrees of obligation, and this division also finds its expression in the conflict outlined above between a voluntaristic and a naturalistic conception.

Under these circumstances, it may be no surprise that the use of the term 'Law(s) of Nature' can be shown to be inconsistent and contradictory:

67 Parkin 1999: 80ff. and 168ff.

68 Toronto, Buffalo 1971, reprint of the edition of 1652.

69 Cf., for example, the choice of words in the two definitions of lex naturae in: DLN V: 185, § 1 and DLN I: 1, § 1.

70 DLN IV: 173f., § 1.

71 Specht 1959: 235.

72 Ibid.: 241; Suárez, *De legibus* II, 6, 13.

73 Specht 1959: 239 and 251.

(a) The term lex/leges (law, laws) is quite clearly (from the context and/or from references to particular authors) used in the sense of a physical concept of law (as in the case of the leges motûs), for example in the following passage:

> *Lastly*, If we consider this *visible World*, with *Des-Cartes* and others, as a most exquisite *Machine*, we may perceive, that this our Vortex is no otherwise daily preserv'd, than by *resisting* some *contrary Motions* of the neighbouring Vortices; by *changing* or *removing Bodies of Figures or Motions less agreeable*; ... But I am determin'd, not to insist upon such *Hypotheses*, altho I know, that we may fairly reason from them, provided the natural Laws of Motion be exactly observ'd in them; and I dare affirm, that has been perform'd by *Des-Cartes*, with great Care and Exactness, in most Parts of his *Hypothesis*. Howbeit, whatsoever *Hypothesis* be assum'd, in order to explain the *Phaenomena* of Nature, such Laws of Motion must of necessity be allow'd, as, amidst all natural Changes, preserve the State of the *System of the World*, by such Methods as I have mention'd ... But all these Theorems, or Laws of Motions, may be deduced from this *Supposition*, 'That Motion is not annihilated, after it has been impress'd upon Matter by the first Cause.' And for this very Reason, 'That it exists in a World that admits no *Vacuum*, it is necessarily still further propagated, till it return into it self': And, on the contrary, the Truth of this *Supposition* is demonstrated, by all the Theorems of Motion observ'd in Nature, by the help of the Senses. (DLN I: 70f., § 25; original DLN I: 41, § 25)

As Cumberland expounds, the leges motûs naturales for their part point to the 'principia Physiologiae Mechanicae generalia'[74] (Principles of Mechanical Philosophy). To this extent, this exposition of Cumberland's sets out a view reflecting that of Descartes which can be described as 'mechanistic': 'It is mechanistic both in a broader sense, because it considers matter and motion in general to be the first and only causes of all natural phenomena, and also in a narrower sense because the forms of motion are determined by the principles of a specific discipline, namely mechanics.'[75] If one wished to express this mechanistic view more precisely, the 'active element of motion' is opposed to the 'passive element of matter that is merely shaped'.[76] Furthermore, elements of the early modern physical concept of law and some of its preconditions can be identified in this passage: abstraction in the form of the reduction of the complex visible world to simple ultimate principles (theorems), the mathematical-logical processing of matter, which is viewed as existing in calculable magnitudes (in the sense of geometrical properties), and of its forms of motion (in the sense of kinematical properties) in accordance with experience (when the phenomena are carefully observed), linked to the demonstration that the leges motûs naturales apply without exception to the entire history of all physical nature.[77] However, as Cumberland draws upon a variety of sources for his 'concept of law', he is not able to endow it with internal conceptual consistency. On the one hand Cumberland follows Descartes' concept of law, which is ultimately anchored in fundamental metaphysical and theological assumptions and does not require to be

74 DLN II: 101, § 15.

75 Schiemann 1997: 21 and 24.

76 Ibid.: 83.

77 DLN I: 40f., § 3: '... to shew the History of the whole corporeal System exactly conspiring with the Laws of Matter and Motion.'

tested against experience.[78] On the other hand, he draws upon the leges motûs debate that is in progress in circles close to the Royal Society, the aim of which is to produce a regular description, in terms of the laws that govern it, of the motion of two bodies after a collision (depending on their motion beforehand), the testing of which by experience (experiment) is envisaged, or at least aspired to. Finally, the theory of rewards and punishments that he formulates assumes a conception of regularity that is accessible to direct observation, i.e. can be attained to on an inductive basis.

(b) For the 'leges naturae', the laws of nature, Cumberland presents two definitions. The first is in the first chapter (§ 1, p. 1 or p. 39), the other at the beginning of the fifth chapter (§ 1, p. 185 or p. 189). The first of these definitions of lex naturae is as follows:

> Intelligimus Propositiones quasdam immutabilis veritatis quae Actiones voluntarias citra Bonorum Electionem, malorúmque Fugam dirigunt, ac Obligationem ad actus externos inducunt: etiam citra Leges Civiles ... (DLN I: 1, § 1)[79]

The second definition, from the fifth chapter, has already been quoted, and runs as follows:

> Lex Naturae est propositio à natura rerum ex Voluntate Primae Causae menti satis apertè oblata vel impressa, actionem indicans Bono Rationalium communi deservientem, quam si praestetur praemia, sin negligatur, poenae sufficientes ex naturâ Rationalium sequuntur. (DLN V: 185, § 1)[80]

In both of these definitions, lex naturae is defined using the term 'propositio'. The first definition could be rendered into modern language as an unchangeable (since 'true') 'ethical maxim' which imposes an absolute obligation, even without invoking (positive) law as embodied in the 'leges civiles'. In the definition presented in the fifth chapter, the imposition of a binding obligation arises out of the fact that the will of God is shown to be the source of this obligation, including whatever sanctions he may impose (although it is noticeable that there is no longer any mention of 'obligatio' here). This voluntaristic moment seems to reflect the time-honoured view that nature too obeys the will of the Creator; just as the idea that God reacts to deviant behaviour with punishment also reproduces the traditional belief that those who violate the laws of God will suffer retribution. As has already been explained, Cumberland understands the observable rewards and punishments to be reliable indicators, with the aid of which, and of the understanding of the 'nature of things' that is afforded by the laws of motion, it is also possible to determine reliably the will of the 'First Cause'. As the various types of reaction which emanate from the divine will also obey the laws of nature or of motion, Cumberland finds himself in

---

78 Steinle 1995: 326; Garber 1992: 197–305.

79 In translation.: 'For we ... understand thereby, certain Propositions of unchangeable Truth, which direct our voluntary Actions, about chusing Good and refusing Evil; and impose an Obligation to external Actions, even without Civil Laws ...' (DLN I: 39, § 1).

80 This is the longer version of the text.

a trap. He attempts to escape from it by assuming that while God does indeed have free will, he will not in fact act inconsistently and to this extent will bind himself to the order of nature that he himself has prescribed.[81] This, however, leaves unsolved the problem that, if a prescription of conduct is elevated to a law of nature, it cannot in fact be violated. This problem thus stands in the way of a consistent analogy.

The fact that Cumberland is constantly a prey to contradictions and inconsistencies is also made clear by the following quotation:

> The Knowledge (or Ideas form'd in the Mind) of *Human Actions*, of Consequences good or evil to human Nature, but, especially of *Rewards* and *Punishments* naturally connected with such Actions, and those Ideas reduc'd into the Form of *Practical Propositions*, ... are all that is *essential* to a *Law*. Such Ideas may be produc'd, by Observation, in the Minds of those who are born *Deaf*, tho, they form no notion of the sound or force of Words; and so the Laws of Nature will become known, even to them. (DLN V: 191, § 1)

Cumberland speaks here of 'practical propositions' or dictates (propositiones practicae), which on the one hand rest upon experience that is accessible even to the deaf (who learn the laws of nature – leges naturales – through observation), while on the other hand having all the attributes essential to a law (lex). As he includes amongst these the divine rewards and punishments that occur with nothing short of predictable regularity, but these in their turn, as he argues elsewhere in the work, are subject to the laws of motion, to which indeed they owe their predictability, there are numerous contradictions and obscurities particularly with regard to the distinctions made between different terms.

(c) The decision as to whether to observe such practical rules of conduct (propositiones practicae) dictated by prudence and (the knowledge gained from) experience Cumberland attributes to 'comparative Dictates of Reason' in the sense of an evaluation of the end and the means or an assessment of cause and effect by *practical reason*, whereupon he comes up with an interesting formulation:

> Nobis qui Legum naturalium Generationem tantùm quaerimus, non est necessarium asserere hujusmodi dictamina, etiam postquam ea Legum vim habere novimus, semper homines ad actus determinare; sufficit ut jus dicant determinationi futurae. (DLN IV: 173f., § 1)[82]

Thus in the case of the 'practical dictates' (to which he gives varying designations: 'propositiones' or 'dictamina') Cumberland does not seek to demonstrate any absolute obligation with a deterministic attitude of expectation, which, as he has explained in his fourth chapter, is something quite foreign to the practical dictates. He contents himself with pointing out that they may indicate the existence of a law and so point to a strictly prescribed manner of behaviour. Drawing upon Suárez's

---

81 Parkin 1999: 168ff.

82 In translation: 'For us, who are engaged in enquiring into the very origins of the laws of nature, it is not necessary to prove that dictates of this kind, once we know that they possess the force of law, always determine the actions of men; it is sufficient that they indicate what the law is for future determination.'

distinction between 'lex obligans' and 'lex indicans', the following interpretation might be offered: mere knowledge of the matter that is to be observed does not create an obligation, but does indicate that a latent obligation may be assumed, which – as should presumably be added – becomes manifest when it is made into law. The translator, who draws directly upon the explanations with which Cumberland underpins his distinguishing of 'Three Forms of practical Dictates of Reason', quite obviously treats what he calls 'practical propositions' as such dictates that tell us how we ought to behave (and decide).

But Cumberland also uses the term 'propositiones' to designate the 'leges naturae', which he generally regards as being identical with the immutable 'leges motûs naturales'. The following passage in particular, which also introduces a modified version of the 'Golden Rule', demonstrates in a particularly vivid way how Cumberland constructs affinities with the help of 'unsuspected similarities' (Helmholtz), while also reminding his readers that the power of thought (vis intellectûs) generally operates in this way:

> It is sufficient, that 'To *perceive* in Men a Likeness of Nature and Condition with respect to Necessaries,' and 'To *infer* from what is done to others, what we are to hope or fear will be done to our selves,' are Acts *Natural* and Universal, and not of *less* Efficacy to *influence* Men, than mutual *Contact* between Bodies moving and moved, is to *communicate Motion* among the Parts of a corporeal System.[83]

At times Cumberland also uses the expression 'principium (principii)' for 'propositio', which the translator renders as 'rule(s)', just as he also uses 'proposition' and 'rule' synonymously. Cumberland also knows the expression 'regulae', but for the most part he uses it when he is talking about, for example, arithmetical rules. If a list is made of the most important terms that Cumberland uses – (natural) laws of Motion (leges motûs naturales); laws of Nature (leges naturae); (general) precepts (praecepta generalia); (general) principles (principia generalia); propositions (propositiones), rules (regulae), theorems (theoremata) – it will be found to be more or less identical with the stock of terms that Friedrich Steinle has identified as being current in the young Royal Society;[84] the synonymous use of these terms is also conspicuously similar.

IV

To conclude, attention should be drawn to that one among all those factors that could have favoured the adoption of a physical concept of law which may to some

---

[83] DLN II: 116, § 14. In the original: 'Sufficit quòd vis intellectûs similitudinem naturae, statûsque, quoad necessaria, inter omnes homines percipiens, quódque ratiocinari à factis erga alios, ad similia facienda aut speranda, aut metuenda planè naturale sit, & perpetuum, nec minùs efficax ad homines commovendos quàm contractus [sic!] mutuus est inter moventia & mobilia ad communicandos motus inter partes systematis corporei' (DLN II: 100, § 14).

[84] Steinle 2001: 78–84; and see Steinle, Chapter 13 in this volume.

extent be regarded as self-evident. Through his access to the Royal Society[85], which was also assured by personal contacts and the bonds of friendship, Cumberland was constantly able to equip himself with the latest ideas, especially as the Society, thanks to the diligence of its secretary and his periodical, had developed into a veritable exchange and mart of information and theories. The advantage that this represented becomes clear if a comparison is made with the 'learned household' of such a one as Bernegger.[86] Although the latter, as was customary in the culture of learned humanism, also corresponded with an extensive network of other scholars (including people of the calibre of Grotius and Kepler), it was a more or less homogenous one,[87] and was at any rate shut off from the outside world.[88] Oldenburg, as secretary of a permanent institution, by printing letters received and/or solicited in whole or in part in a regularly appearing periodical, transformed such material into publicly accessible treatises which invited others to comment or to contribute their opinions. A pluralistic network created in this way and fundamentally susceptible to expansion provides an ideal framework both for the collection of information and for the dissemination of new theories; a framework within which processes initiated by a sequence of actions and reactions and developing a dynamism of their own, and which may be stimulated by 'ambivalent orientations of interests',[89] arouse additional attention, and are even capable of giving rise to something like a 'public domain of activities' in the field in question.

---

[85] Parkin 1999: 116: Cumberland 'was part of a circle of ex-St. Paul's students including Samuel Pepys, an old school friend and later President of the Royal Society; John Hollings, a doctor of medicine, who provided some of the medical references of the Royal Society ...'

[86] Hall 1981: 178.

[87] In Bernegger's network of correspondents, the rough extent of which has been determined on the basis of the volume of letters published by Reifferscheid (1889) and taking into account Boecler's (1640) funeral oration for Bernegger, theologians were underrepresented; his correspondents were predominantly of his own age group and possibly shared with him the predilections and accustomed thought processes that were peculiar to that generation. At any rate, homogeneity is furthered when a group is shut off from the outside world, such separation being often deliberately exploited as a technique to promote that very quality.

[88] Weber 1976: 23, § 10.

[89] Mayntz and Nedelmann 1987: 656ff. The fact that the Fellows of the Royal Society were called upon both to co-operate with each other and to exercise mutual criticism makes them potential partners in activities, but also potential competitors, a typical constellation of an ambivalent orientation of interests, which, as indeed occurred, can lead to disputes about the priority of claims. A well-known example is Huygens' controversy with Robert Hooke over who had priority in the invention of the 'balance-spring watch' in the year 1675.

Chapter 11

Leibniz's Concept of jus naturale and lex naturalis – defined 'with geometric certainty'

Klaus Luig[1]

I Basic Tenets

I.1 The Unity of jus naturale *and* lex naturalis

This essay examines three issues related to jus naturale and lex naturalis in the writings of Leibniz. First of all, did Leibniz believe that legal rules or judicial laws could be drawn up with a claim to absolute truth in the sense of natural law ('with geometric certainty')?[2] If so, the second question that arises is how he intended to draw up the rules in particular. Thirdly, the essay intends to elucidate, on the basis of the theory of compensation, what Leibniz regarded as the specific contents of natural law within the legal system.

Leibniz's notions of law and justice can best be understood by bearing in mind that his most ambitious aim as a jurist was not the creation of a scientific system of legal rules, but the formation of a comprehensive code of law for the German Empire. This codification was never undertaken because, at the time when Leibniz was working intensively on these plans – between 1677 and 1681 – the empire was under threat from the Ottoman Turks, and in Vienna his proposals fell on deaf ears.

Leibniz planned a codification that would comprise all the rules of law corresponding to human nature. Whether and to what extent Roman law would be of assistance to him was of only secondary importance. First and foremost, Leibniz sought to determine legal rules that corresponded to the human nature created by God. This was to be transposed into positive law by the legislature. According to this programme, positive law was to be based on a theologically founded theory of natural law. However, in Leibniz's view, it was the law of nature that humans should

1 Translated by Ishbel Flett.

2 Gottfried Wilhelm Leibniz, *Sämtliche Schriften und Briefe*, ed. Berlin-Brandenburgische Akademie der Wissenschaften und Akademie der Wissenschaften zu Göttingen, Sechste Reihe Philosophische Schriften, Vols. VI 1 – VI 4, Darmstadt 1930 – Berlin 1999; hereafter cited as 'A VI 1 etc.' page, line. Leibniz 2003. A VI 4 361 13: 'Lib III. Elementa jurisprudentiae universalis, quibus vera explicatur natura justitiae tum quid sit meri juris, et quomodo omnes quaestiones meri juris Geometrica certitudine possint definiri, tum etiam quid sit aequitatis ...'

obey God's commandment of neighbourly love in order to work together for the common weal.

The natural law of justice derived, for Leibniz, from observation of humankind. The rules deduced from this had the same degree of certitude (certitudo) for Leibniz as the rules of mathematics and physics. Not only could they be drawn up according to strictly logical factors, as for example the doctrine of conditions,[3] but they could also be developed with a claim to certainty, and thus 'mathematically' proven.

In the thesis of the unity of jus naturale and lex naturalis in Leibniz's *Scientia generalis nova* it was not only a question of orienting jurisprudence towards the exact natural sciences. Instead, there was also mention of 'Sitten-Artzney-Kunst', 'Sitten-Naturforschung', and 'Physiologia Moralis'.[4] Leibniz said of this unity: 'Natural law (jus naturale) which comprises the theory of all those means that people, through their communality or joint endeavours, are able to effect in order to achieve the highest good.'[5]

One of Leibniz's major projects was the production of a work known as an 'Encyclopedia' or 'Scientia Universalis',[6] which was to be able to promote true happiness (felicitas).[7] One of the three books of the encyclopedia, to be published under the title *Elementa iurisprudentiae universalis* (sometimes also referred to as rationalis), was to be devoted to law,[8] the association of which with the aim of promoting happiness Liebniz had always stressed.[9] Leibniz envisaged the other two books of this particular section of the encyclopedia as being about geometry and mechanics.

In this plan, it was clear right from the start that it was not only a question of absolute truth (absolute determinetur veritas[10]), but that there were also things for which only a maxima probabilitas[11] could be demonstrated (demonstretur). Accordingly, Leibniz described universal jurisprudence as follows:

> The elements of a universal jurisprudence in which the true nature of justice is elucidated and proved, both that which is pure law and by which all questions of law can be defined with geometric certainty, as well as that which is termed equity ('aequitas'), or if it is necessary to deviate from pure law for the sake of a higher good.[12]

Such discrepancies left enough room for manoeuvre in the legislator's decision-making.

---

3 Armgardt 2001; Leibniz 2002.

4 A VI 4 2738 15.

5 A VI 4 25.

6 A VI 4 133; A VI 4 442.

7 A VI 4 134.

8 A VI 4 443.

9 A VI 1 465 23: 'Iustitia est habitus amandi omnes'. A VI 1 466 11: 'Amamus eum cuius felicitate delectamur'. A VI 1 466 15: 'Felicitas est status personae optimus'.

10 A VI 4 359 13.

11 A VI 4 359 15.

12 A VI 4 361 13.

As for the terms used by Leibniz, ius naturae (occasionally ius naturale) and lex naturae (occasionally lex naturalis) tend to be employed as synonyms. However, in connection with nature, the term lex is used more frequently, whereas ius occurs more often in connection with law. There are some differences of content as well. According to Leibniz,[13] whatever one facit ex lege naturae suae summo iure naturali facit – meaning that whatever one does according to the law (lex) of nature, one also does by right of nature, in the sense of a subjective entitlement. In other words, ius is the right of the individual that results from lex.

I.2 The Vulnerability of Natural Law

With regard to the relationship between Leibniz's concept of ius naturale and lex naturalis, it should be borne in mind that the laws of human cohabitation, in contrast to the actual laws of nature, can be violated. In this respect, they are not so much a natural law in the way that, for instance, gravity is a law of nature, but more in the sense of the law of nature by which the consumption of alcohol leads to loss of control.

The connection between ius naturale and lex naturalis becomes clear when one considers that it is a violation of both ius naturale and lex naturalis to use one's arms to injure others or one's tongue to slander others, rather than for eating, drinking or speaking. According to Leibniz,

> Or il faut prendre garde que Dieu agit toûjours par les voyes les plus simples, et que les loix de la nature doivent être générales: et qu'ainsi nous ayant donné le pouvoir de remüer nôtre bras et nôtre langue, il ne doit pas nous ôter celuy de frapper un homme injustement ou de le calomnier.[14]

In other words, one may move one's arms against the natural laws of mechanics, but one will then miss the intended aim of orderly human cohabitation.

A violation of lex naturalis is thus also a violation of ius naturale. One of the examples Leibniz uses to illustrate this is that of conditional inheritance: 'Titus shall be heir if he kills Sempronius' is a legal impossibility, since the condition cannot be fulfilled even according to the law of nature.[15]

However, this also means that the content of the rule of natural law has absolute validity like the norms set by the laws of nature. Even a judicial rule or law has to be thus and not otherwise if everything is to be just and right. The laws of human cohabitation are conditional rules. They can be violated, but should not be violated, as this would destroy the natural order of things. Inversely, individuals can pursue their aims more effectively by respecting the laws of nature – for instance, when building a mill or founding an insurance company.[16]

---

[13] A VI 3 270 25.

[14] A VI 4 1919 24.

[15] A VI 1 400 20. Armgardt 2001: 66.

[16] A VI 4 1994 15.

The differences in content, however, cannot be overlooked. For Leibniz, lex, including lex naturae, is oriented towards the human spirit. It is 'dictamen propositio animi, ubi animus non est, jus nullum est'. This is the case among wild animals.

Thus, the law of nature that guides animals is not jus naturale.[17] This explains why, in many places, the term lex naturae is used exclusively in the modern sense of law of nature.[18] What is not entirely compatible with the above is the fact that, elsewhere,[19] Leibniz maintained that the leges naturae would remain intact even if humankind had no rational mind (mens), for then the laws would apply to humankind in the same way as they apply to animals. This elucidates the meaning of the phrase 'jus naturale, quod natura omnia animalia docuit'.[20] Animals follow it by instinct, humans ex recta ratione.[21]

God gave us both ius naturae and lex naturae,[22] and follows them both.[23] However, this means[24] that the law of nature is what the nature of things has produced with the human species – 'ius naturale quod cum ipso genere humano rerum natura prodidit'.

In other words, man can only act and follow the law based on ius naturae because God has given him the ability to act according to the law of nature.[25]

God permits evil, violation of law, unjustified action, but he does not wish it – otherwise he would change the content of the law.[26] However, the individual who violates the law of nature is worse than an animal – 'bestiis deterior est'.[27] The fact that man violates the law of nature may also be due to a lack of awareness. Leibniz taught that excusable lack of awareness of the law of nature meant that acting against the law of nature was not a sin.[28]

I.3 Material Principles

It is the universal law of human nature that no one neglects the opportunity of contributing beneficially to his own welfare, and causes no harm, except in the hope of thereby achieving benefit or out of fear of even greater harm.[29]

According to Leibniz, a successful course of human cohabitation in accordance with the laws of nature is only given if the bonum commune is assured and the veneration of God observed.[30] Leibniz wrote:

17 A VI 1 84 10–15. A VI 4 2778 10.
18 A VI 2 159 3. A VI 2 337 20. A VI 3 216 7.
19 A VI 4 1367 10.
20 A VI 4 2929 20–25. Ulp. Dig. 1.1.1.3.
21 A VI 4 2778 9–21.
22 A VI 4 1182 3. A VI 4 1621 12.
23 A VI 4 1575 10.
24 A VI 4 2930 3.
25 A VI 4 1936 10.
26 A VI 4 1539 15. A VI 4 1560 9.
27 A VI 4 2935 21.
28 A VI 4 2602 5. A VI 4 2700 10.
29 A VI 3 271.
30 A VI 4 1994.

> The law according to which we live is the science of love, and justice is the love (charity) of the wise, or the virtue, that guides the attitude of people to one another according to the laws of reason. Love, however, is the willingness to love all. And he who possesses this is described as a good person. Moreover, wisdom is the awareness of happiness. Happiness consists in our living in the grace and love of God, whose abilities and perfection are the greatest. Because he is the wisest of all, he has generally undertaken to achieve the perfection of all things and, in particular, of his most outstanding creatures, who use reason. Therefore, he who loves God, i.e. he who is wise, will love all, but each individual all the more, the clearer the traces of divine virtue shine within him, and the more he will be able to put his hope in him as a willing and resourceful companion in working for the common weal and that which contributes to it, and for the greater glory of God, the source of all good.[31]

The supreme principle, then, is that justice is the love of the wise – 'iustitia est amor sapientis'. This means that one must not only respect the rights of others and do them no harm (neminem laedere), but also that one must support others to the best of one's ability (prodesse). In principle, this means that refusal to give help where it is possible is as great an injustice as causing harm. Not helping means harming.[32]

II The Proof of Principles

II.1 The Supreme Principle

The supreme principle 'justice is love of the wise' can be proven in two ways: theologically and anthropologically (or judicially). The theological proof consists of two quotes from the Bible – that is, quotations from what Leibniz would term an 'authoritative source'. First of all, the sentence 'Therefore all things whatsoever ye would that men should not do to you, do ye even not to them' – which is the principle of neminem laedere – and secondly the sentence 'And as ye would that men should do to you, do ye also to them likewise'.[33] This is the commandment to help others and to be useful to them.

The anthropological proof is based on the insight into the fundamental significance of the three elements fear, hope and pleasure in one's own perfection as the elements that trigger willingness to help. It is the fear that the other will not help me if I do not help him as well, the hope that others will help us if we help them and, thirdly, pleasure in one's own perfection, as observed in God. It is this pleasure that means one finds one's own happiness first and foremost in the happiness of the community.[34]

---

31 *De tribus gradibus*, A VI 4 2861 15.

32 Buschc 1993: esp. 113 with ref. to A VI 1 433 18.

33 Matthew 7:12; Luke 6:31.

34 Mollat (1885) 1972: 59. Cf. also Riley 1996.

II.2 Further Principles

Further principles are without formal proof derived purely on the basis of the evidence. This also applies to the decisive principle in the field of law, that God wants what is good because it is good. And it is not simply good because God wants it. The conclusion to be drawn from this is that good is to be rewarded and wrong is to be punished. Leibniz was able to employ this premise, which is not proven and requires no proof, as a means of proving the immortality of the soul. The idea behind it was this: God wants what is good. Nevertheless, he allows the existence of evil people who can live happily on earth. In turn, there are also good people who suffer misfortune. But it would be incompatible with the rules of good government such as the government of God, if there were no consolation for this. Such consolation, however, can only be granted in a life after death. Therefore, there must be a life after death granted by God, otherwise crimes would remain forever unpunished and good deeds would go unrewarded.[35]

III The Proof of Conclusions

III.1 Types of Arguments

In proving further conclusions of the supreme principles a distinction may be made between four different types of arguments of scientific certainty (certitudo) – albeit with some unclarity and overlaps. This certainty is assured, on the one hand, by applying the rules of mechanics (see III.2) and on the other hand by the scientific processing of empirically given material (see III.3) as well as by applying logic (see III.4) and, finally, by means of the combinatorial method of developing the individual premises (see III.5).

III.2 Mechanics or 'leges motus'

(a) One derivation of a legal rule that is perfect in terms of natural science and mathematics can be found in the *Specimina iuris*.[36] The legal rule to be proven is Concursu fiunt partes, which means that 'If in law several persons are linked to one another in relation to one and the same thing, on grounds of equal cause, the thing is divided in such a way that each is apportioned an equal part'.[37] In terms of positive law, this results, for Leibniz, from a number of texts in Digest 45.1 *De verborum obligationibus*.[38] The natural scientific proof ('habet enim ea res principium quoddam physicum ex natura motus') can thus be freely translated as follows:

'Given a body A, on which bodies B and C exert an equal force at the same time – one along the axis BA and the other along the axis CA – the angle BAC is divided into

35 Mollat 1972 (1885): 51.

36 A VI 1 392 22. Cf. also A VI 4 1556 1; A VI 4 1558 19; A VI 4 2053 7.

37 A VI 1 393 16.

38 Dig. 45.1.56.

equal parts on the outside by the two forces B and C, and the axes are lengthened: BA to E, and CA to F. I maintain that as a result, object A will move along axis AD. For, if the object set in motion continues to move along the line of the force that set it in motion, which, in this case, would be the line AE and AF, then, given that A is set in motion only by B, A would continue to move along line AE. On the other hand, if A were set in motion only by C, the line would be AF. However, if A is set in motion by both, though not in exactly opposite directions, the object will not move on either of the lines of the bodies that set it in motion, and if both have an equal force, there is no reason why A should move more in one direction than in the other, for nothing happens for no reason. Nor would the object move in both directions, for nothing can be in several places at one and the same time ('nihil simul potest esse in pluribus locis'). Therefore A moves precisely along the line AD, which divides the angle into equal parts.'

Leibniz transposed this theory to law ('ad scopum juridicum applicemus'), resulting in the legal premise cited above. The two rivals are the movements ('motus') BA and CA. The object of the rivalry is the direction ('inclinatio') of the movement of A, which is divided between B and C, given an impetus of equal force.

(b) Another example of a legal premise derived directly from a law of nature is based on a principle of the laws of nature that is diametrically opposed to the above. It goes like this:

Given the fact, already mentioned in the first example, that, according to the laws of nature, two bodies cannot be in the same place ('an duo corpora possint esse in eodem loco')[39] – Leibniz deduces direct conclusions for the judicial theory of ownership: to wit, that two persons cannot own one and the same thing at the same time. Leibniz described his method of drawing conclusions on the basis of natural science as 'analogy': 'Unde patet elegans inter possessionem et positionem seu situm corporum in loco Analogia'.[40] For Leibniz, this proof was derived 'ex principiis iuris naturalis' in contrast to evidence based on empiricism, that is, on the positive Justinian law,[41] which would have been based on the fact that this complied with the teachings of the Roman jurist Paulus, according to Dig. 41.2.3.5.

III.3 Scientific Processing of Empirical Material

Legislation and judicature provide empirical material for scientific conclusions. An empirically founded theory of law is, first and foremost, the dogma of positive law.[42] Leibniz believed in the premise that everything that was in accordance with natural and divine law should also apply in state law: 'Quicquid iuris naturae ac divini est,

39 A VI 1 78 29.

40 A VI 1 79 8; Busche 1997: 95.

41 A VI 1 78 27.

42 *Nova Methodus*, Pars II, A VI 1 293.

etiam iuris civilis haberi debet.'[43] In fact, however, natural law had no need for state legislation: 'Ius naturale est quod legibus non indigent.'[44] Nevertheless, Leibniz observed that even Jesus Christ had taught and prescribed additions to eternal natural law.[45] Therefore, natural law may also be complemented and altered by positive law: 'ius legitimum naturali aliquid detrahere potest'.[46] And what is vague in natural law is concretized according to Leibniz through positive law.[47] The legislator can decree laws that deviate from natural law: this is possible, in particular, in cases where the subject of a right can renounce this right: 'Leges juri naturae contrariae condi possunt circa illa omnia in quibus aliquis juri suo renuntiare potest.'[48] Natural law does, however, take precedence where state law is lacking or incomplete: 'Cessante legi civili pronuntiandum est secundum jus naturae.' But, in contrast to natural law in the narrowest sense, the norm of natural law can be flexible if this is deemed equitable. In other words, natural law may be changed in the interests of fairness: 'Aequitas est quiddam quod ius naturale immutat'.[49]

These statements by Leibniz indicate that, in his view, there were legal premises that could not be derived from natural law, but only from positive Roman law. The crucial factor here is that such a legal premise can also have a 'ratio' and that this ratio has a part in the certainty (certitudo) guaranteed by science (scientia). This applies, for example, to the rule that, in the case of two persons bound to one another by verbal agreement, it is assumed that when one party is no longer present, the other will take their place. An example of this is the will and testament reading: 'I bequeath to Titius and Caius a piece of land in equal parts'. If Titius then dies, Caius receives his share as well.[50] Empirical material is found not only in the lawbooks and their commentaries, but also in the 'customs of the courts'.[51]

The ratio of natural law can thus be approached through the scientific commenting and expounding of positive law. Lawyers trained according to the principles outlined in the *Nova Methodus* are urged to take this approach. Leibniz described such a lawyer as follows:

> He will be able to make his own judgment in the face of controversy, he will read the authentic books – law books – and will be able to cite Justinian law, he will deduce from this what is necessary in deciding controversy, and will establish new rules and new principles that others have overlooked, he will draw upon commentaries and understand the rationes of the laws and will gradually learn the science of legislation. He will then stride through the sea of controversy and will observe the customs of the courts and the precedents of previous decisions. He will determine differences of opinion and disagreement resulting from the situation of different nations and the differences between

---

43 A VI 4 2753 15.

44 A VI 4 2908 9.

45 A VI 4 2384 5.

46 A VI 4 2909 20.

47 A VI 4 2909 23.

48 A VI 4 2753 17–19.

49 A VI 4 2909 13.

50 A VI 1 396 1.

51 A VI 1 362 22.

> states. And he will also learn, by constant comparison, to deduce firm legal premises from the unchanging principles of natural law ('continuo nexu firmas demonstrationes deducere') while bearing in mind the interests of the common weal and will thus wield the sword of invincible science to cut through the undergrowth of unnecessary subtleties and citations by those who practise law and the confusion of contradictions based on presumed authority and inappropriate use of proverbs.[52]

Thus, it is not a question of natural law that God has written into the hearts of men, but of the development of rules of natural law by scientific means on the basis of statutory provisions, the opinions of the commentators and the decisions of the courts. This, then, is the natural law derived from precise – scientific – observation. It was to form the basis for a treatise entitled 'Juris naturalis elementa demonstrative tradita'.[53]

III.4 The Role of Logic

Logic predominates in the theory of Leibniz's *Doctrina conditionum*.[54] In his view, the rightness of legal rules was assured by the fact that they could be developed and drawn up according to the laws of logic and he made this insight the basis for this treatise of conditions. Evidence that Leibniz was correct in doing so can be demonstrated, as Armgardt has done,[55] by the fact that the individual rules of the *Doctrina conditionum* can be expounded with the aid of the techniques of modern logic. In the *Doctrina conditionum* Leibniz was interested less in drawing up new material than in proving that there is 'mathematical evidence and the concomitant certainty in law'.[56] Leibniz found his material – the individual material rules – in the texts of the ancient Roman jurists. Looking to them, he wrote, 'I would rather make the effort of reiteration and would rather put in order their legal commentaries, which are based on extremely certain and even mathematical evidence, than add anything to their inventive prowess'.[57] Thus, if the legal rules existing in Roman law could be formulated strictly according to the laws of logic, they would be valid not on grounds of the authority of the jurists who formulated them in the first place, but on grounds of their logical consistency.[58] Leibniz was serious about the 'mos geometricus'; he wanted to provide evidence. Providing evidence and the security thus achieved is the prime characteristic of the mathematical method.[59]

---

52 A VI 1 362 12ff.
53 A VI 1 364 13.
54 A VI 1 369–430.
55 See Armgardt 2001.
56 Ibid.: 2–3.
57 *Doctrina conditionum*, Prooemium, A VI 1 370 6. Armgardt 2001: 12.
58 Armgardt 2001: 3.
59 Ibid.: 125.

III.5 Ars combinatoria

The field of application of Leibniz's Ars combinatoria is the formation of case studies in the preparation of legislative texts.[60] This hardly points directly to a method of deducing the norms of natural law.[61] On the other hand, combinatorial analysis is not to be regarded as worthless.[62] For Leibniz, at least, whose personal views are the subject of the present essay, the value of these methods derived from geometry lies in the fact that they provided the legislature with an overview of all cases requiring legal regulation.[63] Leibniz was convinced that the legislature could not always foresee the cases that would have to be subsumed under the law. However, he believed that, as Plato had already said, as little as possible should be left to the opinion of the judge, and that it was therefore sensible to apply combinatorial analysis in collating possible cases when formulating the law, so that later restrictions or amendments to the law would not be left to chance.[64]

The art of collating or discovering cases is based on Leibniz's theory of 'complexiones': the combination of various elements in every new constellation. A prerequisite for this is that jurisprudence – in this respect similar to geometry – works with simple elements ('elementa simplicia') and cases ('casus'). Simple elements are persons, things, deeds and omissions as well as rights. Among individuals, a distinction can be made between, say, man, woman, boy, old person.[65] Among things, a distinction must be made between animal, water, land, sea and so forth.[66] Similarly, among deeds or action – possession, handover, damage, words, conditions, and so on;[67] and concerning rights – material and personal rights, property, indentures and so on. Cases are combinations of these elements. There is an infinite number of such combinations. Thus, the Ars combinatoria is indeed worthless at first glance as Leibniz himself had to concede. On the other hand Leibniz believed that it was possible to sort out the irrelevant variations.[68] As he was forced to admit, the strictly mathematical method of combinatorial analysis also involved unrelated elements. Leibniz said: 'The nature of things and moral decency (decus) rarely allow all possible variations to be of use.'[69] Indeed, he succeeded in implementing this consideration of the nature of things and of decency in the most important example concerning the application of his method – the *Elementa iuris naturalis*.[70] It can therefore be said

60 A VI 1 189 12–16.

61 According to Busche 1997: 335, 339. Busche 1993: 113: '... quasi mathematische Grundlegung des Naturrechts' [... quasi mathematical basis of natural law]; 'Kombinatorik als Normfindungs-Methode der Wissenschaft vom Gerechten' [combinatorial analysis as a method of determining legal norms in jurisprudence]; see also ibid., 137.

62 Otte 1983: 8: 'Sie ist wertlos' [It is worthless].

63 *De arte combinatoria*, A VI 1 189 17: 'Ars casuum formandorum'. Otte 1983: 6.

64 A VI 1 189 12–16.

65 A VI 1 189 27.

66 A VI 1 189 32.

67 A VI 1 190 1–5.

68 A VI 1 190 28.

69 A VI 223 8.

70 A VI 1 431–485. Leibniz 2003: 91.

that the *Elementa iuris naturalis* elucidates the usefulness of the Ars combinatoria, as Leibniz had hoped, when it comes to finding the fullest and most logical solutions on the basis of a complete overview of the problems to be resolved. With this in mind, the following outlines the ideas behind the first sections of Leibniz's *Elements of Natural Law*.

IV Elements of Natural Law

Leibniz took as his starting point the two most important principles of the theory of justice: namely, that justice means, first of all, causing damage to no one, and secondly, that one supports one's fellow man in so far as this is possible without detriment to oneself.[71] In what follows only the theory of damage is portrayed in the application of combinatorial analysis.

The term damage has been used in a broad sense that might be more aptly described as hindrance. The most serious form of hindrance is suffering damage in the narrower sense. This is what Leibniz treats first. Later, he considers the hindrance involved in not having possession of a thing to which one is entitled, and then the hindrance involved in the threat of danger.

IV.1 Damage (in the narrower sense)

The term damage can be combined with the elements of blame or guilt and non-blame or non-guilt, whereby a distinction must be made between damage caused deliberately or through negligence. If the damage is deliberate, a further distinction must be made and corresponding cases noted. Yet the legal consequences remain the same: The damaged party has a reason to begin war, a 'jus belli' in the sense of Hugo Grotius.[72]

IV.2 Negligence

Leibniz then turned his attention to damage caused by negligence. The variety of possible legal consequences resulting from the various combinations are of greater significance here:

> There follow the cases in which one person causes damages to another through negligence.[73] The prevention of gain plays no role in this. It is a question of whether the person who causes the damage seeks to damage the physical health or material wealth of the other, i.e. that damage would also be caused if chance did not intervene or if the perpetrator did not do everything in his power to prevent the damage occurring.

In the case of negligence, Leibniz emphasizes the legal consequences. The first legal consequence is the duty to provide security:

---

71 A VI 1 433 18ff.

72 A VI 1 434 1.

73 A VI 434 10.

> Whoever does so is duty bound, 1. to prove his innocence insofar as this is possible, 2. to provide security for orderly behaviour in future. However, a person who cannot prove his innocence or cannot at least present a credible case as far as possible to prove his innocence, is duty bound, as is anyone who has deliberately caused damage, to provide assurance of his future good will.

The possible further legal consequence is an obligation to compensate for the damage:

> With regard to the question as to whether the person is obliged to pay a fine in addition, as is anyone who has deliberately caused damage, it is my opinion that a distinction must be made.
> (a) For either he is unable to provide security for our wealth, in which case it is permitted to cause him such damage that at least the memory of it will deter him from causing further damage.
> (b) But if he is able to provide security for our wealth without damage to himself, then he is to be punished in some way with a view to others, so that these others will not cause us damage when they see that one can inflict damage upon us with impunity, fearing no consequences but that of having to desist from further causing damage, as would be the case if calm prevailed.[74]

IV.3 Without Blame

There follow the cases in which one person causes damage to another without intent and without negligence.

This concerns first and foremost the legal consequences that are to be taken into consideration against the background of the principle of positive law that one is liable to compensation only if one is to blame. Leibniz rejected this principle and developed his own ideas based on natural law. According to these, the following applied: As long as the damage continues, the person who has suffered damage may defend himself against the perpetrator even if this involves causing damage to him.

This complied with the generally accepted right of self-defence. Leibniz's own principle was: 'When the damage is ended, the perpetrator is liable to compensation, but only in so far as this is possible without forfeit.' This duty of compensation in so far as it does not damage the innocent perpetrator, is one example of the application of Leibniz's principle of 'innoxia utilitas' (being of use for others without own disadvantage).[75]

If the perpetrator himself were to suffer damage in compensating for damage, the damage would have to be shared. This sharing of damage in a case in which neither the perpetrator nor the victim is to blame is by no means a new and independent idea of Leibniz's. It is a principle that is also applied to shipping collisions, and can be found in Grotius' *Indleidinge*[76] *and his De iure bellli ac pacis*.[77] Even in the Old Testament it says: 'And if one man's ox hurt another's that he die; then they shall

---

74 A VI 1 434 19.

75 A VI 1 447 22.

76 Grotius 1965: 3.38.18, p. 314.

77 Grotius 1720: 2.17.21. Cf. Luig 1969: 225, notes 176 and 177.

sell the live ox, and divide the money of it; and the dead ox they shall divide.'[78] The justification posited by Leibniz for this rule is not derived from the Ars combinatoria that aids only the legislature in determining the relevant cases and considering them in advance. Leibniz's justification is:

> If you weigh up the matter with care, then, in order to avoid displeasure and envious looks [schehle augen][79] and inimicable attitudes … it will be just that we share the damage, whereby each shall think that he has unfortunately damaged the other or suffered damage. For if both are free of blame, the other has as much reason to complain that my interests were an obstacle for him as I have to think that he has confounded my interests.[80]

IV.4 Loss

In the next step, Leibniz treats the obligation to hand over a thing. In this case, the damage lies in the fact that the person who is entitled to have the thing does not have what he should legally possess. In such cases, blame also plays a role – the blame of the entitled person himself, who has lost the thing through his own fault, and the blame of the person in possession of the thing, who has acquired it either innocently or knowingly, to complete the number of possible combinations, from the thief.

Expenses incurred by the owner in respect of a thing, the fruits of the thing and, ultimately, the results of any altering or processing of the thing, must also be taken into account.

IV.5 Expenses

Leibniz's subtle combinatorial analysis even brings him to consider the case of a person being in possession of a thing that he has knowingly acquired from the thief in order to secure it for the rightful owner. In this case, Leibniz again proposes sharing the damage, even though it would be justified for the person who has acquired the thing on behalf of the rightful owner to have all his expenses reimbursed. This case shows again that, although combinatorial analysis serves to highlight all manner of possible constellations, it does not necessarily lead to answers. The following text provides another good example of this:

> But what is valid in the law of property, i.e. in respect of some thing of mine or some thing to which I have a right of lien? Whether and how the handover of such a thing can be demanded of a third party; unconditionally, so that I do not compensate him for damage if he has unknowingly and blamelessly purchased the thing from a thief? And I do not believe that,[81] nor do I see, on what grounds; but rather, if I have lost it through my own fault, then, on the return of the thing that is mine, I must reimburse the person in possession of it for all his expenses, for I have caused him damage through my own fault. I therefore have a full title to precisely the thing itself, as long as no other suffers damage; for it may be that the thing has an affective value for me that cannot be taken from me,

---

78 Exodus 21:35.

79 A VI 1 435 25.

80 A VI 1 435 27.

81 A VI 1 436 8–14.

> whereas it is enough for the other to suffer no damage, and for me to suffer none either. But if he himself is at fault, he will bear the damage alone; though it is a different matter if he has knowingly purchased the thing from a thief, not to retain it, but to save it for me, or without any particular reason, and I could not otherwise have regained possession of the thing in good order, then the damage is to be shared.'

IV.6 Fruits

For the fruits the following shall apply: [82]

> What applies with regard to the fruits of the thing? In my opinion, one must make a distinction; if the fruits could have been generated in full by me, they are owed to me in full. If other fruits, albeit of equal value, could have been generated, I have a claim to compensation of the value.[83] If the fruits would otherwise not have been generated by me – possibly because the person in possession of the thing has made improvements to it – then I have no claim whatsoever to them, but must deduct the value of those fruits on reclaiming the thing, and this must be done in such a way that loss and profit are equal.

Leibniz posits the following principle regarding the processing or alteration of a thing belonging to another:[84]

> If I unknowingly alter a thing belonging to another, then, if I have improved it, I have a right to the new thing. And if the material has no emotional or ideal value, as for example when I have written something on your paper, then your paper is secondary to the thing that is mine. But if both have an emotional or ideal value, the question arises as to who should be allowed to keep the thing; the one who first had an emotional or ideal interest in it, or the one whose interest is greater, and if both have an equal interest, the one who was there first. And it cannot be said that, in the case of equal value, the one who was there first should take precedence, or that, given the same duration of possession, it should be the one who has the greater interest. The one who has the greater interest should take precedence over the one who came first, and the opposite applies if neither the value nor the duration are the same, for these characteristics cannot be offset against one another. Moreover, only the damage is to be charged to account. However, if the damage is the same, it is, in my opinion, the one who came first who should take precedence, because the surplus of the other thus gives him a right of retention. And under otherwise identical conditions, the person who came first has the greater right. And this simply because, under otherwise identical conditions, the earlier condition must always be reinstated.[85]

IV.7 Risk

In the list of possible detriments, damage caused and retention (non-possession) of a thing is followed by the added aspect of threatened risk and the means of defence permitted to prevent or avoid such risk.[86]

---

82 A VI 1 436 22.
83 A VI 1 436 24.
84 A VI 1 436 26.
85 A VI 1 436 35.
86 A VI 1 437 14.

Possible reactions to the threat of risk are: self-help, and assistance in emergency. Assistance in emergency is in the first instance assistance in an emergency that involves my helping one person without harming another. The one who is not helped suffers a disadvantage in so far as he is cut off from a benefit in the form of the help that is not accorded to him. This is always the case when only one of two parties in need of assistance can be helped. On this, Leibniz said:

> We now come to a question of more considerable import. Given that there are two people in danger of drowning, and only one of them, but not both, can be saved: is it now left to my free judgment to save one and leave the other unaided? And is it not so, that the one I have left unaided, should he indeed be saved by chance, can complain about me? Certainly, he will have no reason to love me, but nor will he have any reason to hate me. I therefore believe that in this case there is only an obligation to act kindly and equitably, and that, strictly according to the law, no help can be demanded, unless one leaves both parties unaided. Admittedly, if someone leaves me unaided even though he could have come to my assistance without endangering himself, I have a right to take action against him. And this is also the case if he can save me only at risk of harm to himself, as long as he does not die himself.[87]

Leibniz considers the questions arising from such a case to be unresolved.[88] Yet in his own opinion, the mathematical combination of possible cases obviously does facilitate the quest for just solutions:[89]

> 'It certainly seems just that the better of the two be chosen, being the one who is of more use to the community, e.g. someone who has many children who would be unable to survive without his support, as opposed to a widower or an idler. Also, the one whose loss would be a loss for the state, such as a hostage, or one who can be sold at a high price.[90] But it is doubtful whether that can be taken into consideration. As to the question of whether I can save a rich man rather than a poor man, this is more a question of my own financial gain, for the rich man can offer me more. It is no small matter, for it is a question of the life and well-being of one or the other. What applies to a father, what to a close friend, what to a master or lord (rector), what applies if the master meets with the friend, or the prince with the father? Who is to be helped? What if the father meets with the friend? What role does gratitude play? Is such an important matter to be excluded from regulations and left to chance or fate? Should the matter be left to a stroke of chance or fate that does not come from outside, but is rooted in the matter itself?[91] I believe we have to come to the aid of the one to whom our aid is most accessible, and do what we can, and that which offers the speediest assistance. A different question is: if, of two swimmers, one grasps towards me first, whether I can cruelly reject him because I am outraged by this. Or, whether the sheer physical strength of the wicked or idle person can save him, while the physical weakness of the wise man is his undoing. This would be admissible if it were a matter of elements without reason, but not in the case of persons endowed with reason. Supposing

87 A VI 1 439 21.

88 A VI 1 439 33.

89 A VI 1 440 17. Cf. Leibniz 2003.

90 A VI 1 440 9.

91 A VI 1 440 15.

> the king cannot be freed without the sacrifice of a citizen.[92] What if a bridge can be built with the bodies of the injured, across which I can save the king, my father, a friend or a charitable man? All these questions must ultimately be answered. Preference is certainly to be given to the individual whose death would involve the death of many others. But in the face of misfortune, all men are equal.[93] Supposing I have a potion against gout that is almost finished and cannot be replaced for the benefit of someone to whom I owe a debt. If I myself have gout, I shall think first of myself, even if others could rightly take the potion from me. Moreover, for instance, on a ship, if I alone have hidden enough victuals, there is no reason to show them openly. Rather, I may use them to nourish myself until the harbour is reached. But if others learn of this, they will rightly demand that I share my victuals with them rather than they should die. And so, in these cases, the necessity results in a just war (bellum justum) for both parties. Whatever the situation, I do not doubt that I can choose which person I shall help first. But there must be a reason. Therefore choose: above all the one with whom your fate[94] is linked, then the one upon whom the well-being of the greatest number of others depends, i.e. first and foremost the common weal. Father, spouse and son will be secondary to the prince upon whom the public weal depends.[95] But if one does not act thus, there is no reason for the party who is left unaided to complain, for the peasant and the philosopher may be of equal value to him, and it would be unjust to demand of you that you value your salvation less than mine. It is quite simply unjust to demand of anyone that he should put my salvation before the salvation of others. But what if that person owes his well-being to me, as the son does to the father? Yet I believe that even then I have no legally grounded right ('actio') to complain. But a distinction must be made. For I believe that the one who supervises the observance of fairness can also penalise what is done against himself, insofar as he could penalise it had it been done against others. Therefore a father, unless he is otherwise entitled to exercise punishment, will not justly punish his son for giving preference to another. The king, however, has this right.[96]

This brief outline may eludicate the way in which Leibniz believed that combinatorial analysis according to the rules of nature which are valid in all fields of human knowledge could be placed in the service of lawmaking.

92 A VI 1 440 21.

93 A VI 1 440 24.

94 'Salus sua'. 'Sua' refers to the party which has to choose. Cf. also Leibniz 2003: 137.

95 A VI 1 440 33.

96 A VI 1 441 4.

Chapter 12

Controversies on Nature as Universal Legality (1680–1710)

Sophie Roux

Introduction[1]

Two distinct interests can justify a study of the emergence and the development of the notion of Nature's law. This notion is omnipresent in moral and political texts in the eighteenth century, so its origin can perhaps be sought by supposing, as is suggested by these texts, that this notion was in fact developed in the field of physical science from which it was later exported.[2] It is clear that this direction is rich in illusions if we do not maintain sufficient distance from the object studied, which in this case is particularly ideological. Ill-controlled retrospection has also paved the way of the second direction, that taken by historians working on the origins of modern science. Two types of preconceived assumption have defined their studies: first, a historical assumption which holds that the seventeenth century experienced a scientific revolution that gave science its modern form;[3] second, a philosophical assumption which holds that law is the epistemological entity at the heart of physics.[4] These two types of prejudice come together in the thesis that the invention of a new concept of law, or even a new idea of Nature as universal legality, constituted the foundation of the new science.[5] This thesis was particularly represented by Ernst Cassirer, who noted in Leonardo da Vinci, Johannes Kepler and especially in Galileo Galilei, an idea of Nature as an immanent whole, totally determined by laws whose universality and necessity were the prerequisites of understanding.[6]

---

[1] I thank Marc Naimark, who translated this essay. The first paragraphs of the introduction summarize Roux 2001.

[2] Casini 1976. Dufour 1980. Regarding these exportation phenomena, see LARRÈRE (Chapter 15 in this volume).

[3] Oakley 1961a: 433 and Oakley 1961b: 78–79, oppose Nature of the Greeks and Nature of the Renaissance. Milton 1981: 183, deems that the emergence of the notion of law cannot be separated from the abandon of substantial forms.

[4] Zilsel 1942a: 245; Milton 1981: 173; Ruby 1986: 341. This assumption goes back to the nineteenth century: the reign of law is apparent there in both science and philosophy (as in, for example, John Stuart Mill and Auguste Comte).

[5] Needham 1951: 518, 542; Chevalley 1995: 128–129; Milton 1998: 680.

[6] Cassirer 1906: 248, 285–287, 307–309. This thesis takes as given the Kantian definition of Nature (for example *Kritik der reinen Vernunft* (hereafter *KRV*), A 216/B 263, AK III: 184). Chevalley 1995: 169–187, analyses the concepts of Nature and law in Kant.

Although the neo-Kantian idea of Nature as universal legality is always more or less lurking in the background of studies on the history of science, these studies rarely come to the same conclusions. It has been held that the emergence of the notion of Nature's law in the modern period was linked to the replacement of local feudality by a monarchy unified in the person of the Sovereign;[7] that voluntarism formed the intellectual context that had allowed the appearance of an empirical concept of law;[8] that the word 'law' appeared prior to the seventeenth century in scientific contexts with no reference to a divine legislator;[9] that there was no single concept of law in the works of Galileo Galilei, René Descartes, Francis Bacon, Robert Boyle, Baruch Spinoza, Christiaan Huygens, Godfried Wilhelm Leibniz or Isaac Newton, but rather mutually exclusive concepts;[10] and finally, that quantum mechanics invalidated the concept of Nature's law that characterized classical physics.[11]

The divergences among these conclusions arise in large part from the fact that these studies dealt in fact with distinct propositions. In particular, the following four propositions must be distinguished:

1. Seventeenth-century scientists discovered certain regularities in phenomena, for example what we now know as the 'law of falling bodies', 'Boyle's Law', or the 'law of universal attraction'.
2. The word 'law' becomes increasingly frequent in scientific texts of the modern period.[12]
3. One or more concepts of law emerged in the sciences of the seventeenth century.[13]
4. Classical science introduced the idea of Nature as universal legality.[14]

Because terminological variations are clues to conceptual variations, the raw material of historians of ideas consists of the words they find in texts: it is therefore reasonable to begin with the second of these four propositions. This is why in a recent article I studied the appearance of the metaphor of law in the sciences, or, more precisely, the generalization of the classical meaning of the word 'law' in the common language of science.[15] From the outset, I characterized the *classical* meaning of the word 'law' by the encounter of the two following usages: (a) A law reveals a natural regularity; this regularity concerns an abstract phenomenon and is expressed in the form of a relation between quantities (*physico-mathematical* usage); (b) The laws of Nature, which apply without exception to all natural bodies, are the laws by which the divine legislator creates and orders Nature (*metaphysical* usage).

---

7 Zilsel 1942a: 277–278.

8 Oakley 1961a: 433; Oakley 1961b: 82; Oakley 1984: 77–78; Milton 1981.

9 Ruby 1986: 341–343.

10 Casini 1976: 418 and 428; Steinle 1995: 318–319 and 357–363; Milton 1998: 692–699.

11 Chevalley 1995:187–223.

12 Zilsel 1942a; Ruby 1986.

13 Oakley 1961a; Oakley 1961b; Steinle 1995; Milton 1998.

14 Chevalley 1995.

15 Roux 2001.

In the first part of the article in question, this characterization allowed me to understand how the classical meaning of the word 'law' had been formed. In contexts concerning the sciences or the description of Nature, at least three usages of the term 'law' had existed before the seventeenth century, each associated with a semantic field (*specific* usage; *disciplinary* usage; *mathematical* usage). All three contributed to the formation (and to the ambiguities) of the physico-mathematical usage of the word 'law': a law concerns an abstract phenomenon and describes specific beings; it is the foundation of a discipline and orders the things of Nature; it expresses a regularity and has a mathematical form. As to the metaphysical usage, it certainly existed before the seventeenth century, in particular in morals, but the occurrences of 'Nature's law' in a strictly physical context were exceptional, with the inalterable order of a Nature created by God more often described by other metaphors: 'order' itself, 'decrees', 'disposition', 'constitution' and 'system'.

In the second part of the article, this semantic approach was complemented by a quantitative analysis. Before 1660, the word 'law' is rare in contexts relating to science or to the description of Nature, and the few authors who use it, do so in the singular. Its use spread in the period 1660–80 when it coexisted with other terms that it did not replace rightaway, such as 'rule', 'principle', 'hypothesis' or 'theorem'; the members of the Royal Society in particular use it in the singular. Finally, dictionaries and on-line data bases show that the term enters general use at the end of the seventeenth century in texts where the physico-mathematical and the metaphysical usages are found together. These are the texts I propose to study in the present article, concentrating on continental Europe.[16]

To present them briefly, we can divide them into two constellations. The first relates to the polemic between Antoine Arnauld and Nicolas Malebranche which arose from the publication of the *Traité de la nature et de la grâce* (1680). The debate was opened by Arnauld on the question of the nature of ideas. One of its goals as of 1685 was to determine how God rules over the kingdom of Nature and over the kingdom of Grace: for Malebranche, God acts through general laws, for Arnauld, God acts by particular wills. In 1686, Bernard Le Bovier de Fontenelle and Pierre Bayle intervened in this debate, Fontenelle opposing Malebranche's occasionalism and Bayle supporting it.[17] Jacques-Bénigne Bossuet took position against Malebranche and encouraged François de Salignac de la Motte-Fénelon to do the same. Yet other

---

[16] On the English debates, see Westfall 1958 and Steinle (Chapter 13 in this volume). The similarity of the controversies in Britain and on the Continent should demonstrate that the problem was not one of rivalry among Protestant denominations in Britain, and among Catholic orders on the Continent, but rather in the assimilation of the idea of universal legality.

[17] In fact, Bayle was involved in the polemic via his reviews as of 1684; see in particular Bayle 1684–1687, Apr. 1684, art. 2: 25–26; May 1684, art. 4: 49–50; Sept. 1684, art. 2: 119–121; March 1685, art. 4: 242; May 1685, art. 3: 282–284; Jul. 1685, art. 8: 333–335; Aug. 1685, art. 3: 346–349; Dec. 1685, art. 1: 426–427; March 1686, art. 3: 507–508; Apr. 1686, art. 3: 531–533. As to the nuances of Bayle's 'Malebranchism' in this period, see Mori 1999: 109–118.

protagonists intervened (Pierre-Sylvain Régis, Henri Lelevel and Dom François Lamy) and the polemic would end only with the death of Malebranche in 1715.[18]

The second constellation is organized around Leibniz and Bayle. In his *Dictionnaire historique et critique* (1696), Bayle took position on a Malebranchist basis both against the Leibnizian system of pre-established harmony, publicized in Leibniz's *Système nouveau de la nature et de la communication des substances* (1695), and against the plastic natures and vital principles defended by Jean Le Clerc, the translator of Ralph Cudworth and Nehemiah Grew. The exchanges between Bayle and his two opponents lasted until 1702 and 1707 respectively.[19] With *De Ipsa natura* (1698), Leibniz had in the meantime taken position in a controversy that Boyle's *Free Inquiry into the Vulgarly received Notion of Nature* (1686) had ignited between two German professors, Johannes Christoph Sturm (a partisan of Bayle) and Gunther Christoph Schelhammer (a defender of Aristotle): he attacked once again the occasionalist thesis that God is active everywhere, and that creatures are not true causes.[20]

This presentation would be incomplete if I did not mention the work of Benedictus de Spinoza. His *Tractatus theologico-politicus*, published in 1670 and censored in Holland, was known in a French translation (1678) which was clandestinely distributed under a variety of titles; the *Opera posthuma*, including the *Ethica*, were published in 1677. However uncertain and partial, the contemporary reception of Spinoza's work was both a reference and a foil, the proof of the excesses to which the Cartesian premises can lead.[21]

The turn of the eighteenth century was long considered as the moment of a 'crise de la conscience européenne', the womb of Enlightenment thinking.[22] I will take as given the work in the history of ideas relating to this turning point, the better to concentrate on the notion of Nature's law. Such a focus is obvious, for this particular notion is omnipresent, in so far as it allows questioning of the relations between three terms – the things of our world, a Nature defined in terms of universal legality, and God, creator, legislator and guarantor of a particular providence. This presents, however, certain difficulties, the first of which comes from the density of the polemic field. It is difficult to isolate the notion of Nature's law in systems in which everything is connected, and in controversies which constantly shift from one problem to another: any position is subject to so many objections that one comes to feel that none of them is tenable. The second difficulty in putting these polemics in their context lies in avoiding two temptations: first, to project the various positions on a temporal axis that would lead to the identification of the scientific with progress

---

18 On this first constellation, see Bouillier 1868, vol. II: 178–207, 236–243, 267–276; Toccane 1978: 97–106; Moreau 1999.

19 On this second constellation, see Roger 1993: 418–426; Toccane 1978: 106–114; Nadler 1993; Mori 1999: 89–154.

20 In the highly favourable report he gave of Boyle's theses on Nature, Bayle highlights their proximity with those of Malebranche (Bayle 1684–87, Dec. 1686, art. 3: 705–708). On the genesis of *Free Inquiry*, see Davis and Hunter 1996. On *De ipsa natura*, see Wilson 1987; Palaia 1990; Gaudemar 1995.

21 On this first reception, see Vernière 1954, vol. I.

22 Hazard 1961; Toccane 1978; Roger 1993.

and the religious with the retrograde; second, to see in these polemics only one form of the timeless question of the autonomy of Nature with respect to its creator.[23]

To mitigate these difficulties, the texts will be broken up into elementary kernels so as to isolate the terms of the problem and the possible alternatives.[24] For each problem, I will begin by presenting the thesis of Malebranche because he manifested the idea of universal legality, and thus structured the polemic. In so doing, I am perforce giving his adversaries the last word: this does not mean that they refuted Malebranche, for the controversies on the idea of legality are metaphysical, and thus one cannot in truth speak of resolution.

Three general questions will be addressed in turn, with the second and third each being broken down into two sub-questions. The first question is that of the *modality* of the laws of Nature: are they necessary, arbitrary or contingent? The second question is that of the *universality* of the laws of Nature: is the Malebranchist principle of the simplicity of the ways (1) metaphysically satisfying and (2) reconcilable with the notion of particular providence? The third question is that of the *efficacy* of the laws of Nature: (1) what is the relation, *a parte Dei*, between law, will and power, and (2) are creatures able to respect the laws of Nature?

The Modality of the Laws of Nature: Necessity, Arbitrariness and Contingency

The question of the modality of the laws of Nature does not depend solely on the introduction of the idea of universal legality; the two opposing traditions most often cited go back in fact to the Middle Ages. According to the voluntaristic tradition, the principal attribute of God is his will, it is by a free decree that he institutes revocable laws, known only by experience and not founded on the nature of things. According to the intellectualist tradition, the primary attribute of God is understanding, his ideas constitute an eternal order on which the nature of things depends and which our reason can know.[25] We can of course classify our authors as belonging to one or the other of these traditions: Arnauld and Fénélon are more voluntaristic, while Malebranche and Leibniz are more intellectualist. The former observe that a God acting according to principles imposed by an eternal order would lose all freedom, and more importantly, all goodness: invincibly obeying an inviolable Order, or even occasional causes, he would be impotent.[26] The latter reply that the choice of the better does not arise from necessity and that as Order is only the understanding of

[23] Against the first temptation, see Moreau 1999: 258–262, 316–321, who does not escape all retrospective illusion, since he treats Arnauld or Bossuet as visionaries. Wilson 1987 gives in to the second temptation.

[24] This procedure has already been tested in Roux 1996.

[25] Oakley 1961a and 1961b; Oakley 1984; Courtenay 1990; Osler 1994.

[26] Arnauld 1685a, 2: 686–687; Arnauld 1685b: I 2, I 3, II 26 3, 8–10, II 25, II 27: 204, 212, 584, 593–595, 598–600, 603; Fénelon 1687: 2, 6, 8, 18, 326–328, 336–338, 341–345, 370–371; Bayle 1704a: 106, 114, 336a, 348a; Bayle 1704b: 151, 165, 166, 811–812, 848, 850; Bayle 1707: 13, 16, 57–58, 62–63.

God, he is not giving in to an outside force, but rather setting laws for himself.[27] The principal references for them all are nonetheless not so much William Ockham or Thomas Aquinas as the Cartesian doctrine of the free creation of eternal truths and Spinoza's necessitarianism.

According to Descartes, God freely created the so-called eternal truths just as he created other creatures: as a king who makes laws in his kingdom, he could make 2 + 2 = 5 or choose not to enact the principle of non-contradiction. But this does not imply that these truths are not necessary: God has made them necessary, and has imprinted this necessity in our minds.[28] In a word, they are necessary without being necessarily necessary.[29] The theological question of the creation of truths and the metaphysical question of their status were thus dissociated: in particular the laws of Nature, while being arbitrarily created by God, nonetheless allow for knowledge whose certainty is at least equivalent to that characterising the understanding of mathematical truths.[30]

Spinoza had denied the specificity of the contingent and reduced the possible to the necessary: things cannot be produced in another way or in another order than they have been; everything that can be, from necessity is.[31] As to what are commonly called the 'laws of Nature', he affirmed in particular that they arise from the nature of things, and gave a *more geometrico* demonstration of the Cartesian laws of motion.[32] In the period 1680–1710, the problem becomes that of avoiding the Cartesian doctrine of eternal truths without falling into Spinoza's necessitarianism. For Malebranche and Leibniz for example, there exists an eternal order of ideas consubstantial with the understanding of God,[33] but the laws of Nature do not arise from this order and are not necessary in a mathematical or logical way.

---

27 Leibniz 1710: 191, 228–230; Malebranche 1680: I 21, II 51: 34, 110.

28 Letters to Mersenne, 15 April 1630, 6 May 1630, 27 May 1630, in Descartes 1964–74, I: respectively, 145–146, 149, 152.

29 For the distinction between 'necessary' and 'necessarily necessary', see the letter to Mesland, 2 May 1644, in ibid., IV: 118–119. More generally, see the letters to Gibieuf, 19 January 1642; to Arnauld, 29 July 1648; to Morus, 5 February 1649; and to Voetius in ibid., respectively: III: 476–478, V: 223–224, V: 272–273, VIII–2: 60. On the eternal truths, see, in the vast secondary literature, Frankfurt 1977; Beyssade 1979; Marion 1981; Curley 1984; Bennett 1994; Barnes 1996. The three laws of Nature set out by Descartes are surely among the eternal truths; they nonetheless present a specific problem: as they are founded on the nature of God, they cannot be described as arbitrary in the same way as, for example, 2 + 2 = 4. For an analysis of this problem, see Roux 1999.

30 An heir to this dissociation is Jean Le Rond d'Alembert, for whom, the theological question having lost all meaning, there remained only the metaphysical question (D'Alembert 1758, 'Discours préliminaire': xxiv–xxvi). The question as to whether physical laws are necessary or contingent had been proposed by the Berlin Academy in 1756; for a few references, see Tonelli 1959.

31 Spinoza 1677, I 33 and scol., I 35 : 341–346.

32 Spinoza 1670, 4: 722–723. Spinoza 1663, II 13–II 31: 269–288. I describe here the way in which Spinoza was perceived; Mason 1996 reckons, to my mind correctly, that for Spinoza legality was secondary with respect to causality.

33 Malebranche 1674–75, écl. 8, écl. 10: III 85–86, 131; Leibniz 1710, 20: 114–115.

As we understand neither the Creator's designs nor the relation between his nature and his attributes, writes Malebranche, the laws of Nature seem to depend on a purely arbitrary will, and we only know them by the sort of revelation constituted by experience.[34] The signification of this arbitrary will in a system otherwise built upon divine Wisdom could be debatable, but Malebranche's empiricism is not a concession to scientific advances: as things do not truly have a nature, the laws of Nature are known to us only as constant relations. This arises from the distinction made by Malebranche between miracles and events conforming to the laws of Nature. An event is miraculous if it is produced from a particular will of God: something that appears ordinary may nonetheless arise from a particular will of God, and only divine revelation can allow it to be identified with certainty as a miracle.[35] In practice, nonetheless, the constant correlation of two events is always the mark of a general law: when we observe that the collision of two bodies is always followed by the same effect, that a certain thought of the soul is always accompanied by a certain motion of the body, we can conclude that these are the result of general laws. Whatever the arbitrariness of God, according to Malebranche, the laws of Nature are known to us only by the constancy of certain relations.

Leibniz explicitly presented his position as a means of escaping from the arbitrary (represented by Descartes, Bayle or Malebranche) and from necessity (represented by Spinoza).[36] Defining miracles, as did Thomas Aquinas, as that which is beyond all created substance and beyond the understanding of all created mind,[37] Leibniz insists that the frequency of an event is only an external accident.[38] If he stigmatizes Malebranche's occasionalist system, the Newtonian notion of universal gravitation and Locke's hypothesis of a thought added to matter as miracles, it is because the constancy of a link is not enough to define a law of Nature: a law of Nature must express the nature of things and be appropriate to our reason.[39] But the laws of Nature are nonetheless not necessary as are logical or mathematical truths: this is the meaning of the difference between essences and existences, between the examination of the possibles and the choice of the best of all possible worlds, between the principle of non-contradiction and the principle of sufficient reason, between, on the one hand, logical or mathematical necessity and, on the other hand, moral or metaphysical necessity. Because our world is the best of all possible worlds, the consideration of the ends and the final causes may also facilitate their apprehension.[40]

---

[34] Malebranche 1958–84 XVII–1: 55. Also the letter to abbé Catelan, Apr. 1687, in ibid.: 44.

[35] Malebranche 1686a, II 1: 695–699; Malebranche 1688, 12 12: 294.

[36] Leibniz 1710: 349: 321.

[37] Leibniz 1687, 17: 441–442. Leibniz 1687, 7: 432, is Malebranchist in the conciliation of general and particular wills. Leibniz 1710, 206–207: 240–241, refuses, however, to define miracles as the product of a primitive particular will of God: anything God wants, he wants in general.

[38] To Arnauld, 30 April 1687, in Leibniz 1686–90: 93–96.

[39] Leibniz 1686–1690: 93–94; Leibniz 1695: 483; Leibniz 1698–1702: 520, 587–588, 594–595; Leibniz 1710: 355: 326. For a more thorough examination of the theses of Malebranche and Leibniz, see Rutherford 1993.

[40] Leibniz 1697: 303–304; Leibniz 1710: 344–351, 318–323.

The Universality of the Laws of Nature: the Principle of Simplicity of the Ways

According to Malebranche, when God created the world, he considered not only the perfection of his work, but the perfection of his action. For his action to be perfect, it had to conform to his attributes, and in particular to his wisdom. To act wisely is to act not in a composite manner, but with simplicity, universality and generality, hence what Malebranche calls the principle of the simplicity of the ways: God determined to produce the world that he could produce and preserve according to simple, universal and unchanging laws.[41] The principle of simplicity of the ways constitutes a theological formulation of the idea of universal legality, the generalization by the intermediary of God of the concept of the law of Nature formulated by Descartes in regard to the motion of a matter everywhere identical.[42]

The adjectives with which Malebranche qualifies laws vary, but can nonetheless be organized into distinct groups. Laws are uniform in time (constant, unchanging) or in space (universal, general); they cannot be broken (inexorable, invincible); they are simple, and 'simplicity' may here be numerical (there is a small number of fertile laws), refer to the things themselves (laws concern basic entities) or to the manner in which we understand them (laws are easy to understand).[43] From these characteristics, it is obviously impossible to deduce the two laws that Malebranche supposes to be sufficient to explain all physical phenomena.[44] In truth, they impose no constraints on content, but merely on form: any utterance can be a law, if it has the appropriate form.[45] Legality is here metaphysical, in that it does not refer to a specific type of being, but defines the mode of action of God in every domain, including that of Grace. It is thus that the controversies of the 1680–1710 period concerned the metaphysical notions mobilized by the principle of simplicity of the ways: simplicity, wisdom and perfection.

For Arnauld, the simplest action has two distinct meanings, depending on whether the action is considered in absolute terms or relative to a certain end. Yet, if the simplest means to obtain a given result must be preferred to more complex means, in absolute terms, it is better to have a perfect circle drawn with a compass than an imperfect circle drawn more simply, that is to say without an instrument.

---

41 Malebranche 1674–75, écl. 8 § 1: 86; Malebranche 1680: I 12–14; II 51, 27–30, 109–110; Malebranche 1688: 9 10, 213–214.

42 Compare the definitions of Nature given in Malebranche 1680, écl. 1 § 3: 148, and in Kant, *KRV*, A 216/B 263, AK III: 184.

43 According to Malebranche, these characteristics do not, however, imply a perfect regularity in phenomena (Malebranche 1674–75: III II 10; VI I 4: 479, 276–278). On the irregularity of meteorological phenomena, see Daston (Chapter 14 in this volume).

44 These two laws state that motion is conserved in straight lines, and that it is communicated by the lesser pressure (Malebranche 1674–1675: écl. 16, § 19: 304–305; Malebranche 1680, I 15: 30).

45 The laws mentioned after those regulating the communication of motions, the union of the soul and the body, and so on, can raise doubts as to what exactly this form is (Malebranche 1688: 13 9: 319–321). Hence perhaps the remark that there are 'plutôt vagues que générales et plutôt incertaines et hasardeuses que véritablement fécondes' (Bossuet 1687: 447).

Malebranche's error is thus, according to Arnauld, in surreptitiously moving from the relative to the absolute, in taking the simplicity of the ways as a quality in and of itself, forgetting that the ways are for the work, not the work for the ways.[46] Similarly, Fontenelle underlines that fact that it is better to act wisely than simply, 'se servir de moyens imparfaits, que de manquer quelquefois sa fin': a watch with ten gears that keeps time is better than one with only five gears that does not. 'On a fait le monde imparfait, pour le faire simple. Il fallait le faire parfait, et puis le faire le plus simple qu'il eût été possible.'[47]

Arnauld and Fontenelle do not want to reduce wisdom to simplicity; Fénelon, taking as his own the notion of perfection that Augustine had opposed to the Manicheans, refuses to apply any process of maximization to divine creation. All creatures, even an inanimate atom, surely bear the mark of the infinite perfection of God in the very fact that they were created, that is to say drawn from nothingness, yet for all that, creation is not determined by the search for maximum perfection. To suppose that creating a world is better than creating an atom is to differentiate among degrees of perfection, and thus to attribute reality to evil, when in fact it is nothingness.[48] To suppose that there exists a best of all possible worlds is to give limits to the power of God.[49] Moreover, the multiplication of rules for the work cannot alter the intrinsic simplicity of the action of God: the distinction between particular will and general will, between composite work and simple work, between exception and rule, is not real for him.[50]

The Universality of the Laws of Nature and the Particular Will of God

The principle of simplicity of the ways is the theological generalization of the idea of universal legality. At the moment it was expressed, this idea presented a general problem: could it be reconciled with the particular providence which had thus far been supposed by the Christian religion? This problem applied to three topics in particular: monsters, miracles and the creation of animate beings and the world in general.

---

[46] Arnauld 1685b: I 1 7, I 8 5, II 1, II 24, II 25, II 26 6: 179–182, 188–190, 244–245, 583, 587, 597–598. Malebranche indicates that God takes into consideration both the perfection of the work and the perfection of the ways, but these are two independent parameters, between which God must choose, and it is because he sometimes prefers the perfection of the ways that evil exists (Malebranche 1688: 9 10–11: 213–220). Leibniz insists to the contrary that God is able to manage both the ends and the means (Leibniz 1710: 208: 241).

[47] Fontenelle 1686: 542–545. Malebranche 1686b: 581–582, justifies the imperfections of our world not as the consequence of the principle of simplicity of the ways, but as a means for the eternal Temple.

[48] Fénelon 1687: 3, 9: 328–331, 345–346.

[49] Ibid.: 7, 16: 363–364.

[50] Ibid.: 4, 16: 331–333, 360–364.

Monsters pose the problem of evil: how can evil exist in a world created by a good and all-powerful God?[51] According to Malebranche, the existence of evil cannot be denied, nor its reach minimized: disorder is everywhere present, and there exist in the physical world monsters, and in the moral world, the damned.[52] Yet, he insists, evil is not desired as such: it results indirectly and by accident from the general laws which God himself cannot break without undermining the principle of simplicity of the ways; God allows it to exist without making of it the object of direct and particular wills.[53] Malebranche thus recognizes the existence of evil, adding, however, that God did not expressly wish it.

For Arnauld, this was Malebranche's first renunciation of the notion of particular providence, by which God creates each creature and continues afterwards to look after each of them by his particular will. Monsters do not constitute in and of themselves disorders, but are only bad in relative terms, he explains, adopting Augustine's analysis of evil. They are imperfect relative to more perfect creatures; they are imperfect relative to our powerlessness to know God's designs. In our inability to judge things, we must therefore affirm in general that each creature is directly willed by God and conforms to his designs.[54]

The problem posed by miracles is to know how to preserve their metaphysical possibility once the idea of universal legality is accepted.[55] Arnauld, Fénelon or Bossuet observe that to insist on the universality of the laws of Nature as does Malebranche is to risk casting doubt on generally accepted miracles.[56] In fact, Spinoza had deemed that it was not reasonable to dissociate the power of God and the power of Nature to seek proof of the existence of the former in the apparent deviations from the order of the latter. First, the laws of Nature are decrees that flow from the nature of God, who cannot produce anything that contradicts them without contradicting himself. Second, miracles are by definition beyond our understanding,

---

[51] For a long history of the *praeter naturam*, see Daston and Park 1998. The controversies which took place at the Académie des Sciences in the eighteenth century were the direct heirs to the conflict between Malebranche and Arnauld: monsters are considered either as the result of rare or random combinations of the general laws of Nature, or as the direct products of the will of a fanciful God (on these controversies, see Roger 1993: 397–418; Tort 1997; Monti 2000).

[52] On the reality of evil as a fundamental theme for Malebranche, see Gouhier 1926: 71; Moreau 1999: 88–95, 110–126. As monsters are to the physical world what the damned are to the moral, in the question of monsters, there is a theological issue which I will here ignore.

[53] Malebranche 1680: I 18, 19, 22: 31, 32, 35–36; Malebranche 1685: 8 § 8: 522; Malebranche 1686a: I 1 3, 4, 7, I 1 11, II 3, III: 651, 653–655, 662, 683, 720, 764–765; Malebranche 1688: 9 9, 11: 212, 215–216. Bayle at first took the side of Malebranche (Bayle 1682: 66, 230: 44, 139–140); for a genetic analysis of Bayle's positions with respect to Malebranche, see Mori 1999: 89–154.

[54] Arnauld 1685b: I 2: 203–204.

[55] For a summary of the theoretical question of miracles, see Lenoble 1943; Hazard 1961: 207–239; Toccane 1978: 115–134. For an analysis of the practices, see Viguerie 1983. For presentations of the doctrines of Spinoza, Malebranche and Leibniz, see, respectively, Vernière 1954: 164–185, Gouhier 1926: 55–68; and McRae 1985.

[56] Arnauld 1685b: I 7–12, 16–17. For Bossuet and Fénelon, see the references given below in note 74.

and thus cannot let us know God. There is therefore no point in seeking the power of God elsewhere than in legality: the laws of Nature manifest in their own way the infinite, eternal and unchanging nature of God.[57]

Leibniz and Malebranche diverged both on the subject of miracles and on the correlative notion of the laws of Nature; they nonetheless adopted similar strategies to deal with the possibility of miracles in the context of universal legality. They distinguish first between miracles in the philosophical sense (that which goes beyond the forces of creatures for Leibniz, that which God wants from particular will for Malebranche) and miracles in the popular sense (monsters and prodigies that surprise us).[58] This allows them to disqualify certain miracles as merely popular, and to drastically reduce their number.[59] They then establish a hierarchy between two types of legislation: miracles violate certain subordinate maxims of Nature, but they nonetheless conform to the general order; what seems to be extraordinary only appears so relative to particular and subordinate rules.[60]

Malebranche denied the existence of particular wills for monsters, he reduced their number in the case of miracles, but multiplied them liberally in regard to creation. Whereas Descartes had asserted that the laws of Nature could explain the formation of our world from an initial formless state of matter, Malebranche affirmed that these laws began to rule the world only once it had been formed, differentiating the first creation and its subsequent maintenance.[61] Likewise, he pruned off a great deal from the essays in which Descartes attempted to explain mechanically the genesis of living beings: the laws of Nature are supposed to regulate only the growth of creatures; this is the theory of pre-existent germs.[62]

A recurring argument raised against him from then on is that there is no reason that God should act *sometimes* or *rarely* by particular wills. A choice must be made: either God, favouring the perfection of his action, will always act by general wills at the risk of imperfection in his work, or, in order to achieve the greatest perfection of his work, he will not hesitate to resort to particular wills, notably to save the damned.[63] Malebranche's error is to have sought an untenable compromise, wisdom and simplicity alternating in primacy in a system 'bigarré'.[64]

---

[57] Spinoza 1670, 6: 751–758. Spinoza then demonstrates that what the Scriptures call Providence is only the order of Nature and that the so-called miracles to be seen there can be explained by natural causes.

[58] Malebranche 1680: I 20–21: 33–34; Malebranche 1686a: II 1: 695–696; Leibniz 1698–1702: 520.

[59] According to Malebranche, the miracles described in the Old Testament are only prodigies carried out by angels, and most acts of Grace can be attributed to Christ. Leibniz seems to favour such a solution in the letter to Clarke, August 1716, Leibniz 1715–1716: 117.

[60] Leibniz 1687: 6–7: 431–432.

[61] Malebranche 1688, 10 17: 247; Malebranche 1674–75, VI II 4: 341 ff.

[62] Malebranche 1688: 10 4–5, 11 9–10: 225–232, 264–268. On this theory, see Roger 1993: 325–463.

[63] Arnauld 1685b: I 4 à 6, II 25: 214–230, 588–590; Arnauld 1685c: 2, 3: 28–30, 42–43; Fénelon 1687: 12, 13, 16: 349–353, 354–356, 361–363; Bayle 1707: II 17: 64–65.

[64] Fontenelle 1686, 4: 544; Bayle 1684–87: August 1685, art. 6: 533; Bayle 1704a: 110, 339.

The Efficacy of the Laws of Nature and the Wills of the Creator

Once the idea of universal legality is accepted, the existence of monsters, the possibility of miracles and the creation of animals pose *a parte Dei* a sole and self-same problem: can the order of the particular wills and acts of God subsist, or is it subsumed by the universal legality? Yet again, the terms of the problem can be decoded in the reactions raised by the theses of Malebranche.

According to Malebranche, for something to exist, a general law of God is sufficient: the laws of Nature are only the general wills of God;[65] his power and his will are identical when they are general; a general will is always practical, that is to say is followed by an effect.[66] On the contrary, it may be that a particular effect does not result from a particular will, but may come into existence as the indirect consequence of general laws (this is the case for monsters). In this sense, God has certain particular wills that are not followed by effects and he can be said to be impotent; this is the meaning of the distinction between 'vouloir' and 'vouloir faire', between 'avoir des volontés particulières' and 'agir par volontés particulières'.[67] General laws are thus sufficient for the production of particular effects, while particular effects do not require wills. In other words, Malebranche's first assertion is that general laws are identical to general wills and thus sufficient to produce particular effects; his second assertion is that there are particular effects resulting from general laws independently from general wills. The second assertion implies however that God is impotent; moreover, it raises an unsolved question: how can a law, that is not a will, be efficient?[68]

Against these theses, Arnauld began by distinguishing between laws and wills.[69] Certainly, by definition laws are general, but they are only the order by which things are done: what ensures that an event takes place is not a law but an act of will. Yet any effective will, will followed by an effect, is particular. Thus 'tout ce que l'on peut dire pour parler exactement est que Dieu agit par volontés particulières en conséquence des lois générales'.[70] As a result, if God does all, it is not from having willed the world in general: for anything to be, he must have willed it in particular, and this will is sufficient.[71] It is only by impotence and imperfection that our kings govern by general orders, that they choose to build a palace less costly but less beautiful than it might be: the details of things do not weary God, nothing is taxing for him, it is enough that He wills something for it to be.[72] If this were not the case, God would not strictly speaking want anything: he would not want monsters, but nor would he want perfect animals;

[65] Malebranche 1686a: I 1 4, II 3: 654, 723.

[66] Malebranche 1680: I 12: 27; Malebranche 1674–75: VI II 4: 316.

[67] Malebranche 1685: 525–527; Malebranche 1686a: 650–655.

[68] Arnauld 1685b: II 18, 22: 539, 566, insists that the centre of Malebranchism is the negation of particular wills.

[69] Arnauld 1685b: I 1 2, 6: 175, 179.

[70] Arnauld 1685a: 7: 737; Arnauld 1685b: I 1 2: 175.

[71] Arnauld 1685b: I 1 2, I 2 2, I 2 5, I 8: 175, 192, 203, 237. This position concerning Nature has its theological corollary: the heart of Jansenism is that Grace is always effective, that is to say that God saves all those he wants to save, and consequently he did not want to save the damned.

[72] Arnauld 1685b: I 1 5, I 2 1: 178, 189–190; Fénelon 1687, 16: 362–363: Bayle 1704b: 155, 825–826. This remark is particularly pertinent against the presentation of the principle

he would not want rain on a sterile Earth, but nor would he want it on a fertile earth: he would be satisfied with following his laws, he would be indifferent to creatures.[73]

In fact, Arnauld, and later Bossuet and Fénelon, only distinguish between the order of legality and the efficacy of wills so as to guarantee the possibility of their co-occurrence; this is what is demonstrated in particular by the 'hidden miracles' of the biblical tradition, miracles that conform to the general laws, but are nonetheless willed by God to fulfil a particular plan. According to them, to deny the possibility of such an over-determination is to eliminate any reason to pray to God or to believe in Providence, it is to make all things equally natural and to become an Epicurean.[74] That we are in general powerless to know one of the co-occurring terms (God's plan) must not lead us to doubt its existence; it may even be possible that the purpose of the general laws is to hide from us the perpetual operation of God behind the veil of the regular course presented by the operations of Nature.[75]

The Obedience of Creatures to the Laws of Nature: Causality and the Nature of Things

If the metaphor of laws is taken seriously, laws are not relations, but the commandments of a lawmaking God. There then arises the problem of determining how material things can conform to these laws when they lack the intelligence to understand them. To this problem must be added, in the context of Malebranche' occasionalism, the problem of knowing how material things can execute these laws when they lack force. Indeed, occasionalism consists in the thesis that creatures are but occasional causes, and that God is the true cause of all that occurs in the world; Malebranche bases this thesis on two arguments.[76] The first is the incomprehensible character of causality in regard to Cartesian ontology – in the elementary case of colliding bodies, one cannot understand the communication of the force of motion, whether it is a mode or a substance. There is however a necessary link between the will of an omnipotent being and the real motion of a body, insomuch as our idea of an omnipotent being implies the efficaciousness of his wills.[77] The second argument is that God cannot divest himself of his essential power to make all that is real in

of simplicity of the ways given in Malebranche 1675–76: 504–509. On the Malebranchist impotence of God, see the references given above in note 26.

[73] Arnauld 1685b: I 8 4: 243–244.

[74] Arnauld 1685b: I 1 4, I 8 2–3, I 10, I 13 I 14 66 3–4: 176–178, 238–241, 257–264, 280–288, 294–302; Fénelon 1687: 15, 18: 358–360, 367–371; Bossuet 1687: 444. See also the commentaries of Moreau 1999: 241ff.

[75] Arnauld 1685b: I 2 2, 4: 191, 199–201; Fénelon 1687: 14: 356–357.

[76] Malebranche 1675–76: VI II 3: 312–316; Malebranche 1685: 7–8: 513ff.; Malebranche 1686a: II 1: 700–704; Malebranche 1686b: 584. For a recent summary of the historical significance of occasionalism, see Nadler 1993.

[77] Which is not to say that we still do not know the means of action of the will of God (Malebranche 1683: IX 2: 96; Malebranche 1686b: 581). On the obscurity of the divine will according to Malebranche, see Moreau 1999: 227–232.

creatures, and that we honour him better by supposing him to be the cause of all things than do the pagans with their secondary causes.

The adversaries of occasionalism sought first of all to define causality so as to distinguish it from legality. Causality can be presented in the form of logical necessity: the cause implies the effect, the effect cannot be without the cause.[78] But Malebranche showed the specificity of the causal link: it can be confused neither with an empirical regularity, nor with logical necessity.[79] One thus seeks to hem it in with supplementary clauses: the effect must take place promptly, says Arnauld;[80] the true cause must contain its effect, be proportional to it, be able to produce it, says Villemandy.[81] But in drawing attention from legality to causality, from the observation of regularities to their effectiveness, the principal reaction against occasionalism was to rehabilitate the notion of individual nature and moving force.

Fontenelle remarks that universality can be expressed in three distinct manners depending on the relation between the action and the subject on which it acts. The action can be indifferent to the nature of the subject (it is indifferent to pieces of metal to be transformed by a machine), the action can conform to the nature of the subject (a machine is made to be set in motion); an action can go beyond the nature of the subject (it is not in the nature of a machine to be constantly repaired). What makes for the perfection of an action is not uniformity as such, but uniformity in so far as it manifests wisdom (not to ask of a subject more than it can produce) and intelligence (to put in the appropriate disposition to produce the wanted effect). A world like that of Malebranche, in which bodies cannot themselves communicate motion to each other, will thus not be endowed with the most perfect uniformity, that in which reign laws that conform to the nature of subjects and such that they can execute them themselves. To endow a world with general uniformity, it is necessary to entrust the execution of laws to subjects so that they do no more than obey the instituted laws: that is to say that they have a nature, that God has endowed them with the means to move, that is to say, with moving force.[82]

It is with the support of his new dynamics, which established the conservation of quantity of force and motive action, that *De Ipsa natura* pursues the rehabilitation of the scholastic forms made public in the *Discours de métaphysique*. If the laws decreed by God were only extrinsic denominations, things could not conform to them; they must therefore have kept some trace, however vestigial, of this first commandment, and have the inherent force to execute it: this force is what is called nature or form.[83] Alongside the general laws that Leibniz qualifies as 'maximes subalternes', individual laws must be added: each substance acts uniformly in so far

78 Arnauld 1685a: 2: 701; Arnauld 1685b: I 1 3: 176; Fontenelle 1686: 3: 533.

79 Malebranche 1675–76: III II 3: 426–428; Bayle 1686: 569–571.

80 Arnauld 1685a: 2: 701; Arnauld 1685b: I 1 3: 176.

81 Bayle 1684–87: August 1686, art. 6: 623, quotes and approves the definition of Villemandy.

82 Fontenelle 1686: 5: 542–558.

83 Leibniz 1698: 503–507; Leibniz 1698–1702: 548. Bayle 1740: art. 'Rorarius' (rem. L): IV 920, having objected that it is difficult to lay out lines in simple and immaterial substance, Leibniz responds that this is what happens in the case of relations, expressions, representations (Leibniz 1698–1702: 551).

as it has a law, that is to say a series of relations that determine the sequence of its actions.[84]

Except perhaps for Leibniz himself, the nature of this force was, however, not easy to grasp. Bayle remarked that regular, or least determined, actions imply an intelligence that establishes laws, but also an intelligence that executes them. Creatures that cannot know how or when or where to apply the laws they are given cannot follow them: without knowledge, we are incapable of building a machine, of sewing a button, or of writing a poem; if it occurs that beings without intelligence act in a determined fashion, it is because they are directed by intelligent causes.[85] Two solutions are then possible: either this intelligence is within God, and we adopt the system of Malebranche; or this intelligence is in creatures, and we are dealing with the hylarchical principles of Henry More, the seeds of Daniel Sennert, the plastic faculties of Jean Le Clerc, the forces of Leibniz, and other intermediate intelligences useful for not keeping God toiling at the spinning wheel, but that are just as apt to let us do without him once the world is created, thus taking us back in practice to the atheism of Straton.[86]

Conclusion

Not only do these texts not produce any science, they are behind the science of their own time: the only example of 'law' they give it that a stone falls when it is released. They nonetheless cannot be dissociated from certain changes induced by the new sciences, in particular by the Cartesian claim that there exist rules of motion that are full-fledged laws of Nature, and that thus determine all the effects that can consequently be observed.[87] The knowledge of universal laws that regulate the path of motion allows the 'new philosophers' to set themselves apart from the ancient atomists, who supposed that everything happens by chance.[88]

The reach of the Cartesian statement cannot however be reduced to the determination of certain effective laws of motion. Because the laws of motion are laws of Nature, it installs in the physical domain the idea of universal legality: Nature is everywhere homogeneous, it is regulated by constant and uniform laws. It is this idea that Malebranche takes as a theme and extends beyond the strictly physical; it

---

84 Leibniz 1698–1702: 520.

85 Bayle 1686: 574; Bayle 1704a: 110–111, 340a–341a; Bayle 1706, 4: 995–996. To respond to this argument, Leibniz advances the theory of little perceptions: we do not truly know what we will do in ten years' time, but we can perceive it in a dim and confused way (Leibniz 1698–1702: 521, 550). On the discussion of Bayle and Leibniz, see Lennon 1993.

86 Bayle 1704a, 110–111: 339ff.; Bayle 1704b: II 179–181: 882–890; Bayle 1740: art. 'Morin, J.–B.' (rem. M.), art 'Plotin' (rem. G.), art. 'Ricius' (rem. C), art. 'Sennert' (rem. C, rem. F): IV 264, IV 705–706, IV 875, V 113, V 116. According to Mori 1999: 142–146, Bayle 1704a: 106, 114: 336a, 348a, would imply agreement on the position of Straton.

87 Descartes 1633: 37, 47. For an analysis of the Cartesian concept of the law of Nature, see Roux 1999.

88 Lamy 1683: 256–257. For a parallel between the notions of limit in ancient atomism and of law in seventeenth-century mechanism, see Wilson (Chapter 1 in this volume).

is the consequences of this idea that the controversies of 1680–1710 analyse. In fact, the historical paradox of these texts is that they stabilized the use of the metaphor of law in the sciences when their ostensible purpose was to question its pertinence and limits.

For us, aware of more recent research on the notion of the laws of Nature, these controversies echo strangely: the terms used are the same as those employed today (causality, universality, necessity, simplicity and so forth), but they are linked to theological problems which are foreign to us. One can certainly think that the theological formulation of these problems renders them inseparable from a theological context. Should not the task of our Godless, and moreover, post-critical, period, therefore be to forget them as quickly as possible?[89] And yet, it is not certain that we have finished with the three questions we have discussed: what is contingency and physical necessity? What are the characteristics of the paradigm of legality and can it be extended from the physical to other fields of knowledge, or even to the entire human experience? What are the prerequisites imposed by the idea of universal legality on the nature of things and the way in which we can know them?

[89] See on this subject, Van Frassen 1989.

Chapter 13

From Principles to Regularities: Tracing 'Laws of Nature' in Early Modern France and England

Friedrich Steinle[1]

Laws of Nature in the Seventeenth Century

The concept of laws of nature already had a long tradition in the seventeenth century, both in natural philosophy and legal thinking. 'Natural law' had long been treated as a specific type, juxtaposed beside divine and eternal law. In ancient and medieval natural philosophy, the talk of 'laws of nature' occurred – if rather rarely – in at least two different traditions. In astronomy and 'mixed mathematics', 'laws' counted as the central principles within a deductive system of theorems – a use still found in Copernicus and Kepler [GRAßHOFF].[2] In theology, by contrast, with Ockham as prominent proponent, emphasis was put on divine voluntarism [ARMOGATHE], while the axiomatic character and the position within a larger system played no major role.[3] Both in natural philosophy and juridical thought, the situation changed profoundly and rapidly in the second half of the seventeenth century. Within a few decades, the law-concept came into much wider use, and its meaning shifted and was significantly broadened. In this paper, I shall focus on natural philosophy and trace the use and meanings of the concept of 'laws' and related terms in both France and England.[4] A few emblematic figures provided important stimuli for establishing and developing the concept of laws of nature.

One of the most influential programmes for a 'new science' was presented in Francis Bacon's 1620 *Novum Organum*. Bacon here used a concept of laws of nature that was closely connected to his idea of 'form' and was thus not more sharply defined than the latter.[5] Rather than stressing theological considerations,[6] Bacon emphasized

[1] I thank Lorraine Daston and Sophie Roux for many stimulating discussions.

[2] Ruby 1986; Schramm 1981; Graßhoff and Treiber 2002.

[3] Oakley 1961a; Oakley 1981; Crombie 1994, I: 402–403.

[4] For previous studies, see Zilsel 1942b; Schimank 1949; Needham 1956: chap. 18; Milton 1981; Steinle 1995; Roux 2001.

[5] For example *Novum Organum* II, 5: 'leges fundamentales et communes, quae constituunt Formas'(Bacon 1858: I, 232.

[6] Thanks to Sachiko Kusukawa for pointing out that Bacon, in his *De Augmentis,* well included theological aspects; see Bacon 1858: I, 567. For the Royal Society, however, the *Novum Organum* would become far more important.

the analogy to the legal realm. He spoke of 'law and its paragraphs' and even drew a distinction between 'consuetudines naturae' – observed regularities in specific domains – and 'leges fundamentales et communes' that applied for a wide range of effects.[7] The analogy to the 'common law' tradition, so important in England, is striking. It was largely based on 'customary' and 'municipial laws' and customs of particular regions were sometimes called 'laws of the land', with no reference to a commanding authority.[8] Bacon – lawyer and politician, after all – dealt with those questions and acted as a proponent of authoritative legislation.[9] In transferring these legal concepts to natural philosophy, he was careful to differentiate between different types of statements that played different roles and had to be established in different ways. 'Consuetudines naturae' could only be recognized by empirical means and were valid even without being derived from more general principles. 'Laws', by contrast, were central parts of a larger structure of argumentation. It is striking to realize that Bacon, being one of the few to draw an explicit analogy between natural philosophy and matters of legislation, did exactly *not* refer to the tradition of natural law, but to the separate common-law tradition, so prominent in England.

It was another author, however, who for the first time gave 'laws of nature' an absolutely central and prominent place within a system of natural philosophy. René Descartes, in his 1644 *Principia philosophiae*, launched the exposition of his mechanical system of the universe with three principles of how the state and motion of bodies were conserved and transmitted. He founded those principles on considerations about the immutability of God and called them 'regulae quaedam sive leges naturae' or 'règles certaines, que je nomme les loix de la nature'.[10] As the careful wording indicates, Descartes was well aware of how unusual the concept was in this context. Moreover, he brought different traditions together here. Cartesian laws had both a quasi-axiomatic status within a deductive system and at the same time reflected the voluntaristic tradition: Descartes emphasized that God could have created different laws. It is significant, moreover, that Descartes reserved the law-concept for those three principles: no other theorem, rule or principle was called a 'law' in his system.

I shall not analyse the intricacies and background of Bacon's and Descartes' law-concepts in detail.[11] Rather, my procedure will be to take these two most influential seventeenth-century authors as starting points, and trace the further use of the law-concept until the end of the century. One should keep in mind here that it is one thing to have the concept of a certain type of statements, and another to call it 'laws of nature'. Concept and terminology of laws were not necessarily connected, and indeed have their own separate contexts and histories. The case of Galileo, who sometimes is regarded as indicating the historical transition from the search for

[7] *Novum Organum*, II, 2 and 5.

[8] See OED, s.v. 'law', sect. II, 14.

[9] Pocock 1987: 103.

[10] *Principia Philosophiae*, II, § 37–42: Descartes AT, VIII/1: 62 and IX/2: 84.

[11] For Bacon, see Steinle 1995 or Krohn 2001. For Descartes, see Loeck 1986; Knebel 1992; Steinle 1995; Roux 1999; Specht 2001.

causes to the search for laws, is instructive here.[12] While the type of statements he made about the fall of bodies may well fit into the concept that later was labelled 'law', he never talked of 'laws' in presenting his research.[13] The idea of empirically based statements that express regular behaviour of things was certainly present in the early modern period, if not earlier. But it was not at all clear that, and why exactly, they should be called 'laws'. My study aims at illuminating that historical process.

Mid-century Terminologies

Among Descartes' contemporaries it was the French polymath Marin Mersenne who played a core role as communicator of scientific research throughout Europe. Mersenne deployed the concept of 'loy naturelle' or 'loy de nature' in a juridical and moral sense, when talking about the naturalness of Abraham having his concubines, for example.[14] It is hence all the more significant that he never spoke of laws in questions of natural philosophy. The topic of falling bodies and of the trajectory of projectiles, widely discussed in the Mersenne circle of the late 1630s and early 1640s, is indicative. In those rare cases in which the statements discussed were labelled at all (usually they were not),[15] the traditional terminology of mathematics prevailed, such as 'la proposition des chutes des corps pesants', the 'demonstration des chutes', or the 'mesure de la chute des graves'.[16] Only in very rare cases was the terminology of laws used, always with explicit reference to Descartes. The young Christiaan Huygens, for example, alluded to Descartes' 'loy de la nature' by which bodies continued in their motion with the same speed.[17] Descartes' terminology was adopted, but not transferred to other contexts or developed further.

A similar attitude can be observed in other mid-century publications that took up Descartes' ideas. The first and immediately problematic case was Henri de Roy (Henricus Regius), Professor of Medicine at the University of Utrecht who, as a propagandist for Descartes, nearly got expelled from his chair at Utrecht, but later distanced himself from Descartes with his 1646 *Fundamenta physices*, in which he placed Cartesian ideas within the context of scholastic metaphysics.[18] But even then Regius maintained Descartes' talk of laws, presenting, for example, a conservation principle of matter under the label 'lex immutabilitatis naturae' or 'lex universalis' and deducing a principle of conservation of motion from it.[19] Like Descartes, Regius did not speak of laws when it came to more specific propositions about light, planetary motions, or the earth. Similar observations hold for more straightforward accounts of

[12] Stilman Drake 1983: 143, even made Galileo speak of 'laws' in some fictive dialogue.

[13] As already observed by Zilsel 1942b: 262–263; for the few exceptions, see Steinle 1995.

[14] Mersenne 1624. See also Mersenne, *Correspondance*, 1932–88: IX, 372, for example.

[15] Mersenne 1932–88: VIII, 232, 421, 696.

[16] Ibid.: XIII, 126; XIV, 527 and 613.

[17] Ibid.: XIV, 569.

[18] Regius 1646; for Descartes' sharp reaction, see Descartes 1648: AT, VIII: 337–369.

[19] Regius 1646: 7–8.

Descartes' ideas. In one of the earliest textbooks of Cartesian philosophy, published in 1653, the Paris writer Jacques Du Roure adopted the terminology of Descartes' *Principia* directly. When it came to motion, he presented the three general 'loix de la nature', and emphasized, against the Aristotelian tradition, that 'les pierres ... ne suivent pas moins les loix de la Nature lors qu'eles [*sic*!] montent, que lors qu'eles [*sic*!] descendent'.[20]

Stimulated by Descartes' approach, Christiaan Huygens started to work on the motion and collision of bodies and finished an extended manuscript in 1656.[21] It was structured along mathematical lines, with 'Hypotheses', 'Propositions', 'Demonstrations', and 'Lemmata'. Only once did Huygens speak of the 'laws according to which bodies impelled each other'.[22] In his extended correspondence on the subject – with the Liège bishop René-François de Sluse, for example – the statements, if they were labelled at all, were called 'regles': 'Cartesii regulae circa corporum occursus', 'regulae impulsus', 'meae regulae', 'Axioma Cartesii de conservatione motus', and so on. Again only in rare cases did Huygens also speak of 'motus leges' or 'lois de mouvement'.[23] Huygens' terminology was not systematic and, like most others, he did not discuss his terminology explicitly. I take it as significant that Huygens, who relied so much on Descartes' ideas, was reluctant to adopt the talk of laws. In the rare cases in which he used it, moreover, he deviated from Descartes' (and his own early) use, speaking no longer of 'laws of nature' in general but, more specifically, of 'laws of motion'. But still 'laws' stood for highly abstract and most general principles, placed at the top of a deductive system.

In research fields pursued more independently of Descartes, the terminology of laws did not occur. Blaise Pascal, for example, did not talk of 'laws of nature' at all in his work on pneumatics and hydrostatics, conducted in the 1640s and 1650s. In his final synthesis, posthumously published in 1663, Pascal presented his deductive structure along the line of 'principes', with the 'principe de la Pesanteur de la masse de l'Air' as the most prominent case.[24] Pascal was, however, perfectly well acquainted with natural law in the juridical sense. In his *Pensées*, he talked about 'les lois naturelles communes en tout pays', contrasting them to the ever-changing laws and customs of particular regions. Although he regarded those natural laws as the best foundation of human societies, he doubted whether human reasoning, always corrupted, could ever achieve a full knowledge of them.[25] This sceptical stance might be the background for his refusing – *pace* Descartes – to use such a terminology in natural philosophy. Moreover, different research traditions come into play here. Hydrostatics and pneumatics had been treated in mathematical terminology ever since Archimedes. Simon Stevin had organized his 1586 *Beghinselen des*

---

[20] Du Roure 1653: 49, 50, 52; later, however, in Du Roure 1665, there was no talk of 'laws'. I thank Dan Garber for pointing me to Du Roure and Regius.

[21] Posthumously published in 1703: Huygens, Oeuvres, 1888–1950: XVI, 30–91.

[22] Ibid.: XVI, 33.

[23] Ibid.: II, 79, 115.

[24] Pascal 1663; reprinted in Brunschvigg and Boutroux 1904–14, see III: 194, 281.

[25] Pascal 1670: §60, p. 53.

waterwichts with definitions, postulates, explications, and propositions,[26] and both Galileo and Torricelli had worked in the same spirit. That tradition in hydrostatics, on which Pascal's studies were essentially based, provided no stimulus whatsoever to introduce a concept of laws of nature.

When the Paris writer and Royal historiographer Charles Sorel published, in 1664, a book-length review of philosophical books in France, he included natural philosophy. He discussed Descartes as most prominent in departing from the scholastic tradition, and mentioned Du Roure's work as being much in Cartesian spirit (even as belonging to the Cartesian 'sect').[27] But, though Sorel spoke well of 'loix de la nature' as moral laws,[28] such a terminology was absent in the natural philosophy part. Sorel's presentation illustrates a general reluctance to use law-talk in France.

In mid-seventeenth-century England, the situation was more complex. The group of philosophers who aimed at reforming natural philosophy was not yet widely visible. Descartes' impact was strong, though not immediate; likewise his concept of laws of nature filtered in only slowly. When Henry More, then a young cleric in Cambridge who had welcomed Descartes' approach enthusiastically, corresponded with Descartes in 1649 on physical questions of the *Principia*, the talk of laws occurred rarely, and then only with explicit reference to Descartes.[29] A quite different account, by contrast, can be seen in the writings of Walter Charleton, physician to King Charles II, and talented expositor of philosophical systems. Entirely devoted to Helmontian chemistry in his youth,[30] Charleton turned his perspective in the 1650s towards a mechanistic approach. In his 1654 defence of Epicurean atomism, explicitly based on Pierre Gassendi [WILSON],[31] he often used the terminology of laws, in a shifting and varied manner. In contrast to Descartes, whose law-talk he knew well and quoted explicitly, Charleton's 'Laws of Nature' were statements about causality, and how it acted in natural processes: namely merely mechanically by motion, and only between contacting bodies. Charleton also had 'Fundamental' or 'Universal Laws of Motion', stipulating how the motion of macroscopic bodies depended on those of the constituting atoms.[32] In other passages, by contrast, his use of 'Lawes' pointed to something like generalized observations and was almost indistinguishable from his concomitant use of 'Rule'. In a section on the loadstone, Charleton even spoke of 'Laws of Magnetick Energy', 'Laws and Experiments Magnetical', and 'Laws of Magnetical Attraction'.[33] Significantly enough, moreover, Charleton used still another term here, without further explication. He labelled statements such as the assertion that armed magnets held stronger than unarmed, that the strength of a magnet was not necessarily related to its bulk and volume, or that each of the two pieces of a cut magnet showed its own polarity, as 'Observables'. And he even ascribed some

26 Stevin 1586.

27 Sorel 1664: 33.

28 Ibid.: 47, 50.

29 Descartes AT, V: 385. For More, see Hall 1990 or Crocker 1990.

30 Kargon 1966.

31 Gassendi 1649.

32 Charleton and Gassendi 1654: 445, 343, and 270, 435.

33 Ibid.: 343, 348, 388, 391, 397.

explanatory power to that sort of generalized observations in stating that all effects of magnetic attraction could 'conveniently be referred to' those observables.[34]

Vague and unexplicated as Charleton's separation of 'laws' and 'observables' remained, it is clear that he drew from sources other than Descartes. Strikingly enough, there was nothing parallel to Charleton's terminology in Gassendi, of whose study Charleton gave a more or less close paraphrase,[35] nor in William Gilbert's work on magnetism, to which Charleton often referred.[36] It was rather Bacon (whom Charleton praised repeatedly) who served as an important model here, with his talk of laws of particular realms of phenomena rather than of nature in general. As a sort of blend between Baconian and Cartesian uses, the law-concept in England became wide and vague at the same time. The talk of laws in natural philosophy differed substantially between France and England already in the 1650s.

Expanding the Law-talk: the Early Royal Society

The situation of natural philosophy changed drastically from the 1660s on. In England, the foundation of the Royal Society in 1660 attracted public attention to the new approaches, with all the various effects attendant upon publicity. As to the law-concept, the case of Henry More is most instructive. Fellow at Christ's College in Cambridge, More had become a famous writer, defending the new approaches of natural philosophy against suspicions of atheism, and was early elected Fellow of the Royal Society in 1662. In the late 1660s, his attitude to the law-concept changed drastically. In contrast to his former reluctance, he not only fully adopted Descartes' use, but also extended it widely. In his pro-Cartesian *Epistola ad V.C.* of 1664, he spoke not only of 'leges Naturae', but also of 'leges mechanicae', 'leges motus', 'Materiae Motusque Leges', and even of 'Magnetismi leges', as he did in his very popular *Enchiridion Ethicum* of 1667.[37] Despite his fierce opposition to Epicurean atomism, so strongly promoted by Charleton, the latter's study provided a direct and main source for More's talk of laws. The concept even survived More's anti-Cartesian turn of the late 1660s. In the very subtitle of one of his main anti-Cartesian texts, the 1671 *Enchiridion Metaphysicum*, More announced his intention to 'consider' ('expendere') natural phenomena with respect to 'Leges Cartesii Mechanicas', but at the same time to demonstrate the 'Vanitas' and 'Falsitás' of Descartes' attempt at explaining the universe by purely mechanical causes. His explicit opposition to mechanistic explanations contrasts with his neutral stance with respect to laws. In the text of the work, More mentioned 'leges mechanicae' in many places.[38]

More set important signals for the talk of laws in the Royal Society. He never participated, however, in what was to become the Society's central programme:

---

34 Charleton and Gassendi 1654: 388, 393–397.

35 What Charleton called 'General Laws of Nature', for example, had been discussed by Gassendi as 'modus agendi & patiendi': Gassendi 1649: 348.

36 Gilbert 1600.

37 More 1679, reprint 1966, vol. II, 1: 109, 110, 112, 113; for example, More 1667: 38.

38 More 1671: 246, 248, among others; English translation by Jacob, More 1995.

an 'experimental philosophy' in a Baconian understanding.[39] That programme, with its empiristic and inductivistic ideal, differed essentially from the Cartesian, rationalistic approach. Beyond that programmatic claim, however, the Royal Society was extremely heterogeneous, and indeed some of the approaches did not have much to do with the Baconian ideal. That heterogeneity was reflected in the development of the concept of laws of nature.

In the late 1660s, the collision of bodies became an important topic in the Royal Society, and it was in this context that the talk of laws visibly crystallized, already when Henry Oldenburg, the Society's secretary, proposed in 1667 'that the experiments for making out a theory of the laws of motion ... should be prosecuted'.[40] In the correspondence between Oldenburg, Huygens, Wren, Wallis, Neile and Gregory, 'laws of motion' were mentioned again and again, in most cases equivocally with 'principles of motion', 'rules of motion', 'rules & axioms' or the like. The background stimulus of the whole enterprise clearly showed up in references such as 'the Lawes of Motion, given by Des Cartes, (divers ingenious Mathematicians looking upon them, as false)'.[41] Cartesian or not, the collision of bodies was fundamental within every mechanical philosophy. The law-talk also was used in the published papers in the *Philosophical Transactions*, with titles such as John Wallis's 'Summary Account … of the General *Laws* of *Motion*' or Christopher Wren's 'Lex Naturae de Collisione Corporum'.[42] Wallis spoke of 'principia de motibus' interchangeably with 'Generales Motuum Leges'. These laws were fundamental principles, even kinematic ones, such as the statement that something which moves in the period T along the distance L would move along the distance nL in the period nT. In Wren's paper, the 'Lex Naturae' stated that in collisions the loss of motion (combined from the bulk and velocity) of one body was equal to the gain of motion in the other. Wren used the law-concept for quite particular cases, comparable to the level of Descartes' seven 'rules' of collision. This points to a significant expansion of the terminology: Descartes had been most careful *not* to call those rules 'laws'. The discussion of the collision of bodies was the first in which the talk of laws was broadly used, first in England, but soon all over Europe.

Not all contributors, however, showed the same usage. While Oldenburg, Wren and Wallis used the terminology of laws quite freely,[43] Huygens, the only one with strong commitments to Cartesianism, remained reluctant. Almost without exception, he responded to Oldenburg's talk of 'loix du mouvement' by speaking of 'regles et theoremes' or the like. His contribution to the competition, submitted in French in early 1669, had the title 'Regles de mouvement', and in the whole paper law-talk occurred only once.[44] When Oldenburg published a Latin translation of Huygens'

---

[39] Sprat 1667; Hunter 1989.

[40] Council meeting of 16 January 1667: Birch 1756–57: II, 140. See Hall 1981: 189–191.

[41] Oldenburg 1965–86: V, 103, 117, 125, 341, 358, among others. For a compilation of relevant passages, see Graßhoff and Treiber 2002.

[42] Wallis 1669; Wren 1669: 867.

[43] Oldenburg 1965–86: V, 103, 117, 358.

[44] Huygens 1669; reprinted in Huygens 1888–1950: XVI, 179–181.

text, he mainly adopted Huygens' terminology of rules, principles and propositions. Significantly enough, however, he changed terms in the very title and presented Huygens' treatise as 'A summary account of the *Laws of Motion*'.[45] It is difficult to imagine that Oldenburg did not register these changes. He was determined to give the law-concept a more prominent place than Huygens.

Discussion of laws occurred also in other fields. John Wallis, in a 1666 paper on tides, considered how the motion of particular bodies should be explained from '*Mechanick* Principles'; that is, 'according to the *Laws of Motion* and *Statick Principles*'. One of those principles was 'that a Body in motion is apt to continue its motion, and that in the same degree of celerity, unless hindered by some contrary Impediment'. Another 'Law of *Staticks*' stated that the common centre of gravity of two bodies was always on the line between them.[46] By means of principles of this kind, Wallis aimed to account for the observed regularities of tides, which themselves were not called 'laws', but tidal 'periods': daily, mensual and annual. These regularities were not called laws: they were rather to be explained by laws. In yet another field – hydrostatics – Robert Boyle often spoke of the 'Principles and Laws of Hydrostaticks' or the 'known laws of hydrostaticks'.[47] He also mentioned 'optical laws', 'mechanical laws' and 'magnetical laws', or even the 'laws of refraction'. Like Wallis and Wren, he used the terms 'Principle' and 'Law' synonymously, oftentimes even with 'rule'.[48] A similarly broad use can be seen in the work of the young Isaac Newton. In his early (unpublished) research notes on collision, he adopted Wallis's and Wren's use of 'Lawes of motion'.[49] Likewise he spoke, in his 1672 paper on light and colours, of the 'received laws of refraction', but also called them 'Hypotheses'.[50] In the long controversy following this publication, the term 'Laws of Refraction' was used by all parties synonymously with 'rule of refraction'.[51] Even earlier, Erasmus Bartholin, in presenting the extraordinary refraction of the Iceland spar, had spoken of the 'ordinary Laws of Usual Refraction'.[52] Again recall the fact that Descartes had been eager *not* to call the sine-relation a 'law'. In London, the talk of laws embraced not only many more subject fields than in France, but also lower-level principles.

---

[45] Huygens and Oldenburg 1669; original emphasis. See also the alphabetic index of the volume.

[46] Wallis 1666: 264, 268, 272.

[47] Boyle 1666a, cf. Boyle 1772 II: 742–745; or Boyle 1663, cf. Boyle 1772 II: 36; or *Philosophical Transactions*, 1 (1666): 233–234. See also the review in *Philosophical Transactions*, 1 (1666): 174.

[48] Boyle 1674 and Boyle 1671, cf. Boyle 1772: IV, 68, 69, 71, 72, and III, 430.

[49] Herivel 1965.

[50] Newton 1672a: 3076–3077; Newton 1958: 48–49.

[51] *Philosophical Transactions*, 7 (1672): 4081, 4089, or 9 (1674): 218, 501; Newton 1958: 79, 81, 149, 152.

[52] Bartholin 1670: 2045.

New Meanings

Along with that gradual expansion of the law-talk, however, a shift in meaning occurred that perhaps was barely noticed. Robert Hooke, in his 1665 *Micrographia*, not only named the sine-relation in optical refraction the 'law of refraction' (and was probably the first to do so), but also emphasized that he had found the law 'experimentally'.[53] That was a new perspective indeed. Empirically established regularities had not been called 'laws' before. Even more distinctly, Hooke mentioned, in discussing his newly invented baroscope, the 'very odd laws' of the change of the pressure of the air.[54] Again, he had in mind empirical regularities, those moreover, which he could not (yet) situate within a larger deductive system. To call them 'laws' was to turn round the Cartesian use. No longer were laws the central principles, but the particular phenomena and regularities which traditionally were to be derived from them: no longer the traditional *explanans*, but the *explanandum*! The position of 'laws' within the explanatory structure had been turned upside down here.

Oldenburg, in reviewing Hooke's book, took up his law-talk unchanged.[55] Later on, in a paean to the usefulness of the new natural philosophy, he even mentioned, 'an Instrument to measure the Refractions of Liquors of all kinds, for establishing the Laws of Refraction'.[56] That laws could – and perhaps should – be established by *instruments*, indicates the change of perspective most strikingly: such an idea would have been unthinkable in Descartes. And when Newton, in discussing optical theory, raised the problem 'What is the Law according to which each ray is more or less refracted?'[57] he did not have the sine-relation in mind, but rather a regularity describing how different colours were refracted – we call it a dispersion-rule. He was fully aware that such a relation could only be found empirically – any explanation from general principles was far away. It is instructive that Newton, after discussing the diverse refrangibility of rays, asked himself 'Where that diversity originates: In some uncertain and irregular cause, or in a certain law [certâ lege] according to which any ray is inclined to suffer a determinate refraction?'[58] The contraposition of an 'uncertain and irregular cause' and a 'certain law' reveals much about what laws had come to mean. Empirical regularities obtained the status of laws if they represented a *distinct* and *regular* outcome. Not only were they not principles in a Cartesian sense, but their status as 'laws' did not even depend on inclusion in deductive systems; it was secured by their certainty and regularity alone – a point that philosophers of law would quickly take up [MOHNHAUPT].

Neither Newton nor Hooke, however, were consistent in their terminology, nor were they inclined to discuss it in its own right. And it is not even clear whether they realized how significant a step they had taken: the new use could appear as just another step within the ongoing broadening of the terminology. Boyle was more

---

53 Hooke 1665: preface, p. xxv in my counting. Ruby 1986 (reprint p. 297) ascribes the term 'lex refractionis' already to Roger Bacon, but gives no reference.

54 Hooke 1665: preface, p. xiv in my counting.

55 *Philosophical Transactions*, 1 (2) (1665): 31, 32.

56 *Philosophical Transactions*, 4 (1669): 894.

57 Newton 1672d; Newton 1958: 93.

58 Newton 1672c; Newton 1958: 100. Also Newton 1672b: 5093.

reflective here. Probably as a response to what he realized as a shift of meaning, he discussed the concept of laws of nature explicitly, and introduced a whole scale of laws. At the one end, there were the 'fixt laws of nature, or rules of action and passion among the parcels of the universal matter',[59] being general rules with broad scope. At the other end, he found empirical regularities, which he compared to 'municipial laws ... that belong to this or that particular sort of bodies'. While only the former were really 'laws of nature, more properly so called', he called the latter ones also 'customs of nature'.[60] Boyle took up here, in verbal translation, Francis Bacon's distinction between 'consuetudines naturae' and 'leges fundamentales et communes'. While Bacon had restricted his concept of laws to the latter statements, Boyle included even the 'customs of nature' within a now much more capacious concept of law.

The Paris Academy: Laws and 'principes d'expérience'

In Paris, as in England, the situation for research in natural philosophy changed dramatically in the 1660s. With the foundation of the Académie Royale des Sciences in 1666, experimental research received a firm institutional backing and, with royal patronage, a widely acknowledged reputation. The academy quickly developed into France's centre for conducting research and exchanging natural philosophical results. Even in those changing times, the talk of laws remained as rare as before, both in books and in the early volumes of the *Journal des sçavans*. As one of the rare cases, the astronomer Auzout opened a treatise on comets with the remark that the motions of comets had been regarded as too irregular as to be captured 'sous des Loix'.[61] Even Cartesian writers were reluctant. Gerard de Cordemoy, in his 1666 study on the relation between mind and body, mentioned the 'loix de la nature' at only one place, directly adopting Descartes' terminology.[62] The same holds for Rohault's famous Cartesian textbook *Traité de physique* (1671).[63] Both the rare use and the specific meaning of the law-concept still directly reflected the Cartesian approach. As already mentioned, this held even for Christiaan Huygens – soon to become one of the academy's most prominent members – and his work on the collision of bodies. In his survey article of 1669, even statements such as the conservation of the overall motion (m•v) in collision (§5), or the conservation of the sum of m•v^2 (§6), were called 'règle', 'proposition' or 'principe'. Only in one case did Huygens use the term 'loy admirable de la Nature',[64] referring to the extremely general principle that the motion of the common centre of gravity of colliding bodies was not affected by the collision.

---

59 Boyle 1663; Boyle 1772: II, 37.

60 Boyle 1686: sect VII, §II: Boyle 1996: 107; cf. Boyle 1772 V: 217. Printed in 1686, the book had already been drafted in 1665–66. See also McGuire 1972.

61 Auzout 1665/6: first page of the preface. The law-talk did not occur elsewhere in the study. Oldenburg adopted the terminology immediately: Oldenburg 1665: 4.

62 Cordemoy 1666, reprinted Cordemoy 1968: 125.

63 Rohault 1671: vol. 1, chap. 11 (p. 69 in the fourth edition of 1681).

64 Huygens 1669; reprinted 1888–1950: XVI, 181.

Among Huygens' fellow academicians, it was probably Edme Mariotte who worked most extensively in experimental natural philosophy – Condorcet would later praise him as the one who brought experimental physics to France. In Mariotte's early writings,[65] there was no talk whatsoever of laws of nature. Even when he studied the collision of bodies (1673) and referred to Descartes and 'some other modern writers', doubtless Wren, Wallis and Huygens, he did not adopt the talk of laws, but used – significantly enough, and much like Huygens – the fine-grained terminology of mathematics: Règle, Proposition, Lemme, Problème.[66] Being more attentive than others to discriminating different types of statements, he introduced, however, a special type of propositions under the name of 'Principe de l'expérience'. The statement that weights, when they fell on a support, made a larger impact than when they rested, provided an illustrative example.[67]

Five years later, in his *Essay de Logique*, Mariotte presented a systematic account of those 'Principes'. Among all propositions about the sensible world, he divided those that could be proved by direct induction ('verités premieres sensibles', such as the statement that fire is hot), from those that could only be argued for by means of certain 'principes', be they 'intellectual' (as in mathematical reasoning) or 'sensibles'.[68] The latter ones were central for empirical research. Mariotte called them 'Maximes ou règles naturelles, ou principes d'expérience' and mentioned, on the one hand, very general statements such as the rectilinear propagation of light, the unequal action of equal weights at unequal distances at the balance, the motion of iron towards magnets and the heating effect of friction, but also, on the other hand, specific regularities such as the refraction of light from air into water towards the perpendicular or the proportionality of compression and weight of the air (later called 'Mariotte's law').[69] Most of those empirical generalizations (as we would call them) were supported by experiment and not embedded in a larger theoretical framework. Mariotte knew well, moreover, that statements of this type were sometimes called 'laws of nature' by his contemporaries. In one case, referring to a relativity principle in collision (of Huygens' type), Mariotte even explicitly spoke of 'un principe d'expérience, ou loy de la nature'.[70] Already earlier, in presenting his famous proposition on pneumatics in 1676, he had introduced it as 'une règle certaine ou loi de la nature'.[71] It is important to note that the reliability of the statement rested on experiments, carried out by Mariotte and the instrument-maker Hubin, and that there was no explanation provided from principles such as the microscopic properties of air. Mariotte did indeed aim at such an 'explication' in the long run, but admitted that, for the time being, it could not be achieved.[72] The status of the proportionality

[65] Mariotte 1666; Mariotte 1923.

[66] Mariotte 1673: 28, 239, 280.

[67] 'second principe d'experience': ibid.: 267, cf. 179.

[68] Mariotte 1678; reprinted Mariotte 1992: 89–90.

[69] Ibid.: 91–93, 127, 132.

[70] Ibid.: 99; cf. Mariotte 1686: 79.

[71] Mariotte 1923: 8.

[72] Ibid.: 38. Opposing the idea that the expansion of air was caused by increasing distance between its particles, he favoured an analogy to the behaviour of cotton wool, an

as a 'principe d'expérience', however, remained unaffected by the lack of a 'deeper' explanation.

Mariotte thus provides a peculiar picture concerning law-talk. On the one hand, he was probably the first to introduce a proposition, established by himself, as a 'law of nature', thus emphasizing and furthering that terminology. On the other hand, he remained very reluctant in general to speak of laws.[73] Finally, he introduced a category – the 'principes d'expérience' – as a sort of empirical generalization, and he explicitly connected this type of statements – that had exactly not been named 'laws' by Descartes – to the now much broadened talk of 'laws'. His approach forms a unique attempt to keep these meta-concepts somewhat sharp, in contrast to what he realized to be widening usages, particularly in England

Metaphysics and Theology

The concept of laws had, of course, many connotations, some of which raised serious problems. Boyle registered them explicitly:

> I must freely observe that, to speak properly, a law being but a notional rule of action according to the declared will of a superior, it is plain that nothing but an intellectual being can be properly capable of receiving and acting by a law. For if it does not understand, it cannot know what the will of the legislator is, nor can it have any intention to accomplish it, nor can it act with regard to it, or know when it does, in acting, either conform to it or deviate from it.[74]

Such an observation made it necessary to explicate the status of those 'laws' and the mode in which they – or their 'author' – were considered to affect the workings of nature. In Boyle's account, the world, once created by God, would run purely mechanically on its own, '*according to mechanical laws*' ordained by God.[75] Given this state of affairs, it appears surprising, however, that Boyle himself used and even propagated the terminology of laws. He argued that the analogy between 'regular motions of inanimate bodies' and the lawful acting of people led many (including himself) to use the notion of laws, 'for brevity's sake or out of custom' – a custom that he obviously observed when looking around in the Royal Society milieu. But he hastened to emphasize that such a talk was only metaphorical: what was really acting in natural processes was just brute inanimate matter and mechanic causes [Wilson].

---

idea probably taken from Pascal (without mentioning his name): ibid., 47–48; cf Pascal 1663 in Brunschvigg and Boutroux 1904–14: III, 197–198.

[73] This also holds for his posthumously published study on hydrostatics and –dynamics: Mariotte 1686: 74, 76, 79, 85, 113.

[74] Boyle 1996: 24–25, or Boyle 1772: V, 170–171. The quoted passages were added in 1680.

[75] Boyle 1674; Boyle 1772: IV, 68–69. See also Boyle 1666b; Boyle 1772: III, 48.

Boyle here reacted to the Cambridge philosopher Ralph Cudworth who – much opposed to Descartes' mechanistic philosophy – conceived God's rule of nature in term of 'laws' and proposed a verbal interpretation:[76]

> Though it be true that the Works of Nature are dispensed by a *Divine Law* and *Command*, yet this is not to be understood in a *Vulgar Sence*, as if they were all effected by the mere Force of a *Verbal Law* or *Outward Command*, because Inanimate things are not *Commandable* nor *Governable* by such a *Law*; …

Whereas Boyle and Cudworth concurred in this point, Cudworth, in strictly voluntaristic mood, proceeded to very different consequences:

> and therefore besides the Divine Will and Pleasure, there must needs be some other Immediate *Agent* and *Executioner* provided, for the producing of every Effect.[77]

Cudworth had in mind a 'Plastick Nature' here, acting as mediator between God's will and brute matter. Much in the same vein, Henry More had argued for the existence of an immaterial substance – the 'spirit of nature'. Boyle did his best to argue against those hylozoist positions, proposing a view of mechanistic action [Wilson].[78] Their dispute, pointing to the metaphysical and theological problems of law-talk, was quickly taken up in France, as Sophie Roux discusses in detail [Roux]. But those problems did not stop the rise of the terminology in all its ambiguity and anthropomorphism.

Towards the End of the Century

In the last decade of the seventeenth century, talk of laws became increasingly common. Whereas in the early years of the *Philosophical Transactions* and the *Journal des Sçavans* the term occurred rather rarely, many papers later inserted it it into their very titles. A significant landmark was the publication of Newton's *Principia* in 1686. Although seldom read in detail, the work became an icon of the 'new' natural philosophy. At the outset of the book, Newton placed his three 'Axiomata, sive Leges Motus', as a deliberate response to Descartes' three 'Laws of nature'. But the concept was also present in many other places, and with other meanings. Newton mentioned the 'laws of planetary motions', 'of the oscillating pendulum', 'of condensation' of an elastic fluid, or 'of gravitation'.[79] The whole spectrum of uses was present in the widely visible work of one author. At the same time, it became clear how fuzzy the concept had become. 'Laws' could mean axiomatic principles, or more or less empirically established regularities, or anything in between. Nor was

[76] I thank Andreas Hüttemann for pointing me to Cudworth. For more details, see Hüttemann 2001.

[77] Cudworth 1678: 147; original emphasis.

[78] Cf. Oldenburg's summary, *Philosophical Transactions*, 7 (92) (1673): 5198–5199.

[79] Newton 1972: 54, 428, 521, 569, 577, 759. For details, see Steinle 1995.

the terminology consistent: for example, Newton called Kepler's three discoveries both 'laws' and 'Phaenomena'.[80]

Newton set an example for many. Edmond Halley, in his review of the *Principia*, fully adopted Newton's terminology in all its variations.[81] That was significant since Halley, in his previous articles on different fields, had never talked of laws, but had preferred a language of mathematical structures: Propositions, Corollaries, Lemmata, and so on. The use quickly went beyond the academic realm, moreover. In his popular sermons against atheism in the early 1690s, the cleric Richard Bentley spoke of 'Laws of Nature', 'laws of motion', 'Laws of Vegetation and Life', 'Laws of mechanism', and so on.[82] Newton, who had provided Bentley with all necessary astronomical information, applauded. From the 1690s on, the notion was firmly established both in England and elsewhere.[83] Even the formerly reluctant Huygens used it more freely now, as his 1690 review of his researches in collision and centrifugal force strikingly shows.[84] In the prominent debates between Malebranche, Leibniz and Newton, the terminology of laws was ubiquitous [Roux]. And in Pierre Regis's 1691 important Cartesian textbook, talk of laws was much in evidence, both as 'loy de la nature' and 'loix de mouvement', indicating a significant widening of Descartes' use.[85] Moreover, Regis intensely treated the natural law in the juridical meaning and emphasized a terminological separation between 'loy de la nature' (for natural philosophy) and 'loy naturelle' (for the moral realm).[86] Together with the English bishop Richard Cumberland [Treiber], he was one of the very few to bring these two law-concepts together explicitly.

It is indicative that many of the great successes of the 'new sciences' in the seventeenth century came to be called 'laws' late in the century. Both Descartes and Snellius had introduced the sine-relation in optical refraction as a 'proposition', but Hooke, in 1665, referred to it as the 'law of refraction'.[87] Galileo had never used law-talk in presenting his research, but Boyle, in 1674, spoke of the 'laws of acceleration of heavy bodies descending'.[88] Kepler had presented his three famous results (1609 and 1615) as 'propositions', but Newton called them the 'laws of planetary motions, detected by Kepler' in 1686.[89] Boyle had introduced the inverse proportionality between pressure and volume of gases as a 'Hypothesis' (1662),[90] but by the end of the century the statement had been dubbed 'Boyle's law' in England. Only Mariotte, in 1676, had been the first to call a proposition established by himself a 'law of nature', and he was quickly followed by Hooke with the proportionality between the

---

80 Newton 1972: 556–63 and 569.

81 Halley 1687: 291, 292, 295.

82 Bentley 1693a; Bentley 1693b; cf. Newton 1958: 348, 368, 369, 387, 388.

83 Zilsel 1942b: 270–273 ; Roux 2001: 565–566.

84 Huygens 1888–1950: XVI, 202–208.

85 Regis 1691: I, 362–389.

86 Ibid., III, chap. 7 of the first book on morals.

87 Hooke 1665: preface, p. xxv in my counting.

88 Boyle 1674; Boyle 1772: IV, 71.

89 *Principia* III, prop.4, scholium: Newton 1972: 569.

90 Boyle 1662: 50, 58; in Boyle 1999: III, 50, 58.

elongation and restituting force of a spring.[91] Within half a century, the concept of laws of nature had been given a firm and visible place in natural philosophy. It was no longer debated, but could be used without further explanation or justification. At the same time, it had lost all sharpness, and the broadness of its meanings – from a-priori insights to empirical regularities – allowed the most divergent writers to invoke its authority.

Laws of Nature and the Rise of the New Sciences

The general picture becomes more differentiated by specific characteristics of, and differences between the developments in France and England. Not only was law-talk much more reluctantly used in France than in England, but the terminology was also much less varied. Whereas in France 'loix de la Nature' were taken in a nearly uniform sense, there was an abundance of more specific 'laws' in England, such as 'mechanical', 'magnetical', 'optical' laws, and laws of 'motion', of 'collision', of 'refraction', of 'gravitation', of 'falling bodies', of 'the change of air pressure', of 'the oscillating pendulum', and of 'planetary motions'. Finally, the epistemic roles of 'laws' tended to be more sharply defined in France. There was either the Cartesian notion of a-priori laws, or (if much more reluctantly) the understanding of laws as generalized empirical results, a notion that was explicitly discussed and preferably treated under the term 'principes d'expérience'. In England, by contrast, the epistemic status of laws was barely discussed, but at the same time varied widely, from axiomatic statements with the character of definitions, to empirical regularities with rather restricted scope, and everything in between.

What is the background of such a remarkable development? Newton himself suggested a first clue by emphasizing that new concepts were needed in order to indicate causation after substantial forms had been discarded.[92] But that can only be a part of the story. Not everyone identified causality with laws, and there had been obvious alternatives to the talk of laws. Wider historical perspectives must be included here. It is significant that it was exactly the protagonists of new approaches to natural philosophy who propagated a wider use of the law-concept. However, the settings in which those programmes began to work varied widely. In England, the activities of the Royal Society were challenged and attacked from early on, and from different angles. In response, many of the early papers were framed as apologies – some of the already cited quotes from Oldenburg are illustrative here.[93] Thomas Sprat's 1667 *History of the Royal Society* – commissioned by the Royal Society expressly for the purpose of gaining public support – was full of considerations showing the usefulness of the new experimental philosophy.[94] One of the most serious questions was that of the relation of those new sciences to religion and divine authority. Fellows felt compelled to show that experimental philosophy was supportive of rather than dangerous to religion. The cleric and FRS Samuel Parker

---

91 Gunther 1923: VIII, 333–334, 336.

92 *Principia*, Auctoris Praefatio, in Newton 1972: 15.

93 Hunter 1989; Hunter 1990.

94 Sprat 1667; cf. Wood 1980.

discussed (and aimed to refute) the objection 'that Philosophy is the Apprenticeship of Atheisme',[95] and Boyle's treatise on the *Usefulness of Experimental Natural Philosophy* was written to the same purpose. Oldenburg characterized the Royal Society as:

> not taking up old fame, or flying Reports, upon too easie trust; nor straining for other kinds of wonders, than the most wise Author of Nature hath allowed, but attending closely to the strict measures of *Natural Truth*, and to the useful contrivances of *Art*.[96]

The emphasis of the 'Author of Nature' was certainly deliberate. In such a context the terminology of laws of nature was extremely useful: it always pointed to the author of those laws. This was probably one of the strongest reasons why it was so much given an increasingly prominent place.

However, the concept of laws inevitably referred to theology and metaphysics, and in those respects the Royal Society was all but homogeneous. In order to instrumentalize law-talk, it had to be explicated in different ways. And here it was convenient that such different authorities as Bacon and Descartes could serve as a resource. Those researchers who envisaged a deductive system à la Descartes (More), or after the model of mathematics and astronomy (Wren, Wallis) could adopt Descartes' use and call the central principles of their domains 'laws'. The experimentalists, on the other hand, such as Charleton, Hooke or Boyle, could allude to the less strict Baconian usage to give their results higher dignity: empirical regularities were nothing but an expression of God's will, even more directly given than the difficult and much debated central principles. It was the explicit voluntaristic aspect of such a use that made even a doubter like Boyle retain the concept, despite all its obvious problems. That the law-concept became so greatly expanded, heterogenized, and weakened, was a reflection of the enormous variety of those programmes which had come together under the common roof of the Royal Society.

The contrast between England and France is most instructive. While the general programmes for renewing natural philosophy had much in common, the specific settings of the Paris academy differed drastically from those of the Royal Society. The fellows were paid for doing research, and some could even make their living that way. The small group of about thirty was supposed to form a coherent body (in contrast to a loose assembly of individual researchers); so much so that in the first years of the *Journal des sçavans* even the individual authors' names were suppressed. In addition to its own library, observatory, chemical laboratory, botanic garden, and instruments, the academy had money for excursions, hiring assistants and publications.[97] In London, there was nothing comparable; rather members had to pay fees. Although both academies enjoyed royal patronage, it was only in Paris

---

95 Parker 1665; cf. Oldenburg's review: *Philosophical Transactions*, 1 (18) (1666): 324–325. Parker was one of the few to emphasize close connexions between moral/ juridical issues and those of natural philosophy: Parker 1681.

96 *Philosophical Transactions*, 2 (23) (1667): unpaginated page at the beginning of the issue.

97 Stroup 1990: pt. 2; Hahn 1971.

that such patronage resulted in funding, and relatively generous funding at that. All these factors suggest that the status and legitimacy of new approaches to natural philosophy was much more easily and quickly accepted in France than in England. The Paris Academy was not under such acute pressure to justify its existence to a broader public, and there is much less of an apologetic mood visible, at least in the early decades. Likewise, there was no strong need for a term like 'law of nature', pointing to the theological innocuousness of the whole enterprise. Moreover, the closer interaction, sometimes cooperation, between the Paris fellows, may well have contributed to a more homogeneous terminology.

In the eighteenth century, and even more in the nineteenth, laws of nature were understood as more or less general empirical regularities, in contrast to theoretical explanations from a-priori principles or microscopic mechanisms [DASTON]. Such a concept was, as I have shown, already present in many seventeenth-century authors, often implicitly, and even in unexpected places [KUSUKAWA, MACLEAN]. Bacon had labelled it 'consuetudines naturae', Charleton 'observables', and, much more clearly, Mariotte 'principes d'expérience'. Boyle was one of the first to subsume it under the overarching category of 'laws', while others consciously refused to do so. That it was exactly that terminology that eventually carried the day and became inseparably attached to the concept of empirical regularities, can only be understood from the particular historical situation of early modern natural philosophy.

Chapter 14

Unruly Weather: Natural Law Confronts Natural Variability

Lorraine Daston

Introduction

In the late seventeenth and early eighteenth centuries, it became a cliché in works of natural philosophy and, especially, of natural theology, to hold up inquiry into the laws of nature as a model for all knowledge. Natural laws, in both jurisprudence and natural philosophy, laid claim to universality and uniformity; positive laws (and religious doctrines) varied widely as to time and place. In his highly influential *Analogy of Religion, Natural and Revealed* (1736), Anglican bishop Joseph Butler recommended that rational Christians concentrate on 'the Conduct of Nature with respect to intelligent Creatures; which may be resolved into General Laws or Rules of Administration, in the same way as many of the Laws of Nature respecting inanimate Matter may be collected from Experiments', in the hopes of discovering a uniform doctrine amidst the Babel of sects.[1] The English natural philosopher Robert Boyle thought God preferred uniformity even to benevolence:

> And, that having, when all these things were in his prospect, settled among his corporeal works general and standing laws of motion suited to his wisdom, to prefer (unless in newly excepted cases) catholic laws, and higher ends, before subordinate ones, and uniformity in his conduct before making changes in it according to every sort of particular emergencies: and consequently, not to recede from the general laws he at first most wisely established, to comply with the appetites or needs of particular creatures, or to prevent some seeming irregularities (such as earthquakes, floods, famines, & c.) incommodious to them, which are no other, than such, as he foresaw would happen ...[2]

It was universality and uniformity that in Boyle's mind distinguished these 'laws of nature' that pertained to 'the fundamental and general constitutions of bodily things' from mere 'municipal laws (if I may so call them) that belong to this or that particular sort of bodies'.[3] Francis Bacon, writing as a jurist, observed a similar order of precedence when he defended monarchy as the only natural and therefore best

1 Butler 1736: viii.

2 Boyle 1966: 5.252.

3 Ibid.: 5.219.

polity: 'for as the common law is more worthy than the statute law; so the law of nature is more worthy than them both'.[4]

Yet late seventeenth-century writers on natural law in both the human and natural realms recognized the fact of variability and the enormous difficulty of untangling the interlaced effects of uniform 'catholic' and diverse 'municipal' laws. The Académie Royale des Sciences in Paris voted at its first meeting of 22 December 1666 that the mathematical and physical classes should hold joint meetings because 'the laws of motion' should in principle determine all natural phenomena in a precisely calculable fashion; yet there were many processes in which 'it is not that the same mathematics does not rule, but that it becomes obscure and almost impenetrable by the too great complication of motions and shapes'.[5] The great diversity of human customs and mores made John Locke doubt that norms of conduct could be innately 'imprinted on the minds of all men as a law', although he still clung to the belief in 'a law of nature ... that we, being ignorant of, may attain to the knowledge of, by the use and due application of our natural faculties'.[6]

If there was a common epistemological turn in natural law doctrines in both natural philosophy and jurisprudence in the late seventeenth centuries, it was a growing scepticism concerning the intuitive self-evidence of such laws. Samuel Pufendorf's *De jure naturae et gentium* (1672) shifted the foundations of natural law from a transcendental morality revealed by the light of nature to a more pragmatic (and secular) principle of sociability and civil welfare – arguably in response to the implacable confessional conflicts, each side claiming divine inspiration, of the Thirty Years War.[7] Similar associations between Cartesian doctrines of natural laws revealed by the light of nature and religious enthusiasm may also account for the wariness with which many natural philosophers approached such claims after c. 1660, especially in Restoration England.[8] French natural philosophers also retreated from the position that natural laws could be known *a priori* through the inspection of clear and distinct ideas. In his programme of botanical investigations proposed to the Parisian Académie in 1667, Charles Perrault for example emphasized that 'quite a large number of experiments' would be necessary to extract 'general truths, whose necessity is subsequently shown by reason to be necessary, or at least to be linked to other truths'.[9] Even necessary truths of reason could be discovered only by the laborious methods of observation and experiment. Moreover, these 'general truths' or 'principles' could be recognized as such only post hoc, by their universality and constancy, not by their intuitive self-evidence.

The challenge of deriving universal and uniform natural laws from the bewildering variability of observed phenomena was nowhere greater than in studies of the weather. Notoriously local and changeable, it seemed the worst possible candidate for the discovery of simple, universal, and constant natural laws. The intrinsic difficulties

4 Bacon 1825–34: 5.116.

5 Académie Royale des Sciences 1733: 1.14–15.

6 Locke 1959: 1.77–78.

7 Hunter 2001: 126–131; Hochstrasser 2000: 83–95, 106–107.

8 Heyd 1995: 159–160 et passim.

9 Académie Royale des Sciences 1733: 1.20.

of investigating fickle meteorological phenomena like temperature, air pressure, rainfall, and wind direction and force were further compounded by idiosyncratic instruments wielded by equally idiosyncratic observers. No two barometers or thermometers were exactly alike; observers took measurements at different hours in different situations and described the sky in vocabularies that not only differed from language to language but from region to region within the same country. No sooner did a generalization appear to emerge from the piles of data then it was contradicted by the next report. Yet from the very beginnings of scientific academies in the mid-seventeenth century through the end of the eighteenth century, ambitious programmes of meteorological observations aimed at ferreting out stable regularities remained a preoccupation, not to say an obsession, among European naturalists. From Florence to Leipzig, Upminster to Zurich, Paris to Peking, far-flung observers rose daily at dawn to read their thermometers and barometers (deliberately placed in northern exposures and unheated rooms), note the wind direction, squint at cloud formations, and jot down the results in diaries or in multi-columned tables. They posted their data to scientific societies, which sifted the columns of entries in search of some rule or correlation – be it with the configurations of planets, sunspots, epidemics, the tides, or simply instrument readings in other locales. Whenever one network of observers dissolved for lack of time, interest, or palpable results, another sprang up in its place. The early Enlightenment search for the natural laws of weather was as futile and interminable as the task of Sisyphus, but it was apparently undertaken with enthusiasm and pursued with tenacity.

My aim in this essay is to explore the efforts of these late seventeenth- and early eighteenth-century weather observers from the standpoint of how conceptions of natural law were put into practice. The qualification 'into practice' is important for my purposes: although the philosophical reflections of Bacon, Descartes, Malebranche, Boyle, Locke, Leibniz, Newton, and other seventeenth-century luminaries are of indisputable importance in establishing the new vocabularly and concepts of natural laws [Roux], and although their influence on natural philosophical practice was significant, there was no straightforward connection between the theory of natural law and its practice. This holds even in those cases in which theorist and practitioner were one and the same person, for example Robert Boyle or John Locke. The reasons for concentrating on the period c. 1660–1740 are twofold: first, these were the decades in which the terminology of natural laws spread throughout natural philosophy [Steinle] and the search for natural laws became the principal goal not only of natural but also moral philosophy [Larrère]; second, the period witnessed no notable successes in attempts to discover natural laws of weather either empirically or through mathematical models.[10] It is precisely this mismatch between programme and results that applied pressure to conceptions and practices of natural philosophers in search of natural laws, forcing modifications. Conceptions drifted away from self-evident truths akin to those of mathematics towards complicated empirical correlations that more closely resembled rules-of-thumb and proverbs;

[10] On later eighteenth-century attempts at mathematical models of meteorological phenomena (not necessarily successful) by d'Alembert, Euler, Lambert, and Laplace, see Frisinger 1977: 128–140; Feldman 1983: 213–229, 259–265.

practices developed in the direction of increasing standardization of both observers and instruments and of the visual representation of data in tables and symbols that highlighted the sought-for regularities.

Implicit in these shifting conceptions and practices was a new metaphysics and epistemology of natural law. No longer understood as divine edicts to be intuited through the light of nature, natural laws became more like the rules of artisans, to be discovered through long practice and observation. Moreover, as the scope of natural laws contracted, their number expanded. The Cartesian (and Newtonian) vision of natural laws as a small set of axioms from which a wide range of phenomena might be derived, preferably by deduction, gave way to a crowd of regularities, each of restricted range [Roux, Steinle]. In principle, the option was left open as to whether these regularities might ultimately be reduced to a few, general, underlying laws, but in practice natural variability proved ineluctable. Uniform natural laws did not always produce uniformity. Instead of revealing a handful of universal laws responsible for the patchwork of climates, early Enlightenment meteorological investigations transformed natural laws into something more like the weather: local, complex, and only partially calculable.

A Natural History of Weather in Practice

Among the six sample natural histories published with Bacon's programmatic *Historia naturalis et experimentalis* was included a 'History of Winds', which listed observations, proposed experiments, and conjectured causes and connections under some thirty-three headings, including 'Winds in General', 'Qualities and Powers of Winds', and 'Extraordinary Winds'. Bacon emphasized the provisional nature of the undertaking, meant to supply examples of how to put the precepts of the *Novum organum* (1620) into practice and to encourage others to greater efforts: 'We set down works and things impossible, or at least which are not yet found out, as they fall under each title; and withal those which are already found out, and are in men's power; and we add to those impossible, and not yet found out things, such as are next to them, and have most affinity to them, that we may stir up and withal encourage human industry.'[11] Although Bacon's vision of a philosophical inquiry into the causes and nature of the winds based on vast collections of data that taxed human industry to the limits of the possible inspired investigations of weather throughout the seventeenth and eighteenth centuries, the concrete ways in which that vision was realized had changed significantly by the latter half of the seventeenth century. Bacon's own method of culling and summarizing observations from literary sources was replaced by schedules of particular observations specified by time, place, and named observer; the observations were increasingly carried out with newly invented instruments like the thermometer and barometer; Bacon's 'tables' – actually numbered lists of items – were replaced by two-dimensional tables arranged in multiple columns of variables indexed to time of observation; instead of a state-financed, centralized, and hierarchically organized corps of investigators as described in Bacon's *New*

[11] Bacon 1825–34: 10.11; 14: 240.

Atlantis (1627), networks of volunteer observers that extended over generations in time and much of the globe in space were projected and intermittently established. Hence, although much of the weather-watching reported in learned journals during the early Enlightenment might be loosely described as Baconian in spirit, the actual business of making observations was by 1660 quite different from anything Bacon had imagined. Because these changes at the level of practice reverberated in attempts to discern regularities and frame explanations, they merit some attention.

In 1704 the *Philosophical Transactions of the Royal Society of London* published an article by Locke containing his weather observations, made at Oates in Essex, for the year 1692.[12] Locke's register was neither the first nor the most comprehensive of such reports published in the annals of early scientific societies, but since it was unusually explicit about its method of construction, and because the manuscript commonplace book on which it was based is still available for consultation, it is particularly informative about the practices of making meteorological observations, and thus serves as a useful introduction to who observed what and how.

In his fragmentary 'The General History of the Air', Boyle had called upon everyone 'who hath leisure, opportunity, and time' to keep a diary of 'his own observations of the change and alteration of the air from day to day', emphasizing the utility of such mundane 'histories'.[13] The annals of scientific societies in the seventeenth and eighteenth centuries are peppered with attempts to recruit and maintain networks of weather observers. In 1654, the Florentine Accademia del Cimento – exploiting the connections of the Grand Duke of Tuscany Ferdinand II and his Jesuit secretary Antinori – organized a network of stations at Florence, Vallombrosa, Cutigliano, Bologna, Parma, Milan, Warsaw, Innsbruck, Osnabruck, and Paris, which kept daily records until the Cimento itself collapsed in 1667.[14] Robert Hooke proposed in 1663 a model form or 'scheme' in which to record notes on the appearance of the sky and 'the Notablest Effects';[15] Edmund Halley issued an appeal to all mariners for information on the prevailing winds in the world's seas and oceans, for '[i]t is not the work of one, nor of a few, but of a multitude of Observers, to bring together the experience requisite to compose a perfect and compleat History of these Winds'.[16] In 1723, James Jurin, in his capacity of Secretary to the Royal Society of London, issued a Latin invitation to potential observers, offering to provide instruments and giving detailed instructions as to when, where, and how to deploy them.[17] For about a decade thereafter, the Royal Society printed responses to Jurin's call from correspondents from Finland to Italy, India to New England. Other short-lived correspondence networks, lasting at most a decade, were organized by Johannes

---

12 Locke 1704.

13 Boyle 1966: 5.642. Locke may have begun his programme of observations with Boyle's encouragement; Boyle includes some of Locke's tables and a letter from him about noxious gases in mines in the 'General History of Air'.

14 Khrigian 1970: 71–72.

15 Sprat 1667: 173–179.

16 Halley 1686b: 162.

17 Jurin 1723; see Rusnock 1999 on Jurin's other correspondence networks.

Kanold in Breslau,[18] Daniel Bernoulli at the St Petersburg Academy of Sciences,[19] *The Gentleman's Magazine* in England,[20] and local improving societies at Leipzig and elsewhere in the German lands.[21] The most ambitious and successful eighteenth-century initiatives to establish dense, reliable, well-equipped, and standardized networks of meteorological observers were both state-subsidized: the commission (after 1778, the Société Royale de Médicine) established by Comptroller-General of France A.J.R. Turgot in 1776 under the leadership of Félix Vicq d'Azyr,[22] and the Societatis Meteorologica Palatina founded in 1780 by Elector Karl Theodor of Mannheim and directed by Johann Hemmer.[23]

The diverse sponsorship of and participation in these observer networks inhibit any prosopographical generalization about the correspondents who made and reported observations: they included country gentlemen, physicians, sea captains and peripatetic Jesuits, erudite abbots and naturalist curates, university professors and academicians, travellers, and almost anyone who kept a regular diary. The varied contexts in which the observations were made often shaped what was observed and how. A provincial parson eager to win the patronage of the lord of the manor in his parish would often focus on local peculiarities and remarkable 'meteors' that would redound to the fame of the district;[24] a learned humanist might relate his observations to (and draw his Greek and Latin vocabulary from) classical texts;[25] navigators keeping the ship's log attended closely to prevailing winds;[26] physicians focused on possible links with outbreaks of plague and other diseases.[27] Hence what was observed varied with who was observing, and the possibilities were dizzying. As one enthusiast for keeping weather 'Calenders' wrote to the Royal Society in 1672, the observations might be correlated with 'deaths or Famines, Epidemical Diseases & c.', or 'the Positions of the Planets', or 'the cause of Heat and Cold, coasting Rain and coasting Winds', or 'the highest and lowest price of Wheat, Rye, Barley, Pease, Beans, Oats, as they are sold in some chief Market in *London*'.[28] Methods of observation varied accordingly: country naturalists were frequently also local antiquarians who applied similar techniques to registering both artificialia and naturalia; seamen preferred time-honored skills for identifying and registering winds to new-fangled (and delicate) instruments and tables; diarists with astrological interests noted the position of the planet Mercury more assiduously than the level of the mercury in the thermometer.

There was therefore little that was standard or standardized in what and how Locke observed about the weather in Oates. However, the intersection of contexts

---

18 Hellmann 1883; Hellmann 1926.

19 Khrigian 1970: 73–74.

20 Sherbo 1985: 23–24.

21 Lowood 1991: 117–118, 121–123.

22 Desaive et al. 1972: 9–20.

23 Kington 1974; Hellmann 1883: 889ff.; Traumüller 1885.

24 Jankovič 2000: 78–89.

25 Telelis 1998.

26 Halley 1686b.

27 Musschenbroek 1732.

28 Anon. 1672: 5141.

in which his observations were situated – medical training, natural philosophical pursuits, membership in the Royal Society, keeper of commonplace books on diverse topics, rural residence but cosmopolitan experience – were not atypical of other early Enlightenment weather correspondents. As recommended by Hooke, Locke recorded his observations in tabular form, although not exactly according to Hooke's scheme.[29] Locke's table consisted of seven columns, headed Day, Hour, Thermoscope, Baroscope, Hygroscope, Wind, Weather. His observations thus combined quantitative thermometer, barometer and hygrometer readings with qualitative remarks on wind direction and force, and the appearance of the sky, all taken daily but not all at regular hours.

All of these entries required explanation and calibration, the instrument measurements perhaps most of all. Boyle had pointed out that moderns had 'an advantage given us in this age, beyond what most ages ever had, by the use of those rare instruments, that they call the thermometers, or weather-glasses'.[30] As Locke and other observers were to discover, these instruments were a mixed blessing. Locke was careful to specify the construction and maker of his thermometers, as were almost all observers during this period. His 'Hygroscope' was contrived from 'the beard of a Wild Oat, of which each turn was divided into fifteen degrees'.[31] Instruments varied greatly in construction, some using mercury, others alcohol as their liquid; it has been estimated that more than forty different thermometer scales were in use during the eighteenth century.[32] Philippe de La Hire, who conducted meteorological observations over decades at the Paris Observatory, complained that no two thermometers were alike.[33] In order to insure comparability of his own measurements, he used the same thermometer for over forty years, and when Parisian savants wanted to discover whether the extreme cold spell of 1776 surpassed the frigid winter of 1709, they had to search for a thermometer that had been calibrated to La Hire's.[34] The extreme individuality of instruments, as well as protracted controversies over scales, bedevilled all attempts to interpret and compare meteorological measurements throughout the eighteenth century, with important implications for attempts to draw generalizations from data accumulated by several hands in dispersed locales.

The more qualitative observations also posed problems of comparison. Locke admitted that his wind direction readings were approximate, 'because the Weathervane visible out of my Window was stiff, and turn'd not easily, nor was the House it stood on situate exactly East and West', and had devised his own wind force scale, from one ('When it just moved the Leaves.') to four ('When it blew a storm.').[35] He also

[29] Hooke's table was intended for naked-eye observations only; Locke added columns for instrument readings and omitted the columns for phases of the moon and 'Notablest effects'.

[30] Boyle 1966: 5.642.

[31] Locke 1704: 1918.

[32] Landsberg 1980: 640. On the history of meteorological instrument construction, see Middleton 1964; Middleton 1966; Middleton 1969; Frisinger 1977.

[33] La Hire 1710: 142.

[34] Feldman 1983: 251.

[35] Locke 1704: 1918; Jurin adopted a scale similar to Locke's in his 'Invitatio': Jurin 1723: 425.

attempted to specify the colloquial terminology of sky description more precisely, noting that the difference between 'cloudy' and 'fair' hinged on whether more or less than half the sky was covered, and that 'Between' signified 'whether it was uncertain whether more of the Sky was cover'd or clear'.[36] When Petrus van Musschenbroek, professor of mathematics and natural philosophy at the University of Utrecht, sent in his weather journal for the years 1729–31 to the Royal Society, he went one step further and developed symbols for various weather conditions. From the annotations in the manuscript versions of the tables which Locke, for at least some years, kept at the back of his commonplace book entitled 'Adversaria physica', it is possible to follow the development of his weather observations and recording methods from September 1666 to April 1703. On the final page of the volume, Locke kept a kind of key to his tables, entitled 'Explication of my Register of Air', with dated entries for when he adopted new instruments or decided upon a term of art, for example, '1692 May 23 Fair from henceforward signifies more of the skie (as far as it was to be seen out of my chamber window) clear of clouds than coverd with them', or '1695 Apr 19 *A few drops* signifies rain but not soe much as makes the houses drip'.[37]

These definitions represent the crystallization of *termini technici* out of everyday language, but less in the interests of the standardization of techniques and vocabulary for a collaborative network of observers that extended over continents and generations (and who could hardly be expected to know how much of the sky could be seen from Locke's chamber window), than to serve the standardization of the self – of perceptions, descriptions, and memories. Locke had devised an elaborate method for organizing his commonplace books, a kind of multiple indexing system,[38] and the fact that his tables of weather observations were kept in the same volume of a commonplace book containing excerpts mostly from works on medicine and natural philosophy that employed this system hints at an affinity between the activities of excerpting from books and observing from nature. Because the habit of excerpting and quoting, also familiar from florilegia and collections of adages, tended to decontextualize the commonplace entry, there is a certain analogy with the fragmentation of experience into observations. There is also some evidence that the practice of keeping commonplace books led to the kind of combination and recombination of items that Bacon had foreseen for the facts of natural history[39] – independent and even in defiance of the intentions of the original author.[40] Although it is a leap from reading practices to observing practices, the engrained habits of excerpting, ordering, and recombining the entries of commonplace books offer a suggestive parallel for at least the recording of facts about nature. In both cases items must be selected, reclassified, and systematically arranged for the purposes of forming new comparisons and clusters. In Locke's case at least, both kinds of practices served to methodize and homogenize memory; it was perhaps not accidental that Locke's philosophy of personal identity depended on the unity of

---

36 Locke 1704: 1918–1919.

37 MS. Locke d.9, n.p. (final page of volume).

38 Locke 1686.

39 Bacon 1825–34: 2.48.

40 Blair 1997: 65–75.

consciousness over time.[41] However idiosyncratic Locke's own methods may have been, the practice of interweaving weather and other natural history observations with a personal diary in the early modern period was widespread,[42] and suggests that weather observations as a genre owed as much to the diary and the commonplace book as to the astronomical ephemerides.

The intertwining of weather observation with personal routines, and of weather registers with diaries, created an unusually close connection between the quality of the observation and the person of the observer. This connection went beyond the anodyne guarantees of the skill and character of the reporters, who were variously described as 'sagacious', 'diligent' and 'curious' (in the sense of 'careful' as well as 'inquisitive'). What an observer chose to record about the weather and its possible correlates, whether the report took the form of a single striking episode or a series of tabulated measurements, whether the weather served to accentuate the peculiarities of a certain locale or demonstrate general trends – all of these elements were left to individual discretion, despite repeated efforts to create networks that would yield standardized observations at standardized times using standardized instruments. Some observations were presented in tables like Locke's, some as running diary entries,[43] some as concise summaries,[44] some as maps and charts,[45] and others – perhaps the majority – as dramatic eye-witness accounts of 'remarkable meteors' (a blizzard, a whirlwind, an aurora borealis).[46] (Tables had the disadvantage of being boring to read and the devil to print – unless engraved, an expensive undertaking.) There were also hybrid forms: tables supplemented by narrative observations and/or accounts of extraordinary weather. Equally heterogeneous were the weather correlates chosen for observation: phases of the moon, outbreaks of disease, magnetic inclination and declination, the flourishing and withering of crops, the return of the swallows (this last faithfully noted by Locke in his manuscript tables). These highly variable practices of observation and recording exacerbated the difficulty of discovering hidden regularities in the capricious phenomena of the weather.

Laws, Rules, Prognostics

Locke had hoped that registers like his own, if only kept long enough throughout all of England, might eventually divulge the secrets of the weather:

---

41 Locke 1959: 1.460–461.

42 Telelis 1998: 54; Fothergill 1974: 14, 29.

43 For example, Cunningham 1699: 323: '*15th* [October 1698]. Fair and clear Weather, with small Gales at *North-east*, in the Morning the Mercury's Altitude 29 15/20 Digit, at Noon 29 14/20; and at ten of night, being cold, rising to 29 16/20.' But cf. Cunningham 1704 for seagoing observations in tabular form.

44 For example, La Hire 1708: 61: 'Mais il seroit ennuyeux de rapporter ces Observations jour par jour; c'est pourquoy je n'en donneray icy que le resultat dans chaque mois.'

45 For example, Halley 1686b: 168ff. (n.p.).

46 Jankovič 2000: 33–54.

> I have often thought that if such a Register as this, or one that were better contriv'd, with the help of some Instruments that for exactness might be added, were kept in every County in England, and so constantly published, many things relating to the Air, Winds, Health, Fruitfulness, & c. might by a sagacious man be collected from them, and several Rules and Observations concerning the extent of Winds and Rains, & c. be in time establish'd, to the great advantage of Mankind.[47]

In the late seventeenth and early eighteenth centuries, several savants tried their hands at sifting and distilling the accumulated data in search of Locke's 'rules and observations': La Hire for wind and rain; Musschenbroek for weather and magnetism; Derham for rainfall and barometric data; Halley for the winds; and Maraldi for the timing of barometric variations in distant locales. Despite the neo-Hippocratic tendency in this period to regard weather topographically, as peculiar to a given locale, almost all of these efforts envisioned 'the air' as a unified, global entity in principle subject to universal laws. Natural theological considerations [KUSUKAWA, TREPP] reinforced natural philosophical confidence in the orderliness of the atmosphere: 'The Atmosphere, or Mass of Air, Vapours and Clouds, which surrounds our Globe, will appear to be a matter of Design, and the infinitely wise Creator's Work, if we consider its Nature and Make and its Use to the World.'[48] Yet these attempts to divine the 'Rules and Observations' of the weather met at best with middling success, spoiled by exceptions and hedged about with caveats. Although no uniform vocabulary or sustained philosophical reflections about natural regularities emerged from these meteorological investigations, it is possible to detect an implicit hierarchy of kinds of regularity, descending from laws to rules to prognostics, that corresponded to a decline in expectations among early Enlightenment weather watchers.

The word 'law' was rarely invoked in specific attempts to penetrate the hidden regularities that governed the weather, in contrast to more programmatic declarations about the natural history and natural philosophy of the air. Indeed, the more specific and voluminous the empirical inquiry, the more elusive even 'rules' appeared to investigators. Stable regularities and patterns were inversely correlated to the quantity and exactitude of the data surveyed by early Enlightenment naturalists. Increases in instrumental precision, number of observed variables, and breadth of the observer network usually fragmented rather than solidified tentative generalizations.

Hence the most ambitious (and arguably the most successful) attempt during this period to discern stable weather patterns, Halley's 1686 analysis of prevailing winds in the world's oceans, was also the least dependent on specific observations and measurements. In a list reminiscent of Bacon's *Historia ventorum* in its short numbered entries, its summaries of information (mostly without sources) and its scrupulous separation of the 'matter of Fact' from putative explanations, Halley set forth what European navigators knew about ocean winds. In comparison with daily weather tables like those kept by Locke, these 'facts' were already digests of many individual observations, generalizations in their own right, of the form:

---

[47] Locke 1704: 1919.

[48] Derham 1716: 4.

> 3. That the limits of the *Trade* and *Variable Winds*, in this Ocean, are farther extended on the *American* side than the *African*: for whereas you meet not with this certain *Wind* till after you have passed the *Latitude* of 8 *degrees* on this side; on the *American* side it commonly holds to 30, 31 or 32 *degrees* of *Latitude*; and this is verified likewise to the *Southwards* of the *Equinoctial*, for near the *Cape of Good-Hope* the limits of the *Trade Winds*, are 3 or 4 *degrees* nearer the Line, than on the coast of *Brazile*.[49]

Having listed these 'principal Observables' (along with a few exceptions, 'as there is no general Rule that admits not of some exception', and with the caveat that his information might 'be not in all parts Accurate'[50]) for the known oceans, Halley summarized the results with a map showing the major wind patterns, and then focused on those phenomena most notable 'by reason of the constancy of the effect, and of the immense extent thereof', such as that the Trade Winds north of the equator blow northwards of east, and those south of the equator, southwards of east. Such a constant effect or 'General Rule' implied a constant cause, which Halley found in the diurnal heat of the sun as the earth rotated, and in the particular configuration and topography of the continents. Reasoning from the 'Laws of *Staticks*' and the westward, warming motion of the sun, Halley explained the formation of the prevailing easterly wind, with northward and southward variations near the equator because of the greater solar heat and therefore greater rarefaction of the air. Further variations from the 'general Rule' of the prevailing easterlies were caused by the situation, mountains, and soils of interposed continents (for example, the deserts of Libya create greater heat and hence rarefy the air still more).[51]

Halley cleanly distinguished between what he called 'matters of fact' or 'observables', 'general rules' and 'laws'. The last term was not applied to the weather phenomena in question, but to their underlying cause – that is, the 'Laws of *Staticks*' which dictate that colder air is less rarefied and therefore 'more ponderous' than hotter air, and hence moves towards the more rarefied parts until an equilibrium is reached. Although it is possible that Halley had Boyle's experiments concerning the relationship between the temperature, volume, and 'springiness' of air in mind here,[52] the reasoning seems more obviously Cartesian in its appeal to hydrodynamic pressure gradients in a plenum and equilibria. The wind patterns themselves never ascend beyond the level of 'general rules', but they are nonetheless solidified beyond the bare statement of observation by putative causes. The causes themselves are of two kinds, those that produce the constant effect (the laws of statics), and those responsible for variations (the configuration and composition of land masses). This is at first glance a puzzling distinction: as far as Halley knew, the action of the land masses would have been as unchanging as that of the sun's warmth. But it seems that Halley reserved special status for causes that were not simply constant, but also partook of laws, which in turn (if they were indeed taken from Descartes' account in

---

[49] Halley 1686b: 154.

[50] Ibid.: 155, 162.

[51] Ibid.: 165–166.

[52] Boyle himself never dignified the relationship now known as 'Boyle's Law' with the term 'law', nor expressed it mathematically: Shapin 1988, 36–43.

the *Principia philosophiae*) were founded on a kind of self-evidence, as well as the accidental facts of the matter, however permanent these might be.

Some light is shed on the meaning of the term 'rule' by a comparison with another investigation carried out by Halley in 1686 on the use of the barometer to determine elevation above sea level. In his *De la nature de l'air* (1679), Edmé Mariotte, through a combination of experiment (to ascertain the thickness of the lowermost 'layer' of the atmosphere), simplifying assumptions (about the average thickness of an atmospheric layer depending on its altitude and the total number of such layers) and calculation (to determine the relationship between atmospheric pressure, and hence barometer readings, and elevation) had concluded that atmospheric pressure decreased arithmetically as elevation increases geometrically (which Mariotte himself could compute only by approximating the geometric progression with an arithmetic one).[53] Mariotte and others referred to this relationship as a 'rule'; he employed the same term (*règle de la nature*) for what came to be known as the Boyle-Mariotte Law relating the pressure, temperature, and volume of air, published in the same work.[54] So, for example, Maraldi reported on how his experiments in tropical Batavia on the dilation of the air in a thermometer seemed to deviate from 'the rule of M. Mariotte'.[55]

Halley also adopted this usage in his title: 'A Discourse of the Rule of the Decrease of the Height of Mercury ...' As he makes clear from the outset of his article, Halley considered the rule concerning the 'Elastick Property of the *Air*' to be 'made out, by Experiments', rathered than deduced from first principles.[56] Using logarithms and the method of indivisibles to calculate the geometric progression Mariotte could only approximate, Halley condensed his 'Rules', based on a combination of experiment and calculation, in a handy table giving altitude as a function of mercury level in the barometer. Yet he was forced to admit that experiments seemed 'to disturb the Geometrical accuracy of these Conclusions',[57] and set about summarizing, in a numbered list and in digested form, the known 'principal Observations' about the effects of weather on barometer readings. The details of his attempts to explain variations (which he attributed mostly to variable winds in the temperate zones) in mercury level are of less interest in this context than the strategy: a general rule is derived from experiment and calculation, and explained by a constant (but in this case experimentally derived) cause (rarefaction and condensation of air due to a compressing weight or force); exceptions are then collected and attributed to variable causes (uncertain winds). The language of 'law' is entirely absent, perhaps because none of the putative causes achieves the fundamental status of the self-evident. Mathematical calculation alone does not suffice.

---

[53] Mariotte 1717: 1. 148–182.

[54] Ibid.: 1. 153. Mariotte also used the term 'rule' for practical procedures; for example, his 'Règles pour les jets d'eau': Mariotte 1717: 1.486. He tended to reserve the word 'principle' for more fundamental regularities, but these were also proved by experience, for example, in 'Du mouvement des pendules': Mariotte 1717: 1.560–600.

[55] Maraldi 1709: 242.

[56] Halley 1686a: 104.

[57] Ibid.: 109.

Even 'rules' of the Mariotte-Halley variety eluded investigators who, like Maraldi, Musschenbroek, and Derham, attempted more fine-grained analyses of the weather data that had begun to accumulate in tables from Paris, Zurich, Essex, Utrecht, and other locales. Maraldi was keenly aware of the risks of conflating particular causes specific to a particular place with general causes that held for 'the entire mass of air'; hence the importance of gathering and comparing observations from far and wide.[58] Starting with a series of barometric observations conducted daily in Paris and Genoa in 1707, Maraldi hazarded the conclusion that 'in a short time there occur large variations in the height of the barometer in Paris as well as in Genoa, and there is a great conformity in these variations which occur at the same time in quite distant lands'.[59] However, as soon as further sets of observations from other locales were taken into account (those of Johann Jakob Scheuchzer from Zurich during the same period), the regularity evaporated. Maraldi attempted to save his rule by variable causes: the places where 'this rule' held tended to be close to sea level, which Zurich evidently was not. But after turning to the aforementioned deviations from Mariotte's rule in the tropics, Maraldi concluded his article with a cautionary remark about the need to be 'circumspect in basing a general system on particular experiments [*expériences*], however certain and numerous these experiments may be'.[60] This was an alarming prospect for those who, like Newton, had hoped that the universality of natural laws (for example, in optics) might vouchsafe the general validity of one or two well-performed experiments.

Derham proceeded in a similar fashion to Maraldi, collecting detailed weather registers from hither and yon, and reached similar conclusions about the mirage-like quality of weather 'rules'. In addition to keeping his own daily weather table at Upminster (Essex), Derham for some years attempted to digest all other weather observations sent in to the Royal Society from other locales, and to discern general patterns. Beyond affirming that a great deal more rain fell annually in Lancashire than in Essex (a result that he admitted surprised no one), all other candidates for regularities could not withstand the assault of more data. Concerning the claim that the mercury of the barometer '*ascendeth and descendeth in all places at the same time, and in the same proportion*', Derham was quick to point out deviations and exceptions.[61] And when there did seem to be some steady correlation, as between the cold weather observed by Scheuchzer in Zurich and, with a five-day time-lag, by Derham in Upminster, Derham was loath to speculate about possible common causes: 'An Indication that (as shall be farther observed hereafter) the Weather in both Places was influenced by the same Causes, whether the Alpine Hills and Cold, or the Influx of the Moon and other heavenly Bodies, or any other Cause, I shall not enquire.'[62] Even on the more unequivocal ground of the much greater annual rainfall observed in Zurich as compared to in Upminster and Pisa, Derham was hesitant to

58 Maraldi 1709: 233.

59 Ibid.: 235.

60 Ibid.: 246.

61 Derham 1703: 1445; Derham 1708: 339.

62 Derham 1708: 344.

generalize: 'But whether it constantly doth so or not, if God spare them Life, the future Observations which Dr. Scheichzer [*sic*] and Dr. Tilli promise us will demonstrate.'[63]

A similar reluctance can be discerned in the weather diary kept by Musschenbroek for Utrecht. All of his attempts to correlate weather with health and disease, or with magnetic measurements, yielded only uncertain results. He despaired of reducing the fluctations of magnetic declinations to 'certain Rules' and, although he seconded Jurin's appeal to keep faithful weather 'ephemerides' so as to eventually 'find the fabrick and Nature of the whole Atmosphere', he was moved by large barometric fluctuations in January 1731 to exclaim: 'How cautiously should we reason on the future condition of the Atmosphere from the highth of ye Mercury in the Barometer!' His only confident conclusions tended to be negative ones, and even those were surrounded with some ambiguity: although he discounted on the basis of his own observations the proverb that a corona around the moon presages a storm or high wind, he nonetheless believed that the phases of the moon strongly influenced terrestrial weather.[64] Martin Lister similarly took exception to the old saw 'that a Green Christmas makes a fat Church-yard' after keeping track of the correlation between barometric readings and sickly seasons.[65]

Despite the contempt of Musschenbroek and other early Enlightenment savants for the 'superstitions' of the vulgar, the scant and qualified harvest of weather regularities from the piles of observations they amassed often resembled the prognostics of peasants and sailors. This may in part explain the rehabilitation of 'shepherd's wisdom' and ancient weather proverbs by mid-eighteenth-century weather watchers.[66] Even critics of folk superstitions admitted that these venerable forms of 'natural divination' might be accurate, or at least as accurate as anything established with the help of barometers and thermometers. In his *Traité des superstitions qui regardent les sacramens* (1741), Jean-Baptiste Thiers was careful to exonerate such 'natural auguries' from any theological reproach: 'Natural auguries are permissible, provided they are not abused, since they ordinarily have solid and invariable foundations.'[67] These foundations were presumably long experience, rather than the causal explanations of natural philosophy. In their dedication to a natural philosophy of the air based on a thorough natural history, early Enlightenment naturalists risked losing sight of even the constant effects summed up in country proverbs, much less the constant causes that could stabilize these effects into rules, if not laws.

Conclusion: Observations and No End

The only rule that seemed to hold without exception for early Enlightenment weather rules was that every rule had its exceptions. And the more plentiful and painstaking the observations, the more profuse the exceptions. Every tentative correlation, for example between wind and thermometer readings, stimulated a flurry of new

63 Ibid.: 341.

64 Royal Society, Miscellaneous Papers 1660–1740: 4(2).MS.6.58, 59, 79, 33, 6.

65 Lister 1684: 793.

66 Jankovič 2000: 135–140.

67 Thiers 1741: 1:195.

observations and experiments, almost always with equivocal results.[68] New data more often than not brought new uncertainty. This situation was not unique to the study of the weather during this period; electricity, magnetism, and luminescence displayed similarly capricious phenomena, and provoked analogous frustration among natural philosophers. As Charles Dufay remarked apropos of his inconclusive experiments on the luminescence of gemstones, 'I see all too many facts, which seem to me almost impossible to explain and even to be contradictory ...'[69] No matter how carefully he repeated his experiments under meticulously controlled conditions, Dufay could discern 'no Rule, [not even] an imperfect appearance of a Rule'.[70]

The search for 'rules' was in principle underwritten by the search for causes. Seventeenth and eighteenth-century meteorological investigations were, however, littered with causes tried and discarded. Boyle had thought astral influences would hold the key to the weather;[71] Maraldi for a time pinned his hopes on sunspots.[72] Causal explanations of the sort posited by Halley for prevailing winds in terms of the earth's rotation, the westward movement of the sun's warmth, and the 'laws of statics' were rare; more often explanations had the ad hoc, unsteady quality of Halley's 'variable' or 'uncertain' causes. It is notable that even the more modest attempts to discover 'rules', whatever the underlying causes, succeeded best when reporters deliberately coarsened the fine-grained detail of the observations they had gathered or received. Many of the observers had received training in medicine and/or natural history, two disciplines celebrated for exacting and voluminous attention to the individual particulars of a myriad of phenomena. The practices they cultivated, like the daily weather diary and the minute description of 'remarkable meteors', tended to hone their microscopic eye for fine differences still further. Louis Cotte, the Oratorian and Corresponding Member of the Académie Royale des Sciences who summarized the meteorological observations submitted to the Académie since 1688 in his *Traité de météorologie* (1774), admitted that many readers would be disappointed to find that this mass of data yielded no knowledge of causes and underlying regularities. Cotte could only hold out the hope for a probabilistic science of effects: 'natural effects are so multiple, so complex, that it seems to me impossible ever to make meteorology into a certain science'. Cotte called for evermore and evermore detailed observations, even if such minutiae bordered on the 'puerile'.[73] But in practice, only by summarizing, taking means, attending only to the most robust effect, omitting swarms of detail and otherwise smoothing out the particularities of the data did early Enlightenment natural philosophers take the first step towards a generalization. Although none of their efforts in this direction compared with Galilean idealizations in either boldness or brilliance, the escape from what Dufay had called 'too many facts' represented perhaps the only possibility to end what was otherwise an endless process of observation.

---

68 La Hire 1706; Cassini 1710.

69 Dufay 1735b: 371.

70 Dufay 1735a: 3.

71 Boyle 1966: 5.641ff.

72 Maraldi 1720: 5ff.

73 Cotte 1774: xxxiii, viii.

The Galilean strategy of idealization depends on an ontology similar to that assumed by Halley in his treatment of the winds: a strong, constant cause (for example, uniform accelerated motion towards the centre of the earth) with small deviations due to a crowd of minor, variable causes (cross-section of the falling body, air currents, and so forth.). Mariotte expressed this idea of subordination of causes in his *Essai de logique*: 'There is not at the same time an infinite subordination of natural causes to the same effect, but each effect may have one or several primary causes, or at least, one cannot proceed infinitely to find the natural causes of the same effect.'[74] Galileo himself thought certain phenomena, for example air currents, were too irregular ever to be the subject-matter of a science.[75] In the optimal case, the strong, constant causes might be intuited by appeal to self-evident ideas, intuition perhaps prodded by a few well-chosen observations and experiments, which were however more illustrative than probative. This path, pursued so triumphantly in seventeenth- and eighteenth-century mechanics, remained blocked to investigators of the weather and many other natural phenomena of perplexing variability, which seemed instead to hint at a more egalitarian ontology of innumerable weak and wavering causes that interacted in inscrutable ways. In this predicament, the notion of a law as a necessary connection, transparent to the light of reason, must have seemed increasingly unattainable. Stable rules were the best that could be hoped for. I do not know whether David Hume, like Locke, kept a weather diary. But his dilute conception of a natural law as invariable, observable uniformities, with no further appeal to causal underpinnings, might be regarded as the philosophical expression of the early Enlightenment weather watchers' retreat to rules.

[74] Mariotte 1717: 1.617.

[75] Galileo 1968: 8.275f.

Chapter 15

In Search of the Newton of the Moral World: The Intelligibility of Society and the Naturalist Model of Law from the End of the Seventeenth Century to the Middle of the Eighteenth Century

Catherine Larrère[1]

Montesquieu appears to have moved away from the normative field of natural law to turn instead to a positive description of facts and to search for their empirical regularity, thus making him the founder of sociology. This well-established idea[2] owes much to the interpretation put forward by Auguste Comte in his *Cours de philosophie positive* and developed by Emile Durkheim in his Latin thesis.[3] According to them, Montesquieu perceived political phenomena as 'inevitably subjected to invariable natural laws just as much as any other phenomena'.[4] This is a typical example of the positivist history of the sciences and its teleological views. Comte and Durkheim transplanted back to the eighteenth century a positivist concept of physical law that was not elaborated until the nineteenth century, while the idea of Montesquieu as a sociologist was based on a view of science that did not exist at the time he wrote *L'Esprit des lois*.

However, the idea brought to light by Montesquieu of the existence of a regularity in the political world of men, similar to the one discovered by physicians in the universe, did not wait until the nineteenth century to be formulated.[5] As soon as *L'Esprit des lois* was published in 1748, the naturalist Charles Bonnet praised its author in the following terms: 'Newton discovered the laws of the material world, you, Sir, have discovered the laws of the intellectual world.'[6] Such comparisons were not reserved for Montesquieu alone. After reading *Emile*, Kant identified Rousseau

---

1 Translated from French by Nieves Claxton.

2 See Althusser 1964: 5–21; Binoche 1998: 31–71.

3 Entitled *Quid Secundatus politicae scientiae instituendae contulerit* (1892). See Larrère 1989 and Larrère 2002.

4 Comte 1969: 193.

5 See Larrère 1999.

6 Bonnet, letter to Montesquieu, 14 November 1753, in Montesquieu 1950–55, vol. III, p. 1478.

as 'the Newton of the moral world', and in this regard he drew the same parallel as Bonnet between the notions of 'order and regularity', as demonstrated by Newton, and 'the secret law' of human nature as discovered by Rousseau.[7]

The list of candidates for the honour of being 'the Newton of the moral world' did not stop there. Hume and Smith certainly laid claims to this title but it was finally Smith who won it, if one agrees with the opinion expressed by Hegel in his *Principles of the Philosophy of Right*.[8] The Scottish historian David Millar had preceded him by attributing to Montesquieu and Smith their respective merits: 'The great Montesquieu pointed out the road. He was the Lord Bacon on this branch of Philosophy. Dr. Smith is the Newton.'[9]

All this clearly demonstrates the deep significance given in the second half of the eighteenth century (and subsequently) to the analogy between the physical and moral worlds, and the idea that the regularity discovered in the former is a model of intelligibility for the latter. For this reason, the expression 'the Newton of the moral world' is appropriate to describe the reactions to the major political and social works written by the leading thinkers of the Age of Enlightenment. But does this imply that the analogy is based on an explicit reference to the laws of motion, to the new scientific concept of natural law? This is how it is understood implicitly nowadays when referring to the expression 'the Newton of the moral world', and this is also what gives a certain consistency to positivist interpretation. Everything appears to have been centred on the notion of law, on a new idea of natural law, which was no longer borrowed from theological or juridical traditions but from physics. And after having searched for models, physics in turn became a reference.

But, to go back to the period when the ambition was taking shape to apply the models of intelligibility elaborated by natural philosophy to human matters, it is clear that this approach was not necessarily a search for laws. The idea that the new science should not be confined to physical phenomena only, but should also encompass morals, was an objective as old as the intention of Descartes to include moral philosophy in the tree of knowledge. During more or less the same period, Hobbes was determined to construct his political philosophy on the foundation of the principles of motion. These ideas made progress and it can be asserted that, by the end of the seventeenth century, the notion of the new science as a model of intelligibility for all phenomena was deeply rooted, thus making it possible to lay down a solid foundation for a veritable moral science.

Abbé de Saint Pierre was a worthy representative of this project, which he described with great clarity and sought to implement throughout his long life. He is therefore the starting point for our investigation. By looking beyond the broad idea of the regularity of the moral world, along the lines of the model for the physical world, and focusing more precisely on what it led to, it turns out that a project on the intelligibility of the social world did indeed exist. However, it was not inspired by a model of law but borrowed more from arithmetic than from mechanics or physics.

7 Kant, in Cassirer 1987: 52.

8 Hegel 1975: 220.

9 Millar 1812: 429–430, n.

To understand how natural law, in the sense of the law of physics, became a positive reference, it is necessary to explore another direction. In his *Traité de la nature et de la grâce* (1680), Malebranche expounded a philosophy of law that placed natural law, or the law of nature, as Descartes described the name and concept, at the heart of his philosophical and theological thinking. It was, in fact, the laws of motion regulating the course of nature that enabled Malebranche to characterize divine action, even in the area of grace (this will be the second phase of our investigation). In consequence, an inversion can be observed in the directions of the transfers, from one area to the other. The way of naming empirically-noted regularities while observing physical phenomena remained in abeyance for a long time. Furthermore, in order to acquire a dominant position in the field of science, natural law was forced to borrow its matrix from other disciplines – older and more prestigious, and mainly from theology [Armogathe, Roux]. Despite these two factors, there appears to have been a reversal of the movement at the end of the seventeenth century, with the scientific view of law serving as a model for theological and philosophical reflection. In reality, this process turned it into a model for political action and not for the intelligibility of social facts.

By going back along the trail in search of 'the Newton of the moral world', one therefore comes across two different methods of elaboration. The first is a project for the intelligibility of society, with references to scientific knowledge but no model of law. The second is a political model of law, constructed on the basis of the laws of motion, but which does not lead to an understanding of social phenomena. By making a clear distinction between the two, it is easier to understand why Montesquieu did not fit into the framework outlined for him. This will be the third phase of our investigation.

Abbé de Saint-Pierre: Political Arithmetic and Government by Law

In one of his *Pensées*, Montesquieu, after noting that the great success of the 'physical sciences' in his time appeared to have discredited 'the admiration for political and moral knowledge' elevated by the Greeks and Romans into a kind of cult, nevertheless found a soul mate among his contemporaries in the person of Abbé de Saint-Pierre. 'Since I was not born in the right century, I have decided to become a disciple of the excellent man, Abbé de Saint-Pierre, who has written so much on Politics these days.'[10]

Abbé de Saint-de Pierre appears to have conceived this project at a very early stage, around 1681–83, after he left college and had followed a few lessons in Physics. On reading Pascal, he decided to concentrate on moral studies, then on politics, but without losing the benefits of the scientific education he had already received.[11] Abbé de Saint-Pierre was guided along this path by his concern for usefulness. He abandoned the physical domain for the moral and then the political domain because, as he himself explained: 'I understood that the progress I could make through it

[10] Montesquieu 1991: no. 1940, p. 590.

[11] Saint-Pierre 1912: 32.

would be more useful in increasing my own happiness and the happiness of my fellow citizens than what I could achieve through physics.'[12] He discarded the sciences he considered as merely 'speculative' or 'curious' ('astronomy, chemistry, mechanics, anatomy, geometry and botany'[13]). This is because he had transferred to moral and political research the practical concern expressed by Descartes to place the new science at the service of the good and well-being of humanity. It is not surprising, therefore, that, in addition to moral philosophy, jurisprudence and politics or the science of government, Abbé de Saint-Pierre included medicine, navigation, trade and military skills among 'the most useful spheres of knowledge to diminish the evil and increase the good'[14] in human life or, as he stated on so many occasions, 'to contribute to the greatest usefulness for the largest number of families'.[15] Thus, the conflict is not between knowledge of the physical and moral sciences, but between the spheres of knowledge based on speculation or curiosity and those – medicine as well as moral philosophy – that are directed 'towards a perfection of the arts and towards the greatest usefulness'.[16]

Having adopted the final goal of the Cartesian project to develop knowledge, Abbé de Saint-Pierre also took over its methods. He resorted principally to a method based on clear and distinct ideas because he admired their formative qualities.[17] He focused in particular on mathematical evidence: 'The geometric method is certainly the only appropriate one to form solid and unshakeable demonstrations in political and moral philosophy.'[18] This is what induced him to give preference to arithmetical proof over rhetoric as a foundation for his political thinking.

This opposition is typical of all those who sided with the Moderns during that period. Fontenelle, for instance, made negative comparisons between the rather narrow rhetoric rules of the Ancients (eloquence and poetry) and the progress of science that 'depends on the accuracy of reasoning'. This remark provoked the criticism of Gottsched, the German translator of *Digression sur les Anciens et les Modernes*, who sided with the followers of the Ancients. He expressed doubts as to whether there was anything comparable to set against the rhetoric of the Ancients.[19] Extricating political theory from the rhetoric of the Ancients was therefore tantamount to applying to it the principles of the new philosophy as defined by Descartes. The author of the Preface to Dudley North's *Discourses Upon Trade* (1691) explained that the subject was handled philosophically, according to a method described as

---

12 Saint-Pierre 1733–41: vol. 13, p. 3.

13 Saint-Pierre 1912: 252 (year 1714).

14 Ibid.: 252.

15 Ibid.: 256 (year 1715).

16 Ibid.: 179.

17 Saint-Pierre 1733–41: 3: 'The habit I had adopted to base my reasoning on clear and distinct ideas did not permit me to reason at length on theology, but I abandoned physics to apply myself to morals …'

18 Saint-Pierre in Perrot 1992: 42; and Saint-Pierre 1733–41: vol. 6, Comment XX, p. 82.

19 Lecoq 2001: 301–302 (Fontenelle), 324–325 (Gottsched).

'Cartesian' or 'mechanical', in other words, 'built upon clear and evident truths', which was introduced by the New Philosophy.[20]

However, this reference applies more specifically to William Petty, given the way he described the method followed in his *Political Arithmetick*:

> The method I take to do this, is not very usual; for instead of using only comparative or superlative words, and intellectual arguments, I have taken the course (as a specimen of a Political Arithmetick I have long aimed at) to express myself in terms of number, weight, or measure;[21] to use only arguments of sense, and to consider only such causes, as have visible foundations in nature; leaving those that depend upon the mutable minds, opinions, appetites and passions of particular men to the consideration of others.[22]

Abbé de Saint-Pierre was very familiar with the works of William Petty and referred to them on several occasions.[23] Like Petty, he was persuaded of the usefulness of 'counting' or of quantitative surveys 'on anything pertaining to the science of government',[24] for instance, demographic estimates (calculation of population based on the number of births and deaths, comparative studies of the populations of major cities such as London and Paris)[25] or economic and financial surveys, such as those undertaken by Vauban in *Dîme royale* (1698).

Political estimates do not record empirical data only but can also incorporate forecasts. Thus, on the basis of a monetary estimate, and by evaluating what one is willing to pay to avoid pain or to obtain pleasure, it is possible to compare the usefulness of various projects. Abbé de Saint-Pierre outlined a project to calculate pleasure and pain in order to evaluate the cost or benefits of social reforms, what he called a 'règlement' – in other words, a calculation based on the possibility of comparing pleasure and pain by attributing a price to them, as a common measurement:

> We already know the price in money for certain daily pleasures and the exemption of certain pains and we know of it through our daily and annual expenditures. Since we are able to compare one pleasure with another, one pain with another, and one expenditure with another, we can consequently estimate in terms of annual income the enjoyment of new annual pleasures and exemption from new annual pains that an effective adjustment would procure because we can easily have points for comparison that are themselves already well calculated by an estimate of annual income in money.[26]

---

20 Dudley North (1691), *Discourses Upon Trade*; quoted by Berry 1994: 102.

21 See Descartes, *Le Monde*, AT, XI, p. 476: 'God has taught us that he has arranged everything in number, weight and measure '; and, for the biblical reference, ARMOGATHE.

22 Petty, 1899: vol. 1, p. 244.

23 See, for example, Saint-Pierre 1733–41 vol. 5, p. 224; vol. 10, p. 278.

24 'De l'utilité des dénombrements', Saint-Pierre 1733–41: vol. 4, p. 263.

25 Questions debated at the Academy of Science. See 'Memoires of the Academy of Science' in Rozier 1775.

26 'Projet pour perfectionner le gouvernement', Saint-Pierre 1733–41: vol. 3, pp. 97–98.

'Everything can be reduced to calculation and extended even to matters that are purely moral,' wrote Melon in his *Essai politique sur le commerce* in 1734.[27] He clearly expressed the key idea of Abbé de Saint-Pierre to develop the science of government. Everything can be measured, and Abbé de Saint-Pierre summarized his plan to select the best governors and administrators through a kind of hierarchical co-optation among candidates to these functions (what he called a 'scrutin'), claiming that it would serve as an excellent 'anthropometer'.[28]

However, elaborate and coherent though this project may have been, it did not include a search for laws. This can be seen, for example, in the 'Plan to improve medicine' (vol. 5 of *Ouvrajes de politique*), in which it was a question of interconnecting the various Medical Academies to broaden the collection of information and multiply exchanges and comparisons between the collected data. The aim was to set up quantitative archives, not to search for laws on the basis of experience. The only feasible certainty produced by this kind of investigation is arithmetical evidence. It is only possible to obtain 'reliable demonstrations by reducing all proof to simple arithmetic based on counting'.[29] The truth of knowledge therefore relies on the accuracy of calculation: 'when the counting is accurate, proof can be submitted to arithmetical demonstration for confirmation'.[30]

The target was well and truly political arithmetic and not social physics. The intention was not to discover laws. It is not that all references to law were excluded from the reflections of Abbé de Saint-Pierre. However, it is necessary to look for them elsewhere, not in the sphere of the knowledge required by the science of government but in the introduction of laws necessary for its functioning.

The calculation of pleasures and pains, which in the opinion of Abbé de Saint-Pierre lay at the heart of the science of government, presupposed that only individual interest motivates behaviour. As he said on several occasions, it is 'the fear of being worse and the hope of being better'[31] that drives human beings. It is unwise to count on virtue or on dedication to the public good because it is intrinsically human nature 'to seek to increase their property by reducing public property, even considerably'.[32]

Interest alone motivates humankind, but this interest is not directed spontaneously at the public good, on the contrary it tends to run counter to it. This is why consent needs to be built up. Abbé de Saint-Pierre believed this was the role of laws: 'the political corps is formed, and it preserves and strengthens itself only through laws, which are rules governing the behaviour of members of this corps'.[33] The high importance attached to laws is what makes the thinking of Abbé de Saint-Pierre so original. Those who since the time of Machiavelli and Guichardin have stressed the importance of self-interest (nothing durable can be accomplished without it) and

27 Melon 1847: 809.

28 *Sic*: 'Projet pour perfectionner le gouvernement', p. 33.

29 'De l'utilité des dénombrements', Saint-Pierre 1733–41: vol. 4, p. 265.

30 Ibid.: p. 266.

31 For example, 'Observations qui regardent le ministère général', Saint-Pierre 1733–41: vol. 6, p. 4.

32 Saint-Pierre 1738: 60.

33 'Observations qui regardent le ministère général', Saint-Pierre 1733–41: vol. 6, p. 32.

its resistance to the public good (nothing durable can be accomplished against it), generally believe that consent should be the result of a skilful and prudent policy or a wise manipulation of specific interests: 'the strongest hold one can exert over men is to know their inclinations, movements, passions and habits, and to use these levers to lead them to wherever one wants,' affirmed Monchrestien.[34] For Abbé de Saint-Pierre, it was the legislative framework that fulfilled this role.

It was, in fact, a question of constructing a veritable edifice. Abbé de Saint-Pierre often added the word 'establishment' to law or regulations to demonstrate that it was not enough to write regulations but that it was also necessary to create institutions to apply them or, as he put it, 'some kind of permanent construction that works constantly at supporting and perfecting the various rules and establishments to achieve its objective'.[35] This prompted him to compare the political corps, formed by laws, to a machine. If the legal framework is well constructed, that is to say, if it succeeds in channelling individual interests towards the public good by finding a motivation that is likely to cause good,[36] then one will have more or less discovered perpetual motion: the machine functions on its own, it winds itself up on its own, 'as long as the members are sufficiently united by their specific interest to contribute to public interest'.[37]

'There is nothing worse than a divided authority',[38] according to Abbé de Saint Pierre who was an absolutist without qualms. This does not imply that he developed a rigidly voluntarist concept of power. On the contrary, he believed that 'the less that is left to be regulated by the whim of a single person'[39] the better. His apology for government by law is in fact an apology for government by reason, government by reasonable men, carefully selected for their intellectual qualities. Even though they only play an advisory role, they are nonetheless the ones who give a government its substance:

> One can therefore say that in general the best governed Kingdom is the one which is governed the most by law, where laws can only be changed by three quarters of the votes of those who, through various polls, have been selected and authorised by the State to serve as legislative counsellors.[40]

---

34 Montchrestien 1999: 192. On these forms of arranged consent over interests, see Hirschman 1980, and Lazzeri 1998.

35 'Observations qui regardent le ministère général', Saint-Pierre 1733–41: vol. 6, Comment XX, p. 82.

36 Abbé de Saint-Pierre based this theory mainly on two reflections. On the one hand, the distribution of rewards for good projects (hence the importance of estimating the advantages in figures) and, on the other, the idea that our interests lie not only in material goods but in reputation and honour. A careful selection of elites should therefore lead to good administrators respected by everyone.

37 'Observations, qui regardent le ministère général', Saint-Pierre 1733–41: vol. 6, p. 33.

38 Ibid.: vol. 6, p. 13.

39 Ibid.: vol. 6, p. 41.

40 Ibid.: vol. 6, p. 41.

Moreover, the law must be known and published, and its motives explained, and there can be no conflict between the laws thus drawn up because 'reason can never be opposed to reason'.[41] It can therefore be affirmed that Abbé de Saint-Pierre had a decidedly rationalist concept of law. He suggested a model based on 'the same laws for all the provinces … by invariably choosing the simplest and clearest, the ones offering the most advantages to the largest number of subjects'.[42]

But, although there is an allusion to the advantage of the largest number, the utilitarian orientation of the political thinking of Abbé de Saint-Pierre – his model of uniformity, simplicity and clarity – has no direct relationship with his political arithmetic. Its introduction is to be found elsewhere.

Malebranche: Natural Law, Divine Action and Political Model

The positions of Malebranche in the area of theology were resolutely rationalist. He disagreed with the Cartesian concept of the creation of eternal truths,[43] and submitted that God can only act according to his reason, which even he cannot avoid; his wisdom prevails over his might, and it is far from being something that was created.[44] Malebranche considered the position of the voluntarists, who attributed greater importance to the almighty power of God than to his wisdom, as if it resulted from an 'anthropology' (in other words, an anthropomorphic distortion of things). Eternal Reason is imposed on God: it 'is still necessary and independent, and we perceive it in a more independent sense than God himself. For God can only act in accordance with this reason; in a way, he depends on it: he needs to consult it and follow it.'[45]

This prompted Malebranche to affirm the universality of law. Nothing can escape it, everybody 'must submit to divine law, to which even God submits himself, so to speak'[46]. As Malebranche repeated frequently, God 'never dispenses with the law'. And what is true for God is also true for all creatures and the created world. Since voluntarists look upon the law as a precept, they tend to restrict natural law to moral law only, and they distinguish between natural law (moral) and the law of nature (physical). Thus, according to Suárez, one only speaks metaphorically of the law by which God governs natural things deprived of reason.[47] Since law is reason, there is no justification for restricting its scope, according to Malebranche. Although he made a distinction between three types of law – between the laws of nature (communication of movements, union between the soul and body, and union between the soul and God) and the laws of grace (for angels and Jesus Christ)[48] – this does not preclude the law from being unequivocal [Armogathe].

---

41 Saint-Pierre 1733–41: vol. 6, p. 42.

42 'Raisons pour publier les motifs des lois', Saint-Pierre 1733–1741: vol. 10, p. 210.

43 *Recherche de la Verité* (RV), *Eclaircissement*, VIII, in Malebranche 1958–84: vol. III, pp. 85–86.

44 RV, *Eclaircissement*, VIII, in ibid.: vol. III, p. 85.

45 RV, *Eclaircissement*, X, in ibid.: vol. III, p. 131.

46 Malebranche, *Traité de morale*, II, IX, § XIII, p. 226.

47 See Courtine, 1999: p. 107, and Armogathe (Chapter 16 in this volume).

48 *Entretiens sur la métaphysique et la religion* (EMR), XIII.

The model is all the more uniform in that the reference can be found indisputably in the physical laws of motion or, as Malebranche put it, in 'the Cartesian laws of motion'.[49] Malebranche placed himself in the continuity of the Cartesian definition of the laws of nature[50] by putting nature in the same category as legality, as Descartes had already done:[51] 'Strictly speaking, what one calls Nature is no other than the general laws established by God to preserve his Work by very simple means, by an action that is always uniform, constant and perfectly worthy of an infinite wisdom and a universal cause.'[52]

Malebranche therefore concentrated on the scientific evidence of the laws of nature in his philosophical presentation. It is based on a universal law, without any exceptions and therefore quantifiable, unlike Aristotelian qualitative physics. It is also founded on a general law, not in the Aristotelian sense (of what occurs the most frequently) but because the general is opposed to the particular and the particular is subordinate to the general: specific phenomena are linked together by general and constant laws. This makes it possible to associate law with physical phenomena and think in terms of the laws of nature rather than one single law of nature, as in the case of the Stoics.[53] It is law that makes it possible to discover uniformity and constancy behind the diversity or irregularity of the world.

The scientific model of the law that emerged from the thinking of Malebranche on the Cartesian laws of motion is a model of universal and general laws that are immutable, uniform, simple and fertile. There was a consensus over this model. In a letter to Arnauld, Leibniz wrote of the 'constant laws that we observe in phenomena'.[54] The difference of opinion was not over the concept of law but on its way of functioning. Leibniz criticized the theory of occasional causes put forward by Malebranche, according to which what we perceive as real and mechanical causes (the impact of two bodies, or different movements of the soul apparently caused by physical sensations) are not causes but only occasions. The only active power is divine power; the impact of two bodies does not produce the communication of movement but is merely the occasion of the communication of a movement for which God alone is the cause.

Leibniz criticized this theory of causality, treating is as a voluntarist explanation. To affirm the legality of nature, as Malebranche did, is to affirm its rationality and to exclude (as far as this is possible) the miracle, this being a perfect example of the voluntarist action of God. But, as Leibniz objected, making God intervene on every occasion so that he can communicate his power over the course of nature is to turn

---

49 *Traité de la nature et de la grâce* (TNG), I, § XV.

50 Descartes, Le Monde, AT XI, p. 37: 'The following rules which make these changes, I call the law of nature.'

51 See Descartes, *Discours* V, AT VI, p. 42: Once the world is created, God only 'lends his ordinary assistance to nature and leaves it to act according to the laws he established'.

52 TNG, *Eclaircissement*, I, § III.

53 See the remark by Jane Ruby: 'When the Stoics broke with the Sophistic tradition, not only was their cosmological natural law at once physical and ethical, descriptive and prescriptive, but they almost never associated it with any physical phenomenon smaller than the cosmos itself' (Ruby 1986: 354).

54 Leibniz, letter to Arnauld, 30 April 1687, in Robinet 1955: 293.

it into a permanent miracle. In reality, to exclude the miracle it is not sufficient to set the general (the law, which is natural) against the exceptional (the miracle, emerging from the ordinary course of things). It is still necessary to prove that regularity can be found in the very nature of things. Malebranche believed that, for an action to be natural, it is enough for it to be general, that is to say, in conformity with the intentions of God. This led him to adopt a conventionalist theory of law, according to Leibniz. The criticism of occasional causes made by Fontenelle supported the view of Leibniz. Like him, Fontanelle reproached Malebranche for considering that 'God laid down a decree whereby he himself is obliged to transport something of the movement of one body to another on the occasion of their impact'.[55] Thus, instead of searching for the law governing the nature of things, Malebranche turned it into an arbitrary will of God. He described it as arbitrary in the sense that it depends on him: an effect does not regularly follow upon another effect except by virtue of the general will of God.

These criticisms are not unjustified. Malebranche made a distinction between two hierarchical levels in divine legality. First of all, there are the immutable laws of order. These are not made, and God of necessity follows them and 'does not dispense with them'. Secondly, there are the laws of nature, or the created laws, which are 'arbitrary'. Malebranche stated this clearly in a letter written in April 1686 and published in *République des lettres* in April 1687: 'I must admit that it could be so, because it is arbitrary and depends on the Creator.' He drew the conclusion that 'it is experience that can show us how the Author of nature acts'.[56] From an epistemological point of view, the position of Malebranche is voluntarist: a frequency is observed, and it will not be established through reason (Roux).

This epistemological voluntarism, however, is accompanied by a theological rationalism. Like voluntarism in general, the empiricism of the position adopted by Malebranche relies on an admission that there are limits to knowledge. We are only aware of the action of God by observing its effects. But these limits only concern part of what we are capable of knowing. This is demonstrated in the positions expressed by Malebranche in his reply to Fontenelle: 'I only see things; I perceive the necessary liaison only between divine will and its effects.'[57] It is because the wisdom of God is superior to his power that the latter, linking specific phenomena together, is less familiar to us than his wisdom. It is within our reach; we are not prohibited from trying to penetrate the intentions of God and to seek 'to discover some of his ways in the production of his Work'.[58]

Such statements provoked critical remarks from Arnauld, who took a voluntarist attitude by defending the idea of the mystery of divine ways, beyond the reach of human understanding. But they enabled Malebranche to extend the scientific model of law by drawing it from the model pertaining to nature, where the model of law was established, and transposing it to the supernatural realm of grace. On both sides

---

[55] Fontenelle, *Doutes sur le système physique des causes occasionnelles* (1686), Chap. III.

[56] Malebranche, in Robinet 1955: 251.

[57] In Fontenelle 1990: 581.

[58] Malebranche, TNG, I, I, § VII, 24–25.

are realms in which a perfect legality reigns, all the effects occurring in the two being produced by the interplay between a series of laws triggered off by occasional causes. In the realm of grace, it is Christ who is the occasional cause, acting as an intermediary for the general will of God to save a particular creature. However, the relevant point of this extension is not the content of the law but its form. Laws are described as ways. The general nature of laws shapes the mode of divine intervention. God works through the simplest and most general ways. There is no doubt that the affirmation of legality holds the promise of an intelligibility of the real (when faced by an incomprehensible phenomenon, it should always be postulated that it derives from a law, even if it is unknown). However, Malebranche was not interested in developing an empirical investigation but to reflect on the way in which God acts. Generality defines this mode of action, carried out by a will that is simple, regular, constant, uniform and fertile, and not by a particular will. It is because the scientific model refers to God and qualifies his action that it can become a political model.

The argument put forward by Arnauld was based on this particular point. He did not question the definition of law, on the Cartesian model, as being general and constant. But for him, this definition did not exhaust that of divine will. God, who regulates nature by general laws, can act through a particular will with respect to the living beings he has created.[59] Arnauld's criticism was therefore not aimed at the concept of law but at its application in an area that has nothing to do with the relationship between things but with the relationship between one will and others. A criticism made by Fénelon, in line with the position adopted by Arnauld, specified the field of application. He reproached Malebranche for reducing providence to simple natural legality: 'this providence, which religion teaches us to resort to, cannot consist of the general laws of nature; for general laws are uniform and invariable; they are never in proportion to personal needs; on the contrary they always sacrifice personal interests to general uniformity'.[60]

From legality at work in nature, one has graduated to government by men. It is no longer a question of comparing nature and grace but divine government and human government. Can God reign through general laws that do not take into consideration the particular and are no respecters of people? This was the view submitted by Malebranche and rejected by Fénélon, who based himself on an ancient tradition. Plato criticized government by law 'because a law is never capable of encompassing precisely that which is the better and fairer for everyone at the same time, and to prescribe what is the best for everyone'.[61] Governing by law can only be the second-best solution. Aristotle also believed that law was too general to take into consideration the diversity of circumstances.[62] Since Malebranche searched for a model in physical law, discovering the mode of divine action in it, he felt that the generality of law was not a stopgap or a more convenient method but the right way

59 Moreau 1999: 220–221.

60 Fénélon 1716: XVIII.

61 Plato, *Politics*, 294 a.

62 Aristotle, *Politics*, III, 1285 a, 10.

of governing, the one revealing divine wisdom. The general nature of law can even become a model for political government.[63]

This approach to the question transformed completely the distinction between will and reason, in the way it had been put by legal theologians with respect to law (as in the case of Suárez) or natural law (as in the case of Grotius and Pufendorf) [STOLLEIS]. At first glance, the opposition between wisdom and power seems to be simply another way of describing the opposition between reason and will, and the terms are interchangeable. But, in view of the fact that this opposition is defined in the area of nature and is ascribed to divine action, the opposition between wisdom and power transforms the one existing between reason and will, and also tends to cancel out the latter in order to make it complementary. Law is divine reason, and universal legality is a rationalist affirmation. However, since this rationality is defined by its form, there is no need to make reference to the nature of things. Since rational law depends on general will, there is no question of opposing will to reason at this level.

Power can be another name for will, but in the case of the latter, it does not qualify the source (law proceeds from will) but the taking of action, the accomplishment of law. Power has to do with efficiency, the implementation of ways. The generality of ways illustrates the wisdom of God, and his power rules the relationship with the particular. It is subordinated to wisdom and only serves to execute it. A model (technical) of the subordination of the executive to the legislative can be found in the relationship between wisdom and power.

There is another relationship between the general and the particular. God is not concerned with the particular, he is indifferent to the particular fate of human beings. This is one of the differences of opinion between Malebranche and Leibniz. According to the latter, divine intention, which is global, also takes into account the interest (and, therefore, usefulness or happiness in the meaning used by Abbé de Saint-Pierre) of each person. 'Just as in a republic, care is taken to ensure as much happiness as possible for each individual, likewise the universe would not be as perfect if the interest of every person were not taken into consideration, at least as far as universal harmony permits.'[64] This is why, even though Leibniz referred to political government,[65] it would appear that the universal harmony he presented is more a model of economic harmony. The objective is to maximize the happiness of each person by acknowledging the diversity of interests. The supposition of a pre-established harmony of interests makes it possible to set aside the legislative and political framework by which Abbé de Saint-Pierre sought to arrange individual

[63] On the political secularization of the general will described by Malebranche, see Riley 1986. At that time, all notions of government by law were not necessarily applications of this model: see Larrère, 1997a.

[64] Leibniz, 'De la production des choses prise à sa racine', in Leibniz 1954, p. 91.

[65] See, for example, *Essaies de Théodicée*, I, § 79: 'The following rules which make these changes, I call the law of nature' ' the more a great and good prince takes care of his glory, the more he will think of making his subjects happy and will yet be the most absolute of monarchs.'

interests. And in the harmony of Leibniz, the reference to law disappears, only arithmetic counts.[66]

The reference to law is central to the thinking of Malebranche, whose view of theodicy shaped a political model.[67] Natural law serves as a political model but, since God is the author of law, the edifice thus built can be described as 'spiritual':

> The more machines are simple and their effects different, the more they are spiritual and worthy of being held in esteem. The large number of laws of a State often reveals little penetration and mental scope in those who have established them; it is more the experience of a need than wise foresight that has given them an order. God, whose wisdom has no limits, must therefore use very simple and fertile ways … [68]

This is indeed the political model to which Abbé de Saint-Pierre referred, in other words, a 'political machine' composed of a small number of simple and uniform laws. This highly centralized model, with its absolutist resonance (that is, the lack of boundaries), is unquestionably French. This does not imply, however, that everyone in France accepted it.

Montesquieu: From Nature to History

> There are certain ideas of uniformity that sometimes seize great spirits (for they touched Charlemagne), but that infallibly strike small ones. They find in it a kind of perfection they recognise because it is impossible not to discover it: in the police the same weights, in the commerce the same measures, in the state the same laws and the same religion in every part of it. But is this always and without exception appropriate? (SL, XXIX, 18)

Montesquieu rejected the model based on the uniformity of laws and government, which had attracted Abbé de Saint-Pierre and Malebranche. He had no hesitation in affirming that the simplicity of laws is not an ideal; on the contrary, their complexity is desirable to such an extent that it can 'make an art of reasoning itself' (VI, 1). According to him, their application is never automatic, and the formalities of justice and complications of laws guarantee the freedom of people (VI, 2). This is precisely what Condorcet reproached him for:

> Since truth, reason, justice, human rights, the interest of property, liberty and safety are the same everywhere, it is difficult to see why all the provinces of a State, or even all States, should not have the same penal laws, the same civil laws, the same commercial laws, etc. A good legal system must be good for everyone, in the same way as a true proposition is true for everyone.[69]

---

66 On the theodicy of Leibniz as an economic model, see Elster 1975.

67 Larrère, 1997b.

68 Malebranche, TNG, I, XXXVIII.

69 Condorcet, 'Observations sur le livre XXIX de *L'Esprit des lois*' in Destutt 1992, p. 458.

If it is accepted that natural law, understood as physical law, is a model of uniformity and universality, then it is Condorcet who applied this model to the political world and not Montesquieu.

There are no mechanical models in the theories of the latter. Or, if there is one, it is an anti-model, like that of the impact between bodies or billiard balls, which is the way he described despotic government: 'the prince's will, once known, should produce its effects as infallibly as does one ball thrown against another' (III, 10). Far from being a model of uniformity and constancy, in *L'Esprit des lois* nature appears to be more an indicator of diversity. The reason why it was so difficult to understand the theory of climates may be because it was understood as if it was based on a mechanistic and repetitive view of physical causes (the model of natural law having been so predominant). And yet it was the theory of climates that enabled Montesquieu to interrelate the changing variety of human customs with the graduated diversity of climatic regions.[70] It is noteworthy that, when discussing climate, Montesquieu did not make reference to contemporary scientific concepts that tried to introduce regularity in meteorological variations but instead stuck to an older current of thought that insisted on diversity [Daston].

It is commonly believed that the distinction made by Montesquieu between the 'relation' law [la loi rapport], as he defined it at the beginning of *L'Esprit des lois*,[71] and the 'commandment' law (imposed by the political authority) implies that he abandoned the normative (political and legal) view of natural law in favour of adopting a descriptive, and therefore scientific,[72] model of a physical law applied to human phenomena. There are no reasonable grounds for making this supposition; the opposition is inside natural law. It is a rationalist and anti-voluntarist stance, as Montesquieu stated in his *Défense de L'Esprit des lois*. For him, it was a question of rejecting the position taken by Hobbes that demolished the very existence of moral values by making justice depend on the will of the one who establishes it. 'Relations', as Hume clearly observed, can also be understood as moral relations just as much as empirical regularities. By adopting the definition of the 'relation law', Montesquieu makes no distinction between 'is' and 'ought'.[73]

Montesquieu therefore stuck to the rationalist view of the univocity of law since the law does not have several interpretations [Armogathe]. In his criticism of the 'relation law',[74] Destutt de Tracy condemned this univocity of law in his *Commentaire sur L'Esprit des lois de Montesquieu* (written in 1811). From a voluntarist viewpoint, he objected to the concept of the equivocality of law, which gives priority to law as a precept. 'In its specific and particular meaning,' he wrote, '[the law is] a rule prescribing our actions by an authority that we look upon as having the right to lay down this law.' The laws of nature can only be known as such by extension, and even metaphorically:

---

70 See Larrère 1992.

71 *L'Esprit des lois*, I, 1: 'Laws taken in the broadest meaning are the necessary relations deriving from the nature of things.'

72 Althusser 1964.

73 Hume 1751, Section III, Part II, pp. 55–56 (note).

74 Ibid.: 'A law is not a relation and a relation is not a law.'

> Then, when we note the reciprocal action of all human beings interacting with each other, when we observe the phenomena of nature and those of our intelligence, when we discover that they all function in a constant manner under the same circumstances, we say that they follow certain *laws*. By extension, we refer to the expression of the way in which these phenomena constantly operate as the laws of nature.[75]

Defining law in terms of relations in an unequivocal manner is not so much a matter of choosing the side of science and empirical description as of opting for a normative rationalism represented by both Malebranche and Leibniz. But the way in which Montesquieu interpreted the need for relations, as well as their derivation, led him to move away from the theological model, the one that Charles Bonnet, an admirer of Montesquieu but also a disciple of Leibniz, wanted to prevail. Why not replace 'relations' (a qualification apparently difficult to accept) with 'consequences', he asked?

> You, Sir, have defined them [the laws] as the necessary relations that derive from the nature of things. There is only a slight difference between these two definitions, but we felt that it was more accurate to say consequences than relations. The structure of a magnet is the foundation of its relation with iron; the attraction is an effect, a consequence of these relations; it is a law. Perhaps, Sir, you had the same idea in mind and that the speed of your style did not allow you to express it.[76]

By removing necessity and by replacing 'relations' with 'consequences', Bonnet retained the idea of Leibniz concerning the unity of the world as a chain of human beings and a pre-established harmony. Montesquieu countered this vision of unity with diversity: 'the laws of the universality of human beings are not the consequences of nothing but produce countless consequences'.[77] This is clearly an abrupt rejection of the notion, so dear to Bonnet, of a divine plan whereby everything is a consequence. Montesquieu did not find a model of rationality either in the uniformity of a nature reduced to mechanical relationships or in the unity of divine understanding.

He therefore modified the relationship between the general and the particular. In the way he presented it at the beginning of *L'Esprit des lois*, he seemed to be quite close to Malebranche, holding a view that can be described as 'top-down':

> The law, in general, is human reason in that it governs all the peoples of the earth; and the political and civil laws of each nation should only be particular cases to which this human reason is applied (I, 3).

Yet this implies a shift from divine reason to human reason. Even more than in the thinking of Malebranche, this definition is derived from the Stoic idea, adopted by modern natural law, that humanity participates in the same rational community, the diversity of laws and customs of the different countries being merely specific applications.

---

75 Destutt de Tracy 1992: 1–2.

76 Bonnet, letter to Montesquieu, 1 April 1754; Montesquieu 1950–55: vol. III, p. 1500.

77 Letter of 6 May 1754, Montesquieu 1950–55: vol. III, p. 1500.

But, in reading further on in *L'Esprit des lois*, this relationship is reversed. In the definition provided by Montesquieu of the general spirit of Book XIX, there is a change from a 'top-down' movement to a 'bottom-up' movement. It is not the generality of reason that is imposed from above on the diversity of particular phenomena like a pre-established form, but it is from the latter that a delimited generality emerges:

> Several things govern mankind: climate, religions, laws, the maxims of government; examples of past things, customs, manners; and the result is the formation of a general spirit. (XIX, 4)

Thus, one leaves the sphere of nature to enter that of history. Well before Durkheim and without positivist presuppositions, the Scottish historians of the Enlightened Age learned from Montesquieu that law is a historical phenomenon.[78]

There is no doubt that the expression 'the Newton of the moral world' is pertinent. It reflects the prestige of natural philosophy in the seventeenth century and the importance of the analogy between the physical and moral worlds. But it also encourages a positivist interpretation, which concludes rather hastily on the predominance of the epistemological model of natural law from the eighteenth century onwards. Although the eighteenth century saw the triumph of law, it was in fact the triumph of a political model, of a way of undertaking things rather than understanding them. It is therefore possible to conclude that the adoption of a scientific concept of law, as a description of empirically observed regularities, does not all of a sudden cause the disappearance of the normative, theological or judicial model of natural law. During the eighteenth century, nature unquestionably had a normative dimension, and there is no reason to see only the survival of metaphysics in this.

[78] Haakonssen 1996, p. 249.

Chapter 16

Deus legislator

Jean-Robert Armogathe[1]

John Milton (1608–74), in his great biblical poem in twelve cantos, *Paradise Lost* (published in 1667) depicts the act of Creation. The poet's guide is no longer Dante's Virgil, but Satan himself. Satan invites the demons to accompany him on a guided tour to see the realization of a divine prophecy: the creation of the world and of man. After a long journey, disguised as a curious cherub, Satan comes to visit the new world. He arrives at Mount Niphates, then Eden, where, disguised as a cormorant, he perches himself on the Tree of Life. After different dialogues and the intervention of various angels, the poet describes the creation of a new world and new beings, including human beings. The newly created man begins immediately to pose questions; Adam wants to know

> What neerer might concern him, how this World
> Of Heav'n and Earth conspicuous first began,
> When, and whereof created, for what cause,
> What within EDEN or without was done,

that is to say, *the physical laws of the world.* But the archangel Raphael tells him to learn to be content with his reason alone, cautioning him to make limited use of his curiosity (book 7, vv. 60ff.).

In investigating the history of an expression – *deus legislator* – which is at the root of modern science, we begin with the premise that the concepts which make up the corpus of modern science were created within certain historical matrices, the articulation of which permits us to see not only the genesis of these concepts but also their passage from one discipline to another, from one field of knowledge to another. A theory of a 'matrix of ideas' presents itself as resolutely genetic: on the one hand, several elements come together to inspire and give rise to a new idea, on the other hand, the concept thus conceived preserves in its 'genes' its hereditary origins. The present study belongs to a more general research into these matrices, in particular those which, arising from the juridical concept of the organization of the Universe and knowledge of it, organize the passage from law into epistemology. The thesis of this essay is that one cannot understand the transfer of concepts which have a juridical origin onto the physical world unless one understands the *theological matrix* that undergirds them both. Moreover, the debate about the theological origins of the concept of the 'laws of nature', understood as physical laws, has often been badly formulated, in a double

[1] Translated by Ann T. Delehanty.

error of understanding: first, in its situating itself as a field of research, the debate has neglected the exegetical perspective; and second, in its conceptual situating, its *Sitz im Leben*, it looks more to the imaginary of origins than to the actual relationship that God as Creator has with the world. It is this double aspect that will be clarified here, in the articulation of the theological, the juridical and the physical, referring mainly to medieval theologians, to Francisco Suárez and to the Jesuit exegetical tradition at the turning point of the sixteenth and seventeenth centuries.[2]

Theological Voluntarism

Among the propositions condemned in Paris and Oxford in 1277,[3] several of them deal with an immanentism which was perceived as risking to privilege the intelligibility of the world over divine omnipotence. The influence of the thought of Avicenna and Averroes motivated this fear; some theologians realized that, if you followed the thinking of these authors to its logical conclusion, the universe would possess in itself an intelligibility that could become independent, like an autonomous force of intellection. There would therefore be eternal ideas that coexisted with the creator, perhaps even imposing themselves on his understanding (this will be the position of certain later nominalists). How then does one situate the laws which fall under divine will, laws of nature which govern the world, and human laws which govern men? Faced with this difficult situation, the short Thomistic treaty *De legibus* (questions 90 to 109 of Ia–IIae) constitutes a remarkable effort to provide a synthesis which would balance the two: St Thomas Aquinas proposes a natural law inherent to nature, the ideas being thus like patterns (*exempla*) according to which God proceeded to create the world. This natural law constitutes the expression of divine wisdom, inasmuch as it directs all actions and all movements (q. 93, a. 1, resp.).

The censures of 1277 identified and contested the latent immanentism of this compromise solution. Furthermore, the Franciscan school reacted by defending divine omnipotence and affirming the primacy of the will in the divine intellect. This omnipotence manifests itself by its decrees, which constitute a juridic apparatus of government (*gubernatio*). *Divine voluntarism* (a modern expression) thus entails slippage: one moves from the law produced by divine understanding to the *ratio* of the divine will. It no longer has to do with natural law (*lex naturalis*), but with eternal law (*lex aeterna*). The modern notion of the 'laws of nature' proceeds from the eternal law (*lex aeterna*).

'The objects of the eternal law are the external works of God' (*Lex aeterna habet pro materia opera Dei ad extra*), as Suárez would write much later.[4] *Lex aeterna* therefore applies to creatures, it is the government of things. Later on, in the work of a Louvainist commentator on Aquinas, one finds the expression *lex aeterna* linked to *gubernatio rerum*, in a formula which further clarifies the thinking of the angelic

---

2 See Armogathe 2007.

3 *La condamnation parisienne de 1277* (1999), new edition from the Latin, translated and with introduction and commentary by David Piché. See also Paqué 1985.

4 Suárez, *De Legibus*, II, 3, 6.

doctor: 'eternal law is the order to govern things with the will of binding them to this mode of operation' (*lex aeterna est ordo rerum gubernandarum cum voluntate adstringendi ad illum operandi modum*).[5]

This definition must be analysed carefully: *lex aeterna* is an *ordo*, which means equally the ordering of things as well as the commanding or mastering of them [Stolleis]. The verbal adjective of *gubernare* returns to the 'government of nature', the *gubernatio rerum*, which is a synonym for Providence.[6] The law proceeds from the will of the legislator and it determines the *modus operandi* which will connect the two (*legibus adstringere* is a classic syntagma).

The seventeenth century is far from having forgotten these medieval disputes [Kusukawa]. One need only open the library catalogue of a Puritan scholar such as William Ames to see the host of volumes of *Commentaries on the Sentences* and *Cursus ad mentem Scoti*. A single example from these disputed questions will allow us to see how this debate between the Thomists and the Scotists remained very much alive in the seventeenth century. The example arises from a discussion which opposed an intransigent Scotist to a rigorous Thomist, the conventual Franciscan monk Angelo Volpi[7] and the Dominican Hyacinthe de Ruggieri. For our purposes, it suffices to examine the words of Ruggieri:[8] 'Was Father Volpi right to say that all the Thomists are mistaken in holding, along with Aquinas, that *the eternal law in God is the same for the government of nature?*',[9] that is to say, the Scotist author accused the Thomists, in their intellectualism, of having returned the eternal law to the eternal *ratio* of God.

Ruggieri reproduces the argument of his adversary:

> Duns Scotus, supposing the existence of eternal laws, teaches that the movement of our mind to know the authentic truths is reduced to eternal rules in the divine understanding. He wants to speak of rules as practical as they are speculative which are necessary for

[5] Wiggers 1634: 299.

[6] For example, in Lactantius, *Institutiones* 1, 3: 'tantarum rerum gubernationem mens una possidet'.

[7] Angelo Volpi, OFM. Conv. (Montepelusio?–Naples 1647), Lat. *Pilosius* ou *Vulpes*. A Franciscan monk, he joined the college of Saint Bonaventure in Rome in 1615, and then taught in Assisi and Naples for twenty-five years. He was one of the principal contributors to Scotist studies in his time, as is evident in his vast *Summa theologiae Scoti et commentaria in eamdem, quibus illius doctrina admodum fuse elucidatur, comprobatur, defenditur* (Naples, 1622–46). This work was put on the Index, after a number of attacks, led by the Dominican Giacinto de Ruggieri, of which the *Defensorium doctrinae divi Thomae contra objecta patris magistri fratris Angelis Vulpis* (Naples, 1655: BnF D–2393) is preserved. The Archives of the Congregation for the doctrine of faith (Holy Office) in Rome hold the unedited censure of Father Joseph Scilla, SJ, on the *Summa theologiae* (ff. 403–406 in Prot. D4), and the numerous successive decrees which bring down condemnation ('tomi primi pars I et II, et tomi secundi pars I donec corrig.; ceterae partes operis absolute prohib') on the following dates: 3.02.1659; 5.03.1714; 1.10.1715; 20.01.1716; 16.11.1716; 7.02.1718; 4.12.1719; 26.01.1722; 26.08.1726.

[8] Liber VII, defensio II, cap. 1.

[9] 'an pater Vulpes recte dixerit, decipi Thomistas omnes, opinantes, cum sancto Thomas, legem aeternam esse ipsam rationem gubernationis rerum in Deo.'

eternal truth. But one cannot speak of eternal laws in this manner except for the laws of nature, to be precise, inasmuch as they are the precepts of the first tablet, and, in a general manner, of all the principles of acting things, known by their ends, as well as the conclusions demonstrated as a result of them. … From there, Duns Scotus proves that the theology of necessary things or of things which treat theological truths arising from necessary ends is totally practical, and not speculative, in all understanding, in order for it to precede all acts of the will, according to the kind [*modus*] of rule which is proper to it. It results that all the Thomists are mistaken (among others Vasquez, Suárez, Becanus), in holding with Aquinas that the eternal law is equivalent to the very *ratio* of the government of nature in God. [10]

Ruggieri then presents the defence of the Thomistic point of view:

That the eternal laws would be laws of nature, as Master Volpi says, does not prevent the *ratio* of the government of nature in God from being an eternal law or, on the contrary, knowing that the eternal law is the *ratio* for government in God, as Aquinas says. The law of nature is not said to be eternal in the same way that the eternal law is said to be the *ratio* for government in God. Ultimately, the eternal law is said to be in God, as it is for one who makes the rules [*regulans*], but in nature, as that in which the rules are made [*regulatum*]. Even if one considers it a part of nature to make the rules [*regulans]* for created things, that is to say as the directing and natural rule of created things, that is only the case insofar as it is participating in the eternal law (inasmuch as all things participate according to their own manner in eternal law).[11]

This participation in eternal law, for the rational creature, is the *lex naturalis*, which is moral law ('lex naturalis nihil aliud est quam participatio legis aeternae in rationali creatura'). The Scotist point of view then distinguishes natural law (*lex naturalis*) from (*lex naturae*). *Princeps scotistorum*, the Franciscan Bartolomeo Mastri (1602–73) presents this distinction, when he distinguishes between *lex naturalis*, which possesses all the distinctive traits of a law, and which was put in us

---

[10] 'Scotus in I dist. 36, quaest unica, sup. A, supponit dari leges aeternas: docens, motionem nostri intellectus ad cognoscendum veritates sinceras, reducendam esse ad regulas aeternas in diuino intellectu. Loquitur de regulis tam practicis, quam speculatiuis necessariis aeternae veritatis. Possunt dici eiusmodi leges aeternae, solae leges naturae, presse, ut sunt praecepta primae tabulae ex 3. dist. 37 et universaliter, omnia principia operabilium, nota ex terminis ac conclusiones ex illis demonstratae … Hinc Scotus probat Theologiam necessariorum seu de veritatibus theologicis ex terminis necessariis esse totaliter practicam, non speculativam, in quovis intellectu, ut praecedant omnem actum voluntatis, per modum regulae illius. Ex his patet, decipi Thomistas omnes: Vasquez in expositione articuli; Suárez lib 2 cap. 1; Becanum tract 4, cap 2, q. 1 opinantes cum sancto Thoma, legem aeternam esse ipsam rationem gubernationis rerum, in Deo.'

[11] 'Quod leges aeternae sint leges naturae, ut ait Magister Vulpes, non tollitur quod ratio gubernationis rerum in Dei sit lex aeterna, aut e contra, quod scilicet lex aeterna, sit ratio gubernationis in Deo; sicut ait s Thomas. Non enim lex naturae, dicitur lex aeterna, eomodo quo lex aeterna dicitur ipsa ratio gubernationis in Deo. Nam lex aeterna dicitur in Deo sicut in regulante; in natura autem, sicut in regulato. Vel si consideretur in natura etiam sicut in regulante, regulante scilicet creaturas, id est ut regula, naturaliter directiua creaturarum; non consideratur, nisi ut participata; nimirum, prout omnia suo modo participant aeternam legem.'

by the *lumen naturale*, and *lex naturae*:[12] 'the law of nature is not, properly speaking, a law, and does not have the force of obligation to the law, as it does not command, but indicates.'

The law of nature is on the order of a rule, a measure of all of nature (*mensura totius naturae*) (this is what we find in the astronomers, GRAßHOFF). A precision is necessary here to underscore the importance of this distinction in the Scholastic tradition – the Jesuit Gabriel Vasquez proposes a detailed study in his commentary on Aquinas.[13] Despite the difficulties, he says, the Thomists endeavour to maintain in the eternal law the characteristics of a law. Their reasoning is not flawless: (a) it is not an *imperium* per se, but a *judicium* of a divine *cognitio*, in other words, of an *idea* (and as there are in God some ideas of things which will never be, one could not speak of them as an *imperium* in their own right); (b) there is not a place in God for the intellectual act of commanding *what ought to be*; (c) finally, this supposed law was never promulgated but was imposed and it applies in all ways on all of creation, and not only on rational beings. It, therefore, does not have all of the characteristics of a true law.

Instead of trying desperately to align this supposed eternal law with the definition of law, Vasquez explains that it suffices to renounce the word 'law': 'an idea is a kind of law, but it is not preceptive and does not need promulgation'.

Vasquez is therefore opposed to exegetical interpretations such as that of Proverbs 8 ('When he gave to the sea his decree, that the waters should not pass his commandment') since, he says

> by *decree*, here the Holy Writ does not mean an eternal law, but the law imposed by God in time to the sea and the waters, according to Job 38, 11 *And said, Hitherto shalt thou come, but no further* and Psalm. 103 [Hebr. 104], *Thou hast set a bound that they may not pass over; that they turn not again to cover the earth*. This was no more than the very nature of the waters, created by God with this natural inclination, in order that, locked in this hole of the earth that God created after their creation to close them in as in an uterus, they could not cover the earth . It has been very properly called bi the Holy writer the law of the waters, because it stands as a kind of a rule or a law, without having the ratio of the law [*quia se habet ad modum regulae, et legis, non quia habeat rationem legis*]. (p. 17)

Thus, by way of these examples, we can make the following claim: the medieval and antique formulation of creation, and its insertion into the traditional teachings of Christianity is essential to understand the teaching of the theologians and philosophers of the seventeenth century about the origin and the status of the universe.

The Government of the World

Ultimately, the text of Scripture alone proves to be insufficient as a source for a conceptual apparatus that would allow these phenomena to be explained and to be fitted into the world system in a satisfactory and coherent manner. Neither biblical cosmology nor the allegorizations (or moralizations) of the Lapidaries and Bestiaries

[12] Mastrius 1684: vol. 2, Disp. VI, q. 3, n. 65, p. 368.

[13] Vasquez 1611: vol. 2.

would be up to this task. Another source is needed to articulate and complete an exhaustive (for the epoch and its knowledge) explanation of the world. The scholarly authors looked for such a source, compatible with the biblical data: they understood that they had at their disposal a text which would permit them to fill the Scriptural lacunae: Plato's *Timaeus*.[14]

This dialogue served as an exceptional reference for them (and a unique one, until the discovery of the texts of Aristotle's *Physics* and his Arab commentators). By way of this text, known either through a partial Latin translation done by Cicero (also used by Augustine[15]) or in a translation by the Christian Calcidius (or Chalcidius)[16] which was accompanied by a scientific commentary on *Timaeus* 17 A–53 C3, the *Timaeus* gave to these thinkers, from the age of Scotus Erigenus onward, a scientific authority which was comparable to the Mosaic narrative of Genesis. With Macrobius' commentary on the *Somnium Scipionis*,[17] and the ninth metre of the third book of Boethius' *Consolation*, as well as the commentary of Bovon of Corvey,[18] a Platonic corpus was developed which established the autonomy of nature and paved the way for Peripatetic physics, which itself was known, in the majority of works translated from the twelfth century, through the prism of Arab Platonism.[19]

The diffusion of the *Timaeus* in medieval universities is a well-known fact.[20] One can safely say that it was the Platonic dialogue which had, by way of its Latin translations, the greatest circulation.[21] This included, as well, commentaries and glosses of certain passages (the origin of the world, *anima mundi*, the creation of the soul and the body, *materia prima*), which were often cited in an abridged fashion by Calcidius or William of Conches, still used by Marsilio Ficino in the fifteenth century.[22] The *Timaeus* is really, as its subtitles suggest, a *De Natura liber*, received and distributed as such in the translation of Marsilio Ficino, published by Francesco Zampini, or even a *De Universitate* (in the edition of Cicero and Calcidius, Paris, 1563). Finally, the editions of the scholar Mersius (1579–1639) were widely circulated in the seventeenth century. The Jesuit Athanase Kircher, for example, develops a cosmology that is infused throughout by his exposure to the *Timaeus*.[23] Even if the full history of its reception in the seventeenth century remains to be completed, the

---

14 We follow here the classic work of Tullio Gregory; see Gregory 1958: chap. 4, 'il Timeo e i problemi del platonismo medievale', pp. 53–150; also Gregory 2007.

15 According to Courcelle 1948: 156ff. Carl Andresen has argued, on the other hand, for knowledge of the translation of Calcidius (Andresen 1968: 93ff.).

16 Edition by J.H. Waszink, in *Plato Latinus*, vol. 4, 1962 (BnF: 4–Z–4485 (4)); see also Waszink 1964.

17 Schedler 1916; Duhem 1958: vol. 3, pp. 62–81.

18 Jeauneau 1973.

19 Courcelle 1939; Gregory 1963: 132–133.

20 Grabmann 1936: 197; Gibson 1969.

21 Tigerstedt 1974: *passim*.

22 Marsilio Ficino cites him in the *De voluptate* (*Opera*, 1576, vol. 1, p. 997).

23 Kircher 1669: 154.

Timaeus undoubtedly constitutes an essential element in the formation of modern scientific thinking.[24]

Moreover the studies of medieval Platonism have shown how, in the twelfth century, it engendered a new idea of nature, not solely considered as creation, but also with its own autonomous organization. A passage from the commentary on Boethius' *De Trinitate* by Thierry of Chartres exposes clearly this shift. It is a question of the necessity of the complexion (or order) (*necessitas complexionis* (*ordinis*)) which rules the links between natural causes: 'that which some call natural law, others nature, others soul of the world, others natural justice, others eimarmene. But others still call it fate, parchae, intelligence of God.'[25]

Timaeus' subject, in the eponymous dialogue, is a cosmological treaty, which is presented as the practical application of a political conversation which preceded it.[26] This new dialogue proposes to pass from the ideal of the State previously described to its inception, in other words its origins as a political act. It is in this political context that Timaeus reveals his conception of the genesis of the known Universe, a genesis which comes to be by way of a structure of harmonic relations, put into place by geometry. The tenth book of the *Laws,* where Plato treats the question of blasphemy and thus the role of the gods in the city and the organisation of the world, provides the connection to a juridical structure. 'He who has ordered all things' is called 'our King' (X, 902ff). A study of the reception and dissemination of Plato's *Laws* during the period shows that book 10 is precisely the book that garnered the most sustained interest from Christian readers.[27] Suárez often mentions the connection between the *Timaeus* and the *Laws*, calling attention to the recurrence of the verb *gubernare*: 'Plato etiam in Timaeo quatuor leges distinguens [*Timée* 24b], primam vocat divinam, per quam plane hanc aeternam intelligit, per quam mundum Deus gubernat, ut idem tradit dialogo 10 de Legibus'.[28] Or again when he enumerates the four senses of law for Plato:[29]

> divine law for Plato is the principle [*ratio*] which governs the universe and which exists in the mind of God, a law which the theologians recognize also, but which they call eternal

[24] See, among others, Desplaces 1976. It is worth noting that, at the beginning of his great *Commentary* on Genesis, the eminent Jesuit exegete Benoît Pereire, defending the simplicity of the biblical narrative (or perhaps, he says, its '*gravitas*'), compares it to the narrative of the *Timaeus*, a work which the adversaries of Pereire call 'philosophiae Deus Plato': 'quam multa in Timaeo de hac ipsa mundi generatione & de prima rerum omnium procreatione, nullis argumentorum firmamentis munita, sed nuda tantum oratione simpliciter enarrata et explicata reliquit' (Pereyra 1622:, praefatio, p. 1).

[25] Häring 1971: 273 (on *De Trin.* II, 21): 'quam alii legem naturalem, alii naturam, alii mundi animam, alii iustitiam naturalem, alii ymarmenem nuncupaverunt. At vero alii eam dixere fatum, alii parchas, alii intelligentiam Dei.'

[26] Modern commentators suggest that the reference is to the *Republic*, but as one sees in the work of Suárez, medieval commentators (who would not have known the *Republic*) suggest that it refers to the *Laws*, the political dialogue which they knew.

[27] Desplaces 1962: 216 (also Desplaces 1981: 476).

[28] *De Legibus* II, 1, 2, vol. 5, p. 86. The connection seems to come from Marsilio Ficino, *Dialogo Minos vel De Lege*, (*Omnia Divi Platonis Opera*, Venice 1571 p. 29).

[29] *De Legibus* I, 3, 6.

> law. The divine law can be identified, ultimately, in two different ways – because it is in God himself or because it comes directly from him, at the same time as it is outside of him. Plato calls the first kind of law 'divina' but the theologians, after Augustine,[30] in order to distinguish it from that which comes from God, call it eternal, and we will do the same.

It is helpful to examine here the treatment of the *Timaeus* in the Scotist tradition; one finds a long analysis in the work of the master of the Scotist movement in the seventeenth century, the Franciscan monk Philippus Faber, or Filippo Fabro, called Faventinus, in a work which was widely circulated, his treatise against the atheists (*Adversus impios atheos disputationes quatuor philosophicae*, Venice 1627). Dedicated to his nephew, Cardinal Francesco Barberini, the work attacks atheists and deists in the name of *natura, experientia et ratio* by way of philosophic authorities. The Plato of *Timaeus* (*disputatio tertia*) figures in the first ranks of those who refuse the eternity of the world. Faventinus summarizes (pp. 226–227) the discourse of Timaeus, studies the arguments which are opposed to a Christian Plato (the *materia prima,* the *anima mundi*) and concludes[31] that, even if all is not perfect in the attempt to render Plato a Christian, and even if his teaching remains somewhat ambiguous ('even if Plato was inconsistent and ambiguous in his doctrine and his explanation of the principles of the world', p. 233), he nevertheless clearly teaches the temporal production of the world by God.

This Platonic source allows us to understand the permanence of the juridical notion, despite the rarity of the expression *leges naturae*. Suárez separates inanimate beings from the concept of law (for him, it can be nothing more than a metaphor), but his theological thinking remains infused with the idea of 'divine government'. The *ratio gubernationis rerum* is the *ratio* of divine understanding, where the order of providence presides over the general ordering of nature (a thesis which was discussed, we have seen, between Scotists and Thomists) [Kusukawa; Trepp]. Additionally, Cicero provides this definition in the first book of *De Legibus*: 'est autem lex ratio summa insita in natura, quae jubet ea, quae facienda sunt, prohibetque contraria'.

For Suárez himself, the *lex aeterna*, which is in God (the Thomistic thesis), is the supreme *ratio* for the government of the world. And after having cited the *Timaeus* and the *Laws*, Suárez illustrates the thought of Aquinas by way of the classic citation from Boethius: 'o qui perpetua mundum ratione gubernas',[32] concluding that 'this eternal *ratio* of God has true juridical status.'

The objection which then arises[33] is that this *ratio aeterna agendorum* is nothing other than providence. The debate about this alternative runs thus: either providence is a general design of government, or it is a *ratio aeterna*, that is to say the principles of nature. The *providentia* is not necessarily a law *ab aeterno,* it would be a law

---

30 *De libero arbitrio* I, 6, 14 (PL 32, 1229).

31 With the authority of Augustine, *City of God* X, 31: 'quanquam et de Mundo et de his quos in Mundo Deo a Deo factos scribit Plato apertissime dicat eos esse coepisse, et habere initium, finem tamen non habituros, sed per conditoris potentissimam voluntatem in aeternum permansuros esse perhibeat'.

32 *De consolatione* philosophia,e III, 220, metre 9 (PL 63, 758 ; CSEL 67, 63).

33 *De Legibus*, II, 1, 4.

materialiter (or, more exactly, *quasi materialiter*), but not *formaliter*. Thus Creation can be properly called eternal *materially*, in the sense that it is an idea of God, but *formally* it comes to be in time. However, Suárez, following Aquinas, insists: eternal law is at the same time a law and eternal – divine designs are necessarily directed, the divine project of creation is directed, thus an eternal law presides necessarily over nature. For there exist two kinds of laws, or, perhaps, the concept of law can be understood in two different ways: the *status* which it has in the internal disposition of the legislator, that is in the thought of the lawmaker, on the one hand,[34] and on the other hand, the *status* that it has as it is constituted outside of its existence in the thought of the legislator, in its promulgation to its subjects. *There is therefore an eternal law in God, even though the law which applies to creatures is not eternal.*

The discussion goes further then to culminate in a new distinction, at the heart of our inquiry. One must not hold, Suárez underscores, that this eternal law is not a law, because it is not promulgated but ought to be promulgated ('non est lata, sed ferenda'): it was promulgated, in truth, for all eternity *according to its mode*. The divine *imperium* is as eternal as its will. Suárez enters thus into the same discussion as is under discussion here: certain people, he says, think that this eternal law is that which affects the actions of God *ad extra*, that is to say Creation, and that which is properly the rule and measure (*regula et mensura*) of all that God does. He introduces at this moment an original and very bold distinction between *lex morum*, the moral law, which is proposed to the human consciousness, and *lex artificiorum*, the law of the mechanics, presiding over creation. He borrows this distinction from Plato; at the beginning of *De Legibus*, and aside recalls this division, proposed in the *Minos*, between two kinds of laws, *lex artis* and *lex morum*. One can add, Suárez suggests, a *lex ordinis seu propensionis naturae*, following the four-part distinction of the *Timaeus* (24b) and the *Gorgias* (XIX, 464b and XXXI, 483d)[35] between the divine law, celestial law, natural law and human law (a distinction in which Suárez eliminates celestial law, calling it superfluous or erroneous).[36] In this way, he continues, natural law, *lex naturalis*, is not that which is in men, but that which partakes in all things by inclination, implanted by the author of nature ('eam quae rebus omnibus ex inclinatione ab auctore naturae indita convenit'). Returning to the beginning of book II on this distinction, he is very aware of the novelty of his claims ('non est lex morum, *ut sic dicam,* sed artificiorum'). The use of *ut sic dicam*, 'so to say' (or 'I dare say'), is frequent in Suárez to introduce a new expression, and one has to be careful because it sounds lilke a hint for a bold new proposal. In effect, the classical inventory of laws, as the Jesuit exegete Benito Pereyra, for example, explains in his commentary on Genesis,[37] lists five kinds of laws – natural,

---

[34] *De Legibus*, II, 1, 5: 'quatenus in mente (legislatoris) iam illa lex descripta est, et eius absoluto decreto ac firma voluntate stabilita'.

[35] Suárez's source, indicated by the editors of *De Legibus* in the *Corpus hispanorum de pace* (t. XI, Madrid, 1971), is Marsilio Ficino on the *Minos* (Ficino 1571: 29).

[36] *De Legibus* I, III, 5: 'vel superflua est vel doctrina erronea continet').

[37] There are several editions of the *Commentaria et Disputationes in Genesim*. The following quote from the commentary on chapter 2, verse 16, is taken from the Cologne 1622 edition (p. 140).

supernatural, Mosaic, divine (that of the Gospels) and private – and it seems wrong to substitute for these the four senses of the *Timaeus*. Suárez continues:

> all that God does relates to God as an artifact does to its artisan. In the same way that the idea of the artisan can be called a law which imposes itself to produce artifacts that conform to that idea, this eternal law is the idea by which God as supreme artisan decides how to establish all things for all of eternity.[38]

Thus, all objections fall away – such a law does not have need of promulgation ('haec est necessaria in lege morum, non in lege artificiorum'). It is not addressed to subjects, it does not constitute a government. Suárez's refutation of this precision is weak, because it takes recourse to the weight of authority; such a definition of the law, he says, goes against the opinion of Augustine and of all the theologians, of Cicero and of all the philosophers. The law only applies to morality, applying it to inanimate beings can only be metaphorical and would not pertain to those beings. Suárez's objections about the proper usage of the term should not mislead us [STOLLEIS]. In fact, he has caught a glimpse of the distinction between *lex morum* and *lex artificiorum*, the moral law for men and the law of the mechanics, which presides over all of creation. The *supremus artifex*, the supreme mechanic, is not only the supreme *legislator* for men, superior to Moses, Solon or Lycurgus but also it is the *legifer,* that which establishes the laws for nature. The terminology serves as our guide here: *legifer* is the translation retained by the Vulgate for the passage from the prophet Isaiah (33:22): 'the Lord is our judge, the Lord is our lawgiver (*Dominus legifer noster*), the Lord is our king'. With this, we can see the third and final element of the conceptual matrix: the holy Scripture.

Deus legifer: Exegesis

The Bible is an important reservoir of lexical and conceptual innovations, a veritable herbarium of western thought. The appearance of the juridical notion of law as part of an explanation of the physical world merits further research over the entirety of the biblical corpus [ROUX]. It is instructive here to begin this research by examining one book, and the choice is not Genesis, but Job. Contrary to what one might think at first, the commentaries on Genesis do not contain the most useful topos for these considerations: the exegetes and theologians who comment on the beginning of Genesis are too preoccupied by the creation of the world and its constituents to envision its maintenance and permanence. In several places, by contrast, the commentaries and the paraphrases of the book of Job insist on the juridical character of the divine intervention in nature, in terms of a *lex aeterna*, and a certain number

[38] 'omnia quae a Deo fiunt comparantur ad illum, tanquam artefacta ad artificem; unde sicut idea artificis dici potest lex, quam ipse sibi praescribit, ut juxta illam artefact producat, ita haec lex aeterna est, qua Deus ut supremus artifex omnia condere statuit ex aeternitate'(II, 1, 7). The image of God as an artisan recalls Augustine: for example, *De Genesi contra Manichaeos* I, V ('dicant nobis isti, quomodo iis rebus quae fabricandae sunt, superferatur voluntas fabri').

of discussions come to light with regard to this.[39] These questions are directly posed in the book of Job, by God himself or by the friends of Job. In the discourse of Elihu (Job 36:22, Vulgate), we find an explicit reference to *Deus legislator*: 'Behold, God shall prevail by his strength, and nobody among the Lawmakers is equal to Him' (the Authorized Version follows the Hebrew: *Who teacheth like him*) [*Ecce Deus excelsus in fortitudine sua et nullus ei similis in Legislatoribus*].

Et nullus ei similis in Legislatoribus (the initial capital letter is frequent in the printed texts of the Vulgate): the commentary of verse 36:22 inscribes God in the tradition of *legislators*. Obviously, many commentators understood the word in terms of social organization. The Jesuit Juan de Pineda (1558–1637), in his authoritative and greatly circulated commentary (two folio volumes of commentaries on the biblical text),[40] interprets this verse in the sense of the moral law. He comments on the word *Lawmakers* (*Legislatores*): 'or Doctors' (*vel Doctores*), and tries to set up the portrait of the *just legislator* in this context. He notes at the beginning the polysemy present in the word *hry*, a word that means both 'to rain,' 'to order' and 'to teach'. With regard to Job 22:22, Pineda, who extracts from the root *hry* the word *hrwt*, relates the 'rain' to the *law* as divine teaching, and interprets the metaphor in its moral meaning: the law is that which irrigates and gives drink to souls.[41] *Aequitas*, *sapientia*, *eruditio* – justice, wisdom and knowledge – are traits of the character of the good legislator: Pineda shows how they are present, to the highest degree, in the action of the Creator.[42]

In the same spirit, in his *Job elucidatus* (1646), the Jesuit Balthasar Cordier wonders to which legislators God is compared, since Moses for the Hebrews, Phoronaeus for the Greeks, Mercury Trismegistus for the Egyptians, Solon for the Athenians, Lycurgus for the Spartans, Numa Pompilius for the Romans, are all after the supposed time of the biblical narrative. Which *legislatores* could be the basis for comparison? The profound originality of the *Deus legislator* comes from the comparison with tyrants, who impose hard and unjust laws which are intolerable for the people. The same manner of rule is not found in God who seeks to make the weight of the laws equal to the ability of those who receive them. One sees how, to comment on this verse, the application is more towards the moral sense than towards the cosmological sense.

But other verses call for commentaries which go in a different direction: these are classic verses, which appeal directly to the evocation of physical laws. In what follows, we will analyse two primary examples of this:

(a) *'For [God] looketh to the ends of the earth, and seeth under the whole heaven; to make the weight for the winds; and he weigheth the waters by measure. When he made a decree for the rain and a way for the lightning of the thunder ...* '(Job 28:24–25)

---

39 Zúñiga 1584 (on whom, see Arámburu 1961); Boulduc 1619; Cordier 1646.

40 Juan de Pineda, *Commentaria in Job*. First published in Madrid between 1597 and 1601, Pineda's commentary went through ten editions in thirty years. We refer here to the Cologne edition, 1605 (BnF A–1357).

41 Ibid.: 300–301.

42 Ibid.: 878–879.

The lengthy commentary of Balthasar Cordier takes the entirety of chapter 28 to affirm the voluntarism of a divine wisdom which imposes laws onto nature: 'the Holy Wisdom is therefore the principle and the cause and the procreator and the perfection and the custodian and the end of the created wisdom and of all minds, reasons and senses' (p. 517).

The exegete points to an example which is particularly illuminating in demonstrating this legislative power of God: the control of the winds (Job 28:25: 'to make the weight for the winds'). What does this weight of the winds (*ventis pondus*) mean? In an encyclopedic elaboration of *anemology*, the exegete explains that it has to do with the *force* and the *direction* of the winds. The subject, he says, is of great importance and not in the least a futile source of inquiry. With the Book of Wisdom 7:17 ('He hath given me certain knowledge of the things that are, namely … the violence of winds … and all such things as are either secret or manifest, them I know'), he recalls that this concept is difficult and hard to see: 'it is indeed hard to know what is the nature of winds, whence they come, what causes them, how their speed and violence, their periodicity and their duration proceed from a constant order and a sure law [constanti ordine *certaque lege*]'.[43] He concludes: 'wind is a tiny thing, but to know it is no light glory, nor the smallest part of wisdom'.

Certa lege, a sure law: the divine power imposes weight and measure (*pondus et mensura*) on the most rebellious of elements, the most resistant to all order and all discipline (about *lex certa*, see Mohnhaupt). Even the wind, says Cordier, is not borne as it wishes and cannot go as it might desire: 'God imposes on it a *mandatum*, a commandment. His power manifests itself well in allowing something to which weight and measure is unknown only to move under the determinate weight and measure that he determined [*statuit*]' (p. 518).

(b) *'Where wast thou when I laid the foundations of the earth? declare, if thou hast understanding. Who hath laid the measures thereof, if thou knowest? or who hath stretched the line upon it? Whereupon are the foundations thereof fastened? or who laid the corner stone thereof?'* (Job 38: 4–6)

God interrogates Job about the author of all things, about why he had commanded chaos. Balthasar Cordier paraphrases the divine questions: 'who assigned a place to every thing so that the heavy ones may go down and the light ones go up according to their nature, and that apart from nisus and pondus, a higher force had set a law to the things?' The divine *imperium* permitted this order and arranged all things with *measure and number and weight, mensura et numero et pondere*, an expression of the *Book of Wisdom* 11:22, the modern reception of which also merits being studied.

Conclusion

The theological matrix of the concept of *deus legislator* can be seen through the polysemy that expresses it in the seventeenth century: as juridical law, promulgated

[43] Italics added.

in order to regulate the comportment of men, the *lex naturalis* only applies to rational beings [STOLLEIS]. As *lex morum*, it is the law of the code. A double etymology presents itself here. While Isidore of Seville makes *lex* from *legere*,[44] Aquinas mentions *two* etymologies: 'the law is said from to link, because it binds, or to read, because it is publicly read, according to Isidorus'.[45] *Doctor irrefragabilis*, the Franciscan Alexandre de Halès (c. 1185–1245) had even seen the *two* etymologies in Isidore,[46] an error that Suárez (*De Legibus* II, 1 p. 87) denounces (a false attribution of authority, which shows well that the etymology *lex<legere* was useful and necessary to the Scotist thesis). The sense of the *lex aeterna* maintains itself in the Scotist tradition, as *lex artificiorum*, and not as *lex morum* It is the eternal law that regulates all of creation, *mensura et numero*, *lex* coming here from *ligare*. The double etymology arises out of the polysemy of the term, between the binding law (*ligare*), applied to any creature, and the promulgated law (*legere*), applied only to mankind.

The theological and philosophical currents divide themselves in many ways according to the two possible etymologies: on the one hand, a juridical law, that which is written and read (*lex<legere*) and, on the other hand, an eternal law, a law of nature (given and imposed by nature) which has particular characteristics and which is a rule for all of creation (*lex<ligare*). These currents mark the epistemologic coming into being of the expression, *Deus legislator*. One can see this, for example, in the background of point 8 of the Sixth Objections[47] of Descartes' *Meditations*, where it is clear that Descartes responds with a sharpened understanding of the theological dossier[48] ('God, as the supreme legislator'). *Legere* relates to the political laws, *ligare* to the physical laws: the equivocation remains, a semantic doubling. We find it again in a text which gives important testimony to the ubiquity of its diffusion: in Book XIV of the *Hieroglyphica* of Pierius, a very significant document for the semiotics of early modern Europe, where the icon of the law is a crown, which returns to the political sense, but *a braided crown* (an allusion to the mystical sense of the crown of thorns), affirming thus at the same time the political law (*legere*) and the physical law (*ligare*), because 'it is interwoven by some links, which compel our life to be bound in some way' (*certis est vinculis complicata, quibus vita nostra veluti religata coercetur*).

---

44 *Etymologiarum sive Originum Libri XX*, lib. II, cap. 10, n. 1 (PL 82, 130; ed. W.M. Lindsay, Oxford, 1911): 'nam lex a legendo vocat, quia scripta est'.

45 'Lex dicitur a *ligando*, quia obligat. Vel dicitur a *legendo*, quo publice legatur, secundum Isidorum' Ia–IIae, q. 90, a. 1. In Cicero, at the beginning of *De legibus*, one finds also *delegere* (a fact which is commented upon by Vasquez 1611: vol. 2, p. 5).

46 Alexandre de Halès, *Summa Universae Theologiae* (Venice 1575; Quaracchi 1948), vol. 4, lib. III, pars II, inq. 1, quaestio unica, n. 224, p. 315: 'lex uno modo dicitur a legendo, alio modo a ligando. Secundum quod dicitur a legendo, extenso nomine lectionis non solum ad lectionem temporalem, sed ad lectionem secundum quod legitur in mente, sic lex est in dispositione. Lex autem prout est in promulgatione dicitur a ligando. Primo ergo modo est aeterna, secundo modo non.' The play on words of *ligare*/*legere* had been recognized for a long time: this can be seen in the hesitations of Ovid's copyists, where one finds the same variation in *Métamorphoses* I, 91–92: 'Nec verba minantia fixo aere *legebantur* (vel: *ligabantur*)'.

47 Descartes, *Œuvres*, ed. Adam-Tannery, vol. 7, p. 417.

48 Ibid.: pp. 435–436.

Bibliography

Note: This volume was submitted to the press in 2006. The bibliography reflects the state of the literature at that date.

Primary Sources

Abicht, Johann Heinrich (1792), *Neues System eines aus der Menschheit entwikelten Naturrechts*, Bayreuth.

Académie Royale des Sciences (1733), *Histoire de l'Académie Royale des Sciences depuis son établissement en 1666 jusqu'à 1699*, 11 vols, Paris.

Achenwall, Gottfried (1754), *Observationes iuris naturalis, specimen II: De obligatione et imputatione*, Göttingen.

Achenwall, Gottfried (1774), *Prolegomena iuris naturalis*, 4th edn, Göttingen.

Achenwall, Gottfried and Pütter, Johann Stephan (1750), *Elementa iuris naturae*, Göttingen; republished 1995, with German translation by Jan Schröder, under the title *Anfangsgründe des Naturrechts*, Frankfurt am Main.

Alembert, Jean le Rond d' (1758), *Traité de dynamique*, 2nd edn, Paris.

Alexander of Hales (1575), *Summa universae theologiae*, Venice; reprinted 1948, 2 vols, Quaracchi.

Althusius, Johannes (1649), *Dicaeologicae libri III*, 2nd edn, Frankfurt.

Amyraut, Moyse (1648), *Considérations sur les droits par lesquels la nature a reglée les mariages*, Saumur.

Anon. (1672), 'The Copy of a Letter from Somersetshire, Concerning a Strange Frost, Which Hath Lately Done Much Hurt about Bristol; Together with Some Useful Hints Suggested upon That Occasion', *Philosophical Transactions of the Royal Society of London*, 7: 5138–5142.

Aquinas, St Thomas (1955), *Summa Theologica* I–II (German edition, vol. 10): Die menschlichen Leidenschaften, Heidelberg, Graz, Vienna and Cologne.

Aquinas, St Thomas (1988), 'Über den Lehrer. De magistro. Quaestiones disputatae de veritate', Quaestio XI; *Summa theologiae*, ed. G. Jüssen et al., Hamburg.

Aquinas, St Thomas (2000), *Summa theologiae*, translation in *Thomas Aquinas: Treatise on Law*, trans. Richard J. Regan, Indianapolis.

Argenterio, Giovanni (1610), *Opera ex exemplari Veneto revisa*, Hanau.

Aristotle (1930), *Physics*, trans. R.P. Hardie and R.K. Gaye, Oxford.

Aristotle (1963), *Nicomachean Ethics*, trans. H. Rackman, Cambridge, MA.

Aristotle (1995), *Physik, Vorlesung über die Natur*, in *Aristoteles, Philosophische Schriften*, vol. 6, trans. H.G. Zekl, Darmstadt.

Arnauld, Antoine (1685a), *Dissertation de M. Arnauld sur la manière dont Dieu a fait les fréquents miracles de l'Ancienne Loi*, in Arnauld (1775–83), vol. 18, pp. 675–741.

Arnauld, Antoine (1685b), *Réflexions philosophiques et théologiques sur le nouveau système de la nature et de la grâce*, in Arnauld (1775–83), vol. 19, pp. 1–153.

Arnauld, Antoine (1685c), *Neuf lettres de M. Arnauld Docteur de Sorbonne au R.P. Malebranche*, in Arnauld (1775–83), vol. 19, pp. 154–856.

Arnauld, Antoine (1775–83), *Œuvres*, 43 vols, Lausanne and Paris.

Arndt, Johann (1597), *Ikonographia*, Halberstadt.

Arndt, Johann ([1610] 1851), *Vier Bücher vom wahren Christentum, das ist von heilsamer Buße, herzlicher Reue und Leid über die Sünde und wahren Glauben, auch heiligem Leben und Wandel der rechten wahren Christen nebst desselben Paradies-Gärtlein*, Berlin.

Arnisaeus, Henning (1613), *De iure connubiorum commentarius politicus*, Frankfurt.

Augustine, *De Genesi contra Manichaeos* (Patrologia Latina [= PL] 34, col. 177).

Augustine, *De civitate Dei* (PL 41, 311).

Augustine, *De libero arbitrio* (PL 32, 1222).

Augustine (1912), *Confessiones*, trans. William Watts, Cambridge, MA.

Auzout, Adrien (1665/6), *L'Éphéméride de la comète*, Paris.

Bacon, Francis (1740), *De augmentis scientiarum*, in Bacon (1858), vol. 1.

Bacon, Francis (1825–34), *Lord Bacon's Works*, ed. Basil Montagu, 16 vols, London.

Bacon Francis (1858), *The Works of Francis Bacon*, ed. James Spedding, Robert Leslie Ellis and Douglas Denon Heath, 15 vols, London.

Bacon, Francis ([1620] 1878), *Novum organum*, ed. Thomas Fowler, Oxford.

Bacon, Francis (1996), *Works*, ed. Brian Vickers, Oxford.

Bartholin, Erasmus (1670), 'An Accompt of Sundry Experiments upon a Chrystal-Like Body, Sent to Him Out of Island', *Philosophical Transactions of the Royal Society*, 5: 2039–2048.

Bastit, Michel (1990), *Naissance de la loi moderne. La pensée de la loi de saint Thomas à Suarez*, Paris.

Bauer, A. (1808), *Lehrbuch des Naturrechts*, Marburg.

Bayle, Pierre (1682), *Pensées diverses sur la comète*, in Bayle (1727–31), vol. 3, pp. 3–160.

Bayle, Pierre (1684–87), *Nouvelles de la République des Lettres*, in Bayle (1727–31), vol. 1.

Bayle, Pierre (1686), *Réflexions sur la lettre de l'auteur des Doutes à M. ***, pour répondre à une difficulté qui lui avait été objectée*, in Fontenelle (1686), pp. 569–574.

Bayle, Pierre (1694), *Addition aux Pensées diverses*, in Bayle (1727–31), vol. 3, pp. 161–186.

Bayle, Pierre (1704a), *Continuation des Pensées diverses écrites à un Docteur de Sorbonne*, in Bayle (1727–31), vol. 3, pp. 187–417.

Bayle, Pierre (1704b), *Réponse aux questions d'un provincial*, in Bayle (1727–31), vol. 3, pp. 501–988.

Bayle, Pierre (1706), *Réponse à M. Le Clerc*, in Bayle (1727–31), vol. 4, pp. 989–1009.

Bayle, Pierre (1707), *Entretiens de Maxime et Thémiste*, in Bayle (1727–31), vol. IV, pp. 1–106.

Bayle, Pierre (1727–31), *Œuvres diverses de M. Pierre Bayle*, 4 books in 5 vols, The Hague.

Bayle, Pierre (1740), *Dictionnaire historique et critique*, 4 vols, 5th edn, Amsterdam, Leyde, The Hague and Utrecht.

Bentley, Richard (1693a), *A Confutation of Atheism from the Origin and Frame of the World, Part II*, London.

Bentley, Richard (1693b), *A Confutation of Atheism from the Origin and Frame of the World: the third and last part*, London.

Berlich, Matthias (1739), *Conclusiones practicabiles secundum ordinem Constitutionum divi Augusti*, Cologne.

Bernardus, Joannes Baptista (1605), *Seminarium totius philosophiae*, 3 vols, Geneva.

Bernegger, Matthias (1618), *C. Cornelii Taciti, De vita Julii Agricolae liber*, [expositus à Matthia Berneggero, Historiarum in Argentoratensi Academia Professore], Argentorati.

Bernegger, Matthias (1619), *Hypobolimaea divae Mariae, Deiparae Camera: seu Idolum Lauretanum, eversis Baronii cardinalis, Canisii, Turriani ac Tursellini jesuitarum fulcimentis dejectum; ubi passim ex re natâ contra pseudojubilaeum Petri Roestii, Jesuitae Molsheimensis Academiae, disseritur*, Argentorati.

Bernegger Matthias ([1621] 1624), *Tuba pacis occenta: Scioppiano belli sacri classico, Salpiste Theodosio Berenico, Norico, Historiarum & Patriae Studioso – Pax Optima Rerum, Augustae Trebocorum.*

Bernegger, Matthias (1635), *Systema cosmicum, Authore Galilaeo Galilaei, Lynceo, Academiae Pisanae, Mathematico extraordinario, Serenissimi Magni-Ducis Hetruriae Philosopho et Mathematico Primario: In quo Quatuor Dialogis, De Duobus Maximis Mundi Systematibus, Ptolemaico et Copernicano, Utriusque rationibus Philosophicis ac Naturalibus indefinite propositis, disseritur.* Ex Italica Lingua Latine conversum. Accessit Appendix gemina, qua SS. Scripturae dicta cum Terrae mobilitate conciliantur, Augustae Trebocorum.

Bernegger, Matthias (1636), *Nov-antiqua Sanctissimorum Patrum, & Probatorum Theologorum Doctrina, De Sacrae Scripturae Testimoniis, In Conclusionibus Mere Naturalibus, Quae Sensatâ experientiâ, & necessariis demonstrationibus evinci possunt, temere non usurpandis:* (…) privatim ante complures annos, Italico idiomate conscripta à Galilaeo Galilaeo, (…) Nunc vero juris publici facta, cum Latina versione Italico textui simul adjuncta, Augustae Trebocorum.

Besold, Christoph (1618), *Politicorum libri duo*, Frankfurt.

Beza, Theodorus (1571), *Tractatio de polygamia et divertio*, Geneva.

Biesius, Nicolaus (1573), *De natura libri v*, Antwerp.

Binsfeld, Peter (1596), *Tractatus de confessionibus maleficorum et sagarum*, Trier.

Birch, Thomas (1756–57), *The History of the Royal Society of London: for improving of natural knowledge from its first rise, in which the most considerable of those papers communicated to the society, which have hitherto not been published, are inserted in their proper order, as a supplement to the Philosophical transactions*, London.

Blumblacher, Christoph Andreas (1670), *Commentarius in Kayser Carl des Fünften Peinliche Hals-Gerichts-Ordnung*, Salzburg.

Bocer, Heinrich (1588), *Ad tres priores Pandectarum partes disputationes*, Tübingen.

Boecler, Johannes Heinrich (1640), *In obitum summi viri Matthiae Berneggeri, oratio funebris, publico nomine dicta in Academia Argent.*, [à Joanne Henrico Boeclero, Eloq. Prof. Publ.], Argentorati.

Boecler, Johannes Heinrich (1663), *In Hugonis Grotii Iuris Belli & Pacis. Librum Primum. Commentatio*, Argentorati.

Boecler, Johannes Heinrich (1674), *Institutiones politicae. Accesserunt dissertationes politicae et selecta veterum historicorum loca et libellus memorialis ethicus*, Argentorati.

Boethius, Severinus, *De consolatione philosophiae* III, 220, metre 9 (PL 63, 758 ; CSEL 67, 63).

Böhmer, Johann Samuel Friedrich von (1770), *Meditationes in Constitutionem Criminalium Carolina Codem*, Magdeburg.

Böhmer, Justus Henning ([1704] 1756), *Introductio in ius Digestorum*, I, 9th edn, Halle.

Böhmer, Iustus Henning (1741), *Introductio in ius Digestorum*.

Bossuet, Jean-Bénigne (1687), Lettre à A. d'Allemans, 21 mai 1687, in Malebranche (1958–67), vol. 18, pp. 443–448.

Boulduc, Jacques (Bolducus, Jacobus), OFM Cap. (1619), *Commentaria in librum Iob*, Paris.

Boyle, Robert (1662), A *Defence of the Doctrine Touching the Spring and Weight of the Air*, London.

Boyle, Robert (1663), *Some Considerations Touching the Usefulnesse of Experimental Naturall Philosophy*, London.

Boyle, Robert (1666a), *Hydrostatical Paradoxes, made out by new Experiments*, London.

Boyle, Robert (1666b), *Origin of Forms and Qualities*, London.

Boyle, Robert (1671), *Some Considerations Touching the Usefulnesse of Experimental Naturall Philosophy, the second tome*, part 2, London.

Boyle, Robert (1674), *The Excellency of Theology, compared with Natural Philosophy, to which are annexed Some Occasional Thoughts about the Excellency and Grounds of the Mechanical Hypothesis*, London.

Boyle, Robert (1685), *A Free Inquiry into the Vulgarly Received Notion of Nature*, London.

Boyle, Robert (1686), *On the Vulgarly Received Notion of Nature*, London.

Boyle, Robert (1744), *Works*, 5 vols, London.

Boyle, Robert (1772), *The Works of the Honourable Robert Boyle*, ed. Thomas Birch, 6 vols, London. Reprint 1966, Hildesheim.

Boyle, Robert (1996), *Robert Boyle: A Free Inquiry into the Vulgarly Received Notion of Nature*, ed. Michael Hunter and Edward B. Davis, Cambridge: Cambridge University Press.

Boyle, Robert (1991), *Selected Philosophical Papers of Robert Boyle*, ed. M.A. Stewart, Indianapolis.

Boyle, Robert (1999), *The Works of Robert Boyle*, ed. Michael Hunter and Edward B. Davis, London.

Brosserius, Simon (1546), *Philosophiae naturalis totius epitome*, Paris.

Budaeus, Giuliemus (1557), *Operum tomus III, in quo annotationes in pandectas*, Basle.

Buffon, George-Louis Leclerc, Comte de (1954), *Œuvres philosophiques de Buffon*, ed Jean Piveteau, Paris.

Buffon, George-Louis Leclerc, Comte de (1956), 'Histoire naturelle des animaux', in *Œuvres philosophiques*, ed. Lehez-Cazeneuve, vol. 2, Paris.

Butler, Joseph (1736), *The Analogy of Religion, Natural and Revealed, to the Constitution and Course of Nature*, London.

Calov, Abraham (1676), *Disputatio theologica de polygamia*, Wittenberg.

Calvin, Jean (1961), *Institutes of the Christian Religion*, London.

Camerarius, Johannes Rudolphus (1626–30), *Sylloges memorabilium medicinae et mirabilium naturae arcanorum centuriae duodecim*, Strasbourg.

Cardano, Girolamo (1663), *Opera omnia*, ed. Charles Spon, 10 vols, Lyons.

Carpzov, Benedict (1635), *Practica nova rerum criminalium.*

Case, John (1599), *Ancilla philosophiae*, Oxford.

Cassini, Jacques (1710), 'Experiences de l'effet du vent à l'egard du Thermometre', *Mémoires de l'Académie Royale des Sciences*: 544–552

Chandler, Henry William (1891), *Catalogue of the Aristotelian and Philosophical Portions of the Library of the Late Henry William Chandler*, Oxford.

Charleton, Walter and Gassendi, Pierre (1654), *Physiologia Epicuro-Gassendo-Charltoniana: Or a fabrick of science natural, upon the hypothesis of atoms, founded by Epicurus, repaired by Petrus Gassendus*, augmented by Walter Charleton, London.

Cicero (1922), *Academica*, ed. Otto Plasberg, Leipzig: Teubner.

Cicero (1949), *De inventione; De optimo genere oratorum; Topica*, trans. H.M. Hubbell, London.

Cicero (1951), *De natura deorum*, trans. H. Rackham, Cambridge, MA.

Cicero (1994a), *De legibus*, ed. Rainer Nickel, Darmstadt.

Cicero (1994b), *De re publica. De legibus*, trans. Clinton Walker Keynes, Cambridge, MA.

Claproth, Johann Christian (1749), *Grundriß des Rechts der Natur*, Göttingen.

Clasen, Daniel (1685), *Commentarius in Constitutiones criminales Caroli V.*, Frankfurt.

Commentarii (1593), *Commentarii de regulis iuris antiqui*, Lyons.

Comte, Auguste (1969), *Cours de philosophie positive*, 47e leçon, in *Œuvres complètes* (1830–42), vol. 4, Paris.

La condamnation parisienne de 1277 (1999), new edition from the Latin, trans. with introduction and commentary by David Piché, Paris.

Connanus, Franciscus (1562), *Commentariorum iuris civilis libri X*, bearb. v. F. Hotman, with preface by Bartholomaeus Faius, Basle.

Conring, H. (1643), *De origine iuris germanici*, Helmstadt; German translation 1994, ed. Michael Stolleis, Frankfurt.

Conring, Hermann (1663), *Disquisitio politica de prudentia peregrinandi, proponit Detleff Brockdorff (Respondens)*, Helmstadt.

Conring, Hermann (1695), *De origine Juris Germanici liber unus*, editio quarta, Helmestadt.

Copernicus, N. (1973), 'The Derivation and First Draft of Copernicus' Planetary Theory: A Translation of the "Commentariolus", with Commentary, by Noel M. Swerdlow' *Proceedings of the American Philosophical Society*, 117: 423–512.

Copernicus, N. (1984), *De Revolutionibus*, ed. Heribert M. Nobis, vol. 2, Gesamtausgabe, Hildesheim.

Copernicus, N. (1985), *Minor Works*, ed. Pawel Czartoryski, trans. and commentary by Edward Rosen, with the assistance of Erna Hilfstein. London.

Copernicus, N. (1990), *Das neue Weltbild: Drei Texte*, ed. and trans., with introduction and notes, Hans Günter Zekl, Hamburg.

Copernicus, N. (1992), *On the Revolutions*, ed. Edward Rosen. New York.

Cordemoy, Géraud de (1666), *Le Discernement du corps et de l'ame en six discours*, Paris.

Cordemoy, Géraud de (1968), *Oeuvres philosophiques, avec une étude bio-biobliographique*, ed. Pierre Clair and François Girbal, Le mouvement des idées au XVIIe siècle 6, Paris.

Cordier, Balthasar, SJ (1646), *Iob elucidatus*, Anvers.

Corpus Iuris Civilis (1990), trans. and ed. Okko Behrends, Rolf Knütel, Berthold Kupisch and Hans Hermann Seiler, Heidelberg.

Cotta, John (1612), *A short discoverie of the unobserved dangers of severall sorts of ignorant and unconsiderate practisers of physicke in England*, London.

Cotte, Louis (1774), *Traité de méteorologie*, Paris.

Crusius, David (1615), *Theatrum morborum hermetico-hippocraticum, seu methodica morborum et curationis eorundem dispositio.*

Cudworth, Ralph (1678), *True Intellectual System of the Universe*, London.

Culverwell, Nathaniel ([1652] 1971), *An Elegant and Learned Discourse of the Light of Nature*, ed. Robert A. Greene and Hugh MacCallum, Toronto and Buffalo.

Culverwell, Nathaniel ([1652] 1978), *Discourse of the Light of Nature*; reprinted 1978, New York and London.

Cumberland, Richard (1672), *De legibus naturae disquisitio philosophica, in qua earum forma, summa capita, ordo, promulgatio, & obligatio è rerum natura investigantur; quinetiam elementa philosophiae Hobbianae, cùm moralis tum civilis, considerantur & refutantur*. Translated as *A Treatise of the Laws of Nature* (1978), ed. René Wellek, London.

Cumberland, Richard (1683), *De legibus naturae disquisitio philosophica*, 2nd edn, Lubeck and Frankfurt.

Cunningham, James (1699), 'Some Observations of the Mercury's Altitude, with the changes of the Weather at Emüy in China', *Philosophical Transactions of the Royal Society of London*, 21: 323–330.

Cunningham, James (1704), 'Observations of the Weather, Made in a Voyage to China. Ann. Dom. 1700', *Philosophical Transactions of the Royal Society of London*, 24: 1639–1447.

Damhouder, Jose (1565), *Praxis rerum criminalium*, Antwerp.

Daniel, Gabriel (1732), *Suite du voyage de M. Descartes*, Utrecht.

Darjes, Joachim Georg (1762), *Discours über sein Natur- und Völkerrecht*, Part 1, Jena.

Derham, William (1703), 'A Letter from the Reverend Mr William Derham, F.R.S. to Mr John Haughton, F.R.S. containing his Observations of the Weather, & c. for some years past', *Philosophical Transactions of the Royal Society of London*, 23: 1443–1448

Derham, William (1708), 'Tables of the Barometrical Altitudes at Zurich in Switzerland in the Year 1708. Observed by Dr. Joh. Ja. Scheuchzer, F.R.S. and at Upminster in England, Observed at the Same Time by Mr. W. Derham, F.R.S. as Also the Rain at Pisa in Italy in 1707, and 1708. Observed There by Dr. Michael Angelo Tilli, F.R.S. and at Zurich in 1708', *Philosophical Transactions of the Royal Society of London*, 23: 1443–1448.

Derham, William ([1713] 1716), *Physico-Theology*, 4th rev. edn, London.

Descartes, René (1633), 'Le Monde ou traité de la lumière', in Descartes (1964–74), vol. XI, pp. 3–202.

Descartes, René ([1644], 1982), *Principia philosophiae*, in Descartes (1897–1913), vol. VIII–1.

Descartes, René (1648), *Notae in programma quoddam*, in Descartes (1964–74).

Descartes, René (AT: 1897–1913), *Œuvres*, ed. Charles Adam and Pierre Tannery, 12 vols, Paris; new edn (1964–74), ed. J. Beaude, P. Costabel, A. Gabbey and B. Rochot, 11 vols, Paris.

Descartes, René (1908), *Discours de la méthode pour bien conduire sa raison et chercher la vérité dans les sciences*, ed. Paul Ziertmann, Heidelberg.

Descartes, René (1955), *Die Prinzipien der Philosophie* (1644), trans. and with commentary by Artur Buchenau, Hamburg.

Descartes, René (1976), *Discours de la méthode*, ed. E. Gilson, Paris.

De Soto, Domingo (1569), *Commentarii in quartum sententiarum*, Venice.

Destutt de Tracy, Antoine, ([1817] 1992) *Commentaire sur l'Esprit des lois de Montesquieu*, Caen.

Deutsches Rechtswörterbuch (1974, ed. Akademie der Wissenschaften zu Berlin), Weimar.

Diocles (of Carystius) (1572), *Aurea ad Antigonum regem epistola*, ed. Antoine Mizauld, Paris, apud Federicum Morellum, 8vo.

Diogenes Laertius (1931), *Lives of the Philosophers*, 2 vols, trans. R.D. Hicks, Cambridge, MA.

Donellus, Hugo ([1589] 1801), *Commentarii de iure civili*, I, 6th edn, published by Johann Christoph König, Nuremberg.

Donne, John (1953–62), *The Sermons*, ed. George R. Potter and Evelyn M. Simpson, 10 vols, Berkeley and Los Angeles.

Dufay, Charles (1735a), 'Sur la lumière des diamants et de plusieurs autres corps', *Histoire de l'Académie Royale des Sciences*, 1–4.

Dufay, Charles (1735b), 'Recherches sur la lumière des diamants et de plusieurs autres matières', *Mémoires de l'Académie Royale des Sciences*, 347–372.

Durkheim, Emile ([1892] 1953), *Quid secundatus politicae scientiae instituendae contulerit*, in *Montesquieu et Rousseau précurseurs de la sociologie*, ed. A. Cuvillier, Paris.

Du Roure, Jacques (1653), *La physique expliquée suivant le sentiment des anciens et nouveaux philosophes, et principalement de Descartes*, Paris.

Du Roure, Jacques (1665), *Abregé de la vraie philosophie, lequel en contient. les définitions, les divisions, les sentences, & les questions principales*, Paris.

Ernestus, Johann Rudolph (1718), *Dissertatio iuridica de iuris incertitudine*, Altdorf.

Etymologiarum sive Originum Libri XX (1911), ed. W.M. Lindsay, 2 vols, Oxford.

Fénelon, François de Salignac de la Motte (1687), *Réfutation du système du P. Malebranche sur la nature et la grâce*, in Fénelon (1843), vol. 1, pp. 324–421.

Fénelon, François de Salignac de la Motte ([1688] 1716), *Réfutation du système du P. Malebranche sur la nature et la grâce*, Paris.

Fénelon, François de Salignac de la Motte (1843), *Œuvres philosophiques de Fénelon*, Paris.

Feuerbach, Anselm Ritter von (1847), *Lehrbuch des gemeinen in Deutschland gültigen Peinlichen Rechts*, 14th edn, Gießen.

Fichte, Johann Gottlieb ([1797] 1979), *Grundlagen des Naturrechts nach Prinzipien der Wissenschaftslehre*, Hamburg.

Ficino, Marsilio (1548), *Omnia divini Platonis opera*, Lyons.

Ficino, Marsilio (1559), *Theologia platonica de immortalitate animorum*, Paris.

Ficino, Marsilio (1571), *Omnia Divi Platonis Opera*, Venice.

Ficino, Marsilio (1576), *Opera*, 2 vols, Basle.

Filangeri, Gaetano (1784), *La scienza della legislazione*; trans. T. Vormbaum (1993), *Texte zur Strafrechtstheorie der Neuzeit*, vol. 1, pp. 179–88, Baden-Baden.

Fischl, O. (1913), *Der Einfluss der Aufklärungsphilosophie auf die Entwicklung des Strafrechts*, in *Doktrin, Politik und Gesetzgebung, Strafrechtliche Abhandlungen*, vol. 169, Breslau.

Fontenelle, Bernard Le Bovier de ([1686] 1990), *Doutes sur le système physique des causes occasionnelles*, Paris; reprinted in Fontenelle (1989–2001), vol. 1, Paris, pp. 525–563.

Fontenelle, Bernard Le Bovier de (1989–2001), *Œuvres complètes*, ed. Alain Niderst, 9 vols, Paris.

Fredersdorff, Leopold Friedrich ([1790] 1999), *System des Rechts der Natur auf Bürgerliche Gesellschaft, Gesetzgebung und das Völkerrecht angewandt*, Brunswick.

Frölich zu Frölichsburg, Johann Christian (1741), *Commentarius in Kayser Carl des Fünften Peinlichen Hals-Gerichts-Ordnung*, Innsbruck.

Galen (1821–33), *Opera omnia*, 20 vols, ed. C.G. Kühn, Leipzig: Cnoblauch.

Galileo (1937), *Discoveries and Opinions of Galileo*, ed. Stillman Drake, Garden City.

Garcaeus, Johannes (1584), *Meteorologia*, Wittenberg.

Gassendi, Pierre (1649), *Animadversiones in decimum librum Diogenis Laertii, qui est de vita, moribus, placitisque Epicuri*, Lyons.

Gemma, Cornelius (1575), *De natura divinis characterismis: seu raris et admirandis spectaculis, causis, indiciis, proprietatibus rerum in partibus singulis universi libri ii*, Antwerp.

Gilbert, William (1600), *De magnete magnetisque corporibus, et de magno magnete tellure, physiologia nova, plurimis & argumentis & experimentis demonstrate*, London.

Glafey, Adam Friederich (1723), *Vernunfft- und Völcker-Recht*, Frankfurt/Leipzig.

Gobler, Justin (1543), *Caroli Quinti de capitalibus iudiciis constitution*, Basle.

Goclenius, Rudolph Sr (1591), *Scholae seu disputationes physicae, more academico fere propositae et habitae plaeraeque omnes in schola illustri Cattorum*, Marburg.

Goclenius, Rudolph Sr (1609), *Conciliator philosophicus*, Kassel.

Goclenius, Rudolph Sr (1613), *Lexicon philosophicum, quo tanquam clave philospohiae fores aperiuntur*, Frankfurt am Main.

Goetten, Gabriel Wilhelm (1736), *Das jetztlebende gelehrte Europa oder Nachrichten von den vornehmsten Lebensumständen und Schriften jetztlebender Europäischer Gelehrte*, 2 vols, 2nd edn, Braunschweig and Hildesheim.

Gratarolo, Guglielmo (1554), *Opuscula*, Basle.

Grawerus, Albertus (1614), *Libellus de unica veritate*, Wiemar.

Gribaldus Mopha, Matthaeus (1541), *De ratione studendi*, Lyons.

Gribner, Michael Heinrich (1715), *De iure incerto ex dubia legum, quibus utimur, auctoritate oriundo dissertatio*, Wittenberg.

Grimm, Jacob and Wilhelm, eds (1897), *Deutsches Wörterbuch*, Leipzig.

Grotius, Hugo (1625), *De iure belli ac pacis libri tres*, Paris.

Grotius, Hugo ([1625] 1939), *De iure belli ac pacis*, published by B.J.A. de Kanter-van Hettinga Tromp, Leiden; reprinted 1993 with notes by R. Feenstra et al., Aalen.

Grotius, Hugo (1626), *De iure belli ac pacis libri tres*, Frankfurt.

Grotius, Hugo (1720), *De iure belli ac pacis*, Amsterdam.

Grotius, Hugo (1965), *Inleidinge tot de Hollandsche Rechtsgeleerdheid*, Leiden.

Gundling, Nicolaus Hieronymus (1747), *Ausführlicher Discours über das Natur- und Völcker-Recht*, new edn, Frankfurt and Leipzig.

Gutberleth, Henricus (1613), *Physicae, hoc est naturalis philosophiae compendiosa institutio, accurata conscripta, tribus libris distincta*, Herborn.

Halès, Alexandre de (1575), *Summa universae theologiae*, Venice; reprinted 1948, Quaracchi.

Halley, Edmund (1686a), 'A Discourse of the Rule of the Decrease of the Height of the Mercury in the Barometer, according as Places are elevated above the Surface of the Earth, with an Attempt to discover the true Reason of the Rising and Falling of the Mercury, upon change of Weather', *Philosophical Transactions of the Royal Society of London*, 16: 104–116.

Halley, Edmund (1686b), 'An Historical Account of the Trade Winds, and Monsoons, Observable in the Seas between and near the Tropicks, with an Attempt to Assign the Physical Cause of the Said Winds', *Philosophical Transactions of the Royal Society of London*, 16: 153–168.

Halley, Edmond (1687), 'Account of Isaac Newton's *Philosophiae Naturalis Principia Mathematica*', *Philosophical Transactions of the Royal Society of London*, 16 (186): 291–297.

Häring, N.M., ed. (1971), *Commentaries on Boethius by Thierry of Chartres and His School*, Toronto.

Harpprecht, Johannes (1658), *Commentarii in IV libros Institutionum Iuris Civilis*, I, 2nd edn, Frankfurt.

Harsdörffer, Georg Philipp (1651), *Delitiae mathematicae et physicae: der mathematischen und philosophischen Erquickungsstunden Zweyter Teil*, Nuremberg.

Harvey, William (1653), *Anatomical exercitations, concerning the generation of living creatures*, London.

Hawenreuther, Johannes Ludwig (1594), *ΣΥΝΟΨΙΣ ΤΗΣ ΦΥΣΙΚΗΣ*, Cambridge.

Hawenreuter (1597), see Zabarella.

Hegel, Georg Wilhelm Friedrich ([1821] 1975), *Principes de la philosophie du droit*, trans. R. Derathé, Paris.

Hegel, Georg Wilhelm Friedrich (1902), *Grundlinien der Philosophie des Rechts. Vorrede Hegels vom 25. Juni 1820.* Published with an introduction by G.J.P.J. Bolland, Leiden.

Heineccius, Johann Gottlieb (1738), *Elementa iuris naturae et gentium*, Halle.

Hellerus (1548), *Præfatio, in Epitome totius astrologiæ a Ioanne Hispalensi Hispano astrologo celeberrimo ante annos quadingentos, ac nunc promum in lucem edita*, Nuremberg.

Helmholtz, Hermann von (1862), 'Über das Verhältnis der Naturwissenschaften zur Gesamtheit der Wissenschaft'; reprinted 1968, in H. von Helmholtz, *Das Denken in der Naturwissenschaft*, Darmstadt, pp. 3–29.

Hemmingius, Nicolaus (1564), *De lege naturae apodictica methodus*, Wittenberg.

Hemmingsen, Niels (n.d. [1572?]), *Libellus de coniugio, ripudio et divortio in gratiam fratrum*, Leipzig.

Heydenreich, Karl Heinrich (1794), *System des Naturrechts nach kritischen Prinzipien*, Part 1, Leipzig .

Hobbes, Thomas (1642), *De cive*, London; reprinted 1994 in *Vom Menschen. Vom Bürger*, Hamburg.

Hobbes, Thomas (1647), *Elementa philosophica de cive*, Amsterdam.

Hobbes, Thomas ([1651] 1985), *Leviathan*, ed. C.B. Macpherson, London.

Hobbes, Thomas ([1839–45] 1961), *Opera philosophica quae latine scripsit omnia*, vol. 2, ed. William Molesworth; reprinted 1961, Aalen.

Hobbes, Thomas (1962), 'A dialogue of the Common Law', in *Thomas Hobbes, The English Works*, vol. 6, ed. William Molesworth, reprint Aalen.

Hooke, Robert (1665), *Micrographia*, London.

Hooker, Richard (1975), *The Laws of Ecclesiastical Polity*, ed. A.S. McGrade and Brian Vickers, New York.

Höpfner, Ludwig Julius Friedrich (1780), *Naturrecht des einzelnen Menschen, der Gesellschaften und der Völker*, Gießen.

Höpfner, Ludwig Julius Friedrich (1803), *Theoretisch-practischer Commentar über die Heineccischen Institutionen nach deren neuesten Ausgaben*, 7th edn, ed. Adolph Dieterich Weber, Frankfurt am Main.

Horst, Gregor (1629), *De morbis eorumque causis ac symptomatibus liber, cum declaratione quaestionum controversarum*, Marburg.

Hostiensis [Henry of Segusio] (1537), *Henricus de Segusio Cardinalis Hostiensis, Summa una cum summariis et adnotationibus Nicolai Superantii*, Lyons; reprinted 1962, Aalen.

Hotman, François (1569), *Commentarius verborum juris,* Lyons.

Hucher, Jean (1602), *De prognosi medica libri duo*, Lyons.

Hufeland, Gottlieb (1785), *Versuch über den Grundsatz des Naturrechts nebst einem Anhange*, Leipzig.

Hufeland, Gottlieb (1795), *Lehrsätze des Naturrechts und der damit verbundenen Wissenschaften zu Vorlesungen*, 2nd edn, Frankfurt and Leipzig.

Humboldt, Wilhelm von (1792), *Ideen zu einem Versuch, die Gränzen der Wirksamkeit des Staates zu bestimmen*; reprinted 1969, in *Werke in fünf Bänden*, vol. 1, Darmstadt.

Hume, David (1748), *Philosophical Essays Concerning Human Understanding*, London; reprinted 1986, Hildesheim..

Hume, David (1751), *An Enquiry Concerning the Principles of Morals*, London.

Huygens, Christiaan, (1657), 'De ratiociniis in aleae ludo', in *Exercitationum mathematicarum libri quinque*, ed. Frans van Schooten, Leiden, pp. 521–534.

Huygens, Christiaan (1669), 'Extrait d'une lettre de M. Hugens à l'Auteur du Journal: Regles du mouvement dans le rencontre des Corps', *Journal des sçavans* (18 March): 19–24.

Huygens, Christiaan (1888–1950), *Oeuvres complètes de Christiaan Huygens*, ed. Société Hollandaise des Sciences, The Hague.

Huygens, Christiaan and Oldenburg, Henry (1669), 'A summary account of the Laws of Motion', *Philosophical Transactions of the Royal Society of London*, 4: 925–928.

Indagine, Joannes ab (1603), *Introductiones apotelematicae elegantes in physiologiam, astrologiam naturalem, complexiones hominum, naturas plantarum, cum periaxiomatibus de faciebus signorum et canonibus de aegritudinibus hominum: omnia ob similem materiam accessit Gulielmi Grataroli Bergomatis opuscula de memoria reparanda, augenda, conservanda,; de praedictione morum naturamque hominum; de mutatione temporum, eiusque signis perpetuis. Et Pomponii Gauridi Neapolitani tractatus de simmetriis, lineamentis et physiognomia, eiusque speciebus*, Oberursel.

Ingolstetterus, Johannes (1596), *De aureo dente Silesii pueri, responsio ad iudicium M. Rulandi*, Leipzig.

Isidore of Seville (1911), *Etymologiarum sive Originum libri XX*, ed. W.M. Lindsay, 2 vols, Oxford.

Jacobus, Joannis (1595), *Cornucopia ..., in se continens definitiones*, Prague.

Jurin, James (1723), 'Invitatio ad Observationes Meteorologicas Communi Consilio Instituendas', *Philosophical Transactions of the Royal Society of London*, 32: 422–427.

Kant, Immanuel (1785), *Grundlegung zur Metaphysik der Sitten*, Riga.

Kant, Immanuel (1797), *Metaphysik der Sitten*, in *Werke in zehn Bänden*, ed. W. Weischedel, vol. 7, Darmstadt.

Kant, Immanuel (1798), *Die Metaphysik der Sitten, Part 1: Metaphysische Anfangsgründe des Rechtslehre*, 2nd edn, Königsberg.

Keckerman, Bartholomaeus (1613), *Systema physicum, septem libris adornatum*, 3rd edn, Hanau.

Keckermann, Bartholomaeus (1614), *Opera*, Geneva.

Kepler, J. (1937a), *Briefe 1599–1603*, ed. Max Caspar, *Gesammelte Werke*, vol. 14, Munich.

Kepler, J. (1937b), *Mysterium cosmographicum*, ed. Walther von Dyck, Max Caspar and Franz Hammer, *Gesammelte Werke*, vol. 1, Munich.

Kepler, J. (1945), *Briefe 1590–1599*, ed. Max Caspar, *Gesammelte Werke*, vol. 13, Munich.

Kepler, Johannes ([1609] 1990), *Astronomia nova seu physica coelestis, tradita commentariis de motibus stellae Martis, ex observationibus G.V. Tychonis Brahe* (1609); reprinted as *Neue Astronomie*, trans. and with commentary by Max Caspar, Munich.

Kepler, J. (1991), *Epitome astronomiae copernicanae*, ed. Max Caspar, *Gesammelte Werke*, 2nd edn, vol. 7, Munich.

Kepler, J. (1995), *Briefe 1604–1607*, ed. Max Caspar, *Gesammelte Werke*, vol. 15, Munich.

Kestner, Heinrich Ernst (1699), *Prudentia studendi jura*, Rintelii.

Kircher, Athanasius (1669), *Ars magna sciendi*, Amsterdam.

Kirchner, Hermann (1608), *Respublica*, Marburg.

Kleinschrod, Gallus Aloys (1805), *Systematische Entwicklung der Grundbegriffe und Grundwahrheiten des peinlichen Rechts aus der Natur der Sache und der peinlichen Gesetzgebung*, 3rd edn, Erlangen.

Kling, Melchior ([1542] 1557), *In IV Institutionum iuris principis Iustininai libros enarrationes*, Lyons.

Knorr, Balthasar (1680), *Compendium juris axiomaticum*, Regensburg.

Kreps, M. (1620), *Teutsche Politick oder von der Weise wol zu Regieren in Frieden und Kriegszeitten*, Frankfurt.

Kues (Cusanus), Nikolaus von (1970), *De docta ignorantia*, 2nd edn, ed. Hans Gerhard Senger (Latin–German), Hamburg.

Lactantius (1964, 1965), *The Divine Institutes, Books 1–7*, The Fathers of the Church, Vol. 49, trans. M.F. McDonald, Washington, DC: Catholic University of America Press.

Lactantius (1986), *Institutiones divinae*, Sources chrétiennes 326, Paris.

La Hire, Gabriel-Philippe de (1706), 'Dissertation sur les Barometres et Thermometres', *Mémoires de l'Académie Royale des Sciences*, 432–442.

La Hire, Phillipe de (1708), 'Observations de la quantité d'eau de pluie qui est tombée à l'Observatoire Royal à Paris pendant l'année 1707, & les hauteurs du Thermometre & du Barometre', *Mémoires de l'Académie Royale des Sciences*, 60–63.

La Hire, Phillipe de (1710), 'Observations de la quantité d'eau qui est tombée à l'Observatoire pendant l'année 1709, avec l'état du Thermometre & du Barometre', *Mémoires de l'Académie Royale des Sciences*, 139–158.

Lamy, Bernard ([1683] 1966), *Entretiens sur les Sciences*, ed. François Girbal and Pierre Clair, Paris.

Lecoq, Anne-Marie, ed. (2001), *La Querelle des Anciens et des Modernes, XVIIe–XVIIIe siècles*. Introduction by Marc Fumaroli and Afterword by Jean-Robert Armogathe. Paris.

Leibniz, Gottfried Wilhelm (1686–90), *Correspondance avec Arnauld*, in Leibniz (1875–90), vol. 2, pp. 1–138.

Leibniz, Gottfried Wilhelm (1687), *Discours de métaphysique*, in Leibniz (1875–90), vol. 4, pp. 427–463.

Leibniz, Gottfried Wilhelm (1695), *Système nouveau pour expliquer la nature des substances et leur comunication entre elles*, in Leibniz (1875–90), vol. 4, pp. 471–503.

Leibniz, Gottfried Wilhelm (1697), *De rerum originatione radicali*, in Leibniz (1875–90), vol. 7, pp. 302–308.

Leibniz, Gottfried Wilhelm (1698), *De ipsa natura sive de vi insita actionibus creaturum*, in Leibniz (1875–90), vol. 4, pp. 504–516.

Leibniz, Gottfried Wilhelm (1698–1702), *Eclaircissement des difficultés que Monsieur Bayle a trouvées dans le système nouveau de l'union de l'âme et du corps [et autres textes consécutifs à la publication du Système nouveau]*, in Leibniz (1875–90), vol. 4, pp. 517–595.

Leibniz, Gottfried Wilhelm (1710), *Essais de théodicée*, in Leibniz (1875–90), vol. 6.

Leibniz, Gottfried Wilhelm ([1715–1716] 1957), *Correspondance Leibniz–Clarke*, ed. André Robinet, Paris, Presses universitaires de France, 1957.

Leibniz, Gottfried Wilhelm (1875–90), *Die philosophischen Schriften von G.W. Leibniz*, ed. C.I. Gerhardt, Berlin, 7 vols; reprinted 1961, Hildesheim.

Leibniz, Gottfried Wilhelm (1930), *Sämtliche Schriften und Briefe*, ed. Berlin-Brandenburgische Akademie der Wissenschaften und Akademie der Wissenschaften zu Göttingen, Sechste Reihe Philosophische Schriften, Vols. VI 1 – VI 4, Darmstadt; reprinted 1999, Berlin.

Leibniz, Gottfried Wilhelm (1954), *Opuscules philosophiques choisis*, Paris.

Leibniz, Gottfried Wilhelm (2002), *Des conditions (De Conditionibus)*, trans. and with introduction and notes by Pol Boucher, Paris.

Leibniz, Gottfried Wilhelm (2003), *Frühe Schriften zum Naturrecht, Lateinisch – Deutsch*, ed. and trans. Hubertus Busche, Hamburg.

Lemosius, Ludovicus (1598), *De optimo praedicandi ratione libri sex. Item iudicii operum magni Hippocratis liber unus*, Venice.

Lesser, Friedrich Christian (1735), *Lithotheologie, das ist: Natürliche Historie und geistliche Betrachtung derer Steine, also abgefaßt, daß daraus die Allmacht, Weißheit, Güte und Gerechtigkeit des grossen Schöpffers gezeuget wird; anbey viel Sprüche der Heiligen Schrifft erklähret und die Menschen allesamt zur Bewunderung, Lobe und Dienste des grossen Gottes ermuntert werden*, Hamburg.

Lesser, Friedrich Christian (1740), *Insecto-Theologia, oder Vernunfft- und schrifftmäßiger Versuch, wie ein Mensch durch aufmercksame Betrachtung derer sonst wenig geachteten Insecten zu lebendiger Erkäntniß und Bewunderung der Allmacht, Weißheit, der Güte und Gerechtigkeit des grossen Gottes gelangen könne*, 2nd edn, Frankfurt and Leipzig.

Lessing, Gotthold Ephraim (1778), 'Über den Beweis des Geistes und der Kraft', in *Gesammelte Werke* (1968), vol. 8, Berlin and Weimar.

Lessius, Leonardus (1605), *De iustitia et iure caeterisque virtutibus cardinalibus libri IV*, Löwen.

'Lex naturae est indispensabilis', advertisement for Cambridge disputation 1 July 1650.

Leyser, Johnann (1674), *Discursus politicus de Polygamia*, Freiburg.

Liddel, Duncan (1628), *Ars medica, succincte et perspicue explicata. Accessit eiusdem tractatus de dente aureo pueri Silesii contra Horstium: ex museo Joachimi Morsii nunc primum prolatus. Adiicitur Johannis Jessenii a Jessen historica relatio de rustico Bohemo cultri-vorace*, Hamburg.

Liebler, Georg (1561), *Epitome philosophiæ naturalis*, Basle.

Liebler, Georg (1566), *Epitome philosophihae naturalis*, Basle.

Lipsius, Justus, ([1704] 1998), *Justi Lipsii politicorum, sive civilis doctrinae libri sex, qui ad principatum maxime spectant; Ex Instituto Matthiae Berneggeri cum indice accurato, praemissa dissertatione Joh. Heinr. Boecleri De politicis Lipsianis*, ed. Wolfgang Weber, Hildesheim.

Lister, Martin (1684), 'A Discourse concerning the Rising and Falling of the Quicksilver in the Barometer; And What May Be Gathered from Its Great Rise in Frosty Weather, as to a Healthy or Sickly Season', *Philosophical Transactions of the Royal Society of London*, 14: 790–794

Locke, John, (1686), 'Méthode nouvelle de dresser des recueuils', *Bibliothèque universelle et historique*, 2: 315–328.

Locke, John ([1690] 1959), *An Essay Concerning Human Understanding*, ed. Alexander Campbell Fraser [1894], 2 vols, New York.

Locke, John, (1704), 'A Register of the Weather for the Year 1692, Kept at Oates in Essex', *Philosophical Transactions of the Royal Society of London*, 24: 1917–1937.

Locke, John (1954), *Essays on the Law of Nature*, ed. W. von Leyden, Oxford.

Locke, John (1975), *Essay Concerning Human Understanding*, ed. P.H. Nidditch, Oxford.

Lonicer, Johannes (1540), *De physica auscultatione, De generatione et corruptione, De longitudine et brevitate vitae, De vita et morte animalium, De anima*, Marburg.

Lucretius, Titus Carus (1975), *De rerum natura*, trans. W.H.D. Rouse, revised M.F. Smith, Cambridge, MA.

Ludovici, Jacob Friedrich (1716), *Constitutiones Criminales Caroli V*, Halle.

Ludovici, Jacob Friedrich (1725), *Doctrina Pandectarum*, 4th edn, Halle.

Luther, Martin (1964 [1901]), *D. Martin Luthers Werke*, Kritische Gesamtausgabe 23, unaltered reprint of the 1901 edn, Weimar.

Luther, Martin (1955–76), *Luthers Works*, ed. J. Pelikan and H.T. Lehmann, 55 vols, St. Louis.

Magirus, Johannes (1596), *Artis musicae methodice legibus logicis informatae*, Frankfurt.

Magirus, Johannes (1603), *Anthropologia, hoc est: commentarius erudtissimus in aureum Philippi Melanchthonis libellum de anima*, Lich: C. Nebenius and Frankfurt am Main.

Magirus, Johannes (1642), *Physiologiae peripateticae libri sex*, Cambridge.

Malebranche, Nicolas (1674–75), *Recherche de la vérité*, in Malebranche (1958–84), vols 1–3.

Malebranche, Nicolas (1680), *Traité de la nature et de la grâce*, in Malebranche (1958–84), vol. 5.

Malebranche, Nicolas (1683), *Méditations chrétiennes*, in Malebranche (1958–84), vol. 10.

Malebranche, Nicolas (1684), *Traité de morale*, in Malebranche (1958–84), ???

Malebranche, Nicolas (1685), *Réponse à une dissertation de M. Arnauld contre un Eclaircissement du Traité de la Nature et de la Grâce*, in Malebranche (1958–84), vol. 7, pp. 469–615.

Malebranche, Nicolas (1686a), *Lettres du P. Malebranche (...) dans lesquelles il répond au livre I des Réflexions philosophiques et théologiques*, in Malebranche (1958–84), vol. 8, pp. 619–787.

Malebranche, Nicolas (1686b), *Réflexions sur un livre (...) intitulé Doutes sur le système des causes occasionnelles*, in Malebranche (1958–84), vol. 17, pp. 579–586.

Malebranche, Nicolas (1688), *Entretiens sur la métaphysique et sur la religion*, in Malebranche (1958–84), vol. 12.

Malebranche, Nicolas (1696), *Entretiens sur la mort*, in Malebranche (1958–84), vol. 13.

Malebranche, Nicolas, (1958–84), *Œuvres complètes*, ed. A. Robinet, 20 vols, Paris.

Malvezzi, Virgilio (1635), *Il ritratto del privato politico Christiano*, Bologna.

Maraldi, Giacomo Filippo (1709), 'Comparaison des observations du Barometre Faites en differens lieux', *Mémoires de l'Académie Royale des Sciences*: 233–246.

Maraldi, Giacomo Filippo (1720), 'Observations sur la Quantité de Pluie, sur le Thermometre & sur le Barometre pendant l'Année 1719', *Mémoires de l'Académie Royale des Sciences*: 1–8.

Mariotte, Edme (1666), *Observations sur l'organe de la vision*, Paris.

Mariotte, Edme (1673), *Traité de la percussion ou chocq des corps, dans lequel les principales Regles de mouvement, contraires à celles que Mr Descartes, et quelques autres Modernes ont voulu establir, sont demonstrées par leurs veritables Causes*, Paris.

Mariotte, Edme (1678), *Essai de logique, contenant les principes des sciences, et la manière de s'en servir pour faire de bons raisonnemens*, Paris.

Mariotte, Edme (1686), *Traité du mouvement des eaux et des autres corps fluides*, Paris.

Mariotte, Edme (1717), *Œuvres de Mariotte*, 2 vols, Leiden.

Mariotte, Edme (1923), *Discours de la nature de l'air – De la végétation des plantes – Nouvelle découverte touchant la vue*, Paris.

Mariotte, Edme (1992), *Edme Mariotte: Essai de logique, suivi de l'écrit intitulé 'Les principes du devoir et des connaissances humaines' attribué à Roberval*, ed. Guy Picolet, Paris.

Martianus Capella (1983), *De nuptiis philologiae et mercurii*, ed. James Willis, Leipzig.

Martini, Cornelius (1593), *Programma cum responsione studiosorum Rameae philosophiae*, Helmstadt.

Mascov, Balthasar (1692), *Polygamia legi naturae repugnans*, Greifswald.

Mastrius, Bartholomaeus (1684), *Disputationes in primum [-quartum] librum Sententiarum*, 2 vols, Venice.

Meier, Justus (1657), *Collegium Argentoratense, with notes by Johann Otto Tabor*, Strasbourg.

Melanchthon, Philipp ([1546] 1961), *Philosophiae moralis epitomes libri duo*; reprinted in *Werke, Studienausgabe*, ed. R. Stupperich, vol. 3 (ed. R. Nürnberger), Gütersloh.

Melanchthon, Philip (1581), *Initia doctrinae physicae*, Wittenberg.

Melanchthon, Philip (1834–60), *Corpus Reformatorum. Philippi Melanthonis opera quae supersunt omnia*, ed. C.B. Bretschneider and H.E. Bindseil, 28 vols, Halle and Brunswick.

Melanchthon, Philip (1999), *Orations on philosophy and education*, trans. C.F. Salazar, ed. S. Kusukawa, Cambridge.

Melon, Jean-François (1847), 'Essai politique sur le commerce' (1734), in *Economistes et financiers du XVIIIe siècle*, ed. Eugène Daire, Paris.

Mersenne, Marin (1624), *[L']impiété des déistes, athées et libertins de ce temps: combattue et renversée de point en point par raisons tirées de la philosophie et de la théologie, ensemble la réfutation du 'Poème des déistes'*, Paris.

Mersenne, Marin (1932–88), *Correspondance*, ed. Paul Tannery, Cornelis de Waard, René Pintard and Bernard Rochot, Paris.

Millar, David ([1787] 1812) *An Historical View of the English Government*, London.

Molina, Lodovicus (1614), *De iustitia et iure tomi VI*, Cologne.

Mollat, Georg (1885), *Rechtsphilosophisches aus Leibnizens ungedruckten Schriften*, Leipzig; reprinted 1972 in English as *The Common Concept of Justice*, in *Leibniz. Political Writings*, ed. Patrick Riley, Cambridge.

Mommsen, Theodor (1899*), Römisches Strafrecht*, Leipzig.

Montchrestien, Antoine de ([1615] 1999), *Traicté de l'oeconomie politique*, Geneva.

Montesquieu, Charles de Secondat ([1721] 1923), *Persian Letters*, trans. John Davidson, London.

Montesquieu, Charles de Secondat, baron de ([1748] 1973), *De l'esprit des lois*, ed. R. Derathé, Paris.

Montesquieu, Charles de Secondat ([1748] 1845), *L'Esprit des lois*, Paris.

Montesquieu, Charles de ([1748] 1992), *De l'esprit des loix*, German translation by Ernst Forsthoff, Tübingen.

Montesquieu, Charles de Secondat (1950–55), *Œuvres complètes*, ed. A. Masson, 3 vols, Paris.

Montesquieu, Charles de Secondat, baron de (1991), *Pensées*, ed. Louis Desgraves, Paris.

More, Henry (1667), *Enchiridion ethicum, praecipua moralis philosphiae complectens, illustrata ut plurimum veterum monumentis, et ad probitatem vitae perpetuo accomodata*, London.

More, Henry (1671), *Enchiridion metaphysicum, sive, De rebus incorporeia succincta & luculenta dissertatio. Pars prima: De existentia & natura rerum incorporearum in genere. In qua quamplurima mundi phaenomena ad leges Cartesii mechanicas obeter expenduntur, illiosque philosophiae, & aliorum omnino omnium qui mundana phaenomena in causas pure mechanicas solvi posse supponunt, vanitas falsitasque detegitur*, London.

More, Henry (1679), *Henrici Mori Cantabrigiensis opera omnia*, London; reprinted 1966, Hildesheim.

More, Henry ([1679] 1995), 'Henry More's Manual of Metaphysics. A Translation of the Enchiridion Metaphysicum (1679) with an introduction and notes', ed. Alexander Jacob, *Studien und Materialien zur Geschichte der Philosophie* 38, Hildesheim.

Muschenbroek, Petrus van (1732), 'Ephemerides meteorlogicae', *Philosophical Transactions of the Royal Society of London*, 37: 357–384, 408–426.

'Necessario ponuntur ordes eccentrici', advertisement for Cambridge disputation, 2 July 1639.

Nettelbladt, Daniel (1750), 'Von dem rechten Gebrauch der Wolffischen Philosophie in der Theorie der positiven Rechtsgelahrheit', in D. Nettelbladt (1792), *Sammlung kleiner juristischer Abhandlungen*, Halle; reprinted 1997, in *Gesammelte Werke, Materialien und Dokumente, Vol. 38*, ed Christian Wolff, Hildesheim, Zürich and New York.

Nettelbladt, Daniel (1785), *Systema elementare universae iurisprudentiae naturalis*, 5th edn, Halle.

Nettesheim, Agrippa von (1526), *De incertitudine et vanitate omnium scientiarum*; first anonymous German translation: *Ungewißheit und Eitelkeit aller Künste und Wissenschaften*, Ulm 1534 (first printed: Antwerp 1530).

Newton, Isaac (1661), 'Trinity Notebook', Cambridge University Library, MS Add. 3996.

Newton, Isaac (1672a), 'A Letter of Mr. Isaac Newton, containing his New Theory about Light and Colors', *Philosophical Transactions of the Royal Society of London*, 6 (80): 3075–3087.

Newton, Isaac (1672b), 'Mr. Newton's Answer to Some Considerations upon his Doctrine of Light and Colors', *Philosophical Transactions of the Royal Society of London*, 7 (88): 5084–5103.

Newton, Isaac (1672c), 'Mr. Newton's Answer to the foregoing Letter [of Pardies]', *Philosophical Transactions of the Royal Society of London*, 6 (85): 5014–5018.

Newton, Isaac (1672d), 'A Serie's of Quere's propounded by Mr. Isaac Newton, to be determin'd by Experiments, positively and directly concluding his New Theory of Light and Colours', *Philosophical Transactions of the Royal Society of London*, 6 (85): 5004–5007.

Newton, Isaac (1958), *Isaac Newton's Papers and Letters On Natural Philosophy, and related documents*, ed. I. Bernard Cohen, Cambridge, MA.

Newton, Isaac (1972), *Isaac Newton's Philosophiae Naturalis Principia Mathematica: The third edition with variant readings*, ed. I. Bernard Cohen, Alexandre Koyré and Anne Whitman, Cambridge.

Newton, Isaac (1978), *Papers & Letters on Natural Philosophy and related documents*, 2nd edn, ed. I. Bernard Cohen, Cambridge, MA, and London.

Nicholas of Cusa (1983), *Opera omnia, vol. 5: Idiota de mente*, ed. Renate Steiger, Hamburg.

Obrecht, Georg (1603), *Disputationes ex variis iuris civilis. materiis*, Oberursel.

Oldenburg, Henry (1665), 'The Motion of the late Comet praedicted', *Philosophical Transactions of the Royal Society of London*, 1: 3–8.

Oldenburg, Henry (1965–86), *The Correspondence of Henry Oldenburg*, ed. Alfred Rupert Hall and Marie Boas Hall, Madison, Milwaukee and London.

Oldendorp, Johannes (1548), *Lexicon iuris. Epitome definitionum et rerum*, Frankfurt.

Paalzow, C. Ludwig (1781), *Versuch über die Gesetze. Erster Theil*, Breslau.

Parker, Samuel (1665), *Tentamina physico-theologica de Deo: sive Theologia scholastica ad normam novae & reformatae philosophiae concinnata, & duobus libris comprehensa*, London.

Parker, Samuel (1681), *A demonstration of the divine authority of the Law of Nature and of the Christian Religion*, London.

Pascal, Blaise (1663), *Traitez de l'équilibre des liqueurs et de la pesanteur de la masse de l'air, contenant l'explication des causes de divers effets de la nature qui n'avoient pas esté bien connus jusques ici, & particulièrement de ceux que l'on avoit attribuez à l'horreur du vuide*, Paris.

Pascal, Blaise (1670), *Pensées de M. Pascal sur la religion et sur quelques autres sujets, qui ont esté trouvées après sa mort parmy ses papiers*, Paris.

Pascal, Blaise (1904–14), *Œuvres de Blaise Pascal, publiées suivant l'ordre chronologique*, ed. Léon Brunschvigg, Pierre Boutroux and Felix Gazier, Les grands écrivains de la France, Paris.

Pascal, Blaise (1991), 'Reflexions sur la géométrie en général', in *Oeuvres complètes* vol. 3, ed. Jean Mesnard, Paris.

Pereyra, Benito (1593–94), *Prior [secundus] tomus Commentariorum et disputationum in Genesim*, 2 vols, Lyons; 1622 edition in 1 vol., Köln.

Petty, William (1899), *The Economic Writings of Sir William Petty*, ed. Charles Henry Hull, Cambridge.

Peucer, Caspar (1580) *Commentarius de praecipuis generibus divinationum*, Wittenberg.

Piccolomini, Francesco (1600), *De rerum definitionibus*, Frankfurt.

Pineda, Juan de (n.d.), *Commentaria in Job*, first published in Madrid between 1597 and 1601.

Plato (1962), *Timaeus a Calcidio translatus*, ed. J.H. Waszink, in *Plato Latinus*, vol. 4, London and Leyden.

Pliny (1938), *Pliny: Natural History*, ed. W.H.S. Jones and H. Rackham, London and Cambridge, MA.

Polybios (1963), *Geschichte*. Gesamtausgabe, 2 vols, trans. Hans Drexler, Zurich and Stuttgart.

Polybius (1960), *The Histories*, 6 vols, with an English translation by W.R. Paton, London and Cambridge, MA.

Porta, Giambattista della (1593), *Physiognomonia*, Hanau.

Porzio, Simone (1598), *De rerum naturalium principiis libri duo*, Marburg.

Project des Corporis Juris Fridericiani (1750), 2nd edn, Halle.

Ptolemy, Claudius (1984), *C. Ptolemy's Almagest*, ed. G.J. Toomer, London.

Pufendorf, Samuel (1660), *Elementorum jurisprudentiae universalis libri duo*, The Hague.

Pufendorf, Samuel (1672), *De jure naturae et gentium libri octo*; reprinted 1998 in *Gesammelte Werke*, vol. 4 , ed. Frank Böhling, Berlin.

Pufendorf, Samuel (1673), *De officio hominis et civis juxta legem naturalem libri duo*; reprinted 1997 in *Gesammelte Werke*, vol. 2, ed. Gerald Hartung, Berlin.

Pufendorf, Samuel (1682), *De officio hominis et civis juxta legem naturalem*, London.

Pütter, Johann Stephan (1767), *Neuer Versuch einer Juristischen Encyclopädie und Methodologie*, Göttingen.

Quistorp, Johann Christian (1796), *Grundsätze des deutschen peinlichen Rechts*, 6th edn, Leipzig.

Régis, Pierre Silvain (1691), *Cours entier de philosophie ou systeme general selon les principes de M. Descartes, contenant la logique, la metaphysique, la physique, et la morale*, Amsterdam.

Regius, Henricus (1646), *Fundamenta physices*, Amsterdam.

Remus, Georg (1594), *Nemesis Karulina Karuli V.*, Herborn.

Reifferscheid, Alexander, ed. (1889), *Quellen zur Geschichte des geistigen Lebens in Deutschland während des 17. Jahrhunderts. Nach Handschrift*en vol. 1, *Briefe G.M. Lingelsheims, M. Berneggers und ihrer Freunde*, Heidelberg.

Reinkingk, Theodor (1651), *Tractatus de regimine seculari et ecclesiastico*, 5th edn, Frankfurt am Main.

Rheticus, G. J. (1982), *Narratio prima*. Edition critique, traduction française et commentaire par Henri Hugonnard-Roche, Studia Copernicana. Warsaw.

Rist, Johann ([1638] 1982), 'Philosophischer Phönix. Das ist: Kurtze / jedoch Gruendliche vnnd Sonnenklare Entdeckunge der waren vnd eigentlichen Matery deß Aller-Edelsten Steines der Weisen [.]', in *Sämtliche Werke* 7, ed. Eberhard Mannack, Berlin, pp. 3–29. .

Rist, Johann (1648), Holstein vergiß eß nicht: Daß ist Kurtze, jedoch eigentliche Beschreibung Des erschreklichen Ungewitters, Erdbebens und überaus grossen Sturmwindes, welcher In der Fastnacht dieses 1648 Jahres, am Tage Valentins, [.] entstanden und an vielen Oertern in Holstein, sonderlich aber am Elbstrohm [.] Den feurbrennenden Zorn Gottes, [.] vor die Augen gestellet, Hamburg.

Rist, Johann ([1652] 1978), *Neuer Teuetscher Parnass, auff welchem befindlich Ehr' und Lehr, Schertz und Schmertz, Leid und Freuden Gewaechse*, Hildesheim.

Rist, Johann ([1663a] 1972a), 'Das AllerEdelste Nass der ganzen Welt/Vermittelst eines anmuthigen und erbaulichen Gespraeches/Welches ist dieser Ahrt die Erste/

und zwahr Eine Jaenners-Unterredung/ Beschriben und fuergestellet von Dem Ruestigen', in *Sämtliche Werke* 4, ed. Eberhard Mannack, Berlin, pp. 1–120.

Rist, Johann ([1663b] 1972b), 'Das AllerEdelste Leben der ganzen Welt/ der gantzen Welt/ Vermittelst eines anmuthigen und erbaulichen Gespraeches/ Welches ist dieser Ahrt Die Ander/ und zwahr Eine Hornungs-Unterredung/ Beschriben und fuergestellt von Dem Ruestigen', in *Sämtliche Werke* 4, ed. Eberhard Mannack, Berlin, pp. 121–305.

Rist, Johann ([1666] 1974), 'Die AllerEdelste Belustigung Kunst- und Tugendliebender Gemuether/ Vermittelst eines anmuthigen und erbaulichen Gespraeches Welches ist dieser Ahrt/ Die vierte/ und zwahr Eine Aprilens-Unterredung/ Beschrieben und fuergestellet von Dem Ruestigen', in *Sämtliche Werke* 5, ed. Eberhard Mannack, Berlin, pp. 183–411.

Rist, Johann ([1667] 1976), 'Die allerdelste Erfindung Der Gantzen Welt/ Vermittelst eins anmutigen und erbaukichen Gespraeches/ Welches ist dieser Art/ die Fuenffte/ Und zwar eine Maeyens-Unterredungen/ Beschrieben und fuergestellet Von Dem Ruestigen', in *Sämtliche Werke* 6, ed. Eberhard Mannack, Berlin, pp. 1–240.

Rist, Johann ([1668] 1976), 'Die allerdedelste Zeit-Verkuertzung Der Gantzen Welt/ Vermittelst eines anmuthigen und erbaulichen Gespraeches/ Welches ist dieser Art die Sechste/ Und zwar eine Brachmonats Unterredungen/. Beschrieben und fuergestellet Von Dem Ruestigen', in *Sämtliche Werke* 6, ed. Eberhard Mannack, Berlin, pp. 241–448.

Rohault, Jacques (1671), *Traité de physique*, Paris.

Royal Society of London, *Miscellaneous Papers 1660–1740*, vol. IV (2): Physiology, Meteorology, Pneumaticks (manuscript source).

Rozier, abbé F. (1775), *Nouvelles tables de matières de l'Académie des sciences de sa fondation à 1770*, 4 vols, Paris.

Saint-Pierre, Charles Irénée Castel de, abbé, (1733–41), *Ouvrajes de politique*, later *Ouvrajes de morale et de politique*, 14 vols, Rotterdam.

Saint-Pierre, Charles Irénée Castel de, abbé, (1738), 'Nouveau plan de gouvernement des États souverains', in *Ouvrajes de politique*, 2nd edn, Rotterdam, vol. 3.

Saint-Pierre, Charles Irénée Castel de, abbé (1912), *Annales politiques (1703–1738)*, ed. Joseph Drouet, Paris.

Scaliger, Julius Caesar (1592), *Exotericarum exercitationum liber xv, de subtilitate*, Frankfurt.

Schaumann, Johann Christian Gottlieb (1792), *Wissenschaftliches Naturrecht*, Halle.

Scheffer(us), Johannes G. (1670), *Index in libros Grotii de iure belli ac pacis a Boeclero 1657* ed. sine nomine auctoris, Amsterdam.

Scheffer(us), Johannes G., (1693), *H. Grotius enucleatus sive Hug. Grotii De jure belli ac pacis. Libri tres in compendium olim redacti a viro cl. Jo. Scheffero, & nunc primum editi*, Sedini (Stettin).

Schickhard, Martin (1615), *Logica juridica*, Herborn.

Schmalz, Theodor (1795), *Das reine Naturrecht*, 2nd edn, Königsberg.

Schmauss, Johann Jacob (1754), *Neues Systema des Rechts der Nature*, Göttingen.

Schmidt, Eberhard (1968), *Einführung in die Geschiche der deutschen Strafrechtspflege*, 3rd edn, Göttingen.

Schneidewin (Oinotomos), Johannes (1575), *In quatuor Institutionum Imperialium D. Iustiniani libros commentarii*, ed. Matthaeus Wesenbeck, Strasbourg.

Scribonius, Gulielmus Adolphus (1584), *Idea medicinae secundum logicas leges informandae et describendae*, Lemgo.

Sennert, Daniel ([1650] 1676), *Opera omnia*, 3 vols, ed. Charles Spon, Lyons.

Severinus, Petrus (1571), *Idea medicinae philosophicae, fundamenta continens totius doctrinae Paracelsicae, Hippocraticae et Galenicae*, Basle.

Snellius, Rudolf (1596), *In aureum P. Melanchthonis de anima librum*, Frankfurt am Main.

Solnon, Jean-François (1994), *Sources d'histoire de la France moderne*, Paris.

Sorel, Charles (1664), *[La] bibliothèque françoise de M. C. Sorel, ou Le choix et l'examen des livres françois qui traitent de l'éloquence, de la philosophie, de la dévotion et de la conduite des moeurs*, Paris.

Spiegelius, Jacobus (1569), *Lexicon iuris civilis*, Basle.

Spinoza, Baruch (1663), *Renati Des Cartes Principiorum philosophiae, more geometrico demonstratae*, in Spinoza (1954), pp. 203–299.

Spinoza, Baruch (1670), *Tractatus theologico-politicus*, in Spinoza (1954), pp. 662–964.

Spinoza, Baruch (1677), *Ethica ordine geometrico demonstrata*, in Spinoza (1954), pp. 365–652.

Spinoza, Baruch (1954), *Oeuvres complètes de Spinoza*, ed. Roland Caillois, Madeleine Francès and Robert Misrahi, Paris.

Sprat, Thomas (1667), *The History of the Royal Society of London, for the Advancement of Experimental Philosophy*, London.

Stevin, Simon (1586), *De beghinselen des waterwichts*, Leyden.

Stigelius, Johannes (1570), *De anima commentarii clarissimi ... D. Philippi explicatio*, Mühlhausen.

Strigelius, Victorinus (1590), *In Philippi Melanchthonis libellum de anima*, Leipzig.

Struve, Georg Adam (1663), *Syntagma juris civilis*, Jena.

Stryck, Samuel (1706), *Tractatus de Successione ab intestato*, Frankfurt.

Suárez, Francisco ([1644] 1944), *Selections from Three Works (De legibus, ac Deo legislatore, 1612; Defensio fidei catholicae, et apostolicae adversus anglicanae sectae errores, 1613; De triplici virtute theologica, fide, spe, et charitate, 1621)*, ed. James Brown Scott, 2 vols, Oxford and London.

Tafinger, Wilhelm Gottlieb (1794), *Lehrsätze des Naturrechts*, Tübingen.

Thiers, Jean-Baptiste (1741), *Traité des superstitions qui regardent les sacremens*, 4th edn, 4 vols, Paris.

Thomas, Anton (1803), *Lehrbuch der natürlichen Rechtswissenschaft*, Frankfurt am Main.

Thomas von Aquin (1955), *Summa theologica 1–11* (German edition, vol. 10): *Die menschlichen Leidenschaften*, Heidelberg/Graz/Vienna/Cologne.

Thomas von Aquin (1988), 'Über den Lehrer. De magistro. Quaestiones disputatae de veritate', Quaestio XI; *Summa theologiae*, Pars 1, quaestio 117, articulus 1, ed. G. Jüssen (et al.), Hamburg.

Thomasius, Christian (1685), *Vom Laster der zwiefachen Ehe*, Leipzig.

Thomasius, Christian ([1688] 1730), *Institutionum jurisprudentiae divinae libri tres*, 7th edn, Halle an der Saale.

Thomasius, Christian (1705), *Fundamenta juris naturae et gentium ex sensu communi deducta*, in usum auditorii Thomasiani, Halae et Lipsiae; 1718, 4th edn, Halle and Leipzig.

Thomasius, Christian (1710), *Cautelae circa praecognita jurisprudentiae in usum auditorii Thomasiani*, Halle an der Saale.

Thomasius, Christian (1713), *Notae ad singulos institutionum et pandectarum titulos varias juris Romani antiquitates*, Halle an der Saale.

Thomasius, Christian (1720), *Institutiones jurisprudentiae divinae libri tres*; reprinted 1963, Aalen.

Timpler, Clemens (1605), *Physicae seu philosophiae naturalis systema methodicum*, Hanau.

Titelmans, Franciscus (1530), *Libri de consideratione rerum naturalium earumque ad suum creatorem reductione*, Antwerp.

Titelmans, Franciscus (1552), *Compendium physicae*, Paris.

Titelmans, Franciscus (1572), *Compendium naturalis philosophiae, sive de consideratione rerum naturalium lib. xii*, Venice.

Tittmann, Carl August (1800), *Grundlinien der Strafrechtswissenschaft und der deutschen Strafgesetzkunde*, Leipzig.

Toletus, Franciscus (1615), *Commentaria una cum quaestionibus in octo libros Aristotelis de physica auscultatione*, Cologne.

Valerius, Cornelius (1567), *Physicae seu de naturae philosophia institutio*, Antwerp.

Vasquez, Gabriel (1611), *Commentariorum ac disputationum in Primam Secundae ... tomus primus-secundus*, Ingolstadt.

Vasquez, Gabriel (1620), *Commentariorum ac disputationum in primam secundae Sancti Thomae tomus 2*, Lyons.

Vattel, Emer de (1747), *Essai sur le fondement du droit naturel. , ibid: Le loisir philosophique ou pièces diverses de philosophie, de morale et d'amusement* (Part 1), Dresden.

Velcurio, Johannes Bernhardi (1537), *In philosophiae naturalis partem omnium praestantissimam ... de anima libros*, ed. W. Bigot, Basle.

Velcurio, Johannes Bernhardi (1538), *Epitome physicae libri quatuor*, Erfurt.

Velcurio, Johannes Bernhardi (1540), *Commentarii in universam phyiscam Aristotelis libri quatuor*, ed. S. Hauwenreuter, Tübingen.

Vicomercatus, Franciscus (1596), *De principiis rerum naturalium libri tres*, Venice.

Vigelius, Nicolaus (1603), *Constitutiones Carolina Codee publicorum juridicorum*, Basle.

Vitoria, Francisco de (1557), *Relectiones theologicae*, Lyons.

Vultejus, Hermann (1614), *Jurisprudentiae Romanae a Justiniano compositae libri II*, 4th edn, Marburg.

Waldung, Wolfgangus (1611), *Publica de monstris disputatio, resp. Joannes Saubertus*, Altdorf.

Wallis, John (1666), 'An Essay, of Dr. John Wallis, exhibiting his Hypothesis about the Flux and Reflux of the Sea', *Philosophical Transactions of the Royal Society of London*, 1: 263–289.

Wallis, John (1669), 'A summary account of the General Laws of Motion', *Philosophical Transactions of the Royal Society of London*, 3: 864–866.

Weinrichius, Martinus (1595), *De ortu monstrorum commentarius, in qua essentia, differentiae, causae et affectiones mirabilium animalium explicantur*, Leipzig.

Wesenbeck, Matthaeus (1582), *In Pandectas iuris civilis et Codicis Iustinianei lib. IIX. commentarii*, Basle.

White, Thomas (1657), *Euclides physicus seu de principiis naturae staecheidea*, London.

Wiggers, Johann (1634), *In Primam Secundae divi Thomae Aquinatis commentaria*, Louvain.

Wildenberg, Hieronymus Gürtler von (1548), *Totius naturalis philosophiae epitome*, Paris.

Winkler, Benedict (1615), *Principiorum iuris libri quinque*, Leipzig.

Wolff, Christian (1716), *Mathematisches Lexicon*, Leipzig.

Wolff, Christian (1733), *Ausführliche Nachricht von seinen eigenen Schrifften, die er in deutscher Sprache von den verschiedenen Theilen der Welt-Weißheit heraus gegeben*, Frankfurt am Main.

Wolff, Christian (1735), *Ratio praelectionum Wolfianarum mathesin et philosophiam universam*, 2nd edn, Halle an der Saale.

Wolff, Christian (1736), *Philosophia prima, sive ontologia, methodo scientifica pertractata*, Frankfurt and Leipzig.

Wolff, Christian (1738), *Philosophia practica universalis, pars prior*, Frankfurt and Leipzig.

Wolff, Christian (1750), *Institutiones juris naturae et gentium*; reprinted 1969, Hildesheim.

Wolff, Christian (1751), *Vernünfftige Gedanken Von Gott, der Welt und der Seele des Menschen, Auch allen Dingen überhaupt, Den Liebhabern der Wahrheit mitgetheilet*, new edition, Halle an der Saale.

Wolff, Christian (1978), 'Vorbericht von der Welt-Weisheit', in *Gesammelte Werke*, I. Abteilung: Deutsche Schriften, vol. 1: *Vernünftige Gedanken*, ed. Hans Werner Arndt, Hildesheim and New York.

Wolff, Christian (1754), 'Grundsätze des Natur- und Völkerrechts', in *Gesammelte Werke*, ed. M. Thomann, vol. 19, Magdeburg; reprinted 1968, Hildesheim.

Wren, Christopher (1669), 'Dr. Christopher Wren's Theory concerning the same subject [i.e. the Laws of Motion]', *Philosophical Transactions of the Royal Society of London*, 3: 867–868.

Zabarella, Jacopo (1586–87), *Opera logica*, ed. Giulio Pace, [Heidelberg].

Zabarella, Jacopo (1590), *De rebus naturalibus libri xxx*, Cologne.

Zabarella, Jacopo (1597), *Opera logica*, preface by Joannes Hawenreuter, Cologne.

Zachariae, Karl Salomon (1829), 'Ueber den Zweck dieser Zeitschrift. Statt einer Vorrede', in *Kritische Zeitschrift für Rechtswissenschaft und Gesetzgebung des Auslandes*, ed. C.J.A. Mittermaier and K.S. Zachariae, vol. 1, Heidelberg.

Zanchius, Hieronymus (1602), *De operibus Dei intra spacium sex dierum creatis opus*, 3rd edn, Neustadt.

Zasius, Ulrich (1550), *Opera omnia* I, Lyons.

Zedlers Grosses vollständiges Universal aller Wissenschafften und Künste (1740), vol. 23, Leipzig and Halle.

Zeiller, Franz Edler von (1806), 'Nothwendigkeit eines bürgerlichen, einheimischen Privat-Rechts. Grundzüge zur Geschichte des Oesterreichischen Privat-Rechts. Eigenschaften eines bürgerlichen Gesetzbuches', in F.E. von Zeiller, *Jährlicher Beytrag zur Gesetzkunde und Rechtswissenschaft in den Oesterreichischen Erbstaaten*, vol. 1, Vienna.

Zincgref, Julius Wilhelm (1993a), *Emblemata ethico-politica, Erster Teilband, Text*, ed. Dieter Mertens and Theodor Verweyen, Tübingen.

Zincgref, Julius Wilhelm (1993b), *Emblemata ethico-politica, Zweiter Teilband, Erläuterungen und Verifizierungen*, ed. Dieter Mertens and Theodor Verweyen, Tübingen.

Zúñiga, Diego, OSA ([1584]1691), *In Iob Commentaria*, Rome.

Secondary Sources

Affolter, Albert (1904), *Naturgesetze und Rechtsgesetze*, Munich.

Albert, Hans (1991), *Traktat über kritische Vernunft*, 5th edn, Tübingen.

Althusser, Louis (1964), *Montesquieu la politique et l'histoire*, Paris.

Alunni, C. (1982), 'Codex Naturae et Libro della Natura chez Campanella et Galilée', in *Annali della Scuola Normale Superiore di Pisa*, serie III, vol. XII, 1, Pisa: 189–239.

Amari, Emerico (1857), *Critica di una scienza delle legislazione comparate*, II, Ristampa (1969), Palermo.

Andresen, Carl (1968), 'Gedanken zum philosophischen Bildungshorizont Augustins vor und in Cassiciacum', *Augustinus*, 13: 93ff.

Anstey, Peter (2002), 'Boyle on Seminal Principles', *Studies in the History of the Biological and Biomedical Sciences*, 33: 537–630.

Arámburu Cendoya, Ignacio (1961), 'Fr. Diego de Zúñiga: biografía y nuevos escritos', *Archivo Augustiniano*, vol. 55, no. 163, pp. 51–103; no. 165, pp. 329–384.

Aries, Philippe (1984), 'Überlegungen zur Geschichte der Homosexualität', in P. Aries, A. Bejin, M. Foucault et al., eds, *Die Masken des Begehrens und die Metamorphosen der Sinnlichkeit. Zur Geschichte der Sexualität im Abendland*, Frankfurt am Main, pp. 80–96.

Armgardt, Matthias (2001), *Das Rechtslogische System der 'Doctrina conditionum' von Gottfried Wilhelm Leibniz*, Marburg.

Armogathe, Jean-Robert (2007), *La nature du monde. Science neuve et exégèse au XVIIe siécle*, Paris.

Arndt, Hans Werner (1971), *Methodo scientifica pertractatum. Mos geometricus und Kalkülbegriff in der philosophischen Theorienbildung des 17. und 18. Jahrhunderts*, Quellen und Studien zur Philosophie, vol. 4, Berlin and New York.

Arndt, Hans Werner (1978), 'Einführung des Herausgebers', in Christian Wolff, *Gesammelte Werke*, I. Abteilung: Deutsche Schriften, vol. 1: *Vernünftige Gedanken von den Kräften des menschlichen Verstandes*, Hildesheim and New York.

Arnold, Wilhelm (1865), *Kultur und Rechtsleben*, Berlin.

Asch, Ronald G., ed. (1996), *Der Absolutismus – ein Mythos. Strukturwandel monarchischer Herrschaft in West- und Mitteleuropa*, Köln.

Asendorf, Urich (1982), 'Eschatologie VII: Reformations- und Neuzeit', *Theologische Realenzyklopädie*, 10: 310–334.

Axmacher, Elke (1989), *Praxis Evangeliorum. Theologie und Frömmigkeit bei Martin Moller (1547–1606)*, Göttingen.

Barker, Peter (1997), 'Kepler's epistemology', in *Method and Order in Renaissance Philosophy of Nature*, ed. Daniel A. Di Liscia, Eckhard Kessler and Charlotte Methuen, Aldershot, pp. 355–68.

Barnes, Jonathon (1996), 'Le Dieu de Descartes et les vérités éternelles', *Studia Philosophica*, 55:163–192.

Barnes, Robin B. (1988), *Prophecy and Gnosis. Apocalypticism in the Wake of the Lutheran Reformation*, Stanford.

Barnes, Robin B. (1999), 'Der herabstürzende Himmel: Kosmos und Apokalypse unter Luthers Erben um 1600', in *Jahrhundertwenden. Endzeit- und Zukunftsvorstellungen vom 15. bis zum 20. Jahrhundert*, ed. Manfred Jakubowski-Tiessen, Göttingen, pp. 129–145.

Bastit, Michel (1990), *Naissance de la loi moderne. La pensée de la loi de saint Thomas à Suárez*, Paris.

Bauer, A. (1808), *Lehrbuch des Naturrechts*, Marburg.

Bauer, C. (1951), 'Melanchthons Naturrechtslehre', *Archiv für Reformationsgeschichte*, 42: 64–100.

Behrends, O., ed. (1993), *Privatrecht heute und Jherings evolutionäres Rechtsdenken*, Cologne.

Bellucci, D. (1998), *Science de la nature et Réformation*, Rome.

Ben-Chaim, Michael (2002), 'Empowering Lay Belief: Robert Boyle and the Moral Economy of Experiment', *Science in Context*, 15: 51–77.

Bennett, Jonathan (1994), 'Descartes's Theory of Modality', *The Philosophical Review*, 103: 639–667.

Bernhardt, Reinhold (1999), *Was heißt 'Handeln Gottes'? Eine Rekonstruktion der Lehre von der Vorsehung*, Gütersloh.

Berry, Christopher J. (1994), *The Idea of Luxury, A conceptual and historical investigation*, Cambridge.

Beutin, Wolfgang (1990), *Sexualität und Obszönität, Eine literaturpsychologische Studie über epische Dichtungen des Mittelalters und der Renaissance*, Würzburg.

Beyssade, Jean-Marie (1979), *La Philosophie première de Descartes*, Paris.

Binoche, Bertrand (1998), *Introduction à De l'esprit des lois de Montesquieu*, Paris.

Blair, Ann (1997), *The Theater of Nature: Jean Bodin and Renaissance Science*, Princeton.

Blair, Ann (2000), 'Mosaic Physics and the Search for a Pious Natural Philosophy in the Late Renaissance', *Isis*, 91: 32–58.

Blickle, P. (1998), *Der Bauernkrieg. Die Revolution des Gemeinen Mannes*, Munich.

Blumenberg, Hans, (1996), *Die Genesis der kopernikanischen Welt: Die Zweideutigkeit des Himmels. Eröffnung der Möglichkeit des Kopernikus*, 3rd edn, 3 vols, Frankfurt am Main.

Bobzien, Suzanne (1998), *Determinism and Freedom in Stoic Philosophy*, Oxford.

Bona, Ferdinando (1987), 'La certezza del diritto nella giurisprudenza tardo-repubblicana', in *La certezza del diritto nell'esperienza giuridica romana*, ed. Manlio Sargenti and Giorgio Luraschi, Padua.

Bono, James J. (1999), 'From Paracelsus to Newton: The World of God, the Book of Nature, and the Eclipse of the "Emblematic World View"', in *Newton and Religion. Context, Nature, and Influence*, ed. James E. Force and Richard H. Popkin, Dordrecht, pp. 45–76.

Bouillier, Francisque (1868), *Histoire de la philosophie cartésienne*, 3rd edn, 2 vols, reprinted 1972, Hildesheim and New York.

Braun, Christina von (1989), 'Die Blutschande', in C. von Braun, *Die schamlose Schönheit des Vergangenen*, Frankfurt, pp. 81–113.

Brecht, Martin (1993), 'Das Aufkommen der neuen Frömmigkeitsbewegung in Deutschland', *Geschichte des Pietismus 1: Der Pietismus vom siebzehnten bis zum frühen achtzehnten Jahrhundert*, ed. Martin Brecht, Göttingen, pp. 113–203.

Brett, Annabel S. (1997), *Liberty, Right and Nature: Individual Rights in Late Scholastic Thought*, Cambridge.

Brooke, John Hedley (1991), *Science and Religion. Some Historical Perspectives*, Cambridge.

Brooke, John Hedley and Cantor, Geoffrey (1998), *Reconstructing Nature: The Engagement of Science and Religion*, Oxford.

Buchholz, Stephan (1987), 'Erunt tres aut quattuor in carne una. Aspekt der neuzeitlichen Polygamiediskussion', in *Zur Geschichte des Familien- und Erbrechts. Untersuchungen und Perspektiven*, ed. H. Mohnhaupt, Frankfurt, pp. 71–91.

Buck, A. (1985), *Machiavelli*, Darmstadt.

Bünger, C. (1893), *Matthias Bernegger. Ein Bild aus dem geistigen Leben Strassburgs zur Zeit des Dreissigjährigen Krieges*, Strasbourg.

Busche, Hubertus (1993), 'Die drei Stufen des Naturrechts und die Ableitung materialer Gerechtigkeitsnormen beim frühen Leibniz – Zur Vorgeschichte der "caritas sapientis"', in *Realität und Begriff, Festschrift für Jakob Barion*, ed. Peter Baumanns, Würzburg, pp. 105–149.

Busche, Hubertus (1997), *Leibniz' Weg ins perspektivische Universum – Eine Harmonie im Zeitalter der Berechnung*, Hamburg.

Cantimori, D. (1976), 'Introduzione', in N. Machiavelli, *Il Principe e le opere politiche*, Garzanti.

Cartwright, Nancy (1983), *How the Laws of Physics Lie*, Oxford.

Casini, Paolo (1976), 'La Loi naturelle : réflexion politique et sciences exactes', *Studies on Voltaire and the Eighteenth Century*, 151(27): 417–432.

Caspar, Max and van Dyck, Walther, eds (1930), *Johannes Kepler in seinen Briefen*, 2 vols, Berlin, vol 1.

Cassirer, Ernst (1906), *Das Erkenntnisproblem in der Philosophie und Wissenschaft der neueren Zeit*, Berlin.

Cassirer, Ernst (1987), *Le problème Jean-Jacques Rousseau* (1932), Paris.

Céard, Jean (1996), *La Nature et les prodiges: L'Insolite au XVIe siècle*, Geneva.

Chevalley, Catherine (1995), 'Nature et loi dans la philosophie moderne', in *Notions de philosophie*, ed. Denis Kambouchner, 3 vols, Paris, vol. 1, pp. 127–230.

Courcelle, Pierre (1939), 'Étude critique des commentaires sur la *Consolatio Philosophiae* de Boèce (IX–XVè siècles)', *AHDLMA* 14.

Courcelle, Pierre ([1943] 1948), *Les Lettres grecques en Occident, de Macrobe à Cassiodore*, 2nd edn, Paris.

Courtenay, William J. (1990), *Capacity and Volition: A History of the Distinction of Absolute and Ordained Power*, Bergame.

Courtenay, William J. (1995), 'Was there an Ockhamist School?', in *Philosophy and Learning: Universities in the Middle Ages*, ed. M.J.F.M. Hoenen, J.H.J. Schneider and G. Wieland, Leiden and New York, pp. 263–292.

Courtine, Jean-François (1999), *Nature et empire de la loi, Etudes suareziennes*, Paris.

Cox, Virginia (1992), *The Renaissance Dialogue. Literary dialogue in its social political contexts, Castiglione to Galileo*, Cambridge.

Crocker, Robert (1990), 'Henry More: A biographical essay', in *Henry More (1614–1687): Tercentenary Studies*, with a biography and bibliography by Robert Crocker, ed. Sarah Hutton and Robert Crocker, Dordrecht, pp. 1–17.

Crombie, Alistair C. (1994), *Styles of Scientific Thinking in the European Tradition: The history of argument and explanation especially in the mathematical and biomedical sciences and arts*, London.

Crowther-Heyck, K. (2003), 'Wonderful secrets of nature: natural knowledge and religious piety in Reformation Germany', *Isis*, 94: 253–273.

Cunningham, A.R. (1991), 'How the *Principia* got its name; or, taking natural philosophy seriously', *History of Science*, 29: 377–392.

Curley, E.M. (1984), 'Descartes on the Creation of the Eternal Truths', *The Philosophical Review*, 93(4): 569–597.

Daston, Lorraine, (1988), *Classical Probability in the Enlightenment*, Princeton.

Daston, Lorraine (1992), 'Baconian Facts, Academic Civility and the Prehistory of Objectivity', *Annals of Scholarship*, 8: 337–363.

Daston, Lorraine (1998a), 'The Nature of Nature in Early Modern Europe', *Configurations*, 6: 149–172.

Daston, Lorraine, (1998b), 'Wunder und Beweise im Frühneuzeitlichen Europa', in *Die ungewisse Evidenz. Für eine Kulturgeschichte des Beweises*, ed. Gary Smith and Matthias Kroß, Berlin, pp. 13–68.

Daston, Lorraine (2000a), *Eine kurze Geschichte der wissenschaftlichen Aufmerksamkeit*, Munich.

Daston, Lorraine (2000b), 'Natural laws and the problem of variability, 1660–1730', Natural Law Conference paper, Berlin.

Daston, Lorraine and Park, Katharine (1998), *Wonders and the Order of Nature, 1150–1750*, New York.

Davis, Edward B., and Hunter, Michael (1996), 'The Making of Robert Boyle's Free Inquiry into the Vulgarly Received Notion of Nature (1686)', *Early Science and Medicine*, 1(2): 204–270.

Davis, N.Z. (1966), 'Publisher Guillame Rouillé: businessman and humanist', in *Editing Sixteenth-Century Texts*, ed. R. J. Schoeck, Toronto, pp. 72–112.

Deason, Gary B. (1986), 'Reformation Theology and the Mechanistic Conception of Nature,' in *God and Nature, Historical Essays on the Encounter Between Christianity and Science*, ed. David C. Lindberg and Ronald L. Numbers, Berkeley, pp. 167–191.

Desaive, Jean–Paul, Goubert, Jean-Pierre, Ladurie, Emmanuel Leroy, Meyer, Jean, Muller, Otto and Peter, Jean-Pierre (1972), *Médecins, climat et épidémies à la fin du XVIIIe siècle*, Paris.

Des Chene, Dennis (1996), *Physiologia: Natural Philosophy in Late Aristotelian and Cartesian Thought*, Ithaca and London.

Desplaces, Edouard (1962), 'La tradition indirecte des *Lois* de Platon (livres VII–XII)', in *Studia patristica*, 5, Berlin; reprinted 1981 in E. Desplaces, *Études platoniciennes (1929–1979)*, Leiden.

Desplaces, Edouard (1976), *Platonismo e tradizione cristiana*, Milan.

Diestelkamp, Bernhard (1977), 'Das Verhältnis von Gesetz und Gewohnheitsrecht im 16. Jahrhundert', in *Rechtshistorische Studien, Hans Thieme zum 60. Geburtstag zugeeignet*, Cologne and Vienna, pp. 1–33.

Dölemeyer, Barbara (2000), 'Kodifizierung/Kodifikation', in *Der Neue Pauly. Enzyklopädie der Antike*, ed. Manfred Landfester, Bd. 14, Stuttgart and Weimar.

Drake, Stilman (1983), *Telescopes, Tides and Tactics: a Galilean dialogue about the 'Starry messenger' and systems of the world*, Chicago.

Dreier, H. (1999), 'Die Natürlichkeit des Menschen und die Künstlichkeit des Rechts', in *Streitsache Mensch. Zur Auseinandersetzung zwischen Natur- und Geisteswissenschaften*, ed. H.M. Baumgartner et al., Stuttgart, Düsseldorf and Leipzig, pp. 281–303.

Drouet, J. (1912), *L'Abbé de Saint-Pierre, l'homme et l'œuvre*, Paris.

Dufour, Alfred (1980), 'L'Influence de la méthodologie des sciences physiques et mathématiques sur les fondateurs de l'École du Droit Naturel moderne', *Grotiana*, 1: 33–52.

Duhem, P. (1958), *Le Système du monde*, vol. 3, *L'Astronomie latine au moyen âge*, Paris.

Eastwood, B. and Graßhoff, G. (2003), 'Planetary Diagrams – Descriptions, Models, Theories: From Carolingian Deployments to Copernican Debates', in *The Power of Images in Early Modern Science*, ed. W. Lefèvre, J. Renn and U. Schoepflin, Basle.

Ebel, Wilhelm (1988), *Geschichte der Gesetzgebung in Deutschland*, reprint of 2nd edn (1958), Göttingen.

Eckart, Wolfgang U. (1992), 'Antiparacelsismus, okkulte Qualitäten und medizinisch-wissenschaftliches Erkennen im Werk Daniel Sennerts', in *Die okkulten Wissenschaften in den Renaissance*, ed. August Buck, Wiesbaden, pp. 139–158.

École Française de Rome (1991), *Théologie et droit dans la science politique de l'état moderne*, Rome.

Ehrard, Jean ([1963] 1994), *L'Idée de nature en France dans la première moitié du XVIIIe siècle*, 2nd edn, Paris.

Eisler, Rudolf (1910), 'Gesetz', in *Wörterbuch der philosophischen Begriffe*, vol. 1, Berlin.

Elster, Jon (1975), *Leibniz et la formation de l'esprit capitaliste*, Paris.

Erle, Manfred (1952), *Die Ehe im Naturrecht des 17. Jahrhunderts*, Göttingen.

Feingold, Mordechai (2002), 'Science as a Calling? The Early Modern Dilemma', *Science in Context*, 15: 79–119.

Feldman, Theodore Sherman (1983), 'The History of Meteorology, 1750–1800: A Study in the Quantification of Experimental Physics', unpublished Ph.D. dissertation, University of California, Berkeley.

Fischer, Michael W. (1985), *Rationalisierung der Gesetzgebung. Historische Bemerkungen mit einem wissenschaftskritischen Kommentar*, Frankfurt am Main.

Foster, Michael (1934), 'The Christian Doctrine of Creation and the Rise of Modern Natural Science', *Mind*, 43: 446–58.

Fothergill, Robert A. (1974), *Private Chronicles: A Study of English Diaries*, London.

Frankfurt, Harry (1977), 'Descartes on the Creation of the Eternal Truths', *The Philosophical Review*, 86: 36–57.

Freedman, Joseph S. (1988), *European Academic Philosophy in the Late Sixteenth and Early Seventeenth Centuries: The life, significance, and philosophy of Clemens Timpler (1563/4–1624)*, 2 vols, Hildesheim, Zürich and New York.

Freedman, Joseph S. (1997), 'The Career and Writings of Bartholomew Keckermann', *Proceedings of the American Philosophical Society*, 141: 307–64.

French, R.K. and Cunningham, R. (1996), *Before Science: The Invention of the Friars' Natural Philosophy*, Aldershot.

Frey, Christopher (1994), 'Natur und Übernatur', *Theologische Realenzyklopädie*, 24: 107–113.

Frisinger, H. Howard (1977), *The History of Meteorology: To 1800*, New York.

Funkenstein, Amos (1986), *Theology and Scientific Imagination: From the Middle Ages to the seventeenth century*, Princeton.

Gagnér, Sten (1960), *Studien zu Ideengeschichte der Gesetzgebung*, Uppsala.

Gamm, Gerhard (1994), *Flucht aus der Kategorie. Die Positivierung des Unbestimmten als Ausgang der Moderne*, Frankfurt am Main.

Garber, Daniel, (1992), *Descartes' Metaphysical Physics*, Chicago and London.

Garber, Daniel and Ayers, Michael, eds (1998), *Cambridge History of Seventeenth-Century Philosophy*, 2 vols, Cambridge.

Gaskell, P. (1979), 'Books bought by Whitgift's pupils in the 1570s', *Transactions of the Cambridge Bibliographical Society*, 7(3): 284–93.

Gaudemar, Martine de (1995), 'Nature individuelle, nature essentielle et lois naturelles', *Studia Leibnitiana* – Sonderheft 24: *La Notion de nature chez Leibniz*, ed. Martine de Gaudemar, Stuttgart, pp. 143–155.

Gawlick, Günter (1994), *T.H.: Vom Menschen. Vom Bürger*, 3rd edn, Hamburg.

Georges (1972), *Ausführliches Handwörterbuch Lateinisch–Deutsch*: 'crimen', vol. 1, 13th edn, Hanover.

Geyer, Hermann (2001a), *Verborgene Weisheit: Johann Arndts 'Vier Bücher vom Wahren Christentum' als Programm einer spiritualistisch-hermetischen Theologie*, 3 vols, Berlin.

Geyer, Hermann (2001b), '"die pur lautere Essenz und helles Licht": Verschmelzung von Alchemie und Theologie in Johann Arndts "Vier Büchern vom Wahren Christentum" (1605/10)', in *Antike Weisheit und kulturelle Praxis. Hermetismus in der Frühen Neuzeit*, ed. Anne-Charlott Trepp and Hartmut Lehmann, Göttingen, pp. 81–101.

Gibson, Margaret (1969), 'The Study of the "Timaeus" in the Eleventh and Twelfth Centuries', *Pensamiento* 25.

Gigerenzer, Gerd, Swijtink, Leo, Porter, Theodore, Daston, Lorraine, Beatty, John and Kruger, Lorenz (1990), *The Empire of Chance*, Cambridge.

Gilbert, Neil W. (1960), *Renaissance Concepts of Method*, New York.

Gilly, Carlos (1977–79), 'Zwischen Erfahriung und Spekulation: Theodor Zwinger und die religiöse und kulturelle Krise seiner Zeit', *Baseler Zeitschrift für Geschichte und Altertumskunde*, 77 (1977): 57–137; and 79 (1979): 125–223.

Globig, Hans Ernst von and Huster, Johann Georg (1969), *Abhandlung von der Criminal-Gesetzgebung*, Frankfurt.

Glück, Christian Friedrich (1797), *Vollständige Erläuterung der Pandecten nach Hellfeld. Ein Commentar*, Part 1, 2nd edn, Erlangen.

Glucker, John (1995), 'Probabile, veri simile and related terms', in *Cicero the Philosopher*, ed. J.G.F. Powell, Oxford, pp. 115–144.

Goldammer, Kurt (1991), *Der göttliche Magier und die Magierien Natur. Religion, Naturmagie und die Anfänge der Naturwissenschaft vom Spätmittelalter bis zur Renaissance*, Stuttgart.

Gouhier, Henri (1926), *La Philosophie de Malebranche et son expérience religieuse*, Paris.

Grabmann, M. (1936), 'Eine für Examinazwecke abgefasste Quaestionensammlung der Pariser Artistenfakultät aus der ersten Hälfte des XIII. Jahrhunderts', in *Mittelalterliches Geistesleben*, II, Munich.

Graßhoff, Gerd (2000), 'Keplers Naturgesetz der Planetenbewegung', Natural Law Conference paper, Berlin.

Graßhoff, Gerd and Treiber, Hubert (2002), *Naturgesetz und Naturrechtsdenken im 17. Jahrhundert. Kepler – Bernegger – Descartes – Cumberland, Fundamenta Juridica*, Beiträge zur rechtswissenschaftlichen Grundlagenforschung 44, Baden-Baden.

Grawert, Rolf (1975), 'Gesetz', in *Geschichtliche Grundbegriffe*, vol. 2, ed. O. Brunner, W. Conze and R. Koselleck, Stuttgart, pp. 863–922.

Gregory, Tullio (1958), *Platonismo medievale. Studi e ricerche*, Studi storici 26–27, Rome.

Gregory, Tullio (1963), *Giovanni Scoto Eriugena. Tre studi*, Florence.

Gregory, Tullio (2007), *Speculum naturale. Percorsi del pensiero medievale*, Rome.

Greschat, Martin (1968), 'Die Funktion des Emblems in Johann Arnds "Wahrem Christentum"', *Zeitschrift für Religions- und Geistesgeschichte*, 20: 154–174.

Greyerz, Kaspar von (1999) 'Die Konfessionalisierung der Apokalyptik', in *Zeitstruktur und Apokalyptik. Interdisziplinäre Betrachtungen zur Jahrtausendwende*, ed. Urban Fink and Alfred Schindler, Zurich, pp. 163–179.

Greyerz, Kaspar von (2001), 'Wissenschaft, Endzeiterwartungen und Alchemie im England des 17. Jahrhunderts', in *Antike Weisheit und kulturelle Praxis. Hermetismus in der Frühen Neuzeit*, ed. Anne-Charlott Trepp and Hartmut Lehmann, Göttingen, pp. 205–217.

Gros, Karl Heinrich (1815), *Lehrbuch der philosophischen Rechtswissenschaft oder des Naturrechts*, 3rd edn, Tübingen.

Gruebner, Birgit (1998), *Gott und die Lebendigkeit in der Natur. Eine Interpretation des Dritten und des Vierten Buches von Johann Arndts 'Wahrem Christentum'*, Reinbach.

Grunert, Frank (2000), *Normbegründung und politische Legitimität. Zur Rechts- und Staatsphilosophie der deutschen Frühaufklärung*, Tübingen.

Gundlach, F. (1927), *Catalogus professorum Academiae Marburgensis 1527–1910*, Marburg.

Gunther, R.T., ed. (1923), *Early Science in Oxford*, Oxford.

Haakonssen, Knud (1996), *Natural Law and Moral Philosophy, From Grotius to the Scottish Enlightenment*, Cambridge.

Hacking, Ian (1975), *The Emergence of Probability. A philosophical study of early ideas about probability, induction and statistical inference*, London and New York.

Hahn, Roger (1971), *The Anatomy of a Scientific Institution: The Paris Academy of Sciences, 1666–1803*, Berkeley.

Hall, Alfred Rupert (1990), *Henry More: magic, religion and experiment*, Oxford.

Hall, Marie Boas (1970), *Nature and Nature's Laws*, New York.

Hall, Marie Boas (1981), 'Salomon's House Emergent: The Early Royal Society and Cooperative Research', in *The Analytic Spirit: Essays in the History of Science in Honor of Henry Guerlac*, ed. Harry Woolf, Ithaca, pp. 177–194.

Hampe, Michael (2000), 'Gesetz, Natur, Geltung – Historische Anmerkungen – ', in *Philosophia naturalis*, vol. 37/2, ed. Peter Mittelstaedt and Gerhard Vollmer, Frankfurt am Main, pp. 241–253.

Harrison, Peter (1998), *The Bible, Protestantism and the Rise of Natural Science*, Cambridge.

Hazard, Paul (1961), *La Crise de las conscience europèene*, Paris.

Hellmann, Gustav (1883), *Repertorium der deutschen Meteorologie*, Leipzig.

Hellmann, Gustav (1926), 'Die Entwicklung der meteorologischen Beobachtungen in Deutschland, von den ersten Anfängen bis zur Einrichtung staatlicher Beobachtungsnetze', *Abhandlungen der Preussische Akademie der Wissenschaften, Physisch-Mathematische Klasse*, 1: 1–25.

Hellyer, M. (2005), *Catholic Physics: Jesuit natural philosophy in early modern Germany*, Notre Dame.

Helm, J. and Winkelmann, A., eds (2001), *Religious Confessions and the Sciences in the Sixteenth Century*, Leiden, Boston and Cologne.

Hempel, C.G. and Oppenheim, P. (1948), 'Studies in the Logic of Explanation,' *Philosophy of Science*, 15: 135–175.

Henry, John (2004), 'Metaphysics and the Origins of Modern Science: Descartes and the Importance of Laws of Nature,' *Early Science and Medicine*, 9: 73–114.

Herberger, Maximilian (1981), *Dogmatik: zur Geschichte von Begriff und Methode in Medizin und Jurisprudenz*, Frankfurt am Main.

Hergemöller, Bernd Ulrich (2000), *Sodom und Gomorrha. Zur Alltagswirklichkeit und Verfolgung Homosexueller im Mittelalter*, 2nd edn, Hamburg.

Herivel, John, ed. (1965), *The Background to Newton's Principia*, Oxford.

Hermelink, H. and Kaehler, S.A. ([1927] 1977), *Die Philipps-Universität zu Marburg 1527–1927*, Marburg.

Herrmann, F. (2001), *Das Standardwerk. Franz von Liszt und das Völkerrecht*, Baden-Baden.

Hervada, J. (1983), 'The Old and the New in the Hypothesis "Etiamsi daremus" of Grotius', in *Grotiana*, new series, 4: 3ff.

Heyd, Michael (1995), *'Be Sober and Reasonable': The Critique of Enthusiasm in the Seventeenth and Early Eighteenth Centuries*, Leiden and New York.

Hirschman, Albert O. ([1977]1980), *Les Passions et les intérêts*, French trans. Paris.

Historisches Worterbuch der Rhetorik (1994), ed. Gerd Ueding, vol. 2, Tübingen.

Hochstrasser, T.J. (2000), *Natural Law Theories in the Early Enlightenment*, Cambridge.

Hochstrasser, T.J. and Schröder, P., eds (2003), *Early Modern Natural Law Theories: Contexts and Strategies in the Early Enlightenment*, Dordrecht.

Hoffbauer, Johann Christoph (1804), *Naturrecht, aus dem Begriffe des Rechts entwickelt*, 3rd edn, Halle.

Hofmann, Hasso (1986), *Recht-Politik-Verfassung. Studien zur Geschichte der politischen Philosophie*, Frankfurt am Main.

Horowitz, Maryanne Cline (1998), *Seeds of Virtue and Knowledge*, Princeton.

Hotson, H. (2000), *Johann Heinrich Alsted, 1588–1638: between Renaissance, Reformation and universal Reform*, Oxford.

Hügli, A. (1984), 'Naturrecht IV. 1–3', in *Historisches Wörterbuch der Philosophie* 6 (1984), ed. J. Ritter and K. Gründer, col. 582 et seq.

Hugo, Gustav (1817), *Juristische Encyclopädie*, essay 5, Berlin.

Hunter, Ian (2001), *Rival Enlightenments: Civil and Metaphysical Philosophy in Early Modern Germany*, Cambridge.

Hunter, Ian and Saunders, David, eds (2002), *Natural Law and Civil Sovereignty: Moral Right and State Authority in Early Modern Political Thought*, Houndmills.

Hunter, Michael (1989), *Establishing the New Science: The experience of the early Royal Society*, Woodbridge.

Hunter, Michael (1990), 'First Steps in Institutionalization: The Role of the Royal Society of London', in *Solomon's House Revisited: The Organization and Institutionalization of Science*, ed. Tore Frängsmyr, Canton, pp. 13–30.

Hüttemann, Andreas (1998), 'Scientific Practice and the Disunity of Physics', *Philosophia Naturalis*, 35: 209–222.

Hüttemann, Andreas (2001), 'Über den Zusammenhang zwischen plastic natures, spirit of nature und dem Naturgesetzbegriff bei Cudworth und More', *Studia Leibnitiana* – Sonderheft 31*: Kausalität und Naturgesetz in der frühen Neuzeit*, ed. Andreas Hüttemann, Stuttgart, pp. 139–53.

Ilting, Karl-Heinz (1978), 'Naturrecht', in *Geschichtliche Grundbegriffe* 4, ed. O. Brunner, W. Conze and R. Koselleck, pp. 245ff.

Ilting, Karl-Heinz (1983), *Naturrecht und Sittlichkeit. Begriffsgeschichtliche Studien*, Stuttgart.

Jakob, Ludwig Heinrich (1802), *Philosophische Rechtslehre oder Naturrecht*, 2nd edn, Halle.

Jankovič, Vladimer (2000), *Reading the Skies: A Cultural History of the English Weather, 1650–1820*, Manchester.

Jeauneau, Edouard (1973), *Lectio philosophorum. Recherches sur l'École de Chartres*, Amsterdam.

Jensen, K. (1990), 'Protestant Rivalry – Metaphysics and Rhetoric in Germany c. 1590–1620', *Journal of Ecclesiastical History*, 41(1): 24–43.

Kaltenborn, Carl von (1848), *Die Vorläufer des Hugo Grotius auf dem Gebiete des Ius naturae et gentium sowie der Politik im Reformationszeitalter*, Leipzig; reprinted 1965, Frankfurt am Main.

Kantorowicz, Ernst H. ([1957] 1970), *The King's Two Bodies. A Study in Medieval Political Theology*, Princeton.

Kargon, Robert Hugh (1966), 'Introduction', in *Physiologia Epicuro–Gassendo–Charltoniana: Or a fabrick of science natural, upon the hypothesis of atoms, founded by Epicurus, repaired by Petrus Gassendus, augmented by Walter Charleton*, ed. Robert Hugh Kargon, New York, pp. xiii–v.

Kaufmann, Thomas (1998), *Dreißigjähriger Krieg und Westfälischer Friede: kirchengeschichtliche Studien zur lutherischen Konfessionskultur*, Tübingen.

Kaufmann, Thomas (1999), '1600 – Deutungen der Jahrhundertwende im deutschen Luthertum', in *Jahrhundertwenden. Endzeit- und Zukunftserwartungen vom 15. bis zum 20. Jahrhundert*, ed. Manfred Jakubowski-Tiessen and Hartmut Lehmann, Göttingen, pp. 73–128.

Kaulbach, Friedrich (1984), 'Natur', in *Historisches Wörterbuch der Philosophie*, vol. 6, Darmstadt.

Kemper, Hans-Georg (1981), *Gottebenbildlichkeit und Naturnachahmung im Säkularisierungsprozeß*, 2 vols, Tübingen.

Khrigian, A.K. ([1959] 1970), *Meteorology: A Historical Survey*, trans. and ed. Ron Hardin, Jerusalem.

Kiefner, H. (1990), 'Rezeption (privatrechtlich)', in *Handwörterbuch zur Deutschen Rechtsgeschichte*, vol. 4, col. 970–984.

Kiesow, Rainer M. (1997), *Das Naturgesetz des Rechts*, Frankfurt.

Kington, J.A. (1974), 'The Societatis Meteorologica Palatina', *Weather*, 29: 416–426.

Kirchhoff, A. (1889), 'Lesefrüchte aus den Acten des städischen Archivs zu Leipzig', *Archiv für Geschichte des Deutschen Buchhandels*, 12: 120–127.

Kirk, Linda (1987), *Richard Cumberland and Natural Law. Secularisation of Thought in Seventeenth-Century England*, Cambridge.

Kisch, G. (1967), *Melanchthons Rechts- und Soziallehre*, Berlin.

Klippel, Diethelm (1976), *Politische Freiheit und Freiheitsrechte im deutschen Naturrecht des 18. Jahrhunderts*, Paderborn.

Knebel, Sven K. (1992), 'Necessitas moralis ad optimum (III): Naturgesetz und Induktionsproblem während des zweiten Drittels des 17. Jahrhunderts', *Studia Leibnitiana*, 24: 182–215.

Koch, Elisabeth (1983), 'De polygamia', *Rechtshistorisches Journal*, 2: 266–276.

Kolb, R. (1987), *For All the Saints: Changing perceptions of martyrdom and sainthood in the Lutheran Reformation*, Macon.

Kopp, Hermann ([1886] 1971]), *Die Alchemie in der älteren und neueren Zeit*, Hildesheim.

Korn, Dietrich (1957), *Das Thema des Jüngsten Tages in der Literatur des 17. Jahrhunderts*, Tübingen.

Koselleck, Reinhart (2000), *Vergangene Zukunft. Zur Semantik geschichtlicher Zeiten*, 4th edn, Frankfurt am Main.

Koyré, Alexandre (1998), 'Der Beitrag der Renaissance zur wissenschaftlichen Entwicklung', in A. Koyré, *Leonardo, Galilei, Pascal. Die Anfänge der neuzeitlichen Naturwissenschaft*, Frankfurt am Main, pp. 57–69.

Krafft, Fritz (1999), *'Denn Gott schafft nichts umsonst!' Das Bild der Naturwissenschaft vom Kosmos im historischen Kontext des Spannungsfeldes Gott – Mensch – Natur*, Münster.

Krajewski, Władysław (1968), 'Das Naturgesetz als notwendiger Zusammenhang', in *Der Gesetzesbegriff in der Philosophie und den Einzelwissenschaften*, ed. Günter Kröber, Berlin.

Krause, H. (1952), *Kaiserrecht und Rezeption*, Heidelberg.

Krause, Otto Wilhelm ([1949] 1982), *Naturrechtler des sechzehnten Jahrhunderts. Ihre Bedeutung für die Entwicklung eines natürlichen Privatrechts*, legal dissertation, Göttingen; Frankfurt am Main.

Krause, Peter (1988), 'Naturrecht und Kodifikation', in *Die Aufklärung und die Schwärmer*, ed. Norbert Hinske, Hamburg.

Krawietz, Werner (1974), 'Gesetz I.'', in *Historisches Wörterbuch der Philosophie*, 3, ed. J. Ritter and K. Gründer, col. 480–493.

Kretzmann, Norman (1982), 'Syncategoremata, exponibilia, sophismata', in *The Cambridge History of Later Medieval Philosophy*, ed. N. Kretzmann, A. Kenny and J. Pinborg, Cambridge, pp. 224–231.

Kretzmann, Norman, Kenny, Anthony and Pinborg, Jan, eds (1982), *The Cambridge History of Later Medieval Philosophy*, Cambridge.

Krohn, Wolfgang (2001), 'Das Naturgesetz zwischen Formbegriff und Handlungsregel bei Francis Bacon', *Studia Leibnitiana* – Sonderheft 31: *Kausalität und Naturgesetz in der frühen Neuzeit*, ed. Andreas Hüttemann, Stuttgart, pp. 47–64.

Krolzig, Udo (1988), *Säkularisierung der Natur: Providentia-Dei-Lehre und Naturverständnis der Frühaufklärung*, Neunkirchen-Vluyn.

Kuhn, Thomas (1977), 'Mathematical and Experimental Traditions', in T. Kuhn, *The Essential Tension: Selected Studies in Scientific Tradition and Change*, Chicago.

Kunkel, W. and Schermaier, J. (2001), *Römische Rechtsgeschichte*, 13th edn, Köln, Weimar and Vienna.

Kunz, Erhard (1980), *Protestantische Eschatologie. Von der Reformation bis zur Aufklärung*, Freiburg.

Kusukawa, S. (1995), *The Transformation of Natural Philosophy: The case of Philipp Melanchton*, Cambridge.

Kusukawa, S. (1997), '*Vinculum Concordiae*: Lutheran method by Philip Melanchthon', in *Method and Order in Renaissance Philosophy of Nature: the Aristotle commentary tradition*, ed. Daniel A. Di Liscia, Eckhard Kessler and Charlotte Methuen, Aldershot, pp. 337–354.

Kusukawa, S. (2002a), 'The Reception of Melanchthon's Textbooks in Sixteenth-century Cambridge and Oxford', in *Melanchthon und Europa*, 2. Teilband. WestEuropa, ed. G. Frank, Sigmaringen, pp. 233–254.

Kusukawa, S. (2002b), 'Mediations of Zabarella in Northern Europe: The preface of Johann Ludwig Hawenreuter', in *La presenza dell'Aristotelismo Padovano nella filosofia della prima modernità*, ed. G. Piaia, Rome and Padua, pp. 199–213.

Lamb, Hubert Horace (1982), *Climate, History and the Modern World*, London.

Landsberg, Ernst (1898), 'Winkler, Benedict', in *Allgemeine Deutsche Biographie*, 43, p. 449.

Landsberg, Helmut E. (1980), 'Past climates from Unexploited Written Sources', *Journal of Interdisciplinary History*, 10: 31–642.

Lang, H.S. (1992), *Aristotle's Physics and Its Medieval Varieties*, Albany.

Lantella, Lelio (1987), '"Ius certum", in D. 1. 2. 2.', in *La certezza del diritto nell'esperienza giuridica romana*, ed. Manilio Sargenti and Giorgio Luraschi, Padua.

Larousse (1982), *Grand Dictionnaire du XIX Siecle*, vol. XI (2), Geneva and Paris.

Larrère, Catherine (1989), 'Montesquieu républicain? De l'interprétation universitaire de Montesquieu pendant la troisième République', *Dix-huitième siècle*, 21: 1499–161.

Larrère, Catherine (1992) 'Galiani, lecteur de Montesquieu', in *Eclectisme et cohérence des Lumières. Mélanges offerts à Jean Ehrard*, ed. Jean-Louis Jam, Paris.

Larrère, Catherine (1997a) 'Le Gouvernement de la loi est-il un thème républicain?', *Revue de synthèse*, 2-3: 237–258.

Larrère, Catherine (1997b), 'Divine Dispense', *Droits*, 25: 19–32.

Larrère, Catherine (1999), 'Tradition et modernité', in *1748: année de L'Esprit des lois*, ed. Catherine Larrère and Catherine Volpilhac-Auger, Champion.

Larrère, Catherine (2002), 'Montesquieu and the Republican Heritage in Nineteenth-Century France', in *Montesquieu and the Spirit of Modernity*, ed. David Wallace Carithers and Patrick Coleman, Oxford, pp. 235–250.

Lazzeri, Christian, (1998), 'Peut-on composer les intérêts?', in *Politiques de l'intérêt*, ed. C. Lazzeri and D. Reynié, Besançon.

Lehmann, Hartmut (1980), *Das Zeitalter des Absolutismus: Gottesgnadentum und Kriegsnot*, Stuttgart.

Lehmann, Hartmut (1986), 'Frömmigkeitsgeschichtliche Auswirkungen der "Kleinen Eiszeit"', in *Volksreligiosität in der modernen Sozialgeschichte*, ed. Wolfgang Schieder, Göttingen, pp. 31–50.

Leinkauf, Thomas (2000), 'Der Natur-Begriff des 17. Jahrhunderts und zwei seiner Interpretationen', *Berichte zu Wissenschaftsgeschichte*, 23: 399–418.

Leinsle, U.G. (1985), *Das Ding und die Methode. Methodische Konstitution und Gegenstand der frühen protestantischen Metaphysik*, Augsburg.

Lennon, Thomas M. (1993), 'Mechanism as a Silly Mouse: Bayle's Defense of Occasionalism against the Preestablished Harmony', in Nadler (1993), pp. 181–196.

Lenoble, Robert (1943), *Mersenne ou la naissance du mécanisme*, Paris.

Lenoble, Robert (1968), *Esquisse d'une histoire de l'idée de Nature*, Paris.

Lesser, Andreas (1992), *Friedrich Christian Lesser (1692–1754) und seine Vorfahren, insbesondere die Pfarrerfamilien Maior, Rothmaler und Sagittarius und die Familien Neefe und Stromer*, Munich.

Lindberg, David C. (1986), 'Science and the Early Church', in Lindberg and Numbers (1989), pp. 19–48.

Lindberg, D. and Numbers, R.L., eds (1989), *God and Nature: Historical essays on the encounter between Christianity and science*, Berkeley.

Linden, Stanten J. (1984). 'Alchemy and Eschatology in Seventeenth-Century Poetry', *Ambix*, 31: 102–124.

Lines, D.A. (2008), 'Teaching Physics in Louvain and Bologna: Frans Titelmans and Ulisse Aldrovandi', in *Scholarly Knowledge: Textbooks in Early Modern Europe*, ed. E. Campi et al., Geneva, pp. 183–203.

Link, Christoph (1987), 'Das Gesetz im späten Naturrecht', in *Zum römischen und neuzeitlichen Gesetzesbegriff*, ed. O. Behrends and C. Link, Göttingen, pp. 150ff.

Loeck, Gisela (1986), *Der cartesische Materialismus: Maschine, Gesetz und Simulation*, Frankfurt am Main.

Lohr, C.H. (1988a), *Latin Aristotle Commentaries* II. *Renaissance Authors*, Florence.

Lohr, C.H. (1988b), 'Metaphysics', in *The Cambridge History of Renaissance Philosophy*, ed. C.B. Schmitt and Q.R.D. Skinner, Cambridge, pp. 537–638.

Lohr, Charles (2000), 'The Arabic Backbround to Ramon Lull's Liber Chaos (ca. 1285)', *Traditio*, 55: 159–170.

Long, A.A. (1977), 'Chance and Natural Law in Epicureanism', *Phronesis*, 22: 63–88.

Lotze, Hermann (1856–64), *Mikrokosmus. Ideen zur Naturgeschichte und Geschichte der Menschheit*, 3 vols, Leipzig.

Lowood, Henry E. (1991), *Patriotism, Profit, and the Promotion of Science in the German Enlightenment: The Economic and Scientific Societies, 1760–1815*, New York and London.

Luethy, Christoph (1997), 'Thoughts and Circumstances of Sebastien Basson. Analysis, micro-History, questions', *Early Science and Medicine*, 2: 1–73.

Luhmann, Niklas (1978), *Legitimation durch Verfahren*, 3rd edn, Frankfurt am Main.

Luhmann, Niklas (1992), *Funktion der Religion*, 3rd edn, Frankfurt am Main.

Luig, K. (1969), 'Überwiegendes Mitverschulden', *Jus commune*, 2: 225.

Luig, K. (1983), 'Conring, "das deutsche Recht" und die Rechtsgeschichte', in *Hermann Conring (1606–1681). Beiträge zu Leben und Werk*, ed. M. Stolleis, Berlin, pp. 355–395.

Luig, Klaus (1998), *Römisches Recht, Naturrecht, nationales Recht*, Goldbach.

Lüpke, Johannes von (1999), 'Schöpfer/Schöpfung VII', *Theologische Realenzyklopädie*, 30: 305–326.

McGuire, J.E. (1972), 'Boyle's Conception of Nature', *Journal of the History of Ideas*, 33: 523–542.

McGuire, J.E. and Tamny, M. (1983), *Certain Philosophical Questions: Newton's Trinity notebook*, Cambridge.

MacIntosh, J.J. (1991), 'Boyle on Epicurean Atheism and Atomism', in *Atoms, Pneuma, and Tranquillity: Epicurean and Stoic Themes in European Thought*, ed. Margaret J. Osler, Cambridge, pp. 197–220.

Maclean, Ian (1984), 'The Interpretation of Natural Signs: Cardano's *De subtilitate* versus Scaliger's *Exercitationes*', in *Occult and Scientific Mentalities in the Renaissance*, ed. Brian Vickers, Cambridge, pp. 231–252.

Maclean, Ian (1992), *Interpretation and Meaning in the Renaissance: The case of law*, Cambridge.

Maclean, Ian (1996), *Montaigne philosophe*, Paris.

Maclean, Ian (1998), 'Foucault's Renaissance Episteme Reassessed: An Aristotelian counterblast', *Journal of the History of Ideas*, 59: 149–166.

Maclean, Ian (2000a), 'Evidence, Logic, the Rule and the Exception in Renaissance Law and Medicine', *Early Science and Medicine*, 5: 227–257.

Maclean, Ian, (2000b), 'Humanismus und Späthumanismus im Spiegel der juristischen und medizinischen Fächer', in *Späthumanismus. Studien über das Ende einer kulturhistorischen Epoche*, ed. Notker Hammerstein and Gerrit Walther, Göttingen, pp. 227–244.

Maclean, Ian (2002a), *Logic, Signs and Nature in the Renaissance: The Case of Learned Medicine*, Cambridge.

Maclean, Ian (2002b), 'Mediations of Zabarella in Northern Germany, 1586–1623', in *La presenza dell'Aristotelismo Padovano nella filosofia della prima modernità*, ed. G. Piaia, Rome and Padua, pp. 173–98.

McRae, Robert (1985), 'Miracles and Laws', in *The Natural Philosophy of Leibniz*, ed. K. Okruhlik and J. Brown, Dordrecht.

Mager, Inge (1998), 'Johann Arndts Bildfrömmigkeit', in *Pietas in der Lutherischen Orthodoxie*, ed. Udo Sträter, Wittenberg, pp. 41–60.

Mandelbrote, Scott (2001), *Footprints of the Lion: Isaac Newton at work*, Cambridge.

Mannack, Eberhard (1995), 'Die Stellung der Pegnitzschäfer in der deutschen Barockliteratur', in *Der Franken Rom: Nürnbergs Blütezeit in der zweiten Hälfte des 17. Jahrhunderts*, ed. John Roger Paas, Wiesbaden, pp. 132–145.

Marion, Jean-Luc (1981), *Sur la Théologie blanche de Descartes*, Paris.

Mason, Richard (1996), 'How Things Happen: Divine-natural law in Spinoza', *Studia Leibnitiana*, 28: 17–36.

Mauthner, F. ed. (1912), *Jacobis Spinozabüchlein nebst Replik und Duplik*, Munich.

Mayntz, Renate and Nedelmann, Birgitta (1987), 'Eigendynamische Prozesse. Anmerkungen zu einem analytischen Paradigma', *Kölner Zeitschrift für Soziologie und Sozialpsychologie*, 39: 648–668.

Medick, Hans and Krusenstjern, Benigna von (1999), 'Einleitung: Die Nähe und die Ferne des Dreißigjährigen Krieges', in *Zwischen Alltag und Katastrophe. Der Dreißigjährige Krieg aus der Nähe*, ed. Hans Medick and Benigna von Krustenstjern, Göttingen, pp. 13–36.

Meinel, Christoph, (1988), 'Early Seventeenth-Century Atomism. Theory, epistemology, and the insufficiency of experiment', *Isis*, 79: 68–103.

Middleton, W.E.K. (1964), *The History of the Barometer*, Baltimore.

Middleton, W.E.K. (1966), *A History of the Thermometer and Its Uses in Meteorology*, Baltimore.

Middleton, W.E.K. (1969), *Invention of the Meteorological Instruments*, Baltimore.

Mikat, Paul (1984), 'Polygamie', in *Handwörterbuch zur Deutschen Rechtsgeschichte*, vol. 3, Berlin, pp. 1813–1820.

Mikat, Paul (1988), 'Die Polygamiefrage in der frühen Neuzeit', in *Rheinisch-Westfälische Akademie der Wissenschaften* – Vorträge G 294, Opladen.

Miller, Jon (2003), 'Spinoza and the Concept of a Law of Nature,' *History of Philosophy Quarterly*, 20: 257–276.

Milton, John R. (1981), 'The Origin and Development of the Concept of the "Laws of Nature"', *Archives Européennes de Sociologie*, 22: 173–195.

Milton, John R. (1998), 'Natural Law', in *The Cambridge History of Seventeenth-Century Philosophy*, ed. Daniel Garber and Michael Ayers, Cambridge, vol.I, pp. 680–701.

Mittelstrass, J. (2000), 'Historical and Epistemological Aspects of the Concept of Nature', in *Changing Concepts of Nature at the Turn of the Millennium*, ed. R. Hide, J. Mittelstrass and W.J. Singer, Pontificae Academiae Scientiarum Scripta Varia 95, Vatican City, pp. 3–19.

Mohnhaupt, Heinz (1972), 'Potestas Legislatoria und Gesetzesbegriff im Ancien Régime', *Ius Commune*, 4: 188–239.

Mohnhaupt, Heinz (2000), 'Von den leges fundamentales' zur modernen Verfassung in Europa. Zum begriffs- und dogmengeschichtlichen Befund (16.–18.Jahrhundert)', in H. Mohnhaupt, *Historische Vergleichung im Bereich von Staat und Recht*, Frankfurt, pp. 35ff.

Mohnhaupt, Heinz, ed. (2003), *Prudentia legislatoria*, Munich.

Mohnhaupt, Heinz and Grimm, Dieter (2002), *Verfassung. Zur Geschichte des Begriffs von der Antike bis zur Gegenwart*, 2nd edn, Berlin.

Monti, Maria Teresa (2000), 'Epigenesis of the Monstruous Form and Preformistic "Genetics" (Lémery-Winslow-Haller)', *Early Science and Medicine*, 5(1): 3–32.

Moravia, Sergio (1977), *Beobachtende Vernunft. Philosophie und Anthropologie in der Aufklärung*, Frankfurt.

Moreau, Denis (1999), *Deux Cartésiens. La polémique Arnauld–Malebranche*, Paris.

Mori, Gianluca (1999), *Bayle philosophe*, Paris.

Morrison, James C. (1977), 'Philosophy and History in Bacon', *Journal of the History of Ideas*, 38: 585–606.

Müller, Severin (1973), 'Gesetz', in *Handbuch philosophischer Grundbegriffe*, ed. Hermann Krings, Hans Michael Baumgartner and Christoph Wild, vol. 3, Munich.

Münkler, H. (1982), *Machiavelli. Die Begründung des politischen Denkens der Neuzeit aus der Krise der Republik Florenz*, Frankfurt.

Nadler, Stephen, ed. (1993), *Causation in Early Modern Philosophy*, University Park.

Needham, Joseph (1951), 'Human Laws and the Laws of Nature in China and the West', *Journal of the History of Ideas*, vol. 12, 3–32: 194–231; reprinted 1956 in *Science and Civilization in China* , Cambridge, vol. 2, section 18, pp. 518–583.

Needham, Joseph (1956), *Science and Civilisation in China*, Cambridge.

Needham, Joseph (1969), *The Grand Titration: Science and Society in East and West*, London.

Newman, W.R. (1996), 'Robert Boyle's Corpuscular Philosophy,' *Annals of Science*, 53: 567–585.

Oakley, F. (1961a), 'Christian Theology and the Newtonian Science: the Rise of the Concept of the Laws of Nature', *Church History*, 30-4: 433–458.

Oakley, Francis (1961b), 'Medieval Theory of Natural Law', *Natural Law Forum*, 6: 65–83.

Oakley, Francis (1981), 'Natural Law, the Corpus Mysticum, and Consent in Conciliar Thought from John of Paris to Matthias Ugonius', *Speculum: A Journal of Mediaeval Studies*, 56: 786–810.

Oakley, Francis (1984a), *Omnipotence, Covenant and Order: An Excursion in the History of Ideas from Abelard to Leibniz*, Ithaca.

Oakley, Francis (1984b), *Natural Law, Conciliarism and Consent in the Late Middle Ages: Studies in Ecclesiastical and Intellectual History*, London.

Oakley, Francis (1999), *Politics and Eternity: Studies in the History of Medieval and Early Modern Political Thought*, Leiden.

Oberman, H.A. (1987), 'Via antiqua and via moderna. Late medieval prolegomena to early Reformation thought', in *From Ockham to Wyclif*, ed. Anne Hudson and Michael Wilks, Oxford, pp. 445–463.

Oestmann, P. (1998), 'Die Grenzen richterlicher Rechtskenntnis', in *Colloquia Academica*, (Akademie der Wissenschaften und der Literatur zu Mainz): 37ff.

Oestmann, P. (2002), *Rechtsvielfalt vor Gericht. Rechtsanwendung und Partikularrecht im Alten Reich*, Frankfurt.

Osler, Margaret J. (1994), *Divine Will and the Mechanical Philosophy. Gassendi and Descartes on Contingency and Necessity in the Created World*, Cambridge.

Oster, Malcolm (1994), 'Millenarianism and the New Science. The case of Robert Boyle', in *Samuel Hartlib and Universal Reformation. Studies in Intellectual Communication*, ed. Mark Greengrass, Michael Leslie and Timothy Raylor, Cambridge, pp. 137–148.

Otte, Gerhard, (1970), 'Zwanzig Jahre Topik-Diskussion: Ertrag und Aufgaben', *Rechtstheorie*, 1: 183–197.

Otte, Gerhard, (1971), *Dialektik und Jurisprudenz. Untersuchungen zur Methode der Glossatoren*, Frankfurt am Main.

Otte, Gerhard (1979), 'Der sogenannte Mos Geometricus in der Jurisprudenz', *Quaderni Fiorentini per la storia del pensiero giuidico moderno*, 9, Milan, pp. 179–196.

Otte, Gerhard (1983), 'Leibniz und die juristische Methode', *Zeitschrift für Neuere Rechtsgeschichte*, 5: 1ff.

Palaia, Roberto (1990), 'Naturbegriff und Kraftbegriff im Briefwechsel zwischen Leibniz und Sturm', in *Leibniz's Auseinandersetzung mit Vorgängern und Zeitgenossen, Studia Leibnitiana*, Supplementa 27, Stuttgart, pp. 157–172.

Paqué, Ruprecht (1985), *Le Statut parisien des nominalistes: recherches sur la formation du concept de réalité de la science moderne de la nature: Guillaume d'Occam, Jean Buridan et Pierre d'Espagne, Nicolas d'Autrecourt et Grégoire de Rimini*, trans. from German by Emmanuel Martineau, Paris.

Parker, Geoffrey and Smith, Lesley M., eds (1978), *The General Crisis of the Seventeenth Century*, London.

Parkin, Jonathan Bruce (1999), *Science, Religion and Politics in Restoration England: Richard Cumberland's De legibus naturae*, Woodbridge.

Patrides, C.A., ed. (1969), *The Cambridge Platonists*, Cambridge.

Perrot, Jean-Claude (1992), *Une Histoire intellectuelle de l'économie politique*, Paris.

Petersen, P. (1921), *Geschichte der Aristotelischen Philosophie im protestantischen Deutschland*, Leipzig.

Peterson, Claes (1992), 'Rechtsvereinheitlichung durch Naturrecht? Zur Frage des Naturrechts in der schulphilosophischen Rechtstheorie des 18. Jahrhunderts', *Quaderni Fiorentini per la storia del pensiero giuridico moderno*, 21: 7–35.

Pfister, Christian (1985), *Klimageschichte der Schweiz 1525–1860*, 2 vols, 2nd edn, Bern.

Pocock, John Greville Agard (1987), *The Ancient Constitution and the Feudal Law: A study of English historical thought in the seventeenth century*, Cambridge.

Pollock, Frederick (1922), *Essays in the Law*, London.

Prechtl, Peter and Burkard, Franz-Peter (1999), *Metzler Philosophie Lexikon. Begriffe und Definitionen*, 2nd edn, Stuttgart and Weimar.

Press, Volker (1991), *Kriege und Krisen. Deutschland 1600–1715*, Munich.

Radbruch, G. (1938), 'Die Natur der Sache als juristische Denkform', in *Festschrift zu Ehren von Prof. Dr. jur. Rudolf Laun, Rektor der Universität Hamburg: anlässlich der Vollendung seines 65. Lebensjahres am 1. Januar 1947*, Hamburg, pp. 157–176.

Reeds, Karen (1991), *Botany in Medieval and Renaissance Universities*, New York.

Reif, P. (1969), 'The Textbook Tradition in Natural Philosophy, 1600–1650', *Journal of the History of Ideas*, 30: 17–32.

Rein, Siegfried (1993), *Friedrich Christian Lesser (1692–1754). Pastor, Physicotheologe und Polyhistor*, Erfurt.

Riley, Peter, (1986), *The General Will before Rousseau. The transformation of the divine into the civic*, Princeton.

Riley, Peter (1996), *Leibniz' Universal Jurisprudence*, Cambridge MA.

Robinet, André (1955), *Malebranche et Leibniz. Relations personnelles*, Paris.

Rockwell, W. (1904), *Die Doppelehe des Landgrafen Philipp von Hessen*, Marburg.

Röd, Wolfgang (1970), *Geometrischer Geist und Naturrecht*, Munich.

Roeck, B. (1984), *Rechtsystem und Reichsherkommen*, Stuttgart.

Roger, Jacques (1993), *Les Sciences de la vie dans la pensée française au XVIIIe siècle*, 2nd edn, Paris.

Roger, Jacques (1997), *The Life Sciences in Eighteenth-century French Thought*, trans. Robert Ellrich, ed. Keith R. Benson, Stanford.

Roux, Sophie (1996), 'La Philosophie mécanique (1630–1690)', unpublished doctorate thesis, École des Hautes Études en Sciences Sociales, Paris.

Roux, Sophie (1999), 'Les Lois de la nature au XVIIe siècle: idée, concept, métaphore polémique', paper presented to the Workshop Natur – Gesetz – Naturgesetz: Historische und zeitgenössische Perspektiven, Bad Homburg (unpublished manuscript).

Roux, Sophie (2001), 'Les lois de la nature à l'âge classique: la question terminologique', *Revue de synthése*, 4: 531–576.

Rublack, Ulrika (1995), '"Viehisch, frech und onverschämpt", Inzest in Südwestdeutschland, ca. 1530–1700', in *Von Huren and Rabenmüttern Weibliche Kriminalität in der Frühen Neuzeit*, ed. Otto Ulbricht, Cologne, pp. 171–215.

Ruby, Jane E. (1986), 'The Origins of Scientific Law,' *Journal of the History of Ideas*, 47: 341–359.

Ruby, Jane (1995), 'The Origins of Scientific Law', in *Laws of Nature: Essays on the Philosophical, Scientific and Historical Dimensions*, ed. Friedel Weinert, Berlin and New York.

Rusnock, Andrea (1999), 'Correspondence Networks and the Royal Society, 1700–1750', *British Journal for the History of Science*, 32: 155–169.

Rutherford, Donald P. (1993), 'Natures, Laws, and Miracles: The Roots of Leibniz's Critique of Occasionalism', in Nadler (1993), pp. 135–156.

St Leger, J. (1962), *The 'Etiamsi daremus' of Hugo Grotius. A Study in the Origins of International Law*, Rome.

Scattola, Merio (1999a), *Das Naturrecht vor dem Naturrecht. Zur Geschichte der 'jus naturale' im 16. Jahrhundert*, Tübingen.

Scattola, M. (1999b), '*Notitia naturalis de Deo et de morum gubernatione:* die Naturrechtslehre Philipp Melanchthon und ihre Wirkung im 16. Jahrhundert', in *Melanchthon und die Marburger Professoren (1527–1627)*, ed. Babara Bauer, 2 vols, Marburg, vol. 2, pp. 865–882.

Schedler, M. (1916), *Die Philosophie des Macrobius und ihr Einfluss auf die Wissenschaft des Mittelalters*, Beiträge zur Geschichte der Philosophie des Mittelalters, 12, 6, Munster.

Scheible, H., ed. (1997), *Melanchthon in seinen Schülern*, Wiesbaden.

Schiemann, Gregor (1997), *Wahrheits- Gewissheitsverlust. Hermann von Helmholtz, Mechanismus im Anbruch der Moderne. Eine Studie zum Übergang von klassischer zu moderner Naturphilosophie*, Darmstadt.

Schiemann, Gottfried (1998), 'Usus modernus und Gesetzgebung', in *Gesetz und Gesetzgebung im Europa der Frühen Neuzeit*, ed. Barbara Dölemeyer and Diethelm Klippel, Berlin.

Schilling, Heinz (1994), *Aufbruch und Krise. Deutschland 1517–1648*, Berlin.

Schilling, Heinz (1999), *Die neue Zeit*, Berlin.

Schimank, Hans (1949), 'Der Aspekt der Naturgesetzlichkeit im Wandel der Zeiten', in *Das Problem der Gesetzlichkeit II: Naturwissenschaften*, ed. Joachim Jungius-Gesellschaft der Wissenschaften, Hamburg, pp. 139–186.

Schindling, Anton (1977), *Humanistische Hochschule und Freie Reichsstadt. Gymnasium und Akademie in Strassburg 1538–1621*, Wiesbaden.

Schmitt, C. (1950), *Der Nomos der Erde im Völkerrecht des Jus Publicum Europaeum*, Köln.

Schmitt, C.B. (1983a), *Aristotle and the Renaissance*, Cambridge, MA.

Schmitt, C.B. (1983b), *John Case and Aristotelianism in Renaissance England*, Kingston, Ont.

Schmitt, C.B. (1988), 'The Rise of the Philosophical Textbook', in *The Cambridge History of Renaissance Philosophy*, ed. C.B. Schmitt and Q.R.D. Skinner, Cambridge, pp. 792–804.

Schmitz, Ulrich (2000), *Der Unterhaltsanspruch des nichtehelichen Kindes gegen seinen Erzeuger*, Frankfurt.

Schneider, Hans (1991), 'Johann Arndts Studienzeit', *Jahrbuch der Gesellschaft für Niedersächsische Kirchengeschichte*, 89, pp. 133–175.

Schneider, Hans (1995), 'Johann Arndt als Paracelsist', in *Neue Beiträge zur Paracelsus-Forschung*, ed. Peter Dilg and Hartmut Rudolph, Rottenburg and Stuttgart, pp. 89–110.

Schneider, Hans (1999) 'Die unerfüllte Zukunft. Apokalyptische Erwartungen im radikalen Pietismus um 1700', in *Jahrhundertwenden. Endzeit- und Zukunftserwartungen vom 15. bis zum 20. Jahrhundert*, ed. Manfred Jakubowski-Tiessen and Hartmut Lehmann, Göttingen, pp. 187–212.

Scholz, Johannes-Michael (1973), *Der brandenburgische Landrechtsentwurf von 1594. Eine Studie zu Rechtsetzungslehre der Rezeptionszeit*, Cologne and Vienna.

Schott, Clausdieter (1983), 'Einfachheit als Leitbild des Rechts und der Gesetzgebung', *Zeitschrift für Neuere Rechtsgeschichte*, Vienna, pp. 121–146.

Schott, Clausdieter (2001), '"Interpretatio cessat in claris" – Auslegungsfähigkeit und Auslegungsbedürftigkeit in der juristischen Hermeneutik', in *Theorie der Interpretation vom Humanismus bis zu Romantik – Rechtswissenschaft, Philosophie, Theologie*, ed. Jan Schröder, Stuttgart.

Schramm, Matthias (1981), 'Roger Bacons Begriff vom Naturgesetz', in *Die Renaissance der Wissenschaften im 12. Jahrhundert*, ed. P. Weimar, Zurich, pp. 197–209.

Schröder, Jan (2001), *Recht als Wissenschaft. Geschichte der juristischen Methode vom Humanismus bis zur historischen Schule (1500–1850)*, Munich.

Schulze, Winfried (1987), *Deutsche Geschichte im 16. Jahrhundert*, Munich.

Schwab, Dieter (1995), 'Ehe und Familie nach den Lehren der Spätscholastik', in *Schwab, Geschichtliches Recht und moderne Zeiten*, ed. D. Klippel, Heidelberg, pp. 141–177.

Schwarz, Andreas B. (1951), 'Das strittige Recht des römischen Juristen', in *Festschrift Fritz Schulz*, ed. Hans Niedermeyer and Werner Flume, vol. 2, pp. 201–225.

Sciences et religions de Copernic à Galilée, 1540–1610: actes du colloque international organisé par l'École française de Rome, en collaboration avec l'École nationale des chartes et l'Instituto italiano per gli studi filosofici, avec la participation de l'Università di Napoli 'Frederico II', Rome, 12–14 décembre 1996 (1999), Paris.

Scriven, Michael (1961), 'The Key Property of Physical Laws – Inaccuracy', in *Critical Issues in the Philosophy of Science*, ed. H. Feigel and G. Maxwell, New York, pp. 91–101.

Scriven, Michael (1962), 'Explanations, Predictions and Laws', *Minnesota Studies in the Philosophy of Science*, 3: 170–230.

Seelmann, Kurt (1997), *Theologie und Jurisprudenz an der Schwelle zur Moderne. Die Geburt des neuzeitlichen Naturrechts in der iberischen Spätscholastik*, Baden-Baden.

Sellert, Wolfgang and Rüping, Hinrich (1989), *Studien- und Quellenbuch zur Geschichte der deutschen Strafrechtspflege*, vol. 1, Aalen

Shapin, Steven (1981), 'Of Gods and Kings: Natural Philosophy and Politics in the Leibniz–Clarke Dispute,' *Isis*, 72: 187–215.

Shapin, Steven (1988), 'Robert Boyle and Mathematics: Reality, Representation, and Experimental Practice', *Science in Context*, 2: 23–58.

Shapiro, Barbara J. (1983), *Probability and Certainty in Seventeenth-Century England. A Study of The Relationships Between Natural Science, Religion, History, Law and Literature*, Princeton.

Sharples, R.W. (1995), 'Causes and Necessary Conditions in the *Topica* and *De Fato*', in *Cicero the Philosopher*, ed. J.G.F. Powell, Oxford, pp. 247–271.

Sherbo, Arthur (1985), 'The English Weather, The Gentleman's Magazine, and the Brothers White', *Archives of Natural History*, 12: 23–29.

Siraisi, Nancy G. (1994), 'Vesalius and Human Diversity in *De humani corporis fabrica*', *Journal of the Warburg and Courtauld Institutes*, 57: 60–88.

Siraisi, Nancy G. (1997), *The Clock and the Mirror: Girolamo Cardano and Renaissance Medicine*, Princeton.

Siraisi, Nancy G. (2000), 'Anatomizing the Past: Physicians and History in Renaissance Culture', *Renaissance Quarterly*, 53: 1–30.

Skinner, Q. (1981), *Machiavelli*, Oxford.

Specht, Rainer (1959), 'Zur Kontroverse von Suarez und Vasquez über den Grund der Verbindlichkeit des Naturrechts', *Archiv für Rechts- und Sozialphilosophie*, 45: 235–255.

Specht, Rainer (1984), 'Naturrecht III. 4. und 5.', in: *Historisches Wörterbuch der Philosophie*, ed. J. Ritter and K. Gründer, vol. 6, col. 576–582.

Specht, Rainer, (2001), 'Regulae quaedam sive leges naturae', in *Kausalität und Naturgesetz in der Frühen Neuzeit*, ed. Andreas Hüttemann, Stuttgart, pp. 65–75.

Stafleu, M.D. (1999), 'The Idea of Natural Law', *Philosophia reformata*, 64: 688–104.

Stebbins, Sara (1980), *Maxima in minimis. Zum Empirie- und Autoritätsverständnis in der physikotheologischen Literatur der Frühaufklärung*, Frankfurt am.Main.

Steiger, Johann Anselm (1999), 'Ästhetik der Realpräsens. Abendmahl, Schöpfung, Emblematik und mystische Union bei Martin Luther, Philipp Nicolai, Valerius

Herberger, Johann Saubert und Johann Michael Dilherr', in *Von Luther zu Bach*, ed. Renate Steiger, 2nd edn, Sinzig.

Steinle, Friedrich (1995), 'The Amalgamation of a Concept. Laws of Nature in the New Sciences', in *Laws of Nature. Essays on the Philosophical, Scientific and Historical Dimensions*, ed. Friedel Weinert, Berlin and New York, pp. 316–368.

Steinle, Friedrich, (2001), 'Von a-priori-Einsichten zu empirischen Regularitäten: Der Gesetzesbegriff und seine Alternativen in der frühen Royal Society', in *Kausalität und Naturgesetz in der Frühen Neuzeit*, ed. Andreas Hüttemann, Stuttgart, pp. 77–98.

Stephanitz, Dieter von (1970), *Exakte Wissenschaft und Recht. Der Einfluß von Naturwissenschaft und Mathematik auf Rechtsdenken und Rechtswissenschaft in zweieinhalb Jahrtausenden. Ein historischer Grundriß*, Berlin.

Stiening, G. (1999), '*Deus vult aliquas esse certas noticias*: Philipp Melanchthon, Rudolph Goclenius und das Konzept der *notitiae naturales* in der Psychologie des 16. Jahrhunderts', in *Melanchthon und die Marburger Professoren (1527–1627)*, ed. Babara Bauer, 2 vols, Marburg, vol. 2, pp. 757–787.

Stollberg-Rilinger, Barbara (1986), *Der Staat als Maschine. Zur politischen Metaphorik des absoluten Fürstenstaats*, Berlin.

Stolleis, Michael (1987a), 'Reichspolizistik – Politik – Naturrecht im 17. und 18. Jahrhundert,' in Stolleis (1987b), pp. 9–28.

Stolleis, Michael, ed. (1987b), *Staatsdenker im 17. und 18.Jahrhundert. Reichspublizistik – Politik – Naturrecht*, Frankfurt am Main.

Stolleis, Michael (1988), *Geschichte des öffentlichen Rechts in Deutschland*, vol. I, *Reichspublizistik und Policeywissenschaft 1600–1800*, Munich.

Stolleis, Michael (1990), 'Condere leges et interpretari. Gesetzgebungsmacht und Staatsbildung in der frühen Neuzeit', in M. Stolleis, *Staat und Staatsräson in der frühen Neuzeit*, Frankfurt.

Stolleis, Michael (1996) 'Die Idee des souveränen Staates', in *Entstehen und Wandel des verfassungsrechtlichen Denkens*, Beiheft 11 zu *Der Staat*, Berlin, pp. 63–85.

Stolleis, Michael (1997), *Rechtsgeschichte als Kunstprodukt. Zur Entbehrlichkeit von 'Begriff' und 'Tatsache'*, Baden-Baden.

Sträter, Udo (1995), *Meditation und Kirchenreform in der lutherischen Kirche des 17. Jahrhunderts*, Tübingen.

Stroup, Alice (1990), *A Company of Scientists: Botany, Patronage, and Community at the Seventeenth-Century Parisian Royal Academy of Sciences*, Berkeley.

Swerdlow, N.M. and Neugebauer, O. (1984), *Mathematical Astronomy in Copernicus's 'De Revolutionibus'*, New York.

Szlezák, Thomas A. (1993), *Platon lesen*, Stuttgart and Bad Cannstatt.

Tamm, D. (1983), 'Nolo falcem in alienam messem mittere. Der dänische Theologe Nils Hemmingsen aus juristischer Sicht', in *Gerichtslauben-Vorträge, Freiburger Festkolloquium zum 75. Geburtstag von Hans Thieme*, ed. K. Kroeschell, Sigmaringen.

Telelis, Ioannis (1998), 'The Climate of Tübingen A.D. 1596–1605, on the Basis of Martin Crusius' Diarium', *Environment and History*, 4: 53–74.

Thomas, Yan (1991), 'Imago naturae: note sur l'institutionnalité de la nature à Rome,' in École Française de Rome (1991), pp. 201–227.

Thorndyke, Lynn (1931), *History of Experimental Science*, 8 vols, New York.

Tierney, Brian (1997), *The Idea of Natural Rights. Studies in Natural Rights, Natural Law and Church Law 1150–1625*, Atlanta.

Tigerstedt, Eugène-Napoléon (1974), 'The Decline and Fall of the Neoplatonic Interpretation of Plato', in *Commentationes Humanarum Litterarum*, vol. 52, ed. Societas Scientiarum Fennica, Helsinki, pp. 31–38.

Toccane, Bernard (1978), *L'Idée de nature en France dans la seconde moitié du XVIIe siècle. Contribution à l'histoire de la pensée classique*, Paris.

Toellner, Richard (1982), 'Die Bedeutung des physiko-theologischen Gottesbeweises für die nachcartesianische Physiologie im 18. Jahrhundert', *Berichte zur Wissenschaftsgeschichte*, 5: 75–82.

Tonelli, Giorgio (1959), 'La nécessité des lois de la nature au XVIIIe siècle et chez Kant en 1762', *Revue d'histoire des sciences*, 12(3): 225–241.

Tort, Patrick (1997), *L'Ordre et les monstres. Le débat sur l'origine des déviations anatomiques au XVIIIe siècle*, 2nd edn, Paris.

Traumüller, Friedrich (1885), *Die Mannheimer meteorologisches Gesellschaft (1780–1785)*, Leipzig.

Treiber, H. (1998), 'Zur Physiologie des Rechts oder Der Muskel als Scharnierbegriff', in *Physiologie und industrielle Gesellschaft. Studien zur Verwissenschaftlichung des Körpers im 19. und 20. Jahrhundert*, ed. P. Sarasin and J. Tanner, Frankfurt, pp. 170–203.

Trepp, Anne-Charlott (1999), 'Religion, Magie und Naturphilosophie: Alchemie im 16. und 17. Jahrhundert', in *Im Zeichen der Krise. Religiosität im 17. Jahrhundert*, ed. Hartmut Lehmann and Anne-Charlott Trepp, Göttingen, pp. 469–489.

Trepp, Anne-Charlott (2001), 'Im "Buch der Natur" lesen: Natur und Religion im Zeitalter der Konfessionalisierung und des Dreißzigjährigen Krieges', in *Antike Weisheit und kulturelle Praxis. Hermetismus in der Frühen Neuzeit*, ed. Anne-Charlott Trepp and Hartmut Lehmann, Göttingen, pp. 103–143.

Trepp, Anne-Charlott (2005), '"Nature" as Religious Practice in Seventeenth-Century Germany', in *Religious Values and the Rise of Science in Europe*, ed. John Brooke and Ekmeleddin Ihsanoglu, Studies and Sources on History of Science 13, Istanbul, pp. 81–110.

Trepp, Anne-Charlott (in press), *Natur als religiöse Praxis. Zum Verhältnis von Natur und Religion in der Frühen Neuzeit*, Göttingen.

Tuck, Richard (1979), *Natural Rights Theories: Their Origin and Development*, Cambridge.

Tuck, Richard (1987), 'The "Modern" Theory of Natural Law', in *The Languages of Political Theory in Early-Modern Europe*, ed. Anthony Padgen, Cambridge, pp. 99–119.

Turnbull, C. (1984), *The Forest People. The celebrated portrayal of life among the pygmies*, London.

Van Fraassen, Baas C. (1989), *Laws and Symmetry*, Oxford.

Vernière, Paul (1954), *Spinoza et la pensée française avant la Révolution*, Paris.

Viguerie, Jean de (1983), 'Le Miracle dans la France du XVIIe siècle', *XVIIe Siècle*, 35: 313–331.

Voet, L. (1969–72), *The Golden Compasses: A history and evaluation of the printing and publishing activities of the Officina Plantiniana at Antwerp*, 2 vols, Amsterdam.

Voet, L. (1982), *The Plantin Press (1555–1589): A bibliography of the works printed and published by Christopher Plantin at Antwerp and Leiden*, 5 vols, Amsterdam.

Vollmer, Gerhard (2000), 'Was sind und warum gelten Naturgesetze?', in *Philosophia naturalis*, vol. 37/2, ed. Peter Mittelstaedt and Gerhard Vollmer, Frankfurt am Main, pp. 205–239.

Wagner, Gerhard, (1996), 'Transversale Vernunft und der soziologische Blick. Zur Erinnerung an Montesquieu', *Zeitschrift für Soziologie*, 25: 315–329.

Wallmann, Johannes (1990), *Der Pietismus*, Göttingen.

Wallmann, Johannes (1995), 'Pietismus und Chiliasmus. Zur Kontroverse um Speners 'Hoffnung auf bessere Zeiten"', in *Theologie und Frömmigkeit im Zeitalter des Barock: gesammelte Aufsätze*, ed. Johannes Wallmann, Tübingen, pp. 390–421.

Wallmann, Johannes (1999), 'Reflexionen und Bemerkungen zur Frömmigkeitskrise des 17. Jahrhunderts', in *Krisen des 17. Jahrhunderts*, ed. Manfred Jakubowski-Tiessen, Göttingen, pp. 25–42.

Walsham, A. (1999), *Providence in Early Modern England*, Oxford.

Waszink, J.H. (1964), *Studien zum Timaioskommentar des Calcidius*, Leiden.

Wear, Andrew (1995), 'Epistemology and Learned Medicine in Early Modern England', in *Knowledge and the Scholarly Medical Traditions*, ed. Don Bates, Cambridge, pp. 151–73.

Weber, Edmund (1978), *Johann Arndts Vier Bücher vom Wahren Christentum als Beitrag zur protestantischen Irenik des 17. Jahrhunderts. Eine quellenkritische Untersuchung*, 3rd edn, Hildesheim.

Weber, Max, (1973), *Gesammelte Aufsätze zur Wissenschaftslehre*, 4th edn, Tübingen.

Weber, Max (1976), *Wirtschaft und Gesellschaft*, 5th edn, Tübingen.

Webster, Charles (1975), *The Great Instauration. Science, Medicine, and Reform 1626–1660*, London.

Webster, Charles (1982), *From Paracelsus to Newton. Magic and the Making of Modern Science*, Cambridge.

Webster, Charles (1986), 'Puritanism, Separatism, and Science', in *God and Nature: Historical Essays on the Encounter between Christianity and Science*, ed. David C. Lindberg and Ronald L. Numbers, pp. 192–217.

Weinert, Friedel, ed. (1995), *Laws of Nature. Essays on the Philosophical, Scientific and Historical Dimensions*, Berlin.

Welzel, Hans (1962), *Naturrecht und materiale Gerechtigkeit*, 4th edn, Göttingen.

Wesel, Uwe (1985), *Frühformen des Rechts in vorstaatlichen Gesellschaften*, Frankfurt.

Westerman, Pauline C. (1998), *The Disintegration of Natural Law Theory, Aquinas to Finnis*, Leiden.

Westfall, Richard (1958), *Science and Religion in Seventeenth-Century England*, New Haven.

Westman, R.S. (1980), 'The Astronomer's Role in the Sixteenth Century: A preliminary study', *History of Science*, 18: 105–47.

Whitehead, Alfred North (1933), *Adventures of Ideas*, New York.

Wieacker, Franz (1967), *Privatrechtsgeschichte der Neuzeit*, 2nd edn, Göttingen.

Wilson, Catherine (1987), '*De Ipsa Natura*: Leibniz on Substance, Force and Activity', *Studia Leibnitiana*, 19: 148–172; reprinted 1991 in V. Chappell, ed., *Essays on Leibniz*, Hamden.

Wilson, Catherine (1995), *The Invisible World: Early Modern Philosophy and the Invention of the Microscope*, Princeton.

Wintzer, Friedrich (1979), 'Auferstehung III.: praktisch-theologisch', *Theologische Realenzyklopädie*, 4: 529–547.

Wolf, Armin (1981), 'Gesetzgebung und Kodifikationen', in *Die Renaissance der Wissenschaften im 12. Jahrhundert*, ed. Peter Weimar, Zurich.

Wood, P.B. (1980), 'Methodology and Apologetics: Thomas Spratt's History of the Royal Society', *British Journal for the History of Science*, 13: 1–26.

Wyduckel, D. (1979), *Princeps Legibus Solutus. Eine Untersuchung zur frühmodernen Rechts- und Staatslehre*, Berlin.

Zilsel, Edgar (1942a), 'The Sociological Roots of Science', *The American Journal of Sociology*, 47: 545–567.

Zilsel, Edgar (1942b), 'The Genesis of the Concept of Physical Law', *The Philosophical Review*, 51: 245–279.

Zumkeller, A. (1980), 'Aegidius Romanus', in *Lexikon des Mittelalters*, vol. 1, col. 178.

Index